D1551796

Nuns Without Cloister

Sisters of St. Joseph in the Seventeenth and Eighteenth Centuries

Marguerite Vacher

Translated by Patricia Byrne and the United States Federation of the Sisters of St. Joseph

UNIVERSITY PRESS OF AMERICA®, INC.

Lanham • Boulder • New York • Toronto • Plymouth, UK

Copyright © 2010 by
University Press of America,® Inc.
4501 Forbes Boulevard
Suite 200
Lanham, Maryland 20706
UPA Acquisitions Department (301) 459-3366

Estover Road
Plymouth PL6 7PY
United Kingdom

Library of Congress Control Number: 2008939272
ISBN: 978-0-7618-4342-9 (paperback : alk. paper)
eISBN: 978-0-7618-4343-6

Front cover photos: Hands of Sr. Marie-Augustin Laliron (1897–1995)
Back cover photo: Constitutions 1694

♾™ The paper used in this publication meets the minimum
requirements of American National Standard for Information
Sciences—Permanence of Paper for Printed Library Materials,
ANSI Z39.48—1992

To the Sisters of St. Joseph,
the inheritors of Father Médaille
spread today
throughout the world.

. . . nous sommes comme des religieuses or la cloture.

. . . we are like nuns outside the cloister.

Mother Jeanne (Marguerite) Burdier, 1683

Contents

Illustrations

Following page 124

Sister of St. Joseph, Ex Voto Painting, Seventeenth Century

Sister Antoinette Bresse, Ex Voto Painting (1707)

Habit of the Sisters of St. Joseph (1714)

Sister of St. Joseph between Two Nuns (1792)

Widow of La Tour d'Auvergne, Mid-Nineteenth Century

Former Kitchen of the Hôpital des Orphelines, Le Puy-en-Velay

"The Old Convent," First House of Sisters of St. Joseph, Le Cheylard

House of Sisters of St. Joseph in Saint-Julien-Vocance (1675)

House of Sisters of St. Joseph and Village, Saint-Julien-Vocance

Abbreviations

ORIGINAL MANUSCRIPTS OF THE SISTERS OF ST. JOSEPH

Manuscript A	A
Apinac Manuscript	Ap
Manuscript B	B
Bas-en-Basset Manuscript	Ba
Boisset Manuscript	Bo
Manuscript C	C
Manuscript D	D
Gap Manuscript	G
Saint-Hilaire Manuscript 1	H1
Saint-Hilaire Manuscript 2	H2
Lyon Manuscript	L
Montferrand Manuscript	M
Saint-Didier Manuscript	S

ARCHIVAL AND PUBLISHED SOURCES

TP 1981	*Sœurs de Saint-Joseph. Textes primitifs*, Clermont, 1981
CP	Constitutions primitives
R	Règlements
MI	Maximes du Petit Institut
MP	*Maximes de Perfection*
PD	Petit Directoire
AR	Avis et Règlements

CM	Conférence de Monseigneur de Maupas
LE	Lettre Eucharistique
CV 1694	*Constitutions pour la Petite Congregation des sœurs de Saint-Joseph* (Vienne, 1694)
ACMND	Archives de la Compagnie de Marie-Notre-Dame
AD	Archives Départementales
AHC	Archives des Hospices Civils
AHD	Archives de l'Hôtel-Dieu
AM	Archives Municipales
AMM	Archives Maison-Mère
ARSI	Archivum Romanum Societatis Iesu
Tolos. 2^I	Tolosan. Epist. General, 1636–1646
Tolos. 2^{II}	Tolosan. Epist. General, 1646–1656
Tolos. 5	Tolosanae Catalogi Breves, 1609–1647
Tolos. 6	Tolosanae Catalogi Breves, 1651–1680
Tolos. 9	Tolosanae Catalogi Triennales, 1587–1642
Tolos. 10^I	Tolosanae Catalogi Triennales, 1645–1651
Tolos. 10^{II}	Tolosanae Catalogi Triennales, 1655–1660
Tolos. 11	Tolosanae Catalogi Triennales, 1665–1675
BM	Bibliothèque Municipale
BN	Bibliothèque Nationale
ACSS	Voyer d'Argenson, *Annales de la Compagnie du Saint-Sacrement* (Marseille, 1900)
ASSM	Raoul Allier, *La Compagnie du Saint-Sacrement de l'Autel à Marseille, Documents* (Paris, 1902)
CSJ 1970	*The Constitutions of the Society of Jesus* (St. Louis, 1970)
DAF 1694	*Dictionnaire de l'Académie Francaise*, 1st ed. (Paris, 1694)
FDU 1690	Antoine Furtière, *Le Dictionnaire universel* (The Hague, 1690)
RSI 1620	*Règles de la Compagnie de Jésus* (Paris, 1620)
PDL	Georges Guigue, *Les papiers des dévots de Lyon* (Lyon, 1922)

Note: French terms are generally translated into English or explained within the text. In cases where the names of institutions or terms had no satisfactory English equivalents or the French was very familiar, the French terms are retained and explained in the glossary.–Trans.

Foreword

The Sisters of St. Joseph, "spread today throughout the world," remain a body of independent congregations, all tracing their origins to 1650 in Le Puy-en-Velay, all recognizing in each other the same roots and the same vocation. As a type they belong to the non-cloistered women's congregations of seventeenth-century France who established the pattern of active, apostolic religious life for women that would become so prominent in nineteenth-century Catholicism. Female congregations like the Sisters of St. Joseph at that time played an effective role in the massive drive toward universal literacy demanded by an industrializing era and in the development of organized health care and social services spurred by attending rural-urban migrations. Between 1800 and the mid-1960s such communities indisputably formed the backbone of the Catholic Church's vast network of institutional presence in Western countries. In the United States alone they conducted the largest private school system known to history. By the 300th anniversary of their foundation in 1950, and near their numerical peak, there were approximately 60,000 Sisters of St. Joseph worldwide, roughly half of them in the United States and Canada. Their greatest relative growth today is in India, Egypt, and parts of Africa, followed by Brazil.

The historical profile of Catholic women's congregations is familiar. Numerous readers hold part of it as living memory. Beyond the barest facts, however, the beginnings of the Sisters of St. Joseph have remained obscure. In contrast to the French orders examined by Elizabeth Rapley (Ursulines, Visitandines, and others), early communities of St. Joseph preserved no detailed records of their internal life. This dearth of evidence resulted in part from the relatively minor social standing of the women who were Sisters of St. Joseph and the lack of a centralized organization to generate correspondence. It had to do as well with the life they led as "hospitallers." Directed primarily toward work with the poor rather than expressly to teaching, it left little leisure for writing. A critical history of their origin demanded the prolonged and disciplined study of documents scattered over a wide variety of private and public archives in France, as well as a developed understanding of the historical situation that produced them. That has been achieved for the first time in Marguerite [Sister Thérèse] Vacher's *Des "régulières" dans le siècle: Les sœurs de Saint-Joseph du Père Médaille aux XVIIᵉ et XVIIIᵉ siècles*, published in 1991 and translated in the present volume as *Nuns Without Cloister*.

Vacher's work investigates a group of women living a religious life that was by design engaged with the society of its day—in the words of Mère Jeanne Burdier, "*or la cloture*" (outside the cloister). It explores not only facets of Catholic life in south-central France during the ancien régime, but also the contested translation of Ignatian inspiration into a feminine idiom. Against that background, the evolution of the Congregation of St. Joseph before the French Revolution leads to the question of whether and to what degree succeeding generations grasped the original inspiration.

Marguerite Vacher states plainly in the preface that she undertook her scholarly study in the hope of providing some illumination for present-day Sisters of St. Joseph. The result has been a definitive history of their origins that succeeds, for a far wider audience, in bringing the foundations of a major women's religious congregation out of the shadows and placing its development squarely within the context of post-Tridentine Catholicism and the varied social conditions of the southeastern quarter of France.

Patricia Byrne, CSJ
Trinity College, Hartford
June 29, 2007

Preface

Sisters of St. Joseph, the heirs of Fr. Jean-Pierre Médaille spread today to every continent, have tried over the past twenty years to gain a better knowledge of their origins in order to have a better grasp of their vocation. For that reason, federations of St. Joseph in the United States, Canada, Italy, and France have all created research teams.

The French congregations bear a uniquely challenging responsibility in this pursuit of further knowledge, since they possess most of the archives relative to the origins in the seventeenth and eighteenth centuries. Conscious of this responsibility and of these resources, the need to return to the earliest stage of the institute in order to understand the particular patterns of growth and change operative at that time spurred me to undertake deeper research on the communities of St. Joseph as a whole, from the origins at Le Puy around 1650 until the Revolution. The present work aims to comprehend the relationship between the normative texts and the historical realities of the communities of St. Joseph in a way that might provide some light for the congregations today.

Based on archival analysis, my research was done principally in the dioceses of the southeastern quarter of France, since the Sisters of St. Joseph did not go beyond that region during the ancien régime. It must be noted that the nearly complete destruction by fire of the municipal archives of the city of Le Puy deprived me of one of the primary sources of information on the beginnings of the Sisters of St. Joseph, making my research both more demanding and more far-flung. Finally, the Jesuit archives, in Rome as well as for the Toulouse Province, have added to the all too rare data on the person of Fr. Médaille.

In this work, done at the Université Lumière-Lyon 2 and at the Centre André Latreille, the regional inter-university center for the study of religious history, I was fortunate to profit from the help and competence of Jean-Pierre

Gutton, professor at the Université Lumière, to whom I express my sincere gratitude. I also thank the motherhouses of the French Congregations of St. Joseph who opened their archives to me, and particularly that of Le Puy. My gratitude to all those sisters for their interest, their welcome, and their generosity. Finally, I thank my congregation of Clermont-Ferrand which, along with me, committed itself to this research.

May this work, like a return to the source, serve the Sisters of St. Joseph of Fr. Médaille as a means of renewed vitality.

Marguerite Vacher
Sisters of St. Joseph of Clermont-Ferrand, [1990]

Acknowledgments

This translation has involved the commitment of numerous persons under the aegis of the United States Federation of the Sisters of St. Joseph. Mary Beth Ingham, CSJ, Loyola-Marymount University, laid the foundation. Marie-Louise Murphy, Isabel Chevillard Evelein, and Veronica O'Reilly, CSJ, supplied long hours and expertise in the initial stages. Jane Frances Morrissey, CSJ, edited the manuscript, expertly proofed by Helen Barrett, CSJ and Maureen Dougherty, CSJ. Paula Drass, CSJ, kindly contributed photographs. Barbara Hecht kindly rescued the graphics, and David Tatem of Trinity College, the photographs. I am indebted to President James F. Jones, Jr., Professors Leslie Desmangles, Alden Gordon, Dori Katz, Kenneth Lloyd-Jones, A. D. Macro, and Mark Silk of Trinity College for their scholarly advice; to Dr. Jeffrey Kaimowitz, Head of Trinity's Watkinson Library, for help with Latin translations; and to librarians Patricia Bunker, Mary Curry, and Sally Dickenson for proficient and patient assistance. Brian DeRocoo of Rowman and Littlefield provided guidance throughout the publication process.

Sincere thanks to Dame Olwen Hufton for her comment on this translation and inspiration over the years. The Sisters of St. Joseph of Baden generously allowed me the time for this work. The Benedictine nuns of the Abbey of Regina Laudis prayed, hoped, and befriended. Barbara Baer, CSJ, has offered invaluable assistance at every step. Without the unfailing and intelligent collaboration of Marcia Allen, CSJ, the translation would never have been completed, and her community at Manna House of Prayer in Concordia, Kansas, provided, time after time, warm welcome and an ideal place to work. The financial and moral support of the United States and Canadian Federations of Sisters of St. Joseph, and a generous Faculty Grant from Trinity College have been indispensable. The Sisters of St. Joseph at Saint-Étienne furnished gracious hospitality and the author, Sister Thérèse Vacher, has given friendship, encouragement, and honest criticism throughout. She has also answered innumerable questions and been a tenacious partner in pursuing the meanings of old and elusive terminology.

Introduction: Religious Life for Women in Seventeenth-Century France

The emergence of apostolic religious communities of women during the seventeenth century in France took place in the historical environment shaped by implementation of the Council of Trent (1545–1563). Although the Council aimed exclusively at strengthening the monastic model, the reforms it initiated in the sixteenth century directly affected the subsequent birth of apostolic, non-cloistered religious congregations of women. In the seventeenth century, the term "religious" or "regular" signified one who professed solemn vows, and in the case of women, observed strict enclosure. The following introduction explains that women's communities whose members professed simple vows and whose apostolic purpose precluded enclosure were not perceived as "religious" (or nuns) in the accepted sense of that term. They represented something new. The Congregation of St. Joseph belonged to this new movement. Marguerite Vacher therefore begins her study with a presentation of the influence in France of reforms decreed by the Council and the reaction of the French kings. The introduction concludes with the variety of ways women found to pursue their goal of apostolic service as an expression of their consecration to Christ. The context so richly developed underscores the freshness of approach taken by Father Jean-Pierre Médaille, SJ, and the first women in Le Puy, who together founded the Congregation of St. Joseph. —Trans.

RELIGIOUS LIFE AND THE COUNCIL OF TRENT

The Council of Trent was in session, with frequent interruptions, from 1545 until 1563. Several times in the course of those eighteen years it tackled the serious problems, stemming from lax discipline and the need for spiritual reform, that were plaguing monasteries. As the Council drew to a close in November of 1563, it dealt with essential issues concerning monastic life. The resultant decree, *De regularibus et monialibus* (On Regulars and Nuns), was issued during the Council's last session, December 3–4, 1563. Chapters of this decree concerned exclusively with women's monasteries put the greatest emphasis on two points: the enclosure of nuns and women's freedom in entering religious life. Chapter 5, "On the Enclosure of Nuns," cited *Periculoso*, the constitution issued by Pope Boniface VIII in 1298 forbidding all nuns to leave their monasteries except in the case of serious contagious illness.[1] The Council of Trent specifically reinforced that prohibition, "by the judgment of God to which it appeals and under threat of eternal malediction." It commanded bishops to re-establish the practice of enclosure wherever it had been abandoned and to preserve it where maintained: "restraining with ecclesiastical censures and other penalties, every appeal being set aside, the disobedient and gainsayers, even summoning for this purpose, if need be, the aid of the secular arm." The decree also forbade all outsiders to enter the enclosure under pain of excommunication. In exceptional and legitimate cases, however, permission to do so could be obtained, but only from the bishop or ecclesiastical superior and in writing.

The chapter on enclosure takes an exceptionally harsh and menacing tone. Twice it mentions the use of coercion, if necessary, to force nuns into compliance. Twice it threatens them or others who opposed their enclosure with ecclesiastical sanctions and excommunication. Lastly, and above all, it threatens recalcitrant bishops with "eternal malediction." Such severity was necessary due to the complicity of some families of abbesses in resisting monastic enclosure. It was also undeniably linked to the status of women in sixteenth-century Europe. Nowhere does the decree use equally strong language in regard to monasteries of men; strict enclosure for them was exceptional in the western world.

The status of women also underlies Chapters 17 and 18 of *De regularibus et monialibus*, which contain legislation "having in view the freedom" of women and girls entering religious orders.[2] A girl could not take the religious habit before the age of twelve, nor without examination by the local bishop. Prior to profession, he had to examine her again in order to verify that she did so freely, with full knowledge and the qualifications necessary to keep the rule. In the same concern for freedom, "the holy council anathematize[d]" anyone who either forced a woman to enter religious life or prevented her from doing so. No similar regulations applied to men's communities, since the external pressures to enter religious life were not the same for men. The last few points clearly reveal the pervasive influence of societal norms on the differences in the treatment of men's monasteries from that of women's. If the council's chief or most pointed concerns regarding men's monasteries had to do with delimiting their power, in the case of women's, they were rather to assure them protection and maintain their dependence upon ecclesiastical and male authorities. Given the historical context, it could not have been otherwise.

The Council hardly considered the possibility of forms of life consecrated to God other than monastic. *De regularibus* speaks only once, in Chapter 18, of "women called penitents or convertites [*convertitae*]," noting that they are exempt from the regulations given for nuns and governed by their own constitutions. These women belonged to various third orders, especially, as noted by Joseph Creusen, "the numerous members of the Third Order of St. Francis, who lived in community without solemn vows . . . commonly referred to as sisters of penance." Other women, attached to the Dominican Order, had been authorized by Pope Julius II to live in community and to make the three vows of poverty, chastity, and obedience, but without the obligation to observe enclosure or sing the Divine Office in choir.[3] Such groups without solemn vows seemed of so little importance that the Council fathers scarcely adverted to them.

Implementation of the Council in the Church

Pius V, who became pope in 1566, added radical measures to the enforcement of religious enclosure for women. In the constitution *Circa Pastoralis*, promulgated May 29, 1566, he rigorously reaffirmed and expanded the provisions for enclosure decreed by Trent, making them universal. *Circa Pastoralis* addressed "each and every nun, present and future" including those "who are called lay sisters." It also imposed enclosure on all "women who are in third orders or . . . called [sisters] of penance living in community, regardless of the order to which they belong." Unlike the Council of Trent, *Circa Pastoralis* superseded the proper law of congregations, directing all those "who have made profession, either openly or tacitly, even if they are not obliged by their constitutions to observe enclosure," to submit themselves to it immediately and to observe it in perpetuity. Bishops and ecclesiastical superiors of women belonging to third orders (who would not have pronounced solemn vows) were to "exhort them in like manner." If communities of women did not make public profession and accept enclosure, they would no longer have the right to accept novices.[4]

These injunctions were accompanied by threats and sanctions against the "rebels and incorrigibles," who must be forced "by all the means available to law and to faith to submit absolutely to the mandated enclosure. . . . If they have refused, let them be punished in the most severe manner."[5] The Council of Trent dealt only with "regulars and nuns," but the constitution *Circa Pastoralis* targeted with the same rigor all forms approaching consecrated life: tertiaries, lay sisters, and others. Like the conciliar decree, the constitution of Pius V commanded ecclesiastical authorities to make sure that enclosure was actually observed, and this "under oath of judgment by God and the threat of eternal damnation." The pope implored "by the bowels of the mercy of Our Lord Jesus Christ, all princes of this world, other nobles and civil magistrates," for the remission of their sins, that they "assist all patriarchs, primates, archbishops, bishops, and other [male] superiors of nuns . . . and even use temporal punishments on the rebellious."[6] The constitution employs extremely severe terms throughout, scarcely softened by the invocation of the "mercy of Our Lord Jesus Christ." Even on the assumption that great evil and abuses existed within religious orders, it is difficult today to comprehend the extraordinary severity of such language.

Following the death of Pius V in 1572, Gregory XIII continued to promote reform of the older religious orders, but he also authorized new ones. As pope, he vigorously upheld the sanctions regarding enclosure and solemn vows for regulars. At the same time, he granted approval on December 24, 1582, for the founding of Ursulines in the diocese of Milan under St. Charles Borromeo as an association of women who made simple vows and led a common life.[7] Gregory gave particular support to new forms of consecrated life for men. He endorsed societies of clerics who did not claim to be religious, such as the Barnabites and the Oratorians of St. Philip Neri. In the Bull *Ascendente Domino* (May 25, 1584), he also confirmed previous decrees in favor of the innovation by which scholastics and coadjutor brothers of the Society of Jesus were considered real religious, even though they made only simple perpetual vows. This decision contained in principle the entire future evolution of canon law for religious.[8] Requested by Ignatius Loyola for the spiritual coadjutors of the Society—and granted by Paul III in 1546, confirmed by Julius III in 1550, and finally by the Council of Trent in 1563—it conferred on simple vows the character of public vows received by the authority of the church and recognized those who pronounced them as belonging to the religious state. Despite the support of Gregory XIII, however, this point was long and actively contested. In the post-Tridentine world, it was hardly possible to imagine authentic religious life in men's orders, much less women's, without solemn vows.

In summary, the Council of Trent's decree on religious orders and monasteries placed the authority and responsibility for reform in the hands of bishops, together with the male superiors of orders or other ecclesiastics in charge of monasteries. This meant that the foundation of new monasteries required permission from the local bishop and should occur only where resources and alms were sufficient to support them. Bishops were to enforce enclosure, using the power of civil authorities if needed. It was up to them to judge the legitimacy of any temporary absence from the monastery, for which they had to give written permission. The same conditions, enforced under pain of excommunication, held for permission to go inside a monastery of nuns. The bishop or other male superior presided at the election of the abbess or female superior. In case of need, in monasteries that were directly subject to the pope, the metropolitan or the local bishop had the right to intervene as delegate of the Holy See. Bishops and other male superiors were responsible for providing the nuns with ordinary and extraordinary confessors. The bishop or his delegate was to examine candidates before they took the habit or made profession. He was also to verify a woman's freedom in entering or her reasons for leaving the monastery. Finally, bishops were to implement without delay all the council's directives concerning monasteries.

In his history of this era in France, Léopold Willaert argued that the Coun cil of Trent "brought about a remarkable renaissance among the monks and nuns of older orders."[9] There is consensus among some scholars that the Council can be credited with saving religious life. Its decrees were certainly decisive in the renewal of existing religious orders. That renewal was based upon an older understanding of religious life, however, concerned more with restoring the past than moving into the future. For several centuries, Pius V's uncompromising decree, which meant effectively that non-monastic congregations were doomed to disappear, caused considerable problems for groups of women trying to find a way toward new forms of consecrated life. In spite of this, congregations such as the Ursulines survived, and others were created. Even the Holy See exercised tolerance, and several bishops allowed the establishment of non-cloistered congregations in response to the pastoral and social needs of the people. The excessive severity of *Circa Pastoralis* rendered it to some extent ineffective.

Proscriptions against congregations of simple vows without enclosure eventually lost their force in face of the spiritual and apostolic vitality of new congregations. It is well known that Francis de Sales, a theologian and doctor of canon and civil law, had to subject the monasteries of Visitation nuns he had founded at the beginning of the seventeenth century to enclosure. He nevertheless contributed, directly and indirectly, to the foundation of several women's communities requiring only simple vows without enclosure. He wrote the rule for the Daughters of the Cross in Paris, founded by Madame Marie L'Huillier de Villeneuve, which was based on the rule of the first Visitation and later approved by Jean-François de Gondi, Archbishop of Paris. Saint Vincent de Paul, too, was involved in the efflorescence of non-monastic women's congregations during the first half of the seventeenth century. Although they retained intact the essence of consecrated life, such congregations had the juridical status of secular communities. This status suited local church authorities, who could keep control over them. It also suited the king, at least for a time, but for different reasons.

Reception and Implementation of the Council in France

Several European countries gave the decrees of the Council of Trent and the obligation to apply them a cold reception.[10] Among those most opposed were the kings of France. The chief impediment to applying the decrees lay in the profoundly intertwined powers of church and state. The French kings regarded Rome's decrees as laws from a foreign legislator. After all, the council had affirmed the absolute authority of the pope in the church. It denied princes the right to intervene in strictly ecclesiastical affairs. On the contrary, it seemed to assert the right of the pope to interfere in the administration of the kingdom of France. In that case, what became of the absolute power of the king? The content of the required reforms, moreover, undermined critical royal interests. The most important had to do with the practice of *commendam*, assigning revenues from a religious office or ecclesiastical benefice to a cleric or a lay person who did not exercise the spiritual authority connected with it. Reform in this area meant that kings could no longer dispose of the church's goods—bishoprics, abbeys, or monasteries—for their own material and political gain.

The *parlements*, even more than the kings, expressed growing opposition to the publication and implementation of the conciliar decrees. At first the *parlements'* resistance was polite, but their opposition gradually hardened toward Rome and the Council, which they perceived as undermining the Gallican character of the French church. Determined to restrain the pope's authority in favor of that of the bishops and the king, the *parlements* continued to view Tridentine decrees as not promulgated and therefore not applicable in France.

The decrees of the Council of Trent never received official recognition in the kingdom of France. Instead, they were introduced gradually as the bishops came to accept them. In the mid-sixteenth century a considerable number of bishops did not reside in their dioceses and were little concerned with pastoral duties. Some led scandalous lives or were suspected of heresy. Little by little, however, the bishops' initial resistance gave way to a desire to follow the Council's decrees. In 1615 the French church decided to accept them as its law, despite opposition on the part of the *parlements*. Despite their decision, the French bishops could not implement the Council of Trent, nor did they want to, in opposition to the king. On May 6, 1616, Louis XIII responded to their decision from Blois, voicing "disapproval of the conduct of the clergy in promulgating the Council of Trent." The kings did not refuse to work toward Christian reform as prescribed by the Council; they preferred putting it into effect on their own initiative, when it suited them, without submitting to any other authority, even that of the pope. Caught between popes and kings, the French clergy struggled to honor both loyalties. If the bishops in general were obliged to maintain this balancing act throughout the reign of Louis XIV (1643–1715), neither king nor pope could enforce ecclesiastical reform in France, especially that of monasteries and other religious communities, without their active collaboration.

RELIGIOUS LIFE AND THE KINGS OF FRANCE

Although kings issued injunctions to bishops for spiritual reform throughout the seventeenth century, resistance to the restoration of monastic observance was strong. In addition to opposition from lax religious who had no true vocation and from some families of religious, bishops and kings alike had to deal with the problems caused by exemption. Certain religious orders and monasteries that were directly under Roman jurisdiction were by that fact free, or exempt, from dependence on their immediate ecclesiastical superior, the bishop of the diocese. Bishops saw Rome's practice of granting exemption as a restriction to their episcopal jurisdiction. The kings and *parlements* perceived it as an ultramontane tendency posing the threat of rival power — but only when it came to monasteries of men.

The practice of exemption, like the governance of monasteries, was a gendered issue. Women's monasteries could also enjoy the same freedom of direct recourse to Rome, but in a different way. According to an eighteenth-century canonist, Durand de Maillane: "[T]here are in the kingdom several monasteries of women under the direction and special government of the male religious of the same order, whose rule they observe as adapted to their sex: this constitutes an authentic exemption from episcopal jurisdiction."[11] Only through connection with the male branch of the same order did these nuns participate in the exemption of religious orders. Durand asserted that the Council of Trent did not alter this usage, but rather confirmed it.[12] Nuns of some exempt monasteries, in contrast, asked to transfer to episcopal jurisdiction. It was not always easy to identify the competent ecclesiastical superior. The introduction of the Carmelite nuns in France at the beginning of the seventeenth century is a good example of the complexity in determining the ecclesiastical superiors of certain monasteries. Depending on their establishment, the Carmelite monasteries were divided, and the nuns subject to two jurisdictions: the Oratorians and the discalced Carmelite men.

Women's monasteries, even those that were exempt, rarely presented the same risk of independence from royal or episcopal authority as the men's, simply because they did not enjoy comparable power. Durand put it succinctly, ". . . in the religious life, women differ from men in that they can be governed only by men."[13] In the seventeenth century it was taken for granted that women religious possessed only the limited power delegated to them by a bishop or male religious superior. This viewpoint produced skepticism about the exemption of women's monasteries, evident in a collection of canonical jurisprudence of 1771:

> It must be noted . . . that nuns are ordinarily not presumed exempt because such concessions have been made to this sex only recently, since their needs, necessity, and seemliness require greater subjection. It is therefore expedient that they be under the watchful eye, not of a distant authority, but of one nearby to guide them, lest they fall into laxity and license. Such were the words of M. Bignon, Solicitor General, in the case between the Religious of the Rule of Limoges and the Bishop, 6 March 1653.[14]

Taken at face value, this ruling suggests that monasteries of nuns under male authority, whether episcopal or regular, exercised much less influence than those of monks. In reality, the role of women became increasingly broad. It is well known that legislation always comes into play after the fact, to account for the reality that has preceded it. Canonists, who explained the conventions of law, did not necessarily describe the actual place of women's monasteries in society. Their existence was certainly important enough to command the concern of French kings when it was a question of their own interests or those of the kingdom.

Royal Legislation for Monks and Nuns

Royal legislation throughout the seventeenth century restricted the establishment of monasteries and other communities. Three successive edicts show increasingly detailed requirements, intended as safeguards against the instability of new monasteries. In 1629, Louis XIII prohibited "the establishment of any regular and religious monastery, house, or community of either sex without express permission of the king."[15] On June 7, 1659, Louis XIV reaffirmed this principle in his declaration "bearing regulations on the establishment of religious communities, seminaries, confraternities, etc."[16] He renewed the prohibition against foundations without letters patent registered in the royal courts, adding a requirement for approval by diocesan bishops and municipal governments.

Ten years later, in the edict of December, 1666, the king further expanded the requisites for a new foundation to obtain letters patent. The requirements included "the approbation of the diocesan archbishop or bishop, or of the vicars general . . . the statement of the judicial officer of the place . . . containing the opinions of the mayors, municipal magistrates, consuls . . . pastors of parishes and [ecclesiastical] superiors of religious houses." These were accompanied by threats and sanctions against anyone who might "allow a foundation without all the said formalities having been observed."[17] The kings were preoccupied about conditions for the establishment of monasteries and other communities primarily because they wanted to avoid foundations without sufficient resources, which would later be "obliged to abandon their convents."[18] Such fears were well grounded. From the second half of the seventeenth century on, many hasty foundations failed for lack of sufficient material means and recruits. It was in the interests of royal authority, since it ultimately had to assume the debts of these communities, to preclude the problem.[19]

Legislative texts also revealed increasing apprehension about the accumulation of property by certain ecclesiastical communities, both religious and secular. The central concern was that "In many places, the communities have and possess the best part of lands and revenues," to the detriment of family assets.[20] The king wanted to put an end to these disorders, and to watch "carefully . . . over the conservation of properties in the families." To ensure that goods and property stayed in the hands of families, two decrees of Louis XIV (April, 1691 and April, 1693) regulated the dowries paid for women entering monasteries.[21] Monasteries, abbeys, or priories that claimed "not to have enough resources to sustain the number of nuns who are there [must] present accounts of their revenues and their expenses to the archbishops and bishops," who would then try to cover their needs through "pensions, sums . . . of money or endowments," without despoiling families in the process.

Nearly sixty years later, in August, 1749, Louis XV referred to the very large portion of the kingdom's territories held by persons in mortmain, who could transfer it in perpetuity without having to pay the usual taxes to the state. Among these establishments, he mentioned "colleges . . . religious houses or communities . . . congregations, confraternities, hospitals, or other bodies and communities, whether ecclesiastical, secular, religious, or lay."[22] In order to "reconcile as much as possible the interests of families with the protection of establishments which truly serve the public interests," the king recapitulated and renewed the royal mandates and prohibitions enacted by his predecessors. All institutions established without letters patent he declared null and deprived of all rights their members and anyone who had formed or directed them. The 1749 edict protected not only the patrimony of families, but also the interests of the state. By placing on the market properties confiscated through this law, the king was able to recover lost revenue and taxes. By preventing the concentration of wealth and properties in monasteries, abbeys, and orders of regulars—and this was most important—he could prevent the formation of a rival power in religious orders of men, especially those with papal exemption.

Royal Legislation for Secular Communities

In contrast to recognized religious orders, which constituted a separate state of life and could amass considerable property and wealth, secular communities were small associations formed for various activities. Due to their relative insignificance, they were largely ignored in royal legislation during the first half of the seventeenth century. At that time, community was an ordinary way of life, fundamental for both men and women as a means of survival. Communities were common throughout France in every arena. Furtière's *Dictionnaire Universel* (1690) defines the term "community" generically as "a society of people who reside in the same place." Furtière mentions "cities, towns, villages, [or] parishes," all of which were spoken of as a community of inhabitants.[23] In a narrower sense, he says "community also refers to certain individuals who have placed their goods in common, whether for business or to live a more peaceful life, or who possess or have goods shared in common." Furtière also indicates that "community" refers to

> pious sites founded to support and sustain several persons in a certain type of
> life, religious or secular. These include convents, abbeys, conventual priories,
> seminaries, *hospices*, and all kinds of religious houses. It also applies to persons
> who come together voluntarily to fulfill all the charges of a parochial benefice,
> or to devote themselves to pious works.

He identifies a "secular" as a "lay person who lives in the world without being obligated by vows and to the specific rules of a community, and without being bound in ecclesiastical orders." A secular community was therefore not a group of men or women under vows and thereby subject to particular rules, but rather a group of persons gathered together voluntarily for a type of life or service ("seminaries, *hospices*, and all kinds of religious houses," according to Furtière's definition). Royal legislation concerning religious profession during the seventeenth century treated secular communities somewhat apart from "regular" communities, precisely because they had nothing to do with formal commitment to religious life. Instead, laws touching the secular communities covered primarily the type of service they provided.

From the end of the sixteenth to the middle of the seventeenth centuries, new congregations in France wove connections between various services to others and commitment as religious. A parallel evolution in legal language increasingly connected secular and religious communities, without, however, assimilating one to the other. This at times raised questions about where secular communities stood before the law. In 1675 the *parlement* of Grenoble had to determine, in connection with a donation made to the Oratorians, "whether secular communities are included in the prohibition of the ordinances which declare as null and void donations made to monasteries where one makes profession."[24] A detailed examination of the Oratorians' status revealed, that although they did have one year of formation, they had neither novitiate nor vows and did not live apart from their families. The *parlement* consequently concluded that they were, in the eyes of the law, "priests voluntarily assembled" and not subject to the ordinance regulating donations to monasteries.

Until the end of the seventeenth century, royal declarations concerning houses of religious sometimes expressly associated secular communities with them or simply referred to "communities" as such. For example, an edict in August 1661 forbade "the donation of any monies in kind, inheritances, or annuities to ecclesiastical communities, whether regular or secular . . . on condition of an annual income for life."[25] This decree treats both types of community under the same rubric, as does that of December, 1666, dealing with the formalities necessary for the establishment "of colleges, monasteries, communities religious or secular, even under pretext of *hospice*." A shift appeared in April of 1693, in the declaration of Louis XIV "concerning the reception and endowment of persons entering monasteries to embrace religious profession."[26]

Although the title of the decree implicitly assimilates secular communities to monasteries and other religious houses, the text actually deals with them separately. After addressing monastic communities and the financial requisites for the reception of new members who intended to make religious profession, the decree turns to secular communities, making particular mention of certain aspects of their customs and resources. The king prohibited "widows and unmarried women who commit themselves in secular communities, where, under the authority of the superior, they maintain holding and ownership of their goods, from giving more than 3000 *livres* in dowry, apart from life annuities as indicated." The dowry permitted in secular communities, capped as it was at 3000 *livres* in real property, was more modest than the 6000 or 8000 *livres* allowed to monasteries. The edict of 1693 also required that secular communities thereafter fulfill the same conditions for establishment as religious houses, that is, obtaining royal letters patent in accordance with the edict of December, 1666. It also required that "the formalities that must be observed for the establishment of communities, secular or religious" be promptly executed. The decree clearly echoes the note of concern sounded in previous legislation about properties transferred permanently to communities.

The edict of August, 1749, mentioned above, aimed at limiting the concentration of property held in mortmain, and had little to do with secular communities. It introduced a major shift, however, in explicitly granting free operation to groups of a different type. Although the edict confirmed earlier legislation regarding the establishment of any kind of "body and community whether ecclesiastical, secular, religious, or lay," it added the following exception:

> We do not intend to include in the two preceding articles the particular foundations that neither seek to establish a new body, college, or community, nor attempt to create a new right of benefice, and whose only objectives are . . . the marriages of poor women, charitable schools, relief for prisoners and victims of fire, or other pious works of the same kind and similarly useful to the public. Such foundations need not obtain our letters patent; they need only have their acts or the provisions they contain officially recognized by our *parlements* and superior councils."[27]

The allotment of goods for various charitable works was obviously not seen as a threat to the balance of wealth in the kingdom. Many pious women could undertake such charitable works, even as a group, without needing letters patent, but under two conditions: they could neither establish any "new body (*corps*), college, or community" in order to perform these charitable works, nor could they create "a new right of benefice."

A *corps*, or body, refers to a group of persons formed for their own common good and, simultaneously, for the pursuit of goals that benefit the public interest. For instance, the *corps de ville* refers to the group of officials in the town; the *corps du clergé* refers to members of the clergy as a whole. "Bodies" are moral persons and, as such, they can enter into contracts, possess patrimony, and sue in court. The term *corps* can be applied to any community having its own powers, rights, and privileges. According to the edict of 1749, therefore, men or women could gather together to undertake works for the public good; they could receive funds for such endeavors as long as they made no effort to expand, to accumulate property, or to exert powers belonging to corporate bodies. This type of association could not be called a community, not even a secular community. It needed no letters patent from the king because it did not constitute a body. Legally, it had no recognized juridical existence and could pose no financial or political threat. When compared to religious orders and secular communities, these groups looked like poor relations without money or power. They laid claim only to living a fully Christian life, completely available for service to the neighbor.

THE IMPETUS TOWARD NEW FORMS
OF RELIGIOUS LIFE FOR WOMEN

The Council of Trent had distanced what it considered religious life properly speaking from confraternities, various third orders, and charitable groups. New forms continued to develop, nonetheless, in an impetus to reconcile what the council had presented as irreconcilable—authentic consecrated life and the exercise of charitable and apostolic works. Women belonging either to monastic orders or to voluntary associations provided initiative for this movement. Some, wishing primarily to be religious and officially recognized as such, also desired to open the monastery to active service of the neighbor. Others, already belonging to pious and charitable groups, wanted to live a life fully consecrated to God. The question here is to understand how these two directions appeared, the goal of each, and the way they embodied both consecrated life and the apostolic dimension. The constitutions and other normative texts of a few typical foundations provide examples that illuminate this topic. They also reflect the effects of the Council of Trent and royal legislation, as well as the various levels of concern on the part of each group to conform to them.

In Monasteries: Trends toward Apostolic Service

Whether seeking reform or newly created, women's religious communities in the late sixteenth and early seventeenth centuries had to accept the conditions laid down by the Council of Trent. To preserve the law of enclosure, therefore, any charitable work assumed by women religious had to be done within the house. Church regulation in this matter echoed the mores of the age, which required women to live for the most part inside the house. The education of girls, for example, took place inside the house; whether in the family or in a religious community, it always happened within a type of enclosure. The same cultural norm applied to services given in hospitals. The practice of *enfermement*, of confining the homeless, the poor, and the sick in hospitals to care for them and to help them more effectively to "save their souls," increased throughout the seventeenth century.[28] This meant that hospital personnel also lived in an enclosed environment, though not necessarily a cloister. Given in an enclosure, such works seemed compatible with the juridical forms of life proper to a religious community. It was therefore through activities taking place in the house that monastic life was about to attempt an apostolic aperture on the world—in particular, through the education of girls.

The most famous example of the juncture of enclosure and apostolic openness was the Visitation Order founded by Francis de Sales in 1610, but it did not succeed, or at least not in the way he anticipated. Other orders had better support from ecclesiastical authority, among them, the Company of Mary Our Lady (Compagnie de Marie Notre-Dame), founded at the beginning of the seventeenth century in Bordeaux by Jeanne de Lestonnac. A widow, she first tried monastic life with the Benedictines, but poor health forced her to relinquish it, leading to the creation of a new order, the Company of Mary Our Lady.

The founders of the Daughters of the Company of Mary Our Lady clearly wanted the new congregation to be regarded and confirmed by the pope as a "vrai corps de Religion," a real religious institute.[29] The Constitutions repeatedly express concern that the forms of life be monastic, in compliance with the Council of Trent, particularly in regard to enclosure and solemn vows. The subject of enclosure appears at the very beginning of the Constitutions in article 3, immediately after directives about the goal and purpose of the order: "They shall maintain enclosure with great care . . . from which they may not depart except in cases permitted by law." Enclosure was to be maintained specially as indicated "above, in the formula of the Instutute."[30] This refers to the "The Summary or Form of the Institute," submitted in 1606 to Cardinal François de Sourdis, Archbishop of Bordeaux, and inserted before the text of the Constitutions. The "Summary" stipulated, that in order to observe enclosure properly, and to combine it with

> welcoming the young girls who will attend their school or college . . . they will erect a separate building . . . to receive the extern or outside students . . . and above [that] . . . the rooms . . . [of] girls who will come to live as boarders, who will not have anything in common with the members or the community of the nuns of the said order.[31]

The chapter of the Constitutions entitled "Formulary for Classes or Schools and the Constitutions for the Girls" offered further specifications. Approval of the Holy See would require the nuns "above all to ensure that carrying out this responsibility [education] in no way compromises the enclosure of regular orders so earnestly enjoined by the Council of Trent."[32] The same chapter also spells out precautions to be taken in opening and closing the doors between the street and the classrooms, and between the classrooms and the sisters' house; it describes how to transfer keys from the Sister Portress or domestic *Tourière* to the Mother Prefect or the Directress of Classes, and to the external *Tourière* or Guardian of the classes. Rules pertaining to relations with the outside were essentially the same as those found in greater detail in enclosed monasteries. The spirit of this enclosure suggests a religious life that genuinely sought separation from the world and was, at the same time, attempting and effecting the introduction of a new element into cloistered conventual life through the project of educating girls.

The education of girls as an apostolic activity was so integral to the Company of Mary that it displaced the ordinary monastic practice of chanting Divine Office in choir. The Constitutions are explicit that this modification was necessary in order to allow the time required for the education of girls, because

> this function . . . [is] fundamental to this Institute for the greater glory of God, the public good and the salvation of souls . . . even His Holiness, in consideration of this, abolished . . . without having been asked for it, any obligation to recite the Divine Office or Breviary, whether privately or in public, for the religious of this Company.[33]

The "Summary of the Institute" reaffirms the same view:

> Even though the choir is praiseworthy in itself and appropriate for other women religious . . . this congregation cannot and should not be obliged [to the Divine Office] since this is incompatible with the ordinary, daily instruction of young girls.[34]

Because they could not say the Divine Office, its says, "the sisters will recite the Little Office of the Glorious Virgin Mary Our Lady in private, every day, according to the Council of Trent."[35] They could chant it on Sundays and solemn feasts only if there were enough sisters "to attend to both the classes and the choir."[36]

All sisters, choir or lay, professed "the same vows of poverty, chastity, obedience, and enclosure."[37] These were solemn vows to which the choir sisters added the "special vow to teach or provide for the instruction of young girls."[38] The formula of vows recapitulated the sisters' vocation: "to seek diligently their own salvation and perfection along with that of the neighbor" by means of vows, enclosure, and the Christian education of girls.

The entirety of the Company of Mary's apostolic project began with the core of consecrated life. Its originality lay in the commitment to the education of young girls. That was its outstanding point, what specified it and brought about two important shifts in the monastic life: opening the monastery for classes and suppressing the Divine Office in choir. All the other aspects of an ordinary conventual life were retained. The new Company wanted to have papal approbation, and for this they needed more than their constitutions. Any newly created monastery was obliged to adopt an already existing rule, because the Fourth Lateran Council in 1215 had forbidden the foundation of new orders. Jeanne de Lestonnac and her companions had asked to follow the rule of an approved Institute—the Society of Jesus, whose texts inspired their own Constitutions. Paul V, however, in the brief dated October 7, 1607, left the choice of an order to Cardinal de Sourdis. He chose the Benedictine Rule, and Jeanne de Lestonnac acquiesced.[39]

In Charitable Groups: Trends toward Religious Life

Despite its focus on the reform of existing religious orders, the Council of Trent was well aware of the inclination on the part of certain charitable associations toward forms of life consecrated to God. It had mentioned, if only once, members of third orders and other groups of pious and secular single women, exempting them from its regulations on enclosure. Some of these groups were trying to move closer to strictly religious life, either because they wanted a more complete consecration of their lives to God and the neighbor, or simply in order to benefit from the spiritual and material resources granted to religious communities. One of the more typical forms of such groups were the women drawn together in city hospitals to serve the poor and the sick. Often called "sisters" or "daughters," occasionally, "religious," they sometimes lived together, but without forming a monastic or religious community in the exact sense of the term. The women called Sisters of the Hôtel-Dieu of Lyon exemplify this type of organization.

Charitable women had long come to the Hôtel-Dieu of Lyon to care for the sick. In 1502, for example, twenty prostitutes were converted during a Lenten mission. The bishop authorized them to work for the poor at the Hôtel-Dieu in a semi-cloistered life that would remove them from the dangers of the streets. During a severe famine in 1531, prominent citizens formed an organization of women, "la Police de l'Aulmosne de Lyon," to assist the poor, who were very numerous that year. A book about this organization published in 1539 reveals the same group of women caring for the poor at the Hôtel-Dieu:

> . . . to serve the sick poor at the said Hôtel-Dieu, there are eighteen or twenty [women] religious, penitents as well as others, who have entered there for the honor of God and to serve the poor. . . . And when they have given dinner and supper to the said poor, they retire to the chapel where they say grace, and all the said poor give thanks to God as well, and pray for the benefactors of the said Hôtel-Dieu. And for their wages and reward they have the grace of God and will have paradise at the end.[40]

In the eyes of the author, these women were religious—pious women who lived together under the authority of a superior, "who is called the Mother." Supported by the Hôtel-Dieu, they performed all the duties of piety and Christian charity, prayed together, and sought no remuneration other than the grace of God and paradise at the end of their days.

In 1589, the archbishop's vicar-general attempted to attach these women to a religious order, provoking strong opposition from the rectors of the Hôtel-Dieu and the city council. They thought, in order to care for the poor, that it was "more expedient to have women free from monastic rules than religious continuously at prayer and contemplation."[41] It was therefore better if these women were not nuns. As the years passed, however, struggles continued between the ecclesiastical authorities and the rectors over the status of these sisters. A deliberation recorded in the register of the Hôtel-Dieu on April 19, 1598, reveals the different aspects of the dispute. The point was

> to ascertain whether these women, who are received at the Hôtel-Dieu to care for the sick poor, are considered as professed nuns or as servants, and if, when they . . . are admitted to wear the habit . . . they make any vow and religious profession before any ecclesiastical religious superior or another who has authority in this regard.[42]

The rectors of the Hôtel-Dieu had the register searched and "discovered that the said women assigned to the care of the sick poor at the said Hôtel-Dieu . . . are received . . . as ordinary domestics to serve the said sick poor."[43] They were received in the church of the Hôtel-Dieu by the rectors, who explained their duties and obligations. During a high Mass the women took an oath to fulfill them and were then "received and vested in a long linen dress and a veil of white cloth, without further ceremony, and without making profession of any rule in the hands of any cleric or superior other than before the said rectors who hold the entire governance and administration of the affairs of the said Hôtel-Dieu."[44]

The rectors may have wanted to clarify the secular status of the women at the Hôtel-Dieu of Lyon in 1598 to deflect interference from the archbishop. Whatever the reason, from the beginning until the middle of the seventeenth century, the rectors no longer employed religious, but rather simple servants or chambermaids. In 1664, however, lifetime commitments and formulas of reception again turn up in registers of the proceedings of the *bureau*.[45] Numerous candidates appeared at that time, offering to dedicate themselves for life to service of the sick poor. On August 21, 1667, seven servants of the Hôtel-Dieu asked the rectors to receive them. Rules were then prepared, "stable

and certain for the reception and establishment of *filles* of this station, [dated]
On Sunday, the first day of January, sixteen hundred sixty-eight after noon."
The rectors admitted those whom they judged "the most capable" and suited
to the needs of the Hôtel-Dieu. If the women provided satisfactory service,
they could

> be given the gray habit with the small cincture. Afterwards their zeal and health
> will be further tested for one whole year before giving them the final sign of
> their reception and secure establishment as sisters of the house, which will be a
> small silver cross imprinted with the image of Our Lady of Mercy. . . . And be-
> cause, in all these proceedings, there is no vow, but a simple promise which con-
> tains no absolute commitment on either part, should it come to pass for what-
> ever reason that the administration chooses to dismiss the said sisters thus
> received and established in the house, it will be obliged to compensate them on
> the basis of their time of service and of the wages ordinarily paid to other ser-
> vants.[46]

Despite lifelong service to the poor and a special form of dress, the women at
the Hôtel-Dieu of Lyon in 1668 were no more true religious than their predecessors.

From the beginning of the sixteenth century until 1668, the goal of the sisters of the "Grand Hôtel-Dieu" seems to have varied somewhat. In 1539, they
lived there "for the honor of God and to serve the poor." They were "fed and
clothed at the expense of the said Hotel-Dieu . . . and for their wages and reward they have the grace of God and will have paradise at the end."[47] The rectors' deliberation on April 15, 1598, has a slightly different resonance:
"moved by devotion and charity toward the poor . . . [these women] decide to
leave the world and to withdraw for their whole life in the service of the
poor."[48] It is no longer said that they are there "for the honor of God." The
rectors' words may not have reflected the desire of the sisters, however, since
they gave this particular definition only to clarify "whether these women,
who are received at the Hôtel-Dieu to care for the sick poor" should be considered as religious or simply as servants. This question raised by the rectors,
as well as the intrusion by the archbishop's vicar general in 1589, echoes the
unmistakable repercussions of the Tridentine decrees: no religious life outside
the cloister and without solemn vows.

After a hiatus, in the middle of the seventeenth century some girls and
women again presented themselves to the rectors asking to be accepted
"among the number of those who are entirely dedicated to the service of the
sick poor . . . [with] the design of spending the rest of their days there . . .
[without] any salary or other recompense that that which they hope to receive
from God in heaven."[49] The rule of 1668 written as a result of this request in-

dicates their status of servants of the poor, but is careful to add, just as in 1598, "in all these proceedings, there is no vow . . . no absolute commitment on either part." These women could therefore leave if they wished, or the *bureau* could dismiss them, paying them for the time of their service. They were not nuns.

In the course of the eighteenth century, however, the women concerned definitely moved in the direction of religious consecration. In the "Formulary for the Reception of the Habit" of 1762, a woman expresses her desire, "to give myself to Jesus Christ in the service of the poor."[50] Although the commitment included no vows, the women began to promise to live a life of poverty, chastity, and obedience, making it explicit that the following of Jesus Christ was their primary choice, to be lived in service to the poor.[51] This tendency toward a religious commitment offered the advantage of increased stability on the part of the sisters, without constituting religious life in the juridical sense of the term. Their commitment was only a private promise and thus did not violate the Council of Trent. Neither was it contrary to royal legislation since these women at the Hôtel-Dieu had their subsistence assured and had not formed a community, either religious or secular. In this arrangement, everybody had something to gain—the rectors, the sisters, and the poor.

The Emergence of New Groups

Despite all the prohibitions and problems encountered, new religious groups were emerging almost everywhere in France. Through all their diversity, the guiding impulse in each of these new communities is discernable. They gave priority either to the following of Christ in a life consecrated to God or to a life dedicated to charitable and apostolic pursuits. Rather than famous examples of this new movement, such as the Daughters of Charity of St. Vincent de Paul, this study focuses on two lesser-known groups: the Sisters of St. Charles of Le Puy, founded around 1624 by Just de Serres, Bishop of Le Puy, and the Filles du Travail, or de l'Union, of Rodez, established in the Rouergue during the second half of the seventeenth century.

The goal of the Sisters of St. Charles of Le Puy, as expressed in their earliest constitutive texts, *The Rules for the Company of Virgins and Chaste Widows*, was primarily a gift of self to God.[52] Inspired by the Ursuline Rule, they wanted "to live a holy and chaste life in the world," through consecration to God in "holy virginity and chastity," accompanied by "the continual exercise of the works of charity toward all."[53] Their principal goal appears as a desire to live the life of authentic religious, although without the external forms that distinguished it in that era. Their Constitutions, the Bull of Gregory XIII approving the Ursulines in 1582, and the prologue written by Just de Serres all state clearly that neither the Ursulines nor the Sisters of St. Charles were religious in the monastic sense of the term. This point would have been clear enough to their contemporaries of the sixteenth or seventeenth centuries because they wore no religious habit, lived in the homes of their families or masters, did not recite the Office in choir, and did not profess solemn vows. Because these new "Companies" affirmed unmistakably that they did not belong to the monastic way of life, they and their rules were able to gain the approval of two popes, allowing them all the material and spiritual advantages pertaining to religious orders. For example, when they entered this new form of consecrated life, the sisters could acquire and transfer to the Company "all legacies [and] donations" just as if they had "taken the religious habit, made profession, or contracted marriage."[54] They also participated in all spiritual privileges "as if they were members and sisters of religious orders." In the mind of Just de Serres, these women were not religious in the canonical sense of the term. For the Sisters of St. Charles as for the Ursulines, however, their commitment was first and foremost consecration to God and to the following of Christ—the fundamental goal of religious life. Living this consecration in "the continual exercise of the works of charity,"[55] they represent the first type of new communities mentioned above.

The other movement, in which apostolic and charitable service to the neighbor predominates, is epitomized by the Filles du Travail, or de l'Union, at Rodez. During the second half of the seventeenth century, a number of secular communities took shape in the Rodez diocese under the titles of Filles du Travail, Filles de l'Union, Filles du Travail Manuel, or Filles Régentes. Whatever their similarities or their differences, rules from the various houses of these communities have one point in common: the definition of the group always begins with the precise apostolic objective that brought them together, whether the Christian formation of *nouvelles converties*, educating girls, giving spiritual help to women, or forming a community of Christian women that might influence the neighborhood.[56]

The raison d'être of the Filles du Travail and others was first and foremost the apostolic and charitable works they wished to accomplish in their milieu, not religious consecration, since they had none. Their commitment consisted in sharing everything in common, even their clothing, without making any vow or promise of poverty. In the three manuscripts of the rules for the Filles du Travail examined, there is no reference to chastity, apart from a few recommendations relating to good manners, modesty, and prudence when going out, and to kindness and gentleness within the house. These women made neither promise nor vow of obedience, but "tried to practice it as promptly and as cordially as if it had been vowed."[57] The customary triad of poverty, chastity, and obedience expressing commitment as religious never appears in the Rules of the Filles du Travail or de l'Union. At the time of her reception, each sister promised "to live together as the early Christians lived, having but one heart and one soul, to keep the rule given by his Excellency the Bishop and Count of Rodez, and to care for the young girls of the parish."[58]

Enclosure was no more a consideration for these groups than the vows. A single line in the rule stipulates that a sister should never go out without a companion or without permission.[59] Lacking vows and enclosure, the sisters knew very well that theirs was not a religious community, and that the decrees of the Council of Trent did not apply to them. They saw themselves in the tradition of the Daughters of Charity, given over completely to multiple services of the neighbor, with no pretense to religious life as it existed at that time. In deference to the requirements of royal legislation, the sisters were under the authority of the bishop, who vouched for their particular vocation.

Most of the groups initiating new forms of consecrated life for women had some difficulty in defining themselves, or at least in situating themselves clearly. This was very much the case for the Ursulines. In 1535, in Brescia, Italy, Angela Merici founded a "company of virgins" consecrated to God, living without enclosure and evangelizing their own milieu, without any special dress or communal life. For practical reasons involving mutual support and apostolic work, several of these women regrouped into communities that were officially authorized after the Council of Trent for the dioceses of northern Italy by St. Charles Borromeo. Following the arrival of their Rule in France at the end of the sixteenth century, local pressures gradually forced the Ursulines into a more traditional mold. The house in Paris was converted into a monastery with enclosure and solemn vows, and Paul V recognized it as such on June 13, 1612. Although several houses mounted long-term resistance to this monastic transformation, by the mid-seventeenth century all the Ursulines in France had become cloistered.[60]

At the same time, Anne de Xaintonge established her first house of Ursulines in 1606 in Dôle, a town of Franche-Comté, then ruled by Spain. With the help of Jesuit Father Stéphane Guyon, she adapted the rule of the Ursulines of Ferrara, published in Tournon in 1597, to form a congregation living consecrated apostolic life in the world. She wanted to form her Company of St. Ursula on the model of the Society of Jesus and stoutly refused enclosure in order to be able to attend to girls and poor women in their own environment. She kept the name "Company of St. Ursula" and the reference to the Ursuline Rule, approved by Gregory XIII and Sixtus V, because this connection facilitated the new foundation. Her spirituality, however, remained fundamentally Ignatian.[61]

Neither the Ursulines nor the ecclesiastical or administrative authorities of the time always had a clear understanding about precisely how to connect the two elements of a life consecrated to God and to apostolic activity. In the rule she composed at Tulle in 1623, Mother Micolon, founder of several Ursuline houses in the Massif Central, indicated "that the principal aim and primary goal of this Institute is to instruct girls in Christian doctrine and good morals."[62] Yet the course of action described in her manuscript, through the trial and error of successive foundations, reveals very clearly that her primary concern was the search for an authentic life of consecration to God. Nevertheless, this consecration does not appear as a priority in the text defining their vocation. This ambiguity reveals not only the difficulty of that era in assigning apostolic activities an integral place within consecrated life; it also affirms the necessity, in order to understand the living reality of a particular vocation, of considering how the concrete facts of a life correspond with the normative sources.

This brief glance at several new forms of apostolic consecrated life for women in the seventeenth century gives a sense of the spiritual dynamic of each, as well as the wide variety of ways by which they reckoned with the prescriptions of the Council of Trent and with royal legislation. In order to exist as an officially recognized religious institute, certain foundations such as the Company of Mary Our Lady explicitly conformed to this legislation, simultaneously requesting some modifications of enclosure or the form of prayer in order to allow apostolic works. Others, like the Daughters of Charity or the Filles du Travail and Filles de l'Union, made no claim of living a religious life. The decrees of the Council of Trent had nothing to do with them, and they could, as did monastic orders, benefit from royal recognition. They could also choose the modes of life suitable to them, without worrying about enclosure or solemn vows. Finally, other groups, such as the Company of St. Ursula founded by Anne de Xaintonge, aspired to live a genuine religious consecration with simple and therefore private vows, but without obligation of enclosure in light of their apostolic works. In certain cases, such as the Sisters of St. Charles of Le Puy, the members made vows but did not live under the same roof. By contrast, the Filles du Travail and de l'Union, who did live in common in the same house, had, strictly speaking, no religious commitment.

The diversity in forms of life and types of personal commitment that emerged in the new groups confounded all the traditional classifications, making it difficult to position the mutual correlation of consecrated life and apostolic works accurately. It is not surprising that most of the men and women engaged in this evolution, even while living some aspects of it, were not always able to specify its central core and its periphery. Canon law did not recognize consecrated apostolic life theoretically until the beginning of the twentieth century, even though it had existed in reality for more than three hundred years.[63]

Amid this diversity, and coming after so many new and illustrious congregations, what is the unique place of Father Médaille's "Little Congregation of the Sisters of St. Joseph"? The examples given above demonstrate that constitutive texts were inadequate in themselves to communicate the reality of life in any of the new foundations. To gain a clear understanding of the vocation of the Sisters of St. Joseph and the various forms it took would require bringing the texts and the actual history face to face. Thorough research into all aspects of that history exceeded the time constraints for this work; it was necessary to focus more narrowly. For that reason, it was equally important, and in this case more urgent, to grasp the concrete forms of the life lived by the Sisters of St. Joseph in order to understand its significance and scope.

NOTES

1. *Clausurae monialium,* in *Concilium Tridentinum, Diariorum, Actorum, Epistolarum, Tractatuum, nova collectio,* 13 vols. (Freiburg: B. Herder, 1901-1938), 9:1080. English translation from J. Waterworth, ed. and trans., *The Canons and Decrees of the Sacred and Oecumenical Council of Trent* (Hanover Historical Texts), The Twenty-Fifth Session: On regulars and nuns, 232-53, http://history.hanover.edu/texts/trent/ct25.html.

2. *Concilium Tridentinum,* 9:1083 and 1084; and Waterworth, 247-49.

3. Bull *Considerante,* March 14, 1509, in Joseph Creusen, SJ, "Les Instituts religieux à vœux simples," *Revue des communautés religieuses* (May, 1940): 57.

4. *Magnum Bullarium Romanum,* vol. 2, *A Pio IV Ad Innocentium IX (1560-1591)* (Luxembourg, H. A. Gosse & Soc., 1742), 196, §1-3.

5. Ibid., 2:196, § 2-3.

6. Ibid., 2:197, § 8.

7. Teresa Ledóchowska, *Angèle Merici et la Compagnie de Saint-Ursule,* 2 vols. (Rome: Ancora, 1969), 2:140 and 408. Just de Serres, bishop of Le Puy, would invoke this same Bull of Gregory XIII to authorize the establishment of the Sisters of St. Charles and the rules which he gave them in 1632 (Archives des Sœurs de Saint-Charles, Le Puy).

8. Robert Lemoine, OSB, *Le Monde des Religieux,* vol. 2 of *L'Époque moderne 1563-1789* (Paris: Éditions Cujas, 1976), 6-7.

9. Léopold Willaert, *Après le Concile de Trente: La Restauration catholique, 1563-1648,* vol. 18 of *Histoire de l'Église, depuis les origines jusqu'à nos jours,* ed. Augustin Fliche and Victor Martin (Paris: Bloud et Gay, 1960), 146.

10. This review of the most important aspects of the reception of the Council of Trent in France is taken principally from Victor Martin, *Le Gallicanisme et la Réforme catholique: Essai historique sur l'introduction en France des décrets du concile de Trente 1563-1615* (Paris: A. Picard, 1919); and Léopold Willaert, *Après le Concile de Trente*; and *Les Mémoires du Clergé de France,* 1716-1750, 12 vol.

11. Pierre Toussaint Durand de Maillane, *Dictionnaire de Droit canonique et de pratique bénéficiale*, 4 vols. (Lyon: Benoît Duplain, 1770), 2:429. [Durand de Maillane was later an important redactor of the Civil Constitution of the Clergy. –Trans.]

12. Ibid., 4:330.

13. Ibid., 4:329.

14. Guy du Rousseaud de La Combe, *Recueil de Jurisprudence canonique et bénéficiale*, Nouvelle édition revue et corrigé et augmentée, Paris, chez Despilly, 1771, 300-301; Rousseaud refers to *Anciens Mémoires du Clergé*, 1:944.

15. "Déclaration de Louis XIII le 21 novembre 1629," in François André Isambert, Athanase Jourdan, Decrusy, et al., *Recueil général des anciennes lois françaises, depuis l'an 420 jusqu'à la révolution de 1789,* 29 vols. (Paris: Belin-Le-Prieur, 1822-1833), 16:347.

16. Ibid., 17:369.

17. Ibid., 18:94.

18. Ibid., 17:369.

19. Robert Mandrou, *La France aux XVIIe et XVIIIe siècles* (Paris: Presses Universitaires de France, 1970), 164.

20. Isambert et al., 18:94.

21. Ibid., 20:127 and 177.

22. Rousseaud de La Combe, 269-70.

23. Antoine Furtière, *Le Dictionnaire Universel*, 3 vols. Rotterdam, Chez A. et R. Leers, 1690, s.v. "communauté."

24. *Recueil des Actes, Titres et Mémoires concernant les Affaires du Clergé de France*, vol. 4, *Des ministres de l'Église qui sont réguliers*, À Paris, Chez Guillaume Deprez, 1768, 1071.

25. Rousseaud de La Combe, 127.

26. Ibid., 180-82.

27. Ibid., 270, art. 3.

28. Jean Pierre Gutton, "L'enfermement à l'age classique," in *Histoire des Hôpitaux en France*, ed. Jean Imbert (Toulouse: Privat, 1982), 164; see entire chapter, 161-93.

29. ACMND, "Abrégé ou forme de l'Institut des filles Religieuses de la glorieuse Vierge Marie Notre-Dame . . . le 7è jour du mois de mars 1606," art. 4, § 1.

30. ACMND, *Constitutions et Règles de l'Ordre des Religieuses de Notre-Dame*, Bordeaux, 1638, art. 3, "La Clôture," 46.

31. ACMND, "Abrégé ou forme de l'Institut," art. 9

32. ACMND "Formule des Classes ou Ecoles et Constitutions des filles," 351 ff.

33. ACMND, *Constitutions et Règles de l'Ordre des Religieuses de Notre-Dame*, 350.

34. ACMND, "Abrégé ou forme de l'Institut," art. 8.

35. Ibid.

36. ACMND, *Constitutions et Règles*, 48, art. 4.

37. ACMND, "Abrégé ou forme de l'Institut," art. 11.

38. ACMND, "Abrégé ou forme de l'Institut," art. 6.

39. ACMND, *Constitutions et Règles*, Receuil de titres et documents, 25 and 33.

40. *La Police de l'Aulmosne de Lyon*, Chez Sébastian Gryphe, 1539, cited in Auguste Croze, *Les sœurs hospitalières des Hospices Civils de Lyon* (Lyon, 1933), 23.

41. AM Lyon, BB 124, Registre, fol. 273.

42. AHD Lyon, Délibération du 19 avril 1598.

43. Ibid.

44. Ibid.

45. AHC Lyon, E H-D 44, "Mandats 1664-1667."

46. Ibid., 57 ff.

47. *La Police de l'Aulmosne de Lyon.*

48. Ibid.

49. AHC Lyon, E H-D 45, "Mandats 1667-1761," 57 ff.

50. *Formulaire pour la Prise d'habit des nouveaux Frères et Sœurs, dans l'Église du Grand Hôtel-Dieu de la ville de Lyon, par M. Prin, prêtre, œconome*, À Lyon, mille-sept-cent-soixante-deux, 15.

51. Ibid., 39.

52. Archives Sœurs de Saint-Charles, le Puy, *Règles de la Compagnie des Vierges et Chastes Veuves, instituées par l'illustrissime cardinal Charles Borromée . . . Traduites et accommodées de l'autorité du reverendissime Just de Serres, évêque du Puy*, Lyon, chez François La Bottière, 1632.

53. Sœurs de Saint-Charles, *Nos Textes Fondateurs, Règles de la Compagnie des Vierges et Chastes Veuves* (Le Puy, 1984), 56.

54. Bulle de Grégoire XIII in Sœurs de Saint-Charles, *Nos Textes Fondateurs*, 48.

55. Sœurs de Saint-Charles, *Nos Textes Fondateurs*, 70.

56. Archives Sœurs de Saint-François de Sales, dîtes de l'Union, Rodez. In 1841 this congregation amalgamated twenty-one communities of Sœurs du Travail established in the Rouergue. References are chiefly to *Règlements* from the houses of Pomayrols, Rodez and Chirac.

57. AD Aveyron, "Règlement pour les filles Régentes de Saint Geniez," art. 10, in *Semaine Religieuse de Rodez* (1974).

58. Archives des Filles du Travail Manuel de Lunet, près Saint-Chély d'Aubrac (Aveyron), Registre des réceptions, 20 juin 1730, 1.

59. Archives Sœurs de Saint-François de Sales, MS Règlement de Pomayrols, no. 32.

60. See Marie de Chantal Gueudré, OSU, *Histoire de l'ordre des Ursulines en France*, 3 vols. (Paris: Éditions Saint-Paul, 1958-1963). —Trans.

61. See Marie-Amélie le Bourgeois, *Les Ursulines d'Anne de Xainctonge (1606): Contribution à l'histoire des communautés féminines sans clôture* (Saint-Étienne: Publications de l'Université de Saint-Etienne, 2004). –Trans.

62. *Mémoires de la Mère Micolon 1592-1659: Recueil de la vie de la mère Antoinette Micolon, dite sœur Colombe du Saint Esprit*, Cahier Henri Pourrat hors série (Clermont-Ferrand: La Française d'Édition et d'Imprimerie, 1982), 102. This publication is an edition of a manuscript of the Ursulines of Clermont.

63. Leo XIII, Apostolic Constitution "Conditae a Christo Ecclesiae," December 8, 1900, *Acta Leonis XIII*, 20:317-327. [English trans. in *The States of Perfection*, selected and arranged by the Benedictine Monks of Solesmes, trans. E. O'Gorman (Boston: St. Paul Editions, 1967), 164-165. —Trans.]

Part One

THE GENESIS
OF THE LITTLE DESIGN

Introduction to Part One: Le Puy-en-Velay in the Seventeenth Century

During the first half of the seventeenth century, the period that gave birth to the Sisters of St. Joseph, the Wars of Religion continued to ravage the region of Velay. The city of Le Puy, the provincial capital, was assailed first by Huguenots from Vivarais and Gévaudan, then torn apart by conflicts between Royalists and Leaguers, both Catholic. The city of Le Puy backed the anti-Royalist League, and the rest of the diocese sided almost entirely with the Royalists.[1] Families of the nobility slaughtered one another in war, and the ordinary people, already overburdened by taxes, endured the plundering and violence of marauding soldiers and other groups who devastated the countryside. Intermittent epidemics, particularly the plague, added to this suffering and were a source of constant terror.

Le Puy, nevertheless, maintained the fullness of its prestige throughout Christendom because of its black Virgin and its cathedral, a famous place of pilgrimage on the road to Compostela. Antoine Jacmon, citizen of Le Puy, praised the city in his memoirs: "Of the ninety-five French bishoprics, that of Le Puy is the first in dignity, if not in wealth, and is subject to no other but directly to the Holy Father, the pope, ranking [in ceremonies] immediately after the cardinals."[2] The title of "immediate suffragan of his holiness" appears in official documents of Henry de Maupas and Armand de Béthune, bishops of Le Puy who initially authorized the Sisters of St. Joseph. The city enjoyed another privilege granted by the popes, that of a special jubilee when March 25, the feast of the Annunciation, fell on Good Friday. This celebration attracted very large crowds as well as distinguished visitors. The year 1644, when Bishop de Maupas came to Le Puy, was a Jubilee Year. In addition to these ecclesiastical honors, which, although eminent, lacked financial counterpart, the bishops of Le Puy held other titles that were more materially rewarding. Their titles as "bishop and Lord of Le Puy, Count of Velay," always carried a personal benefice. Henry de Maupas was also the commendatory abbot of Saint-Denys de Rheims, and Armand de Béthune, his successor, that of Notre Dame de la Vernuse. Beyond his spiritual authority, the bishop of Le Puy therefore had administrative responsibilities in regard to the city and the province. He presided over the Estates of Velay. As the owner of large properties, he played an important juridical role, exercising rights of government and supervision over almost every establishment of charity and public assistance. The bishops of Le Puy always gave the impression of very *grands seigneurs*. The various duties of the church within Le Puy were reserved mostly to families of the bourgeoisie, more than likely because these families were active in the city. As a result, financial interests could be advantageous in bolstering those of the spiritual life.[3]

The city administration, partially controlled by the bishop as Lord of Le Puy, was carried out by the consuls. Elected by the citizens of Le Puy, consuls were often selected from the same families—families of merchants and lawyers who had gradually become holders of lands, titles, and annuities. These families constituted a kind of consular caste to the extent that, in order to become a consul, one almost needed to have been one, or at least to belong to a consular family. The Eyraud family is frequently mentioned among this consular circle.[4] Consuls were responsible for all matters concerning the order, poor relief, and general organization of the city for the good of all its inhabitants. They provided for the regulation of trade and were in charge of matters having to do with social assistance and education. Their charitable and educational functions at times put them in a position of either support or opposition to the cathedral canons or the bishop, particularly regarding the hospitals in Le Puy. Such tensions are evident in some deliberations of the governing body of the consular house. Among other things, consuls and administrator-canons argued over the "nomination of the citizens who are entitled to be part of the *bureau* of the hospital and deliberate over its affairs."[5]

The large number of monasteries and other religious houses in Le Puy attested to the church's influence.[6] The oldest were men's houses: Dominicans, present since 1221; Franciscans, established in 1223; and Carmelites, in 1286. The Poor Clares arrived in 1430. After the influx of mendicant orders established in the thirteenth century, another wave of new foundations surged toward the end of the sixteenth. The Jesuits opened their college in 1588. The Dominican Nuns of St. Catherine of Siena established their monastery in 1605, and the Capuchins founded theirs in 1609. The Ursulines came to Le Puy in 1610. Some members of that community later joined the sisters of the Company of Mary Our Lady, daughters of Jeanne de Lestonnac, established in Le Puy in 1618. Just de Serres, Bishop of Le Puy, gave constitutions to the Sisters of Saint Charles in his diocese in 1624. A Visitation monastery was founded in 1630 from Lyon. Such a large number of convents in the one city of Le Puy may have contributed to the honor of Christianity. Most often, it was a source of anxiety for the consuls, who had to ensure the survival of these convents when they lacked the means of support. Fortunately for the townspeople, all of these monasteries were not in need of money all of the time. Among the foundations of the second wave, those with an apostolic purpose made a point of providing themselves with the means for their services. Among the latter were Sisters of St. Joseph.

NOTES

1. Étienne Delcambre, *Une institution municipale languedocienne: Le consulat du Puy-en-Velay des origines à 1610* (Le Puy: Imprimerie de la Haute Loire, 1933), 206.

2. Antoine Jacmon, *Mémoires d'Antoine Jacmon, Bourgeois du Puy, XVIe-XVIIe s* (Le Puy: Augustin Chassaing, 1885), 187.

3. Bernard Rivet, "Une ville au XVIe siècle: Le Puy-en-Velay," *Les cahiers de la Haute-Loire* (1988): 177 ff.

4. Rivet, 267 and 291.

5. AM Le Puy, BB2, Livre des Conseils de la maison consulaire de la ville du Puy, 1er décembre 1639 au 8 octobre 1652, registre 267, fols. 136-137.

6. Andre Chanal, "Vieilles églises et vieux couvents," chap. 11 in *Le Puy, Ville Sainte et Ville d'art* (Le Puy / Paris: Xavier Mappus, 1953), 133-44.

Chapter One

The Founders

The first known house of Sisters of St. Joseph was established by Father Médaille at Dunières, a village about thirty miles northeast of Le Puy, on September 29, 1649. The Le Puy house was not founded officially until the following year. Le Puy, nevertheless, was the one recognized by Bishop Henry
de Maupas and considered by communities subsequently established as the
foundation house. The Le Puy community therefore takes first place in this
history. Although the sources relative to the beginnings are limited, it is possible at least to determine who the first Sisters of St. Joseph were and how
they came to found a new religious congregation.

THE FIRST SISTERS OF ST. JOSEPH
AND THEIR COLLABORATORS

The preface to the first printed constitutions, published in Vienne in 1694, is
fundamentally a summary of the historical origins. Although relatively late, it
is the point of departure for any study of the history of the Sisters of St.
Joseph, providing the only comprehensive account of how they came together. In language stripped of detail it presents a summary of the origins:

> Father Jean-Pierre Médaille, Great missionary of the Society of Jesus . . . met in
> the course of his missions several pious widows and single women who, not
> wanting to marry, planned to leave the world to devote themselves to the service
> of God and to their salvation, but could not enter the monasteries for lack of suf-
> ficient means; this good Father decided to propose to some bishop the estab-
> lishment of a congregation that these devout widows and single women could
> enter, to work for their salvation and to devote themselves to all the exercises of
> which they were capable for the service of the neighbor.[1]

This passage indicates that Father Médaille's project, which he often called the "little design," originated first in the desire of the women he encountered. It was because these women spoke to him about their desire to consecrate themselves to God that he, in response, proposed to establish a congregation corresponding to their request. It was the same for Anne Deschaux at Dunières. She is described as "the first and most intent on taking the habit among the daughters of the Congregation of St. Joseph," as well as being called upon by Father Médaille for this foundation.[2] About the "pious widows and single women" of the house in Le Puy whom Father Médaille met during his missionary travels, the preface to the Vienne Constitutions offers no further information, neither number nor names. Only a contract of association dated December 13, 1651, enabling the sisters to establish a community of goods and habitation, furnishes their names and origins. They were six:

Françoise Eyraud, native of the place of Saint-Privat, diocese of Le Puy;
Clauda Chastel, widow of the late Guilhaume Mazaudier of the city of Langogne, diocese of Mende;
Marguerite Burdier, native of Saint Julien-en-Forez [diocese of Vienne];
Anna Chaleyer, from the place of Saint-Genest-Malifaux, diocese of Lyon;
Anna Vey, from Saint-Jeure [de Bonas, diocese of Le Puy];
Anna Brun, from Saint-Victor [Malescours], diocese of Le Puy.[3]

Father Médaille learned about the desire of the first sisters while he was stationed at the College of Saint-Flour in the Haute-Auvergne. None of these six, however, came from that region. By contrast, the last four listed in the contract were from the area located along the borders of the Le Puy and Lyon dioceses, in the regions of the Velay and Forez. There is undoubtedly some significance to their common geographic origin, but it is not clear precisely what. In addition to understanding their geographic roots, some information about the family origins of the first sisters helps to give them substance.

Françoise Eyraud and Her Family

Françoise Eyraud was born at Varennes, in the commune of Saint-Privat in the diocese of Le Puy, the daughter of Pierre Eyraud and Izabeau Besqueut.[4] The record of her death, found in the parish register of the church of Saint-Georges-du-Puy, provides an approximate date of birth. The entry reads: On May 23, 1683, "Sister Françoise Heyraud [*sic*], superior of the house of St. Joseph of Le Puy, deceased the previous day at the said house of Saint Joseph at the rue de monferrant [*sic*] at the age of about seventy-two years . . . was buried inside the church."[5] That implies that Françoise was born in

1611. She was probably the fourth of five children: Delphine, born January 23, 1605; Anne, born January 20, 1607; and Catherine, born January 2, 1611. She also had a brother, André, whose date of birth is not mentioned in the parish registers.[6]

The Eyraud family enjoyed a certain prestige. Very old and widespread throughout the region of Saint-Privat d'Allier near Le Puy, they had a long history with the Hôtel-Dieu, whose records often mention dealings with various branches and generations of the Eyrauds.[7] For example, there is a reference to Pierre Eyraud, *curé* and prior of Chaspuzac and former administrator of the Hôtel-Dieu. On September 22, 1641, he completed a transaction with the Hôtel-Dieu, "by which each party renounces any debt to the other incurred during the period when the said Pierre was administrator of the Hôtel-Dieu."[8] He may have been an uncle or great uncle of Françoise, although the precise relationship is difficult to identify.

The most famous member of the Eyraud family in the seventeenth century was Barthélemy Eyraud (1620–1690), Lord of Chaumarès and secretary to Queen Anne of Austria from 1646 until her death in 1666.[9] He most likely studied with the Jesuits of Le Puy, as he wrote a first will in their favor in 1642. Later, in a will dated October 2, 1682, since he had no children, he designated the Jesuits of Le Puy as his universal heirs on condition that each year in perpetuity they would preach a mission in one of the parishes of the Le Puy diocese. There must have been a falling-out between them, or perhaps the Jesuits failed to honor the proviso in his will, because on January 27, 1690, two days before he died, Barthélemy prepared a new will that made no mention of the Society of Jesus. Instead, he left legacies to convents in Le Puy: the Franciscans, Carmelites, Capuchins, and Poor Clares; to his niece Marie Eyraud; to the *curé* of Le Vernet, the parish closest to his property of Le Poux, where he wished to be buried; and to his servants and maids. To his wife he bequeathed "all the furniture of his house in the rue Pannessac and that in the Pavillon du Poux, the ownership of this apartment, and, beyond the *augment* that appears in the marriage contract, three thousand *livres* and a significant amount of grain." Finally, he named as his universal heirs "the poor who are perpetually present at the Hôpital Général and at the Hôtel-Dieu Notre-Dame of the city of Le Puy," leaving them his immense fortune.[10]

Among the heirs of Barthélemy Eyraud, particularly the convents and hospitals in Le Puy, the Hôpital des Orphelines of Montferrand is conspicuously absent. Barthélemy was well aware of its existence because Françoise, his relative, had written to him on January 28, 1673, asking his help in collecting an annual income in favor of the poor girls in Montferrand: "Even though I have not had the honor of your acquaintance, I take the liberty . . . of offering you the opportunity to extend your charity." She continued, "I do not ask you as a relative, but only want to ask this charity for the love of Jesus Christ and on behalf of a number of poor girls who live here and who are in need."[11] There is record neither of Barthélemy's answer nor of any action he took in favor of the Montferrand orphans. Exactly how Barthélemy was related to Françoise is unclear. He may have been her nephew, as Canon Bois suggests, since Barthélemy's father and grandfather—like Francoise's father and brother—were named Pierre.[12] Pierre, however, was a name passed through generations in the Eyraud families, so Françoise may also have belonged to a different line, the Eyrauds of Vergezac, a younger branch of the Eyrauds of Le Poux, not quite four miles northeast of Saint-Privat d'Allier.[13] Although not so prosperous as their immensely rich relatives, they enjoyed substantial material wealth.

Apart from Barthélemy, Lord of Chaumarès, whose social standing was far above the others, the family of Françoise Eyraud included persons of substance who exercised functions recognized in the city: "notary of Vergezac . . . lawyer of Saint-Privat . . . procurator[s] of Le Vernet . . . *curé* of Chaspuzac . . . merchant of Le Puy."[14] It was therefore a family influential both in number and in services rendered. It was also a prosperous family, where people knew how to organize and manage their assets. It was a family, furthermore, that handed down a tradition of involvement in charitable and social works. This is most evident in the connection of various members with the Hôtel-Dieu of Le Puy. While Françoise was at Montferrand, another Pierre Eyraud was named "forester of the Hôtel -Dieu" on September 13, 1657. According to records of the Hôtel-Dieu, this position offered "annual wages of twenty-four cartons of rye and twelve silver *livres* per year, and the said Eyraud will live in the house of the said poor which they have in Ramourouscle."[15] Although one could earn a living from these duties, they required sacrifice, and the person in charge of providing such service needed to be able to discern the human capacities and Christian values of those he hired. Although we know nothing about the personality of Françoise or her life before she came to the rue Montferrand, this glance at the Eyraud family and its links to the poor helps to explain why, in 1645 or 1646, at approximately thirty-five years of age, she became the head of the orphanage, then in the midst of complete reorganization.

Clauda Chastel

Clauda Chastel, whose name appears second on the contract of association, was the "widow of the late Guilhaume Mazaudier of the city of Langogne, in the diocese of Mende." Born in Langogne on April 20, 1612, she may have belonged to the well-known families of the Chastel de Congres or of the Chastel de Servières.[16] A notarized account dated January 14, 1653, tells us that "the said *demoiselle*," who still owned some property, wished to benefit "*Sieur* Jean Chastel, master apothecary of the town of Langogne, her brother," and also to recognize "the good and gracious services she received from *Sieur* Guilhaume Grioule, merchant of the said Langogne, her brother-in-law, and of *damoiselle* Marie Chastel, her sister, wife of the said Grioule."[17] The same document records that "the said Mazaudier" left the company of his wife "to serve in the King's armies where he died." Clauda was already a widow in June, 1647, according to a receipt drawn to the order of the same *Sieur* Grioule and notarized in Langogne by *Maître* Issartel. It mentions "the late *sieur* Guilhaume Mazaudier" and also to the "*dame* de Chastel."[18]

The Chastels were known in Langogne as *chaudronniers*, or wealthy owners of a foundry producing iron or copper pots.[19] The titles and possessions of the Chastel family and their in-laws suggest a privileged place in society. Among the six founding sisters, only Clauda Chastel was able to bring a dowry, and that, the considerable sum of 800 *livres*. She was also the only one who knew how to sign at the bottom of the notarized contract of association, which indicates that she had a better education than the others. Clauda returned to her home region in 1662 or 1663 along with Marie Reboul of Yssingeaux in order to establish a house of Sisters of St. Joseph to serve at the hospital in Langogne.[20] If one can trust the accuracy of the "catalogue of deceased sisters from the house of St. Joseph in Yssingeaux after 1657," Clauda Chastel and Marie Reboul returned to Yssingeaux and died there at an unknown date before 1670.[21]

Marguerite Burdier

According to the contract of association of 1651, Marguerite Burdier was born in Saint-Julien-en-Forez, later known as Saint-Julien-Molin-Molette. This parish belonged at times to the diocese of Lyon, at others, to that of Vienne. The *Dictionnaire topographique du Forez* specifies, that at the end of the ancien régime, Saint-Julien-Molin-Molette was a "market town, parish, chateau and domain at the outermost borders of the Forez, diocese of Vienne, deanery of Bourg-Argental, *élection* of Saint-Etienne."[22]

A parish register of Saint-Julien contains the act of baptism for Marguerite Burdier in 1626: "Today [October 23] Marguerite was baptized, daughter of Guy Burdier and of Marg . . . [?] de Plauder; present, godfather, Jehan Baroigne and godmother, Marguerite Jullin [or Jullier?]."[23] The same register contains baptismal records of three other children of Guy Burdier. The first after Marguerite was Janne, baptized "this first day of January 1630 . . . Claude du Plaudier was godfather, and Janne [illegible] godmother." The next, Jehan, baptized "the 2nd day of the month of September" in 1633, had for godfather "Anthoyne Burdier [perhaps an uncle] . . . and his godmother Benoiste de Plodier." The fourth child, Anthonin, was baptized "this 4 August one thousand six hundred forty-one," with Anthoine Guillot and Janne [illegible] as godparents.

In the 1633 baptismal record of Jehan, Marguerite's brother, the title "Mr" (*Monsieur*) appears before the name of Guy Burdier, connoting a social status above the ordinary. Similar honorifics appear in Marguerite's will, written in 1695, which refers to the "late *sieur* Guy Burdier and *damoiselle* Gabrielle [*sic*] Deplade, her father and mother." The will also names "*Sieur* André Burdier, her nephew, student in the city of Lyon."[24] A confusion of names makes the identity of André Burdier perplexing. "André," the student at Lyon, fits (in all but name) the description in Mother Burdier's papers of Jean-Claude Burdier, "son of Antoine Bourdier, taylor of Colombe Vourlat," baptized on April 2, 1668.[25] While a priest in the city and diocese of Lyon, Jean-Claude obtained a degree as bachelor of theology at the University of Valence on July 9, 1694. He then transferred to the Vienne diocese, becoming *curé* of Saint-Pierre de Bournay, and subsequently, *curé* of Arzay, near the Côte-Saint-André. He kept up a regular correspondence with his aunt, some of which has been preserved in the municipal archives at Vienne.[26] He was the brother of Jeanne Burdier, Marguerite's niece, who entered the Sisters of St. Joseph of Vienne, where she made her profession on September 21, 1695.[27] There was also a "*Messire* André Beurdier, of Saint-Julien," who was named *curé* of Lupé, near Saint-Julien-Molin-Molette, on January 20, 1709, and installed there on February 1. If Jean-Claude Burdier was also known as André, it is possible that the student at Lyon in 1694 and the *curé* at Lupé in 1709 were one and the same person. All that can be stated certainly is that he (or both?) belonged to Marguerite Burdier's family.

The Saint-Julien parish register for 1614–1693 also lists the name of Jean Burdier, *marguiller* of Saint-Julien, on January 17, 1668. This meant that he was responsible for the temporal management of the parish. Jean Burdier was also *procureur d'offices* (an agent or solicitor for the parish) from 1669 to 1684, when his signature appears in that record for the last time. This Burdier, *marguiller* and *procureur d'offices* in his parish for almost twenty years, was most likely Marguerite's brother. Her brother's position, the presence of an educated priest in the family, and the titles attached to the names of male and female relatives, all confirm that the Burdier family, like the Eyrauds and the Chastels, belonged to an upper level of society, influential and active in the third estate.

In 1668, at the request of the archbishop of Vienne, Mother Burdier was sent by the bishop of Le Puy to establish a house of St. Joseph in Vienne.[28] At that time she took the name of Jeanne, the first name of her younger sister.[29] She was instrumental in establishing numerous and important houses throughout the southeastern quarter of France. Endowed with a strong personality, she appears among the six founding sisters as the one who had the greatest influence on the other houses as a whole up to the end of the seventeenth century. She died in Vienne on February 12, 1700, "having been ill and stricken by fever and extraordinary suffering for about six months."[30] A letter announcing her death, dated February 13 and signed by "Sister Anne Félix, superior of the Sisters of St. Joseph of Vienne," recalls, in language without flourish or extravagant praise, the important aspects of her life and her character:

> She always loved her state of life so much that she lived it in an exemplary way and worked unremittingly for the growth of her congregation through the large number of houses which she established in the neighboring provinces. Before she died, she urged the sisters of her congregation very particularly to love their vocation and to work with all their strength to maintain it for the glory of God, for their own perfection, and for the service of the neighbor. . . . [T]he last words she said to her confessor were these, "By the grace of God my soul is very much at peace, because I no longer want anything but what God wants; if he wants me to suffer longer, I want it, and if he wants me to die, I want that too with all my heart."[31]

At the end of the letter, a line written by a different hand notes: "This is the testimony of the Reverend Father Baltazard, her long-time director."[32]

Anna Chaleyer and Anna Brun

Anna Chaleyer was from Saint-Genest-Malifaux in the Lyon diocese. Anna Brun came from Saint-Victor-Malescours in the diocese of Le Puy. The only information known about them comes from the records of their deaths in the parish register of Saint-Georges in Le Puy.

On January 25, 1685, "Sister Anne [*sic*] Brun, Sister of Saint Joseph, deceased the previous day at their house of St. Joseph in the rue de Montferrand at about fifty years of age, having received all the Sacraments, and being the said Sister Superior of the said House of St. Joseph, was buried inside the church."[33] That means that Anna Brun must have been about fifteen years old when the Sisters of St. Joseph were officially founded in 1650. The absence of any mention of her parents at the time of this commitment, despite her young age, could indicate that she came from the group of orphans. She brought no money, but only her work and her promise for the future.

On September 7, 1694, the same register notes the death of Anna Chaleyer, "Sister of St. Joseph, about 90 years of age." She died the preceding day,

September 6, at the rue Montferrand, and was buried in the Chapel of St. Joseph.[34] Anna Chaleyer would therefore have been born around 1604 and forty-six at the time of the foundation. Some wording in the decennial records of the parish, referring to her as "Chalaÿer Anne, sister of the Third Order," raises a question about the precise nature of her relationship to the community.

Anna Vey

We have seen that Anna Vey came from Saint-Jeure in the Le Puy diocese, but there is no trace of her before or after the act of association, suggesting that she may not have remained in the community. The notarized act shows that her father, Jacques Vey, promised to pay 500 *livres* "in the event that she join the said association and community." Whether she joined the community, died, or left are unanswered questions. Anna Vey is the only one whose father is mentioned in the act. That implies, that except for Anna Brun, who was fifteen, and Anna Vey, all the other sisters were able to speak for themselves.[35]

Two more women were allied with these first six sisters in the foundation of the Sisters of St. Joseph: Lucrèce de La Planche, Dame de Joux, and Marguerite de Saint-Laurans.

Lucrèce de La Planche

After the first "pious widows and single women" exploring their vocation, the preface to the Vienne Constitutions speaks of Lucrèce de La Planche as an invaluable help to the first Sisters of St. Joseph:

> When they arrived in Le Puy, all of them stayed several months with a very virtuous *demoiselle* named Lucrèce de la Planche, wife of *Monsieur* de Joux, nobleman of Tence, who was then living at Le Puy. Not only did this pious *demoiselle* contribute everything in her power to the establishment of these daughters, but she also worked until her death with an extraordinary zeal and charity for the advancement of their congregation.[36]

Various interpretations have been given about the part played by Lucrèce de La Planche at the beginning of the community. At one extreme, Mother Gaucher, a Visitation nun, in her *Vie de Monsieur de Lantages*, assigns her the role of foundress. At the other, Abbé Gouit completely rejects her active presence in the nascent congregation.[37] Neither appears to be correct.

Lucrèce de La Planche belonged to the house of Fugy de La Planche, whose chateau is in the parish of Grazac, near Yssingeaux (Haute-Loire).[38] The sparse written records left by the La Planche family indicate that Lucrèce married Daniel du Ranc, Lord de Joux, on November 16, 1624.[39] He was the son of François Durranc, Lord of Baffre in Vivarais, and Gasparde de Joux. Like his father, he was Protestant.[40] In a region such as Tence, bitterly torn by wars of religion, it was neither easy nor well received for a Protestant and a Catholic to marry. Daniel and Lucrèce had a son, Jean Durranc, who was not baptized until March 19, 1634, when he was two and a half years of age.[41] The child's delayed baptism may reveal a glimpse of religious tensions between the parents, if Lucrèce had to wait for her husband's consent in order to have their son baptized.

Another event, however, suggests harmony between the spouses in spite of their differences. Problems had arisen among three landholders: "*Messire* Just de Serres, Bishop of Le Puy, Count of Velay," who owned some property in the parish at Tence; the "reverend Jesuit Fathers of the College of the Holy Trinity in the city of Lyon, priors and joint lords of Tence"; and the "noble Daniel du Ranc, Lord de Joux," who was constituted *seigneur* over the same parish.[42] As a consequence of these multiple claims, certain boundaries overlapped and some tenants no longer paid manorial dues. In order to avoid going to court, the three parties first agreed to have experts verify on site the properties they claimed to own. Then "in order to live in peace, they and their successors" they required only a "contract of amicable settlement" drawn up in writing. Each party named a representative: the bishop sent *Messire* Jean Verrac (or Veriac?), notary of Monistrol; the Jesuits named Father Pierre Brunet, "procurator for the said College of Lyon and prior of the said Tence"; the Lord de Joux delegated "*demoiselle* Lucrèce de la Planche, his wife . . . and his agent specially equipped as representative of his power and proxy." The amicable contract was passed on May 23, 1640, with the representatives of the three parties. It was later signed by all three landowners and their delegates in Le Puy, Lyon, and Tence. Daniel du Ranc said that he approved the agreement and declared that he was "satisfied with all that his agent had done." Her signature appears next to his on the contract.

Why did the Lord de Joux choose to send his wife when he could have sent a steward or a lawyer? Perhaps, since his properties in the Velay came from his wife, she knew their value better than he or anyone else. Or, because this was an agreement with the bishop and the Jesuits, the Dame de Joux, as a Catholic, would be more at ease with the other parties than her Protestant husband.[43] Whatever the reasons, it is obvious from his tone that Daniel du Ranc had complete confidence in his wife. This Catholic-Protestant couple worked together to take part in a conciliatory agreement and to facilitate peace in a situation where several parties shared an interest. In a place like the town of Tence, where religious tensions remained strong, this example of peacemaking would not have passed unnoticed. Without knowing it, Lucrèce was already putting into effect Father Médaille's advice for the Sisters of St. Joseph—to work toward the union of persons with one another and with God.

The little known about Lucrèce de la Planche substantiates the information found in the preface to the Vienne Constitutions. There is good reason to believe that Lucrèce de La Planche contributed with all her power to the establishment and progress of the Congregation of St. Joseph.

Lucrèce de La Planche died on November 22, 1653, "having received all the sacraments," and "was buried in her tomb in the church of Tence." During her lifetime, she did not have the consolation of seeing her husband's conversion. Daniel du Ranc died less than a month after his wife, on December 17, 1653, "having made profession of faith and received extreme unction . . . [unable] to receive the sacrament of the Eucharist due to his illness." He too "was buried in his tomb in the church of Tence, according to his request," completely reconciled with the Catholic Church.[44]

Marguerite de Saint-Laurans

This mysterious woman, referred to in documents of secondary importance and never mentioned in the official acts of the foundation of the Sisters of St. Joseph, was nevertheless a major actor in those events. Her name first appears in the records of the meeting on March 3, 1648, of the administrators of the Montferrand Hospital, who were looking for "some *fille* who knows how to read and write in this house." Five days later, on March 8, 1648, they noted the arrival of "Marguerite who was recommended to help to educate the said girls" and who asserted "a great desire to serve in the said house."[45]

The name "Margot" appears once again in a different event dated October 15, 1654, reported by Gabriel Lanthenas, a citizen of Le Puy and friend of the Sisters of St. Joseph. He refers to her several times as "superior" of the community and designates Françoise Eyraud as "mistress of the orphan girls." At the end of his account, he introduces "Margot de St. Laurans . . . from Chaudes-Aigues in Gévaudan." He reports that she made

> this holy foundation [of the Sisters of St. Joseph] in the year 1650 with the Reverend Father Médaille, a Jesuit, who was her director. She followed him in his missions. She did not remain long with these religious after founding them. After that, she made many sojourns in Saint-Flour during the time of the last bishop. . . .[46] After his death she became a recluse near a parish five leagues from Saint-Flour where she knew a *curé* who was a great servant of God.[47]

There she lived as a hermit in a cave, sleeping on straw, living on bread and water, and writing "incessantly . . . about the duties of ecclesiastics."

Gabriel Lanthenas was clearly full of admiration for Margot, but he says nothing precise about her background. She may have belonged to the family of Chateauneuf-Saint Laurans (or Laurens), an illegitimate branch of the Chateauneuf-Randon. In 1661, Pierre de Chateauneuf, *Sieur* de Saint-Laurans, married "*demoiselle* Benoïte Richard." He is described as the "illegitimate son of the high and powerful Lord *Messire* Anne Guerrin de Chateauneuf de Randon . . . and of *Demoiselle* Jeanne de Bonnel."[48] According to the *Armorial du Gévaudan*, Anne-Guérin de Chateauneuf-Randon married Anne de Cruzy de Marcillac, niece of the bishop of Mende, on September 9, 1635, and they had ten children.[49] Jeanne de Bonnel, mother of Pierre de Chateauneuf, was therefore not his wife. Illegitimate offspring obviously were not listed among the children, so Marguerite de Saint-Laurans could have been the sister, or a more distant relative, of Pierre de Chateauneuf, *Sieur* de Saint-Laurans. It remains an open question.

The effort to bring the humble women who formed the first community of Sisters of St. Joseph out of the shadows has also disclosed a little of the familial background from which they emerge. At least three of these women—Françoise Eyraud, Claude Chastel, and Marguerite Burdier—belonged to a middle class of upwardly mobile families: people in legal professions, prosecutors, attorneys, practitioners and notaries, wealthy merchants. There were nephews who rose from the ranks for a promotion. Anna Vey certainly belonged to a family in comfortable circumstances, since her father promised a dowry of 500 *livres*. Well-situated in the hierarchy of office within the third estate, those who exercised such professions had considerable power, on various counts, in regard to their fellow citizens. They held positions in society where they could get things done. The first Sisters of St. Joseph benefited in their mission from the capabilities acquired from their families. Only Marguerite de Saint-Laurans belonged to another social class. She possessed a significant level of culture and spiritual formation. Probably from an illegitimate line of the high nobility, she was identified as the first superior of the community, even though she had not signed the contract of association of goods. It is not clear, then, if and to what extent she belonged to the group. Called to another vocation, Margot did not remain long with the community. At the other end of the social spectrum in the group is the young girl of fifteen, Anna Brun, who made her commitment on her own, without her parents, and who would, in her turn, become superior of the community.

The community in its origins has the stamp of a group both solid and diversified. At least half the group were mature women, seasoned in action and experience. Two were younger, about twenty years of age or less. At twenty-four, Marguerite Burdier occupied the mid-point among the group in terms of age. Claude Chastel, a widow, who died around 1665, was thirty-eight years old. Françoise Eyraud was thirty-nine, and Anna Chaleyer, forty-six. Their places of origin are also diverse, since they belonged to four different dioceses: Le Puy, Vienne, Mende, and Lyon, as well as Saint-Flour, which was Margot's home. To bring the group together at its beginning, Lucrèce de La Planche, Dame de Joux, a "very virtuous *damoiselle*," according to the preface, lodged them in her house. Up to her death, she continued an active collaboration with the sisters for "the advancement of their congregation."

FATHER JEAN-PIERRE MÉDAILLE (1610-69)

Jean-Pierre Médaille, a little known Jesuit, was the primary instrument in bringing the first sisters together and with them founding the Little Congregation of the Daughters of St. Joseph. Despite his crucial role in the foundation, he never held a prominent place in the histories of the Sisters of St. Joseph until in the second half of the twentieth century. Before the Revolution, the Sisters of St. Joseph showed little interest in recording information about the man who inspired their foundation. Hélyot's *Histoire des Ordres Monastiques, Religieux et Militaires et des Congrégations Séculières* published in 1714 takes its description of the Congregation of Sisters of St. Joseph entirely from the Constitutions printed in Vienne in 1694, particularly the preface. Its single reference to Father Médaille presents him only as a "great missionary of the Society of Jesus," who started the foundation during his missionary journeys in several dioceses. The second edition of Hélyot in 1792 provided no additional information.[50]

At the end of the nineteenth and beginning of the twentieth centuries, several congregations of St. Joseph wanted to preserve and transmit something of their history. Abbé Rivaux's 1878 biography of Mère du Sacré-Cœur (second superior general of the Sisters of St. Joseph of Lyon) mentions Father Médaille only in passing as author of the Eucharistic Letter, which it reproduces in part.[51] There is not a word about Father Médaille as a person. In 1879, Sister Augustine Battut wrote *Origine et développement de la Congrégation de St Joseph du Bon Pasteur*, the history of her congregation in Clermont.[52] The congregation acquired the title of "Bon Pasteur" (Good Shepherd) because of its first work in Clermont in 1723, which was an institution known at that time as a *maison de Refuge*, a type of reformatory. In the first two chapters of her book, which explain how the first community was founded in Le Puy, Sister Battut attempts a "biography of our founders," Father Médaille and Bishop de Maupas. She speaks, however, only of Jean-Paul Médaille (not Jean-Pierre), and confuses many dates and places—errors discovered by her assistant in 1899 through correspondence with Jesuit Father

Ernest-Marie Rivière of Toulouse.⁵³ Most of these works, especially those written in the twentieth century about congregations of St. Joseph that had been established during the nineteenth, provide very little information about Jean-Pierre Médaille. Bishop de Maupas, the official founder, receives far more attention and notice. Sisters at that point were probably more interested in the history of their own particular congregations than in their common origin.

The identity of the founder of the Sisters of St. Joseph was not, in any case, clear-cut. In the Toulouse Province of the Society of Jesus during the seventeenth century, there were three Jesuits named Médaille, all virtually contemporary. The Jesuit archives in Rome and Toulouse sometimes confused the first names of these three men. It is hardly surprising that the work or writings of each are at times incorrectly attributed to Pierre, Jean-Pierre, or Jean-Paul. It was not until 1930 that Father Ferdinand Cavallera's careful study of the Society's catalogues finally sorted out these attributions.⁵⁴ We now know that the foundation of the Sisters of St. Joseph was the work of Father Jean-Pierre Médaille, the elder brother of Jean-Paul, and no relation to their fellow Jesuit, Pierre Médaille.⁵⁵

Research by a series of historians has finally succeeded in bringing Father Médaille into the light. Published in 1950, *Les Sœurs de Saint-Joseph* by Canon Albert Bois helped to lift the veil from Fr. Médaille's life. It contained information on Jean-Pierrre Médaille that Bois knew to be and regretted as very summary, particularly regarding his childhood and youth.⁵⁶ The sources used by Bois were documents that had been sent to Auguste Achard, a local historian working at the turn of the twentieth century, by Adrien Carrère, superior of the Jesuit house in Toulouse where the province archives were kept.⁵⁷ Marius Nepper, a Jesuit, subsequently discovered new information about Father Médaille in the Catalogues of the Toulouse Province and in the correspondence of Jesuit fathers general in the Society's archives at Toulouse and Rome.⁵⁸ In 1988, Anne Hennessy, a Sister of St. Joseph of Orange, California, provided a study of the historical and spiritual context for Médaille in her doctoral thesis, "In Search of a Founder: The Life and Spiritual Setting of Jean-Pierre Medaille, SJ, Founder of the Sisters of St. Joseph."⁵⁹ Sister Pierangela Pesce, of the Congregation of St. Joseph of Cuneo, Italy, made a definitive inventory in 1983 of the Roman Catalogues of the Society of Jesus, published in 2000 as *Jean-Pierre Médaille, dati biografici*.⁶⁰ Her study, ordering pertinent documents from the Roman archives chronologically, affords the possibility of following the life and activities of Father Jean-Pierre Médaille from his entrance to the Jesuit novitiate at Toulouse until his death. Studies by Adrien Demoustier establishing the historical reliability of the Society's Catalogues of the late sixteenth and early seventeenth centuries confirm them as a sound basis for research.⁶¹

Who Is Father Médaille?

Jean-Pierre Médaille was born in Carcassonne on October 6, 1610, as recorded in the Jesuit archives. His baptismal record, dated October 10, provides the names of his parents, Jean Médaille, *avocat du roi*, and Phelippe d'Estéveril.[62] He was the oldest of three boys: his brother Jean-Paul, born January 29, 1618, also became a Jesuit, and Jean, like his father, was a lawyer.[63] Little is known of Médaille's childhood and adolescence, or of his preparation in humanities at the Jesuit College of Carcassonne, except that his parents had been instrumental in its foundation in 1623.[64]

Jean-Pierre entered the Jesuit novitiate in Toulouse on September 16, 1626, shortly before his sixteenth birthday. The reports of Father Pierre Verthamont, master of novices during this two-year period of formation, reveal the young novice's character.[65] He was outstanding among his twenty-five classmates by reason of his exceptional intelligence, a quality noted in only one other novice. His self-denial, unmatched among his fellow novices, was equally distinguished and noteworthy.[66] This would presume a degree of self-discipline extraordinary in a youth of seventeen.

From 1628 until 1632 or 1633, he pursued his studies in rhetoric, logic, physics, and metaphysics at the College of Toulouse, evidently with rather great success. Equipped with these intellectual tools, he was sent to teach grammar at the College of Carcassonne for two years before doing theological studies at the College of Toulouse from 1635 to 1637.[67] He studied theology for only two years, not four, as normally prescribed by the Jesuit Constitutions. They do, however, permit certain students displaying remarkable qualities to be exempt from a portion of their theological studies, allowing even that "some outstanding persons could be admitted also to the profession of four vows" without having completed four years of theology.[68]

After his ordination in 1637, Father Médaille went to the College of Aurillac in the Massif Central. There he was a consultor and "minister," that is, an assistant to the rector responsible for the discipline and material order of the house. Soon he became "prefect of the *Grande Congrégation*" or Marian Sodality, a group of young Christian men with the purpose of deepening their spiritual life. He fulfilled these diverse duties until 1642. During 1641–1642, the last year he is listed among the fathers of the College of Aurillac, Médaille was also companion to the preacher of Saint-Flour (*socius concionatoris Sancti Flori*) in the Haute-Auvergne.[69] That preacher was Father Jérôme Sauret, from the College of Le Puy, named as *concionator sancti Flori* for that year. Father Médaille must have been in Saint-Flour during June of 1642, because a report left by a treasurer of the College of Le Puy for his successor in 1644 notes, "on June 14, 1642, a mission was preached in Saint-Flour; Father Médaille paid 10 *sols* for mending."[70] How long he stayed there, or what he did during the rest of that year is unknown.

Father Médaille was again in Toulouse during 1642–1643 for what the Jesuits call tertianship, a "third year" sometime after the two years of novitiate, a time to grow deeper spiritually in preparation for the definitive commitment of perpetual vows. A letter of the father general in Rome, dated May 27, 1643, approved Father Médaille for the profession of four vows.[71] He pronounced his solemn vows on October 11 of that year, possibly in Saint-Flour, since he was appointed to the college there.[72] Another priest made them the same day at Carcassonne. At Saint-Flour, beginning in the autumn of 1643, Father Médaille again fulfilled the functions, as at Aurillac, of minister and consultor. In addition, he was catechist and confessor for persons outside the house. He remained at Saint-Flour from 1643 to 1649, exercising at times the duties of minister (two years), at others, those of procurator (two years), in addition to being spiritual prefect (two years), admonitor (three years), and, every year, a consultor, or councilor to the superior, responsible for communicating to Rome his impressions on everything that concerned the college: the men, the events, and the physical plant.

In 1649, Father Médaille was thirty-nine years old. What kind of man was he? Marius Nepper's research in the Jesuit catalogues revealed Médaille's intellectual gifts, successful studies, poor health, and his "bilious and melancholy" temperament.[73] A closer look at the roles he filled and at his superiors' evaluations in the annual catalogues yields an impression of his personality at this period. On the whole, Father Médaille held stationary positions until 1649. Starting in 1637, apart from his tertian year (1642–43) when in principle he would have had no other occupation, Father Médaille fulfilled the office of minister: for four years in Aurillac and for two more in Saint-Flour. There is no information about 1647–1648, as the annual catalogue is missing. From the end of 1646, however, while still at Saint-Flour, he was named procurator, responsible to the superior for the financial and legal interests of the college. This position led him to travel frequently in order to collect outstanding debts. According to the triennial catalogues for 1649 and 1651, he filled this post for three years before 1650.

Since Father Médaille held the onerous duties of minister and procurator for so long a time, his superiors must have judged him capable and competent.[74] The *Rules for the Society of Jesus* provide a description of these positions and the spirit in which they should be carried out.[75] The minister occupies a vital role in the house. He is the superior's right arm, replacing him when he is absent. At meals "when the superior cannot take his place at the head table, he will be replaced by the minister."[76] The minister oversees "the observance of the Constitutions, rules, orders, and approved customs of the house or college."[77] He makes sure that the various tasks in the house are carried out properly, especially in regard to the community's meals, clothing, and health. He notes in writing "the things he encounters that are appropriate to good government" or the "shortcomings, if he perceives any in the house." In a word, he is responsible for the disciplinary and material order of the house. He acts as far as possible in accord with the intentions of the superior and is accountable to him for his actions in the house.

The duties of procurator, similar to those of minister because they deal with "temporal things," are distinct insofar as the procurator deals mainly with external affairs and the minister, with the internal. The duty of procurator "will be to request and receive all revenues of the college . . . and the alms."[78] He keeps the college's accounts and prepares a "summary of contracts and rentals." He stores the money in a safe place and has a written record of all financial dealings, informing the rector of any "active or passive debts of the college." He represents the college or chooses a representative in any lawsuits, frequent occurrences in the seventeenth century. These two posts of minister and procurator have many aspects in common and require the same spirit. The Jesuit Rules say the procurator should take "care to speak and act in an edifying manner toward all he meets, and keep the good will of those whose assistance he needs in order to expedite all affairs." He therefore needs to have organizational and administrative qualities, and at the same time, a feeling for human relations. He must be able to act but also to know how to obtain the help of competent people. He should avoid court cases as much as possible. If it is impossible to do otherwise, if it "is necessary to go as far as litigation, he must remember to maintain great peace, interior and exterior, always making it clear to the opposing party that he is ready to reach a just settlement at any time." Finally, "in all his dealings, he will keep perpetually" in mind the purpose of the Society, "which is seeking the glory of almighty God and attending to the salvation of souls."

The two positions of minister and procurator could allow time for activities of a more directly spiritual nature. This was certainly true for Father Médaille. When he was minister in Aurillac he also served as prefect of the Marian Congregation. In Saint-Flour, while serving as minister, he was also "spiritual prefect" (that is, "spiritual father"), "confessor for day students," "cathechist," or "confessor for Ours [Jesuits]." He continued as "spiritual prefect" when he became procurator. In addition, almost without interruption in the twelve-year period between 1637 and 1649, Father Médaille also had the responsibility of consultor.[79] The annual catalogues indicate that he held this important office continuously for ten years, except during 1641-42, when, as companion for the preacher in Saint-Flour, he was absent some of the time, and during his tertian year in Toulouse, (1642-43). This sensitive appointment, held for so long, is a strong indication of the confidence his superiors placed in him. From 1645 to 1646, he was also admonitor, the one who has the delicate task of informing the superior of his own lapses or of complaints from the other men. The roles of consultor and admonitor require someone who is sufficiently present to the college and to the community to see what is happening and to take appropriate action. They also imply good judgment, tact, spiritual discernment, and apostolic sensibility, especially if the assignment is prolonged. The qualities of "remarkable judgment" and "great and completely religious prudence," noted by the superior of Saint-Flour in 1645 in his assessment of Father Médaille, explain why the provincial of Toulouse appointed him to such difficult tasks.[80] Obviously, Médaille was widely recognized as a person valuable in every sphere, and most particularly for his "great talent for instructing and directing souls."[81]

Beginning in 1649, the triennial catalogues indicate that something was changing for Father Médaille. For the first time, we find among his tasks: "missionarius: 6 menses" (missionary, 6 months), and in a supplemental catalogue, the comment: "natus ad missiones" (born for the missions). Despite his practical and relatively sedentary activities, his God-given gift "for instructing and directing souls" had come to light. On the same page, the evaluations concerning prudence and experience are surprisingly full of reserve. Something must have happened in Father Médaille's life that led the rector to change his tone to this degree. Father Médaille had, in point of fact, become very involved with matters issuing from a group of women who wanted to consecrate their lives to God, and who were destined to cause him trouble before they could begin to exist as Sisters of St. Joseph.

The Encounter between Father Médaille and the First Sisters of St. Joseph

Correspondence in 1647-48 from the Father General Vincent Caraffa to Father Médaille and to the rector of the College of Saint-Flour shows that the first association of the Sisters of St. Joseph occurred several years before the official date of foundation, given in the 1694 Constitutions as October 15, 1650.[82] The correspondence from Father Caraffa is at present the only source revealing the existence of an initial group of women brought together by Father Médaille prior to 1650. It is, nevertheless, reliable and convincing enough to establish the reality of a beginning before 1650. It offers no information, however, of how that came about. Father Nepper, who discovered this correspondence, sees a relationship between the first Règlements of the Sisters of St. Joseph and the Company of the Blessed Sacrament.[83] That, and other possibilities, will be the subject of this research.

The Preface to the Constitutions of Vienne, 1694The preface to the Constitutions printed in 1694, as mentioned above, explains the role of Father Médaille in launching the first community of Sisters of St Joseph:

> The Little Congregation of the Sisters or the Daughters of Saint Joseph had its origins in the city of Le Puy-en-Velay, where it was established by His Excellency, the Most Illustrious and Most Reverend Henry de Maupas, Bishop of the said city, because of the plan inspired in him by the Reverend Father Jean-Pierre Médaille, great missionary of the Society of Jesus, who spent his life fruitfully in giving missions, not only in the diocese of Le Puy, but also in those of Clermont, Saint-Flour, Rodez and Vienne.
>
> Having met in the course of his missions several pious widows and single women who, not wanting to marry, planned to leave the world to devote themselves to the service of God and to their salvation and could not enter the monasteries for lack of sufficient means, this good Father decided to propose to some bishop the establishment of a congregation which these devout widows and single women could enter, to work for their salvation and to devote themselves to all the exercises of which they were capable for the service of the neighbor.
>
> For this reason he appealed to the said Lord de Maupas, Bishop of Le Puy, and, from what he knew of the sublime virtue and extraordinary zeal of this great prelate for the glory of God and the salvation of the neighbor, he firmly believed that he would not reject the proposal he wished to make. Indeed, as soon as he had done so, His Excellency approved it and found it so advantageous for the increase of the service of God and of the neighbor that he had the daughters called to Le Puy whom the said Father had found disposed to leaving the world and to the service of God.[84]

Before relying on this text as a source, there are critical questions to be raised about its credibility. What is its source? Archbishop Henri de Villars of Vienne authorized the preface, but who could have provided him the information for it? At the time of its composition, were there any living witnesses of the initial foundation? Who were the principal architects of the Constitutions printed at Vienne in 1694?

A first clue to the answers occurs in the biography of Monsieur de Lantages, the first rector of the Sulpician seminary at Le Puy.[85] Charles-Louis de Lantages came to the seminary in Le Puy in 1653, a year after it had been founded by Jean-Jacques Olier. He devoted himself not only to the seminary and the Visitation monastery, but also to the Sisters of St. Joseph. According to his biographer,

> [H]e continued to direct the sisters for a long time, sparing nothing to help them establish themselves solidly. . . . For their part, the Sisters of St. Joseph always turned to this wise director as their counsel and their light, and because of this profound respect for his advice, shortly before his death, several sisters from the

principal houses of various dioceses held an extraordinary gathering in Le Puy to consult with him on several important questions regarding their congregation.[86]

Since *Monsieur* de Lantages died in Le Puy on April 1, 1694, this assembly of sisters could have taken place during 1692 or 1693. The "important questions regarding their congregation" raised at this meeting—even if they had been discussed prior to the assembly and with no connection to the actual writing of the constitutions—would certainly have been included in the final version of the constitutions printed at Vienne. The Archbishop of Vienne, moreover, had given permission for printing the constitutions to *Sieur* Laurens Cruzi on November 24, 1693, a date completely consistent with the extraordinary gathering of the Sisters of St. Joseph.

With *Monsieur* de Lantages as a faithful and prudent counselor, the most important witness to the life and history of the Sisters of St. Joseph from the beginnings up to this time was Mother Jeanne Burdier, superior of the community of Vienne. She was also known as Marguerite Burdier, one of the first six women whom Bishop de Maupas assembled at the Montferrand Orphan Hospital on October 15, 1650. Sent to Vienne around 1667 to establish that important house, she remained its superior from 1668, when the community was approved by the archbishop, until shortly before her death on February 12, 1700.[87] Her testimony about the origins of the Daughters of St. Joseph would have been accurate in general and in its meaning, even if some details were questionable.

There is an apparent mistake, for example, in the preface where it presents Armand de Béthune, actually named to the see of Le Puy in 1661, as succeeding Bishop de Maupas only after the latter's death, which occurred in 1680. This could be construed as an intentional mistake, a tactic in face of the king's displeasure at the end of Maupas' tenure in Le Puy. On the contrary, the letters patent of Louis XIV given to the communities of Le Puy, Saint-Didier, and other places in 1674 refer in the same way to "the late Lord de Maupas du Tour, Bishop of Le Puy." In both cases, terminology about the "late" Henry de Maupas signifies merely that he was no longer Bishop of Le Puy.[88] The language is figurative, rather than erroneous, and in no way discredits the memory of the early witnesses. It is entirely plausible that Marguerite Burdier, at the end of her life, remembered perfectly well the details of her own vocation, of her first meeting with Father Médaille, and of the official gathering of the community by Bishop de Maupas on October 15, 1650. There are events in life that one does not forget.

In 1693, Anna Chaleyer, also one of the first sisters, was still alive. As she was very advanced in age, eighty-nine years old by then, she may not have been clear in her mind. Yet even when the mind is muddled, the elderly often retain memories of their youth. Other contemporaries of the early foundation, including *Monsieur* de Lantages, still lived in Le Puy and could provide an account of the early days. The historical summary of the preface of the 1694 Constitutions of Vienne is consequently a sufficiently reliable source to support historical argument.

The preface states that the origin of the first houses of St. Joseph can be traced to the missionary work of Father Médaille. During these missions, he met the widows and single women who desired to leave the world "to work for their salvation and to devote themselves to all the exercises of which they were capable for the service of the neighbor." Determining the circumstances of the foundation, since it was linked to Father Médaille's missions, involves identifying those times before 1650 when his other duties would have allowed him to do such work. In 1633, at the beginning of his ministry, he taught in Carcassonne. In 1646, while he was at Saint-Flour, the new group was already started.[89] Thanks to data from the catalogues of the Society of Jesus in Rome, as well as Adrien Demoustier's studies on the ministries of seventeenth-century Jesuits, it is possible to deduce approximately those periods between 1633 and 1646 when Father Médaille's other apostolic responsibilities would have permitted missionary activity.[90]

Father Médaille could not have exercised any sustained work as a missionary during the two years he taught in Carcassonne (1633-35) or during his studies in theology in Toulouse (1635-37). He then spent four years in Aurillac as minister, a demanding assignment that required his constant presence. He could not have preached long missions during those four years. The most he could have done at that time would have been to give short occasional sermons in the surrounding area. Nevertheless, as mentioned above, during 1641-42, the last time his name appears on the list for the College of Aurillac, the annual catalogue of the Toulouse Province notes that he was companion for an unknown length of time to a preacher in Saint-Flour, Father Jérôme Sauret from the College of Le Puy. The following year (1642-43) Father Médaille was in Toulouse for his tertianship, the last formal period of formation in the Society of Jesus. The tertianship lasted at most six months, and its activities were not thoroughly decided in advance.[91] According to Pierre Delattre, "Except for the long form of the Exercises, which takes thirty days, the tertians are available for many ministerial opportunities."[92] One of the apostolic experiences of the tertians in Toulouse was preparing condemned prisoners for death. Above all, however, tertians preached missions. Because there was no house specifically designated for the tertians in Toulouse, they stayed in groups, either at the novitiate there or at the colleges in Rodez or Cahors.[93] It is probable that Father Médaille was sent on mission, perhaps in Rodez. He later returned to Rodez several times, according to records of the

College in Le Puy: boots were sent either by or for him from Rodez to Le Puy and from Aurillac to Rodez.[94] In the fall of 1643, he was sent to Saint-Flour as minister, a post he held until the fall of 1645, one that would be difficult to combine with long missionary trips. He might, however, have participated in missions at certain times of the year or for services during Advent or Lent.

On March 8, 1647, Father General Vincent Caraffa wrote to Father Médaille (and also to Father Degieu, his rector at the College of Saint-Flour) concerning a "pious association of women which you report you have founded."[95] Both of these letters came in response to those sent by the rector and his consultors, Father Médaille among them. We know from the Jesuit Rules that the rector's consultors were required to write to the father general each year in January.[96] Because mail between Rome and Saint-Flour took about three months, the letters from Rome on March 8 could have been sent in response to one written by Father Médaille, as required, in January of that same year, 1647. In any case, the events Father Médaille's letter reported — among other things, that he "had prescribed rules for a group of women" — would have taken place in 1646.[97] Since this group was already prepared to accept rules in 1646, it must have begun some time before that year.

When could Father Médaille have met the women he brought together? The first allusion to missionary work on his part, and perhaps his first connections with the future Sisters of St. Joseph, was in 1642 at Saint-Flour. While giving the mission, the two priests (Médaille and Jérôme Sauret from Le Puy) presumably worked to prepare the transfer of the college that already existed in Saint-Flour to the Jesuits. The contract was signed December 31, 1642, in the presence of Bishop Charles de Noailles, by the city consuls, and by Jesuit Fathers Louis Molinier and Jean Jallat from the college in Le Puy, officially representing the Vice-Provincial of Toulouse, Father Arnauld Bohyre.[98] It is conceivable that both Fathers Médaille and Sauret spent a good part of 1642 in Saint-Flour preparing for this transfer. The same had happened elsewhere. In those circumstances, they would have been able to extend their missionary activity beyond the town. At the end of 1642, Father Médaille was back in Toulouse for his tertian year. During this time he was probably sent out on mission to Rodez or elsewhere and could have met devout women who were candidates for religious life. For many reasons, this tertian year would be significant for Médaille and would mark him profoundly.

Father Médaille's Tertian Year
and the Company of the Blessed Sacrament

Founded in Paris in 1630 by Henri de Levis, Duc de Ventadour, the Company of the Blessed Sacrament was a completely secret association that included lay Christians of high social rank, secular priests, and in its early years, male religious. The members of the Company wanted to revive the Christian spirit through sanctity of life and good works. The Blessed Sacrament was their principal devotion. Secrecy was their political tool for getting things done unobtrusively, without interference.

Father Jean Suffren, a Jesuit from the College of the Trinity in Lyon and confessor to Louis XIII, was among the earliest members of the Company in Paris in 1630.[99] A year later, when he and Henri de Pichery, an officer of Louis XIII's household, were both in Lyon with the king, they thought it would be opportune to form a Company there. According to the Company's annals, they gathered several virtuous people in the Jesuit novitiate, "which also served as house for the tertians, and Father Suffren gave several conferences to stir up their hearts. . . . Someone then suggested forming an Assembly of Ladies and giving them statutes like those of the Company. But this idea came to nothing."[100] The proposal for a women's branch, repeated on December 7, 1645, was again rejected. *Les Papiers des Dévots de Lyon*, assembled by Georges Guigue, testify to the Jesuit participation in the early years of the Company of the Blessed Sacrament in Lyon:

> In its beginnings, the Company was readily revealed to various religious, such as [Capuchins, Minims, monks and particularly to Jesuits] who were not supportive of Companies that were not subject to them; they even confided their plan to Father [Milieu], who had the ear of the said bishop and, after him, to [Father Gibalin].[101]

The words in brackets were crossed out on the manuscript but can be deciphered nonetheless. Father Milieu was the Jesuit provincial in Lyon in 1642, and Father Gibalin served as rector of the House of St. Joseph, the tertian residence, in 1645.

Nearly a decade after its formation in Lyon, the Company of the Blessed Sacrament established a group in Toulouse in 1641.[102] There is no indication about the exact place where it began, but Father Suffren was again present at this foundation, a sign that the Jesuits were actively involved. Father Médaille came to Toulouse for his tertian year at the end of 1642, having spent part of that year close to Charles de Noailles, bishop of Saint-Flour, who had been a member of the Company of the Blessed Sacrament from its origins. [103] In Toulouse Father Médaille could not have helped being influenced by the recent foundation of the Company there, connected as it was with the Jesuits. With his confreres he certainly participated in its charitable and apostolic activities, particularly since missions were one of the works effectively supported by the Company. Very quickly, as in Lyon, a group of Ladies wanted to form their own group. Alphonse Auguste's work on the Company of the

Blessed Sacrament in Toulouse identifies an undated document, *Mémoire de la distribution des bouillons* (Record of the distribution of soup), as belonging to the first years of the Company there.[104] This manuscript places the Company of Ladies at the very beginnings of the Company in Toulouse, since it shows them in charge of a specific, already well regulated work. "In any case," Auguste concludes, "the establishment of the *Bouillons des Pauvres* would have been at least . . . somewhat before 1645."

At the same time, the Company of the Blessed Sacrament was making its presence felt in Toulouse through many other works, particularly the transformation of the Hospital of St. Sebastian for poor victims of the plague. It became an *hôpital général* for admitting and confining all the poor and was called the Hôpital de la Charité Saint-Joseph de la Grave, a change authorized by the *capitouls* in 1647. Auguste notes, even before this date, the "charitable role of certain Ladies who stepped in to procure some relief for the women confined in the Hospital of St. Joseph," acknowledging, "We do not know whether these were Ladies of the Blessed Sacrament."[105] One of these Ladies was Jeanne de Juliard, *Dame* de Mondonville, foundress of the Filles de l'Enfance (1662) who, after her "conversion" in 1641, went to care for the sick in the hospital and prepare the bodies of deceased women for burial.[106]

Although there is no direct evidence about Father Médaille's role in the activities of the Company of the Blessed Sacrament in Toulouse, particularly in the foundation of the women's group of the Company, he was undoubtedly in contact with this Company and influenced by it. The care given by the charitable Ladies to the sick and the poor at the Hôpital Saint-Joseph brings to mind what Father Médaille said regarding the works of the Sisters of St. Joseph at the beginning of the Congregation: "God has deigned to inspire the foundation of their little congregation precisely for the relief of the sick poor."[107] Even if these "sick poor" were not those at the Hôpital Saint-Joseph in Toulouse, possibly associated with the Ladies of the Company of the Blessed Sacrament in that city, Father Médaille himself clearly connects both the Blessed Sacrament and care of the sick with the beginnings of the "little congregation." In two passages in the original manuscript Constitutions, he reminds the sisters that "the Holy Sacrament of the Eucharist . . . gave beginning to their very little Congregation" and that it "must also maintain it and help it grow more and more in every kind of grace and virtue."[108]

It is curious that the preface to the Vienne Constitutions makes no mention of any link to the Company of the Blessed Sacrament in its account of the foundation of the Congregation of St. Joseph. In 1693, the Company still existed and was active in Vienne, as well as in Lyon and Grenoble. Mother Jeanne Burdier was in contact with the members of these different Companies.[109] More than forty years had passed, however, since the foundation of the Sisters of St. Joseph. If the early foundation had any connection to the Ladies of the Company of the Blessed Sacrament, it no longer existed. Although continuing, here or there, to collaborate with the Company of the Blessed Sacrament, the congregation needed to establish its own identity. Perhaps too much stress on the Blessed Sacrament, still too fresh in memory and sometimes in life, would risk creating some confusion. Referring to the Blessed Sacrament would also have been seriously impolitic. Since the *parlement* in Paris had officially dissolved that Company in 1660, and the provincial Companies survived only by their secrecy and the tolerance of the other *parlements*, it was preferable not to draw the attention of authorities to any possible link. Most of the authors of the preface of the 1694 Constitutions belonged to the generation of sisters who came after Father Médaille's missionary work, rather than to the first, which had come into being in connection with the Company of the Blessed Sacrament. For all these sisters, the congregation had taken shape and developed above all from the activities of Father Médaille, "great missionary of the Society of Jesus."[110] Nevertheless, in Father Médaille's mind, the congregation did not originate in his work as a missionary, but rather under the impetus "of the Blessed Sacrament." An understanding of the exact meaning of this expression, still to be achieved, could indicate both the historical circumstances of the birth of the congregation and its true spiritual roots.

Father Médaille returned to Saint-Flour after his tertian year in the fall of 1643 and took up the role of minister, which he had previously exercised at the College of Aurillac. When he became procurator in 1646–1647, his duties would have given him more latitude for missionary work, whether giving missions as such, or merely Lenten or Advent sermons. He actually did preach during Lent in the cathedral of Le Puy in 1648 at the invitation of Bishop de Maupas.[111] The bishop obviously appreciated the Jesuit. The appreciation was mutual, for it was to Maupas that Father Médaille would address his request for the official establishment of his "little design," the new Congregation of St. Joseph.

BISHOP HENRY DE MAUPAS DU TOUR (1606-80)

In comparison with Father Médaille, the Jesuit of modest local repute circulating in the poor rural areas of the Massif Central, Henry de Maupas creates the impression of a more renowned personage.[112] With the nobility of his family and its courtly connections on the one hand and his episcopal functions on the other, Henry de Maupas was bound to leave his mark on the historical record.

The preface to the 1694 Constitutions states that the Congregation of St. Joseph "was established by His Excellency, the Most Illustrious and Most Reverend Henry de Maupas, Bishop of the said city [Le Puy], because of the plan inspired in him by the Reverend Father Jean-Pierre Médaille." It was certainly because Father Médaille knew "the sublime virtue and extraordinary zeal of this great prelate for the glory of God and the salvation of the neighbor" that he asked him to back the nascent association of pious women with his authority. It was a conscious choice. For new communities to realize their own vision in the middle of the seventeenth century, particularly a group of women of unimpressive social status, it was important to have the support of a well-known figure or the protection of a bishop capable of understanding and respecting their inspiration. Without such support, they could simply be abolished by civil authority or forced to adapt to the interests of local bishops. The Visitation nuns experienced this with Archbishop de Marquemont in Lyon, and the Hospitallers of Saint-Joseph de la Flèche in the diocese of Angers fell victim to the divisive intervention of their bishop, Henri Arnauld, Jansenist and brother of Antoine, "le Grand Arnauld."[113] Father Médaille approached Bishop de Maupas because he knew he was a friend of the Jesuits and would be open to the originality of his project.

Henry de Maupas du Tour was born in 1606 in Champagne at the chateau of Cosson, six miles from Rheims. Henry IV, who wanted to show his esteem for his former comrade in arms, Charles de Maupas, was godfather to his new son, Henry. In 1600 Charles Cauchon de Maupas, Baron du Tour and advisor to Henry IV, married Anne de Gondi, eldest daughter of Jérôme de Gondi, *chevalier d'honneur* to the queen, Marie de Medici. According to the customs of the time, Henry's parents steered their youngest son very early into an ecclesiastical career. At the age of ten he received the tonsure and was named by royal privilege as commendatory abbot of the Monastery of Saint Denys at Rheims. In 1618, after his older brother died, Henry—following the example of St. Charles Borromeo—renounced his rights as heir in order to begin preparing for the priesthood. During this time he studied with the Jesuits at the College of Rheims and later, at the University of Pont-à-Mousson. He obtained the degrees of bachelor of philosophy in May of 1622 and of doctor of theology on December 13, 1623.[114]

Ordained in 1629, Henry immediately received the important post of vicar-general of Rheims. In 1634, while remaining vicar-general, he was named to the formidable position of first chaplain to Queen Anne of Austria, a ministry requiring him to make frequent trips to court. These visits to Paris put him in contact with the most important masters of the French School after Bérulle: Charles de Condren, Jean Eudes, Jean-Jacques Olier, and above all, Vincent de Paul, the apostle of charity. Father de Maupas regularly attended his famous

"Tuesday Conferences," which deepened his desire to live in accord with the holiness of his vocation. He was not merely influenced by Vincent de Paul; he also became his disciple and friend. With good reason, then, the honor of giving the funeral oration for *Monsieur Vincent* fell to him in 1660. During these years Henry de Maupas came into contact with the Company of the Blessed Sacrament and became an active member. In a letter he wrote to the Archbishop of Arles on January 20, 1640, he informed him, on behalf of the Company of the Blessed Sacrament of Paris, "that there are pious persons in your town of Arles who desire to form a Company of the Most Blessed Sacrament, such as ours."[115] Henry de Maupas therefore belonged to the Company before 1640 and was even entrusted with certain missions on its behalf. This association is another sign of his constant concern to promote the Christian spirit in all the levels of society.

Another important figure, Francis de Sales (†1622), helped to form Bishop de Maupas. The writings and example of this holy bishop and his living work, the Visitation Order, all had a profound effect upon the seventeenth century, and in particular, upon the future bishop of Le Puy. His admiration and friendship for the Visitation Order earned him the honor of giving the funeral oration for Jeanne de Chantal following her death on December 13, 1641. As early as 1644, Maupas published the *Vie de la Vénérable Mère Jeanne-Françoise Frémiot de Chantal*, a work dedicated to Queen Anne of Austria that enjoyed significant success. Later, in 1657, he published the *Vie du Vénérable Serviteur de Dieu, François de Sales*, which he dedicated to Pope Alexander VII. In the latter work he voiced his profound admiration for the Visitation Order: "I respect them [religious orders], I honor them . . . but I confess that the Order of the Visitation has my particular blessing for their exact observance of the most sacred laws of humility and charity."[116]

In 1641 Louis XIII named Henry de Maupas as bishop of Le Puy. According to this appointment, he retained his duties as chaplain to the queen. He had to wait, however, for the papal bulls that conferred canonical investiture. The new bishop was consecrated only on October 4, 1643, in the Jesuit church in the rue St. Antoine in Paris—a detail that demonstrates his regard for the Society of Jesus.

During the two-year lapse between his nomination to the bishopric in 1641 and his consecration in 1643, Maupas corresponded with his first secretary about the progress of affairs in Le Puy and frequently recommended that he take the advice of the rector of the Jesuit college there. His remarks about the Jesuits in this correspondence are always favorable. At last, as reported in The *Memoirs* of Jacmon, a citizen of Le Puy, "this Wednesday the 27th day of the month of January in the said year 1644," Henry de Maupas was welcomed to the city of Le Puy. Jacmon describes the bishop's entrance and installation:

The following day, Thursday, January 28 . . . the said Lord bishop went to hear Mass at [the cathedral of] Notre Dame. . . . It is also noteworthy that the following day, Friday the 29th of the said month, the said Lord bishop went to the house of the Jesuit fathers where he said a low Mass, the first which he celebrated in the said city of Le Puy.[117]

On January 30, he was solemnly received by the *"messires* the canons of the choir and the choir boys," before whom he took "the oath."[118] The bishop set to work without delay in his diocese. Jacmon notes a number of his activities during the year 1644.

Already a member, Bishop de Maupas surely had something to do with the establishment of the Company of the Blessed Sacrament in Le Puy in 1644.[119] Along the same lines, on September 20, 1644, he commissioned Maurice Dasquemie, canon of the cathedral of Le Puy, "to establish canonically the Confraternity of the Blessed Sacrament of the Altar in all parishes of the diocese."[120] In 1652, he asked Jean-Jacques Olier, founder of the Sulpicians, to establish a seminary in Le Puy. When his biography of Francis de Sales was published in 1657, the papal court put Henry de Maupas in charge of the inquiry leading to the Bishop of Geneva's beatification. It was also Maupas to whom the king, the Assembly of the Clergy, and the Visitation Order entrusted the office of postulator for the canonization. After some routine delays, he had the joy of hearing the sanctity of Francis de Sales proclaimed on February 25, 1665, and on April 19 of the following year, of being present in Rome for the celebration of his canonization.

By that time Henry de Maupas was no longer Bishop of Le Puy. He had engaged in bloody conflicts with the Lord of Polignac, governor of the Velay, a fractious neighbor who impinged on the bishop's authority. As a result, Louis XIV rendered judgment in favor of the governor, transferring the bishop of Le Puy to the see of Evreux in 1662. This royal decision was very bitter, especially for one who had so faithfully served the king and still remained chaplain to Queen Anne of Austria.[121] In his new diocese, Henry de Maupas continued the same apostolic zeal as in Le Puy. He established a seminary for the formation of clerics, visited parishes, and preached sermons. To promote devotion to the Blessed Sacrament of the Altar as he had done in Le Puy, he established perpetual adoration in all parishes of his diocese.

Toward the end of his life, poor health made his pastoral ministry more difficult. Bishop de Maupas died as a result of an accident, when the horses bolted as he was getting out of his carriage during a visit. He suffered a fractured skull and died two days later on August 12, 1680. An excerpt from the funeral oration, preached by Father de Saint-Michel, a priest from the Seminary of Lisieux, summarized the quality of Henry de Maupas' life: "The heart of our bishop was that of an apostle; his mouth, that of a prophet; his hand, that of a wise and generous father. . . . His words were good; his deeds, even better."[122]

The Hôpital des Orphelines in the Montferrand Quarter

One of the works that Bishop de Maupas actively took in hand upon his arrival at Le Puy in 1644 was the Montferrand hospital, a very old establishment, where there were now orphan girls and widowed women. The bishop exercised significant authority in this house.

In the perspective of the Council of Trent, which desired to effect the reform of hospitals, the bishops—not lay people of high rank, judges, or citizens—were to act as reformers, overseeing the appointment of administrators and the correct use of funds. This was completely contrary to the royal position. Until the end of the seventeenth century, the kings of France issued decrees that incrementally excluded ecclesiastical administration from the various sectors of charitable establishments and activities.[123] In April of 1695, a royal edict separated the temporal jurisdiction, which was yielded to royal judges, from the spiritual jurisdiction that would from then on belong to ecclesiastical tribunals. The church thereby lost temporal jurisdiction over charitable works, which fell entirely to the king.[124] The legislation lacked adequate precision and coherence, resulting in great diversity in the organization of hospitals and sometimes conflicts of authority. Hospital chaplains retained all their prerogatives when it came to spiritual responsibility, and there was no question of replacing brothers or women religious working in the hospitals with lay people. In the beginning of the seventeenth century, all the hôtels-dieu, hospitals, and other places connected with relief were under the jurisdiction of the grand almoner of France. In 1622, Cardinal de La Rochefoucault, then grand almoner, with the king's consent, asked Pope Gregory XV for a bull placing all women religious in France involved in charitable works under the authority of their local bishop, rather than that of the grand almoner. [125] The only exception were those in the city and suburbs of Paris.

In Le Puy before the arrival of Bishop de Maupas, the Montferrand hospital was administered by the consuls, "to whom belong all supervision, direction, and management of the said hospital."[126] On April 1, 1635, in order to appoint the *dame hospitalière* in charge of the house, they had "consultations . . . with His Excellency the bishop of Le Puy and other principal officers, bourgeois, and inhabitants of the present city," but it was the consuls who made the decision. They appointed "Jehanne Comport," a native and inhabitant of Le Puy, who "thanked . . . God and the said *sieurs* consuls and community of this town, who gave her the honor and favor of calling her to this holy and meritorious ministry." She did not thank the bishop because she was not under his authority. The rest of the contract and mutual commitments were made between "the aforesaid Comport, hospitaller" and the consuls. The contract was signed "at Le Puy, in the house of *Messire* Hugues de Fillère . . . counselor of the king and his *juge-mage* in the *sénéchaussée* of Le Puy." Apparently, the bishop had only the right of inspection, but no real power over what happened at the Montferrand hospital.

Upon his arrival, however, Bishop de Maupas started immediately to see to the improvement of this hospital. Antoine Jacmon recounts in his memoirs that "in the said year 1644 . . . the said Lord Bishop brought nuns from [a blank] to form and instruct the poor girls without father or mother in the said Le Puy, sent to Montferrand."[127] Jacmon's manuscript has in the margin next to this paragraph a note written in another hand that looks old, possibly from the eighteenth century, which reads: "Establishment of the Sisters of St. Joseph."[128] This notation, added after, but probably rather close to, the event, may have projected into the past what occurred later at the Montferrand hospital. Perhaps the blank spaces that Jacmon left in his manuscript reveal some confusion on his part. He did not know where the "nuns" came from, and with good reason, because, if they were future Sisters of St. Joseph, they were not nuns, nor recognized as such. On June 20, 1644, the bishop established an administrative council in this house and appointed Canon Pierre Le Blanc as its head.[129] The canon was also involved during 1644 with the Maison du Refuge, founded in 1637 by Saint John Francis Régis and his friend, the same Pierre Le Blanc. The following year, with the bishop's consent, *Messire* Claude Spert de Volhac, priest of Saint Pierre la Tour, brought Augustinian nuns from Avignon to the Refuge.[130]

It was also in 1644, as noted above, that Bishop de Maupas established a Company of the Blessed Sacrament in Le Puy. Pierre Le Blanc belonged to this Company, and Hugues de Fillère, the king's *juge-mage* who signed the contract with Jeanne Comport in 1635, was a member before 1646, although how long before is unknown.[131] Ordinarily, a special focus of the Company was work with women of ill repute, or those in danger of falling into prostitution. Although there is nothing to affirm it with certainty, these coincidences suggest some connection between the presence of the Company in Le Puy and the renovations of these two hospitals, each protective institutions for girls or women.

The Hôpital des Orphelines had to be enlarged for better organization. On July 15, 1644, the syndic of the Montferrand hospital bought a house situated near it from Claude Charantus for sixty-eight *livres*. Charantus is recorded as having "sold [it] to His Excellency Henry de Maupas du Tour, Bishop of Le

Puy . . . who will pay the said sum to expand the rooms of the said Montferrand hospital, to care for and to house the poor." The adjoining land was also purchased on January 14, 1645.[132] In December of 1646, a quarrel erupted over the hospital: "Certain individuals are claiming to assume by authority the direction of the Montferrand hospital in this town and have taken over its administration without the knowledge of the consuls."[133] In the future, it was decided, "the *sieurs* consuls should not tolerate and not permit any person other than those who will be established by their order to hold the said administration and direction." One might suspect that these intrusive "individuals" were members of the Company of the Blessed Sacrament. There is also evident tension between the authority of Bishop de Maupas, who had appointed the administrative council, and that of the consuls, who were more directly in charge of the hospital.

Improvements and renovations continued at the orphanage. From April 7, 1646, Etienne Treveys, procurator and syndic of the orphanage, kept account of what he had furnished "to build rooms and raise the roofs."[134] In a record dated January 12, 1647, he mentioned "la Françoise," who had "to pay a workman," and noted that he had "given twenty-one *sous* to the mistress Françoise to get some plaster."[135] On March 3, 1648, during a meeting of the administrators, they

> read an ordinance for the said house, given by Monsieur de Montauban, Official and Vicar-General of His Excellency, the bishop of Le Puy . . . [after which] it was proposed that it would be very useful to have some *fille* who knows how to read and write in this house. The mistress Françoise Eyraude [*sic*] having said that she knew of one, was charged with having her come to see if they should accept her.[136]

They then asked the mistress the number living in the house. She replied that "there were two servants and thirty-nine girls." Five days later, on March 8, a certain "Marguerite" presented herself "to help to raise the said girls." She demonstrated a "great desire to serve in the said house and to keep a record of the alms given there and of the expenditures."[137]

The chronological parallels between the actions of Bishop de Maupas in restoring the Hôpital des Orphelines and those of Father Médaille in bringing the first Daughters of St. Joseph together are so striking that one has to ask whether these two projects had points of convergence. Could Father Médaille, for example, have been in collusion with Bishop de Maupas in organizing the hospital? Was Françoise Eyraud, the future superior of the community in Le Puy, who appears for the first time at Montferrand in the report of January 12, 1647, part of the earlier group for whom Father Médaille had written the Règlements around 1646? Were the two servants mentioned in the memo of March 3, 1648, members of the original group or would they be among the first six sisters gathered around Françoise Eyraud in 1650 by Bishop de Maupas? The available evidence gives no definitive answers, but so many coincidences strongly suggest that these events were interconnected.

The mention of Marguerite de Saint-Laurans presents other issues. Françoise Eyraud's spontaneous proposal to the administrative council that she call upon someone she knew who could keep the accounts implies that the two women already knew each other. "Margot," as she was called, was not far from Le Puy at that time, since it took her only five days to arrive. Chaudes-Aigues, her native town, would have been too far away for her to get to Le Puy in five days. According to Gabriel Lanthenas, citizen of Le Puy and friend of the Sisters of St. Joseph, Marguerite had Father Médaille as her spiritual director and followed him on his missions.[138] In the early days of March, 1648, Father Médaille was in Le Puy because Bishop de Maupas had given him faculties to preach at the cathedral during Lent.[139] Margot was definitely in the vicinity. Perhaps she was staying with Lucrèce de La Planche, the "virtuous *demoiselle*" who welcomed the sisters in her home at Le Puy for several months before they could officially become a community at the Montferrand hospital. At that time no one knew it, but there is an impression that some type of synthesis was underway. After 1648, the hospital was called the "Maison de la Charité des Filles Orphelines de Saint-Joseph." The new title of the house could have meant that the women who worked there were already living according to the Règlements Father Médaille had given the Daughters of St. Joseph in 1646, or simply that Bishop de Maupas had a special devotion to St. Joseph. A letter written to "his very dear and incomparable sister" on May 4, 1648, refers to a young boy whom he needed as a footman. "If he has not yet been confirmed . . . I hope he will take the name of St. Joseph at confirmation. This great saint, who is my special patron this year, deserves my particular veneration for many reasons."[140] Among those reasons, perhaps one was the Daughters of St. Joseph.

Bishop de Maupas could not have been ignorant of Father Médaille's activities in his diocese. Since he knew Françoise Eyraud, the bishop very likely also made the acquaintance of the widows and pious women whom Father Médaille had encountered, who wanted to consecrate themselves to God and to the service to the neighbor, and for whom the Règlements had already been written. Was there, as Father Nepper thought, a first attempt at foundation between 1645 and 1650, a "first St. Joseph" that would not continue, and a second, official foundation around 1650 that alone gave birth to the "Little Congregation of St. Joseph"? The history of the first houses of St. Joseph offers a key to these questions.

NOTES

1. *Constitutions pour la Petite Congrégation des Sœurs de Saint-Joseph*, à Vienne, chez Laurens Cruzi, 1694.

2. AMM Le Puy, Communauté de Dunières.

3. AD Haute-Loire, 12 H, Filles de Saint-Joseph, Hôpital de Montferrand, liasse 1 (1651-1692), Permission donnée aux filhes de S. Joseph par le Seigr de Maupas evesque du Puy touchant leur établissement. The words in brackets do not appear in the contract.

4. Michel Pomarat, "Barthélemy Eyraud, Seigneur de Chaumarès, secrétaire de la reine Anne d'Autriche," *Bulletin historique . . . de la Société académique du Puy et de la Haute-Loire* 60 (1984): 21 n.

5. AM Le Puy E 67, Livre des Mariages et mortuaires de l'Eglise paroissiale Saint-Georges-du-Puy, (15 nov. 1654-29 déc. 1683), fol. 35v.

6. AD Haute-Loire, 6 E 246.1, Registres paroissiaux Saint-Privat d'Allier. The registers stop in May 1611 and resume in 1642.

7. AD Haute-Loire, H suppl. Hôtel-Dieu, vol. 1: 1B 455; and H suppl. Hôtel-Dieu, vol. 2, Papiers de famille: Eyraud, 157.

8. AD Haute-Loire, Fonds de l'Hôtel-Dieu, 1 B 38, 1641.

9. Pomarat, "Barthélemy Eyraud."

10. Ibid.

11. Ibid. The original of this letter would be in the Archives of the Hôtel-Dieu; it appears as an appendix in Albert Bois, *Les Sœurs de Saint-Joseph, les Filles du petit dessein, de 1648 à 1949* (Lyon: Éditions et imprimeries du Sud-Est, 1950).

12. Bois, 343.

13. AD Haute-Loire, H, suppl. Fonds de l'Hôtel-Dieu, vol. 1, 1 B 445, 1692.

14. Ibid., H, Fonds de l'Hôtel-Dieu, Papiers de famille: Eyraud, 157.

15. Ibid., Fonds de l'Hôtel-Dieu du Puy, 1 E 1, Registre des délibérations du bureau de l'Hôtel-Dieu, 1651-1660, fol. 79.

16. AM de Langogne, Registre B 1610-1632, "Clauda Chastel, nee le 20 avril 1612 à langogne; père Mes. Simon Chastel, mère: Philippe Bongiraud, parrain: Claude Gibelin, marraine: Claude Bongiraud," from material supplied by author, May 16, 2005. –Trans.

17. AD Haute-Loire, 3 E 224, 9, Arcis Ne, 1651-1653, fols. 571 ff.

18. AD Lozère, 3 E 4391, Issartel, 1647-1649.

19. Félix Viallet, *Langogne* (Mende: Société des Lettres Sciences et Arts de la Lozère, 1982).

20. Viallet, 77.

21. AMM Le Puy, Communauté d'Yssingeaux, "Catalogue des Sœurs défuntes de la maison de Saint-Joseph d'Yssingeaux puis l'année 1657." This twelve-page notebook begins with a list of names, including "Clauda Chastel, Superior" and "Marie Reboul."

22. J. E. Dufour, *Dictionnaire topographique du Forez et des paroisses du Lyonnais et du Beaujolais, formant le département de la Loire* (Mâcon: Impr. Protat frères, 1946), col. 885.

23. AM Saint-Julien-Molin-Molette, Registres paroissiaux, 1er registre (1614-1693).

24. BM Grenoble, R 8372, "Registre des Religieuses de Saint-Joseph de la Ville de Vienne a commencer en l'année mil six-cent-soixante-huit," Testament de la Mère Jeanne Burdier, 46.

25. AM Vienne, H 75, Papiers de la Mère Burdier.

26. Ibid.

27. AD Isère, 21 H 1, Sœurs de Saint-Joseph, Registre de professions (1681-1792).

28. BM Grenoble, R 8372, "Registre des Religieuses de Saint-Joseph de la Ville de Vienne a commencer en l'année mil six-cent-soixante-huit," 1.

29. Perhaps her sister Jeanne had died.

30. BM Vienne, Hôpital, GG 42, État-civil 1680-1733, fol. 75v.

31. AMM Sœurs de Saint-Joseph, Saint-Vallier (copy preserved without reference), Lettre d'Anne Felix annonçant le décès de Marguerite Burdier.

32. BM Grenoble, R 8372, Registre des Religieuses de Saint-Joseph de la Ville de Vienne a commencer en l'année mil six-cent-soixante-huit, Table alphabétique des matières, lettre V (Vierge Marie), "Le R P. Balthasard Gelas de la Vierge Marie, augustin déchaussé de Vienne . . . confesseur des Religieuses de Saint-Joseph à l'hopital."

33. AM Le Puy, E 68, Paroisse Saint-Agrève-Saint-Georges, Mariages et mortuaires, 1684-1700, fol. 47.

34. Ibid.

35. Jean Pierre Gutton, *La Société villageoise de l'Ancienne France* (Paris: Hachette, 1979), 46: "Children had to ask their parents' consent in order to marry, up to 25 years for women and 30 years for men. . . . This was in theory; often, there was greater freedom among the common people in rural environments." [Translation mine. –Trans.]

36. *CV* 1694, Preface.

37. [Étienne Michel Faillon], *Vie de Monsieur de Lantages, pretre de saint-Sulpice, premier supérieur du séminaire de Notre-Dame du Puy* (Paris: Imp. A. le Clère et Cie, 1830), 115; and F. Gouit, *Une congrégation Salésienne; Les sœurs de Saint-Joseph du Puy-en-Velay, 1648-1915* (Le Puy: Impr. de l'Avenir de la Haute-Loire, 1930), 36.

38. Gaston de Jourda de Vaux, *Le nobiliaire du Velay et de l'ancien diocèse du Puy (noms féodaux)* (Le Puy: Impr. Peyriller, Rouchon & Gamon, 1925), 3:61.

39. AD Haute-Loire, J 237, no. 166, Famille du Ranc de Joux.

40. Marie Brioude, *Recherches historiques sur une partie du Velay, principalement la ville et la paroisse de Tence* (Le Puy: A. Prades-Freydier, 1900), 76.

41. Ibid.

42. AD Haute-Loire, J 237, no. 213, Transaction à l'amiable, du 23 mai 1640.

43. Brioude, 76.

44. AD Haute-Loire, E Dépôt, 112, Tence, registre S. 1623-1672. Contrary to Bois, 43, Lucrèce de la Planche was never widowed.

45. AMM Le Puy, Délibération des Administrateurs de la maison de la Charité des Filles orphelines de Saint-Joseph, du 3 mars 1648.

46. Jacques de Montrouge, bishop of Saint-Flour from 1647 until his death in 1664.

47. Archives privées de monsieur Charles Bayon de la Tour, Le Puy, "Memoyre d'ung grand miracle arrivé à St Joseph."

48. AD Lozère, P 351, Mariage de Pierre de Chateauneuf et de demoiselle Benoite Richard, 29 octobre 1661.

49. Marie-Henri-François-Charles de Lescure, *Armorial du Gévaudan* (Lyon: A. Badiou-Amant, 1929), 49.

50. Pierre Hippolyte Hélyot, *Histoire des Ordres monastiques, religieux et militaires, et des Congrégations séculières*, 8 vols., Nouvelle éd., revue et corrigée (Paris, Louis, 1792), 8:186.

51. Abbé [Jean-Joseph] Rivaux, *Histoire de la Révérende Mère du Sacré-Cœur de Jésus, Supérieure Général de la Congrégation de Saint-Joseph de Lyon* (Lyon: Briday, 1878).

52. [Mère Augustine Battut], *Origine et développement de la Congrégation de Saint-Joseph du Bon Pasteur* (Clermont-Ferrand: Imp. de Vve Petit, 1879).

53. AMM Clermont, Correspondance de Mère Sainte-Agathe Dupuy de la Grand'Rive avec le P. [Ernest-Marie] Rivière, SJ, 1899-1913. Father Rivière was then working on vol. 11, the supplement to Sommervogel's work, published as *Corrections et additions à la Bibliothèque de la Compagnie de Jésus: Supplément au "De Backer-Sommervogel"* (Toulouse: Chez l'auteur, 1911-1917). His correspondence with Mère Saint-Agathe explains why in that volume he attributes the "Constitutions pour la Congrégation des Sœurs de St. Joseph du Bon Pasteur" to Jean-Pierre Médaille (11:col. 573, no. 1712).

54. Ferdinand Cavallera, "L'héritage littéraire des Pères Médaille," *Revue d'ascétique et de mystique* 11 (April 1930):185-95.

55. For information on Pierre Médaille (1638-1709) and Jean-Paul Médaille (1618-89), see Bois, 33 and 35. [Marie-Louise Gondal, although her conclusions demand extreme caution, provides new archival information about the Médialle family and about the college of Carcassonne, *Les origines des sœurs de Saint-Joseph au XVIIe siècle: Histoire oubliée d'une fondation: Saint-Flour - Le Puy (1641-1650-1661)* (Paris: Les Éditions du Cerf, 2000), 36-51. –Trans.]

56. Bois, 33-50.

57. The author identifies Adrien Carrère as superior from 1887 to 1893 at the Residence de la rue des Fleurs, Toulouse, where the archives of the Toulouse Province were kept; see *Bibliothèque de la Compagnie de Jésus: Nouvelle edition*, ed. Carlos Sommervogel, SJ (Bruxelles: O. Schepens / Paris: A. Picard, 1890-1909), s.v. "Carrère".–Trans.

58. Marius Nepper, SJ, *Origins: The Sisters of St. Joseph*, trans. commissioned by the Federation of the Sisters of St. Joseph, USA [Erie: Villa Maria College, 1975], 3-6 and 64-67. [See also *Dictionnaire de spiritualité ascétique et mystique, doctrine et histoire*, s.v. "Médaille, Jean-Pierre," by Marius Nepper. –Trans.]

59. Anne Hennessy, "In Search of a Founder: The Life and Spiritual Setting of Jean-Pierre Médaille, SJ, Founder of the Sisters of St. Joseph," PhD Thesis (Berkeley: Graduate Theological Union, 1988). –Trans.

60. Sister Pesche's original work, intended as an audio-visual presentation, was quickly communicated to all the Federations of Congregations of St. Joseph originating from Father Médaille. [Subsequently published as M. Pesche, *Jean-Pierre Médaille, dati biografici dai documenti dell'archivio Romano della Compagnia di Gesù* (Cuneo, 2000).–Trans.] See Appendix 2.

61. Adrien Demoustier, SJ, *Les catalogues du personnel de la province de Lyon en 1567, 1606 et 1636*, thèse de doctorat (Rome: Archivum historicum societatis Jesu, Ext., 1974), 59-60 ff, and 163-64.

62. AD Aude, Registres de la paroisse Saint-Michel à Carcassonne, Acte de baptême du Père Jean-Pierre Médaille, année 1610.

63. Bois, 35-36.

64. ARSI, FG 1382.8, Primus contractus fundationis Collegii Carcassonens. 16 Martii 1623.

65. ARSI, Tolos. 5, fol. 177.

66. ARSI, Tolos. 5, fol. 179 v : "Ingenium: eximium"; "mortificatio: magna et eximia."

67. ARSI, Tolos. 5, fols. 202, 215, and 239. Years in the Roman Catalogues generally run from one feast of St. Luke (October 18) to the next in regard to assignments.

68. *CSJ* 1970, part 5, chap. 2, no 519.

69. ARSI Tolos. 5, fol. 420. The triennial catalogue for 1642 also erroneously listed Jean-Pierre Médaille at the college of Montauban, but the contextual information identifies his brother, Jean-Paul. See Appendix 2.

70. Arch. Pr. Toulouse, Père Cros, D 9 1212. [The archives of the former Toulouse Province of the Society of Jesus are now located at Archives de la Province de France de la Compagnie de Jésus, 15 rue Raymond Marcheron, 92170 Vanves, France. –Trans.]

71. ARSI, Assistencia Galliae, Epistolae General. 40, 55v.

72. This date appears in all the triennial catalogues following 1643.

73. Nepper, *Origins*, 4-5.

74. Demoustier, *Les catalogues du personnel de la province de Lyon*, 42 ff.

75. *Règles de la Compagnie de Jésus*, à Paris, chez Jean Fouët, MDCXX, French version of the *Regulae Societatis Jesu*, which round out and clarify the Constitutions and were drawn up in part during the lifetime of St. Ignatius.

76. *RSI* 1620, Règles du Supérieur, 134.

77. Ibid., Règles du Ministre, 241 ff.

78. Ibid., Règles du Procureur du Collège et de la Maison de Probation, 347 ff.

79. Although the annual catalogue for 1647-48 is lacking, a letter addressed to Médaille by Father General Caraffa on April 15, 1648, alludes to his duty of writing about affairs in the house ("de re domestica scriberet"), indicating that he was certainly a consultor (Tolos. 2II, 260).

80. ARSI, Tolos. 10I, 95, Cat. Sec. Collegii Sanflorani - Anni MDCXLV.

81. Ibid.

82. ARSI, Tolos, 2II, 241 v and 260; see Nepper, *Origins*, 7-13.

83. Nepper, *Origins*, 1-11.

84. *CV* 1694, Preface.

85. [Faillon], *Vie de Monsieur de Lantages.*

86. Ibid., 116.

87. BM Grenoble, R. 8372, "Registre des Religieuses de Saint-Joseph de la ville de Vienne, a commencer en l'année mil-six-cent-soixante-huit," 1; and BM Vienne, GG 42, Registre des décès de l'Hôtel-Dieu de Vienne, 76.

88. The reference to the bishop as "dead" corresponds to the ancient usage that considered a church widowed at the loss of a bishop; see Canon 25 of the Council of Chalcedon in Henry R. Percival, ed., *The Seven Ecumenical Councils of the Undivided Church : Their Canons and Dogmatic Decrees* (New York: Edwin S. Gorham, 1901), 285. –Trans.

89. Nepper, *Origins*, 11-12, referring to the Jesuit archives in Rome previously cited.

90. Demoustier, *Les catalogues du personnel de la province de Lyon.*

91. Pierre Delattre, *Les Établissements des Jésuites en France depuis quatre siècles*, 5 vols. (Enghien: Institut Supérieur de Théologie, 1949-1957), 2: col. 1579.

92. Ibid., 2:col. 1579.

93. Ibid., 4:cols. 1243 and 1318.

94. AD Haute-Loire, Fonds du Collège du Puy, cited in Bois, *Les Sœurs de Saint-Joseph*, 46.

95. ARSI, Tolos. 2II, fol. 241v.

96. *RSI* 1620, chap. 15, "La forme d'escrire," 262-63.

97. The *RSI* 1620 allows for exceptions: the provincial consultors could write other than in January "if something pressing occurs and they deem it necessary to write outside the normal time." Father Médaille, though not a provincial counsultor, may have done so.

98. Delattre, 4:cols. 680-81.

99. *ACSS*, 12.

100. *ACSS*, 20; on the tertian residence, see Delattre, 2:col. 1579.

101. Georges Guigue, *Les Papiers des Dévots de Lyon, Recueil de textes sur la Compagnie du St Sacrement 1630-1731* (Lyon: Librairie ancienne Vve Blot, 1922), 66.

102. Delattre, 4:col. 1305.

103. Ibid., 4:14.

104. AD Haute-Garonne, MS 1E 973, Mémoire de la distribution des bouillons; and Alphonse Auguste, *La Compagnie du Saint Sacrement de Toulouse, notes et documents* (Paris: A. Picard / Toulouse: E. Privat, 1913), 26-38.

105. Auguste, 101.

106. Delattre, *Les Établissements des Jésuites en France*, "Toulouse, 2: Hostilités jansénistes et gallicaines-Affinités jansénistes, Les Filles de l'Enfance," 4:cols. 1244-47.

107. *TP* 1981, CP, 29, no. 95.

108. Ibid., CP, 26, no. 80, and 73, no. 354.

109. AD Rhône, 50 H 115 (1682-1690) and 50 H (1694-1699), Registre des délibérations de la Compagnie du Saint-Sacrement de Lyon; and AD Isère, R 5765,

Registre des délibérations de la Compagnie du Saint-Sacrement de Grenoble, du 28 novembre 1652 au 8 avril 1666.

110. *CV*, Preface.

111. Bois, 45.

112. Biographical information about Bishop de Maupas is taken mostly from Bois, chap. 1, utilizing documents from BN, MS français 20636 and Fonds Henry de Maupas G2782, which the author also consulted.

113. Etienne-Louis Couanier de Launay, *Histoire des Religieuses Hospitalières de Saint-Joseph (France et Canada)*, 2 vols. (Paris: V. Palmé, 1887), 2: chaps. 1-2.

114. BN, MS français 20636, fols. 2-3, "Documents inédits de la Compagnie de Jésus," concerning the University of Pont-à-Mousson: "l'illustrissime Henri de Maupas . . . fut promu au doctorat" and received the doctoral hood on March 28, 1635.

115. BN, MS français 20636; and Fonds Henry de Maupas G2782, fols. 11-12.

116. Henry de Maupas, *La vie du Vénérable Serviteur de Dieu, François de Sales*, Paris, Jacques et Emmanuel Langlois, MDCLVII, 309.

117. Antoine Jacmon, *Mémoires d'Antoine Jacmon, Bourgeois du Puy*, ed. Augustin Chassaing (Le Puy: Impr. Marchessou, 1885), 205-206.

118. Ibid., 206.

119. *ACSS*, 93.

120. Jean-Baptiste Payrard, "Les Pénitents du Saint-Sacrement à Chomelix," *Nouveaux mélanges historiques* (1885-1886): 187-89.

121. BN, MS français 20636, no. 72, Lettre de Mgr de Maupas à sa nièce, la Comtesse de Coligny, 27 février 1662.

122. Pierre Collet, *Vie de Henri Marie Boudon, grand-archidiacre d'Evreux* (Paris: Hérissant, 1754), Cited by Sœur Marie du Saint-Esprit Saravia, Notice sur Mgr de Maupas, Maison-Mère St. Joseph de Lyon, 1980.

123. Jean Imbert, "Les prescriptions hospitalières du Concile de Trente et leur diffusion en France," *Revue d'Histoire de l'Église de France* 42 (1956): 5-28.

124. André Latreille, Etienne Delaruelle, and Jean-Rémy Palanque, *Sous les rois très chrétiens*, vol. 2 of *Histoire du Catholicisme en France*, 3 vols. (Paris: Spes, 1960), 378.

125. *Recueil des Actes, Titres, Mémoires concernant les Affaires du Clergé de France* (Paris, 1716-1750), 4:col. 1689.

126. AD Haute-Loire, 12 H, Filles de Saint-Joseph, Hôpital de Montferrand, Le Puy.

127. Jacmon, 205.

128. BM Le Puy, Manuscrit des Mémoires d'Antoine Jacmon, 324.

129. Bois, 51; and AM Le Puy, 1 G7 1, Livre de la maison consulaire, 20 juin 1644, Nomination du Conseil d'Administration de l'Hopital de Montferrand.

130. "Some say Augustinians, others[,] Ursulines, who will soon merge with the Sisters of Notre-Dame," Nepper, *Origins*, 77, n 26.

131. "Decedz en la ville du pui . . . Mr de Filère, Juge-mage au Sénéchal du Roy, 6 juillet 1646," *ACSS*, 93.

132. Bois, 52.

133. AM Le Puy, BB 2, Registre, fols. 136-137.

134. AD Haute-Loire, H. suppl. 8 A1, Comptes d'Etienne Treveys, 7 avril 1646 à mars 1648; and AMM Le Puy, Montferrand.

135. AD Haute-Loire, H. suppl. 8 A1, Comptes d'Etienne Treveys, 7 avril 1646 à mars 1648.

136. AD Haute-Loire, H. suppl. 8 A2, Délibération du Conseil d'Administration de l'Hôpital de Montferrand, 3 mars 1648.

137. AMM Le Puy, Montferrand.

138. Archives privées de monsieur Ch. Bayon de La Tour, Le Puy, "Mémoyre d'ung grand miracle arrivé à St Josepf le 15 octobre 1654."

139. Bois, 45.

140. BN, MS français 20636, G 2782, fol. 13.

Chapter Two

Beginnings

By 1648 Father Médaille and Bishop de Maupas were simultaneously working toward the organization of the first Sisters of St. Joseph and the Hôpital des Orphelines where they would serve. Father Médaille's correspondence with his superior general in Rome attests that the sisters had already received rules before 1647. Exactly what these rules were is uncertain, but the oldest known texts belonging to the Sisters of St. Joseph contain allusions to the Blessed Sacrament and to secret groups of women, pointing to the possible influence of the Company of the Blessed Sacrament. From the earliest days of the Company, designed exclusively for Christian men (clergy and especially laymen), women had tried to organize analogous groups.

In 1631 and 1645, as mentioned above, two unsuccessful attempts had been made to form a women's Company of the Blessed Sacrament in Lyon. The *Annales* of the Company record grudging forbearance: "All we will do is to write to all the Companies to urge them to establish in their cities an Assembly of Ladies, similar to the one at the Hôtel-Dieu in Paris."[1] Baron Gaston de Renty, an influential member of the Company, assisted by the Ursuline Mère de Saint-Xavier, did establish a Company of Ladies in 1643 in Dijon, "as in several cities of the kingdom," according to the annals. The "statutes which are observed in Paris" were recommended for this new company, which continued in existence at least until 1665.[2] In 1645, the Company in Marseille developed statutes for a Company of Ladies that were also based on material sent from Paris, specifically, the "booklets of the rule written for the devout ladies in Paris who help the poor of the Hôtel-Dieu and the sick in their parish."[3] Beginning in 1644, the Company in Paris had published for distribution in other cities a text referred to as "The directive for the practice which the Ladies of Charity observe in visiting the poor at the Hôtel-Dieu."[4]

In his work on the documents of the Company in Marseille, Raoul Allier reports the existence of a draft of the "Statute and Rules of the Company of Ladies associated in honor of the most Blessed Sacrament for the practice of good works."[5] This draft seems to correspond rather closely to the one the Company in Marseille had to develop in 1645 according to instructions received from Paris, which they interpreted freely. The folder containing the document is dated 1666. Around the same time, in 1660, when the Company of *Messieurs* was suppressed in Paris, its members produced a text, "The Spirit of the Company of the Blessed Sacrament," and sent it to all the provincial companies as a kind of last will and testament.[6]

FATHER MÉDAILLE'S NEW ASSOCIATION
AND THE COMPANY OF THE BLESSED SACRAMENT

The texts of the Company introduced above, although quite different, one for men and the other for women, show interesting parallels in some aspects to the earliest documents of the Sisters of St. Joseph: the Règlements, the Constitutions, and a letter to an anonymous sister called the Eucharistic Letter.

A Sister of St. Joseph reading "The Spirit of the Company of the Blessed Sacrament" is inevitably struck by the concern for the perfection and sanctity of all the members of the Company, as well as the universal scope of their apostolic service:

> This study and this work of personal perfection in the whole body and in the members of the Company are preferable to anything done for the neighbor because the primary charity has to do with us, and all we do for the neighbor in the spirit of the Company is impure if not accompanied by purity of spirit.
>
> The seventh means that forms the foundation of the Company's works is to do all the good possible and to avoid all evil possible at all times, everywhere, and in regard to everyone. . . . The Company has no limits, no measures, no restrictions, except those which prudence and good judgment ought to impart in the works. It labors not only for the poor, the sick, prisoners, and all who are afflicted, but also for missions, for seminaries, for the conversion of heretics, and for the propagation of the faith in every part of the world; to preclude all scandal, all impiety, and all blasphemy: in short, to prevent all evil or to secure its remedy, to bring about all good, both general and specific, to embrace all those works that are difficult, onerous, neglected, [or] abandoned and to exert oneself for the needs of the neighbor, in the full compass of charity.[7]

The "Statute and Rules of the Company of Ladies" also introduces their principal goal, expressed early in the text as "the renewal of the spirit of the first Christian women who followed Our Lord and the apostles . . . trying as far as possible to advance his glory." Like the men of the Company, they embraced "the practice of all the works of mercy," but those could not be so comprehensive for the Company of Ladies, since they could undertake only activities "compatible with their social position and their sex."[8]

In the Constitutions of the Sisters of St. Joseph, Father Médaille very often emphasizes the call to great holiness. The novice mistress is to remind the sisters that "the distinctive character of the Daughters of St. Joseph is to profess in all things and everywhere, in great joy and gentleness of heart, the greatest perfection."[9] He describes the congregation as "a community that professes the greatest perfection in all things." In the Rules for the Superior, and in the Summary, he encourages the sisters to live in such a way that their congregation "may bear the name of congregation of the great love of God."[10] The sisters' zeal, although there was no question of going all over the world (they were only humble country women!) was nonetheless universal, since "through zeal for souls," the sisters should "provide for all spiritual and temporal needs of the dear neighbor."[11] To accomplish this, they were to practice "all the holy spiritual and corporal works of mercy of which women are capable."[12] Father Médaille echoes his Ignatian calling to promote the greater glory of God in everything and everywhere when he tells the sisters to engage in all their exercises of zeal "in such a way that God is not offended and to foster the greater glory of God in everything and everywhere."[13] Despite the similarities, one need not look to the Company of the Blessed Sacrament for the source of this language in the St. Joseph documents. A comparison of texts reveals, furthermore, that Father Médaille did not hesitate to propose to the women of pedestrian social status who were the first Sisters of St. Joseph the highest spiritual and apostolic aspirations, something the more reticent gentlemen of the Company did not do for the noble women associated with it. Granted, the *Dames* of the Company were married women who had to fulfill, as their Statute declared, the "obligations of marriage and family."[14]

In addition to this quest for the perfection of the group and the universal apostolic goal, another characteristic of the Company of the Blessed Sacrament was "to honor and to make honored the Most Blessed Sacrament of the altar . . . to adore a hidden God and to draw from this union all its strength, its grace, and its light."[15] The "Statute and Rules of the Company of Ladies" also proposed that the women of the Company "have [the women] of our times enter into the attitude of veneration and love for Jesus Christ hidden in the most Holy Sacrament that his holy women had for him when they conversed with him on earth." Among their various tasks, two Ladies were to accompany "for the period of two weeks, the most Blessed Sacrament when it is carried to the sick."[16]

The Company of *Messieurs* and the Company of *Dames* did not understand their connection with the Blessed Sacrament in exactly the same way.

Pertaining to the men, "The Spirit of the Company of the Blessed Sacrament" affirms that "since the Company is hidden . . . it must therein be continually united [to the Blessed Sacrament] to adore in it a hidden God and to derive from this union all its strength."[17] The mutual hiddenness of the Company and of the divinity leads it to union with God hidden in the Blessed Sacrament to find in him its strength. For the Company of Gentlemen, the Eucharist is principally a source of strength to act in a hidden manner. In contrast, the Company of Ladies saw the Blessed Sacrament as a model:

> To honor the hidden state of victims which is [that of Jesus] in the most Blessed Sacrament and the infinite charity which he proclaims to all, this society must be of the utmost secrecy and its members must work faithfully to sacrifice their senses and inclinations and to practice all the works of mercy.[18]

By contemplating Jesus in "the hidden state of victims" in the Blessed Sacrament, as well as his great love for humanity, the Ladies are led to perfect self-sacrifice and to practice the works of mercy. The connection between the Sisters of St. Joseph and the Blessed Sacrament formulated by Father Médaille is much more in line with that of the Company of Ladies than of the Company of Gentlemen. In the Eucharistic Letter, as in the *Règlements*, Father Médaille presents the Blessed Sacrament as "the true model of their institute, completely emptied of self."[19] In the original Constitutions, he recalls that the Eucharist gave birth to the congregation and must continue to make it live and grow. The Eucharistic devotion of the Sisters of St. Joseph was similar to that of the Ladies of the Company, but it went even farther because it was intended to lead the sisters to the fullness of union with Christ.

The Secret

The most distinctive aspect of the Company of the Blessed Sacrament was its character as a secret association. Secrecy was necessary in the mind of the Company because it provided the means "to undertake important works with more prudence, indifference to success, and fewer contradictions."[20] The main reason for secrecy was a concern for effectiveness. To circumvent obstacles, each member appeared to act under his own name, but he was in fact acting by order of the Company, which was the real, yet invisible, moving force. In order to achieve its universal apostolic goal, the Company had to remain hidden. The immense ambitions of its endeavors encroached upon all kinds of domains. Had it become public, it would have been condemned to disappear.[21] The meaning of secrecy within the Company evolved over time, however. The desire for effectiveness, preponderant at the beginning (1630), gradually changed to a mystical sense of imitation of the God hidden in the

Blessed Sacrament. According to Yves de La Brière, "The mystical rapprochement between the constant hiddenness of the Company and God hidden in the Eucharist was a result of the discipline of secrecy. It did not precede it. The joy of the members of the Company from then on was to be clothed in the livery of a God truly hidden."[22]

The results of this evolution among the *Messieurs* appear in the "Rules for the Little Company of the Blessed Sacrament in Small Towns," where it says, "The Society will remain very secret, as it should have no foundation other than profound humility and charity, in imitation, as far as possible, of O[ur] L[ord] in the Blessed Sacrament, where he is hidden."[23] The same thought is evident in the "Rules for the Little Company of the Blessed Sacrament in the Country," which states, "Secrecy is the soul of this Company, along with humility and charity; this is what Our Lord shows us in this adorable Sacrament where we must imitate him, doing good without revealing the Company."[24] From the beginning, the "Statute and Rules of the Company of Ladies," as seen above, presented secrecy as the way to imitate Christ in the Eucharist. To honor this divine obscurity and "this infinite charity . . . the society must be very secret." Its members must imitate the abnegation and the charity and mercy of Christ. For the Company of Ladies, the purpose of secrecy was never efficacy, but mystical identification.

A similar evolution in the understanding of secrecy seems to appear in the different manuscripts of the Règlements for the Sisters of St. Joseph. Of the thirteen original manuscripts kept in Le Puy, Lyon, and Clermont, eight contain the complete text of the Règlement, which consists of the schedule for various exercises, a general presentation of the new association, and instructions about practices regarding the neighbor.[25] These Règlements manuscripts describe the association as "a very secret Congregation which professes a life . . . wholly consecrated to the pure and perfect love of God, in the practice of profound humility." The congregation bears the name of St. Joseph. Its members live in restricted numbers in small houses, without distinctive dress or monastic enclosure. The aim of the association "will be for them to lead a life of holiness that is lowly and empty of self in human eyes."[26] All eight Règlements manuscripts, plus two others, include the same schedule of exercises (daily, weekly, monthly, yearly). There, the Blessed Sacrament is presented as "the true model of their Institute, completely emptied of self and completely hidden, established entirely to procure the total union of souls with God and among themselves."[27] Rather than a sense of mystery for the sake of increased effectiveness, the secrecy of the Congregation (as for the Company of Ladies), its littleness, its invisibility to human eyes, its consecration to the perfect love of God, all clearly have a mystical meaning of resemblance to the Blessed Sacrament, "a true model of their Institute completely empty of self."

Only the Lyon manuscript includes passages in the Règlements that give secrecy a different connotation. These passages allude to other secret groups, directing the sisters "to instruct persons of the secret associations who will come to see them." In addition, the Lyon manuscript says, "They will also take care of secret associations of the neighbor which will be spoken of later." An explanation of the secret associations to be conducted by the Sisters of St. Joseph does appear at the end of the Règlements, in the section dealing with exercises regarding the neighbor:

> Finally, [the sisters] will organize and admit to the secret Association the persons who come to them, exhorting them to have a weekly spiritual conference according to the rule that will be written down for them. Moreover, these associations should be only in groups of three, so that they may act with greater secrecy and confidence and less danger of ridicule from persons who criticize everything having to do with the holy service of God.[28]

The caution in this passage echoes "The Spirit of the Company of the Blessed Sacrament," written for men, and does not occur in the "Statute and Rules of the Company of Ladies." The Lyon manuscript contains an additional text, immediately following the Règlements, entitled "What is suitable for the three souls, united in heart and in that of Jesus, and in memory of the earthly Holy Trinity." It opens with some brief exhortations and develops an agenda for meetings of the three associated women, in order to help one another "in this great design of being only for God, in the heart of God," and of being so both in their personal life and in their duties toward their family.[29]

It is obvious that the secret societies discussed in this single manuscript are different from the associations of Sisters of St. Joseph described in all the other texts of the Règlements. They were made up of persons responsible for families who came to the sisters. Their meetings focused on spiritual conversation about their personal and family lives. There is no reference to works of mercy. The secrecy, designed to facilitate action, is reminiscent of the Company of the Blessed Sacrament. The group of three in the Lyon manuscript is clearly different from the Company of Ladies of the Blessed Sacrament, however, because it includes only three members (or a small number of women), and there is no mention of "the practice of good works." These "secret associations for the neighbor" were one way for the Sisters of St. Joseph to accomplish a directive presented earlier in the Règlements, under duties toward the neighbor: "to give spiritual formation and direction of life to all those of their sex, in accordance with their social status, age, and occupation in life."[30] The description of these groups does not appear to be related to the Company of the Blessed Sacrament, either that of the Gentlemen or of the associated

Ladies. The word "secret" does not surface anywhere during the meetings, either to facilitate action or mystic imitation of Christ in the Eucharist.

The meeting of the three women, focused on mutual help in deepening their spiritual life and better fulfilling "the duties of their office and social rank," is much closer to meetings organized by the Jesuits for the Marian Congregations (or sodalities) established in their colleges than to Companies of the Blessed Sacrament. Elements included in the text on "Three Associated Souls" appear prominently in the various booklets communicating the rules of these Marian Congregations: the goal proposed; sanctifying the day through the morning offering, some beneficial reading, and the particular examen, as well as concern for the sanctification of the family. The same holds true for frequent communion, at least every two weeks, and devotion above all to the Blessed Virgin and Saint Joseph, and finally to the patron saint for the month.[31] Marian Congregations were flourishing at the College of Le Puy and the College of the Trinity in Lyon.[32] Father Médaille had been prefect of the Marian Congregation at Aurillac from 1639 to 1641.[33] The Company of the Blessed Sacrament, furthermore, had strong links to the Marian Congregations, because they formed a basis of recruitment for the main group and branches in the provinces. Despite repeated prohibitions by successive generals of the Society of Jesus against members' working with women, some Congregations of Ladies, and others that were mixed, were organized in several European countries as a way of influencing family life.[34] In Lyon, during the episcopate of Alphonse de Richelieu († 1653), enemies of the Jesuits protested against what they described as an invasion by Jesuit Associations or Congregations: "there were some for the rich, there were some for the poor . . . there were some for married people, there were some for adolescents, there were some for children, there were even some for women."[35]

If these groups were so common, the insistence of the Lyon manuscript on secrecy for the associations of women is puzzling, particularly when it was never mentioned during their meetings. In 1645 or 1646, the danger of ridicule was very real for simple women who claimed to provide spiritual guidance for other women, just as Jesuits did for their sodalities. Stress on secrecy in the Lyon text may indicate that it was an older document, and with time, it became unnecessary in the other manuscripts to speak of secret gatherings. The Lyon manuscript undoubtedly provides the best evidence of the influence of the Company of the Blessed Sacrament on the first communities of St. Joseph. In it Father Médaille proposes to the sisters, for the spiritual formation of the "associated souls," means inherited from the Company of the Blessed Sacrament and the Marian Congregations. It is the only document, however, to provide such evidence.

In every manuscript without exception, the Règlements delineates for the sisters a way of life that is unquestionably a distinctive form of apostolic religious life. It is not simply an association of pious and charitable women, like the "Company of Ladies Associated in honor of the most Blessed Sacrament and for the practice of good works." Details of the way of life found in the Règlements—house, dress, "a type of enclosure"—all express apostolic presence to a life situation in a secrecy that is humility, the absence of prestige, and not mystery. The name of St. Joseph given to the new group of women has sometimes been misinterpreted.[36] Seven manuscripts state that the name was chosen because of the "virtue hidden *in* this great saint" (*la vertu cachée en ce grand saint*). Only the Lyon document refers to the "hidden virtue *of* this great saint" (*la vertu cachée de ce grand saint*).[37] The latter expression, "the hidden virtue" of Joseph, read as equivalent to humility, reinforced mystery and secrecy. Virtue (*vertu*), however, an important term here, must be understood in keeping with the strong meaning it had in the seventeenth century of physical or moral vigor. Consequently, St. Joseph is the man who carries within him a holiness both vigorous and inconspicuous. The sixth point of the summary in the Règlements confirms this interpretation: "In honor of St. Joseph . . . they will be all union and charity among themselves and toward every kind of neighbor."[38] This is the fullness of sanctity, even though no more visible than that of the Blessed Sacrament.

The Eucharistic Letter, to be examined later, is addressed to an unknown sister and develops the mystical dimension of the Règlements.[39] Quite probably written after the Règlements, it contains the same language of humble and unobtrusive presence, in the image of Christ in the Blessed Sacrament, in order to "bring about this two-fold union of the sisters and of the dear neighbor among themselves and with God."

"The Blessed Sacrament gave beginning . . ."

A comparison of the manuscripts of the Règlements for the Sisters of St. Joseph with the texts of the Company of *Messieurs* and the Company of *Dames* sheds some light on Father Médaille's assertion that "the Holy Sacrament of the Eucharist . . . gave beginning to their very little congregation."[40] It may also lend some accuracy to our understanding of when the first sprouts of the Congregation of St. Joseph began to appear.

Father Médaille's correspondence with Rome, showing that he had already given the sisters rules in 1646, revealed that the congregation's origins could have occurred between 1645 and 1646. At approximately the same time, several attempts were being made to form Companies of Ladies of the Blessed Sacrament in various French cities. Such an attempt was rejected in Lyon on

December 7, 1645.[41] Correspondence from the Company of Paris to Marseille dated April 11, 1645, reports that they had sent "booklets of the rule prepared for the devout women of Paris who help the poor of the Hôtel-Dieu and the sick of their parish."[42] The Parisian Company had been having the booklets printed since 1644. A reversal of former policy, transmitted from Paris to Marseille on March 13, 1646, forbade "the Company of Paris and all the others to have any communication, liaison, and correspondence with any Company of Ladies, under any pretext whatever."[43] The ban on communication with Companies of Ladies, meant to protect the secrecy of the men's groups, certainly created problems for the formation of groups of women.

If the first Sisters of St. Joseph actually did want to participate in the Companies of Ladies of the Blessed Sacrament, this prohibition could have caused them to change direction and deepen their desire for the total gift of themselves to God and to the neighbor. Marguerite Burdier, from the Vienne diocese, with family connections to that of Lyon, always, throughout her life had relationships with the Company of the Blessed Sacrament. In becoming a Sister of St. Joseph, it is plausible that she continued, but in a different way, what she had done prior to coming to the hospital at Montferrand. Following this line of conjecture, one might posit several possibilities about where the earliest beginnings took place. The first devout women could have met Father Médaille in Toulouse while caring for the sick poor at the Hôpital de la Charité Saint-Joseph de la Grave. Or it may have been in Rodez. It could also have happened at Saint-Flour, under the protection—before his nomination to Rodez in 1646—of Bishop Charles de Noailles, a member of the Company of the Blessed Sacrament. Or they may have gathered in Le Puy where Bishop de Maupas, also a member of the Company, arrived in January 1644 and brought "nuns" to the Orphan Hospital of Montferrand.[44] Speculation is the only thing possible at this point. Beyond Father Médaille's correspondence with Rome, there is simply no precise information about the earliest phase of the congregation.

Four of the first six sisters at Le Puy were from the same area on the borders of the Velay and Forez regions. The first house of Dunières was located in the same area. None of the sisters came from the Haute-Auvergne. The only one from that region was Marguerite de Saint-Laurans, from Chaudes-Aigues, on the border of the regions of Auvergne and Gévaudan, but she was not a sister. Like Marguerite, Clauda Chastel, who was from Langogne in Gévaudan, could have encountered Father Médaille during his missions. Supported by the Company of the Blessed Sacrament, several missions were preached in the Cévennes, particularly in 1639 and 1651. The absence of women from the Auvergne among the first sisters, nevertheless, leaves little room for the possibility of a beginning in Saint-Flour. On the other hand, the appearance of Françoise Eyraud's name at Montferrand in 1647 and the origins of three of these women in the diocese of Le Puy support the conclusion that the initial group came together in the diocese, if not the city, of Le Puy.

It is equally uncertain whether the first rules that Father Médaille gave to the "pious group of women" (and that worried the Father General) were identical with the existing Règlements. Neither do we know what forms of life the first group of women followed when they were brought together by Father Médaille—or perhaps brought together, with Father Médaille, by the Company of Ladies of the Blessed Sacrament. It is very clear, however, that the Règlements for the Sisters of St. Joseph, though related in some way to the Statutes for the Company of Ladies of the Blessed Sacrament, describes a non-cloistered form of religious life that really existed and that was innovative enough to trouble the ecclesiastical or religious authorities of the time. This first group of Sisters of St. Joseph persisted in its early days as an apostolic presence barely discernible in its own milieu. The secret societies for the neighbor disappeared rather rapidly, at least in that form, from texts of the Sisters of St. Joseph. Described only in the Lyon manuscript, they are absent in the others. The Lyon manuscript thereby preserves a hint of the trial and error of the origins, while setting forth, even then, the originality of the first communities of St. Joseph. The survival of relatively numerous manuscripts of the Règlements from the seventeenth and eighteenth centuries testifies that communities of this type still existed during that period. This earliest form of life was therefore not ephemeral. It was well recognized in its time as one of the forms of life for the Sisters of St. Joseph. Only later history, however, clarifies the relation of this proto-community with the community of Le Puy and the others described in the Constitutions.

THE FIRST HOUSES OF ST. JOSEPH

Dunières, 1649

The first known house of Sisters of St. Joseph was in Dunières. In this village about thirty miles northeast of Le Puy, the Jesuits from the College of the Trinity in Lyon appointed the *curé*, since they owned the priory of Saint-Martin de Dunières. Previously a dependency of the Benedictine Abbey of Chaise-Dieu, this priory, with the consent of the abbot, had been ceded to the College in Lyon through a papal bull on May 5, 1577.[45]

The foundation of the house at Dunières is recorded in a notarized act titled "Constitution of a dowry for herself made by Sister Anne Deschaux, Superior of the Congregation of the Daughters of St. Joseph."[46] It shows that Anne Deschaux, from the place of the Chasteaux, parish of Dunières [was] the first and most intent on taking the habit of the daughters of the Congregation of St. Joseph established by her in the said Dunières at the request of the R[everend] F[ather] Médaille of the Society of Jesus, the twenty-ninth day of September, one thousand six hundred forty-nine.

In what is called a "good and praiseworthy design," she hoped for "all sorts of good success and benefits advantageous for the said parish, both spiritually and temporally." She was "assisted by several women," particularly "by Sister Catherine Gagnaire and Marie Blanc, established [*sic: establies*] in the habit in their parish of the said Dunières."[47] The document, dated February 10, 1662, almost thirteen years after the community began, portrays fear on the part of Anne Deschaux that she, or her relatives after her, would be criticized for having used the goods of the house where they lived without having brought anything to it. To allay these fears, she constituted for herself a dowry of 538 *livres*.

The same document reports that Marie Blanc, who "took the habit of the daughters of the Congregation of St. Joseph" a year before in 1661 "on the feast of St. Luke the Evangelist . . . in the house established in the village and parish of Dunières," asked to make "general profession." Sister Anne promised her that her profession would take place before "the feasts of the next Pentecost." In order "to live more suitably," she constituted for herself a dowry of "four hundred *livres* and three baskets of rye wheat, measure of Saint-Didier." These dowries were set up for the benefit of the community, whatever would later become of it, even "if it ceased to exist" for any reason or was transferred elsewhere.

The community of Dunières came into being both from the great desire of Anne Deschaux ("the most intent") and from the entreaty of Father Médaille, who requested the foundation. Although the community was established to benefit the parish both spiritually and temporally, the "Constitution of a dowry" does not mention precisely what the sisters did. The only thing said about the commitment of Marie Blanc is that she was there to "help in the good works" of the community, and that she had already given "good edification in her way of life." In the little known about the Dunières community: spiritual and temporal benefit, good works, and edification of the neighbor, the broad lines of the Little Design are already visible.

Le Puy, 1650

The official beginning of the congregation took place only with the foundation of the Le Puy community in the Hôpital des Orphelines in the Montferrand quarter and its recognition by Bishop de Maupas. Prepared over the course of several years on the part of Bishop de Maupas and the administrators by the restoration of the hospital and by Father Médaille in supporting his directees in their distinct vocation, this community was finally able to come together and obtain the bishop's approval. Father Médaille had made no mistake in turning to Bishop de Maupas and believing that he could support this innovation. Once again, the preface of the Vienne Constitutions provides a description of the event:

> Finally, everything having been prepared by the said Lord Bishop for carrying out such a pious design, His Excellency assembled all these Daughters in the Hôpital des Orphelines of Le Puy and confided its direction to them and [*sic*] the fifteenth day of the month of October, Feast of Saint Theresa, in the year one thousand six hundred fifty. This illustrious prelate gave them an exhortation, completely filled with the unction of the Spirit of God, by which he stirred all these new sisters to a more pure love of God and to the most perfect charity toward the neighbor; and at the end he gave them his blessing with extraordinary signs of cordial affection and paternal kindness toward their congregation. He then placed them under the protection of the glorious Saint Joseph and ordained that their congregation should be called the Congregation of the Sisters or of the Daughters of Saint Joseph; he gave them rules for their guidance and prescribed a form of habit for them; and finally he confirmed the establishment of the said congregation and the rules which he had given them by his letters patent of the tenth of March one thousand six hundred fifty-one.[48]

This account provides the date of the first official assembly of the community as October 15, 1650. Abbé Gouit and, later, Canon Bois contested this date as incompatible with Bishop de Maupas' other responsibilities at that time of year.[49] He would normally have been obliged to leave for the meeting of the Estates General of Languedoc. The *Histoire Générale de Languedoc*, however, asserts that in 1650 the opening meeting of the Estates took place on October 24 in Pézenas, and that the Count de Bioules gave the opening discourse, recorded in the minutes, on that same day.[50] Bishop de Maupas would have had ample time to travel to Pézenas between October 16 and 24, since the trip took only four to five days. Another potential impediment to Bishop de Maupas' departure was the diocesan synod, normally scheduled for the Thursday after the feast of St. Luke (October 18). We know, however, from an entry in the diary of Abbé Aulanier, *curé* of Brignon, that in 1650 the synod was transferred to October 7 in order to allow the bishop "to go to Languedoc, to the Estates General of the Province."[51] Bishop de Maupas could have attended the synod in Le Puy on Friday, October 7, assembled the first Sisters of St. Joseph on Saturday, October 15, and participated in the opening ceremony of the Estates General on October 24. There is every reason to accept the date given in the preface of the Constitutions for the official beginning of the Congregation of St. Joseph.

The main lines of the foundation, recorded in the 1694 Preface, show that the bishop, after the preparations discussed earlier, assigned the women whom Father Médaille had brought together in Le Puy to the Hôpital des Orphelines and put them in charge of it. That did not, obviously, happen overnight. Françoise Eyraud had taken a few years to prepare herself as head of the orphanage, and during the early part of 1650, the first sisters stayed together as guests of Lucrèce de la Planche in the house she owned in Le Puy, which was still standing, according to *Gallia Christiana*, in 1720.[52] After they moved to the hospital, Bishop de Maupas came to see them on October 15 and gave them an exhortation to inspire them to "the most pure Love of God and the most perfect charity for the neighbor." He imparted his blessing and the name of St. Joseph, who was already patron of the hospital. He also gave the sisters rules to live by and prescribed a form of dress. He would confirm their foundation and their rules again in his letters patent of March 1651.

What rules did Bishop de Maupas give the first Sisters of St. Joseph on October 15, 1650? The Preface to the Vienne Constitutions says that Bishop de Maupas gave the sisters "Rules" (*Règles*) on October 15, 1650, and confirmed those "Rules" (*Règlements*) by his letters patent of March 10, 1651. Despite the difference in terminology, the text seems to identify the two. The term *Règlements* is used in the actual letters patent in March, 1651, and it recurs in the contract of association notarized nine months later by *Maître* Arcis on December 13, 1651. Because the letters patent of Bishop de Maupas dated March, 1651, indicate that the sisters at the Hôpital des Orphelines had already begun to observe the *Règlements*, they were probably the same rules as those he gave them in 1650. It is hardly credible that the "Rules" (whether *Règles* or *Règlements*) given to the sisters in 1650 were any but those written by Father Médaille for the earliest beginnings of the Sisters of St. Joseph. Since these initial *Règlements* continued in use by the small communities in the diocese after the Constitutions were drawn up, they must have been confirmed by Bishop de Maupas and officially communicated to those communities.

The portion of the Règlements concerning the schedule was incorporated into five of the six manuscripts of the Constitutions. In the sixth of these manuscripts, that of Lyon, the Règlements appear separately from the Constitutions, and in this manuscript alone they begin with a general presentation of the new association, as one might expect. The Règlements in the Lyon manuscript continue with the organization of life, describing the yearly exercises, then monthly, weekly, and daily. They end with the exercises dealing with the neighbor. All the other manuscripts reverse this order. In them, the Règlements begin with the organization of time: daily, weekly, monthly, and yearly.[53] The purpose of the new association comes afterward, as if it were secondary, or had been written later than the description of daily exercises, which were necessary to begin living a way of life even if its definition had not yet been articulated. It must be noted, furthermore, that all the Règlements manuscripts contain, in a different section, the first three parts of the Constitutions—precisely those that define the new association. In these manuscripts, the overall presentation of the new association in the Règlements therefore loses its purpose and falls to the background. The copy of the Règlements in the Lyon manuscript, which is very detailed and perfectly organized, could well correspond to the document Bishop de Maupas authorized and officially gave to the sisters until the constitutions could be written. By preserving its most official form, the Lyon manuscript, plainly meant as an archival document, reestablishes the integral text of the Règlements.

Bishop de Maupas formally confirmed what he had done to establish the new community on October 15, 1650, through his "Letters of appointment . . . in favor of the daughters of the Congregation of Saint-Joseph of Le Puy, concerning their establishment, 10 March 1651." From then on, the sisters could "assemble and live in community in one or several houses as it will be necessary for them better to spread the fruit of their charity." In addition, "to make the said new congregation prosper," the bishop gave them "rules . . . which they shall observe exactly for the greater glory of God and the edification of the neighbor, as they have begun to keep them at the aforesaid hospital of Montferrand."[54] That same year, on December 13, the sisters ratified a contract of association in the presence of *Maître* Arcis, "royal apostolic notary," by which they constituted a community of life and goods among them.[55] This document provides the names of the first sisters: Françoise Eyraud, Clauda Chastel, Marguerite Burdier, Anna Chaleyer, Anna Vey, and Anna Brun. Only two of them, Clauda Chastel and Anna Vey, brought a dowry. Clauda Chastel brought 800 *livres*, and Jacques Vey, father of Anna Vey, promised 500 *livres*. Only one, Clauda Chastel, signed the contract; the others declared they did not know how to sign.

Records exist for the first six sisters' taking the habit and forming the contract of association, but there are none concerning the profession of vows. Nevertheless, the Règlements stipulate that the sisters "will make vows of poverty, chastity, and obedience and will possess these virtues . . . in a rather high degree of perfection."[56] These were definitely not solemn vows. In order to comply with civil and canonical legislation, they could only be private, purely devotional vows, without juridical effect. A pattern in archival records of communities of St. Joseph shows that the action signifying the official commitment of the new sister—whether taking the habit or the profession of vows—was always associated with placing goods in common through a notarized act. The first sisters at Le Puy did not place their goods in common when they received the habit on October 15, 1650. The community of goods was notarized by Arcis only on December 13, 1651, and this date probably marked the approximate time of their profession. In addition to the community of goods, they would by then have had more than one year of novitiate, fulfilling the canonical requirement.

The new community had finally been established at the Hôpital des Orphelines of Montferrand. It took several years for the women to find their own way, between the Ladies of the Company of the Blessed Sacrament and the monastic life. Father Médaille guided them in these complexities through spiritual direction, practical advice, and finalizing their rule of life. The Jesuit incurred blame from his superiors for giving rules to this group of women, and there was also trouble about the restoration of the hospital by Bishop de Maupas. The sisters risked bearing the brunt of rivalries between the city consuls and the bishop, not to mention the invisible gentlemen of the Company of the Blessed Sacrament, each party wanting to appoint persons of their own choice to manage the hospital. It appears that that Bishop de Maupas never engaged in the dialogue with the consuls and other city leaders necessary for the establishment of this new religious community.

An incident reported by Gabriel Lanthenas, "merchant of the present city of Le Puy," tends to confirm some problems in communication, and above all, the lack of any kind of recognition for the new group on the part of civic leaders. On October 15, 1654, Lanthenas happened to be with the "The *messieurs* the seneschal's magistrates, the officers of the communal court, and the consuls . . . assembled in the chamber of *monsieur* the chief justice for some business." A leader among these three bodies complained about the excessive number "of convents of nuns that the community has permitted to be established in this city," because they would cause "a shortage of food." Then, he began to say that

> with impunity, on their own authority, without having asked permission from the community of the city or having observed any of that which should be observed in order to establish a convent of nuns in a city, and to the great detriment of the Hôpital des Orphelines, a convent of nuns who are outsiders was established in the house and hospital of the orphan girls, without having asked any permission. . . . [T]o which the entire assembly agreed . . . that they should be driven from this house, and out of the city. . . . And in order to implement this decision, they deputized two persons from each of the three groups . . . who departed at once with great zeal to carry out their mission.[57]

Gabriel Lanthenas interpreted this decision, generated by the discourse of a single person, as an evil "plan which the devil had placed in his mind." Because he had a "special affection for these holy daughters" and had great veneration for Marguerite de Saint-Laurans, he ran ahead to warn them. While these notables came in through a door and rudely accosted "the mistress of the orphan girls," he went to the room where the sisters "were making ribbon" to inform them of "the intentions of these men" and to offer them his own house. He told the superior (as he called Marguerite de Saint-Laurans):

> "Alas! My good sister, do not be alarmed; they are coming to throw you out of here. But you will not be in need of a house, because God has given me one large enough to shelter you." [She] said to me in response: "Ah, Sir, if that is so, then it is an act of Providence that should cause us not to be alarmed, but to adore." At that moment, these *messieurs* came in, but God so changed the minds of all of them by his Providence that their entire behavior and conversation were nothing other than a proper and very civil visit, as if they had been sent to call on them on behalf of the community, and they left in the same manner.[58]

Of course Lanthenas was embarrassed for having made these remarks and offered his house for no apparent reason. He still wanted to know what the delegation would report to the city officials. To his astonishment, he saw them return to their respective homes as if there were nothing to report. He finishes his account: "When I recounted this event to a great servant of God, he told me it was a greater miracle than having raised from the dead someone who had been in the ground for fifteen days. I certify the above to be true; in testimony whereof I sign, Lanthenas."

From the report of Lanthenas, it would appear that the city officials knew nothing about this new community of women. If Bishop de Maupas had not considered it necessary to inform the consuls and local authorities of Le Puy about the beginning of the little community of St. Joseph, the question is why. True, the first sisters had come together gradually, as the orphanage expanded, and Bishop de Maupas' visit to the community on October 15, 1650, might have looked to an outsider like one of the numerous visits he had had to make during the hospital's restoration. In his letters patent, the bishop himself did not refer to the group as a convent or a monastery, but rather as a "society and congregation" of "several good widows and single women" seeking to "devote themselves to the laudable works of charity."[59] The absence of a reference to vows in the preface of the Vienne Constitutions (1694), which does mention taking the habit, says quite the same thing. There was no need to refer to these vows—and perhaps no need for the bishop to alert the city officials—since private vows held no formal status before the law.

The magistrates and Consuls of Le Puy accused the Sisters of St. Joseph of settling in the orphan hospital without authorization. At least one document disproves this affirmation, the contract of association of goods among the first six sisters. The end of this document affirms that "the said appearers" declared that they submitted the disposition of their goods "to the courts and conditions of *Monsieur* the Seneschal of Le Puy and to all others of the present kingdom." The authorities could have been informed that these women were living a communal life and that they held their goods in common "in order to devote and dedicate themselves to the education, care, and instruction of the orphan girls."[60] But nowhere does the contract say that the new congregation had any pretensions to religious life. This was probably the real grievance. When the local leaders discovered that the women had been leading an authentic religious life for four years, they felt that they had been duped as to the real nature of the association. If the women were religious, they had not said so and ought to be driven away, because the city could not take care of them. The authorities complained that "the excessive number of convents of nuns that the community has permitted to be established in this city would be the entire ruin of this city."[61] It was quite true that Le Puy had a large number of convents, and that too often, they had to be supported through gifts and alms. The authorities at both national and local levels needed to guarantee that new monasteries would have sufficient resources to sustain themselves so as not to burden the local inhabitants. If the Sisters of St. Joseph were nuns, it would be important to verify their means of subsistence. Like Gabriel Lanthenas, one could suspect the officials of Le Puy of bad faith. Since the authorities knew that these women had formed an association and had held their goods in common for several years, even if they did not know the details of the contract, they could have concluded with a minimum of good will that the arrangement sanctioned by the bishop's authority allowed the new religious group to support themselves. Their suspicion was probably directed more toward the bishop than the Sisters of St. Joseph.

Contact with the community had caused the delegates to change their mind. Françoise Eyraud, long known to them as "the mistress of the orphan girls," absorbed the first shock. Marguerite de Saint-Laurans, "the superior," welcomed the untoward event as sent by Providence and was immediately prepared to welcome it as such. When the men entered the room where the sisters were making ribbon, the community at work made such a strong impression on them that they could no longer say that these women were there "to the great detriment of the Hôpital des Orphelines." They lived as stipulated in their contract, making use of "every kind of work and skill . . . for their livelihood, food, and upkeep."[62] Not only were they not a burden to anyone, but they also had the freedom to apply themselves to the education of poor girls. The men's argument did not stand up. Their aggression gave way spontaneously and immediately, so completely that they showed the sisters "every kind of civility and esteem that they had towards them," and they left "without saying a word on the subject of their deputation." Obviously, after their visit to these "nuns who are outsiders" to the city, these men were speechless; there was nothing more to say. The city authorities believed that they knew something about this community of women, which they had at first thought similar to the communities of *filles dévotes* formed to serve a hospital. They subsequently envisaged it on the model of the other convents in the city of Le Puy. Having seen it, they were surprised to find that it was neither. To understand what really went on in the community, it would have been necessary either to be a member or its ecclesiastical superior.[63] Simply knowing that the new association existed at the orphan hospital was not enough to grasp the reality of its life in its concrete organization and its spiritual depth.

Was the Montferrand community the same one for whom Father Médaille wrote rules around 1646? This amounts to the question raised by Father Nepper, whether there were two consecutive foundations of St. Joseph.[64] As early as 1646, a small group of women in its earliest beginnings tried out the way of life described in the Règlements, but we do not know exactly where. It was intended to be an authentic religious life without having its external forms, as well as an apostolic presence that was simultaneously inconspicuous and effective. In 1648, the Montferrand hospital, under the administration of the *Messieurs* of the Company of the Blesssed Sacrament and directed by Françoise Eyraud, took the name "Maison de la charité des Filles Orphelines de Saint Joseph." Beginning in 1650, under the protection of Bishop de Maupas, the official connection was forged between the small group of women whom Father Médaille had met and the establishment of the first Sisters of St. Joseph at the hospital. This new community introduced by the bishop was, at the very most, a community of *filles séculières* like many others that existed in hospitals. In their own eyes, however, they were living a different reality: that of a religious life in the world, doing charitable works, but without any royal or ecclesiastical approval as a "religious order."

At that time, the community of Le Puy was not the only house of St. Joseph. Others were already established, as at Dunières (1649), or being established, as at Marlhes (1651). They needed official status, which since 1622 could be granted only by the bishop. Bishop de Maupas granted this on October 15, 1650, at the meeting held at the Hôpital des Orphelines, and especially in the letters patent he gave to the new congregation on March 10, 1651. Such official recognition was an important step for the community. A closer look at the authorization of March 10, 1651, explains what sort of recognition they received:

> We, Henry de Maupas du Tour, Bishop and Lord of Le Puy, Count of Velay, Immediate Suffragan of His Holiness, Abbot of Saint-Denis de Rheims, Counselor of the King in his Councils and First Chaplain to the Queen Regent, desirous of

advancing the glory of God and the salvation of souls and the service of charity in our diocese, having learned that several good widows and single women, wishing to devote themselves to the laudable works of charity, both for the service of the principal hospital and of the sick poor of our city and for the education and guidance of the orphan girls of our Hospital of Montferrand, and that to be able to attend with more adequate time to the said works, they desired, with our consent and by our approbation, to form a society and congregation where, living in community, it would be permissible for them without any hindrance to devote themselves to the said services, we considered this design so admirable that we have embraced it with great affection. We have permitted and do permit the said widows and single women to establish their congregation under the name and title of Daughters of Saint Joseph and to come together and live in community in one or several houses as it will be necessary for them better to spread the fruit of their charity and to be able to multiply their said houses in all the places of our diocese where we will judge it appropriate. And so that all things be done with greater order to make the said new congregation prosper, we have drawn up and given rules (*règlements*) to the aforesaid single women and widows, which they shall observe exactly for the greater glory of God and the edification of the neighbor, as they have begun to keep them at the aforementioned Hospital of Montferrand. We henceforward take the said widows and single women and their congregations, present and to come, under our protection and command our vicars and officials to see to it that their praiseworthy enterprise may never cease to obtain new growth and that no one come to trouble the said widows and single women, to whom we give our blessing from the whole extent of our affection, and we ask, with the same affection, the blessing of God the Father, Son and Holy Spirit. At Le Puy, this tenth day of March, one thousand six hundred fifty-one.

Henry B[ishop]. of Le Puy, Count of Velay[65]

The authorization granted to the community of Le Puy makes no reference to what we could call "religious life" in that house. It does refer, several times and in different ways, to "praiseworthy works of charity" and to "spread[ing] the fruit of their charity." It says that to be better able to perform these exercises they ask "to form a society and congregation" with life in community. They receive permission for this, and even for the opportunity to "multiply their said houses . . . to spread the fruit of their charity." Their official name becomes Daughters of St. Joseph. The Règlements, already observed "at the aforesaid hospital of Montferrand," are authorized and officially conferred. Rules were common, however, to all hospital personnel. There is no question of the distinctly religious life of this community. The bishop merely authorizes its existence for better service to the neighbor. He says nothing about aspects of life consecrated to God, because this remained a private matter. He authorizes what lies within his jurisdiction and for the rest, he does not transgress the edicts of the king.

The same is true for the "Permission given to the Daughters of St. Joseph by Lord de Maupas, Bishop of Le Puy, regarding their establishment," or the contract of association of goods, on December 13, 1651. *Maître* Arcis, the notary, restates the essentials of the letters patent concerning life in community for the exercise of charity, specifying that the sisters

> promise . . . to live together on the grounds of the said hospital and to live in community, to keep and observe the rules which were prescribed by the said Lord Bishop for this purpose; and for their livelihood, food, and upkeep, to make use of every kind of work and skill, and to consign to their said community each and every one of their goods, rights, and legal claims.[66]

It goes without saying, this type of document dealing with placing goods in common does not allude to religious life as such, since the very terms of the contract are directly opposed to the legal forms of the vow of poverty in monastic life. The women living in Montferrand could continue to earn money or receive other goods, whereas such things were impossible in a monastery.[67] The notarized act, executed under Bishop de Maupas' authority, could not use language contradictory to that of the letters patent he had already given.

The Règlements provide the only criterion given for the structure of the actual life led by this new group of women. A rule for a group like this was nothing unusual. All charitable operations had their rules, the same as all corporations, confraternities, sodalities—in short, all types of groups. The reaction on the part of Le Puy's prominent citizens when they realized that the new association intended to be a religious community shows clearly that the bishop's authorization had not changed anything in the community's everyday life. The reaction of persons so well informed and highly placed also indicates how the ordinary people of Le Puy would have perceived the Sisters of St. Joseph: as an association of pious women corresponding to the "sisters" in the hospitals, who came together as a means for better service of the neighbor. There was no suggestion of the life of nuns. Their way of life at Montferrand remained ordinary, "in keeping with their condition and social background."[68] The life of this community was in fact essentially the same as that described in the Règlements. It lived the same mystically "secret," or inconspicuous, reality, "in a spirit which should be all humility . . . all zeal, and all union with God, among themselves and with every kind of neighbor."[69]

There were not two foundations of St. Joseph. The community gathered together by Father Médaille, authorized by Bishop de Maupas, then visited and interrogated by the dignitaries of Le Puy, was fundamentally the same as that to which Father Médaille had given the Règlements around 1646. The official recognition by Bishop de Maupas, however, brought a new element. It authorized not only the community of Le Puy, but also other communities who wanted "to assemble and live . . . in one or several houses . . . better to spread the fruit of their charity." The bishop allowed them to "multiply their said houses in all the places of [his] diocese" where he thought it appropriate. By taking "their congregations, present and to come, under [his] protection," he desired to promote, as he said, their "new growth."

THE ORIGINAL DOCUMENTS OF THE LITTLE DESIGN

The Règlements

The first normative texts written for the Sisters of St. Joseph were composed soon after their first experiments in this life consecrated to God in the service of their brothers and sisters, lived fully in the world. As a Jesuit, Father Mé daille lived this vocation. It was he who enabled these women to realize their desire. He also gave them its first written form: the "Règlements of the Daughters of St. Joseph, Assembled in Honor of the Holy Uncreated Trinity of God the Father, the Son, and the Holy Spirit and the Created [Trinity] of Jesus, Mary, and Joseph."[70] The earliest form of this rule, around 1646, most likely began with a program of spiritual exercises, like those used by Marian Congregations of men, according to day, week, month, and year.[71] All but one of the manuscripts of the Règlements begin in this way. Father Médaille may not have added the general introduction, which follows in the manuscripts, until he received the authorization requested from his superiors. The version of the Règlements given to the first sisters by Bishop de Maupas on October 15, 1650, was probably that of the Lyon Manuscript, which originated in Vienne and gives the text its logical structure, beginning with a general presentation of the new association, followed by the prescribed form of the sisters' life, and concluding with the "Exercises regarding the Neighbor." The study of the Règlements in the preceding pages demonstrated the connection between the first communities of St. Joseph and the Company of Ladies of the Blessed Sacrament. It also revealed some distinctive characteristics of these new communities of sisters.[72] Consecrated to God by the three simple vows of religious life, with no particular dress, not even that of widows, and dedicated to every spiritual and corporal service to the neighbor, the daughters of Father Médaille were to live in small "associations" of three to six persons, with the structures and obligations "ordinary for religious orders." Their house and way of life were in keeping with the atmosphere of their social origins. In addition, they kept "a type of enclosure . . . not open to men," which would have offended propriety, and they went out only to go to church and to engage in works of charity. The Règlements nevertheless state plainly:

"contact with the world [should] be ordinary for them according to their Constitutions."[73] This last sentence was certainly added after the Constitutions were written. It shows that the mode of life described in the Règlements was expressly connected to the Constitutions, that it had been recognized, sanctioned, by the Constitutions, and integrated into the constitutional text. The general presentation of the new association in the Règlements already described all the essentials that would characterize the Sisters of St. Joseph in later texts. In particular, it contained a summary of the fundamental spiritual orientations found in the Constitutions.

The Constitutions

The "Constitutions for the Little Congregation of Daughters of St. Joseph" were drawn up by Father Médaille after 1650 and before any major expansion of houses. Towards the beginning, the Constitutions mention the possibility "that this very little Congregation would come to be spread throughout the Church of God."[74] The same eventuality is repeated at the end of the sixth part, in regard to faults against charity: "If God should bless our little Design and there are many houses, sisters of incompatible temperament can be changed."[75] In other words, when Father Médaille wrote the Constitutions, it seems he was writing for the single house of Le Puy, since it was the only one then recognized by Bishop de Maupas. The next time Bishop de Maupas was present at the foundation of a community after that of Le Puy was in 1653 or 1654, at the inauguration of the house of Tence, thereby giving it a certain ecclesiastical recognition. Father Medaille alone was present for the founding of the other small village houses, at Marlhes in 1651, and at Saint-Romain-Lachalm in 1652. The house of Tence, like those of Le Puy and Saint-Didier, would later ask for letters patent, which meant that they had some sort of ecclesiastical recognition by that time.[76] Consequently, the composition of the Constitutions can be placed between March 10, 1651, when Bishop de Maupas authorized the community in Le Puy, and before or a little after the foundation of the community of Tence, around 1653 or 1654, at the latest, 1655. The first official mention of these Constitutions was made by Armand de Béthune, successor of Henry de Maupas as Bishop of Le Puy, in his approbation given to the Sisters of St. Joseph on September 23, 1665, where he makes reference to both the "Règlements" and the "Statutes" of the Sisters of St. Joseph.

The first Constitutions of the Sisters of St. Joseph were inspired on the whole by the Constitutions of the Society of Jesus, and more precisely by the Rules of the Society. The latter, written after the Society's Constitutions, contain a "Summary of the Constitutions," "Common Rules" applying to all members, rules applying to different categories of responsibilities, and prescriptions for specific practices (for example, "Instruction for giving an account of one's conscience").[77] It was not, presumably, by chance that Father Médaille chose his inspiration chiefly from the Rules of the Society rather than the Jesuit Constitutions. He found in the Rules of the Society a more straightforward expression of the essential content of the Constitutions, as well as fidelity to their spirit in proposals for implementation. This type of text, less official than the Constitutions, could be applied to women without provoking opposition from royal or ecclesiastical authorities.

The original Constitutions of the Sisters of St. Joseph were addressed to women "who lack the means to enter religious life [in monasteries] or who are not called to it."[78] In order to open this form of religious life to all social classes, and so that the sisters could be useful to others within their own milieu, the Constitutions divide the sisters into three categories reflecting the society at the era: 1) the *demoiselles de service,* women coming from a higher social class who, having the means to live on their income, could dedicate themselves fully to works of charity; 2) the *demoiselles du travail,* who did not have sufficient means to live on and had to compensate this lack by work; and 3) the *veuves et filles de basse condition,* widows and unmarried women of the poorer classes who had to work to earn a living and would lead a "more frugal life."[79] This differentiation of groups does not indicate the existence of choir and lay sisters. It aimed to provide better service to the neighbor by women of the same social background as the people among whom they worked. In addition to the sisters who together comprised the body (*corps*) of the congregation and took simple public vows, there were others, the *agrégées.* These women were attached to the Congregation by a vow of stability, lived in small communities in towns or villages, and carried out the same exercises as the sisters. The Constitutions suggest that this group could include "noblewomen whose rank or obligations keep [them] in the world against their will."[80] Finally, joined to the congregation were *associeés,* or associates, pious lay women living in their families, who collaborated with the Sisters of St. Joseph and with the Ladies of Mercy.[81] They constituted a type of third order of St. Joseph about whom the text contains little precise information. This diversity of social conditions and ways of life adapted for the sisters the third paragraph of the Jesuit Summary: "The distinctive quality of our vocation is to . . . live wherever we may hope to render greater service to God and greater spiritual help to the neighbor."[82] It was a way of enabling the Sisters of St. Joseph to participate in a universal service of God and neighbor.

Father Médaille did not develop the structures of the nascent congregation from a vacuum. He witnessed a group of women living this vocation, working it out day by day. What he wrote in the Constitutions resulted from reflection on what he observed—he wrote for the future, but began with what he had in front of him. Knowing a little about the family situation of some of the first sisters, we can try to put names on the categories of women listed in the Constitutions. Clauda Chastel, who brought with her a significant dowry, probably belonged to the *demoiselles de service*, who lived from their revenue. Françoise Eyraud could have belonged to the *demoiselles du travail*. If, like her predecessor Jehane Comport, she had contributed any possessions at the time of her appointment as head of the Montferrand Hospital, they would already have been incorporated into the institutional resources, and the only balance required would be her work.[83] Marguerite de Saint-Laurans could have been an *agrégée*, kept in the world against her will because of her "rank or obligations." Gabriel Lanthenas names her as superior of the community, even though she did not take part in the contract of association of goods with the other six sisters. Later history shows that other *agrégées* were superiors of communities. Finally, among the *associées*, a category much more imprecise and difficult to define, was a collaborator of the first rank, Lucrèce de la Planche.

The variety of social origins among the first sisters was evident in the structures of daily life. That, too, recaptures the Jesuit Summary: "For good reasons our outward manner of life is ordinary, and should always be regulated with a view to God's greater service."[84] Despite these differences, the Règlements assert that the "same Institute" (that is, the same collection of rules) served for all the sisters, with "some exceptions however, in their food, clothing, distribution of prayers, schedule, and daily occupations."[85] The diversity among the sisters' personal situations required great flexibility in the organization of daily life and manner of clothing, eating, praying, and working. They dressed as widows because that was the most ordinary attire for women in an era of numerous wars, and also because it allowed them a freedom of action and mobility that safeguarded propriety.[86] The dress of widows could also differ from one region to another according to local custom.

The Constitutions provide no specific directives about the architecture or construction of the houses. If the sisters worked in a hospital or an orphanage, they requested a portion of the building for their community use, and in addition, "some rooms and bedrooms for the various confraternities of mercy," the orphans, or "fallen women in need of help."[87] In the country the sisters lived together "when possible . . . and only in small groups of two or three."[88] The houses were places of welcome, which also contained some private sections where the sisters observed a measure of enclosure. There is, significantly, no mention of a chapel, because the sisters attended the local parish church or other public places of worship. Since they did not recite the Divine Office, they had no need of a chapel. The work they had to do—either to earn a living or to provide spiritual or material help for the neighbor—did not allow for long daily prayers, and even the Office of the Blessed Virgin was prayed "only on Sundays and holy days." The fifth part of the Constitutions ("On their exercises") contains details, particularly for work days, about the organization of the community's life, including times for praying and working. Similar instructions appear in the fourth part, "On various offices and officers, their rules, and rules common to all the sisters."[89]

The Constitutions make no mention of the relationships among communities, perhaps because only Le Puy existed at the time of writing, and Father Médaille did not know for certain if other houses would be established. Another reason is surely the juridical status of the communities. They appear as autonomous, independent from one another, and subject only to the ecclesiastical authority of the bishop or his delegate.[90]

All the aspects of diversity presented in the life of the first communities of St. Joseph coalesce and unite around what defines the congregation itself—its purpose. In the second part of the Constitutions ("Of the end . . . and of the means for achieving it"), where Father Médaille explains this purpose at length, he also draws it together succinctly:

From what is said above, it is clear that the END of our new Congregation is twofold:

> It seeks first to establish and maintain in very high virtue all of its members. Second, to practice all the holy works of mercy, spiritual and corporal, of which women are capable, and at the same time, by means of these works to benefit many souls of the dear neighbor.[91]

This purpose is the same as that specified for the Society of Jesus in the second paragraph of the Summary: "The end of the Society is twofold: to devote ourselves with God's grace to the salvation and perfection of our own members, and with the same grace zealously to exert ourselves for the salvation and perfection of others."[92]

The final part of the Constitutions also presents a synthesis of the vocation of St. Joseph, but from a different angle. The last chapter of Part Six offers "appropriate means of sustaining the very little Congregation" and others "to prevent its decline."[93] It safeguards against things that have been harmful to other "congregations of widows and single women" and proposes remedies to help the congregation continue. This section has to be read in connection with Part Three, which treats the qualities required for persons to be admitted as members. There Médaille says, that for the congregation to remain faithful to its vocation, since it was "a community without enclosure," one had to look for "qualities of mind and body, perhaps rare . . . that women who enter religious

orders do not possess, because the latter . . . are not so openly engaged in
works of zeal for the neighbor."[94] The final chapters of the Constitutions set
forth the major spiritual foundations of the vocation of the Sisters of St.
Joseph, with what should be done and what should be avoided in order to realize it. They are the same spiritual orientations already formulated by Father
Médaille in the Règlements.

Father Médaille alludes in both the Règlements and in the Constitutions to
another document, a summary "of what seems most excellent in the virtues
they should profess": the spiritual Maxims.[95]

The Maxims of the Little Institute

All manuscripts of the Règlements and Constitutions save one contain a copy of
the Maxims, certainly given by Father Médaille to the first Sisters of St. Joseph
in the earliest days of their foundation. The Lyon manuscript of the Règlements,
apparently the oldest form of this text, is the only one where there is mention
within the Règlements of "a hundred spiritual maxims which shed light on the
great virtue which they always profess in a spirit of very exact humility and manifest littleness."[96] These maxims, known as "Maxims of the Little Institute,"
were largely drawn from the Summary of the Constitutions of the Society of Jesus, sometimes word for word, and always in keeping with its spirit. They were
not published by Father Médaille, but handed down within the congregation
along with manuscripts of the Règlements and the Constitutions until they were
published, directly following the text of the Constitutions, at Vienne in 1694. The
Constitutions refer to them as "Maxims of the Great Virtue."[97]

The Maxims of the Little Institute have often been presented as taken from
Father Médaille's *Maxims of Perfection* published in 1657 in Clermont.[98] It is
more likely that the Hundred Maxims of the Little Institute antedated the
Maxims of Perfection. In the former, after an introduction of four maxims that
recall the consecration to the Trinity, Father, Son, and Holy Spirit, the following maxims follow no apparent order, whereas the *Maxims of Perfection*,
which are more developed, are organized and separated into fourteen chapters, with a final concluding chapter. Chapter 13, called "Mixed Maxims,"
gathers together counsels of human wisdom and spiritual pedagogy found
scattered throughout the Hundred Maxims, which obviously did not fit into
any other category. It would make sense if this section were arranged for the
publication of the *Maxims of Perfection* in 1657. Had the "Maxims of the Little Institute" been drawn from the *Maxims of Perfection*, they would have undoubtedly retained the order suggested there, and that is not the case. The
more reasonable assumption, then, is that the Hundred Maxims destined for
the Sisters of St. Joseph are the older version, and that they served as the ba-

sis for the *Maxims of Perfection*. The latter text, also called "The Long Maxims" by the Sisters of St. Joseph, was addressed to all Christian souls "who aspire to the great virtue."[99]

Father Médaille encouraged the sisters to live according to their Maxims, "which," he said, "are the spirit of your little Institute."[100] He hoped that the novice mistress would take "particular care to understand the maxims of the great virtue well and to practice them . . . [so that] all the sisters understand, cherish, and observe them for the greater glory of God."[101] The Sisters of St. Joseph grasped the importance of the Maxims, since every manuscript (except manuscript A, which contains only the Constitutions) includes them. The fundamental spiritual orientations in the other writings of the founder are there, although in a scattered order, throughout the hundred maxims.

A Spirituality of Consecrated Apostolic Life

Father Médaille integrated the important points of the spirituality of the Sisters of St. Joseph in a résumé that he called "Summary of the end of the very little Congregation of St. Joseph," reproduced almost identically in the Règlements and the Constitutions.[102] Despite differences in formulation, all the documents list the three persons of the "uncreated Trinity: Father, Son, and Holy Spirit," and the three persons of the "created Trinity: Jesus, Mary, Joseph," with virtues or attitudes associated with each of these persons. The reference to the created and uncreated Trinities, surprising to us, is not unique to Father Médaille. It occurs in the writings of other seventeenth-century authors, particularly St. Francis de Sales. In a sermon given on the feast of St. Joseph, March 19, 1621, he described the "Trinity on Earth" of Jesus, Mary, and Joseph.[103] The expression "uncreated Trinity," however, presented as a linear concept, in which each person is depicted according to a particular role and from the perspective of the Incarnation, most likely derives from Bérulle and his school.[104] It may also be that Bérulle and Médaille drew from the same sources. Whatever its origin, Father Médaille uses this scheme in his own way, different from Bérulle's. He adds to the "uncreated Trinity," in an analogous and parallel fashion, the "created Trinity" of Jesus, Mary, and Joseph, through whom the Incarnation was realized. Médaille's originality lies with the inclusion of Joseph. Bérulle, Bourgoing, and others, had already spoken of Mary as the mother of grace in the Incarnation ("filled to overflowing with every kind of grace," in Médaille's words), but they never mentioned Joseph.[105] In the "Summary of the End," Médaille sets Joseph in a position analogous to the place of the Holy Spirit. Just as the Holy Spirit "is all love," Joseph is model for the sisters of "the most perfect love and charity among themselves . . . and . . . toward every kind of neighbor."[106]

In this summary and elsewhere, Father Médaille uses terms from the Bérullian vocabulary, particularly "nothingness" (*néant*) and "annihilation" (*anéantissement*), shocking to contemporary readers. These words signify the nothingness of humanity before God and the abasement of Christ in the Incarnation, but they also denote, for Christ as for the sisters, their full identification with humanity. Such negative vocabulary was quite common at the time.[107] Contemporary Jesuit writers like Jean-Baptiste Saint-Jure, for instance, used such language without belonging to the Bérullian school. The discovery of Father Médaille's contacts with the spiritual orientations of Bérulle reveals on close inspection that the "Summary of the End" was both a theological synthesis and a catechetical summary applicable to all Christians, reflecting the language of the time. Nonetheless, Father Médaille wrote this "Summary of the End" first and foremost for the Sisters of St. Joseph in the Règlements, then the Constitutions. Later he suggested it for all Christians in the *Maxims of Perfection* published in Clermont in 1657.

This double enumeration of persons and virtues captures Father Médaille's goal for the sisters. It specifies the purpose that he proposes to the Sisters of St. Joseph from the first paragraph of the Constitutions: "After providing for their own salvation and perfection, they will devote themselves to pious works of mercy. . . . They will try by means of these works to bring about . . . the salvation and perfection of neighbor."[108]

Previous research has shown that Father Médaille did not simply compile a list of virtues in imitation of eminent—and fairly inaccessible—models .[109] Rather, these virtues reveal a network of relations at whose heart the Sisters of St. Joseph are bound together with all Christians and the whole of humanity. Called by God the Father to be his children, they endeavor to enter into this union by welcoming the fullness of life which, in the image of the Son, makes them daughters of God. The experience and dynamism of the life they receive propels them toward their brothers and sisters in the world, so that they might make it known and shared. In union with Jesus as Servant, and in order to communicate this life, they live and work to bring about the restoration of humanity in every way and by every means. The "means" are not only charitable works, but also that "spiritual mercy" which leads to conversion of heart. Those who receive this good news of the Father's life and love communicate it in their turn. The Spirit of Love which unites the sisters with one another constitutes the congregation as a body, just as it gathers men and women together in the church as brothers and sisters. In working for and with the neighbor, the sisters work to bring about the "total union" of all persons with one another, and of "all persons with God" for the greater glory of God.[110] The most perfect human realization of this union in a communication of life and love is presented to the sisters in the life and the community of Jesus, Mary, and Joseph, the "created Trinity," image of the "uncreated Trinity," living from the holiness of God without extraordinary deeds.

The Règlements, even more than the Constitutions, demonstrate that the sisters' manner of life is as apostolic as their works of charity. Their "new way of life," lived at the heart of the world in a "little house," gives witness to their consecration "to the pure and perfect love of God."[111] The text does not say that they are called to frantic activity, but only that "their continual care [should be] to make live in them and in all their houses the dear life of Jesus, Mary, and Joseph in a spirit which should be all humility, all zeal, and all union with God, among themselves and with every kind of neighbor." In that way, those around them are brought to take the same path, that of the "Christians of the early church." In order to "better achieve this end," they undertake, in addition, "all the spiritual and corporal works of mercy" of which they are capable.[112]

From Father Médaille's perspective, which is that of Ignatius Loyola, the sisters' apostolic and charitable actions flow from the consecration of their life to God. Apostolic life becomes the expression of mystical life. Without the external observances of monastic life, but in other ways, they desired to live the profound reality of that life. The community, rooted in the experience of the love received from God, works that this same love might be communicated to others around them. The place of service becomes the place of union with God and with every neighbor, restoring the world to God. The spirituality of the Sisters of St. Joseph, both in its Trinitarian and Christocentric orientations and in the forms of consecrated apostolic life it expresses, is fundamentally Ignatian.

The Little Directory

The Little Directory appears in all thirteen manuscripts. There are a few passages missing in the Le Puy manuscript and some changes in the latest manuscript, which comes from Saint-Hilaire around 1750. The Little Directory nearly always begins with an invocation to the "two Trinities" and invariably ends with an offering of the year to their six persons, fitting perfectly into the spiritual orientations of Father Médaille.

At the beginning of Part Five of the Constitutions, Father Médaille announced the future redaction of a "directory governing the conduct of the Daughters of St. Joseph," as "a separate treatise for their instruction and consolation."[113] He mentions it occasionally in the Constitutions, but the actual text communicated in the manuscripts does not seem to correspond to his stated intent. The Little Directory does not, for example, mention specific hours for "visiting the sick poor," as stated in the Constitutions, nor does it deal with the relations between the professed sisters and the mistress of novices or the superior, recommended by Father Médaille "according to what will be indicated in the directory."[114] The counsels given in the Little Directory almost always deal with the sisters' personal relationship with God, and more precisely, how they are to live this relationship in "the ordinary daily actions and extraordinary actions of the week, month, and year."[115] In fact, daily and weekly practices of the spiritual life are its primary subject, with only three paragraphs devoted to monthly practices, and a few more about yearly practices.

Although some of these exercises are clearly Ignatian, the overall spirit of the Little Directory seems quite different from Father Médaille's. When he speaks of the personal spiritual life of the sisters in the Règlements and Constitutions, Father Médaille always includes some aspects of the sisters' charity among themselves and "toward every other neighbor."[116] For example, in regard to formation of the Sisters of St. Joseph, he insists that the novice mistress should take great care to make them understand "how, profitably and with perfection, to make use of the sacraments and other activities, both ordinary and extraordinary, and how to help the neighbor in all the exercises of zeal proper to their state of life."[117] Nothing of this kind appears in the Little Directory. Only one paragraph, entitled "Concerning recreation and relaxation," deals with charity among the sisters.[118] Although the section on encountering the neighbor "in the parlor" advises the sisters not to allow "the whole time of the meeting to pass without somehow raising . . . their mind to God and saying something useful for souls," it seems that the core concern is directed more toward personal perfection than to apostolic zeal for the neighbor.[119] In the realm of prayer, during thanksgiving after communion, the sisters should pray "for all the needs of the world, especially . . . [the] persons closest [to them], and . . . for the souls in purgatory."[120] One or two references are made to prayer during the Mass "for every type of person," without other details. By contrast, at the end of the document, in the "offering of the year," which repeats the "Summary of the End" written by Father Médaille, the text invites the sisters, with the Savior Jesus, to "live, die, and work tirelessly for the salvation of souls." The apostolic vigor of this last text, in contrast with what precedes it, confirms even more clearly that the Little Directory could not have been written by Father Médaille. The text itself provides some clues to its source.

Passages referring to the Visitation in the text of the Constitutions from Saint-Didier and manuscript A point toward Francis de Sales. A comparison of the Little Directory of St. Joseph with the Spiritual Directory of the Visitation reveals some similarities in their framework, but also great differences in their structure as well as their composition.[121] A more compelling comparison can be made between the directory of the Daughters of the Cross, who, like the Visitation, trace their origin to Francis de Sales. He established them in the diocese of Geneva and he "himself wrote the principal rules."[122] They went to Picardy in 1625, then to the rue de Vaugirard in Paris in 1636. In 1640, Madame Marie L'Huillier de Villeneuve, their foundress, wanted to introduce vows, possibly to transform them into a religious community with solemn vows.[123] Fear of that evidently provoked a division. One group kept its traditional rules and customs. The other followed Madame de Villeneuve and became more conventual, living in Paris at the Hotel des Tournelles under the direction of Louis Abelly, their superior from 1650 to 1664.[124] He gave a new structure to the former Règlements and Constitutions and added a detailed directory for regular exercises, offices in the house, and instruction in the schools.[125]

There is a genuine link between the Directory of the Daughters of the Cross and the Little Directory of Sisters of St. Joseph, even though the former is far more detailed and spans several large volumes. The outline of the Little Directory is similar to the general structure of the "Second Book" of the Directory of the Daughters of the Cross, entitled "Organization of Daily Activities of the Daughters of the Congregation of the Cross." Some chapters of this Second Book were deleted in the Little Directory, while others were added from other parts of the large Directory of the Daughters of the Cross. Overall, the Little Directory is much more condensed, but it is basically a reworking of texts from the Daughters of the Cross.

Jean-Jacques Olier and the Sulpicians he founded in Paris in 1641 were known to have quite close connections with the Daughters of the Cross. It is very likely, then, that Father Charles-Louis de Lantages, a Sulpician, adapted their directory for the Sisters of St. Joseph. He came to Le Puy in 1653 as first superior of the Sulpician seminary there and was, from the beginning, also the ecclesiastical superior of the Sisters of St. Joseph at the Montferrand Hospital. Since he left Le Puy in 1663 at the request of the bishop of Clermont to head the new seminary there, we can assume that the Little Directory had been written before then. It was probably composed even before 1660 or 1661, as suggested by the order of the manuscript of Saint-Didier.[126] Written between 1660 and 1665, the Saint-Didier manuscript places the Little Directory nearly at the end, outside the Constitutions and after the Maxims. In later manuscripts, the Little Directory tends to be integrated into Part Five of the Constitutions or replace it entirely.

A brief glance at the Little Directory of the Sisters of St. Joseph—with the elements retained from the Directory of the Daughters of the Cross—gives some insight about its purpose and scope. As mentioned above, most of the text deals with "ordinary daily actions," probably to supplement the single short paragraph Father Médaille devoted to this subject in the fifth part of the Constitutions.[127] Although the "distribution of time" given in the Règlements is more developed, it, too, could have seemed insufficient, because it merely mentions the daily spiritual exercises without giving specific directions about how to carry them out. By contrast, the Little Directory emphasizes meditation, Divine Office, Mass, and the examen over the other daily exercises. Several of these exercises have Ignatian origins. For instance, the method of meditation in the Little Directory is that of the first week of the *Spiritual Exercises* of Saint Ignatius.[128] The morning and evening examen of conscience also follows the steps of the general and particular examen in the *Exercises*.[129] The Little Directory presents the Mass as daily, confession and communion as weekly.[130] This is the rhythm indicated for the same exercises in the Marian Congregations and in the Constitutions of the Society of Jesus, under the chapter for "the students in their colleges."[131]

The "little conference on virtue" among several sisters prescribed in the Little Directory, replicating in part the text of the "three associated souls" mentioned in the *Règlements*, also comes from the Marian Congregations of the Jesuits.[132] The same is true for the practice of drawing the name of a patron saint for each month.[133] The author obviously wanted to collect various Ignatian methods and practices. One must ask, though, why the Divine Office would be proposed as a daily practice for the Sisters of St. Joseph. *Monsieur* de Lantages certainly knew that according to their constitutions, the sisters recited daily vocal prayers, and the Office of the Blessed Virgin only on Sundays and holy days.[134] The inclusion of the Divine Office may intimate, that even during the earliest years, some Sisters of St. Joseph were drawn toward a more monastic type of life. The redactor of the Little Directory could have repeated what Monsieur Abelly wrote for the Daughters of the Cross (adding the Divine Office from the Visitation Directory) in response to an inclination of the Sisters of St. Joseph themselves. It is doubtful, however, that all the sisters shared that desire. Even so, the prominent insertion of the Little Directory into the fifth part of the Constitutions, precisely because this integrated it with other texts, was enough to temper the influence of its monastic tendencies. One thing is certain: the Divine Office has never been part of the spiritual tradition handed on and lived out in the communities of St. Joseph across the centuries.

NOTES

1. *ACSS*, 20.
2. N. Prunel, "Y eut-il, au XVIIe siècle, des Compagnies de Dames du Saint-Sacrement?"*Revue pratique d'Apologétique* 11, no. 128 (January 15, 1911):607-610,

citing Jean-Marie de Vernon, *La Vie de la Vénérable mère Marguerite de S. Xavier, religieuse ursuline du monastère de Dijon* (Paris: Josse, 1665); original, BN L. 27 n. 5105, réserve.

3. Lehoux, sup., Barreau, directeur, [et] de St Firmin, secrétaire, to Messieurs, a Paris, ce 11e apvril 1645, in *La Compagnie secrète du Saint-Sacrement, lettres du groupe parisien au groupe marseillais, 1639-1662*, ed. Alfred Rebelliau (Paris: H. Champion, 1908), 50-51; see Joseph Brucker, "Hommes d'œuvres aux XVIIe siècle: Nouvelles découvertes sur la Compagnie du Saint-Sacrement," *Études* 121 (1909): 5-30, and 201.

4. "[Le] règlement fait pour les dames dévotes de Paris qui assistent les pauvres de l'Hôtel-Dieu et les malades de leur paroisse," *ASSM*, 179.

5. "Status et règlemans de la Compagnie des Dames associées en l'honneur du tres sainct sacremant pour la pratique des bonnes œuvres," *ASSM*, introduction and 278.

6. "L'Esprit de la Compagnie du Saint-Sacrement," *ACSS*, 193.

7. Ibid., 196.

8. "Status et reglemans de la Compagnie des Dames associées," *ASSM*, 278-79.

9. *TP* 1981, CP, 47, no. 178.

10. Ibid., CP, 38, no. 129; and 31, no. 109.

11. Ibid., CP, 21, no. 44.

12. Ibid., CP, 22, no. 49.

13. Ibid., CP, 30, no. 105.

14. "Status et reglemans de la Compagnie des Dames associées," *ASSM*, 279.

15. "L'Esprit de la Compagnie du Saint-Sacrement," *ACSS*, 196.

16. *ASSM*, 278 and 282.

17. "L'Esprit de la Compagnie du Saint-Sacrement," *ACSS*, 196.

18. "Status et reglemans de la Compagnie des Dames associées," *ASSM*, 278-79.

19. *TP* 1981, LE, 5; and R, 126, no. 54.

20. "L'Esprit de la Compagnie du Saint-Sacrement," *ACSS*, 195.

21. Yves de La Brière, *Ce que fut la cabale des Dévots 1630-1660* (Paris: Bloud, 1906), 22.

22. La Brière, 22.

23. "Règlementss pour la petite Société du Sainct-Sacrement aux petites villes," *PDL*, 149.

24. "Règlements de la petite compagnie du Sainct-Sacrement à la compagne," *PDL*, 154. [See Alain Tallon, *La Compagnie du Saint-Sacrement, 1629-1667* (Paris: Éd. du Cerf, 1990), 117. —Trans.]

25. *TP* 1981, R, 108-127, nos. 20-50; see Appendix 1.

26. Ibid., R, 106, no. 10.

27. Ibid., R, 126, no. 54.

28. Ibid., R, 113, no. 33; 119, no. 41; and 128, nos. 59-60 (MS L).

29. Ibid., "Aux trois âmes," 293.

30. Ibid., R, 128, no. 58.

31. Louis Châtellier, *The Europe of the Devout: The Catholic Reformation and the Formation of a New Society*, trans. Jean Birrell (Cambridge [England] / New York: Cambridge University Press / Paris: Editions de la Maison des sciences de l'homme, 1989), 34-36.

32. Châtellier, 15, 19, 28-30.

33. *ARSI*, Tolos. 5, fols. 369 and 394.

34. Châtellier, 102-103, 141-47.

35. Poullin de Lumina, *Histoire de l'Eglise de Lyon* (Lyon: Berthoud, 1770), 410-411.

36. Marius Nepper, SJ, *Origins: The Sisters of St. Joseph*, trans. commissioned by the Federation of the Sisters of St. Joseph, USA [Erie: Villa Maria College, 1975], 21-22.

37. *TP* 1981, R, 102, no. 2.

38. Ibid., R, 106, no. 16.

39. Ibid., LE, 5-10.

40. Ibid., CP, 26, no. 81.

41. *ACSS,* 20.

42. Rebelliau, ed., 50-51; see Brucker, 201-202.

43. No. 43: Circulaire signée de G. de Renty, supérieur, l'abbé de Gesy (?), directeur, D'Amours, secrétaire, 15 mars 1646, in Rebelliau, 65.

44. Antoine Jacmon, *Mémoires d'Antoine Jacmon, Bourgeois du Puy*, ed. Augustin Chassaing (Le Puy: Impr. Marchessou, 1885), 205.

45. AD Rhône, D 144, Union des prieurés Saint-Martin de Dunières, et Sainte-Marie de Tence au Collège de la Trinité à Lyon.

46. AMM Le Puy, Communauté de Dunières.

47. "Established" (*establies en habit*) has the double sense of being stable and recognized in a situation and of being set up or established in a position either by one's parents, or, as here, by providing oneself with a dowry, *DAF* 1694, s.v. "établir." — Trans.

48. *CV* 1694.

49. F. Gouit, *Une congrégation Salésienne; Les sœurs de Saint-Joseph du Puy-en-Velay, 1648-1915* (Le Puy: Impr. de l'Avenir de la Haute-Loire, 1930), 39 and appendix D; and Albert Bois, *Les Soeurs de Saint-Joseph, les Filles du petit dessein, de 1648 à 1949* (Lyon: Éditions et imprimeries du Sud-Est, 1950), 59-61.

50. Claude de Vic, Joseph Vaissette, and Ernest Roschach, *Histoire générale de Languedoc avec des notes et les pièces justificatives par dom Cl. Devic & dom J. Vaissete*, 15 vols. (Toulouse: Privat, 1872-92), vol. 13, p. 7 of the chronology, and 14: 326-28.

51. Hugues Aulanier, *Moi, Hugues Aulanier, Journal de l'Abbé Aulanier, curé du Brignon, 1638-1691*, ed. Sylvère Heuze, Yves Soulingeas, and Martin de Framond, 6 vols. (Saint-Vidal: Éditions de la Borne, 1987-2005), 2 (1641-50):209.

52. "Hospitium dictis sororibus S. Josephi exhibuit Anicii fuis in aedibus illustris matrona Lucretia de la Planche D. de Joux uxor; deinde Henricus episc. in domo orphanarum S. Josephi Aniciensis in vico de Monte-ferrando," *Gallia Christiana in provincias ecclesiasticas distributa*, vol. 2, *Ecclesia Aniciensis*, ed. Denis de Saint-Marthe and Barthélemy Hauréau (Paris: Ex Typographia Regia, 1720), 2:740.

53. See Appendix 1.

54. AD Haute-Loire, 12 H1, Lettres de provisions données par Mgr Henri de Maupas . . . en faveur des Filles de la Congrégation de Saint-Joseph du Puy . . . 10 mars 1651.

55. AD Haute-Loire, 12 H1, "Permission donnée aux Filles de Saint-Joseph par le Seigneur de Maupas, Evêque du Puy, touchant leur établissement, 13 décembre 1651.

56. *TP* 1981, R, 105.

57. Archives privées de monsieur Ch. Bayon de la Tour, Le Puy, "Memoyre d'ung grand miracle arrivé à St Josepf."

58. "Memoyre d'ung grand miracle."

59. AD Haute-Loire, 12 H1, Lettres de provisions données par Mgr Henri de Maupas, 10 mars 1651.

60. AD Haute-Loire, 12 H1, "Permission donnée aux Filles de Saint-Joseph par le Seigneur de Maupas, Evêque du Puy, touchant leur établissement, 13 décembre 1651.

61. "Mémoyre d'ung grand miracle."

62. AD Haute-Loire, 12 H1, "Permission donnée aux Filles de Saint-Joseph par le Seigneur de Maupas, Evêque du Puy, touchant leur établissement, 13 décembre 1651.

63. *TP* 1981, LE, 5, no. 8.

64. Nepper, *Origins*, 7-22.

65. AD Haute-Loire, 12 H1, Lettres de provisions données par Mgr Henri de Maupas, 10 mars 1651.

66. AD Haute-Loire, 12 H1, Permission donnée aux Filles de Saint-Joseph par le Seigneur de Maupas, Evêque du Puy, touchant leur établissement, 13 décembre 1651.

67. By the solemn vow of poverty, the individual monk or nun could not buy, sell, inherit, or bequeath material goods. As a corporation, the monastery could. —Trans.

68. *TP* 1981, R, 105, no. 6, MS L.

69. Ibid., R, 107, no. 17.

70. Ibid., R, Title in the Lyon MS, 103.

71. *Pratique de devotion et des vertus chrestiennes, suivant les Règles des Congrégations de Nostre Dame*, À Lyon, Chez Jean Baptiste De Ville, MDCLXXXIX, chap. 3, "Pratiques pour tous les jours, semaines, mois et années."

72. *TP* 1981, R, 105-107.

73. Ibid., R, 107 no. 19.

74. Ibid., CP, 16 no 20.

75. Ibid., CP, 87 no. 426.

76. According to archival evidence (AMM Le Puy), the Saint-Didier community began before 1655, but the precise date of foundation is unknown.

77. *RSI* 1620, 230.

78. *TP* 1981, CP, 21, no. 43.

79. Ibid., CP, 17, nos. 23-25.

80. Ibid., CP, 19, no. 33.

81. Ibid., CP, 28, no. 93; 29, no. 99; 57, no. 254; and 59, nos. 273-81.

82. "[L]e propre de nostre vocation est de . . . vivre en tout lieu où on peut esperer de rendre plus grand service à Dieu, et plus grande ayde spirituelle au prochain." *RSI* 1620, Sommaire, 4, no. 3.

83. The contract between the Consuls and Jehanne Comport, whom they named "dame hospitalière" of the Montferrand Hospital on April 1, 1635, stipulates, that should she wish to leave, "the aforesaid Comport will be permitted to take all the furniture and goods which belong to her, which she will have brought into the said

hospital when she started there," AD Haute-Loire, 12H2, Filles de Saint-Joseph, Hôp. De Montferrand.

84. *RSI* 1620, par. 4.
85. *TP* 1981, CP, 18, no. 26.
86. Ibid., CP, 19, no. 34.
87. Ibid., CP, 18, no. 23.
88. Ibid., CP, 18, no. 31.
89. Ibid., CP, 71-75, nos. 339-64, and 16, no. 16.
90. Ibid., CP, 19, no. 38.
91. Ibid., CP, 22, nos. 47-49.
92. *RSI* 1620, Sommaire, par. 2.
93. *TP* 1981, CP, 77-89, nos. 365-443.
94. Ibid., CP, 33, no. 113.
95. Ibid., R, 128, no. 61, MS L; and CP, 35, no. 123, MS S.
96. Ibid., CP, 33, no. 113.
97. Ibid., CP, 35, no. 123 MS S; 37, no. 125; and 47, no. 183.
98. Ibid., *MP*, 189-242.
99. Ibid., 189.
100. Ibid., MI, 170.
101. Ibid., CP, 47, no. 183.
102. Ibid., R, 106, nos. 11-16; and CP, 31, nos. 106-112.
103. François de Sales, St., Entretien XIX: "Sur les vertus de Saint-Joseph," in *Les oeuvres de Sainct François de Sales, revues et très exactement corrigées sur les premiers et plus fidèles exemplaires*, 11 vols. A Paris, chez Frederic Leonard, 1669-1673, 2 (1669): col. 1972.
104. Louis Cognet, "Bérulle et sa synthèse spirituelle," chap. 9 in *L'essor: 1500-1650,* part 1 of *La spritualité moderne* (Paris: Aubier, 1966), 332-46.
105. Cognet, 373.
106. *TP* 1981, CP, Abrégé de la Fin, 31, nos. 109 and 112.
107. Cognet, 451.
108. *TP* 1981, CP, 17, no. 21.
109. Pierre Wolff, "Étude sur les Constitutions Primitives des sœurs de Saint Joseph," Fédération française des Congrégations de Saint Joseph, 1978-1979.
110. *TP* 1981, R, 107, no 17; CP, 25, nos. 74-75, and 31, no. 112.
111. Ibid., R, 105, no. 5.
112. Ibid, R, 107, nos. 17-18.
113. Ibid., CP, 71, no. 339.
114. Ibid., CP, 29, no. 95; 74, no. 361; 48, no. 184; and 74, no. 362.
115. Ibid., PD, 141, no. 1.
116. Ibid., CP, 25, nos. 74-75; 62-63, nos. 290-98; and R, 106-107, nos. 11-18.
117. Ibid., CP, 48, no. 186.
118. Ibid., PD, 154, no. 78.
119. Ibid., PD, 156, no. 91.
120. Ibid., PD, 162, no. 140.

121. François de Sales, *Opuscules*: Vol. 26 of *Œuvres de saint François de Sales, Évêque de Genève et docteur de l'Église* (Annecy: Monastère de la Visitation, 1931), 133 ff.

122. Règles et Constitutions de la Congrégation des Sœurs de la Croix du diocèse du Puy, 1835, Bref historique, 14 ff.

123. Règles et Constitutions de la Congrégation des Sœurs de la Croix, 14 ff.

124. Louis Abelly (1603-1691), bishop of Rodez 1664-66. He resigned the bishopric to return to Paris, where he wrote the first biography of St. Vincent de Paul. — Trans.

125. AMM Filles de la Croix de Paris.

126. See Appendix 1, The Original Documents Presented in Two Tables.

127. *TP* 1981, CP, 74, no. 363.

128. Ibid., PD, 143; and *CSJ* 1970, 40-44, nos. 45-61.

129. *TP* 1981, PD, 151; and *The Spiritual Exercises* 35-38, nos. 32-43.

130. *TP* 1981, PD, 148-50, nos. 49-55; 158-60, nos. 105-128; and 160-63, nos. 129-42.

131. *CSJ* 1970, part 4, chap. 4, 184, no. 342.

132. *TP* 1981, PD, 157, nos. 100-104.

133. Ibid., PD, 163, nos. 144-45. Francis Borgia (†1572) devised the custom of the saint of the month at the court of Portugal. It was used by the Marian Congregations at the end of the sixteenth century, see Jean Crasset, SJ, *Des Congrégations de Notre-Dame, érigées dans les maisons des Pères de la Compagnie de Jésus*, Paris, chez Urbain Coutelier, 1694, 30-34.

134. *TP* 1981, CP, 20, nos. 39-40.

Chapter Three

Early Growth

The ink was hardly dry on Bishop de Maupas' formal authorization in 1651 before the new Congregation of St. Joseph began to grow and spread. At the same time, Fr. Médaille received a new assignment that put him at some distance from the nascent communities.

FATHER MÉDAILLE'S OBEDIENCE
AND THE EMERGENCE OF THE FIRST HOUSES

Father Médaille's personal association with this group of women again provoked rumors and questions, this time among his colleagues in Le Puy. The first to question his activities, however, was Médaille himself. He had written to his superior general, Father Vincent Caraffa, in 1646 or 1647 because he was keenly aware of the Rules of the Society that read: "They will not write the statutes of any confraternity or congregation without the superior's permission, whether it be an old association or if it seems a new one should be organized. They will not act in this matter before asking the superior's advice."[1] In the beginning, Father Médaille had not attached a great deal of importance to the spiritual direction of this little group of pious women who were loosely related to the Company of Ladies of the Blessed Sacrament and whose daily activities were inspired by the Jesuits' Marian Congregations. He thought it required no particular consideration—until the day he realized what direction things had taken. Up to then, he may merely have given these women some concrete suggestions for spiritual direction over the course of days, months, perhaps a year. The force of events, however, led him to give structure to the new group, to define it, to recognize it for what it had started to become. Until then, Father Médaille had kept Father Degieu, rector of the College of Saint-Flour and his superior, informed about the progress of these women. Now, he could not make the decision thrust upon him without consulting a higher authority, ordinarily the Jesuit superior of the Province of Toulouse. Father Médaille chose instead to write directly to his superior general to tell him what was taking shape under his eyes and to submit the matter to him. His reason for appealing to the Society's highest authority is not clear, but he must have sensed that establishing the new group risked going against not only the Rules of the Society, but even more so, against canonical regulations for the religious life of women. In his response to Father Médaille, on March 8, 1647, Father General Vincent Caraffa referred him to the provincial, stating:

> In regard to the pious association of women which you report you have founded, I can only reply that it should not have been begun without the approval of the provincial. Much less should rules have been prescribed for them unless he approved, since both could be liable to much talk, complaints, perhaps even dangers. And so Your Reverence is to take care that I am informed more fully about this entire matter through the provincial, so that if this be for the glory of God, it may be more beneficial for having been accomplished more safely.[2]

The same day, the father general wrote to Father Degieu in a similar vein, "Father Médaille ought not to have prescribed rules for an association of women without the approval of the provincial."[3] Both recipients would have felt keenly the reprimand expressed in these letters. And yet the letter addressed to Father Médaille did not contain a categorical proscription. To the contrary, although he advised prudence and the permission of the provincial, Father Caraffa left the possibility open for the project to continue if it were "for the glory of God." During the following two years the correspondence between Father Médaille, still consultor to the rector in Saint-Flour, and Father Caraffa implies a good relationship. On April 15, 1648, Caraffa's response to Father Médaille had a cordial tone.[4] In a letter to the rector of Saint-Flour dated June 20, 1648, he sent a greeting to Father Médaille.[5]

Father Degieu's triennial report of May, 1649, to the provincial and father general reveals a certain perplexity regarding Father Médaille.[6] According to Father Degieu, Médaille was a man of exceptional intelligence (*ingenium sublimae*) and remarkably gifted for every kind of study (*in superioribus et inferioribus eximius*), at least as far as his ill health permitted (*si liceat per valetudinem*). The rector doesn't know what to think about his judgment. He leaves that space on the form blank. Prudence, that human wisdom and capacity to risk, posed another problem. Seeing how Father Médaille had allowed this group of women to take the lead—had actually followed their impetus—Father Degieu found him excessively credulous (*nimis credulus*) and lacking in prudence.[7] In the light of experience, Father Médaille had not lived up to the rector's expectations (*non ita attendit*). At the same time, he saw clearly the apostolic vigor of Father Médaille's spirit, because, in response to the question concerning talent for ministerial works, he wrote, "born for the missions" (*natus ad missiones*). He found Father Médaille disconcerting.

The provincial's evaluation of Father Médaille has not survived. Although there are no vestiges of it, Father Médaille certainly had contact with the provincial. Antoine Savignac replaced Vital Théron in that office on August 25, 1648.[8] Father Médaille's continued support for the growth of the Congregation of St. Joseph during the years that followed indicates that he must have had some level of approval from his superiors. He was in Le Puy on September 27, 1650, "coming from the professed house," which was in Toulouse.[9] He had presumably seen Father Savignac there, since the first sisters were already together at Le Puy in Lucrèce de la Planche's house and were to receive recognition of their vocation and mission from Bishop de Maupas on October 15. By then, Father General Vincent Caraffa had died in Rome on June 8, 1649. Father Médaille's vigilant confreres at the College of Le Puy hastened to warn his successor, Francis Piccolomini, of what had just happened there on October 15. On February 20, 1651, Father Piccolomini answered the letters of Fathers Gabriel Garreau, rector of the College of Le Puy, and Ignace Gras, probably a consultor. His answers, all directed toward the provincial's point of view, indicate that he did not know everything about the situation and at the same time trusted Father Médaille's communication with his provincial. He may have had some information from earlier letters and reports sent to Rome. The father general wrote to Father Gras: "Your Reverence considered that you thought I should be warned in regard to that new institute ["congregation" has been erased] of women which Father Peter Médaille has in mind. I shall refer the matter to the provincial."[10] To Father Garreau he wrote, "I am writing to the provincial about Father Médaille's plan (*consilio*)."[11] That very day he sent a letter to Father Savignac, provincial of Toulouse:

> Those at Le Puy say that Father Peter Médaille is launching an extraordinary undertaking (*mira moliri*) to establish some type of association of women. I want to know the nature of his plan and from whom he obtained permission to get involved in these matters which are not at all in accord with our Institute.[12]

Whether Father Piccolomini wanted to understand how things had developed in the time of his predecessor, or whether he was satisfied with what he learned from the provincial is not certain.

Father Piccolomini died within the same year. There is no further evidence that other obstacles arose in Father Médaille's path opposing the growth of the new Congregation of St. Joseph. His original obedience, during 1645 and 1646, had been docility to the events that were unfolding. At that time, his superior's reports had noted a great and completely religious prudence.[13] As the situation developed and decisions had to be made, he had recourse to his various superiors, desiring to live what he was then writing for the first sisters: "Be always ready to obey peacefully . . . placing your entire happiness in the accomplishment of the divine will."[14] The successive deaths and replacements, first of the provincial and then of the father general, left Father Médaille in the uncomfortable situation of being the object of blame, remarks, questions, or advice, without being able to obtain either confirmation or condemnation. Taking his own counsel about the Sisters of St. Joseph, he therefore followed "gently and efficaciously" what he "prudently believed to be for God's greater glory."[15] Finally, once the general and provincial superiors could gain mutual clarification about the anxieties of the fathers in Le Puy, they concluded that Father Médaille's "astonishing" actions were for the glory of God and should be continued. He could now pursue his undertaking with more confidence, in so far as Providence left the responsibility to him.

During the year 1650–1651, Father Médaille was appointed to the College of Aurillac, at some distance from the diocese of Le Puy.[16] His duties as preacher outside the city (*extra urbem*) would have kept him on the road, giving him opportunities, at least that year, to guide the newly established communities of St. Joseph. Close by or at a distance, he was able to follow the development of the congregation as it spread throughout the diocese of Le Puy.

Like the community at the Montferrand Hospital, the little house started at Dunières in 1649 evidently gave rise to other foundations. On October 6, 1651, Father Médaille was back in the area. With the permission of Bishop de Maupas, he established the Daughters of St. Joseph at Marlhes, not far from Dunières, and then in the diocese of Le Puy. There he gave the habit to Catherine Frappa, a woman about thirty years of age.[17] Soon after, "Agathe Charroin was taken from the house of Dunières by order of the bishop and *Monsieur* Besantage (probably an error of the scribe; it should read, de Lantages) who was director of the daughters, to be superior of the daughters at Marlhes."[18] The reason is unknown, but there may have been problems in the house that led the bishop himself and the ecclesiastical superior to intervene. The bishop's involvement nevertheless demonstrates his interest in these very small foundations and also reveals the importance of the house in Dunières, since ecclesiastical superiors could appeal to it when need arose.

On October 15, 1652, with Bishop de Maupas' permission, Fr. Médaille was at Saint-Romain-Lachalm, a village close to Dunières and Marlhes, to establish another new house. There he gave the habit to two sisters, Jeanne Perrilhon and Marguerite Montchouvet, both aged twenty-eight.[19] By 1653 a house existed in Tence, a small town located slightly to the south of Marlhes, in the same region where the Lord de Joux and his wife, Lucrèce de La Planche, owned lands and a chateau. At that time, according to a paper acknowledging a debt for manorial dues (*censive et laud*), the sisters in Tence lived in a house that belonged to the Jesuits of Lyon.[20] Another document, found in the papers of the house at Champanhac and dated April 12, 1664, indicates that the community at Tence had been established by the "Most Illustrious and Most Reverend *Monseigneur* de Maupas, bishop of Le Puy," but gives no exact date of foundation.[21] The presence of Bishop de Maupas at this foundation seems to indicate that he considered it a house of some importance. Later, letters patent issued in 1687 gave it the same juridical status as the houses of Le Puy and Saint-Didier. In this sector tinged with Protestantism and surrounded by a Catholic population, one of the apostolic tasks of the sisters at Tence was "the instruction of young girls recently converted" from Protestantism, a work dear to both Bishop de Maupas and the Company of the Blessed Sacrament.[22]

A house was established at Saint-Didier en Velay in the same area and at about the same time as those in Marlhes, Saint-Romain, and Dunières. The approbation later given this house by the Marquis de Nérestang to obtain letters patent from the king reveals that the sisters were at Saint-Didier before 1655.[23] That same year saw still another foundation of the Sisters of St. Joseph, at Aurec, slightly more than a mile northeast of Saint-Didier and probably also under the protection of the Marquis de Nérestang, whose titles and properties included the barony of Aurec.[24]

Soon the Congregation of St. Joseph moved beyond the borders of the Le Puy diocese. In the archdiocese of Vienne, adjacent to Le Puy on the east, two new houses were established with the archbishop's approval, one in Saint-Julien-Vocance, and the other at Bourg-Argental for the hospital there.[25] Archival documents for these two houses suggest that they were founded around 1655, but give no precise details. The first foundation in the diocese of Lyon, bordering Le Puy on the north, was at Le Chambon, near Saint-Étienne. Invited by Gaspard de Capponi, Baron of Feugerolles, and his wife Madeleine du Peloux, the sisters established a house there, according to the Feugerolles records, "on the authority of His Excellency, the Archbishop of the said Lyon, by permission given on the eighth of September, one thousand six hundred fifty-five."[26]

Meanwhile houses were multiplying in the Le Puy diocese. Three new houses opened in 1657: Yssingeaux, Saint-Jeures-de-Bonas, and Saint-Victor-Malescours, followed by Riotord in 1659.[27] The year 1660 surpassed all previous years in the number of foundations. Five new houses began in the Le Puy diocese. Three of them—Montregard, Lapte, and Jonzieux—were in

the same area as Tence and Saint-Didier-en-Velay.[28] The other two, Boisset
and Saint-Georges-l'Agricol, were farther toward the northwest of the diocese.[29] The house at Saint-Jean-de-Bonnefonds certainly existed in the diocese of Lyon prior to 1660, but it is impossible to specify the exact date of
foundation.[30] Around 1660, Father Médaille founded the house of Arlanc in
the diocese of Clermont, neighbor to Le Puy on the northwest, and Sisters of
St. Joseph established another house in the Vienne archdiocese at Satillieu,
approved by Archbishop Henry de Villars in 1661.[31]

SUPPORT FOR THE INITIAL DEVELOPMENT

The concentration of all the first houses of Sisters of St. Joseph in a restricted
geographic area necessarily raises a question. Since Bishop de Maupas had
authorized the Sisters of St. Joseph to establish houses throughout the diocese
of Le Puy, why were these new houses huddled in its northeast corner? One
might suppose that the priests and people of neighboring villages, having
learned about the service given by the new sisters, asked that houses of the
same type be established to provide them in their own parishes. Given the inconspicuous nature of the early communities, however, this explanation
seems unlikely, or at least inadequate. It is more probable that the Sisters of
St. Joseph needed mutual support in order to discover, day by day, how to live
this new way of religious life without its outward signs. The houses were extremely small: Anne Deschaux alone was mentioned when she took the habit
in 1649 at Dunières, and it was the same for Catherine Frappa in 1651 at
Marlhes. There were two sisters at Saint-Romain-Lachalm in 1652, Jeanne
Perrilhon and Marguerite Monchouvet. Their need to help one another was all
the greater since they lived directly under the authority of the local pastor,
who was not necessarily able to understand the nature of their vocation. Other
problems could arise from the temptation to turn the house of the Sisters of
St. Joseph into a community belonging to a certain parish or pastor, which
would have been the ruin of the new congregation.

   Precisely that danger seems to have formed one of the chief preoccupations
of Father Médaille and Bishop de Maupas. Research on the pastors and the
various persons in charge of parishes where the first houses of St. Joseph
were established reveals that these parishes were almost always former priories, by then belonging to Jesuit colleges. It was the Jesuits, therefore, who
appointed the *curé*. The Priory of Saint-Martin in Dunières and the priory of
the same name in Tence had been ceded, with the consent of the Abbott of
Chaise-Dieu, to which they belonged, to the College of the Trinity in Lyon
and consolidated by the pontifical bull of May 5, 1577.[32] Letters patent given

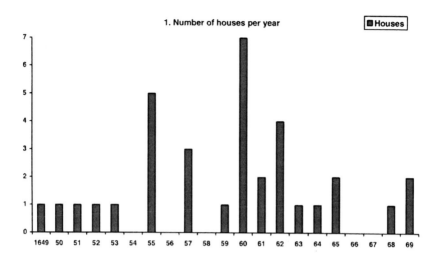

1. Number of houses per year

2. Foundations by Diocese

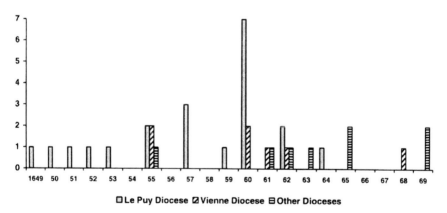

Foundations of House of Sisters of St. Joseph, 1649-69

by Henry III in April of 1580 and recorded at the Parlement of Toulouse on January 20, 1581, confirmed this cession.

The office of *curé* at Saint-Romain-Lachalm, where a house of St. Joseph was established in 1652, and that in the nearby parish of Saint-Victor-Male-scours, where one was established in 1657, were both under the authority of the priory of Dunières.[33] The rector of the College of the Trinity in Lyon and the bishop of Le Puy were alternate proprietors of the pastorship and priory at St. Romain-Lachalm. At the beginning of the seventeenth century, the parish at Marlhes was also under the priory of Dunières. Jehan Prodhome, *curé* of Marlhes, acknowledged his debt to the Jesuit fathers in Lyon, holders of the Priory of Saint-Martin, to whom he was obliged to pay "an annual and perpetual fee for the said parish of Marlhes," as recorded in the "Book of the territory of the Lord prior of Saint-Martin de Dunyères."[34] In 1657 another house of Sisters of St. Joseph was established in Saint-Jeures de Bonas, where the appointment of the *curé* at that time belonged to the priory in Tence, and therefore, once again, to the Jesuits of the College of the Trinity in Lyon.[35] In the Vienne diocese the appointment of the *curé* at the two parishes of Bourg-Argental and Saint-Julien-Vocance, where the Sisters of St. Joseph were established in 1655, belonged to the priory of Saint-Sauveur-en-Rue, which had been ceded to the Jesuit college in Tournon at the beginning of the seventeenth century.[36] The record of the union of the priories at Dunières and Tence states that the parish of Riotord, where the Sisters of St. Joseph established a house in 1659, also came under the College of Tournon through the "priory and domain of St-Sauveur-en-Rue," as indicated by "acknowledgment of the benefice of Riotord to the Jesuits."[37] Nine houses founded before 1660, therefore, were located in parishes where Jesuits appointed the *curé*. Six parishes came under the authority of the College of the Trinity in Lyon through its control of the original priories at Tence and Dunières, and three, under that of the Jesuit College of Tournon, which then held the former priory of Saint-Saveur-en-Rue.

The Jesuits were not the only source of protection for the early houses. Some began in places belonging to the domain of a sympathetic nobleman. An example is the house of Chambon-Feugerolles near Saint-Etienne, mentioned above. It was in a parish where the Jesuits did not control the appointment of the *curé*. Rather, as indicated in records of the pastoral visits of Camille de Neufville, Archbishop of Lyon, "the *curé* is appointed by our [cathedral] chapter of Lyon." [38] Although the parish did not have the support of the Jesuits, a house of St. Joseph was established there and authorized by the archbishop on September 8, 1655. A register of deceased sisters started in 1757 indicates the possibility of an even earlier foundation.[39] The first line reads, "Since 1650 at the beginning of the house of Le . . ." The rest of the sentence is missing. Was it the house of Le Chambon or of Le Puy? The first name on the list is "Françoise de Bourdon, sister superior," followed by five others, including "*Demoiselle* Catherine de Chazau, daughter of Claude de Chazau, a noble lord, and *Damoiselle* de La Grevol, her mother." None of them appears in the contract of association of goods referred to in the sale of a "domain" on February 15, 1659.[40] Does this mean that a group of women may already have come together in Chambon before Gaspard de Capponi and his wife Madeleine du Peloux invited the Sisters of St. Joseph there?

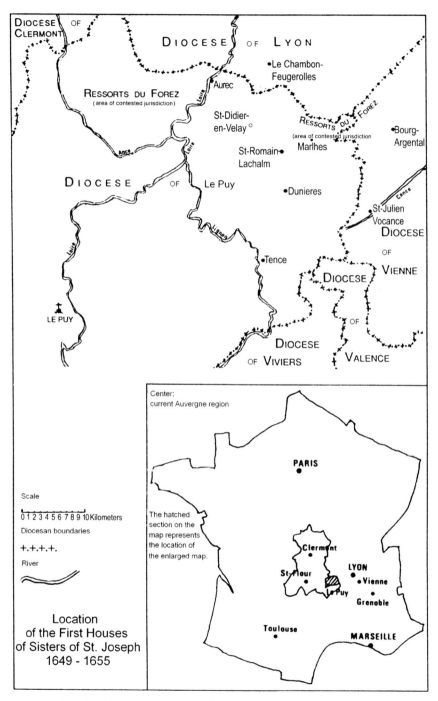

Location of the First Houses of Sisters of St. Joseph, 1649-55

Another question is whether, before their official establishment as Sisters of St. Joseph, they had some connection with the Company of Ladies of the Blessed Sacrament. The very devout family background of the Capponi, their links with the Jesuits (a son, Claude, died at 17 while a novice in Avignon), and the influence of Gaspard's first wife, Isabeau de Crémeaux, who died in 1645, venerated by the poor and considered a saint, were a number of factors situating the Capponi among the Christian elites of their community.[41] Gaspard, baron of Feugerolles, was a member of a "Company of Gentlemen" that had been established in the provinces by the Company of the Blessed Sacrament, as evidenced in the minutes of a meeting held on September 20, 1658.[42] There is still another hint that the Lord de Capponi and the Sisters of St. Joseph at Chambon were involved with the Company of the Blessed Sacrament. In the house he gave the sisters, Gaspard de Capponi had an arcade constructed between the house and the church gallery to make it easier for them to go to the church for adoration of the Blessed Sacrament.[43] Isabeau de Crémeaux, together with one or another of the women from the little group existing before the foundation in 1655, could have been among those who asked the Company of the Blessed Sacrament of Lyon in 1645 to create a women's branch. In one form or another, there was very likely a specific link between the foundation of the Sisters of St. Joseph at Chambon and the Company of the Blessed Sacrament. The barony of Feugerolles, in addition to that of Chambon, included the parishes of Saint-Romain-les-Atheux, Jonzieux, and part of Saint-Genest-Malifaux.[44] The presence and favor of the *Seigneur* de Capponi could facilitate the establishment of houses of St. Joseph in nearby parishes without detracting from whatever protection the Jesuits offered in the same places.

The house in Saint-Didier-en-Velay may have enjoyed similar circumstances. Like his neighbor in the chateau of Feugerolles, the Marquis de Nérestang wanted God to be honored and served in his domain, the poor assisted, and young girls educated, above all poor orphan girls. He is therefore noted as rejoicing at the "project for the establishment of a house of Daughters of the Congregation of St. Joseph" on the outskirts of his city of Saint-Didier.[45] Who controlled the appointment of the *curé* is unknown, but the presence and collaboration of the local *seigneur* provided effective support for the foundation of the Sisters of St. Joseph. Like the Baron of Feugerolles, the Marquis de Nérestang had power over all the surrounding lands, since he qualified as "baron of Saint-Didier-en-Velay, Saint-Victor-de-Malescours, Aurec, Oriol, La Chapelle, Saint-Ferréol, Saint-Just-en-Velay, Saint-Romain . . . and other places."[46]

For any foundation to succeed, several powers had to be aligned. The consent of the Marquis de Nérestang, for example, meant that the Sisters of St.

Joseph would not encounter any serious opposition in establishing their house at Saint-Didier-en-Velay. Only the bishop would have had the power to prevent the foundation, since it could not be made without his consent. Bishop de Maupas, however, as juridical founder of the congregation, had given his approval in principle from the beginning. Henry de Maupas was also a member of the Company of the Blessed Sacrament, to which the first Sisters of St. Joseph were no strangers.

Other bishops remained more suspicious of that secret association. In Lyon, Archbishop Alphonse de Richelieu, brother of the cardinal and first minister of Louis XIII, seemed to have had little regard for the Company. During his episcopate, moreover, he particularly favored the creation of new houses of women religious whose forms of life seemed to him closer to cloistered nuns: the Visitation Nuns, and still more, the Ursulines.[47] Mother Jeanne Chézard de Matel, who founded the Order of the Incarnate Word, authorized by papal bull on June 12, 1633, found him an inflexible opponent. Perhaps he feared that this order, supported by Jesuits, might become a non-cloistered female counterpart to the Society of Jesus.[48] Under these circumstances, it is understandable that the small houses of Sisters of St. Joseph did not risk putting down roots in the Lyon diocese, especially if they had some connections to the Company of the Blessed Sacrament. This may explain why, even if a group of women had already been together in Le Chambon for several years, the house of St. Joseph could be established only after the death of Archbishop de Richelieu in 1653. It was authorized in 1655 by his successor, Camille de Neufville, a friend of the Jesuits, who had confidence in the Company of the Blessed Sacrament.

In the diocese of Vienne, the foundation of the first houses of Sisters of St. Joseph at Bourg-Argental and Saint-Julien-Vocance around 1655 coincided with the nomination of Henry de Villars as coadjutor to his uncle Pierre de Villars, whom he succeeded as Archbishop of Vienne in 1662.[49] The Company of the Blessed Sacrament was also established in 1655 at Vienne, which suggests that the new coadjutor may have helped to open the way for the Company in the diocese.[50] He may even have brought members in his retinue when he arrived in Vienne. In regard to the Sisters of St. Joseph, Henry de Villars could have known about the house in Le Chambon in the diocese of Lyon through connections in his own family. His sister, Louise de Villars, in 1642 had married Balthazard de Charpin, a relative by marriage of the Capponi family.[51] In any case, he most certainly was acquainted with his neighbor, Henry de Maupas, and knew of his personal inclinations and his contacts with the Company of the Blessed Sacrament. Perhaps, at least through the house of Chambon, he knew about the early development of these little groups of women, without import or panache, that had just taken shape in the diocese of Le Puy.

"Favored by men and by circumstance"

The development of the little houses of St. Joseph could not have taken place without the support of the bishops, because, lacking their permission, they could not be established in a diocese. In the beginning, this authorization at times amounted to non-interference. This seems to have been the case for the Archbishop of Lyon, Camille de Neufville. After authorizing the house in Le Chambon in 1655, the bishop, who died in 1693, is never known to have had any other involvement in the foundation or activities of the few small houses that were established in the region of Le Chambon. Apparently, he never invited the Sisters of St. Joseph to Lyon. Bishop de Maupas, on the contrary, welcomed Father Médaille's proposal at once, officially installing the first sisters at Le Puy, and through his letters patent of March 10, 1651, giving them every possibility of expanding within his diocese. Henry de Villars, as coadjutor and eventually archbishop of Vienne, seems to have welcomed the sisters warmly throughout his episcopacy. Whether a bishop was more or less favorable toward the Company of the Blessed Sacrament and the Jesuits was certainly one of the factors which, in the beginning, inclined him to accept or refuse houses of Sisters of St. Joseph. While it is difficult to trace the dealings of the celebrated Company because of its secrecy, its presence and action can be observed or sensed to some extent in the way notables became involved in establishing a house, or in the type of works they favored: the orphan girls at Le Puy, the new converts at Tence, the rehabilitation of fallen women almost everywhere, the evangelization of families, and so forth. The action of the Company is always evident in the establishment of the more important houses, such as those of Le Puy, Tence, or Le Chambon, and never for the small houses scattered throughout the countryside, which were by far more numerous.

The most immediate and day-to-day support for the country houses could only come from the pastor of the parish. The pastor, however, needed to be sufficiently educated and informed that he would not be inclined to alarm these women about their claims to religious life—and that under forms that didn't say so! This is why the first small houses of St. Joseph were established in the diocese of Le Puy under the protection of Henry de Maupas and in parishes under Jesuit authority. This gave the sisters the possibility of support from men who lived essentially the same vocation of apostolic religious life, a vocation the sisters had to devise each day in their life as women. The sisters were rooted in this specific geographic area in part because the priories attached to the Colleges of Lyon or Tournon were situated in that region. Other factors might have operated as well. The various parishes involved were all located in areas where administrative regions and governing powers overlapped, creating zones with indeterminate borders. For example, Marlhes, on the border between the Velay and the Forez, was a parish in the diocese of Le Puy, belonging to the *élection*, or tax district, of Saint-Étienne (Lyon diocese) and under the jurisdiction of the *baillage* of Bourg-Argental (Vienne diocese).[52] The powers of the *baillage* of the parish of Bourg-Argental extended to those belonging not only to the diocese of Vienne, but also to some parishes in the dioceses of Lyon (Saint-Genest-Malifaux, Saint-Sauveur-en-Rue) and of Le Puy (Riotord).[53] In addition, Bourg-Argental was the seat of a deanery which comprised twenty parishes, some in the Forez and some in the Vivarais.[54] Jonzieux-en-Forez belonged to the diocese of Le Puy, the *élection* of Saint-Étienne (diocese of Lyon) and the *baillage* of Saint-Ferréol, united with that of Bourg-Argental. It belonged, moreover, to the barony of Feugerolles.[55] The town of Vanosc was located in the Vivarais, but it incorporated some hamlets in the Forez, and the parish as a whole belonged to the diocese of Vienne in Dauphiné.[56] This entanglement of boundaries, very common in France at the time, is epitomized by the parish of Marlhes. Although it belonged to the diocese of Le Puy, it was adjacent to parishes in two other dioceses: Saint-Genest-Malifaux in the diocese of Lyon and Saint-Sauveur-en-Rue in the diocese of Vienne. These three dioceses intersected at a point still called "Pierre des Trois-Évêques."[57]

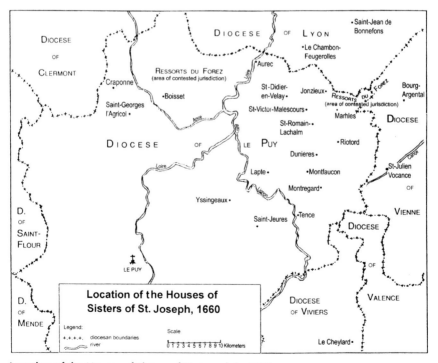

Location of the Houses of Sisters of St. Joseph in 1660

Most of the parishes where the first houses of St. Joseph were established were unimportant places far from centers of influence, whether political or religious. This pattern reflects a strategy used by the Jesuits. As Louis Châtellier notes, "When this was possible and without question of it being a general rule," the Jesuits established their charitable works by preference "in the interstices of power, where the remoteness or confusion of authority rendered it less pressing and more uncertain. It was here that the enterprise of spiritual and moral renewal to which the [Marian] congregations aspired found the most fertile ground."[58] Father Médaille had advised the Sisters of St. Joseph, particularly those engaged in teaching little girls, in the same vein: give service only where no one else is providing it, "in the places where nuns who are already established do not take care of it."[59] The spiritual orientation toward humility and disinterested service dovetailed with removal from places of power. Sisters were situated in places where no one else met the needs, whatever the insignificance or the grandeur of the place or service. In these places, with this approach, they continued to increase.

A CRISIS OF GROWTH: 1660-61

Within a decade, the small congregation established in the Velay had grown considerably, to twenty-two houses in four dioceses: sixteen in the diocese of Le Puy, three in Vienne, two in Lyon, and one in Clermont. Father Médaille had been present in person at the foundation of the earliest houses—Dunières, Marlhes, and Saint-Romain-Lachalm—founded with the approval of Bishop de Maupas. Although he is not mentioned, Fr. Médaille was surely there at the official founding in Le Puy, since he had presented the idea to the bishop and brought together women "found disposed to leaving the world and to the service of God."[60] No information relates whether he was present in Tence in 1653 for the founding of the community by Bishop de Maupas. It is remarkable, however, that during his years at the college in Aurillac (1650-1654), a town rather distant from Le Puy and difficult to reach through mountain roads, he managed to be present at the foundation of the smaller houses in the Le Puy diocese. Father Jean Baillard, rector of the college at Aurillac, may have understood Father Médaille and been favorable toward his enterprise. Unlike the priests at the college of Le Puy, he apparently did not write letters to the father general or the provincial expressing suspicions about Father Médaille. In addition, Father Baillard's evaluations of Father Médaille in the Society's Catalogues remain favorable, even though he alludes to the same credulity that others had ascribed to him. In Father Baillard's eyes, Médaille was far above average. Of remarkable intelligence (*ingenium eximium*), he possessed great judgment (*iudicium magnum*) and great prudence (*prudentia magna*), although this wisdom could at times be seen as inadequately cautious (*sed videtur parum limitata*).[61] The restrictive nuance of this evaluation seems to apply more to how his wisdom was "seen" than its reality. According to Baillard, Father Médaille had great talent for all the works of the society (*talentum magnum ad omnes Societatis functiones*). During his four years at Aurillac, Father Médaille served initially as preacher *extra urbem* (1650-51), then as minister, or assistant to the rector, and consultor (1651-52 and 1652-53), and finally as spiritual prefect, confessor for the priests, and admonitor to the rector (1653-54). All these functions, and even their evolution, point to the growing admiration Father Baillard had for Médaille, and at the same time the possibility of a favorable attitude toward the modest project of the Sisters of St. Joseph.

Archives of communities in the Le Puy diocese, even those preserving some recollection of their origins, do not mention Father Médaille in connection with foundations of new houses of Sisters of St. Joseph after 1653. In 1654 Father Médaille left Aurillac for the College of Montferrand, near Clermont in Basse-Auvergne, where he stayed until 1662, continually involved in missionary work. One might expect that this new appointment, which brought him closer to Le Puy and required constant travel for the missions, would favor his contacts with newly established houses of Sisters of St. Joseph or with those being planned. There is no mention, however, of such an encounter until 1660, when Father Médaille, with the help of sisters from Le Puy, established a house at Arlanc. This community, not quite thirty-five miles from Le Puy in the southeast corner of the present Puy-de Dôme, was the first community of St. Joseph in the diocese of Clermont.

The growth of houses of Sisters of St. Joseph, we know, caused some turmoil among the Jesuits. After all, hadn't Father Médaille given proof of imprudence by being involved for so long with a group of women, contrary to the rules of the Society? In fact the height of imprudence—he had brought together women from every level of society in the same institute, with such diversity in living the rule, and what apostolic freedom! It is no wonder that his local superiors at this period labeled Father Médaille's prudence as "mediocre." For 1660-61, Father Jean Gaillard, rector of the College of Montferrand, wrote, "prudentia simplicior," an ambiguous evaluation with a likely pejorative nuance suggesting naïveté.[62] This expression could also be read, however, as indicating completely evangelical transparency.[63]

The Sisters of St. Joseph experienced just as much turmoil. They had to learn how to find and keep their appropriate place within the various forms of this vocation. How could a *fille de basse condition*, for instance, not hanker after the external signs of greater prestige, such as the dress and manners belonging to women of a different class? Whether in town or country, in a small house or a large one, what was the best way to handle coming in and going out, contacts between the interior of the house and the exterior? How could they learn to integrate prayer and action and not confine themselves to one or the other? Whatever their origin—town or country, noble or humble— they had to develop a personal spiritual life with the help of a spiritual director and the sister superior. Organizing the houses in districts could help this formation process, but it did not happen automatically. The trial and error involved in these early stages entailed some serious and perilous irregularities that had to be remedied. *Monsieur* de Lantages, the sisters' ecclesiastical superior in the diocese of Le Puy, would not, on his own, have been able to untangle this maze of problems, problems connected with the very nature of the vocation and the elasticity of its structures. The sisters had to have recourse to Father Médaille, who had written the constitutions and to Bishop de Maupas who, as the ecclesiastical authority, alone could determine the official criteria. In order to remedy these disorders, Father Médaille composed the Avis et Règlements, and Bishop de Maupas gave the sisters a conference clarifying certain juridical guidelines. Both texts survive in numerous sources.

Avis et Règlements

The seven manuscripts of the Règlements contain both Father Médaille's "Avis et Règlements nécessaries pour mettre l'uniformité et le bon ordre dans les maisons des filles de Saint-Joseph" (Advice and Regulations necessary to introduce uniformity and good order in the houses of the Daughters of St. Joseph) and the "Conférence de Monseigneur de Maupas," which was given May 12, 1661.[64] Among the six Constitutions manuscripts, only two (Gap and B) contain the Avis et Règlements in its entirety. The Lyon manuscript preserves only those parts dealing with the country sisters. The Saint-Didier manuscript, contemporaneous with these events, has a slightly different text, probably written prior to the Avis et Règlements: "Quelques avis pour les Congregations de Saint-Joseph donnés par nos reverand père Médaille" (Advice for the Congregations of St. Joseph given by our Reverend Father Médaille).[65] This is the only Constitutions manuscript that conveys Bishop de Maupas' Conference, copied in its final pages. From so little information it is difficult to deduce which of the two texts is older and which of the two men first came forward to help the sisters. A closer examination of the content of these texts, as well as comparison with the "Quelques avis . . ." (Saint-Didier), indicates that Father Médaille was most likely the first to have intervened, around 1659 or 1660. Bishop de Maupas may have alerted him, or his missionary journeys may have given him the chance to notice the first shaky steps and the problems of the new communities. Parallels in the two documents make it clear, however, that Bishop de Maupas and Father Médaille worked in concert.

The title Father Médaille gave to his "Avis et Règlements" leaves no doubt about its purpose: "to introduce uniformity and good order in the houses of the Daughters of St. Joseph." Confusion must have reigned to some degree in the houses if it was necessary to put them in order. The most urgent need was reorganizing the houses in groups that would allow them to offer each other mutual support. Father Médaille therefore directed that "The city houses should be arranged in districts as soon as possible, and it should be known clearly to which district the country houses belong, so that in doubt and in need, each country house might have recourse to the [sister] superior of the city house on which it depends and to the [ecclesiastical] director of the entire district."[66] He also gave explicit points about the status of the members, especially the country sisters. He reminded them very briefly about specific details concerning their attire. He then explained that the three vows made by the country sisters (which in the Constitutions he had termed the "vow of stability") obliged them only "for the entire time they will live in the congregation."[67] He added that the sisters in towns "will observe the matters above [dress and vows] in the manner which has already been approved."[68] This suggests that instability was a problem primarily in the newest among the houses, those established in the country without semi-conventual forms. Father Médaille, however, gives little emphasis to the differences in the manner of life among the categories of sisters.

Most of the recommendations Father Médaille gives, beginning in the third paragraph, are addressed to "sisters both in the town and in the country" and deal with the sisters' relationships with others both outside and inside the houses (§3-9). Outside the house, the sisters could have contacts for business (§3); communication with their directors and other ecclesiastics (§4); and relationships with family: sometimes it was necessary to take a meal at home or to visit in case of illness or when in the vicinity (§5-6). Whenever the sisters went outside the house, they were to respect the proprieties as all other women did, who never went out alone, but always with a companion (§7). When admitting others to the house, they would follow the same rules of prudence. Men could only enter the house in case of illness among the sisters or "for major necessities regarding temporal affairs" (§8), and then in an appropriate way. For the town houses, this meant in the parlor, or in the country houses, in a "lower chamber" reserved for this use. As a general rule, the sisters did not invite anyone else to take meals with them (§9). As an exception, it might be necessary to welcome lay persons, and then they should be received "in places mentioned above [parlor or lower room], and this should be done very rarely, in case of necessity" (§9). The sisters should also "refuse to take in any kind of woman overnight" (§17). Yet "with permission of the local ecclesiastical superior," they could "sometimes house particularly edifying widows . . . as well as single or widowed candidates," but not others, and never women who were married. As in their dealings with men, all these cautions were in the interest of prudence and propriety.

Aware that precise details about sisters' relations with laity, within their houses and outside them, were not enough to reestablish order, Father Médaille urged the Daughters of St. Joseph to "try with all their power to be worthy daughters of so great a Father" (§12). He reminded the sisters that by reason of their vocation, "they should give good edification to everyone and avoid the least occasion of scandal. For if, unfortunately, one of the houses, either town or country, scandalize the people, their Excellencies the prelates might destroy them all" (§12). For Médaille, what would restore order among the Sisters of St. Joseph was not external uniformity, but rather the desire for holiness and love for their vocation, in whatever house they lived it, in town or country (§13). "In order to become holy," he wrote, the sisters should "school themselves in mortification" so that they might "be given . . . the gift of prayer" (§13–14); they should practice the "virtues which are the perfection, or at least the true character of their congregation" (§15). To maintain balance in all this, "lest the work of mind and body do too much harm to their health" (§16), they could take one afternoon a week for relaxation. Finally, should some disorders again slip into their houses, the sisters should speak to the sister superior or their spiritual director (§18) so that they might be remedied.

The number of special instructions addressed to the country houses among these counsels indicates that they presented the greatest problems in structuring daily life. Father Médaille presents his advice in a way that is clear, not cutting, and never moralizing. He does not make use of the term *agrégées*, which might be heard by those sisters as indicating a certain inferiority in relation to the others. He uses instead the expressions "town sisters" and "country sisters." As with all his spiritual counsels, moreover, he directs invitations to prudence or propriety to every sister without distinction. All are called to enter more profoundly into their single vocation, even if their ways of living it are different. He concludes his advice with a humble request to this little congregation so dear to him: "I pray the good sisters of St. Joseph keep the rules above faithfully, and I remain, after recommending myself to their prayers, their very humble and very affectionate servant in Our Lord, Jean-Pierre Médaille of the Society of Jesus." Had Father Gaillard, rector of the College of Montferrand, seen this text when he described Father Médaille as a man of "prudentia simplicior"? Having read the Avis et Règlements attentively, one can only support his judgment with admiration.[69]

The Conference of Bishop de Maupas

To be fully effective, Father Médaille's counsels of human and spiritual wisdom had to be confirmed by ecclesiastical authority. Bishop de Maupas did so in the conference given to the Sisters of St. Joseph assembled in the house in Le Puy on May 12, 1661.[70] The bishop brought his vicar-general with him, and "it was resolved that . . . all the sisters would maintain uniformity."[71] In order to implement this general resolution, Bishop de Maupas gave the sisters "some rules" dealing with three principal points: founding new houses, organizing houses into districts, and clothing for the different categories of sisters. Wherever new houses were to be established, the bishop required that sisters be sent who had pronounced vows and were "somewhat mature in age" (§2). If the new houses were situated in the diocese, "a small amount of the sisters' revenue" would be sent with them. This was never the case for the houses outside the diocese, "for those who ask them to come are obliged to provide for their living." Bishop de Maupas speaks of the districts as if they were already in place or in the process of organization. The sisters in villages could admit sisters without "the presence of the ecclesiastical superior or the sister superior of the district; they must simply inform them before the reception" (§5). In the small villages, they were "never to place sisters like those in the towns, but only *agrégées*, who will always depend upon the houses established in the towns" (§7). These houses should have "particular concern for the sisters who depend upon them, and the priest who has care of them should visit them from time to time" (§8). Sisters in the villages "will occasionally go to make their retreat at their district house" (§6). Bishop de Maupas described the various sorts of dress in greater detail than Father Médaille.[72] The attire of Sisters of St. Joseph—whether town sisters or "*agrégées* sisters of the villages"—expressed both the social rank of the one who wore it and her membership in the congregation. It could not be assumed, put aside, or changed without permission from the bishop. It was therefore important that the elements of this dress be precisely described. To the two categories, the sisters of the town and the sisters of the country, Bishop de Maupas added a third, "the servants of the sisters of the towns" (§9 and 14), who were employed by the Sisters of St. Joseph, with the administrators' consent, to help in the hospital houses. They were authorized to dress "like the *agrégées*" but without the cross. They could be present for "spiritual conferences and chapter . . . but not at other meetings dealing with the business of the house." The bishop concluded his conference with a directive about the commitment made by the sisters of the villages: "after two years of novitiate, they will make their vows at the foot [of the altar in] their oratory before their parish priest." These were simple vows, made out of devotion, with no juridical status.

In general, Bishop de Maupas gave more prominence to the distinction between sisters in the town and the *agrégées* sisters in the villages than did Father Médaille. The rules he gave the sisters were far more juridical ordinances
than spiritual counsels. At this difficult juncture, the little congregation
needed both stable reference points and complementary principles. Ten years
after the foundation, Father Médaille and Bishop de Maupas joined together
a second time to provide them.

THE LITTLE DESIGN AND FATHER
MÉDAILLE'S LAST YEARS (†1669)

With order replacing the confusion of the Sisters of St. Joseph's early days,
or for some other reason, the College of Le Puy showed itself more favorable
toward Father Médaille's endeavors. Following the example of the illustrious
College of the Trinity in Lyon, it even agreed around 1660 to the establishment of a house of St. Joseph in the parish of Montregard, a priory belonging
to the College of Le Puy since 1620.[73] After 1660, however, foundations in
the diocese of Le Puy diminished somewhat. This slower growth may have
been linked to the departure of Bishop de Maupas for the see of Evreux in
1661. His successor, Armand de Béthune had not yet arrived, and his vicars-
general did not automatically share Bishop de Maupas' sympathy for the Sisters of St. Joseph. Before 1669, only three or four new houses were established: Monistrol-sur-Loire, summer residence of the bishops of Le Puy,
around 1661, Chomelix in 1662, Grazac in 1664, and Saint-Just-Chomelix
(today known as Bellevue-la-Montagne), around 1669 or later.[74] By contrast,
houses proliferated in neighboring dioceses. Three were established in the
diocese of Lyon: Saint-Jean-de-Bonnefonds (around 1660), Saint Marcellin
(1662), and Saint-Genest-Malifaux (1665), and two more in Clermont: Sauxillanges (1665), where Father Médaille, then a missionary in the diocese, was
present and involved, and Dore-l'Église (1669).[75] The first house in the diocese of Viviers opened in 1661 at Cheylard, and the first in the diocese of
Mende, at Langogne, where Clauda Chastel went to establish a house in
1663.[76] In the diocese of Vienne, the house at Satillieu was authorized by
Henry de Villars on December 6, 1661, and that of Vocance began before
1663.[77]

The most important of all the houses established under the ancien régime,
however, was that of Vienne in Dauphiné. Archbishop Henry de Villars asked
for Sisters of St. Joseph to take charge of the Hôtel-Dieu of the city of Vienne.
Two were sent; one, Marguerite Burdier, was among the six founders of the
house at Le Puy in 1650. The archbishop formally authorized the establish-

ment of the Vienne house on September 10, 1668.[78] This foundation represented a critical juridical step, since the protection of the archbishop of Vienne could provide significant assurance for the future of the incipient Congregation of St. Joseph.[79]

Father Médaille continued his missionary activities at the College of Montferrand. In July of 1663, the college was moved to Clermont, with setbacks
and violent opposition from supporters of the Oratory.[80] Father Médaille and
some other priests were not named in the records of this ambitious move, perhaps because he was absent on missionary journeys. During the following
year (1664-65), however, he once again functioned as minister, this time to
Father Guillaume Chabron, who succeeded Jean Gaillard as rector of the College of Clermont.[81] He was also confessor for the day students and consultor
to the rector. Amid the string of problems accompanying the transfer of the
college, Father Chabron may have felt the possibility of a strong and pacific
support in the presence of Father Médaille. The provincial in Toulouse would
have shared this trust in Father Médaille, because it was he who assigned the
office of minister. Lacking the triennial catalogue of the province of Toulouse
for 1665, that remains conjecture.

The charge of minister lasted, surprisingly, only one year. The following
year (1665-66), Father Médaille appears to have left again for missionary
work. Perhaps there were urgent needs in the missions, or the post as minister was too heavy for his poor health. Throughout most of his life, the Society's catalogues note his fragile health (*vires infirmae*). It must have been a
cause, if not the only one, for this change. The catalogues of the Province of
Toulouse again fail to provide details on Father Médaille's activities between
1665 and 1668–1669. It seems as if missionary work did not occupy all his
time. The 1668-69 catalogue notes that he had served as preacher in the
chapel of the College of Clermont for two years.[82] This post implies some degree of presence in the house. Typically, the office of preacher was held by
the rector or "done by someone else well versed in the nature of our institute,"
who was to give "an exhortation to ours every Friday, or every other Friday,
in which he discusses the observation of the rules and constitutions . . . instead of an exhortation, however, he might sometimes give a spiritual conference on the same matters."[83] The rector might have asked Father Médaille
to carry out this function because it was so compatible with poor health and
intermittent external occupations.

During the last ten years of his life, while continuing his missionary work,
Father Médaille kept working on the *Maxims of Perfection*. Nicolas Jaquard,
a friend of the Jesuits, had published the first part of these maxims at Clermont in 1657. The second part, entitled "Exercise for being stripped of self,
and putting on Jesus Christ, and imitating him in his hidden and public life,"

was published, again by Jacquard, only in 1672, three years after Father Médaille's death. This part of the maxims is reminiscent of Bérulle's reflections
on "the states and mysteries which share in the life and public circumstances
of the Son of God."[84] The imitation to which Father Médaille refers borders
on the participation in the very life of God in Jesus Christ which Bérulle
called *adhérence*. The triennial catalogue of the Toulouse Province for
1657–1658 cites Father Médaille's great success in the humanities and philosophy and his talent for literary works.[85] This evaluation is certainly connected with the publication of the *Maxims of Perfection* in 1657. Three years
later, the catalogue for 1660-1661 provides a similar assessment of his gift for
literary works (*talentum ad res litterarias*). Perhaps at this time Father Médaille wrote the second part of the maxims, "Exercise for being stripped of
self." The qualifier "res litterarias" seems ill-chosen for this text, which is
much more prayer and contemplation than literature. It is actually better
suited to another of Father Médaille's writings, drafted as a literary exercise
known as an *emblème,* or symbolic representation, and well known by the
Sisters of St. Joseph: the Eucharistic Letter.

The Eucharistic Letter

The Eucharistic Letter appears in only one manuscript of the Constitutions,
kept in the Motherhouse at Lyon, which contains all the principal early texts
concerning the Sisters of St. Joseph.[86] The status of the Eucharistic Letter
among sisters in the seventeenth and eighteenth centuries is uncertain. It appears to be addressed personally to an unknown sister, yet its studied literary
form makes one think that it was not an ordinary letter intended for strictly
private use. It is a text that could be communicated through one person as intermediary, primarily to other members of the group it refers to, and possibly
to a larger audience. Perhaps to a unit of the Company of the Blessed Sacrament? It was rediscovered at Riotord in 1870, and subsequently, at Lyon in
1878. When Abbé Jean Joseph Rivaux published an edited version of the Letter in his *Vie de la R. Mère du Sacré Cœur de Jesus* in 1878, the Sisters of St.
Joseph recognized it as a summary of their vocation.[87] More recently, we, like
Father Marius Nepper, thought that this letter from Father Médaille was written near 1646, and that it predated the foundation of the Sisters of St.
Joseph.[88] Further study of the historical circumstances and texts regarding the
Congregation of St. Joseph has now led to a different conclusion. It is there-
fore important to clarify the origin and contents of this letter.

A careful comparison of the Eucharistic Letter with the Constitutions establishes that at least the latter part was written after them and therefore, on
even stronger grounds, after the Règlement. When Father Médaille drew up

the Constitutions, he did so for the single house in Le Puy, while hoping for an increase of houses. In the Eucharistic Letter, however, the author refers to an organization of houses. He mentions the diversity of the social conditions proper to each association (community) and refers to "principal daughters" who leave the house for apostolic reasons and "little sisters" who in their works should "so act that the whole world will try . . . to live and serve God in spirit and in truth."[89] Obviously, when the letter was written, there were not only several associations or houses in existence, but these diversified houses were organized as "principal houses" with "principal daughters" and smaller houses where "our little sisters" were employed.[90] This distinction certainly seems to correspond to the districts described by Fr. Médaille in the Avis et Règlements, where small country houses were grouped around a more prominent city house.[91] That leads to the conclusion that the Eucharistic Letter was written after the Avis et Règlements, around the year 1660. This approximate date is confirmed by the Letter's reference to the directory, speaking of the "duties of our little sisters . . . according to their directory."[92] We know that the Little Directory was written shortly before 1659 or 1660. The Eucharistic Letter was therefore not written before 1660.[93]

The identity of the person to whom the letter was addressed also surfaces some points of convergence, if not another confirmation. Internal evidence from the manuscript, now in the Lyon community archives, shows that it was formerly at Vienne. The presence of this manuscript, and therefore the letter, at Vienne suggests that it was addressed to Marguerite Burdier, who was superior of the community in Vienne from 1668 and one of the first founding sisters at Le Puy in 1650. In 1660 Marguerite was superior at Tence, which had helped to establish the house at Riotord in 1659 by sending one sister, Gabrielle Riou, for this foundation.[94] The presence of the Eucharistic Letter at Riotord and Vienne seems to confirm that it was addressed to Marguerite Burdier.

The contents of the letter, a long comparison between the new congregation and the Eucharist, is meant for someone who shared Father Médaille's understanding of the Eucharist, "which is, if I am not mistaken, the source of all our pure and holy loves on earth."[95] Of the first Sisters of St Joseph, Marguerite Burdier is most surely known to have had numerous contacts with various Companies of the Blessed Sacrament, chiefly for the establishment of several communities. If Father Médaille spoke to her in this way, it was most likely because her connections with the famous Company, like his own, had well-established roots preceding the foundation of the Sisters of St. Joseph.

A large part of the letter simply describes the reality of the congregation, expressing the mystical meaning of this description through a comparison with the Eucharist. "A body without a body . . . a congregation without a congregation . . . a religious order without a religious order": this described the actual status of the new association.[96] It could not be recognized as a social body or as a congregation, still less as a religious order in the monastic sense of the term. The Letter describes it as "so hidden in its foundation that only the persons who compose it and their superiors will know about it."[97] The dignitaries of Le Puy had just that experience in 1654 when they visited the Montferrand Hospital: they thought they knew; they were surprised by what they found. This was also the experience of members of the Company of the Blessed Sacrament. When Father Médaille wrote the Letter around 1660, most of the existing houses were very small, with as little outward appearance as Jesus in the Eucharist. This he saw as gain: "how happy our Institute will be if it maintains this spirit of littleness, humility, self-emptying."[98] It was also precisely true that the new association, as the Letter says, had neither founder nor foundress. In the meaning of founder (*fondateur*) at that time, the sisters had none, that is, no eminent person or influential protector who also provided financial security through an endowment (*fonds*). But the Eucharistic Letter is not only a description. Its central section is also a contemplation on the Eucharist as the "model of our love for God and of our charity towards the neighbor," in order to work toward the union of all persons among themselves and with God.[99] If Father Médaille sent his letter to the house of St. Joseph in Tence, a region cruelly tried by the wars of religion, this message and this mission could have assumed their full significance, brought all their influence to bear.

The final part of the Letter alludes to the manner of life in the new congregation in terms of numeric symbols, popular at the time. It describes the community in analogy to the three divine Persons, the apostolic proclamation of the Word through "the sixteen apostles and evangelists," the exercise of compassion "in honor of the seven deacons," and finally the communication of the Gospel in the world by the seventy-two disciples.[100] Symbolic numbers also appeared in certain statutes of the Company the Blessed Sacrament, especially the numbers twelve and sixteen, but without any systematic usage, for example, ". . . twelve founders and confreres, in memory of the twelve apostles of J.C., to increase only up to the number of sixteen."[101] The different parts of the Letter—description, contemplation, and symbolic allusion—are often expressed in the future, as a prophetic vision, "Our incomparable Savior was pleased to communicate to me . . . ," writes the founder. For this "very dear association" Father Médaille expressed a hope: "God grant that it may be established throughout his Church."[102]

The Eucharistic Letter is of fundamentally the same inspiration and spirituality as all the other writings of Father Médaille. Certain formulations nevertheless seem closer to the Règlement than to the Constitutions and other texts. Characteristic expressions occur in the Letter and in the Règlement, particularly "the total double union" of the members of the congregation "with God, among themselves, and with every kind of neighbor."[103] This similarity had contributed, formerly, to the belief that the Règlement had its origin in the Eucharistic Letter, as if it were the implementation of Father Médaille's illumination about the Letter. We can see that it is no such thing. There is indeed an illumination of Father Médaille's vision and of his understanding, but stemming from what he has witnessed for ten years, and whose first development, whose first fruits, he now sees and whose future he can already glimpse. The year 1660 was precisely one of great increase in the number of houses. Father Médaille reviewed what had taken place since the beginning. He did this in light of the first inspiration received and written in the Règlements, and not the more juridical text of the Constitutions. The Eucharistic Letter simply reiterates and expands the mystical aspects of apparent littleness and of union with God and among all persons already expressed in the Règlements. And yet, the letter indirectly confirms what is stated in the Constitutions: "The Blessed Sacrament gave beginning to their little congregation." It is also the Blessed Sacrament which must "maintain it and cause it to grow more and more in every kind of grace and virtue."[104] Through literary forms and comparisons now obsolete, the essential theology of Eucharist in the Letter still remains contemporary.

An expression often repeated in the Eucharistic Letter is the phrase "little design." It appears four times in the original Constitutions, but not in the Règlements.[105] It is used profusely in the Eucharistic Letter, and since its rediscovery at the end of the nineteenth century, Sisters of St. Joseph have often employed the term to designate the congregation founded by Father Médaille. At times it refers to God's plan, "his design" (§ 5), at others, to an objective fulfilled, "this new design" (§ 11) or the "little association of the Little Design" (§ 19). Less often, and only after speaking much about "our dear association," "our institution," or "our dear congregation," etc., Father Médaille speaks of "their design" (§ 26), that is, of the members of the congregation. At the very end of the letter, Father Médaille writes "our little design" (§ 51), as if, little by little, the project of God became simultaneously his and the sisters'. Adrien Demoustier's study of the Eucharistic Letter explains the double usage of the word "design" (*dessein*) in the seventeenth century, when the same word referred to the idea, the linear or pictorial representation, and to the project.[106] Father Médaille's "little design" is therefore both a description of the reality and a plan. What is the origin of this expression? Why did Father Médaille seem to experience such particular delight in using this term? It is as if, for him, there were a contrast between this very "little design" and some large unspecified design. In this context, Father Nepper calls to mind the "great design" that Francis de Sales wrote about to Jeanne de Chantal before establishing the Order of the Visitation.[107] Another hypothesis is suggested by the foundation of the Sisters Hospitallers of St. Joseph de La Flèche in the diocese of Angers.

Around 1630, Jérôme Le Royer de La Dauversière, a pious lay member of the Company of the Blessed Sacrament, felt called by God to a triple mission.[108] He was to found a new community of religious, for a hospital that did not exist, in a city which did not yet exist—the city of Montreal in New France. This vast enterprise would be realized step by step. The Hospitallers of St. Joseph were founded in 1636; the city of Montréal began with a group of lay recruits in 1642; and the Hospitallers went to the Hôtel-Dieu there in 1659.[109] This was obviously an immense program, a very "great design." The Bishop of Angers, Claude de Rueil, approved the Constitutions of the Sister Hospitallers in 1643.[110] According to these constitutions, the new religious were not cloistered and did not make solemn vows. Consecrated to God through simple vows, "in the world without being of the world," the sisters were committed to serving the neighbor, especially the poor and sick.[111] After Claude de Rueil's death, Henry Arnauld, a Jansenist, became Bishop of Angers in 1650. From the time of his arrival, the new bishop wanted to transform the Congregation of the Hospitallers of St. Joseph into a religious order with enclosure and solemn vows. In 1653 he provoked strong opposition from the sisters and sowed division in the community. Jérôme de La Dauversière's great design, the evangelization of New France, risked being derailed. Through an extraordinary and momentary reversal, however, Bishop Arnauld allowed the sisters to leave for Canada on July 2, 1659, taking with them the Constitutions of 1643. Dauversière therefore had the joy of seeing his vision fulfilled before he died in 1659.[112] Nonetheless, the transformation of the congregation into a religious order continued in France. In 1666 Bishop Arnauld obtained a brief from Pope Alexander VII recognizing the sisters as "true religious, maintaining enclosure and forming a religious community, living according to the rule of St. Augustine."

Father Médaille had to be aware of the attempts to evangelize New France, of the Jesuits martyred there, and of the actions carried out by the Company of the Blessed Sacrament at the College of La Flèche. He surely knew of the Congregation of the Hospitallers of St. Joseph, particularly because their texts show that the Jesuits had been involved in writing their constitutions. He must have been struck by the contrast between the vastness of M. de La Dauversière's prospect and the humility of his own little project. The term "little design" appeared in the Constitutions of the Sisters of St. Joseph between 1650 and 1653, during the very period when the Bishop of Angers wanted to bestow the prestige of religious on the Hospitallers of La Flèche. Later, around 1660, in the Eucharistic Letter, Fr. Médaille insisted favorably on the littleness, at once real and mystical, of the "little design." At just this time, the Hospitallers were becoming a cloistered religious order, and the project of M. de La Dauversière had almost been annihilated. One can understand Father Médaille's gratitude for the "miraculous" development of "this new design" (§ 11), not grounded in appearances or prestige, but entirely given over to the hands of God.

Even though the Eucharistic Letter was addressed only to one person, it contained a message for all members of the "very little institute," a message of union of the sisters with God, among themselves, and with every neighbor, the congregation as a whole being called to make "profession of the most pure and perfect love."[113] Written after the Avis et Règlements, this message could help to unify from the inside out the diversity of forms of life in the houses. That union was effected through making littleness, humility, and the absence of legal recognition the basis of the new association and a means of advancing "the glory of God and the salvation of souls."[114] It seems, however, that the message was not received, at least not in this particular form. Apparently, the Eucharistic Letter was not circulated, or very little, among the communities. It might have been perceived primarily as a personal message and therefore more or less rejected for use by the group. Perhaps it was thought to be too close to the Company of the Blessed Sacrament. Some houses might have felt cramped by the notion of not being legally recognized. All that is known is that Marguerite Burdier, in order to work toward "the double union," was content to keep this letter as a treasure in her heart and in her records, without imposing it. In the letter, Father Médaille directed attention toward what was newest, that is, the little houses scattered in the country, rather than toward the more prominent, and already more recognized, city houses. This was also the perspective of the Avis et Règlements. Despite the temptations toward upward social mobility common to small and large houses, the sisters on the whole maintained the differences in their modes of life, with their apostolic meaning of presence to all in love and humility. This diversity, surviving the French Revolution, would undergo several further revolutions.

Father Médaille's Last Years

We have little information about Father Médaille's last years, particularly because the 1665 triennial catalogue of the Toulouse Province is missing. These were the years when he composed the second part of the maxims: "Exercise for being stripped of self and putting on Jesus Christ."[115] This exercise was destined for all Christians and not just for Sisters of St. Joseph. The purpose for "this little book," according to Father Médaille, is what he asks of Christ: "That, by an easy method, you teach me the way to live in you and through you, and have your dear life and adorable virtues live in me."[116] The "little book" might be a collection done by Father Médaille himself of exhortations or private texts written earlier. Father Médaille may not have published the text because it was written in the first person "in the form of prayers and colloquies with the . . . Savior."[117] His confreres published it only it 1672, three years after his death. There may have been other reasons, such as ill health, but we simply do not know. The triennial catalogue of 1669 again mentions Fr. Médaille's literary success.[118] If his writings have interest today, it is admittedly not for their literary value, but rather for the quality of the spiritual experience they attest.

Through the record of Father Médaille's apostolic undertakings through the years, enhanced by notes made by his superiors, a clearer picture of him emerges. During a long first phase in the society, until around 1648, whatever his occupation, his superiors' evaluations contain high praise in all areas except health. He spent a little time as procurator, two years, and a longer period, six years, as minister. Perhaps his superiors believed that for Father Medaille, in the office of procurator, the glory of God had too much to do with looking after other people's concerns, even if he never disregarded the interests of the college. The two positions of procurator and minister, as mentioned above, require administrative and organizational skills and also a knack for human relations. In a certain sense, the minister's responsibility is always secondary, related to the primary authority of the rector. This position seems to have suited Father Médaille well, in regard to both responsibility and relationship, since he held it for a fairly long time. During those years, he was also confessor to the Jesuits or to persons outside the house (5 years), in addition to being consultor (10 years) and admonitor to the rector (3 years). These posts required a great deal of judgment, a recognized gift of spiritual discernment. During the following period of about ten years, until around 1660, in the Colleges of Aurillac, then of Montferrand, this spiritual wisdom became suspect. Father Médaille had entered into events relating to the foundation of the Sisters of St. Joseph with great simplicity, receiving blame and criticism, and trying to benefit from them. In the absence of prohibition on the part of his superiors, Father Médaille continued the endeavor, with all the ambiguity and docility to circumstances that came with it. To move on in uncertainty, however, is not easy—not for oneself, and much less so for others. It became the source of suspicion and anxiety on the part of his confreres, which he had to endure, and which may well have been a great trial for him. In none of the scant information available is he ever seen to try to justify himself. Even in the absence of sources, it is easy to see that he probably understood the good reasons behind the other Jesuits' fears. In the end, however, he did not have to justify himself.

Events quickly took a turn for the better in regard to the progress of the Sisters of St. Joseph. Father Médaille regained the esteem of the Jesuits at the College of Le Puy, due in part, no doubt, to his personal attitude. At the same time, around 1660, he received an illumination from God about the Little Design and the Eucharist, which he explained to Marguerite Burdier in a letter written in an unusual style. In a way, what he wrote about the action of God confirms the opinion that some of his fellow Jesuits had of his abilities: "As for our part in it . . . that amounts to nothing but a real obstacle to his [God's] work."[119] Paradoxically, his statement also testifies to the depth of his spirituality and humility. The last triennial catalogue (1669) to mention Father Médaille praises his intelligence and judgment, his great experience in the missions, a certain literary success, and his particular aptitude for the missions and for hearing confessions (*ad misssiones et confessiones audiendas*). His prudence, however, still remains "middling" (*mediocris*).[120]

Among the evaluations given for Father Médaille by successive superiors over the years, one attribute is constant, the gift for dealing with spiritual matters, especially for spiritual direction. All the catalogues indicate that from the beginning of his ministry in Saint-Flour, he had a talent for teaching and guiding souls (*ad instruendas et regendas animas*), whether large crowds in the missions or individuals in direction. He was born for the missions (*natus ad missiones*) and had a great gift for hearing confessions (*ad confessiones audiendas*). From 1655 on, the triennial catalogues that survive include these various ministries, and beginning in 1658, reference to his literary activities. Even though his superiors did not understand what Father Médaille was doing, or rather, what was happening to him, they always recognized his God-given gift for spiritual direction. Oddly, when this gift was expressed in writing, as in 1658 after the publication of the *Maxims of Perfection for Every Christian Soul*, his superior saw the work only as literary progress. In his written work as in the Little Design, Father Médaille's profound spiritual wisdom remained partially hidden. In what he did, he was not sure of himself and did not conceal it. As he said, his work was "little, both in its own eyes and in reality."[121] God, however, made good use of this quite ordinary wisdom, completely given over to his will, in the words of Médaille, to "accomplish his marvels according to the measure of his good pleasure."[122]

A letter of Father Médaille has survived, written probably during his last years at Clermont, addressed to Sister Fayole, superior of the house in Saint-Didier.[123] "It pains me to see you bearing crosses," he said, "you have them on all sides. . . . The order which divine providence has established for the birth and progress of good works is strewn with crosses." Then he complains of having had no word from her: "I have not received any letter from you in a long time. . . . I would have been very happy to have word of your whole congregation, but God has not willed it." Later he refers to a favor she had requested of him: "Here I have little chance of seeing you, yet if the occasion and opportunity present themselves, I would gladly do everything possible to assist you there. Recommend everything to the glorious St. Joseph. For my part, I will not neglect to pray to God for all your concerns." Then he speaks of his health: "On your part also, pray to God for my health which has been a little diminished for some time. I send greetings with all my affection to your dear congregation, and am with all my heart in Our Lord, my very dear Sister. [signed] Your very humble and very obedient servant in O[ur] L[ord], J. Médaille of the Society of Jesus."

This letter, most likely written at the same time as he wrote the "Exercise for being stripped of self and clothed with Jesus Christ," indicates that toward the end of his life, Father Médaille, whose own heart seemed to be stripped, continued to be full of affection and solicitude for his dear congregation without having news about them. The severe trials he suffered had not dehumanized him. Even when writing lofty and demanding spiritual texts, he remained, very really and warmly, close to those he cared about.

In 1669, probably because of his poor health, he was sent to the College of Billom, which also served as a retirement house for the aged or infirm Jesuits.[124] Named confessor for day pupils, he did not fulfill this ministry for long. He died there on December 30 of the same year, at the age of 59.[125] His obituary makes no reference to the Little Design, but more generally to his apostolic works: "He spent the greater part of his life in the missions of the Province, with such a reputation for zeal and for holiness that here and there he was called 'the saint,' 'the apostle.' The fruits of his apostolic labors were no less than his reputation, so much so that he was always very dear to poor and rich alike, but especially to the bishops in whose dioceses he labored."[126]

After his death, his Jesuit brothers indirectly confirmed the reputation for sanctity that Father Médaille had been accorded by the simple people whom he evangelized. By having his Maxims published in 1672, particularly the second part, "Exercise for being stripped of self and putting on Jesus Christ," they demonstrated, that even if it is not exceptional as a literary work, the contents reveal an uncommon experience of spiritual realities. For his Jesuit brothers, too, Father Médaille was a man of God.

NOTES

1. *RSI* 1620, Règles des Missions, 327
2. ARSI, Tolos. 2^{II}, fol. 241v; see Supporting Documents, 5.
3. Ibid., Tolos. 2^{II}, fol. 241v.

4. Ibid., Tolos. 2^{II}, fol. 260.

5. Ibid., Tolos. 2^{II}, fol. 260.

6. bid., Tolos., 10^{I}, fol. 183r.

7. Ignatius Loyola, although open to appropriate relationships with high born women, did not believe the same possible with women of the lower classes, whose emotional and behavioral instability might cause scandal in regard to those who tried to help them, Olwen Hufton, "Altruism and Reciprocity: The Early Jesuits and Their Female Patrons," *Renaissance Studies* 15.3 (2001): 332-33; see John W. O'Malley, The First Jesuits (Cambridge: Harvard University Press, 1993), 133. –Trans.

8. Pierre Delattre, "Toulouse," in *Les Établissements des jésuites en France depuis quatre siècles*, 5 vols. (Enghien: Institut Supérieur de Théologie, 1940-1957), 4: col. 1255.

9. AMM Le Puy, Citation by A. Achard from a notebook of the procurator of the College of Le Puy, which has since been lost. Delattre notes that at that time, there were only a small number of professed houses in France and they were always related to the more universal activities of a province of the Society. In this case, it could only be the house of Toulouse, Delattre, "Introduction," 1: vii.

10. ARSI, Tolos. 2^{II}, 297v.

11. Ibid., Tolos. 2^{II}, 297v.

12. Ibid., Tolos. 2^{II}, 297v.

13. Ibid., Tolos. 10^{I}, 95.

14. *TP* 1981, MI, 178, nos. 72 and 67.

15. Ibid., MI, 178, no. 67.

16. Archives Sociéte de Jésus, Toulouse, Copy of the annual Catalogue for 1650-51 (nineteenth or early twentieth c.), lacking in the Society's archives in Rome.

17. AMM Le Puy, Communauté de Marlhes, "Contract reçu Sieur Verne, Nre de Marlhes, 6 octobre 1651."

18. AMM Le Puy, Communauté de Marlhes, Registre des réceptions des sœurs de Marlhes, 1.

19. AMM Le Puy, Communauté de Saint-Romain-Lachalm, "Contrat reçu Chapuis, le 15e octobre 1652."

20. AMM Le Puy, Communauté de Tence.

21. Cited in Marie Brioude, *La ville et la paroisse de Tence* (Le Puy, 1900), 121.

22. AMM Le Puy, Communauté de Tence, copie des Letters Patent: Arch. Parlement de Toulouse, registre no. 26, fols. 244 ff.

23. Ibid., Communauté de Saint-Didier, Copie des dons faits par le seigneur de Saint-Didier aux sœurs de Saint-Joseph de lad. ville, 12 septembre 1674.

24. Ibid., Communauté d'Aurec.

25. AMM Aubenas, Communauté de Saint-Julien-Vocance, "Albergement ou assencement de deux pugniers et demi jardin," le 31 mai 1675; and AMM Lyon, Bourg-Argental, Demande d'approbation à l'archevêque de Vienne, le 6 mai 1675.

26. Archives Comte de Charpin-Feugerolles, Notice sur le Chateau de Feugerolles, Lyon 1878, 129.

27. AMM Le Puy, Communautés d'Yssingeaux, Saint-Jeures-de-Bonas, Saint-Victor-Malescours, and Riotord.

28. AMM Le Puy, Communauté de Montregard, approximate date of foundation according to "Quittance donnée à Honneste Claude Ferraton, supérieure des sœurs de Saint-Joseph . . . le 4 mai 1666"; Lapte, approximate date of foundation according to the notes of Abbé Achard; and Jonzieux, Acte de profession de Louise Didier, Anne Brunon et Angélique Bayle, le 1er Février 1664.

29. AMM Le Puy, Communauté de Boisset, Acte d'association [of seven sisters], le 24 mai 1664, Minutes de Bouchet, Copy in the MS Règlement of Boisset; and BMU Clermont-Ferrand, Fonds Paul Leblanc, MS 650, p. 6: Retrait d'Anne Guilhomont du contrat d'association, le 8 aout 1670.

30. AMM Lyon, and AM Saint-Jean-de-Bonnefonds, Registres paroissiaux 1666.

31. AD Puy-de-Dome, 1G 1573, nos. 1 and 2, Religieuses de Saint-Joseph à Arlanc; and AMM Aubenas, Communauté de Satillieu, Confirmation de l'établissement des sœurs de Saint-Joseph à Satillieu par Mgr Henry de Villars, archevêque de Vienne, le 6 décembre 1661.

32. AD Rhône, Série D, 144, Union des prieurés Saint-Martin de Dunières et Saint-Martin de Tence au Collège de la Trinité à Lyon (1496-1581).

33. AD Rhône, Série D, 193, Prieuré de Dunières, cure de Saint-Romain-Lachalm (1669-1747); and D 194, Prieuré de Dunières, cure de Saint-Victor-Malescours (1483-1667).

34. AD Haute-Loire, J 237/149, Curés de Marlhes, copy of a portion of "Livre terrier du Sr prieur de Saint-Martin de Dunyères," fol. VI^{xxv}.

35. AD Rhône, Série D, 175, Prieuré de Tence, cure de Saint-Jeures de Bonas (1462-1611).

36. Delattre, 4: col. 1422.

37. AD Loire, 1 J 136, "Recognoissance de la cure de Riotord a M^{rs} les Jésuites."

38. AD Rhône, 1 G 52, Visites pastorales de Mgr Camille de Neuville, 1656.

39. AMM Lyon, Communauté du Chambon, "Registre Des sœurs qui ont decede Dans notre maisont Depuis les premier." This very important archival document for the community of Chambon begins in 1600, shows no listing between 1600 and 1650, and a partial listing from 1650 until the Revolution.

40. AM Saint-Étienne (Loire), MS 115, pièce 5, "Contrat de vente . . . du 15e Febvrier 1659."

41. Jean-Antoine de La Tour-Varan, *Chroniques des Chateaux et des Abbayes, Étude Historique sur le Forez* (Saint-Étienne: Montagny, 1854-1857; reprint, 2 vols. in one, Marseille: Laffitte, 1976), see Chateau de Feugerolles.

42. *PDL*, "Statuts des Compagnies de Gentilshommes, envoyés par la Compagnie de Paris," le 12 février 1648, 145; and Edmonde Albe, "La Confrérie de la Passion: Contribution à l'histoire de la Compagnie du Saint-Sacrement," *Revue d'Histoire de l'Eglise de France*, 3 (1912): 656-57.

43. AMM Lyon, Communauté du Chambon, Historique, in a small notebook, end of nineteenth c.

44. La Tour-Varan, see Chateau de Feugerolles.

45. AMM Le Puy, Communauté de Saint-Didier, "copie des dons faits par le marquis de Nerestang, Seigneur de Saint-Didier, aux Sœurs de Saint-Joseph de lad. Ville, 12 septembre 1674."

46. Vital Chausse, *Saint-Didier-en-Velay, Actualités, Histoire, Traditions* (Saint-Étienne: Impr. industrielle, 1948).

47. Jacques Gadille, *Histoire du diocèse de Lyon* (Paris : Beauchesne, 1983), 148 and 151.

48. Ibid.

49. Ulysse Chevalier, *Notice chronologico-historique sur les archevêques de Vienne* (Vienne: Savigné, 1879).

50. *ACSS*, 154 and 279.

51. Archives privées comte de Charpin-Feugerolles.

52. AD Haute-Loire, J 237/149, Marlhes, *Chronique du Dimanche*, unsigned newspaper article of July 30, 1905.

53. AD Loire, B, carton no. 130, Bourg-Argental.

54. A. Vachet, *Les paroisses du diocèse de Lyon* (Bourg-Argental: Lérins, 1899), 52.

55. Archives privées comte de Charpin-Feugerolles.

56. J.E. Dufour, *Dictionnaire topographique du Forez et des paroisses du Lyonnais et du Beaujolais formant le départmenet de la Loire* (Macon: Impr. Protat frères, 1946), Introduction, xxxi.

57. AD Haute-Loire, J 237/149, Marlhes, *Chronique du Dimanche*, July 30, 1905. The Pierre des Trois Eveques is now in the confines of the commune of Saint-Régis-du-Coin (Loire).

58. Louis Châtellier, *The Europe of the Devout: The Catholic Reformation and the Formation of a New Society*, trans. Jean Birrell (Cambridge [England] / New York: Cambridge University Press, 1989), 30.

59. *TP* 1981, CP, 28, no. 91.

60. *CV* 1694, Preface.

61. ARSI, Tolos. 10^{I}, 253r.

62. ARSI, Tolos. 10^{II}, 529r.

63. *Simplex* (*simplicior* in the text) can mean "unaffected" or even "transparent." Because it directly follows the response, "Judicium: non firmum," however, indicating that the rector found Father Médaille's judgment less than solid, I find the negative interpretation of *simplicior* more convincing and prefer "excessively simple," or "too naïve." See Appendix 2. —Trans.

64. *TP* 1981, Avis et Règlements, 131-135; and Conférence de Mgr de Maupas, 136-138.

65. Ibid., "Quelques avis," 265-267; the fanciful spelling in the [French] title is due to a poor copyist.

66. Ibid., AR, 131, no. 11.

67. Ibid., CP, 133, no. 32.

68. Ibid., AR, 131, nos. 1 and 2.

69. The author's conclusion depends on a positive reading of "prudentia simplicior." See note 62. —Trans.

70. *TP* 1981, CM, 136.

71. Ibid., CM, 136.

72. Ibid., AR, 137-138, nos. 9-13.

73. "Le 20 juillet 1620, résignation de Me Jean Laurent, doyen de l'église cathé-drale N.D. du Puy," in favor of the College of Le Puy, Delattre, 3:col. 611; and AMM Le Puy, Communauté de Montregard.

74. AMM Le Puy. These dates are uncertain.

75. AMM Lyon; and AMM Clermont-Ferrand.

76. AMM Aubenas; and AD Lozère, H 375, Établissement des sœurs de Saint-Joseph de la ville de Langogne.

77. AMM Aubenas.

78. BM Grenoble, R 8372, Registre MS in fol., 1.

79. Vienne was at this time a primatial see in France, and its archbishop held sig-nificant secular power as well.—Trans.

80. BMU Clermont, Ms 606, fol. 71, Arrivée des Jésuites à Clermont, copie du récit du P. Soubrany, procureur au college de Montferrand.

81. ARSI, Tolos. 6, 171v.

82. ARSI, Tolos. 11, 85, P. Joannes Petrus Médaille: "concionator in nostro tem-plo 2 [years]."

83. *RSI* 1620, Règles du Recteur, 155.

84. Louis Cognet, *L'essor: 1500-1650*, part 1 of *La spiritualité moderne* (Paris: Aubier, 1966), 345, 52, and 54.

85. ARSI, Tolos. 10^{II}, 424r.

86. An analysis of this text shows that it comes from Vienne (Dauphiné), where the community was recognized by the Archbishop in 1668. Archivists date it to the second half of the seventeenth century.

87. AMM Le Puy, Communauté de Riotord, Cahier Ab[bé]. Freycenon; and [Jean Joseph] Rivaux, *Vie de la R. Mère Marie du Sacré Cœur de Jésus* (Lyon, 1878), 13 ff.

88. *TP* 1981, Introduction to the Eucharistic Letter, 3.

89. Ibid., LE, 9, nos. 45-48.

90. Ibid., "Obligations Principales," document of the early eighteenth century, 281, 2nd paragraph.

91. Ibid., AR, 133, no. 11.

92. Ibid., LE, 9, no. 48.

93. The author wishes to indicate that her research following the publication of the French edition has led her to consider it possible that the first part of the Eu-charistic Letter may have been written in the first days of the Institute, and the latter part, which describes the different houses, around 1660. —Trans.

94. AMM Le Puy, Communauté de Tence et Communauté de Riotord.

95. *TP* 1981, LE, 5, no. 5.

96. Ibid., LE, 5, nos. 7, 8, and 10.

97. Ibid., LE, 5, nos. 7, 8, and 10.

98. Ibid.

99. *TP* 1981, LE, 7, no. 25.

100. Ibid., LE, 9, nos. 38-44.

101. *PDL*, "Statuts de la Majour à Marseille," 140.

102. *TP* 1981, LE, 5, no. 8.

103. Ibid., LE, 8, no. 29; R, 107, no. 17.

104. Ibid., LE, 26, no. 80.

105. Ibid., CP, 21, no. 22; 22, no. 50; 73, no. 354; and 87, no. 426.

106. Adrien Demoustier, SJ, "Étude de La lettre Eucharistique du P. Médaille," Fédération française des Sœurs de St. Joseph, 1969.

107. Marius Nepper, *Origins: The Sisters of St. Joseph*, trans. commissioned by the Federation of the Sisters of St. Joseph, USA [Erie: Villa Maria College, 1969], 8.

108. Although the Company of the Blessed Sacrament was established at La Flèche (present Department of the Sarthe) from its origin in 1630, it is not known when M. Le Royer de La Dauversière joined it.

109. "un grand dessein . . . le dessein de Montréal," Camille Bertrand, *Monsieur de La Dauversière, fondateur de Montréal et des Religieuses hospitalières de S.-Joseph, 1597-1659* (Montréal: Les Frères des écoles chrétiennes, 1947), 88-89.

110. Etienne-Louis Couanier de Launay, *Histoire des Religieuses Hospitalières de Saint-Joseph*, 2 vols (Paris: Société Générale de Librairie Catholique / Bruxelles: Société Belge de Librairie, 1887): 2: chaps. 1 and 2.

111. Constitutions de la s Filles de Saint-Joseph établics dans l'Hôtel-Dieu de La Flèche, en l'honneur de la Sainte Famille de Notre Seigneur . . . 20 octobre 1643, chap. 1, §2.

112. On December 3, 1659, the Company of the Blessed Sacrament of Grenoble got word of M. de la Dauversière's death on November 6, 1659, Raoul Allier, *La cabale des Dévots, 1627-1666* (Paris: A. Colin, 1902), 146.

113. *TP* 1981, LE, 8, no. 27.

114. Ibid., LE, nos. 38-40.

115. Ibid., *MP*, 223.

116. Ibid., *MP*, 240.

117. Ibid., *MP*, 223.

118. ARSI, Tolos. 11, 135, "profectus in literis magnus."

119. *TP* 1981, LE, 6, no. 13.

120. ARSI, Tolos. 11, 135.

121. *TP* 1981, LE, no. 9.

122. Ibid., LE, 10, no. 51.

123. AMM Le Puy, Communauté de Saint-Didier, "A ma tres chere Seur en N. S La seur Fayole, supre des Filles de la Congregation de Saint-Joseph a Saint-Deydier."

124. ARSI, Tolos. 6, 229 and 257r.

125. Ibid.

126. ARSI, Tolos. 23, 168v.

Conclusion to Part One:
The Genesis and Its Fruit

When the Little Design came to light in the middle of the seventeenth century, it was by no means the first attempt at consecrated apostolic life open to the world. Previous efforts in that direction had been beset by many juridical and social impediments that had to be recognized, integrated, or circumvented. By the time the Sisters of St. Joseph took root, apostolic freedom, although bold in its forms, was not so new or provocative as it had been fifty years earlier in the days of Francis de Sales. The Sisters of St. Joseph benefited in a certain way from the earlier attempts, whether successes or failures. When Father Médaille died in 1669, the Little Design stood among the apostolic experiments that claimed success, with more than thirty communities in the six dioceses of Le Puy, Lyon, Clermont, Vienne, Viviers, and Mende. At that time, none of its very small houses was affected by any external legislation. Making no claims to be religious or secular communities, they fell under neither the rubrics of the Council of Trent nor the articles of royal legislation. These small groups of women scattered throughout rural areas shared the way of life common to the surrounding population. Existing as independent units, the communities did not form a legal body or claim to exert any powers belonging to one. They were the poor relations of the secular communities. Subject only to the authority of the bishops, they had complete liberty to grow in number.

The very littleness of Father Médaille's project had clearly facilitated its development. In order to care for the people, particularly young girls and women, the first sisters did not want to establish a monastery as Jeanne de Lestonnac had done fifty years earlier. Neither could they form a female counterpart to the Society of Jesus, as did Mary Ward at Saint-Omer or even Anne de Xaintonge in Franche-Comté. Those women belonged to the nobility and had a good education. At the beginning of the seventeenth century, they were

119

impressed by the work of the Jesuits with young boys in their colleges and wanted to give the same Christian and human formation to young girls—in the case of Anne de Xaintonge, especially to poor girls. By contrast, only two of the women brought together by Bishop de Maupas were from a higher social class: Marguerite de Saint-Laurans and Clauda Chastel. The other five, from the lower or middle classes, were illiterate. They knew nothing, or very little, about the Jesuit Constitutions or the education provided in their colleges, and so could not aspire to imitate them. Whatever their social rank, they were conscious of having worked to serve God and their neighbor with whatever means they had. They acted by themselves or with other women, sometimes aided by the Jesuits, especially by Father Médaille or by Jesuits in the Lyon Province. If they could not imagine themselves following the constitutions of the Society of Jesus—much less the Jesuits' work in colleges— they could aspire to live out their spirit fully, as they had experienced it on different occasions: with the Company of Women of the Blessed Sacrament, in the Marian Congregations, or simply through sermons at missions. First and foremost, they desired to commit their entire life to the following of Christ in a more radical way, not merely as in the sodalities, or in the groups of devout women in the hospitals like the *donnades* in the hotels-Dieu, or in their own houses, like the Filles du Travail et de l'Union in Rodez. Father Médaille understood all of this very well. He did not try to impose on them forms of life or action based on those of such groups; less, those of monasteries; and still less, those of the male communities of the Society of Jesus in the South of France. He suggested that they continue to be present to and act in their own environment, but with "a new way of life." They would take simple vows, and their small communities would show that the life of the sisters was "entirely consecrated to the pure and perfect love of God," all "union and charity among themselves and toward every kind of neighbor."[1] Their type of service and their kind of action, inside the house or outside, would be those practiced around them, what they might have done with the Ladies of Mercy before they became Sisters of St. Joseph: serving in hospitals, visiting the poor and prisoners, running orphanages, caring for fallen women, giving spiritual direction to the laity, preparing young women for marriage, and as Father Médaille had pointed out, "even instructing girls in places where those nuns already established are not taking care of that."[2] In short, "they will undertake all the exercises of zeal" appropriate for women, so that the "greater glory [of God] might increase in everything and everywhere."[3]

All the recommendations given to the Sisters of St. Joseph by Father Médaille are wholly Ignatian in spirit, all directed toward seeking God in all things, in action as in contemplation. There are no indications of really marked influence coming from other contemporary spiritual currents. Even if Father Médaille uses Bérulle's Trinitarian model and his vocabulary of *anéantissement*, he gives such terms a meaning slightly different from the French School's. For Father Médaille, the Incarnation and the Paschal Mystery are seen from the vantage point of human salvation and not from the perspective of their attributes in the person of the Incarnate Word. The Salesian expressions of gentleness, moderation, and confidence, which create a particular atmosphere in some of his writings, appear only to reflect the influence of Francis de Sales on the entire seventeenth century. These expressions may sometimes add charm and color, but they do not change the fundamental structure. Nevertheless, a paragraph added later to two manuscripts of the Constitutions, those of Le Puy (MS A) and Saint-Didier (MS S), asks the sisters to mold "their life and spirit . . . on the customs, spirit, and life of the holy Daughters of the Visitation."[4] An almost identical paragraph, found in the Constitutions printed at Vienne in 1694, is clearly superimposed on the text without an organic connection to it.[5] In all likelihood, it comes from the current that gave rise to the more conventual aspects of the Little Directory before 1660.

In 1669, the Little Design was barely twenty years old and seems to have achieved stability along its own lines. How novel was it really? It originated from the Company of the Blessed Sacrament. Its first texts were inspired by those of the Marian Congregations and revised by a Jesuit. Its Constitutions followed in large part the Constitutions and Rules of the Society of Jesus. Its visible forms of life, in hospitals or elsewhere, differed little from those of third orders and other groups of devout and charitable women. Its activities of all kinds were shared with the confraternities of the Ladies of Mercy organized by Vincent de Paul more than forty years earlier. They included every sort of service appropriate to women of the same milieu. All of these elements derived from earlier texts and groups, of both lay people and religious men and women. As Father Médaille stated in the Eucharistic Letter, the Little Design had nothing of its own. It was content to benefit from prior experiences of others as well as from its own. It used freely all ways of Christian and apostolic life devised by others before it. It is quite true that it drew nothing from its own depths, and that it received everything. Its intrinsic littleness was one of the wellsprings of its life. This nothingness that becomes dynamic, this dynamic of nothingness, is undoubtedly one of its most fundamental characteristics. This original nothingness, which tells first of all about Father Médaille's humility of heart, enabled the Little Design to welcome all persons and all means of action that could advance the glory of God through service to the neighbor. This little congregation could accept all levels of society, recognized in their diversity and accepted as they were, in order to contribute to the evangelization of their own milieu. It could make use of every association of Christian life and charitable action. By working in this way toward its double end of the holiness of the sisters and of the holiness and service of every neighbor, the Little Design accepted its vocation of bringing people together and of union, in the congregation itself and in the world. This is its second fundamental characteristic, expressed by Father Médaille especially in the Eucharistic Letter: "The purpose of our congregation . . . tends to promote this total double union: of . . . ourselves and every dear neighbor with God, and of ourselves with every kind of neighbor, and of every dear neighbor among themselves and with us. . . . God grant that we may be able to contribute as a weak instrument to the reestablishment in the church of this total union of souls in God and with God."[6]

Chronology of the History

OF FATHER MÉDAILLE . . .		*. . . AND OF THE LITTLE DESIGN*
Birth of Fr. Médaille at Carcassone	1610	
	1611	Birth of Françoise Eyraud
Admission to the Jesuit novitiate	1626	Birth of Marguerite Burdier
Ordination to priesthood	1637	
Solemn profession of 4 vows	1643	
Appointed to the College of Saint-Flour	—	
Fr. Médaille gives rules . . .	1646	. . . to a pious group of women
Redaction of the 100 Maxims	1648	Françoise Eyraud and Marguerite de
of the Little Institute (between		Saint-Laurans are at the hôpital des
1646 and 1650)		Orphelines in Le Puy
	1649	Foundation of the house at Dunières
Appointed to Aurillac	Oct. 15	Official foundation of the
	1650	Congregation of St. Joseph, at Le Puy
Redaction of the Constitutions		
(before 1653)		
Appointed to Montferrand, near Clermont	1654	Visit by the officials of Le Puy to the
		community of St. Joseph in the rue
		de Montferrand
Publication of the Maxims of Perfection	1657	
at Clermont		
Avis et Règlements	ca. 1659	The Little Directory
The Eucharistic Letter . . .	ca.1660	. . . to Marguerite Burdier
	1661	Conference of Bishop de Maupas
Appointed to the College of Clermont	1662	
Fr. Médaille's letter . . .		. . . to Sister Fayolle, superior of the
		house at Saint-Didier
Death of Fr. Médaille at Billom	1669	
Publication of the second part of the	1672	
Maxims: "Exercise for the stripping		
of self . . ."		
	1674	Royal letters patent for the houses of
		Le Puy and Saint-Didier
	1683	Death of Françoise Eyraud
	1694	Constitutions printed at Vienne
	1700	Death of Marguerite Burdier

NOTES

1. *TP* 1981, R, 166, no. 16.
2. Ibid., CP, Seconde partie de la fin de la Congrégation, 28–30, nos. 90–105.
3. Ibid., CP, 30, no. 105.
4. Ibid., CP, 20, no. 41.
5. *CV* 1694, 7.
6. *TP* 1981, LE, 8, nos. 29 and 32.

Sister of St. Joseph, ex voto painting, seventeenth-century: ". . . rendu a une dame du puy par soeur marie maddeleine. . . ." Cathedral Treasury, Le Puy (Haute-Loire). (Photograph courtesy of Paula Drass, CSJ.)

Mademoiselle Antoinette Bresse, Sister of St. Joseph, Annonay, ex voto painting dated 1707, Cathedral Treasury, Le Py (Haute-loire). (Photograph courtesy of Paula Drass, CSJ.)

Soeur de S.ᵗ Joseph.

25   de Poilly f.

Habit of the Sisters of St. Joseph at the beginning the eighteenth century. The design was undoubtedly based on the Constitutions. (Estampe, Pierre Hélyot, *Histoire des ordres religieux, Paris,* 1714-1719, 8:189.)

Sister of St. Joseph between two nuns; detail from a depiction of eighteenth-century women's religious orders. (Pierre He?lyot, *Histoire des ordres religieux, Paris,* 1792.)

Widow of Latour d'Auvergne (Puy de Dôme) in mourning attire, mid-nineteenth century. The former lay sisters in the Congregation of Clermont wore a similar habit. (Delorieux, *Costumes auvergnats*, Clermont-Ferrand, [1841?].)

Former kitchen of the first Sisters of St. Joseph in the Hôpital des Orphelines, Montferrand quarter, around 1650, preserved in the motherhouse, Le Puy (Haute-Loire). (Photograph by Guillet-Lescuyer, Lyon.)

"The Old Convent," first house of the Sisters of St. Joseph in Le Cheylard (Ardèche), second half of the seventeenth century; surface area of 484.4 square feet. (Photograph by the author.)

House of the Sisters of St. Joseph, Saint-Julien-Vocance (Ardèche), built in 1675. (Photograph by the author.)

House of the Sisters of St. Joseph (with scaffolding) among other houses in village of Saint-Julien-Vocance (Ardèche). House in the foreground with white shutters is eighteenth-century. (Photograph by the author.)

Part Two

NORMATIVE TEXTS AND ACTUAL LIFE IN COMMUNITIES OF ST. JOSEPH

Introduction to Part Two:
Expansion in the Seventeenth and Eighteenth Centuries

Father Médaille's death does not appear to have had an impact on the life and development of communities of St. Joseph. After the crisis that necessitated his intervention and that of Bishop de Maupas around 1660 and 1661, his direct involvement, as before, was only in establishing small houses, such as those in Arlanc (1661) and Sauxillanges (1665) in the Clermont diocese where he resided. From that point on, Monsieur de Lantages, the sisters' ecclesiastical superior in the diocese of Le Puy, assumed responsibility for them. It seems Father Médaille was not much involved with them. He could have helped to install two sisters, one of them Marguerite Burdier, at the hospital of Vienne. It is plausible that he was able to support their undertaking and to facilitate contact with the archbishop through the Jesuits in Lyon or Vienne. If so, there is no record of it. By the time of Father Médaille's death, the houses, even the smallest, were numerous and stable enough to continue growing while accepting the diversity of their forms of life as a strength.

Houses continued to proliferate in the dioceses where they were already present—Le Puy and Vienne in particular, but Lyon and Clermont as well. Nevertheless, after 1674 their growth in the diocese of Le Puy was interrupted for some time.[1] Only two new houses were established between 1674 and 1685 or 1686, at Sainte-Sigolène before 1682 and Saint-Julien d'Ance in 1682. Whatever the cause of this interruption, it could not have occurred because of the bishop. Armand de Béthune confirmed all the existing houses of St. Joseph in his letters of approbation dated September 23, 1665, and expressed the hope "that they continue to advance their praiseworthy design."[2] Unlikely, too, that the hiatus resulted from anxieties raised by the letters patent granted by Louis XIV in January, 1674, to the houses in Le Puy and Saint-Didier, because the letters also speak of the *filles associées* who live in

135

community under the name of Congregation of the Daughters of St. Joseph, established throughout the diocese of Le Puy en Velay." The king recognized that these communities had been authorized by "the late Lord de Maupas du Tour," and that this authorization was "confirmed by the Lord de Béthune, current Bishop of the said diocese of Le Puy."[3] The issue may have originated in the situation of the house in Le Puy. Françoise Eyraud died in 1683. Anna Brun, the youngest of the six founding sisters, who succeeded her, died in 1685 and was replaced by Marguerite Mey. New foundations started almost immediately, with the house in Saint-Hilaire, established before 1687.[4] Françoise Eyraud and Anna Brun might have been worried at the multiplication of small houses throughout the diocese without many safeguards in their external forms. How could they control the profusion of this movement? It is doubtful that the house in Le Puy received no requests for new foundations during this decade. The sisters may have wanted only larger houses established, houses that would be confirmed by letters patent. There is no proof, but the resumption of new foundations just when there was a change of superior at the house in Le Puy gives the impression that the lull in foundations originated there.

In the diocese of Le Puy and in the neighboring dioceses of Lyon and Clermont, foundations continued to be made very close to one another, as if by contagion from one parish to another. Until the early eighteenth century, transition into the diocese of Clermont emanated from the Forez-Livradois region, beginning with community of Arlanc, founded by Father Médaille in 1661 with sisters from Le Puy. Foundations radiated from Arlanc in the Livradois to Marsac and Beurrières in 1674, and to Saint-Anthème in 1679. The same occurred with houses in the Vivarais, which borders on the Forez and Lyonnais regions. At the foundation of a new house, a sister from an already established community went to initiate the candidates into the life of the Sisters of St. Joseph. At Viverols in the Livradois, for example, when three single women wanted to establish a community of St. Joseph in 1686, Antoinette Pissavin, assistant for the community of Arlanc, spent some time there to give them formation as Sisters of St. Joseph.[5]

This living transmission was the general rule in all dioceses for both small and large houses. In Saint-Vallier (Vienne diocese), the abbot of La Croix-Chevrières, Count de Saint-Vallier, asked Henry de Villars, the Archbishop of Vienne, to send several sisters. In 1683, two sisters, Anne Félix from Vienne and Marie de Combes from Satillieu, were sent to establish a community at the Hospital of Saint-Vallier.[6] Very rarely did a priest simply give the Constitutions or the Règlements to a group of pious women of his parish without help from an existing community. One such case is Boisset (Haute-Loire), where the *curé*, Vital Bodet, gathered seven women together and gave them the rules of St. Joseph, apparently without calling upon a sister from another house to form them.[7] It is possible, though not certain, that any of the seven women had previously lived with another community of St. Joseph, since the sisters in Boisset were *soeurs agrégées* and could suspend their commitment in one house of St. Joseph and begin it again in another. The juridical establishment of these small houses, which did not aspire to form a "new body," required only the authorization of the bishop, with approval of the pastor and other leading citizens in the parish, who would meet and record their deliberation in a resolution submitted to the bishop for consent.[8]

The house at Vienne played a large part in the development of the congregation, not only within the diocese, but beyond. The community was recognized by Archbishop Henry de Villars in 1668, and the sisters worked at the city's hospital. Under the archbishop's authority and protection, they were able to establish other communities in hospitals in the chief towns of several dioceses. This expansion was also due in great part to Mother Burdier's zeal. As superior at Vienne, she sent sisters to Gap in 1671, to Sisteron around 1688, to Grenoble in 1694, and to Lyon in 1696.[9] After her death in 1700, the Vienne community continued to establish houses: Avignon in 1707, Marseille in 1716, Apt in 1720, and Clermont-Ferrand in 1723.[10] Such expansion is obviously the result of a deliberate choice. Foundations were made in different dioceses, no doubt in hope of eliciting the protection of the bishops and thereby promoting a better development of communities of St. Joseph in these dioceses. Without evidence it is difficult to measure the success of this strategy. The community in Gap was very fruitful, both in that diocese and in the neighboring dioceses of Sisteron, Embrun, and Die. When houses were established in the cities of Lyon and Clermont, about ten small houses of St. Joseph already existed in these dioceses. Other communities were established afterwards with no apparent link to the more important city house. When the house established in the see city of a diocese was the first, the sisters could hope that if the bishop would welcome the opening of a more important house, he would also approve of several smaller houses. Such was the case of Avignon. The register of professions in Vienne indicates that Sr. Madeleine Levrat (professed in 1731), superior of the house in Avignon, ran free schools and "established a novitiate which supplied several houses in the Comtat."[11] The same notation indicates multiple houses in the Comtat. Presently, however, we know of only one house other than Avignon, that of Carpentras, established quite likely from Avignon in 1734.

The majority of houses of St. Joseph founded from Vienne in new dioceses were in hospitals or in *maisons de refuge*. In Gap the sisters provided the services in the hospital, where according to an agreement made in 1671, they would "admit and receive the poor of both religions."[12] In Grenoble, the

Ladies of the Hospital of Providence signed a contract with four Sisters of St. Joseph, one of whom held the position of surgeon and another, of apothecary.[13] In Lyon, the sisters worked at the *Maison forcée des Recluses*. In Avignon and Clermont, the sisters took charge of houses called *Bon-Pasteur*, or Good Shepherd. In time other works were often added to the principal one within the house or outside it. In Vienne, the sisters added a house of refuge next to the hospital and operated some *petites écoles*. In Clermont, the sisters offered free schooling for poor girls, as in Avignon, as well as a boarding school for the daughters of wealthy families, which provided resources for the free school. The pattern of establishment of new houses because of contagion and proximity to existing communities gave way to a demand for specific skills and frequently for more important houses, regardless of distance. A different sphere, the initiation of young converts from Protestantism, exhibits, if not an appeal for certain competencies, at least mutual aid among houses responding to the same concern. For example, around 1660 the house in Tence provided the first superior for the house of Le Cheylard, located in a Protestant area in the diocese of Viviers. Tence also sent the house of Satillieu a copy of its royal letters patent mentioning the sisters' work with young Protestant converts, to help the community at Satillieu formulate its own petition for the same.[14] When houses were founded near others, prior knowledge of the works done by the sisters influenced the people favorably. These tasks were mainly the upkeep of churches, care for the poor and sick, and all aspects of the education of girls and women—rudimentary instruction, good manners, tasks and responsibilities of women according to their age and social status, some relatively professional training (lace-and ribbon-making), and, always, experience of the Christian life.

By the end of the eighteenth century, the Sisters of St. Joseph had spread throughout the entire southeast quarter of France. The principal area of establishment always remained the diocese of Le Puy, where there were definitely more than fifty houses. The dioceses of Lyon and Clermont each had approximately thirty houses before the Revolution. Growth from the house at Vienne stopped before 1730, but the diocese as a whole counted about twenty communities by the end of the eighteenth century. The other known houses were scattered in the dioceses of Viviers, Valence, Gap, Embrun, Sisteron, Grenoble, Uzès, Die, Avignon, Marseille, Mende, Carpentras, Saint-Flour (the community of Blesle), and Digne. Other houses may yet be discovered. All houses, both large and small, received the same Constitutions, those printed in Vienne in 1694, which reiterated, clarified or altered the manuscript Constitutions of Father Médaille.

The second part of this history examines if and to what degree these printed constitutions continued to transmit the spirit of the founder, or, in reflecting the evolution of the congregation and its mentality in 1694, whether they expressed a mutation that was already in place and would continue throughout the eighteenth century.

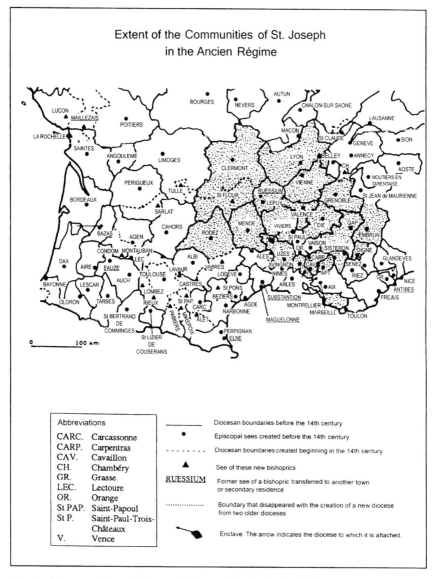

Extent of Communities of Sisters of St. Joseph in the Ancien Régime

NOTES

1. See Appendix 5.
2. AD Haute-Loire, 12 H 1, Lettres Patentes de M3 Armand de Béthune, 23 septembre 1665.
3. See Supporting Documents, 10.
4. AMM Lyon, Communauté de Saint-Hilaire (Loire).
5. AMM Clermont, Communauté de Viverols, established in 1686.
6. AMM Saint-Vallier, Fondation de la communauté de l'Hôpital, 1683.
7. AMM Le Puy, Communauté de Boisset.
8. See Supporting Documents, 17.
9. AD Hautes-Alpes, 3 H suppl. 278, "Conventions faites entre Reverende Mere Jeanne Burdier, supérieure des filles de St Joseph de la ville de Vienne . . . et les sieurs Consulz de la ville de Gap . . . le 17 septembre 1671"; AD Isère, 21 H 1, Registre des professions de la Vienne, 1681-1713, 3; AD Isère, 4 G 23, "Convention entre les Dames directrice de l'hopital de la Providence et les filles de St Joseph, 17 décembre 1694"; and AD Rhône, 44 H, liasse 143, no. 4, Convention des directeurs de la Maison des Recluses avec trois sœurs de Saint-Joseph, 22 décembre 1696.
10. AD Vaucluse, H 44 no. 6, Livre des Contrats depuis 1620, fols. 40v à 44r; AD Isère, 21 H 1, Registre des professions de la Vienne, 1681-1793, 4 and 9; and AD Puy-de-Dome, Bon-Pasteur de Clermont, 1666-1793, "Contrat d'Établissement de trois religieuses de l'hopital de Vienne, en la maison du Bon-Pasteur de Clermont-Fd, du 30 may 1725."
11. AD Isère, 21 H 1, Registre des professions de la communauté de Vienne, 1681-1792, 12, notice nécrologique.
12. AD Hautes-Alpes, 3 H suppl. 278, "Convention . . . le 17 septembre 1671.".
13. "At this time, surgeons were considered as plying a craft, like manual laborers; apothecaries were grouped with grocers, but, at least in Paris, to be received into the organization of sworn apothecaries, one had to be able to read prescriptions," Roland Mousnier, *The Institutions of France under the Absolute Monarchy, 1598-1789,* 1: *Society and the State*, translated by Brian Pearce (Chicago/London: The University of Chicago Press, 1979), 459-63. –Trans.
14. AMM Aubenas, Communauté de Satillieu.

Chapter Four

The First Printed Constitutions: Vienne, 1694

Until the end of the seventeenth century the Constitutions and Règlements of the Sisters of St. Joseph, approved by Bishop de Béthune of Le Puy in 1665, were transmitted as manuscripts from one community to another. Each of these houses, from the smallest to the most important, had a copy of the first parts of the Constitutions, the parts that described the congregation by explaining its goal and the means to attain it. For information on daily life, the smaller houses consulted the Règlements, while the larger houses followed the "Rules for Officers" contained in the Constitutions. Despite their spiritual riches, however, these texts became inadequate. Over time and with growth, new needs were felt, for example, in the areas of the formation of novices or of the juridical status of the congregation. Certain vague passages lent themselves to a variety of interpretations. The time had come to consider printing the Constitutions and completing them by the addition of some indispensable clarifications. The difficulty came with defining the vocation of the Sisters of St. Joseph, deciding which document best captured it, the Règlements or the Constitutions, and determining whether to integrate the Little Directory. What would lead to fidelity?

COMPETING INTERPRETATIONS OF THE VOCATION OF ST. JOSEPH

Tensions already glimpsed in regard to the Little Directory seem to have surfaced again after Father Médaille's death, or simply continued. The vocation of the little Congregation of St. Joseph could be understood in different ways. If the sisters were primarily women who had consecrated their entire lives to

God, even though they lived out this consecration in service to the neighbor, they would probably have to write stricter rules and thus become more like nuns—the women who were considered "true" religious. On the other hand, if they emphasized service to neighbor, then perhaps they should keep the more secular forms of life. It was a question of discernment.

Two Versions of the Vocation

A four-page notebook at the motherhouse of Le Puy contains two texts which, juxtaposed, frame the question of the sisters' vocation.[1] The two texts differ in style and content and are followed by a copy of an accompanying letter attributed to Father Médaille.[2] The first page reads: "The Reverend Father Maidaille [*sic*] advised us with great insistence. . . ." The first text, certainly written after Father Médaille's death and addressed to a group of communities, discusses the spirit in which the candidates should be formed.[3] It deals with the mistress of novices and her task of forming them in the spiritual life. First, it spells out the separation from the world and from self that the vocation of St. Joseph implies, in order to see if the candidates truly wish to commit themselves to it and if they are "really called by God." Next, it explains how the mistress should teach the novices "above all how to receive the sacraments well and how to make meditation," how to understand better "the benefit they draw from it," and how they might "act in times of consolation and in times of dryness in prayer." The mistress must also help them enter into the spiritual combat, and (the text is firm) "if they do not correct themselves, they will have to be dismissed." It was also necessary "to teach them to . . . [open] their soul to the superiors and mistresses of novices, and have [them] give an account of their conscience at the times prescribed by the rule." The mistress ought to govern the novices "with tenderness and love, not being shocked at their faults; she should mortify each according to what her spirit can bear." The mistresses are invited to pray often for the novices, to "give them good example," to "love them tenderly in Jesus Christ and devote themselves earnestly to their formation and the sanctification proper to their institute." Everything in this document echoes passages from the rules for the superior and the mistress of novices in the Constitutions, sometimes in the exact words or with added details.[4] It underscores the serious nature of religious commitment and includes ways to teach novices how to enter into it. The vital and evangelical invitation to freedom in this text manifests its harmony with the other writings of Father Médaille.

The second text included in the manuscript, "Various signs of a truly regular order or congregation," has a different tone. The title speaks of an "order or congregation." An "order" means a religious institute, recognized as such.

Although that was not the case for the little Congregation of St. Joseph, Father Médaille did recommend that the sisters behave "like the most regular religious."[5] In this second document, as in the first, the sisters undoubtedly perceive themselves "to have no less of religious life than the cloistered nuns," in the words of Armand de Béthune, Bishop of Le Puy, in his approbation of 1665. Each text attempts to describe, in its own way, what both call "the infallible signs of the good order—or the good condition—of a religious order." This formulation is typical of seventeenth century language and society, which required order and external points of reference. Although the first text refers to the mistresses of novices and only discusses formation for the spiritual life, the second is addressed to all sisters, including novices and superiors. The communities concerned must have been rather large, because the house represented has a chapel, refectory, and dormitory. The document describes "the good order of a regular (religious) community" and emphasizes important points such as "the good formation of the novices," union "with God from the heart," sisterly charity and "perfect union," preference for the "good of the community . . . over their [own] interests," the sharing of goods, and detachment from all things. All these points are inspired by the rules "for all the sisters, in general and in particular," in the original Constitutions, as well as by the sixth part, dealing with dangers and their remedies.[6] In spite of the merit of the points emphasized, the mode of expression differs markedly from that of the first document, and also from the style of Father Médaille. The second document seems to describe the external appearance of the perfect community of St. Joseph. Apart from passages in the first three paragraphs speaking of the interior dynamic of the community's life, the rest of the text is one-dimensional and moralizing in tone. Certainly, if things went as described, the community was functioning well. The way to arrive there, however, is conveyed in warnings addressed to the superiors and to the sisters: superiors should remember that "they must render a very exact account to God at the hour of death," and the sisters must be "carefully on their guard" in their relationships with persons from the outside. The means to religious perfection amounts to observing the rule, as recommended at the end of the document: "When uniformity is truly kept in all the houses of the same congregation in respect to the rules, observances, and customs, general and particular . . . ," if all of it is "adhered to exactly everywhere, without any deviation," that is the infallible sign of "the good condition of a religious order or devout congregation."

These texts are juxtaposed because both offer criteria, "infallible signs," of authentic religious life. Their juxtaposition is not the result of chance. Perhaps, because the first text deals only with the spiritual education of novices, the second is meant to reflect on matters relevant to the larger community.

The texts, however, do not complement each other. Not sharing the same spirit, they remain side by side. A reading of the first one gives the impression of an apprenticeship in the spiritual life for the vocation of the Sisters of St. Joseph through an appropriate formation. The whole text, like the process of formation, focuses the question of how best to live this life; how to draw the most profit from the time for prayer and from all the "ordinary and extraordinary actions of the congregation,"—in short, how to work by these means "toward the sanctification proper to their institute." In the second text, what is asked of the sisters and the community becomes an inspection, perhaps an inventory, of what one has done or not done, measured against the image of a perfect community. Depending on their response, the recipients might either justify themselves or feel guilty, since the infallible sign of good religious life was observing "all of the above."

It is hard to see how these two approaches can be reconciled, but a further question arises: why are these texts followed by a "copy of the letter of the Reverend Father Médaille written to the Sisters of St. Joseph of Le Puy"?

> My very dear sisters, I should wish, if your superiors permit, that each of your houses have a copy of this text and that it be read from time to time, either at the chapter when you have it or in the refectory during meals. The desire I have for the perfection of your congregation has led me to take the liberty of sending you this reminder. I commend myself to your holy prayers and am in Our Lord [signed] your very humble and very obedient servant, Jean Pière [*sic*] Médaille of the Society of Jesus.[7]

This letter, which seems genuinely from Father Médaille, cannot refer to the two texts that precede it. The first, although very consistent with his style and fundamental spirit, is presented as a recollection: Father Médaille "advised us with great insistence." Obviously, he was not present when the writer recalled this. The second document does not reflect Father Médaille's attitude. He would not have supported these counsels for regimented faithfulness. It does not bear his mark. Furthermore, these two texts were not handed on to other communities of St. Joseph.

It is quite possible that this letter pertained to the Little Directory. Father Médaille may actually have been led to commend the Little Directory to the sisters, even though he had not authored it, and the text was far from what he had told them to expect. In response to the questions, even opposition, of certain sisters disconcerted by the more conventual forms of life advocated by the ecclesiastical authorities, Father Médaille may have sent this hand-written "reminder . . . to the Sisters of St. Joseph in Le Puy," for "each of [their] houses." Without changing anything in his earlier writings—Règlements, Maxims, Constitutions, and Avis et Règlements—he may have accepted this partial distortion of the Little Design, one which actually carried little weight relative to the directions and forms already taken collectively. As recommended in this letter, the Little Directory (Divine Office included) is present in every existing manuscript, that is to say, in every community, large and small, of St. Joseph during the ancien régime. If Father Médaille's accompanying letter refers to the Little Directory, it had the effect, not of integrating the Divine Office into the life of the communities, but of bringing peace to minds and hearts. It allowed the sisters to recognize and accept these differences, but also to understand them as somewhat relative, without changing any of the fundamental orientations of the Little Design.

The two documents placed together after Father Médaille's death reflect the very tension that could have existed among the sisters when the Little Directory was written. If Father Médaille's letter was recopied after these two documents with such opposing points of view, it shows that the sisters who wrote them had in the first place, a conviction about their respective points of view, and then a desire to share them out of mutual respect. What brings these two points of view together is their common reference to Father Médaille. By adding the letter of recommendation for the Little Directory at the bottom of these documents, the sisters indicated that they gave more importance to the example of their founder than to his writings.

Despite the differences in these two texts, both point out what the authors considered important for the vocation of the Sisters of St. Joseph, either by recalling the memory of Father Médaille or simply by describing the ideal of a "truly regular congregation." The texts may have been a first step in preparing for the printing of the constitutions at Vienne. All we know is that around 1693, the Sisters of St. Joseph from different dioceses gathered in Le Puy to consider "several important subjects," and probably to prepare for the printing of their Constitutions. Since the majority of the manuscripts of the Constitutions and Règlements date from the end of the seventeenth century, it seems probable that several of these copies were made in view of the meeting preparatory to printing the Constitutions. At the same time, the provenance of the manuscripts represented in the printed constitutions indicates which communities were represented at the Le Puy gathering: Le Puy, Saint-Didier, Vienne, Gap, and perhaps a few more. The Constitutions were printed, not in Le Puy, but in Vienne, under the protection and authority of Archbishop Henry de Villars, who was very favorably disposed toward the Sisters of St. Joseph.

The Enigma of the Three Editions

Extant copies of the printed constitutions, all claiming to represent the "first edition," but differing in appearance, date, and content, declare an enigma.

Some are dated 1693, others, 1694, and they are not merely reprints of a "first edition," but two quite different editions. There may even have been three different editions: two separate ones dated 1693 and a third, identical to one of the preceding two, dated 1694. The differences among these editions bear traces of the divergence perceptible in the two documents described above. Father Nepper suggested that one of the 1693 editions (which he called 1693 A) is in fact the first.[8] He argued that it proved unsatisfactory, because some of the content was far from the spirit of the Little Design, and a second "first edition" (which he named 1693 B) was then printed to correct the original. In the following year, another edition was published, similar to 1693 B. Sorting out the mystery requires a careful study of these successive editions and determining which version was actually used by the Sisters of St. Joseph under the ancien régime. The primary issue is the purpose of these three different editions. A comparison of their internal differences should bring to light the variations in their contents, and if possible, their meaning. This analysis actually involves only two of the editions (1694 and 1693 A), since those of 1693 B and 1694 are identical.

The first differences appear in the preface and the letters patent from the bishops presented in the preliminary matter.[9] The preface of the 1694 edition describes Father Médaille's project as making consecrated life available to "pious widows and single women who, not wanting to marry . . . could not enter the monasteries for lack of sufficient means."[10] The 1693 A version states instead that Father Médaille wished the Sisters of St. Joseph "to fill the place the Sisters of the Visitation had just vacated by their enclosure." Nowhere in the primitive texts does Fr. Médaille mention such a motive. Each edition describes the assembly of the first sisters, presided over by Bishop de Maupas on October 15, 1650, with the same elements, but presents them in a different order. In the 1694 text, the Bishop came to gave the sisters an exhortation. He then "gave them his blessing, placed them under the protection of . . . St. Joseph, and gave them rules for their conduct." At the end of the assembly, he "prescribed a form of habit for them." In the 1693 A text, at the very beginning of the gathering, after confiding "the administration of the hospital" to the sisters, the bishop "prescribed their form of habit and gave it to them himself." In this edition, emphasis is placed on "their" form of habit and that the bishop himself came to give it to them. The other components of the meeting are mentioned in the same order as that described in the 1694 edition.

Letters patent from the bishops of Le Puy authorizing the congregation follow immediately after the preface. Examination of the letters given by Bishop de Maupas on March 10, 1651, reveals that the 1694 text is true to the original, whereas the version of 1693 A adds that the sisters wished to "create a congregation" in which they could live "in community in the regularity of the cloistered daughters." Bishop de Béthune's letters patent of September 23,

1665, in the 1694 edition are also identical to the original, but the 1693 A version suppresses the passage referring to "those . . . who, for lack of means cannot enter the monasteries, [and] can have no less of religious life than the cloistered nuns." Such mediocre social status was surely considered less honorable. The 1693 A version also omits the entire reference to the zeal of the Sisters of St. Joseph in a variety of services, zeal which causes them

> to live together as a community; to instruct young girls and married women as well as others who are heads or other members of families of the world; to help the sick by their service or by their means, which they bring with them or are earning by the work of their hands in the congregation where they are; to visit, serve, and direct the hospitals entrusted to them . . . .

The 1693 A edition speaks only of "the hospitals entrusted to them." There is no longer any question of being available to families in apostolic and charitable presence. All the changes made to these preliminary texts in the 1693 A edition show by now what inspired them: a desire for conventual forms of life relevant to women of a more privileged social class.

Part One of the Constitutions, which describes "The Nature of the Congregation," makes even clearer the differences between the two editions. In Chapter 1, "Concerning the Origin and Name of this Congregation," the 1694 edition explains that the widows and single women in the congregation would be "few in number and only chosen souls who should live in the manner of religious," that is, live in the manner of religious even though they were not. In the 1693 A text, by contrast, widows and single women should be "rather numerous . . . and live in the regularity of the cloistered daughters." At the end of the chapter, both versions mention the Visitation, stating that the sisters should "try to imitate and follow [their] customs, spirit, and life" and endeavor to "adopt the primitive spirit with which St. Francis de Sales inspired them" (1694, 7). This reference in the 1694 edition is almost identical to the addition inserted in the same place in the manuscript of Saint-Didier. The redactor of the 1693 A edition, however, felt the need to add once again that the Sisters of St. Joseph were "established in the place of these holy daughters, to practice charity following their enclosure."[11] In the following chapter, "Concerning Vows Which Are Made in the Congregation," the 1694 text refers to "three simple vows of poverty, chastity, and obedience."[12] The sisters are obliged "to observe perpetually . . . these three simple vows with as much fidelity and exactitude as if they were solemn." The subsequent paragraphs explain, nevertheless, that the bishop may grant a dispensation and give the conditions for leaving the congregation. The 1693 A version does not specify that the vows are simple vows and adds the adjective "perpetual" to "obedience." Any mention of dispensation from these vows or the possibility of leaving the community has been suppressed.

A remarkable difference between the two editions appears with regard to the sisters' dress. The 1694 text describes a habit similar to that of "virtuous and modest widows" described in Father Médaille's Avis et Règlements and Bishop de Maupas's Conference. In 1693 A, the dress is no longer that of widows. It has become more like the garb of nuns belonging to a higher social status, with "pleated dress, tapered skirt, and train," shoes with buckles, long wool veil, and round guimpe. Another innovation gives the houses *tourières*, as in monastic communities, and describes their habit as well. The 1694 edition contains a chapter entitled "Concerning the Offices and Prayers of the Sisters" stating, in view of service to the neighbor and apostolic availability, that the sisters are not "required to recite or chant the Divine Office." They can, however, chant Vespers on Sundays and holy days in their chapel, if they have one, or in the parish church. This chapter does not appear in the 1693 A version, certainly to maintain the possibility of praying or chanting the Divine Office. Similarly, Chapter 8, "On the *Sœurs Agrégées*," appears in the 1694 edition, but not in 1693 A. In the 1693 A text, the diversity of apostolic activities, already suppressed in the preface, is reduced to diversity of another kind inside the house, between the sisters properly speaking and the *tourières*.

Many other differences are present throughout the editions. They all point in the same direction, to a search for conventual life, and simultaneously, social prestige. All these new prescriptions—whether "the regularity of cloistered daughters" added to Bishop de Maupas' letters patent, the suppression of diversity of apostolic services in those of Bishop de Béthune, monastic modifications of the dress, a larger community singing the Divine Office, or the disappearance of *sœurs agrégées* in the country—completely transform Father Médaille's Little Design. These alterations were motivated by a desire to be recognized as "true religious" and to have the corporate image and prestige that went with it. The 1693 A version omits a telling passage from the chapter "Concerning the Rules for the Superior," directing her to "remember that the role of superior, rather than elevating her, lowers her, being truly the servant of the servants of Jesus Christ, and that thus she should respect all her subjects, and always prefer, as much as good order allows, their contentment to her own."[13] This suppression points to a dangerous transformation, even if the suspicion that it signals actual rejection of humility and service—two fundamental aspects of the vocation of the Sisters of St. Joseph—is tempered by their presence under "Vows Which Are Made in the Congregation."

The comparison of these two editions indicates a will behind the 1694 edition to remain faithful to the original direction given by Father Médaille and Bishop de Maupas. The mystery about the origins of the 1693 Constitutions remains to be solved, and some clues are found in documents from this period belonging to the community of Vienne. A register of professions beginning May 29, 1732, the date of the profession of Sister Marie Pascal, contains the following formula, "in the monastery of the religious of St. Joseph of Vienne."[14] This unexpected term is completely congruous with the monastic forms presented in the 1693 A Constitutions. Another source, the "Register of the Religious of Saint-Joseph of the City of Vienne," contains the collection of a great number of official documents, approvals, letters, and other items. Among them is the copy of the letters patent granted by Louis XV to the community in December 1727, at the request of Archbishop Henry Oswald de La Tour d'Auvergne, "our dear and beloved cousin."[15] These letters authorized the establishment of the "Sisters Hospitallers of St. Joseph" in the House of Providence in Vienne, "belonging to them . . . under the jurisdiction and complete authority of the archbishops of Vienne." Several pages later there is a letter of January 26, 1728, from the archbishop to the vice-legate of Avignon asking for papal recognition of the Sisters of St Joseph of Vienne. That same day, the Vicar General of Vienne, *Monsieur* Didier, wrote to Mother de Bontoux, superior of the community, to communicate to her the archbishop's letter to the vice-legate. He adds, speaking of the royal letters patent just obtained, "Let us have our letters registered, and after that we shall write good rules."[16] This reference to "good rules" certainly implies the preparation of new constitutions: those of 1693 A, in accord with the royal letters patent and the anticipated papal recognition. This information indicates that the 1693 A version had not yet been written in January of 1728. It is not known whether the sisters wanted to wait for Rome's response before drawing them up, but the vocabulary in the register of professions referring to "our monastery" starting in 1732 suggests that the new constitutions had been written prior to that date. They certainly did not wait until the letters patent were recorded, as that happened only on July 9, 1759.[17] The eventful history of the Sisters of St. Joseph in Vienne points to the royal letters patent of 1728 as their official point of departure for functioning as a monastery.

The Constitutions dated 1693 A were therefore doubly antedated; they register neither the correct date of their publication nor even the date of the earlier edition of 1694. At the time it was common to alter the date of later editions or reprints, reproducing the date of the first publication as a mark of respect, as a reminder. This case was nothing of the kind. Apparently the sisters, perhaps the archbishop, wanted this modified version to pass for the first printed edition of the Constitutions of the Sisters of St. Joseph, earlier even that that of 1694. To that effect, even the date of the permission granted by Henry de Villars for printing was altered. The date of approval for the 1694 Constitutions is November 20, 1693, and the permission to print given "to *Sieur* Laurens Cruzi" is dated November 24, 1693. The 1693 A edition advances the date of the permission by one day, to November 23, 1693.[18] This detail would have been sufficient to confirm, if necessary (with Rome, for example) that the so-called 1693 Constitutions were anterior to those of 1694, and therefore more reliable. Under these circumstances of fraud and pretense, the edition called 1693 B, a later edition but one identical to the 1694 text, must have been published in an attempt to counter the fraud. Perhaps this last version was published by a group within the Vienne community who disagreed with the direction set by the archbishop and those in charge of the community. Or this manuscript could have been produced by other communities, perhaps from the diocese or the house in Le Puy. Without further evidence, these suggestions remain hypothetical. At the same time, 1729-30, the administrators of the Maison forcée des Recluses in Lyon had constitutions printed for the Sisters of St. Joseph who worked there.[19] They refer specifically to the 1694 edition, which they reproduce exactly. The edition of 1693 is not in question. The Lyon edition of 1730, too, appears to have been a protest against the 1693 A edition, whether the latter was already published or in process. The edition of 1730, moreover, marks the separation of the Lyon community from that of Vienne, which had founded it in 1696.

There are therefore four successive editions of the Constitutions of the Sisters of St. Joseph: three from Vienne (1694, followed by 1693 A and 1693 B) and one from Lyon (1730). Determining which editions were handed on in the communities can give an idea of where, among these competing rules, Sisters of St. Joseph recognized themselves. An inventory of the old copies of the constitutions found in several motherhouses, above all Le Puy, Lyon, and Clermont, indicates that the versions passed on were those of Vienne 1694 and 1693 B (identical), and Lyon 1730. The latter edition was reprinted in full in 1788. The 1693 A Vienne edition was hardly distributed, except for five copies in Clermont, a community founded by sisters from Vienne in 1723, which broke off relations with its house of origin in 1730. One other copy exists at the Motherhouse in Le Puy. Everywhere else, the editions most distributed were that of Vienne 1694 (8 copies extant), and Lyon 1730 (8 copies extant, of which five are in Lyon). The rarest version is Vienne 1693 B, with only four copies recovered.

On the whole, the Sisters of St. Joseph did not recognize themselves in the Vienne Constitutions of 1693 A. The constitutions handed on in the communities that survived the Revolution, except for that of Clermont, have the same table of contents and the same content: that of the 1694 edition of Vienne, including the chapter on the *Agrégées*. These were the constitutions sent to Turin, Italy, in 1824, by the community of Chambéry, which had received them from Lyon. The same edition, reprinted in Lyon in 1824 and 1827, was taken across the Atlantic by French sisters in 1836, to become the rule for the first American Sisters of St. Joseph at Carondelet, Missouri.

CONTINUITY AND CHANGE IN THE
VIENNE CONSTITUTIONS (1694)

The Constitutions printed in Vienne in 1694 begin with a presentation of the structure of the work almost identical to that of the manuscript constitutions:

> These constitutions will be divided into six parts.
> The first explains the nature of this new congregation.
> The second deals with the end for which it was founded.
> The third, the qualities required of persons who wish to be received.
> The fourth, the particular rules for all the officers and rules common to all the sisters.
> The fifth, the spiritual exercises which the sisters must practice.
> The sixth, the particular means for the survival and growth of this little congregation.[20]

As the material of the 1694 Constitutions is more extensive than that of the manuscripts, each of the parts named above is divided into chapters, and everything is explained in order.

The one hundred maxims of the Great Virtue (Maxims of the Little Institute) are placed immediately after the Constitutions. As in the manuscripts, they are given a place that shows the importance accorded them, and which Father Médaille had attributed to them by presenting them as "the spirit of your little institute."[21] In contrast, the Little Directory, found in Part V of the Constitutions manuscripts, follows the Maxims in this edition, taking its correct place as a supplement providing practical instructions for daily life. The Little Directory preserves the same structure as in the manuscripts: 1) daily actions; 2) weekly actions; 3) monthly practices; and 4) yearly practices. The book closes with the "Manner of receiving and giving the habit to the sisters of St. Joseph," the "Manner of receiving the sisters' profession," and finally, examples "of the act which should be written for the reception of the sisters [and] . . . for the profession."

Despite this overall plan, nearly identical to that of the manuscript Constitutions, the contents of the chapters in the 1694 edition reveal differences whose impetus and meaning are important to grasp in order to gauge their fidelity to the basic direction set by Father Médaille.

The Sisters of St. Joseph and
the "Holy Daughters of the Visitation"

At the beginning of the 1694 Constitutions, in the first chapter of Part One, immediately after the explanation of the origin and name of the congregation and its consecration to the Trinity, there is reference to the "Holy Daughters of the Visitation" whose "custom, spirit and life" the Sisters of St. Joseph should try to imitate.[22] Placed here this paragraph, already encountered in the Le Puy and Saint-Didier manuscripts, seems to take on new significance. Its insertion in the first chapter introducing the congregation puts it on a par with the origin, name, and Trinitarian consecration. It requires careful analysis to determine whether the importance given to the Visitation in the first chapter is born out in the constitutions as a whole.

In Chapter 6 of Part One, "On the [Ecclesiastical] Superiors of the Congregation," the redactor specifies the bishops' responsibility toward the congregation and the way to exercise this responsibility.[23] The chapter ends with a reference to St. Francis de Sales:

> Our Lord Bishops are humbly asked to have paternal charity and a particular care for the preservation and growth of this Little Congregation, out of consideration for the great Saint Francis de Sales, since it was established only to revive the spirit of the first foundation that this blessed prelate made of the Sisters of the Visitation of Holy Mary.[24]

The history of the origins of the Sisters of St. Joseph does not support this assertion. To be sure, Father Médaille advised the sisters to imitate the Visitation in two customs: the practice "of the holy presence of God during the day," found only in the Saint-Didier manuscript, and the "challenge" (*le défi*), found in every manuscript.[25] These were minor customs. As far as is known, neither Father Médaille nor Bishop de Maupas ever made the slightest reference to the Sisters of St. Joseph as replacing the Visitation nuns after their enclosure. Bishop de Maupas' conference in 1661 reaffirmed and specified the original intentions of Father Médaille, without any mention of the Visitation. The reference to Francis de Sales in the recommendation to the bishops may have been intended primarily to shelter the congregation, both spiritually and juridically, in the shadow of an authoritative personage, by speaking of it in the same breath as an illustrious and accepted order. That pretentious plea aside, it remains to establish whether the congregation really did adopt "the customs, spirit and life" of the Visitation.

The chapter, "On the Spiritual Father," which follows that "On the [Ecclesiastial] Superiors of the Congregation," points toward an analogous chapter in the Visitation Constitutions, "Concerning the Spiritual Father of the House."[26] Part Three of the St. Joseph Constitutions (1694), entitled "How to Receive the Sisters and the Qualities Required to be Received in the Congregation" also provides some answers to the question raised above. The chapter "On the Reception of Novices," actually borrows large sections from the definitive Constitutions (1622) of the Visitation.[27] Both texts, however, repeat in large part the questions posed in the General Examen to candidates for the Society of Jesus.[28] The superior of the Sisters of St. Joseph examines the candidate "in particular as to her place of origin, her parents, her age, her disposition, her habits, her health, her strength, what she knows how to do, the conduct of life she practiced, and the motives which make her want to be received in the congregation."[29] The content is indeed taken from the Society of Jesus, but its wording is very close to that of the Visitation. The author killed two birds with one stone: in substance, the text remains faithful to Father Médaille; in form, it is modeled on the Visitation.

The following chapter, "On Qualities Required of Novices," replicates the whole of Father Médaille's text for the same chapter, with only one additional passage from the Visitation texts, dealing with the reception of young widows and the problems they might have.[30] In the section dealing with the novitiate and the education of novices, we find the same "Jesuit and Visitation" amalgam along with some specifically juridical points concerning the ecclesiastical superiors.[31] Again, the principal aspects on the formation of novices are Ignatian, especially in regard to the "experiments": "have them practice all the exercises and serve in all the works of the congregation, as in the kitchen, in serving the sick, in the school for girls . . . sometimes they will accompany the sisters who are going to visit the poor."[32] At the end of the novitiate, as at the beginning, the General Examen of the Society of Jesus is used before deciding whether to admit the novice. The sister superior then convokes the community chapter, as in the Visitation, to make the decision to admit the novice or dismiss her.

The following chapter, "On the Profession and the Vows of the Sisters," begins with remarks about the vows, a summary of the meditations proposed for the Visitation novices during their seven-day retreat before profession.[33] Unfortunately, the chapters on the three vows, taken in part from the Visitation and in part from the pen of the redactor, focus solely on personal sanctity without any mention of the apostolic goal. In the Constitutions manuscripts, Father Médaille spoke very little of the vows. At the beginning, in the presentation of the congregation (First Part), he made a simple reference to the sisters' commitment, consisting of "three simple vows" and the commitment of the *agrégées* through the vow of stability. For him, the sisters' obedience consisted not merely in fulfilling what was asked by superiors, but rather "in the perfect conformity of their will to the divine will, accompanied by a genuine zeal to promote in themselves and in others the greater glory of God."[34] This is also what he expresses in a different manner in the Eucharistic Letter in reference to poverty, chastity and obedience.[35] Inserted in the 1694 Constitutions, the redactor's interpretation changed the very content of the commitment of the Sisters of St. Joseph, and in so doing, distorted the fundamental principles of their vocation. Did the sisters fully appreciate the scope of this change? The entire ceremonial in the Constitutions of 1694 for the clothing and profession of the Sisters of St. Joseph—except the vow formula—is borrowed from the Visitation.[36] The sisters must have had some sort of ritual for taking the habit or for profession before they adopted the Visitation's. It may have been as simple as that indicated in the Constitutions of the Society of Jesus: Bishop de Maupas did suggest that the *sœurs agrégées* would make vows kneeling "at the foot of [the altar or religious image in] their oratory, before their parish priest."[37] In any case, the sisters preferred to adopt the more imposing ceremony of the Visitation. On the other hand, three parts of the Constitutions: "Rules for the Officers," "Spiritual Exercises of the Sisters," and "Means to Support and Spread the Little Congregation," borrow little, and nothing of importance, from the Visitation, merely allusions to the order or its founder.

The Little Directory as it appears in the manuscripts had already been influenced by the Visitation because of its dependence on the directory of the Daughters of the Cross. It, too, was modified in the 1694 edition. The method of mental prayer, although derived from the manuscript of the Little Directory, was developed along the lines of *An Introduction to the Devout Life*, to which it makes explicit reference.[38] Its rather voluntaristic language, however, lacks the Salesian tone, for example (at the beginning of the section on prayer): "You will vividly call to mind that God is present to you. . . . After these considerations, you will stir your heart to good inclinations. . . . You will make strong resolutions to follow all the good sentiments you will have received from God." Finally, it is necessary "to practice the good resolutions faithfully . . . otherwise you will abuse your meditation, and your prayer . . . will be turned into sin." The chapter which follows is no longer entitled "On the Divine Office," as in the Little Directory, but rather, "Concerning the Office and Vocal Prayers."[39] Taken in part from the spiritual directory of the Visitation, this chapter does not focus entirely on the Divine Office, since the Sisters of St. Joseph only recited the Little Office of the Blessed Virgin Mary on Sundays, and said other vocal prayers during the week.[40] In certain aspects, the revised directory seems better adapted to the Sisters of St. Joseph than the first Little Directory.

It is obvious that the references and materials borrowed from the customs and ways of life of the Visitation are quite tangible in the Vienne Constitutions of 1694. Most often the borrowed material deals with practices: important ones such as the admission to the novitiate, or trivial, such as the use of "silver spoons . . . at table, following the example of St. Francis de Sales, who permitted this for the religious of the Visitation."[41] Some additions go beyond the purely formal and yield a spiritual orientation different from that of Father Médaille. (This tendency was evident in the case of the vows.) These modifications could not have failed to influence the whole life of the Sisters of St. Joseph. They may have come from within the group itself, from sisters who wished to transform their community into a "truly regular religious order or congregation," which could have had some positive consequences. It is not certain that these textual additions and alterations were enough to guarantee that the Sisters of St. Joseph would adopt "the spirit . . . of the holy Daughters of the Visitation," as encouraged in Chapter 1. If they were asked to do "all in their power to acquire the primitive spirit which St. Francis de Sales had inspired in his daughters," it was probably because the Sisters of St. Joseph were already living according to a particular (and different) spirit, and to change it would have required some effort. The ceremony for profession borrowed from the Visitation is symbolic of this. The forms of this ritual in the Constitutions of 1694 are Visitandine, but the act of profession itself remained that received from Father Médaille, modeled on the profession of scholastics in the Society of Jesus.[42] Once more, at the very core of a mutation, there is evidence of the desire for fidelity to the founder.

Other additions and changes to the manuscript Constitutions handed on in the Constitutions of 1694 apparently come from a source other than the Visitation. Aside from the confirmation and development of the Ignatian contribution which we have already encountered and will study farther on, a few minor passages from the Constitutions of the daughters of the Cross represent the same Salesian influence in a different form.

The 1694 Constitutions and the Original Texts

Although the general structure of the Constitutions printed in 1694 is the same as that of the manuscripts, the Archbishop of Vienne's approval informs the reader, that before allowing them to be printed, he had them "examined and put in better order."

Among other things, this reorganization meant that fragments of texts were moved from one part of the constitutions to another for the sake of better order. This process is evident in Part Two, Chapter 4: "On the Charity Which the Sisters Should Practice Among Themselves." This chapter, not present in the manuscripts, brings together several paragraphs previously scattered in the "First Part of the End" and in the "Instructions for All the Sisters in General and in Particular."[43] The same pattern applies to the next two chapters, "On the Care for the Sisters Who Are Sick and Dying" and "On the Charity to be Shown the Sisters after Their Death." These chapters rework paragraphs from the original Constitutions and supplement them with others inspired by the Constitutions of the Society of Jesus.[44] This revision attempts to unify the two types of normative texts from the origins, the Règlements and the Constitutions, by integrating the concrete organization of life found in the Règlements into Part Five of the Constitutions, dealing with spiritual exercises. The

Vienne Constitutions do not include the Little Directory, which is placed after the Maxims. In making these changes, the editors referred to the Saint-Didier manuscript, which contains in Part Five Father Médaille's "Special Directions for the Daughters of St. Joseph," but not the Little Directory, which
is in almost all the other manuscripts.[45] In omitting the Little Directory and
replacing it with "Special Directions for the Daughters of St. Joseph," the Vienne Constitutions recover the original form of Father Médaille's text. Following these "special directions" for the practices of the year, the month, the
week, and the day, the 1694 edition adds the organization of the day taken
from the "Regulation of the Sisters of St. Joseph for Work Days," as in the
Saint-Didier manuscript.[46]

The Vienne Constitutions also follow the variations in formulation and
content of the Saint-Didier manuscript, rather than those of Le Puy (Ms A),
as one might have expected. For example, under "Services the Sisters Should
Render to the Neighbor," the Vienne Constitutions restore the earliest reading
of the Saint-Didier text where, under an erasure, it is still possible to read,
"The sisters will see to the instruction of girls in places where nuns already
established are not taking care of it."[47] The 1694 edition also follows the
Saint-Didier manuscript in the listing of officers, and not Manuscript A. The
latter had added offices taken from the constitutions of the Visitation or those
of the Daughters of the Cross: cellarer, cook, linenkeeper, and infirmarian, all
offices appropriate to a larger community.[48] The Vienne Constitutions merely
mention these functions in the chapter "Rules for Other Officers," without
elaboration. This return to the oldest manuscript, and probably the closest to
Father Médaille, reveals the desire of the sisters to return to their source when
it came to printing their constitutions at the end of the seventeenth century.
They preferred the Saint-Didier manuscript to Manuscript A, probably because they did not wish to follow the Jansenistic tendency evident in the latter.[49] They had a consciousness of their own spirit and wanted to be rooted in
it. That being so, the elements borrowed from the Visitation must be seen, not
as essentials, but as supplements to their distinct life style. The sisters hoped,
through these sometimes conventual forms, to be able to express their own
type of commitment, in the same way that the act of profession for the Sisters
of St. Joseph came wrapped in Visitandine ritual.

If the printed constitutions reveal the desire of Sisters of St. Joseph to remain faithful to the vocation articulated by their founder, they reveal, to an
equal degree, signs of evolution over time. The vocabulary is changed. Although the printed constitutions contain elements borrowed from the Visitation, the vocabulary ironically seems much less Salesian than the language of
Father Médaille. There is less gentleness, kindness, and warmth. Certain expressions, such as "the glory of God" or "self-emptying" are more rare. There

is no longer reference to the Little Design or to the Blessed Sacrament which had "given beginning to their little Congregation."[50] Perhaps such expressions were too evocative of the secular forms of apostolic life during the origins. On the whole, the vocabulary evolved with spirit of the times. Modifications also appear in the structure of the congregation. There are no longer "three types of association" reflecting the diversity of sisters' social origins.[51] There is, however, an entire chapter devoted to the *sœurs agrégées*. Among them, one no longer sees "noble ladies whose status . . . keeps [them] in the world," as in the manuscripts.[52] There are only "a number of poor women and peasants in the villages." The large number of the latter must have demanded a better organization of their communities. The chapter therefore gives information on their formation, commitment, and manner of life, borrowed, for the most part, from the Avis et Règlements of Father Médaille and the Conference of Bishop de Maupas.[53] The chapter entitled "On Humility and the Rank of the Sisters," seems to have been added after that on the *agrégées* as a reminder that in the congregation, the primary concern is not the sisters' birth or social rank, but that all sisters be humbly at the service of one another, as they are to the neighbor.[54] As in the manuscripts, there are neither choir nor lay sisters. Only the "elders in the Congregation" merit "particular respect," as well as "those who are old, even if they have been recently received." The sisters are to act "just the same with persons in the world . . . never [scorning] anyone on account of how poor and wretched she might be." Order in the congregation, as in the society of the time, was based on rank: the superior will hold "always and everywhere the first rank," her assistant "will hold the second," and the other sisters will take "rank . . . according to the seniority of their profession." Although in a way different from that of the manuscripts, this text expresses the diversity of social status in the congregation, and at the same time, the sisterly love that should animate it. It seems difficult to find there, as one would in the texts of Father Médaille, the underlying note of the universality of the service to God and the neighbor in every place and in every human situation.

Other modifications and omissions are more perplexing. The first deals with the consecration to the "uncreated Trinity and to the created Trinity." According to the text of the Vienne Constitutions, the congregation "is consecrated to the Most Holy Trinity, Father, Son, and Holy Spirit under the protection of Jesus, Mary, and Joseph."[55] The sisters live this consecration to the Holy Trinity "as did Jesus, Mary, and Joseph when they lived on earth." This formulation raises no theological question, but it does not explain how the earthly trinity is associated with the heavenly. Farther on, the text designated "The Summary of the End" in the manuscripts, consisting of the consecration to the "two Trinities," is no longer set forth as a condensed form of the vocation of the Sisters of St. Joseph. Forty years after its writing, this text no longer held the symbolic meaning it once had. It was no longer seen as a net-work of relations, a living summary of the twofold purpose: love of God and love of humanity, service of God in service of neighbor. Rather, it is presented as a part of the "means which the sisters will take in order to achieve perfection," to a certain degree subsuming service of neighbor under the goal of personal sanctification.[56] It omits indicating that for Father Médaille the reverse was equally true: the sanctification of the sisters is also found in the goal of service of the neighbor. Mentioned in connection with St. Joseph, service to the neighbor in its concrete reality is moved to a position after the Summary, which no longer functions as a recapitulation.

The chapter "On the Services Which the Sisters Should Give to the Neighbor" reflects the same dichotomy as relocating the Summary between personal sanctification and service of others. It begins by presenting Jesus Christ not only "come into this world" as adorer of the Father "by his completely holy and completely perfect life . . . but also" as the servant of humanity. Adoration is placed on one side, as in the preceding chapter, and service on the other. The redactor did not seem to understand the unity of consecrated apostolic life, symbolically synthesized by Father Médaille in the "consecration to the two Trinities." In the manuscript versions, Father Médaille had perfectly situated and expressed the unity of the sisters' vocation. It would seem that the sisters themselves—like some Jesuits who became Carthusians at the end of the sixteenth century—had trouble understanding the unity of their vocation, and in consequence, the forms of life more suitable for realizing it.[57] The tension alluded to at the beginning of this study is obvious here: how to articulate as a coherent whole the two elements of consecration to God and apostolic activity.

Another question pertains to the place of the "Protestations" in the 1694 Constitutions. In the manuscripts, this text, recited by the sisters each month, expressed their communal commitment to live specific aspects of the vocation of St. Joseph. Always presented with the vow formula to demonstrate its importance,[58] the text of the Protestations formed part of the remedies proposed by Father Médaille at the end of the Constitutions to prevent disorders and decline in the communities.[59] In the 1694 Constitutions, the Protestations at the end of Part 6 are replaced by a final chapter, "On the Obligation of the Sisters to Know and Observe Their Constitutions."[60] The rules as a whole are seen as a means for salvation which should contribute "to sustain their little congregation." The actual mention of a communal commitment to live the points expressed in the Protestations becomes part of the chapter on monthly spiritual practices.[61] The Protestations no longer appear as remedies with the potential to prevent deterioration within the communities. They are inserted in the directory, thus losing some of their intensity. The vocabulary and situations had undoubtedly evolved since the early days, and the dangers were not exactly the same. If the sisters did not feel the need to reformulate remedies for threats which had already been eliminated, neither did they see that others may have replaced them, nor that the formula might need to be modified. The Protestations were already becoming an empty ritual. Elsewhere, the 1694 Constitutions stressed the observance of rules in a rather legalistic, even threatening manner, "under pain of serious sin." The replacement of the Protestations by a chapter on the obligation to observe the constitutions was a symptom of this trend.

There are other changes, small but important, in the 1694 Constitutions having to do with spiritual direction. A short passage from Fifth Part in the manuscripts is removed from the printed text: "The professed sisters will communicate with the spiritual coadjutrix or with the superior, according to what the Directory will tell them."[62] Since the Directory says nothing on this subject, and since the rules for the novice mistress refer to apprenticeship in "the manner of communicating and manifesting the interior of their soul . . . to their director, to their superior, and to their mistress," someone may have judged the short paragraph in Part Five to be of little use or out of place, and so deleted it.[63] It was not understood—or it was forgotten—that this paragraph was inserted in the Fifth Part, "On Spiritual Exercises," precisely in relation to these exercises, so that they could learn, through spiritual direction more than through the rules, what would help them to progress. Elsewhere, in the section on the Chapter of Faults, the printed constitutions refer to "the particular communications which [the sisters] should have with their superior to whom they will confidently open their soul . . . [for] their improvement and . . . perfection."[64] The need for a relationship of spiritual assistance between the sisters and the superior is indeed affirmed but without insistence.

The role of the spiritual director seems to be more restricted or perhaps more regulated. In the manuscripts, Father Médaille had sought to remedy the "excessive multiplicity of directors." He believed that if a community had only one good director, that was a grace of God, and one should pray for it.[65] If, however, "for their solace" the sisters "needed to deal with someone else," it should be willingly permitted as long as he was a "man of great virtue" and the rules of prudence and propriety were observed. In the Vienne Constitutions, the tone of this chapter is much sharper and more restrictive. As in the manuscripts, they were to "avoid a multiplicity of directors." To accomplish this, "it is necessary that the sisters choose only one director. . . . And when they have been given one . . . the superiors will not tolerate that the sisters go in search of any others, except for very serious reasons."[66] Nonetheless, in the following chapter entitled "On Means to Avoid the Constraint of the Sisters' Conscience," they were given "the liberty to write to the bishop and to the spiritual father" of the community, in other words, to their ecclesiastical superior. Given the importance of these two men, they certainly would not have done it too often. As in Father Médaille's text, the sisters could also appeal to an extraordinary confessor when the need arose, provided they followed the prescribed rules. These modifications, although restrictive, did not fundamentally change Fr. Médaille's suggestions. He had already noted in the Avis et Règlements that the sisters should avoid "frequent and long communications with ecclesiastics or with male religious."[67] These measures did make the practice of spiritual direction more difficult. In spite of everything, however, in general the 1694 Constitutions, with all their variations, confirm the importance of spiritual direction, the difficulty in choosing and using a good director, and the superior's responsibility in this matter for the spiritual progress of the sisters.

A final sign of the times in the 1694 Constitutions is the appearance of paragraphs and chapters with juridical overtones, principally in connection with the reception of sisters and with vows. The bishop could give dispensations for the reception of women who were illegitimate or had some sort of disability; he also dispensed the vows of a sister who left the congregation.[68] The chapter on the "Vow of Poverty" deals with the possession of goods and alludes to royal legislation and the eventual acquisition of "letters patent of the most Christian King" in favor of one community or another.[69] The mention of these juridical aspects gives evidence of the evolution and growth of the communities of St. Joseph. Their development and increased role in society had made it necessary for them to search out the particular juridical forms suitable for their existence.

The "better order" announced in the approval of the constitutions by the Archbishop of Vienne seems to have had ambiguous results in regard to the fidelity of the new text to the older manuscripts. A desire to return to the sources is detectable in the references to the Saint-Didier manuscript and the choice to integrate the essentials of the other primitive texts in the new document. In addition, some modifications which at times reflected the evolution in society as well as in the sisters' mentality or aspirations managed on the whole to remain rather close to Father Médaille's proposals. The juridical additions, necessitated by the increased number of sisters and by stricter royal legislation, did not in themselves contradict the original texts of Father Médaille. They often need to be understood according to the way they were implemented. On the other hand, moving the "Summary of the End," more or less identified with the means of the sisters' perfection, profoundly modified the understanding of the vocation of consecrated apostolic life of the Sisters St. Joseph in relation to its most fundamental Ignatian roots. The next section therefore examines what the Sisters of St. Joseph received from the Society of Jesus through Father Médaille, and what was kept and passed on in the 1694 Constitutions.

The 1694 Constitutions and the Constitutions and Rules of the Society of Jesus

In the beginning of the manuscript versions of the constitutions, Father Médaille indicates the aim of the congregation: The sisters should devote themselves, "after caring for their own salvation and perfection, to the works of mercy, [and by means of] these works . . . promote . . . the salvation and perfection of the neighbor."[70] The beginning of Part Two reads: "The aim of our new congregation . . . tends, in the first place, to establish and maintain in rather high virtue all of its members; in the second place, to practice all the holy works of mercy, spiritual and corporal . . . and . . . by means of these works [to benefit] many souls of the dear neighbor."[71] The goal of the Congregation of St. Joseph is therefore the sanctity and perfection of the sisters, and at the same time, the sanctity and perfection of every neighbor through the spiritual and corporal works of mercy. The sisters are called to live their preferential and absolute commitment to the following of Christ precisely within their service to the neighbor. The goal is identical to that of the Society of Jesus: "to devote ourselves with God's grace to the salvation and perfection of our own members, and with the same grace zealously to exert ourselves for the salvation and perfection of the neighbor."[72] For the Congregation of St. Joseph, as for the Society of Jesus, the mission is universal. In Father Médaille's plan, the sisters are engaged in every spiritual and corporal work of mercy of which they are capable, wherever they were sent. Although expressed in different words, this mission offered universal apostolic service to simple women who could not aspire to great missionary travels. Father Médaille respected this distinction. He maintained the universal dimension by patterning the congregation's apostolic extension in a series of expanding circles, but without excluding the possibility of wider movement.

At first glance, the purpose of the Congregation of St. Joseph in the 1694 Constitutions seems identical to that found in the Constitutions manuscripts. In both cases, there is a double objective: the sanctity of the sisters and service of the neighbor. A closer analysis, however, reveals an important difference. According to the Vienne constitutions, the sisters should "apply themselves to their own perfection and to service of the neighbor by . . . observing all the rules prescribed for them."[73] Later they assert,

> There are two principal ends for which the Congregation was established. The
> first is that all the [sisters] . . . work . . . toward their own sanctification . . . and

to advance toward the most sublime perfection. The second is to assist the dear
neighbor by all the Works of mercy, both corporal and spiritual.[74]

The aim described in the Vienne Constitutions is no longer that of the manuscripts. It still includes the sanctification of the sisters, but only the assistance of the neighbor in needs "both corporal and spiritual." The sisters live
their religious consecration first and foremost, and to that they add some
charitable works for the neighbor. The mission toward the neighbor is appended to the search for personal sanctity. It consists more in various services than in spiritual companionship for the development of all, both sisters
and the neighbor. In the same chapter of the Vienne text, the wording of the
consecration to the Trinity preserves the search for what is "most perfect and
most agreeable" to God, but it does not continue what follows in the manuscript: "in every kind of work of zeal for the good of souls and relief of the
needy."[75] This suppression is similar to the treatment of Father Médaille's
"Summary of the End" in Part Two of the Constitutions, tilting it completely
toward the means "to acquire perfection" and separating it from apostolic
service to the neighbor. It is coherent, likewise, with the way of presenting
the vows in Part Three solely as means to perfection: "the perfection to
which [the sisters] are committed . . . consists in the perfect observance of
their vows and of their constitutions."[76] Apostolic universality disappears to
some extent. In the 1694 Constitutions the sisters dedicate themselves "entirely to the service of the neighbor," but only in those works listed among
"services which the sisters should render to the neighbor," summarized in
the expression "all the exercises of charity and mercy."[77] Clearly, the modifications put forth in the Constitutions of Vienne go beyond different forms
of living the same vocation. The redactor modifies the vocation itself, in its
most fundamental principles.

    Once the goal of the congregation itself is transformed in the new consti-
tutions, what is left of the early project of Father Médaille in its connection
with the Jesuit texts? Part One of the Vienne text repeats, more or less faithfully, the chief elements found in the manuscripts and develops them. These
elements are all borrowed from the first chapters of the General Examen in
the Constitutions of the Society of Jesus: name and goal of the new congregation, persons to whom it is addressed, their commitment, style of life
(house, dress, prayers), connections with the church (the pope for the Jesuits,
the bishop or his delegate for the sisters). Parts Two and Three sustained the
greatest changes. In the second part, after dealing with the end and means in
the way just described, three chapters were added, all relating to sororal charity. These chapters seem to have been grouped here, after service to the neighbor, to emphasize the sisters' life within the house. They are composed either

of paragraphs taken from Father Médaille's writing or texts inspired by the Jesuit Constitutions. Even when the texts are Father Médaille's or Ignatian in nature, their placement in the structure of the text gives them a different meaning and scope. The community appears more ascetic than apostolic. In Part Three, on the reception of candidates, we have already seen that the chapters added to it are taken from the General Examen of the Society of Jesus, under cover of references to the Visitation, and that the presentation of the profession and the vows has little to do with Father Médaille.

The spirit and style of Father Médaille, nevertheless, are not absent from the first three parts. The description of the congregation in the first part reflects rather closely the community's general way of life as described in the manuscripts: the absence of strict enclosure in light of an apostolic goal, the simple dress of widows, a lighter prayer schedule to allow for "dedication to the service of the neighbor," the *sœurs agrégées* dispersed in rural areas, and the lack of distinction between classes of sisters in the house. All these details are within the perspective of Father Médaille and refer as well to the Constitutions of the Society of Jesus: "[W]ith attention always paid to the greater service of God, in regard to what is exterior the manner of living is ordinary."[78] Through use of passages from the General Examen of the Jesuits, the Vienne text substantially confirms the prudence recommended by Father Médaille in the reception and formation of sisters, given the exposed situation in the world this vocation required. The candidates are scrutinized before admission. Later, however, the text mentions only "sufficient qualities," so that the sisters might "fulfill their assignment" and "maintain . . . constancy in virtue which could . . . edify the neighbor."[79] Father Médaille asked for "qualities a little out of the ordinary" because the sisters were very "openly engaged in the use of zeal to help the neighbor."[80] For him, apostolic audacity required exceptional qualities: it was not enough to edify by good example, although this too was necessary—one needed to show great "zeal to help the neighbor." By reducing the apostolic scope of the vocation of St. Joseph, the redactor of 1694 distorted the spirit of Father Médaille and replaced it with one more timid, not necessarily that of the Visitation, even if it made claim to that. Paradoxically, what is left of the primitive Constitutions in the first three parts of the 1694 text is the configuration of the life of the Sisters of St. Joseph. Although the redactor begins the book with the proposal "to follow the customs, spirit, and life of the Holy Daughters of the Visitation," the customs and life described in these three parts actually remain closer either to the Society of Jesus or to the manuscript documents of St. Joseph.

The last three parts of the 1694 Constitutions continue to describe the form of life of the Sisters of St. Joseph according to Father Médaille, occasionally according to the redactor, and seldom, the Visitation. First, Part Four, "On the

Rules for Officers," describes the internal structure of the community and the way of carrying out various responsibilities. For the most part, these rules came from the Society of Jesus: rules for the superior or rector, for the minister (assistant), for the procurator (treasurer), and so on. Part Five deals with the spiritual exercises of the sisters. The printed text is identical to that of the manuscripts and follows the model for the formation of Jesuit scholastics.[81] The presentation of obstacles to the life of the congregation and the remedies, found in Part Six, are heavily inspired by the last two parts of the Jesuit Constitutions.[82] These last three parts of the Vienne Constitutions, however, were subject to alterations or additions. The activities relative to what Father Médaille calls the spiritual works of mercy have been abbreviated or even eliminated. For example, in service to the neighbor, the Vienne text does retain the duty to work with Congregations of Mercy in which there must be "not only the Works of mercy . . . but also . . . individual direction" of the women who are members "to promote the greater glory of God and the salvation of their family and of the neighbor."[83] The rules for the directress of the Confraternity of Mercy no longer tell her to apply "the rules of the spiritual assistant [the novice mistress] to guidance of the confraternity," nor is she invited to teach the Ladies of Mercy "to give. . . an account of their conscience to their director."[84] Certain expressions have disappeared, such as "with the help of divine grace," "in Our Lord," and "the virtue proper to their institute," as well as passages dealing with this "virtue proper" to the congregation—all expressions or passages which added an Ignatian tone to the text and at the same time characteristics unique to the vocation of St. Joseph. It is impossible not to regret this mutilation of the text. Among the passages added, some chapters and paragraphs only clarify points which require more development, such as the superior's conferences or the chapter of faults, "in order to instruct and correct the sisters."[85] Others envisage new aspects, such as the "Common Rules for All the Sisters" with its details about trips between houses of St. Joseph within or beyond the diocese. The way these aspects are presented is inspired by the "Common Rules" that follow the Summary in the Constitutions of the Society of Jesus.[86] In these last three sections the 1694 redactor often changed the tone of the whole without really altering its content. Hence the last three parts of the constitutions remain fairly faithful to Father Médaille's original texts. The latter parts suggest ways to implement the first three parts, which define the congregation. They therefore handle the customs and life of the Sisters of St. Joseph. Even if the spirit of the Sisters of St. Joseph, set forth in the first three parts, was not really understood by the redactor, the last three, through descriptions of their forms of life, continued to transmit something of the spirit that animated them—that of Father Médaille, inspired by the texts of the Society of Jesus.

At the very end of the Constitutions, in the ritual for profession borrowed from the Visitation, the vow formula of the Sisters of St. Joseph, obviously identical to that of the original texts, is modeled entirely on the formula of vows for Jesuit scholastics.[87] The few additions made to the Jesuit formula in that of the Sisters of St. Joseph signal the vocation proper to the sisters. The evocation of "our Patriarch St. Joseph" next to "the glorious Virgin Mary" speaks for itself in a Congregation of St. Joseph. The presence of the bishop or his delegate at the ceremony makes explicit the juridical situation of the sisters. The most significant addition, however, is the promise of "the most profound humility . . . and the most cordial charity" followed by "the exercise of all the works of mercy." In the formula used by Jesuits who profess four vows, one finds, in the same place, a promise to give oneself "to the education of children" followed by the promise of obedience to the pope "in regard to the missions, according to the same apostolic letters and the Constitutions."[88] The last two points do not appear in the formula for the profession of scholastics. Father Médaille therefore structured the formula for the Sisters of St. Joseph by joining the Jesuit scholastics' commitment with the apostolic aspects of the commitment of the professed, the whole formulated in accord with what the sisters were living: an innate littleness and apostolic accessibility to every neighbor.

THE 1694 CONSTITUTIONS, A MIRROR OF CONFLICTING TENDENCIES

The redactor of the Constitutions printed in Vienne in 1694, who may have been Monsieur de Lantages, certainly played a major role in forming the document. Despite having right before him women imbued with the vocation of St. Joseph like Marguerite Burdier, there were others of equal stature who understood their vocation differently. It is not known which elements in the printed document came from the sisters and which from the redactor. He was endowed with the ecclesiastical power and the prestige of an intellectual and theological formation that asserts itself naturally. It goes without saying that he affected everything in the text, sometimes its content, almost always its form. He readily put his stamp on texts of Father Médaille or the Visitation. His own additions often appear moralizing, sometimes threatening or solemn. For example, Part Six, Chapter 2 of the Constitutions ("On the Means to Destroy Ambition and Intrigue") begins with bombast: "Ambition is the bastard daughter of pride, she is as criminal as her mother."[89] There follow three pages of warnings against ambition before the text returns, in the same chapter, to the much calmer tone of the manuscripts. Nothing is less certain than whether the redactor was aware of his distortion of Father Médaille's project. He undoubtedly wanted to take account of the manuscript texts, the changing needs of the times, and the sisters' desires. Thinking it necessary to modify the customs, spirit, and manner of life, he ended in reality by changing the purpose of the congregation. Although using the same components, the editor presents a structure of consecrated apostolic life different from that proposed by Father Médaille in the primitive texts.

At the same time he referred constantly to the Saint-Didier manuscript, the oldest available manuscript, which he relates almost in its entirety. The redactor borrows new material from the Constitutions and the Rules of the Society of Jesus. He keeps the one hundred Maxims in the right place, immediately after the Constitutions, preserving some lines of introduction: in these maxims "is contained the entire spirit of their little Institute and their Constitutions."[90] Many of these maxims are inspired by, and often repeat exactly, passages from the Jesuit Constitutions. The redactor's insistence on the original manuscripts and on Ignatian orientations could have come from his desire to remain faithful to the origins of the Sisters of St. Joseph. On the other hand, he may simply have utilized Ignatian trappings on a life moving away from them, since the Sisters of St. Joseph were now to live the life of the first Visitandines. It is hard to believe the redactor when he states that the "Little Congregation" of St. Joseph "was only established to take up and continue the spirit of the first" Visitation, when that order had begun almost a century earlier, and the Congregation of St. Joseph had been in existence for more than forty years. Throughout the seventeenth century many other congregations, starting with the Daughters of the Cross of Madame de Villeneuve, were widely known direct heirs of the original Visitation, who wanted to revive its spirit. It can hardly be said that the new spirit proposed to the Sisters of St. Joseph in the 1694 Constitutions was that of the first Visitation. In the first Visitation Constitutions, written between 1610 and 1613, before its enclosure, Francis de Sales defined the goal of his new institute. He wished that "virtuous women and girls" would "dedicate every moment of their life to the love and service of God."[91] To that end, the congregation had "two principal exercises: one, contemplation and meditation . . . the other the service of the poor and sick." Our Lady of the Visitation was chosen as patron because, in the very act "of her charity toward the neighbor," in this case her cousin Elizabeth, she "nonetheless composed the canticle or the Magnificat, the most . . . spiritual and contemplative ever written."[92] Francis de Sales described his version of what other followers of Ignatius Loyola called contemplation in action. This attitude was certainly proposed by Father Médaille in the St. Joseph constitutions, but it does not correspond to that described by the redactor of the 1694 Constitutions. Despite some borrowed material, the spirit of the Vienne Constitutions is not the spirit of the Visitation.

At the close of the seventeenth century, the 1694 Constitutions expressed a mutation of the congregation which would be reinforced in some ways throughout the following century. The new constitutions showed a penchant toward conventual forms under the guise of a search for perfection and sanctity. The new formulation of the goal of the congregation emphasized the means of perfection for the sisters and added apostolic service to the neighbor as secondary. This formulation centered life around the house and gave the whole a conventual orientation. The chapters on charity among the sisters and on the three vows reinforced this tendency. The expansion of the chapter on the *sœurs agrégées* could also have originated from the conventual orientation of the sisters properly speaking (those who were not *agrégées*), but as a counterpart, in the same way that apostolic work was distinguished from what was seen as more direct service of God. The overall framework became more rigid, with rather frequent recommendations about "observing all the rules." The spiritual fathei, who acted as vicar general of the bishop and had authority "over all the sisters of the houses under his jurisdiction," assumed a rather important place.[93] The sisters were to have recourse to him "in all important affairs, whether temporal or spiritual." He was to make sure that houses had the necessary resources and review their accounts.[94] He "will always be watchful that the rules be well kept."[95] His role is specified throughout the Constitutions as one of counsel, often of correction, and especially so, as one might expect, in chapters dealing with dangers and their remedies. The way his role is described, as well as the growing limitation in the functioning of the spiritual director, creates concern that, at times, for the community as for each sister, rules took the place of discernment.

This study of the 1694 Constitutions reveals, once again, the difficulty Sisters of St. Joseph experienced in understanding their own vocation and finding appropriate forms for living it. According to what is written, the Congregation of St. Joseph should be animated by two spirits: that of the first Visitation and that of the Maxims. Taken from the perspective of Francis de Sales, the spirit of the Visitation appears completely compatible with the spirit of the Maxims. Seen from the perspective of the redactor or certain sisters, the two seem more difficult to reconcile. Beyond that, what is involved for the sisters, as for the redactor, is the impossibility of imagining that the vocation of St. Joseph could be lived without the usual forms of religious life. As we have seen, this difficulty appeared almost from the beginning. The first crisis occurred during Father Médaille's time, near 1660, when the Little Directory was composed and introduced into the Constitutions. The second known confrontation originated in different points of view among the sisters themselves, as attested to by the two-document manuscript kept in Le Puy.

At the same time, or a few years later, the Le Puy community wrote a new copy of its constitutions in preparation for the first printing of the Constitutions at Vienne. That manuscript reveals the same conventual tendencies and internal tensions as preserved in the documents mentioned above. The conflicting directions and tensions which appear in these texts could only reflect the real tensions existing in the history of the communities. It could hardly have been otherwise. The sisters who understood their vocation from within did not have the social stature to declare and uphold the external forms of this "ordinary manner of living . . . to the greater service of God."[96] Very few ecclesiastics around them could understand this renunciation of prestige in order to live a life of apostolic consecration more fully. The Jesuits, who might have understood, were not allowed to deal with women religious. In addition, they were not all competent to help such women find their way, even if it was similar to theirs. From 1719 or 1720, the Jesuits in Vienne assisted the Sisters of St. Joseph of that city in their efforts to become enclosed.[97] It comes as no surprise, then, that the St. Joseph communities moved forward as best they could, experimenting in order to find approaches that gave them life, whether in prayer or in service. Apparently the distinction between the *agrégées* and the sisters properly speaking eased tensions and made peace in relationships between the different types of communities and different propensities. Each sister tried, in her own way, to live the life proposed by Father Médaille—a life consecrated to God in universal service to the neighbor. The vocation of St. Joseph, like every Ignatian vocation, directed the sisters toward the search for God in all things. The sisters were not nuns, that is, religious in the precise meaning of the term in that era, because they did not make solemn vows, live in enclosure, or recite the Divine Office in choir. The letters patent of Louis XIV recognized some among them as "associated daughters (*filles associées*) living in community under the title of the Congregation of the Daughters of St. Joseph."[98] Some were thereby recognized as members of a secular community; others existed only as *filles dévotes* under the authority of the bishop, with no other official recognition.

NOTES

1. AMM Le Puy, Communauté du Puy, undated manuscript that appears to be from the second half of the seventeenth century.

2. F. Gouit, *Une congrégation Salésienne: Les sœurs de Saint-Joseph du Puy-en-Velay, 1648-1915* (Le Puy: Impr. de l'Avenir de la Haute-Loire, 1930), 59.

3. See Supporting Documents, 11.

4. *TP* 1981, CP, Règles de la supérieure, 39, nos. 134-38; 40, nos. 144-47; and Règles de la coadjuratrice spirituelle, 46-48, nos. 171-89.

5. Ibid., CP, part 1, 20, no. 41.

6. Ibid., CP, Avertissement pour toutes les sœurs en général et en particulier, 61-69, nos. 282-337.

7. See Supporting Documents, 11.

8. Marius Nepper, S.J., *Origins: The Sisters of St. Joseph*, translated by the Federation of the Sisters of St. Joseph, USA [Erie: Villa Maria College, 1975], 32-33.

9. See Supporting Documents, 13.

10. *CV* 1694, Preface.

11. Constitutions 1693 A, 4.

12. *CV* 1694, 8 ff.

13. Ibid., part 4, chap. 1, "Des règles de la Prieure," 158, § 10, omitted in the same section in Constitutions 1693 A.

14. AD Isère, 21 H 1, Registre de professions des religieuses de Saint-Joseph de Vienne, 1681-1792, 13.

15. BM Grenoble, R 8372, "Registre des Religieuses de Saint-Joseph de la ville de Vienne a commencer en l'année mil-six-cent-soixante-huit" fols. 98 ff.

16. Ibid., fol. 103.

17. Ibid., fol. 167.

18. See Supporting Documents, 13.

19. *Constitutions pour la petite Congrégation des Sœurs de Saint-Joseph*, approuvées par Mgr Camille de Neuville de Villeroy, archevêque de Lyon. A Lyon, chez André Laurens, MDCCXXX.

20. *CV* 1694, 1.

21. *TP* 1981, MI, 170.

22. *CV* 1694, part 1, chap. 1, 7.

23. Ibid., part 1, chap. 6, 23 ff.

24. Ibid., part 1, chap. 6: "Des Supérieurs de la Congrégation," 26.

25. *TP* 1981, CP, 67, no. 321; and 73, no. 353.

26. Constitution 28: "Du Père spirituel de la Mayson," in François de Sales, *Œuvres de Saint François de Sales Évêque de Genève et docteur de l'Église* (Annecy: Monastère de la Visitation, 1931), 25:86-87.

27. *CV* 1694, part 3, chap. 1: "De la réception des Novices," 88 ff; and Constitution 43: "De la première réception de celles qui désirent estre de la Congrégation"; and Constitution 44: "De l'entrée des Novices," in François de Sales, *Œuvres* (Annecy, 1931), 25: 112-113.

28. *CSJ* 1970, "The General Examen and its Declarations," chap. 3, 88-91, nos. 34-52.

29. *CV* 1694, part 3, chap. 1: "De la réception des Novices," 89 ff.

30. Ibid., part 3, chap. 2, 95 ff.

31. Ibid., chap. 3: "Du Noviciat et de l'éducation des Novices," 105-114.

32. Ibid., 109-110; and *CSJ* 1970, "The General Examen and its Declarations," chap. 4, 95-100, nos. 64-79.

33. *CV* 1694, part 3, chap. 4, 115 ff; and François de Sales, *Œuvres* (Annecy, 1931), 25:432 ff.

34. *TP* 1981, CP, 23, no. 58.

35. Ibid., LE, 6-7, nos. 16-24.

36. *CV* 1694: Manière de recevoir et donner l'habit, 540, and Manière de recevoir la profession des Sœurs, 550; and François de Sales, *Œuvres* (Annecy, 1931): "Formulaire de la vêture," and "Formulaire de la Profession," 25:176 and 185.

37. *TP* 1981, CM, 138.

38. François de Sales, *Introduction à la Vie Dévote,* in *Œuvres*, ed. André Ravier and Roger Devos (Paris: Gallimard, 1969), part 2, chap. 2, 82; and *CV* 1694, Directoire, 439.

39. *CV* 1694, Directoire, 451.

40. *Directoire spirituel*, in François de Sales, *Œuvres* (Annecy, 1931), 25:140.

41. *CV* 1694, part 3, chap. 7, "Du vœu de la pauvreté," 142.

42. See Supporting Documents, 14.

43. *TP* 1981, CP 25 and 62.

44. *CSJ* 1970, part 6, chap. 4, 264-66, nos. 595-96, 598, and 600-601.

45. *TP* 1981, CP, part 5, 71-75, nos. 339-64.

46. See Constitutions Manuscripts, Appendix 1.

47. *TP* 1981, CP, part 2, 28, no. 91, and 30, no. 104, with notes; and *CV* 1694, 62.

48. Constitution de la Visitation, in François de Sales, *Œuvres* (Annecy, 1931), 25:106 ff; and Bibliothèque Mazarine, MS 3333, *Constitutions des sœurs de La Croix*, part 2, Constitutions nos. 13-16.

49. See Appendix 3.

50. *TP* 1981, CP, 26, no. 80, and 73, no. 354.

51. Ibid., CP, part 1, 17, no. 22.

52. *CV* 1694, part 1, chap. 8, 34-42.

53. *TP* 1981, AR, 131-35; and CM, 136-38.

54. *CV* 1694, part 1, chap. 9, 43-48.

55. *TP* 1981, CP, chap. 1, 6.

56. *CV* 1694, part 2, chap. 2, 55-59.

57. Louis Cognet, *L'essor: 1500-1650*, part 1 of *La spiritualité moderne* (Paris: Aubier, 1966), 191.

58. See Manuscript Constitutions, Appendix 1.

59. *TP* 1981, CP, part 6, nos. 442-43.

60 *CV* 1694, part 6, chap. 13, 358.

61. Ibid., part 5, chap. 2: "Des exercices de tous les mois," 269.

62. *TP* 1981, CP, part 5, 74, no. 362.

63. *CV* 1694, part 4, chap. 3: "Des règles de la Coadjutrice qui sera maîtresse des Novices," 181, no. 12.

64. Ibid., part 6, chap. 7: "Du Chapitre des Coulpes," 330.

65. *TP* 1981, CP, part 6, 87, nos. 427-29 and 432-33.

66. *CV* 1694, part 6, chap. 9: "Du moyen d'éviter la pluralité des Directeurs," 349.

67. *TP* 1981, AR, 131, no. 4.

68. *CV* 1694, part 3, chap. 2, 104-105; part 1, chap. 2, 9-13.

69. Ibid., part 3, chap. 8, 144.

70. *TP* 1981, CP, part 1, 17, no. 21.

71. Ibid., CP part 2, 22, nos. 48-49.

72. *RSI* 1620, Sommaire, 4, nos. 48-49; see *CSJ* 1970, "The General Examen and Its Declarations," chap. 1, no. 3, 77-78.

73. *CV* 1694, part 1, chap. 1, 2-3.

74. Ibid., part 2, chap. 1, 51.

75. *TP* 1981, CP, part 1, 18, no. 28; and *CV* 1694, part 1, chap. 1, 6.

76. *CV* 1694, part 3, chap. 4, 119.

77. Ibid., part 2, chap. 3, 62.

78. *CSJ* 1970, "The General Examen and its Declarations," 80, no. 8; and *RSI* 1620, Sommaire, 6, no. 4.

79. *CV* 1694, part 3, chap. 3, "Des qualités requises," 96.

80. *TP* 1981, CP, part 3, 33, no. 113.

81. *CSJ* 1970, part 4, chap. 4: "The care and welfare of the scholastics admitted," 184, no. 342.

82. Ibid., part 9: "The Society's head, and the government descending from him," chap 4, 319-20, nos. 773-74; and part 10: "How the whole body of the Society can be preserved and developed in its well-being," 333-37, nos. 816-21.

83. *CV* 1694, part 2, chap. 3, 66-67.

84. *TP* 1981, CP, part 4: "Règles de la Directrice de la Confrérie de la Miséricorde," 59, no. 273; and 60, no. 280.

85. *CV* 1694, part 6, chap. 5, 317 ff.

86. *RSI* 1620, Règles communes, 37-39, nos. 41-46.

87. See Supporting Documents, 14.

88. *CSJ* 1970, 238, no. 527.

89. *CV* 1694, part 6, chap. 2, 297.

90. Ibid., Maximes de la Grande Vertu, 371.

91. Regles et Constitutions de la Congregation des Sœurs dediees a Dieu sous l'invocation de Nostre Dame de la Visitation en la ville d'Annessi, art. 1, in Francois de Sales, *Œuvres* (Annecy, 1931), 25:211.

92. Ibid., 25:214, art. 1.

93. *CV* 1694, part 1, chap. 7, "Du Père spirituel," 29.

94. Ibid., part 6, chap. 7, "Des moyens d'éviter le défaut ou l'excès du bien," 333.

95. Ibid., part 1, chap. 7, 32.

96. *CSI* 1967, p. 16, no. 8. [See English version in *CSJ*, 80, no. 8. –Trans.]

97. BM Grenoble, R 8372, Registre des Religieuses de Saint-Joseph de la ville de Vienne, Table alphabétique des matières, lettre Z (zèle).

98. See Supporting Documents, 10.

Chapter Five

The Superior's Role:
A Key to Life in the Communities

Descriptions of the superior and her role effectively create a thumbnail sketch of the spirituality and life of the community. Because of its potential for communicating a grasp of the pre-Revolutionary communities, this chapter studies the office of superior for the Sisters of St. Joseph in the ancien régime through a comparison of its theoretical presentation in the normative texts and its actual practice in several specific communities. The theoretical superior of the seventeenth and eighteenth centuries is found in the chapter on the rules for the superior in the Constitutions printed at Vienne in 1694, which, like that in the manuscripts, spells out her duties and the authority she has to carry out her mission. The Vienne Constitutions incorporate the entire chapter on the rules for the superior from the Constitutions manuscripts and integrate the first Règlements, as well as juridical details required by the evolution of the communities and by royal legislation. Following the study of theoretical principles and the configuration of the role of superior in the Constitutions, we shall examine how they were actually carried out in the life of the three communities of Vienne, Lyon and Craponne.

THE SUPERIOR IN THE 1694 CONSTITUTIONS

The Vienne Constitutions (1694) treat the superior and her role in Part 4, Chapter 1, which contains "particular rules for the Superior and for all officers . . . and rules common to all the Sisters."[1] This chapter offers nothing systematic or comprehensive about the functions of the superior, either in the Constitutions manuscripts or in the edition printed at Vienne. Rather, it presents general provisions which need to be complemented by material in other chapters, particularly all of Part 6, which deals with the dangers leading to decline and their remedies.

In line with the Constitutions of the Society of Jesus, Father Médaille presents the superior as "lieutenant (*lieutenante*) of God, appointed . . . to lead the entire body of the very little congregation." She "holds the place" (*tient lieu*) of God.[2] She is responsible for the congregation's "felicitous progress" or its decline. The following paragraph immediately warns the superior that this responsibility will always lie beyond her capacity, whatever that might be, since "she cannot maintain by herself a body which professes the greatest perfection in all things and embraces all the exercises of zeal" of which women are capable. Having expressed this impossibility, the text nevertheless indicates, in no specific order, the ways the superior fulfills her responsibility toward each sister, governs the house, and provides for the spiritual welfare of the entire community.

Responsibility for Each Sister

The Vienne Constitutions of 1694 explain the superior's responsibility toward each sister. If she wishes the sisters to attain the "perfection . . . [and] observance of the all the rules," she should surpass them all in the example of her life and by fulfilling "all the orders of the same Institute."[3] Besides praying frequently for all her sisters, she should "be devoted to their direction," considering what they have done well in order to increase it and thank God for it, and what they have done wrong, in order to "apply suitable remedies for it." She takes great care to see that all the sisters are instructed in meditation and are devoted to it so that they might advance "in every kind of virtue . . . [and] edify in Our Lord" all those who "will be in contact with them." When observable faults come to her attention, she should neglect nothing to remedy them, "through public penance," if necessary, for "the edification of the house," or through a personal admonition given with "much demonstration of a truly maternal affection." In addition to this efficacious concern for the sisters' spiritual development, she takes great care to provide for them in all their necessities by "giving them . . . gladly all she can to help them in their needs."

On a more fundamental level, the superior bears the responsibility toward the church and the community to see that the sisters live out their commitment in practice of the simple vows of obedience, chastity, and poverty. She has the power to command the sisters in obedience to do what is advisable "for their perfection or for the temporal or spiritual good of the Congregation," and therefore, to do nothing contrary to the Constitutions.[4] The sisters have the right to express "with humility and respect" their difficulties in obeying. If a sister is obstinate in refusing to obey, the superior must treat her with great patience and charity, inviting the community to support her and pray to help her submit.⁵ If the sister persists, the superior informs the bishop or spiritual father so that he may determine if it is necessary to "put her out of the Congregation." The ecclesiastical superiors and the sister superiors also have the duty to ensure that the sisters observe their vow of chastity. If a sister strays, no matter how, they should warn her, help her to change her ways, and, if necessary, punish her if she does not correct herself, or even exclude her from the congregation.⁶

Regarding the vow of poverty and the use of temporal goods, both personal and communal, sisters could do nothing without the permission of the ecclesiastical and community superiors.⁷ Upon their admission to the community, sisters abandoned "all their goods, leaving them to relatives or to the poor, or . . . in the hands of the superiors of the congregation" in order to detach their hearts from all the goods of the world. Despite the fact that their vows were simple and not solemn, according to the Vienne Constitutions, "the vow of poverty renders them incapable of possessing anything in their own name." The superior consequently had the duty to supply the sisters, whether healthy or sick, with all they need "for food and clothing [according to] the ability of their houses." Through such practices, the sisters avoided the temptation to "obtain anything for their use" under the pretext of necessity. If a superior neglected this duty or "refuse[d] to give the sisters what they need," she should be "severely corrected by the bishop or spiritual father" and even "deprived of her office" if she repeats the offense.

Communities dealt with their goods in various ways. The Constitutions of 1694 affirm that certain houses "confirmed by the Letters Patent of the King" had the "right to possess in common the goods which were given them . . . [or] which the Sisters will have brought." In hospitals or other houses without royal letters patent, the sisters "may make a will and dispose of the goods which they brought there or which will be given to them." They could not, however, make this will without permission of the spiritual father or the sister superior. It must be made in favor of a "sister of the house in which they reside" unless the spiritual father or the sister superior found it more appropriate to make it "in favor of some sister of another house of the Congregation." Finally, the possibility of bequeathing or receiving an inheritance did not exempt the sisters from the observance of their vow of poverty, since all goods were to be placed "always in the hands of the superior who will dispose of them for the good of the community."

The language in passages dealing with the practice of the vows is surprisingly firm, and the measures to be taken or the manner in which they were applied, sometimes harsh. This type of language was not rare for legislative texts of the time. By contrast, in the manuscript constitutions and other related texts, Father Médaille, who also requires that the means necessary for the good health of the sisters and the entire body be taken, does so in a language far more Salesian and in full agreement with his own writings about the sisters' spiritual progress. In addition, the 1694 text rarely mentions the superior alone when describing her different responsibilities toward the sisters. When her authority is mentioned, especially in regard to the vows, one finds the expression *les supérieurs et supérieures*, that is, the ecclesiastical superiors and the sister superiors. This was evident in the examples given above about obedience and chastity, and in the practice of poverty, the sisters could make use of temporal goods only with permission of the *supérieurs et supérieures*. Frequent reference to this double authority may be a way to strengthen the sister superior's authority with that of the bishops and spiritual fathers. In the social order of the time, the superior of a community of St. Joseph suffered a triple handicap: she was a woman, a member of a secular congregation, and often of ordinary social background. Nevertheless, the 1694 Constitutions give her—as Father Médaille had already done—an authority over her sisters similar to that of the ecclesiastical superiors. If the sisters should consider the latter "as veritable lieutenants of Jesus Christ," an identical phrase defined the sister superior.[8] In the Constitutions of the Society of Jesus, Saint Ignatius used similar words to describe the authority of the church and of superiors as "supreme vicar of Christ our Lord, or the superiors of the society, who for them are similarly in the place of His Divine Majesty."[9] Obviously, this equivalence can be perceived only with the eyes of faith, and certainly all the more when it came to sisters who were superiors of the "little Congregation of St. Joseph."

The use of the plural *"les supérieurs et supérieures"* does not refer to a single bishop or single female superior, even though the community superior reports to the bishop and other ecclesiastical authorities in her diocese. The plural term alludes to a group, indicating the basic understanding that the church is a body, and the congregation a body related to the church. The two authorities are inseparable, and the authority of the sister superior operates in that context.

Each authority, nonetheless, influenced certain aspects of the sisters' lives separately. For instance, the sister superior acted alone to help the sisters charitably in their troubles, but the bishop or his delegate had to be involved in executive measures, such as the expulsion of a sister. Most of the chapter on the practice of the vow of poverty has a more imperious tone than the chapters on obedience and chastity. For example, this chapter uses expressions such as "we order . . . we permit . . . we forbid them." The group of sisters and sister superiors who met in 1693 to work out the Constitutions to be printed in Vienne in 1694 may have formulated these expressions, but they must also bear the mark of Henry de Villars, Archbishop of Vienne, who authorized the constitutions and licensed their printing.

The chapter on poverty refers explicitly to a third authority, that "of the most Christian King," whose letters patent gave the communities the right to hold in common whatever goods they received. The juridical status of each house governed the way the sisters practiced poverty in relation to the material goods they needed in order to survive. A few houses, such as those of Le Puy and Saint-Didier, confirmed by royal letters patent in January, 1674, had the right to hold property in common. Other houses in the diocese of Le Puy, far more numerous and smaller, although established with permission of the bishop and implicitly recognized by their mention in the letters patent, could only possess goods by means of individual legal acts on the part of the sisters who formed the community. That is why the Constitutions nowhere mention the sister superior's right to buy or sell property or to receive gifts or inheritances in the name of the community. She could acquire or alienate goods only in her own name and with the permission of the spiritual father. Similarly, each sister could inherit or bequeath property with permission of the sister superior or the spiritual father. Anything that came to her subsequently, she turned over to the superior. The superior was responsible for disposing of these goods to the best spiritual and material advantage of the community, and she was obliged to give an account of her stewardship to the bishop during his official visitation.

In practice, authority over all aspects of a sister's personal life, civil or spiritual, resided in the bishop. The sister superior therefore had recourse to this authority for the juridical matters in her purview. For her work with individual sisters, however, she generally relied upon the counsel of the spiritual father, who no longer served as director of conscience, as in the primitive Constitutions. Rather, as with the Visitation nuns, he became the official delegate of the bishop to a group of religious communities. His position was more juridical and broader than that of spiritual director. The superior collaborated with him to help the sisters through encouragement or sanctions so that they might grow more conscious of their own commitment and maintain the good reputation, as well as the good example, of the community. For their part, the sisters were given freedom to correspond with the bishop and the spiritual father whenever they wished in order to avoid "the serious evils which constraint ordinarily inflicts on consciences."[10] In reality, the extent of this freedom of conscience varied to the extent that the spiritual father preempted the role of the spiritual director. Nevertheless, the rights and duties of the superior toward the sisters could be exercised in a satisfactory way only in respect and collaboration with ecclesiastical authority, as well as respect for the personal responsibility of each sister.

Government of the House and Its Operations

The superior was not only responsible for each member of the community; she was also charged with governing the entire house in its internal and external activities. To fulfill this duty, she was assisted by subordinate officers from whom she should ask information "frequently on the state of the entire house, in order to learn if union and charity, and the observance of the rules" were what they should be.[11] The rules for the officers, inspired by the Rules of the Society of Jesus, explain how each officer participated in the life of the community through the authority received from the superior. The superior's closest collaborators were the assistant, who oversaw the general organization and the "exterior order" of the house, and the "spiritual coadjutrix" or mistress of novices, who assisted in all that concerned "the interior direction of the daughters."[12] The treasurer, too, played an important role by helping "in the administration of temporalities" so that the superior, "relieved of these matters, might more easily devote herself to the spiritual guidance of the house."[13]

The various works of service to the neighbor outside the house were delegated to the directress for the poor, whose duties were similar to those of the treasurer in the house.[14] In addition, she kept track of the needs of the neighbor and organized collaboration between the Ladies of Mercy and the Sisters of St. Joseph in order to supply them with the appropriate remedies. The director of the Confraternity of Mercy played a role in regard to the Ladies of Mercy analogous to that of the mistress of novices in the formation of the sisters. Her role was one of the most important in regard to the apostolic work of the community.[15] Through the services rendered to the neighbor through the competence and apostolic zeal of the two previous officers, the superior was able to exercise real power in her milieu. The sisters undertook "the direction and the service of the poor in the Hospitals, direction of houses of Refuge . . . the care of houses for orphan girls," and they operated "the school for the instruction and education of little girls."[16] Whether in the towns or in the country, all these works conferred power, but also responsibility, for the sisters involved in them, and thus the sister superior who governed and supervised them. The portress was situated between the interior and exterior arenas.[17] She watched over all communication, comings in and goings out, seeing to it that all was edifying. No door could be opened without the superior's permission.

All the sisters attended the conferences of the sister superior, which were directed toward the spiritual and temporal good of the house or the congregation. They expressed their opinion and proposed their own suggestions for the advancement of the community or the congregation.[18] To aid in the government of the house and in the works of charity, the superior had the help of two councilors, who were generally joined in consultations by the assistant and the treasurer.[19] With these councilors, she dealt "with what was going on in her family and with the good order of charity for the poor, which she should have singularly at heart."[20] During council meetings, having prayed and shared their insights on an issue, the councilors let the superior decide as she deemed appropriate. Were she to undertake a dangerous course of action, however, the council would be obliged to warn the bishop or the spiritual father about it discreetly. So that the sister superior might better exercise her authority in a way the sisters had a right to expect, she was given the help of an admonitrix to "advise her . . . of her faults and receive the complaints that the subjects might have against her," an arrangement completely consonant with the Constitutions of the Society of Jesus.[21]

The whole of Part 4 of the Constitutions, which discusses rules for the officers and the rules common to all sisters, defines the structural design of the community. From their beginnings, the various communities of St. Joseph had an overarching structure: the small communities of *"sœurs agrégées"* scattered throughout the countryside were grouped in districts around a larger community nearby, often located in a town. The superior of this community had the "right to watch over" the *agrégées* and "their direction."[22] Attentive to the composition of their community, she made sure, among other things, that at least one sister was literate, in order to do spiritual reading, announce the subjects for meditation, and read the Constitutions. In these small houses "where there are only four or five Sisters . . . the superior alone has the authority to give all the offices to those sisters she chooses," subject to the number of sisters and the needs of the community.[23] In the event of a problem, the superior or members of the small houses could appeal to the sister who was district superior. In that capacity, she exercised authority over a larger geographic sector; otherwise it was the same as the authority she held within her own house. In all communities, whether town or country, each officer undertook specific tasks at her level of responsibility in order to free the sister superior from minor concerns and taking care of details. The object of the rule for superiors was that they would not be burdened with external affairs, but "that they devote themselves to direct their subjectss on the road to great perfection. . . . And for the other tasks in the house, they should choose good officers and see that they fulfil their duties well."[24]

Carrying out the aim of the congregation was a mutual work. For their part, the sisters could contribute to the zeal of the superiors by devoting themselves to their own duties. The admonitrix and councilors, moreover, were to take "care to . . . correct [the superiors] for their negligence and to encourage them in the zeal they should have for the spiritual advancement of their communities."[25] Besides negligence, another danger was the superior's misuse of her authority.[26] In principle she should not do anything of importance without the advice of her councilors, and she was "obliged to follow the plurality of votes."[27] Rarely, however, if "it seemed to her that her judgment was better," she could follow it after after speaking about it with the spiritual father. If she should "commit some scandalous fault . . . the admonitrix and the councilors have the power to depose her . . . in a situation where it is necessary for the good of the house." Through the admonitrix and councilors, it was "to be hoped that the excessive freedom and authority of the superior will be tempered."[28]

By what authority did the officers, including the sister superior, receive their powers and responsibility? How were they chosen? Two successive chapters of the 1694 Constitutions describe two options for designating the officers and the superior herself. The first chapter, entitled "On the Appointment of Officers" states:

> The bishop will always appoint the superiors of our small houses, in which there will be less than six sisters in a community; he may also on his own authority appoint the superiors for other houses, which have communities with many sisters, or indeed he may have them elected by the chapter of the sisters.[29]

The following chapter does not mention appointing but only electing the principal officers and superior and describes how it is done.[30] All members of the community participate in the election, which must always be presided over by the bishop, the spiritual father, or the bishop's delegate. After her election, the superior chooses the sisters "whom she judges according to God to be the most appropriate for assistant and coadjutrix" and proposes them to the chapter, which then proceeds with elections. As for the "lesser officers, the superior takes the advice of the assistant, the coadjutrix, and councilors, names them, and changes them as she chooses."

These passages make it clear that a double current runs through the chapters on elections. The first gives authority to the bishop, who may consult the community. The second gives procedural priority to the community to act freely under the bishop's authority. The second is more faithful to what Father Médaille wrote in the primitive constitutions for the election of the superior.[31] The question is why the the chapter allowing the bishop to nominate was added in 1694. The bishops of Le Puy, Henry de Maupas and subsequently Armand de Béthune, had approved the original constitutions without any need to amend the text in order to reinforce their own authority. Perhaps the Archbishop of Vienne, Henry de Villars, did not share the sentiments of his counterparts in Le Puy. The change could also have been an attempt to minimize the difference in the appointment of superiors in the small houses of *sœurs agrégées* and in the others. Or, the added chapter may have been intended to take royal legislation into account and provide the community more juridical stability by relating it more explicitly to ecclesiastical authority. In that case, the remarks already made concerning the *supérieurs et supérieures* are apropos. The authority of the bishop redounds upon the community, and vice versa. The superior, and through her, the principal officers, hold office both from the church, in the person of the bishop, and from the community, in response to the congregational body.

Development and Life of the Congregation

Above and beyond responsibility to persons, to structures, and to tasks, the superior carried the responsibility for the development and the very life of the community. In the first place, the women received must have the appropriate disposition for the vocation of the Sisters of St. Joseph. The superior therefore was to take "extraordinary care in the choice of the young women who wish to be received into the congregation" and "show herself inexorable toward those who might call for the contrary."[32] During this historical period when families tried to place their daughters advantageously in monasteries and in other religious communities, the superior needed some strength of character to dare turn away daughters of relatives or benefactors because they were ill suited for the vocation. The superior did not act alone in her decisions. The councilors had to give their advice and the sisters had to vote. The candidate, moreover, was "examined by the Lord Bishop or the spiritual father." Nevertheless, the superior held ultimate responsibility for admission to the community. If, in those who had been received, "she discover any one of the serious defects that are forbidden . . . that she dismiss them at the soonest [opportunity]."[33] After their reception, she also saw to it "that during the novitiate the sisters were formed according to the spirit of our little congregation."[34] Both superior and novice mistress had to answer to the community for this responsibility. If it should happen that they "disregard their duty and allow themselves to be prejudiced in favor of a postulant or novice who does not have the required qualities, the sisters who observe this shall inform the spiritual father or bishop about it."[35]

The bishop had authority to establish a novitiate in the communities as he saw fit, particularly in the smaller houses of the *sœurs agrégées*. According to the Constitutions,

> The novices can certainly be received and make their novitiate in any house of the congregation, but if possible, each bishop is required to establish the novitiate in one of the houses of his diocese which has more room and where the community is more numerous so that all the exercises of the congregation be done well there and the novices receive a more regular formation.[36]

In other words, it was desirable that the little houses of the *agrégées* sisters not have a novitiate, so that the novices would receive a "more regular" formation. The bishop retained the juridical authority, both civil and canonical, to establish the novitiate and oversee its operation. The heavier burden of practical responsibility regarding the admission of novices and the quality of their formation belonged to the superior as delegate and representative of the whole body.

The superior's obligation for the life of the community as a whole was to see that the constitutions were observed faithfully. As in any religious institute, the Constitutions of the Sisters of St. Joseph were the principal means "through whose observance [the sisters] should advance from strength to strength . . . if they neglect this means . . . they will lose the path to life."[37] From this perspective, the sister superior occupied the same position as the bishop and spiritual father, who were also to be vigilant "to maintain or put back in force the observance of the constitutions."[38] In the last resort, who was answerable for the substance and the text of the constitutions?

Earlier in this study we found that both ecclesiastical and sister superiors (*les supérieurs et supérieures*) cooperated in the exercise of authority when it came to the vows. As far as the smooth functioning of the community was concerned, authority resided in the bishop or his delegate, the spiritual father, in connection with the sister superior of the community. The bishop approved the constitutions, but he could not modify them at will. In certain cases, the sisters were obliged to remind the bishops or spiritual fathers of the precise norms for the establishment of houses. The sisters were to "prevent the establishment of any of our houses which would not have enough to support at least three sisters," whether in revenue or in work, "for we do not want establishments to be made anywhere where there are fewer than three sisters."[39] Furthermore, "the bishops or spiritual fathers should not accept more sisters in any house than the revenue and work can support; the superiors will always oppose it and resist any pressure in this matter."[40] As to the crucial choice of the spiritual fathers, who answered for the communities to the diocesan authority, the sisters could suggest to the bishop those whom they believed "appropriate for the post " and who would have "the authority as vicars-general of the bishops over all the sisters of the houses under their jurisdiction."[41] Father Médaille had already alluded to the qualities necessary in the Règlements: "Their [ecclesiastical] superior or confessor will be a holy man whom they will choose after offering many prayers and tears to God for this intention."[42]

This tone of cooperation among the sisters and their authority to make certain decisions recurs in numerous passages in the 1694 Constitutions. For example, concerning travel, they state: "We ordain . . . for all the sisters who travel always to stay in the houses of our congregation."[43] At the beginning of Part 5 on spiritual exercises, they read: "We will address in this fifth part all the exercises of piety which should be practiced in our little congregation."[44] Clearly, the voice of authority is not the bishop, the spiritual father, or the redactor. It is the authoritative voice of the body of the congregation in the main houses, speaking on behalf of the entire body. The small communities of sisters or *agrégées*, already scattered over ten dioceses, most of whom had no juridical status and no official connection among them, had the sense of belonging to a single body. They understood that together they bore the responsibility for the life of this body. That is why, with the agreement of their ecclesiastical superiors and under their authority, the sisters revised and updated the primitive Constitutions in order to reflect the evolution of the congregation as a body and to meet the needs of its life. The exhortation in the last chapter of the 1694 Constitutions gives evidence of this sense of responsibility:

> After having given to the sisters of our little congregation in these Constitutions, all the laws and rules needed for their salvation and the perfection of their state, we exhort them on the part of the God who called them and to whom they have made a vow of obedience and fidelity, to study well all the rules of these Constitutions, which God has given them through their [ecclesiastical] superiors, to love them . . . and to practice them all . . . so that, by this means, they may . . . contribute with all their power that their little congregation might live in the state of sublime perfection.[45]

Once again, the text refers to two authorities acting in concert, not just on the level of persons or of communities, but on the level of the body as a whole. First, the authority of the congregational body (*corps congrégation*), giving all the sisters "the laws and rules necessary for their salvation . . . and perfection" and exhorting them to study them well. This same authority of the congregational body in the main houses accepted these Constitutions as coming from God because it was also "given by their [ecclesiastical] superiors," recognized and approved by the representatives of the church. These two authorities were both "lieutenants of God." They exercised different functions, but in order to contribute together toward a better practice of the new Constitutions, which were considered "highly appropriate for the sanctification of everyone . . . and also very advantageous to the salvation and service of the neighbor."[46]

At the conclusion of this study, we have a better understanding of the role of the superior in the communities of St. Joseph and in relationship to the authorities upon whom she depended. Her task was more one of animation and spiritual formation of the sisters than of the organization of the house. Her first and principal duty was therefore to care for the spiritual development of each sister within the general organization of the entire community. She fulfilled this duty by her example, by praying for her sisters, by seeing that they were formed in the spiritual life, and by encouraging them or correcting them as she thought necessary, with courage and a firm hand, but also with "the holy gentleness and humility of the Gospel." In accepting her office, she had to become "the servant of the servants of Jesus Christ."[47]

Within the community she governed, and according to the constitutions, the superior had the duty and authority to ensure that the sisters fulfilled the commitments they had made and to organize the internal life of the community in her own house or in the houses of her district. She was also responsible for overseeing the apostolic service of neighbor. She received her authority from the congregation as a spiritual entity through her community because she was elected by the sisters, and from the bishop because he confirmed her election or had the power to appoint her. The community had the right to check the power of the superior and even to have her deposed in case of very serious faults or abuse through the admonitrix and recourse to the bishop. Both the superior and her community were subject to the congregation as a whole, which formulated its law in the constitutions. The congregation implemented a degree of standardization within a given diocese through the district superiors under the authority of the bishop. The superior of the community was understood as "God's lieutenant" and the intermediary "established by his sovereign goodness to lead the entire body of the very little Congregation of St. Joseph."[48]

From the juridical perspective, the bishops were the primary superiors of the communities. The bishop, like the sister superior, acted as guarantor of the observance of the constitutions. He held juridical responsibility for this observance, while the superior was responsible for implementing it in daily life. Bishops had full power over both sisters and superiors but only according to the constitutions. For example, the bishops could "when they find it useful or necessary, change the sisters and the superiors from one house to another, even send them outside the diocese when other bishops request them."[49] Yet, even if the bishop authorized the creation of new communities and the establishment of the novitiate, even if he received the vows of the novices and dispensed them, he could not give all the care needed for direction of the communities. The spiritual father filled this role through his advice and authority and close collaboration with the sister superior. She would call on him most frequently because he lived nearer the community and was delegated by the the bishop for this role. The sisters could also turn to him "in all important matters, whether temporal or spiritual."[50]

The civil authority gave no recognition to any powers of the sister superior, whether exercised on her own or under the bishop's authority. For the most part the communities of Sisters of St. Joseph—communities of secular sisters with simple vows and no cloister—had no juridical existence. The congregation as a whole, a spiritual assemblage of communities giving itself its own constitutions, existed even less. It could be seen to exist only by those within it. Because they could not be recognized as a religious community and were seldom given the same status as secular communities, the Sisters of St. Joseph did not enjoy any exemptions. In this, they resembled neither the Visitation nor the Society of Jesus. The Sisters of St. Joseph paid taxes on the goods of the community and the superior exercized no personal legal power. Like any sister or lay person, she could inherit or bequeath in her own name, but she could not undertake any official action in the name of the community, since she had no civil power as superior. This apparent non-existence reminded the superior and the entire congregation of what Father Médaille wrote to Marguerite Burdier, ten years after the foundation: "Our cherished association is to be a body without a body . . . a congregation without a congregation . . . nothing in the world and . . . in the eyes of God that . . . [which he] deigns to make of his Institute."[51]

THREE HISTORICAL EXAMPLES: VIENNE, LYON, AND CRAPONNE

Communities of Sisters of St. Joseph under the ancien régime had great variety: in the number and social status of the sisters, in their location in city or country, in different geographic regions with their specific resources, and in the needs of the people and the charitable and apostolic works that met those needs. Despite this diversity, it is possible to form an idea of how communities functioned by looking at those superiors and communities that have sufficient documentation on pertinent issues. The history of three selected communities illustrates how the constitutions could be lived and interpreted, not only by the sisters themselves, but by the administrators and the ecclesiastical superiors who had authority over them. They are the community of Vienne in Dauphiné, introduced to the city's hospital in 1668; that of Lyon, established at the Maison Forcée des recluses in 1696; and the community of Craponne, founded in the diocese of Le Puy in 1723.

The House of Vienne: Player or Pawn?

The house in Vienne was one of the most important communities of St. Joseph during the ancien régime, in both its sphere of influence and its prestige. It had a complex and turbulent history. The considerable archives of the Hospital of Vienne, which have been partially classified and are kept mainly in Vienne, but also in Grenoble and elsewhere, contain very large files on the conflicts experienced during the eighteenth century among the archbishops of Vienne, the rectors and administrators of the hospital, and the community of Sisters of St. Joseph. The totality of these records is fascinating on many accounts, but this study focuses on those documents that mark turning points in the history of the community or supply important details. A careful reading of the evidence will demonstrate who actually held the power and who was being controlled. It also presents a picture of how the superiors and the community fulfilled their tasks and exercised their authority in connection with or opposition to the archbishops and the administrators, in a life more or less consistent with the Constitutions of the Sisters of St. Joseph.

History of the Vienne Community

The community of the Sisters of St. Joseph in Vienne was established at the request of Archbishop Henry de Villars of Vienne who had appealed to the community of Le Puy to take over the Hôtel-Dieu. Bishop Armand de Béthune of Le Puy sent three sisters. During a deliberation on January 26, 1668, the city of Vienne consented "to the establishment of the Sisters of St. Joseph in the hospital, with the approval of the Lord Archbishop of Vienne."[52] One of these three sisters was Jeanne Burdier, also known as Marguerite Burdier, one of the six founding members of the very first community established in Le Puy in 1650.[53] Under her direction, the Vienne community stabilized and grew. Three years later, in May, 1671, Mother Burdier witnessed the misery of the poor at the hospital in Gap. "With the consent of the bishop of Gap and the administrators" of the hospital, she offered to send three sisters "to care for the poor." The bishop and consuls were "asked to write to the Lord Archbishop of Vienne and beg him to send three of these religious to serve the poor."[54] Bishop de Villars gave his consent. The following September a contract was signed between the consuls of Gap, the hospital administrators, and Mother Jeanne Burdier, by which she promised to send three sisters who would receive food and lodging, with the condition that "each of them will be paid annually the sum of 36 *livres* for their clothing." By the time of Mother Burdier's death in 1700, about ten communities serving in hospitals or houses of refuge existed in several dioceses, either with her direct involvement or through communities which she had helped to establish.

In 1686 some charitable high-ranking women of Vienne organized a *maison de Refuge* for fallen girls and women in a house belonging to the Hôtel-Dieu with the support of the Sisters of St. Joseph.[55] Within two years, in 1688, the hospital required the space occupied by the Refuge, so Mother Burdier purchased another house that she put at the disposal of the hospital administrators to replace the first. With the archbishop's permission, the Refuge was transferred to this new building, now called the Maison de Providence. Having only modest resources, it relied on gifts and alms for food and sustenance. A wealthy benefactor, *Demoiselle* Marie Antony, a native of Lyon, came to the aid of this new work. On April 29, 1693, she gave a "donation and endowment . . . in favor of the Sisters of St. Joseph" to support their work with the poor and sick of the Hôtel-Dieu and with the girls and women of the Refuge, as well as for the poor girls in the *petites écoles*.[56] By solving their financial problems, this donation facilitated the charitable work of the sisters. In the contract of donation, however, there was an item worthy of the sisters' attention: *Demoiselle* Antony reserved the right to present the community with novices of her choice. In fact, a novitiate had been planned in the new house so that the formation of the sisters would not burden the hospital. Someone certainly could have thought twice about this very point, since the archbishop's approval was required for the admission of novices.

Soon the Maison de Providence itself was too small. On behalf of the sisters and the penitent women, the new archbishop of Vienne, Armand de Montmorin, in 1696 purchased a larger building, known as the house of Claveyson. After necessary repairs and renovations, the Refuge was once again transferred, to this new house, in 1698. It then became the Maison de Providence and home to the novitiate. The purchase contract stated that this house would be under the direction of the archbishop and the rectors of the hospital, provided that it be "destined in perpetuity to confine fallen girls and women, under the direction of the Sisters of St. Joseph, who will live there, since it was purchased in the name of both and paid for by the latter."[57] A contract uniting the Refuge in the Maison de Providence with the hospital was recommended in view of unifying its administration with that of the hospital. After examining the proposals, "having considered that there would be nothing more advantageous for both the Hôtel-Dieu and for the said house of Refuge," in its deliberation on July 6, 1698, the *bureau* of directors of the Hôtel-Dieu "declared that it accepted the union of the said two houses . . . agreeing . . . that they appeal to the King to obtain his Letters Patent to affirm the said union."[58]

Oddly enough, there is no record of this deliberation and decision in the "Register of the Religious of St. Joseph of the City of Vienne," where all important documents concerning the life of the community were copied. Nor is there any mention of the decision of May 24, 1706, proposing another means for the sisters to own their goods in common under the name of the Hôtel-Dieu. As a matter of fact, the copyist took care to indicate at the beginning of the register that it "lacked many acts held in the archives of the *bureau* of the Hôtel-Dieu, who had them taken from our hands by violence." Farther on, in the "Alphabetical Table of Contents" under the letter *O*, one reads: "Omitted: the transcription of several items in this register according to the order given at the time . . . or because for several reasons it was uncertain whether they should be transcribed."⁵⁹ Whatever the reasons for this omission, there is clearly tension between the sisters and the administrators, and perhaps even tension among the sisters themselves. Deliberations of the *bureau* entered in the registers of the Hôtel-Dieu confirm that problems existed. On September 2, 1699, the administrators noted

> that the hospital will be obliged to feed and support Sister Marguerite Burdier in the hospital, and in case she wishes to go to another house of her congregation, to provide the sum of 40 *livres* per year, and in the event that the said Sister Margtᵉ Burdier should leave the said congregation, or after her death, the said sum belongs to the Hôtel-Dieu.⁶⁰

At this time Marguerite Burdier was ill. She must have been cared for in the hospital among the poor whom she loved and served, because it was there that she "died at the said Hôtel-Dieu the twelfth of February of the year 1700 after having received the sacraments."⁶¹ One has to ask why she desired to leave the community of Vienne to go to another community of the congregation, and even more, to leave the congregation altogether. A decision of this kind for a woman of her age, of her caliber, who did such work for her congregation, could only have been motivated by the gravest reasons.

Between 1706 and 1714 the registers of deliberations of the *bureau* of directors of the Hôtel-Dieu mention no important event linked to the sisters and the Maison de Providence. On April 29, 1714, however, *Monsieur* Perouse, an administrator, made a "representation . . . concerning the abuses which the said Sisters of St. Joseph are starting to introduce in the hospital and in the Maison de Providence and their ambitioned independence from the *bureau*."⁶² That same year, *Monsieur* de Grandval, the "*curé* of the hospital," wrote a memorandum "in favor of the Sisters of St. Joseph."⁶³ The moderate tone of the memorandum does not conceal that it is a series of reports and complaints addressed to the *bureau* of the Hôtel-Dieu on behalf of the sisters. The document first recalls the circumstances of acquisition of the various buildings by the sisters for the good of the confined women and the establishment of a novitiate. It then lists a number of actions which show negligence on the part of the mayors and administrators in the management of the Hôtel-Dieu and the Providence, leaving this responsibility to the sisters, and sometimes neglecting to hand over sums destined either for the penitent women or the Sisters of St. Joseph. The final pages rreminds them of the request for royal letters patent as confirmation of the union of the Maison de Providence and the Hôtel-Dieu, a request never completed because the city of Vienne had refused its consent for "fear of imposition of a small tax . . . on a portion of the house of Claveyson." Finally, the memorandum closes with a request couched in an impersonal style:

The hospital *bureau* is asked in the name of the Sisters of St. Joseph and those concerned, that it maintain the establishment of the Refuge under the name of Maison de Providence and the novitiate of the Sisters of St. Joseph in the house of Claveyson . . . as agreed upon during deliberations on the union of said house to the hospital, and the aggregation and incorporation of the Sisters of Saint Joseph in the above-mentioned house to the said hospital.

After the display of independence by the Sisters of St. Joseph, the administrators of the hospital may have expressed an intention to close the Maison de Providence. That is not certain, but it is clear that this fear did exist and that tensions were growing between the administrators and the community of sisters.

An anonymous document dated 1723, "Report prepared concerning several verbal deliberations of the *bureau* of the Hôtel-Dieu of the city of Vienne," defends the interests of the members of the *bureau* and blames the Sisters of St. Joseph. It recopies the texts of the main contracts made between the directors and the sisters: "The donation given by the late *Damoiselle* Marie Antony of Lyon . . . the union of the Maison de Providence or of the Refuge with the said Hôtel-Dieu . . . [and] the deliberations made in consequence of [those] of March 10, 1699 and May 24, 1706."[64] Point by point, the text catalogues the rectors' and administrators' grievances against the sisters. From the outset, after only a few items about *Demoiselle* Antony's donation, the document contains ten pages of violent diatribe against the abuses and injustices of which the Sisters of St. Joseph were guilty. At the Hôtel-Dieu they do not care for the sick at night, but leave them to two servant girls. They show negligence in carrying out the doctors' orders. The two sisters in charge of the school teach some girls from the town to read and write, but not the poor ones. They have themselves paid or given presents. The mistresses are changed too frequently, without the directors' knowledge, and they are often novices. Eight sisters are too many for the Hôtel-Dieu to support. As for their way of life, they no longer eat at the head of the table with the community of the poor and sick of the hospital, as in the days of the "director Burdier, their first superior." They give too much hospitality "free of charge, for their friends, relatives . . . and . . . other members of their congregation, even for their directors, at the expense of the said hotel-Dieu." They work, sew, or spin only for themselves. Neither do they go "to the mills to have the wheat ground," nor to the oil press,

sending a costly manservant . . . also not doing the laundry . . . but [having it done] by women from the outside . . . relegating to the women and the girls of the Hôtel-Dieu . . . the care of keeping the children clean, scraping and washing the dishes . . . and sweeping their rooms, something the sisters ought to do themselves.

The sister directors failed to give an account of several sources of fixed income, such as the sale of eggs from a number of chickens raised at the expense of the house, the sale of mulberry leaves for two or three years, the sale of the bran from the grain for their bread, or "of the income from the spinning room for the work in hemp or wool done by the poor for people of the town." The sisters were still

> interfering to receive some revenue from the Hôtel-Dieu . . . against the prohibitions of the Lord Mayors. . . . Among others, the director Guillomon in 1704 . . . the director Dixmieu in 1716 . . . and in 1717 . . . [and] Sister Felix during the time she was director [1700-1704] misappropriated things belonging to the house in favor of the sisters.

In closing the indictment, and to assure that the *bureau* be "informed about other abuses which the said sisters perpetrate in the said Hôtel-Dieu, [it] is begged to question in particular the poor . . . and *Messieurs* the mayors and administrators, past and present."

The complaints that follow refer to the implementation of the decisions of the *bureau* dated July 6, 1696, March 10, 1699, and March 24, 1706, dealing in particular with the independent attitude on the part of the sisters. They did not turn in the accounts to the administrators as required. They accepted and released penitents without authorization. They had the Maison de Providence repaired at their own expense, but without consulting the *bureau*. The sister director, who should have been acting in the name of the *bureau*, appealed to that authority about the ownership and management of the community's belongings only when she was forced to do so. She accepted postulants without informing the *bureau*, approving dowries lower than the 1200 *livres* agreed upon. "This is an attack upon the authority of the *bureau*," which needed to be informed of receptions of the sisters, because it received half of their dowries after their death. Obviously, the distance and antagonism between the sisters of the Maison de Providence and members of the the the *bureau* of the Hôtel-Dieu were becoming greater and greater.

The minutes of the deliberations of the *bureau* of the Hôtel-Dieu of December 5, 1728, reveal an unusual and significant event: "Sister Roman, director of the Providence for several years, left her position last January without giving the *bureau* an inventory of the possessions of the penitent women, and no report whatsoever."[65] The following day, Sister de Soulas, in another declaration to the *bureau*, spoke of the intervention of the vicars-general. They had asked Sister Roman for these papers, a request she could not refuse. Why, and by what right, had the vicars-general interfered in reports which the sisters were supposed to give to the mayor-administrator of the hospital and the Providence? The authority of the vicars-general should have been limited to control of the sisters' temporal goods in their own house, the Providence. By this time, however, the community of Sisters of St. Joseph as such in the Maison de Providence was no longer under the authority of the rectors and administrators of the Hôtel-Dieu. Protected by the Archbishop, Henry Oswald de La Tour d'Auvergne and cousin of the king, the sisters had secretly obtained royal letters patent for their Maison de Providence on December 8, 1727.[66]

Henceforth, that house would serve "to confine fallen girls and women, and as a novitiate and refuge for the sisters hospitallers . . . under the jurisdiction and complete authority of the archbishops of Vienne," with no obligation to report to the *bureau* of the Hôtel-Dieu, at least in regard to the admission of novices and the management of the sisters' belongings. The letters patent of Louis XV contained several other clauses which were more restrictive. For example, the sisters were forbidden "to acquire anything for themselves in the houses to which they were called, where they would only accept enough to live on while serving the poor." Consequently they could not "make new acquisitions in our said city of Vienne . . . neither acquiring new endowments nor expanding." Moreover, they could not become cloistered. They could receive "gifts of furniture" and inheritances, but not "claim any mortmain unless it be of the endowments and place where the oratory is built . . . [and the] house and garden," of the Providence, which were in mortmain "as things consecrated to God and singularly dedicated to the service of the poor." In granting these letters, the king acknowledged that he had "expressly derogated" from the existing edicts, declarations, and other laws in effect. These exceptions were applicable "in this case only" and could not be extended to other communities of Sisters of St. Joseph.

Shortly after, on January 26, 1728, the archbishop of Vienne wrote to "His Excellency, the Vice-Legate of Avignon" on behalf of the sisters of the Maison de Providence: "I recently obtained Letters Patent from the King for a house in Vienne. . . . The only thing needed is the apostolic authority to draw upon it more abundant graces through approval by the head of the Church. This, my Lord, is what your Excellency can obtain for them."[67] The history of the Constitutions printed in Vienne has already shown how, on the same day, *Monsieur* Didier, vicar-general of the archbishop of Vienne, had planned with Mother de Bontoux, superior of the Maison de Providence, to prepare what he called "good rules," in other words, new constitutions. After the first 1694 edition, other constitutions, modified and dated 1693, were printed in Vienne, probably at the time of the request for papal recognition. All of the changes in these new constitutions were directed toward a conventual lifestyle and social prestige, not toward the apostolic availability to neighbor intended by Father Médaille. Indicated by the way the superior and sisters had made use of their authority to neglect some of their obligations, and how the bishop had supported them to increase his own power against that of the administrators, it is clear that the community of Vienne was in the process of changing its vocation.

Succeeding Superiors and Their Use of Authority

Mother Jeanne Burdier (1668-1700): A Balance of Powers. Throughout the long disputes that set the Sisters of St. Joseph against the administrators of the Hôtel-Dieu for most of the eighteenth century, the opposing parties occasionally alluded to a common reference, Mother Jeanne Burdier. Both considered her work a solid foundation and her manner of operating constructive, if not ideal. This history has already demonstrated how she fulfilled her function as superior, but extracts from her own memoirs provide more precise insights. On December 8, 1686, she wrote a "Proposal of the Sisters of St. Joseph presented to His Excellency the Archbishop and to the *Messieurs* the Rectors of the Hospital of Vienne."[68] In the name of the sisters and with them, she asked for a stable foundation for the community through royal letters patent, and with this in view, she explained their particular way of understanding the organization of the house, work, and finances, and the sisters' relationship with both the archbishop and the administrators of the hospital.

One of the first objectives, according to this proposal, was to increase the number of sisters. Originally three sisters had come, and they now numbered four. Given the great increase in the number of poor and sick, "they very humbly ask the rectors . . . to increase their community . . . so that in the future there might be eight sisters." To free the hospital of the expense of this increase, and if "their perpetual establishment" were granted, the sisters offered "capital in the amount of four thousand *livres*" and the revenue that would come from it. They would also contribute "all the money and belongings of the daughters who will take the habit of St. Joseph and who will make profession." They "would also donate all their work and all their care to the service of the poor and the sick," in the hope that, after this divestment, "the *messieurs* the rectors would take care to help them when there was need, as well as the other poor." For themselves, the sisters asked "in addition to food, twenty-five *livres* annually for their clothing" for each one. Regarding the organization of the hospital, the sisters "will be completely under the authority of the *bureau* and of *Monsieur* the Mayor-Administrator, and will be obliged . . . to give them an account of their administration of the temporalities and of the supervision of the poor" whenever they wanted it.

In regard to spiritual governance, "the sisters will only be subject to their sole and legitimate superior . . . who is the His Excellency the Archbishop of Vienne or the person he will designate as his vicar for that." Should the rectors have any remarks or complaints concerning the sisters' management, they did not have the right "to punish or correct them juridically themselves." They must take "their complaints either to the superior of the sisters or to his excellency the archbishop." It was also necessary for the sisters to be able to carry out their spiritual exercises. Since these exercises "can only be done well in places a little apart," the sisters asked the rectors that, "without inconveniencing the quarters of the poor, they might have in the hospital some apartment of their own to perform the exercises of their Rules; on this matter, they will take the advice of the rectors." Likewise, concerning the issue of "admitting daughters to [the reception of] their habit," the rectors "only receive the money or belongings that [the sister] is able to give, but it belongs to the sisters alone to test her vocation, to give her the habit and to have her make profession, if His Excellency the Archbishop gives permission for it." The rectors therefore could not admit women whom the sisters or the archbishop would refuse, nor "dismiss those whom His Excellency the Archbishop and the sisters will have found fit for religious life."

The proposal closes with a statement: "What the sisters ask is entirely to the benefit of the good care of the poor and what concerns their interests." Elsewhere, in other hospitals, rectors "had acted to have patents from the King for their establishment." These rectors could therefore obtain them at Vienne as well. Nevertheless, "the said sisters submit to the examination and judgment which his excellency the archbishop and the *messieurs* the rectors will make concerning their proposals and await their decisions with all the respect they owe them."

The archbishop of Vienne and the rectors of the hospital must not have entirely appreciated the proposals made by the Sisters of St. Joseph. It appears that they hardly heard the sisters' request to obtain royal letters patent for a more stable establishment of the community, although the proposal was reiterated in the act of union in 1698. It is unlikely, too, that they really understood the sisters' desire to have more secluded places available in order to facilitate their prayer. When in 1688 Mother Burdier had bought a house placed at the disposition of the administrators for the girls and women of the Refuge (as indicated rather quickly in her 1690 donation) her intention was really that this house "be destined principally . . . for the dwelling of the said Sisters of St. Joseph, and then for the Refuge for the said abandoned girls and women."[69] She probably realized that the sisters had to provide for themselves the space and time necessary for their spiritual exercises, without detracting from the work with the penitent girls. The contract of 1698 regarding the administration of this Maison de Providence carefully distinguished the administration of the penitent women's goods, which the sisters had to report to the *bureau*, and "the administration of their temporal goods in the said house," which they needed to report "only to his excellency, the archbishop, their superior."

Although Mother Burdier was perfectly deferential toward the various authorities, she remained remarkably free in her own speech and actions. She was responsible to the authority of the administrators for her sisters. She took care that the sisters were not crushed by work and that the poor also received good care. She made generous proposals to the administrator of the hospital for the welfare of the poor. She was prepared to render an account of all financial and material affairs. She firmly refused, however, to have these men meddling in what concerned the spiritual life of the sisters. In a letter to an unknown correspondent dated 1683, Mother Burdier wrote about an attempt to establish a community in Valence:

> We are entirely under the authority of the bishops in spiritual matters, the rectors have nothing to do with that . . . you see from that, that we can in no way follow the example of the one of Lyon that you point out to me, for it is absolutely under the authority of the *messires* [rectors], and we are like nuns outside the cloister.[70]

She pursued an active collaboration with the archbishop and ecclesiastical authorities in matters concerning her own community or the creation of new houses in the diocese of Vienne and beyond. We have seen how she proposed to the bishop and to the consuls at Gap that sisters be sent to care for the poor at the hospital. If they wanted sisters, they should direct their request to the archbishop of Vienne, and she herself would supply the sisters. The houses she helped to propagate in this way were structured around the Vienne community like the districts described in the original texts and repeated more discretely in the 1694 Constitutions.[71]

Obituaries appended to the register of professions illustrate that these houses continued to depend upon the Vienne community.[72] Not only were the novices formed in Vienne sent to different dioceses and houses, but they could later be transferred as needed through the intermediary of the archbishop and the sister superior of Vienne. For example, Françoise Alliaud (Sister Madeleine) took the habit at the hospital in Sisteron and made her novitiate in the hospital at Vienne. After her profession, she was sent to Bourgoin in 1693, then as superior to the Maison des Recluses in Lyon, and finally to the orphanage in Grenoble, where she died.[73] In 1691 the community at the hospital of Gap, where several sisters died in an epidemic among the soldiers, appealed to Mother Burdier to send reinforcements, and she did.[74] Vienne also helped its dependent communities with money, habits, and spiritual reading books, always given in relatively close connection with the archbishop or his representative.[75] It was important for the sisters to distinguish carefully between matters appropriately directed to the ecclesiastical authority and those subject to the hospital administrators. Both Mother Burdier and her successor, Sister Anne Félix, seem to have clearly understood the difference. Sister Félix noted in the journal about her own appointment: "On the first of March 1700, His Excellency the Archbishop appointed me superior of the Sisters of St. Joseph and the members of the *bureau* appointed me director of the said hospital."[76] The archbishop referred to here was no longer Henry de Villars, deceased on December 2, 1693, who had greatly promoted the development of the Sisters of St. Joseph. Shortly before his death, he had approved the Constitutions of the Sisters of St. Joseph that Mother Burdier and other sisters belonging to various houses had enhanced and put in better order, with the aim of fidelity to the vocation of their origins. He then ordered the printing of the constitutions, which was completed in the following year of 1694.

In 1693 the Sisters of St. Joseph had also benefitted from the generosity of a rich benefactor, Marie Antony. Her gift, intended to give the community a solid foundation, was accompanied by a condition. She reserved the right to present "ten women" of her choice to Mother Burdier and to other superiors for admission to the congregation to fulfill the obligations attached to the financial endowment. After *Demoiselle* Antony's death, if these places became vacant, the community would be obliged to give preference to candidates who were "her relatives or in-laws," provided they had a good vocation. This clause was included "by the consent of His Excellency the said Archbishop and the said Lord Mayors, consuls, and administrators of the said Hôtel-Dieu."[77] It does not say that Jeanne Burdier gave her assent, although she signed at the end of the contract. It is not even certain that she was consulted about it. The administrators must have been delighted by such great generosity, and there was the warranty of the archbishop for a good choice of novices . . . In spite of that, the agreement contained an extremely dangerous clause. It is likely no accident that the constitutions revised during that same year are adamant, in a new way, that the superior or mistress of novices not "be prejudiced in favor of any postulant or novice who lacks the necessary qualities." Should that occur, it was important to "warn the spiritual father or the bishop."[78]

The qualms expressed in the constitutions were justified. At the time when the donation was made and in the following years, three nieces of *Demoiselle* Antony were admitted. Two of them, Sisters Marie Françoise and Marie Catherine Caillet, daughters of *Sieur* Louis Caillet, *bourgeois* of Lyon, and Jeanne Anthony, would bring suit against the congregation in 1717 over their aunt's inheritance, which had become the endowment of the Vienne community.[79] Two daughters of *Sieur* François Gesse, consul of Vienne when the community began in 1668, were received in 1694 and 1695.[80] Five daughters of *Sieur* Pierre Hervier, royal notary and *procureur d'offices* in Saint-Paul-en-Jarest, were admitted between 1696 and 1704. In 1705, the community received Françoise, "legitimate daughter of the noble Felix de Blisson and Dame Sibile de Barier."[81] Obviously, and certainly in line with the wishes of *Demoiselle* Antony (†1717), the social level of the sisters in the community was rising.

Even before Marie Antony's involvement as benefactor, women of some social standing had been accepted. In 1689 Sister Marguerite Serve-Ponsonet, with the bishop's approval, had admitted a novice to the house of Grenoble. She was Françoise de Vincent de Rambion, daughter of the noble Pierre de Vincent de Rambion, originally from Meizieu in the Lyon diocese.[82] It appears that Françoise de Vincent contributed in some way to the problems Mother Burdier experienced at the end of her life. A deliberation of the *bureau* of the Hôtel-Dieu of Vienne dated December 7, 1699—therefore after their decision of September 2 the same year to grant financial help to Mother Burdier shortly before her death—mentions a claim by Sisters Françoise de Rambion and Françoise Alliot (or Alliaud) concerning the dowries they had turned over to Mother Burdier.[83] They asked the *bureau* what had become of "the said sums." The *bureau* asked Mother Burdier about the matter and communicated the answer. The roundabout communication indicates mistrust on the part of these sisters, toward either the *bureau* or Mother Burdier. Could it be that Mother Burdier allocated the funds without the *bureau's* consent? The sisters knew well, that according to their constitutions, they had to hand over to the superior all the goods they brought with them. Perhaps they were trying to gain support from the hospital administrators against Mother Burdier, but the administrators trusted her. Was this episode the result of a gap between a younger generation and this old superior who had been in office for more than thirty years? Or was the difference in mentality too great between this generous woman with great organizational skills, but of humble social origin, and the daughters of the bourgeoisie and local nobility? The only certainty is that these problems existed and may have been linked to the changing social level of the sisters at Vienne and the other houses under its authority.

Power Struggles between Community and Administrators (1700-1730). After the death of Mother Burdier in 1700, Sister Anne Félix, her assistant, succeeded her as superior at Vienne. Relations between the administrators of the Hôtel-Dieu and the Sisters of St. Joseph seemed to be good. In 1701, the *bureau* took action to oppose a "significant tax on the daughters at the Providence . . . [and] concluded that they should petition the Council."[84] During this period the first important transaction between the sisters and the *bureau* occurred on May 24, 1706. The sisters had petitioned the *bureau* to have the Maison de Providence as the locus for holding their goods in common. The agreement read as follows:

art. 1 – that the sisters would possess their goods, present and future, would protect their rights under the name of the *bureau* and with its consent, without its ever being in charge of them; art. 2 – that the contract of their reception will be made with the *bureau*, that the dowries will be ascribed under the name of the *bureau* to the profit of the said sisters . . .[85]

who would enjoy the entire revenue during their lifetimes. At their death, half the sisters' dowries would revert to the Hôtel-Dieu, the other half to the sisters at the Providence. The same distribution would be made of all the possessions due the sisters through inheritance, gifts *inter vivos*, or otherwise. Everything was to be shared between the sisters and the poor of the Hôtel-Dieu. The *bureau* accepted these terms, which it considered to the benefit of the poor, and renewed the recommendations made in the act of union of 1698, that the sisters could never "draw from from that any pretext to become cloistered, make new acquisitions or a new establishment in this town without the consent of the *bureau* and of the said city." The signatures follow. The first is that of Armand [de Montmorin], Archbishop of Vienne, then those of all the rectors and administrators, and finally those of the eight sisters, beginning with "Sister Guillomon, superior of the said Hôtel-Dieu," and ending with "Sister Thérèse Pellet, Director of the House of Providence."

Who actually formulated these proposals is uncertain. The sisters definitely wanted to find a way to own their goods in common while augmenting the assets of the poor. Because they had confidence in the administrators, they turned to them to ask their support. The arrangement, good in terms of what it did for the poor, seems very ambiguous about the relationship of dependency it inaugurated between the sisters and the men of the *bureau*. The distinction between the different spheres of administration, very clear in the 1698 contract of union, was becoming blurred. The archbishop signed, seemingly without any questions. The sister director of the Providence had to give him an account of the sisters' belongings, but he had no real say in the matter. Perhaps he did not sense any danger—or even wanted to please the *bureau*. The sister in charge of the Maison de Providence and Sister Guillomon, superior of the community, may have felt that they lacked the competence necessary to manage their own affairs and preferred, on trust, to rely on the competence of the members of the *bureau*. In any case, the entire community signed the document, apparently confirming the superior's signature and their confidence in the administration. The superior may well have needed to feel support in this matter. Following Mother Burdier as head of the community was, in all probability, not easy. It is telling that between 1700 and 1710, three superiors succeeded one another, with the third holding office until 1720.

During these two decades, the names of superiors seldom appear in the decisions of the Bureau of the Hôtel-Dieu. For admissions to profession, the *bureau* recorded requests apparently made by different persons: the archbishop in 1708, for a *demoiselle* from Sisteron; the procurator in 1711; the father of a postulant in 1715; the postulant herself in January, 1719; and sometimes anonymous requests, as in January 1718, for "reception of *demoiselle* Claudine Jaquin."[86] In addition, the source of information given before reception of the habit is never indicated. Only once, on January 10, 1719, did the *bureau* say that it added a novice to the number of sisters in the community "after having the agreement of Sister Dixmieu and Sister Roman," superiors of the Hôtel-Dieu and Maison de Providence. Other records make it plain that at least some of the administrators, wary about giving too much control to the community of sisters, kept decisions in their own hands.

Concern about the sisters' independence emerges clearly in 1714 in the "representation made by *Monsieur* Perouse, administrator, concerning the abuses" of the Sisters of St. Joseph in the hospital and in the Maison de Providence.[87] They took too much initiative on their own authority. For example, *Sieur* Perouse discovered that a postulant had been at the Hôtel-Dieu for several months, paying fifty *livres* annually for board and lodging, without the knowledge of the administrators. He insisted that the sisters should not "decide with the postulants on room and board and the dowries without the permission" of the officials of the Hôtel-Dieu. The *bureau* should judge "the birth, class, qualifications, and moral character of the postulants." At the Providence, the two sisters in charge of the house had "long ambitioned not to acknowledge the authority of the *bureau* . . . they render no account . . . they even invest their savings on their own under different names." *Sieur* Perouse presented all this conscientiously, as he had already done, he said, but the *bureau* did not take his reports into consideration, "as if the *bureau* wished to rely on the sisters of this house for the choice of the women who would succeed them . . . which would be absurd; this would give them fuller privileges . . . this sort of congregation only too often proliferates at the expense of the poor, whatever precautions are taken against their enterprise." In his complaint, Perouse spoke with disdain of "this sort of congregation."

The memorandum of *Monsieur* de Grandval written in the same year, undoubtedly in response to these remarks, although not employing such a haughty tone, is precise and firm regarding the accounts of the Providence, the accounts of of the sisters, and the accounts of the girls and women confined there. From what he says it appears that the sisters no longer needed to rely on the administrators to govern their own affairs. They made good use of the freedom allowed them in managing things. By this time, it was the sisters, under the name of *Monsieur* de Grandval, who could reprimand the administrators for negligence they considered abusive and dishonest. It may have been no coincidence that this debate took place when the episcopal see in Vienne was vacant, between the death of Armand de Montmorin on October 6, 1713, and the appointment of his successor, François de Bertons de Crillon, on December 30, 1714.[88] Bishop de Montmorin's vicar-general, Henry Oswald de la Tour d'Auvergne, who probably was the interim administrator, undoubtedly had something to do with these displays of hostility.[89] Once the new archbishop was installed, conflict returned to its normal level. François de Crillon, an unpretentious man, did not try to compete for power with the administrators of the Hôtel-Dieu.

In 1721, the episcopal see was again vacant. This time Henry Oswald de la Tour d'Auvergne requested, and was granted, permission from the king to leave the see of Tours, where he had been appointed, to take the archdiocese of Vienne. He arrived in Vienne on August 20, 1722.[90] It did not take long after his arrival for hostilities between the Sisters of St. Joseph and the Bureau of the Hôtel-Dieu to flare up again. In 1723, reports carefully compiled by the *bureau* virulently describe their complaints.[91] Notes added later in the margins detail and confirm these grievances. The backdrop for this dispute seems to have been the difference in social rank between the sisters under Mother Burdier and those who formed the community in 1720. Complaints against the sisters in these reports portray a way of life belonging to upper class women:

> sending a costly manservant . . . also not doing the laundry . . . but [having it done] by women from the outside . . . relegating to the women and the girls of the Hôtel-Dieu . . . the care of keeping the children clean, scraping and washing the dishes . . . and sweeping their rooms, something the sisters ought to do themselves.

To do the heavy work and menial tasks, the sisters had "a costly manservant . . . women from outside, . . . [and] girls of the Hôtel-Dieu." As the administrators pointed out, "Were they to perform these tasks, like the *bourgeois* directors," they would free up the manservant "who could do farmwork in one of the house's vineyards." The sisters, moreover, had a way of organizing the profitability of the house that foiled the administrators. They would "sell the eggs from the many chickens they raise at the expense of the house . . . sell mulberry leaves and mulberries from the courtyard" of the Hôtel-Dieu; "[they] sell large quantities of bran" from the flour for their bread; and they "sell drugs and medications." These reproaches were mostly inspired by the fact that the sisters did not give an account about any of it to the mayor-administrator and that they were keeping the profit from these initiatives. The

daily life of the community had changed greatly. The sisters no longer ate
with the poor and sick of the hospital. They "had two separate pots, one for
their soup and the other for the soup of the sick and [hospital] community,
whom they had eating very bad meat." There was a change in the way of educating young girls. The two teaching sisters asked for money "to buy what
they call brooms to clean the school . . . not taking the trouble to teach them
to sew or do any other work . . . they make them buy from them *civilités*, cat-
echisms, paper, and pens, yet the young girls are as ignorant when they finish as when they began." Allowing for differing ideas about work and organization of lifestyle is not enough to absolve the sisters from all guilt and
suspicion.

Accusations by the *bureau* against the superior and the community concerning goods and money diverted to the sisters' profit, although not entirely
true, were not completely lacking in foundation. The sisters needed money to
live at a certain level. Under other circumstances, as we have seen, the same
accusations had been made by the sisters against the administrators. Once dis-
trust has settled in, anything can be cause for complaint. The *bureau's* complaints are too formulaic to be totally credible. The most important and well-
founded grievance, however, was something other than money. It had to do
with the sisters' independence in regard to the *bureau*, a complaint made previously in 1714. The same elements are repeated: the director of the Maison
de Providence admitted or dismissed penitents without permission of the the
Bureau of the Hôtel-Dieu; and the director of the Hotel-Dieu, who was the superior, received postulants into the novitiate without informing the rectors,
who could not claim the fifty percent of the dowries to which they were entitled. They perceived the sister director, by contrast, as readily accountable to
the archbishop. Making note of the sisters' submission to his guidance in spiritual matters, their memoir states, "this point is undoubtedly carried out well."
Concerning the report the superior had to give the archbishop on the sisters'
material goods, it reads: "The said director does not fail to fulfill this provision." In the eyes of the administrators, the sisters had become too dependent
upon the archbishop. The suspected evolution was real.[92] Unfortunately, the
archbishop was an ambitious man who liked wealth and prestige—traits
which corresponded with certain trends in the community of St. Joseph. This
concurrence was significantly dangerous for the house.

From 1720, the superior of the community and director of the Hôtel-Dieu
was Anne-Marie de Bontoux, a native of Sisteron.[93] The registers of decisions
of the Bureau of the Hôtel-Dieu seem to indicate that she had a more stable
relationship with the administrators than her predecessors. During the ten-
year period of her position as superior, her name appears more often in the
register than had theirs. It is often associated with that of Sister Roman, di-

rector of the House of Providence, in rendering accounts, presenting novices, and other transactions.[94] In the deliberations of the Bureau of the Hôtel-Dieu, as in her obituary, she was described as a pleasant woman from Provence: "Her kindly zeal gained her God's Blessings and the protection of the men whose assistance she needed . . . she had a very lively, very happy, and most helpful disposition."[95] In the year of her election as superior, on April 3, 1720, she gave the habit to Sister Marie Magdeleine de Mauteville, thirty-three years of age, who was the great grand-daughter of Françoise Bertaut (or Berthaud), *Dame* Langlois de Mauteville († 1689), a close friend and confidante of Anne of Austria.[96] She was a mature woman, "a war widow from Lyon," who took her vows on July 10, 1722, increasing the number of persons of high social rank in the community.

Until 1728, nothing out of the ordinary seems to have occurred between Mother de Bontoux, the administrators, and the archbishop. In reality, the superior was plotting secretly with the archbishop and his vicars-general to obtain royal letters patent without the knowledge of the administrators, either from a sense of self-sufficiency or from fear of encountering opposition. The obituary no doubt alludes to this collusion with ecclesiastical superiors when it mentions "the protection of the men whose assistance she needed." The House of Providence obtained letters patent on December 8, 1727, thanks to the intervention of the archbishop, and without the knowledge of the administrators and civil leaders. Legally, the latter should have been consulted and given their agreement. These proceedings seem to have provoked divisions within the community of sisters. The vicar-general of Vienne, *Monsieur* Didier, wrote to Mother de Bontoux on January 26, 1728, about "the punishment which some of your sisters of N___ deserve for their endeavor."[97] On February 2, he wrote again:

> You responded like an angel to Sister Roman; let us hope she will do as you say, for it is certain that no superior has the right to repay capital without the order of His Excellency the Archbishop's approval; so let these good sisters address their questions to His Excellency who will answer them.[98]

Sister Roman must have expressed disapproval because, promptly sent to another community, she wrote secretly to the Bureau of the Hôtel-Dieu on June 19, 1728:

I beg you to use this advice without naming me . . . have the *bureau* ask Sister de Soullas, who replaces me, for the accounts that I kept. They contain notes about all that belongs to the house of Providence . . . I tell you that all furniture [and] buildings connected to the house, sacred vessels . . . linen, vineyard . . . everything comes from the penitents' money."[99] The repayment

of capital mentioned by *Monsieur* Didier most likely had to do with the goods
belonging to the penitents in the House of Providence, a situation that Sister
Roman, upon reception of the letters patent, considered it necessary to clarify. The mayor-administrator of the Hôtel-Dieu did not request to see the
books of the Providence until December, 1728. On December 5 and 6 two
meetings of the *bureau* took place at which the administrators were unable to
obtain the accounts kept by Sister Roman from Sister de Soullas, who had apparently turned them over to the vicars-general. On December 13, the *bureau*
decided to ask "*Monsieur* le Vibaly as Deputy of the Court to request . . . that
a house search be allowed in the said Maison de Providence for the inventories and accounts left by the said Sister Roman, even the inventory of titles
and documents concerning the said house." Since the search might not be
completed "in one visit, that permission be granted to affix seals until the said
inventory be finished." If the sisters refused "to turn over the keys to the ar-
moires, cupboards, chests, etc. . . . let us have them opened by locksmiths,
closed and sealed" until the inventory was completed.[100] This process lasted
several years.

During this time, as we know, *Monsieur* Didier attempted to write what he
called "good rules," that is, a transformation of the constitutions in line with
the sisters' desire to change their house into a monastic community. With this
end in mind, the sisters and the vicar-general did not hesitate to modify Bishop
de Maupas' letters patent of March 10, 1651 and to shorten those of Bishop de
Béthune of September 23, 1665, in order to direct the community toward "the
regularity of the cloistered daughters" by suppressing the diversity of apostolic
service.[101] These new constitutions, probably printed in 1728 or the beginning
of 1729 (although dated 1693), prescribed a monastic habit having a "skirt
with a train," a long veil and a "round guimpe."[102] The chapter "On the
Agrégées" disappeared from the constitutions, as it no longer had any purpose.
Several paragraphs on the rules for the superior were deleted, among others:

> She shall remember that the office of superior, instead of elevating her, should
> rather lower her and make her in reality the servant of the servants of Jesus
> Christ and that therefore she should always respect her sisters and always pre-
> fer their contentment to her own insofar as good order permits.[103]

Rather than humble service, the revised constitutions emphasize the sisters'
recognition as true religious, enjoying the prestige associated with this status.
Despite all these efforts, there is no evidence that the sisters received papal
approval. If they had, such a document would appear prominently in the Register of the Religious of Saint-Joseph where the titles, legal deeds, and other
important documents of the history of the community are collected. The only
documents it contains from Rome are indulgences.

Mother de Bontoux and her successor, Mother de Mauteville, were satisfied. Now they could speak of the monastery of the *religieuses* (nuns) of St. Joseph of Vienne.[104] What distance between their undertaking and that of Mother Burdier in 1686! For Jeanne Burdier, royal letters patent were only a means to ensure a better legal and financial basis for the community of sisters. Free from cares, the sisters would be able to put all their goods and all their strength at the service of the poor. Her only objective was "to benefit the good care of the poor . . . and what concerns their interests." She addressed her request clearly to both "His Excellency the archbishop and to the *Messieurs* the rectors," without any intention to pit one against the other to her benefit, and she was willing to accept "the examination and judgment . . . [which they] would make about their [the sisters'] proposals." She took no indirect means to obtain what she wanted because she was seeking the good of all, while preserving the sisters' fidelity to their vocation. When met with opposition, she suggested or took other means but remained loyal. It is difficult to say if Mother de Bontoux knew what she wanted. Apart from her dealings with the *bureau*, there are no records of specific acts that reveal who she is. She might have had a pleasant personality, but needed "assistance," as stated in her obituary, being open to manipulation by internal forces from her community and external forces from the archbishop.

The successive shifts within the community, seen as a whole, tend toward arrogant independence and self-sufficiency in opposition to the administrators of the Hôtel-Dieu. These attitudes played into the interests of Archbishop Henry Oswald de la Tour, "Prince d'Auvergne," because, thanks to the sisters, his authority came to dominate. He did not understand the vocation of the Sisters of St. Joseph any more than his vicar-general, *Monsieur* Didier. The sisters did not know how radical their vocation actually was. They desired another, apparently considering their apostolic works an inferior aspect of their vocation. They imparted this attitude to the archbishop, who believed "that they are inclined not only toward the activities of Martha, but also those of Mary," as if they should not learn to live both at the same time and in all things.[105] Under pretext of spiritual ascent, all those involved sought more or less to satisfy their own ambitions under cover of pious discourse. *Monsieur* Didier, all the while working against the interests of the Hôtel-Dieu and the city consuls, spoke a spiritual language to the sisters to absolve and even legitimize this anarchy. Writing to Mother Bontoux about the letters patent, he said:

> I believe that you should lose no time in getting them registered, and do not worry too much about contradictions you may find there; Herod is trying to kill the Infant Jesus; as a true daughter of St. Joseph, save him from this persecution, but according to his example, in silence and patience.[106]

Here the sister superior is falsely transformed into a savior, almost a martyr. The ecclesiastical authorities certainly had a hand in the sisters' misunderstanding of their own vocation. Nevertheless, there were other houses of Sisters of St. Joseph attached to Vienne, either in the Vienne diocese, such as that of St. Vallier, or in others, like those of Lyon and Clermont, that took a completely different path. The community of Vienne, therefore, had already changed direction on its own and had departed from the path of the "Daughters of the Little Design."

After 1730: The "Monastery of the Religious of Saint Joseph of Vienne." The letters patent in favor of the Providence were registered with the Parlement of Dauphiné on March 13, 1728. A notation made in 1780 or after stated, "The sisters never told the *bureau* about their letters patent or their registration."[107] Disputes continued between the sisters and the Hôtel-Dieu. The sisters may have been somewhat troubled about the validity of their own proceedings, because in 1728 they felt the need to seek approval of the bishops in dioceses where the house of Vienne had established other communities. The register relating the important acts of the community contains approbations from the bishops of Gap, Clermont, Sisteron, and Grenoble, as well as those of the archbishops of Vienne and a few vicars-general. There is, however, no approbation from the archbishop of Lyon, merely from his vicar-general.

In 1730, Mother de Mauteville, the noblewoman admitted in 1720, succeeded Mother de Bontoux as superior. She remained in office until 1758. Under her governance, which was very influential, the community continued to strengthen its monastic orientation. Even before obtaining the letters patent, the Vienne community ceased establishing new communities within and outside the diocese. Little by little, it seems that bishops cut the ties between their local communities and the archbishop and community of Vienne. This was the case for the community of the Maison des Recluses of Lyon, which separated in 1729. At the same time, the community at the Refuge in Clermont became autonomous, and the community of the hospital in Saint-Vallier followed suit in 1743.[108] Attempts at reconciliation on the part of the sisters with the *bureau* of the Hôtel-Dieu bore little fruit. In 1753, the *bureau* noted the rebellious attitudes of several sisters.[109] On July 13, 1755, there was a meeting at the Hôtel-Dieu of Vienne:

> The *bureau*, having invited the superior of the sisters [Mother de Mauteville] . . . to explain [a long list of complaints] . . . and having again asked her if she consented to the implementation of the contracts of 1698 and 1706 and to the sharing of dowries and other items of these acts, she replied said she could not uphold them.[110]

Upon hearing her response, the *bureau* "begged and enabled *Sieur* Guiet, the mayor and administrator . . . to recruit and accept in the hospital secular women of good morals and good family . . . and deputized *Sieur* Guiet to thank the sisters for their service and tell them of the *bureau's* decision." The sisters left the Hôtel-Dieu and joined those who lived in the House of Providence.

On July 9, 1759, the letters patent were registered at the Chambre des Comptes. At the end of a manuscript copy of these letters, one reads:

> These said letters were ratified at the Parlement without the Hôtel-Dieu or the city having been heard. And the sisters presented a petition to the Chambre des Comptes in order to have them ratified . . . [but] the Chambre . . . did not want to ratify them because the city had not been heard.

It says that petition had not been presented to the Hôtel Dieu "in order to avoid opposition to ratifying the said letters." In the margin, there is a note in the same hand next to the paragraph prohibiting the sisters' enclosure: "Enclosure—in both the said Hôtel-Dieu and in the said Maison de Refuge, no longer going with the poor to the burials of the city's notables, nor taking part in the procession of the poor . . . during Lent."[111] The superiors who came after Mother de Mauteville accentuated monastic prescriptions even more. On May 10, 1777, they obtained from *Monsieur* Bertolet, vicar-general of Archbishop de Pompignan of Vienne, "permission to construct and arrange a parlor, grille, and a turn in the vestibule of the house."[112] The Sisters of St. Joseph were definitively cloistered in their Maison de Providence in Vienne. No other community of St. Joseph followed their example, however, and the Vienne house did not survive the French Revolution. In the end, having attempted to defend themselves against the administrators and having turned to the archbishop to guarantee their own power, the Sisters of the Vienne community became slaves to it and enclosed themselves within it.

The Houses of Lyon and Craponne: To Command or to Serve?

None of the communities of St. Joseph under the ancien régime, with the exception of Vienne, could be described as "powerful." Even when communities provided services that came with a certain authority and legal status, such as the Maisons de Refuge (in Avignon, 1707; Clermont, 1723) or certain hospitals (Langogne, 1663; Saint-Vallier, 1683), it seems there was no long-term scheming to establish their own power. Disputes did occur now and then with administrators, or between a superior and sisters, in relation to their respective responsibilities and authority. The way of assuming these duties and powers could be very different from one community to another. Ecclesiastical and civil authorities also exercised their authority and responsibility in different ways. For the sisters, it was important that their choices and ways of acting were consistent with their constitutions. Two communities, among many others, appear exemplary in living out this fidelity, as did Mother Burdier: the Maison des Recluses in Lyon and the community of Craponne, near Le Puy.

The Maison Des Recluses of Lyon: Abusive Authority of the Administrators

Located within the confines of the Maison des Filles Pénitentes, where the Sisters of the Visitation worked, the Maison Forcée des Recluses of Lyon had been been sustained and encouraged since 1686 by a Company of Ladies of the Blessed Sacrament.[113] Members of the Company of Gentlemen in Lyon were among the administrators of the house.[114] In 1694 they contacted Mother Burdier, superior of the house in Vienne, and requested several sisters to staff the Maison des Recluses.[115]

Mother Burdier, having given it consideration, accepted. Before the arrival of the sisters at Lyon, she wrote to the administrators on November 6, 1696, to outline the mutual authority and responsibilities of bishops, sisters, and administrators in establishing the new community.[116] Following the customary greetings, the superior of Vienne described in rather quaint language how the bishops proceeded:

> It has to be understood that our Congregation of St. Joseph is not a monarchy where one can gather a general assembly as at the sound of the bell, and have one person act for the whole congregation, in so far as each house is independent of the others and the said houses are subject to the bishop of the diocese where they are located. If bishops want to establish them in their diocese[s], they approach bishops who have the said Sisters of St. Joseph established in theirs and ask them for subjects who are suitable for the work they want them to do . . . and then the bishop who has been asked contacts the superior and asks her if she has some subjects suitable for the work they are wanted to do. And, the superior responding to the bishop that she has them, he gives them obedience and sends them to the one who asked for them, on this condition, that the bishop who asked for them will procure them a solid and permanent foundation and that he will be responsible for all [of them] for their entire life, both in sickness and health.

This passage merely explains and clarifies the text of the 1694 Constitutions relative to the power of the bishops to move superiors and sisters from one diocese to another.[117] Farther into the letter Mother Burdier clarified the authority and responsibilities of the sisters who are sent, as well as the responsibility of the administrators toward them:

The rectors of the hospitals and directors of houses of penitent women and others should contract with the sisters who have been sent to them, with the authority, however, of the archbishop or bishop of the said place. It is true, however, and has always been done in this way, that the bishop who sends them gives power and authority to the said sisters to make a contract, as well as to him who directs them, or to any other person whom he thinks appropriate to help with the contract and sign it on his behalf, so that things be done correctly, since the sisters he sends are still presumed to be under his jurisdiction. . . . Furthermore, it would not be right or even charitable for a sister who has worked in a house throughout her youth . . . to be put out on the street when she becomes old or sickly, or sent to another house which has no less need for work and service than the one from which she comes, since it is true that those who reap the benefits should also bear the burdens.

She also outlined the procedure for making the contract between the sisters and the rectors. It should be done

in conformity with what has been promised . . . or with the act which the sisters, whom His Excellency the Archbishop of Vienne sent recently to His Excellency the Bishop of Sisteron, . . . made with the rectors of the said hospital by the authority of the said bishop of Sisteron. According to the articles of the said act or of the summary, the sisters will be under the said Lord Bishop for all spiritual matters, who will give them a confessor and director whom he thinks suitable. Regarding temporal goods, they will answer to the messieurs the rectors and will be obliged to render an account for said temporal goods when they are asked for it.

Mother Burdier concluded her letter by asking that they kindly "advise us if your *messieurs* of the *bureau* are willing to make the contract in this way." If they did not accept, it would be necessary to "bring the sisters back after they have received the blessing of the said Lord Archbishop of Lyon."

It is no surprise that this letter follows very closely the directions for contracts with the administrators of hospitals in the 1694 Constitutions printed at Vienne, because Mother Jeanne Burdier had unquestionably taken part in their preparation. Because she had contributed thoroughly to the development of the congregation in the neighboring dioceses, she was very well acquainted with the concrete realities and the legal terms and conditions involved in establishing new communities.

In Lyon the administrators agreed to the terms of the contract and the sisters did not return to Vienne. Françoise de Rambion and Françoise Aillaud signed the contract drawn up according to the following conditions:

That in spiritual matters they will submit to the will of the said Lord Archbishop and that of his successors . . . as for temporal belongings, they will be under the authority of the said *Sieurs* directors . . . the said sisters may not receive or dispose of the said temporal belongings without the consent of the said directors. [There were to be three sisters] of an age, health and ability . . . for the said management, and among them there will always be one capable, suitable, and experienced in supervising the manual work that must done there.[118]

When the sisters can no longer carry out their work because of "old age or illness," they will be "provided for by the said *Sieurs* directors of the confined women [according to their] charity and prudence." In their turn, the sisters would rely on the directors "with all the confidence that daughters receive from and should have toward good fathers." The directors were to provide "food, housing, and medicine for the three sisters." They would also engage "a servant for the upkeep of the said house and they will pay her wages and food." This agreement was signed on December 22, 1696, in Lyon. Between the lines one can see that the sisters trusted the directors and demanded little in return for their work, just enough for their living and health.

In 1729, the administrators of the Maison des Recluses and the archbishop introduced a major change in the status of the sisters living there. On June 2 of that year, the four sisters of St. Joseph employed at the Maison des Recluses concluded an agreement with the administrators with the archbishop's approval.[119] The administrators acknowledged the "important services rendered in this house" by Suzanne Gesse, Antoinette de Marcou, Antoinette Jomard, and Jeanne Évrard of the Congregation of St. Joseph, "through the piety and the good management demonstrated in their administration." For one, this was twenty-two years, for another, twenty-one, and fourteen and thirteen years respectively for the others. From then on, these sisters "of the Community of St. Joseph established in the city of Vienne" would be completely cared for, even in illness, old age, and death, by the administration of the Maison des Recluses of Lyon. They would continue to be subject to the archbishop in spiritual matters, and after their death they would be "buried in the choir of the shared church" of the Recluses and Penitents.[120] This act was ratified the next day, June 3, 1729, by François Paul de Neuville de Villeroy, archbishop of Lyon. The sisters of the Maison Forcée des Recluses ceased effectively to belong to the house of Vienne. On July 1, the archbishop approved the establishment of the Sisters of St. Joseph in both the Maison des Recluses and the entire diocese of Lyon. He authorized the opening of a novitiate for admission to profession for those who desired it, whether for the service of the house or for hospitals and other establishments in the diocese.[121] He also emphasized that the sisters should follow "the statutes and *règlements* given to them by

His Excellency, Henry de Maupas, Bishop of Le Puy, and confirmed by His Excellency, Henry [actually Armand] de Béthune, his successor, according to the letters of approval of September, 23, 1665, printed in the city of Vienne in 1694 under the title Constitutions for the Little Congregation of the Sisters of St. Joseph," which he, too, had approved and confirmed. Henceforth the community of sisters at the Maison des Recluses had no further ties with the community of Vienne and belonged solely to the archdiocese of Lyon.

The new status of the community at the Maison des Recluses was closely connected with the events that took place between 1727 and 1728 in the Vienne community. The four sisters in Lyon very probably did not approve of the transformation of the Maison de Providence at Vienne into a monastery, the secret petition for royal letters patent, and particularly the sisters' arrogant opposition to the *bureau*. Although satisfied with the staff of sisters in Lyon, the administrators of the Maison des Recluses may have feared that the outlook prevailing in the house of Vienne might slip little by little into their institution. The archbishop was plainly aware of the falsification of the constitutions antedated 1693, because in the constitutions he approved for printing in Lyon in 1730, he cited the precise date of the letters of approval and the exact title of the first printed Constitutions.[122] There seems to have been a sort of conspiracy between these different partners so that under the authority of the archbishop and protected by the rectors, the community of the Maison des Recluses was set up as the opposite of that in Vienne. The rectors may have wanted to suggest as much in their address to the archbishop, placed at the beginning of the constitutions (identical to those of 1694) that they had printed in 1730. The sisters, they said, "owe to you a regeneration through the novitiate that you . . . granted their institution." The rectors later summarized the vocation of St. Joseph as "love for God, love for the neighbor, detachment from all self love."[123] The latter point apparently received little honor at this time in the community of Vienne.

Throughout the establishment and authorization of the community at the Maison des Recluses, it is the rectors who speak. The sisters are not much in evidence. It is impossible to tell what their authority is. They are looked after because of their invaluable services, but they do not make the decisions. At least in appearance, they have no say. Their power lay entirely in their service. And so, in the general euphoria surrounding the important things that had just taken place, a clause in the royal letters patent of 1710, recalling that "the said Maison des Recluses cannot be staffed by any regular community," seemed forgotten. In fact, this clause did not apply to the Sisters of St. Joseph, because they were not a "regular" community—that is to say, they were not nuns.[124]

The community operated differently in its new status. How it admitted candidates to the novitiate is particularly significant, and eighteenth-century registers record it was the *bureau* that

> determines what it requires for the dowry of each sister, and agrees with her or her relatives, in regard to assets, those things to be given to her by contract which they judge reasonable; no one can be admitted into the house for the first trial of three months, nor to the reception of the habit, nor to profession except as a result of a deliberation by the *bureau*.[125]

This degree of dependence on the administrators for an issue as important as the admission of new members into the community seems to have been rather rare among Sisters of St. Joseph. It was possibly an administrative formality after the community itself had decided upon the admission, but no evidence affirms that. On the following page, the administrators expressed their satisfaction regarding the sisters' management, declaring themselves "always extremely satisfied with the piety, zeal, and good management of the sisters whose selection and support are the most important object of their concern."[126] The following lines appear to confirm the bureau's authoritarian power over the community of the Maison des Recluses. The register reports the "single point that has caused them anxiety":

> These sisters have their own constitutions, and it is to be feared that they claim, by way of observance, to conform to them in everything, constituting a separate religious community in the house, without sufficient subordination to the bureau and to the overall purpose of the work.
>
> It was to prevent such a disorder that, in the first contracts of 1696, it was said expressly, "*It is understood that the sisters may never establish in the Maison des Recluses a separate community for themselves.*"[127]
>
> A dangerous claim erupted in this regard in 1753 concerning the selection of the superior. Upon the death of Sister Gesse, they thought that their constitutions authorized them to choose their superior themselves and consequently to depose her at the end of her three years, or to maintain her as they please. They even tried to inform His Excellency, Cardinal de Tencin, the archbishop, of this provision. Happily, they were wrong and their constitutions leave this authority entirely to the ordinary. The administrators who were aware of the importance of this point wrote memoranda apprising His Excellency the Archbishop, and in the end obtained from him the appointment of the superior whom they would present to him.[128]

The "Cartulary of the Legal Documents of the Community" contains the minutes of the entire deliberation.[129] The cardinal archbishop must have known the *Constitutions of the Sisters of St. Joseph*, especially this proverbial

Chapter 12, which allowed the sisters to elect their superior, since it took "a discussion of more than an hour" for the administrators to convince the cardinal to recognize the "legitimacy of their right." Finally, at the suggestion of the administrators, the cardinal sent an order to the *bureau* to name Sister Antoinette de Marcoux superior of the Maison des Recluses. At the next meeting of the *bureau*, the administrators "had the said Sister de Marcoux appear, to whom they read her appointment as superior . . . and gave her a copy . . . of the said ordinance." The *bureau* had her installed as superior to "the general applause of the entire house, and of all the women and girls confined there, and they began to sing the *Te Deum* and *Laudate* without even waiting until the sisters of the house had been assembled to go to sing it in the choir of the church."

The minutes of the deliberation conclude with an appeal to Chapter 11 of the constitutions, which states, virtually in opposition to Chapter 12, that "the bishop will always appoint the superiors of our small houses" of fewer than six sisters, but that he "can also, on his own authority, appoint the superiors . . . for communities with many sisters." That being so, the sisters had no reason for complaint about how the appointment of their superior took place—it had been done according to their constitutions! The outcome of this affair in its entirety breathes a lack of good faith. The dichotomy between the powers of the bishop and the community described in the 1694 Constitutions, where both were likely to get involved at different levels in the appointment of the superior, could, admittedly, support this hypocrisy in practice. The rectors and administrators of the Maison des Recluses may have been threatened by the community's evolution toward greater autonomy and internal coherence. In 1753 the Vienne community, from which the sisters at the Maison des Recluse had come, was in strong opposition to its own administrators, imperiously asserting its autonomy in face of every civil authority. The rectors of the Maison des Recluses at Lyon surely wanted to protect themselves from a similar situation. As a result, they blocked all means of access for the sisters to what they considered too much liberty. Their action was in truth a real abuse of power.

There is no record of the how the sisters of the Maison des Recluses reacted in the face of this injustice. At the end of the century, even the revolutionaries praised them. In the satiric "Gold-Plated Legend, or Supplement to the Martyrology of Lyon," the author ridicules the Maison des Pénitentes and the Visitation Sisters who worked there.[130] Yet, in his eyes, the Maison des Recluses was almost perfect, very useful for the needs of the city. He has nothing to say about the Sisters of St. Joseph—in itself a compliment. Another document, "Report for the Maison des Recluses in Lyon," whose content appears to be contemporary with the previous, gives high praise to the

Maison des Recluses, its organization, and the way the girls and women were treated, enabling them to learn useful skills.[131] Even if this eulogy was directed to the administrators without mentioning the sisters, it was they who were responsible for giving the house its humane character and for helping the fallen women to reclaim their personal dignity.

A Model Superior: Mother Charlotte de Vinols, Craponne (1747-1771)

The community of Sisters of St. Joseph at Craponne in the Le Puy Diocese was established officially on May 22, 1723, by the act of association concluded between Jeanne-Marie Porrat Delolme and Louise Dupoux.[132] Both women wished to "live in celibacy . . . to consecrate themselves to God in rules and in holy endeavor, feeling a strong inclination to dedicate themselves to the instruction of the youth of their sex." They made their novitiate with the Sisters of St. Joseph of Le Puy, and after their profession on July 3, 1724, with the consent of the bishop of Le Puy settled in Craponne, where they lived in a house donated by the *curé*, Messire Capraix de Vinols. The following year, on April 18, 1725, Charlotte de Vinols was admitted to the novitiate. She made profession on December 4, 1727, at the age of twenty-five, taking the name of Sister Saint-Charles. When she died in 1775, she was venerated as a saint. In the year she died, Abbé Clavel, probably a vicar of Craponne, began her biography.[133] His admiration for her was such that his work could only be hagiography. He was obviously familiar with the chapter from the *Constitutions of the Sisters of St. Joseph* on the rules for the superior, as he followed its outline to demonstrate how Mother de Vinols realized that ideal. His manuscript is the principal source for understanding how the superior of a little community in a small town used the authority of her position for the good of her sisters and all those around her.

In 1731, Sister Saint-Charles was named mistress of novices and assistant to the superior at Craponne. The first of these duties gave her a spiritual responsibility; the second, responsibility for the overall organization and material goods of the house. "She gave preferential care to the sick; she consoled them and helped them draw benefit from their suffering." As assistant, she shared with the superior the burden of purchasing a new house when the first became too small. The motivation for this move was that a "more spacious lodging would welcome more students to instruct, the retreats could be more numerous . . . and people would draw more benefit from the community." They purchased the new house on January 24, 1733.[134]

On April 27, 1747, Sister Saint-Charles was unanimously elected superior. Clavel tells us that her first concern was to practice herself what she would have to ask of others. She often read the constitutions for a better understanding of the vocation of the Sisters of St. Joseph, knowing that she was "truly responsible for guiding the entire community." She respected the personal journey of each sister and never imposed on them something that suited her. For example, "she regretted seeing what was wasted. She would have wished that certain sisters save many things to help the poor. But, as superior, she did not make this an obligation . . . she contented herself with asking wealthy persons to come to the aid of the impoverished."[135] In community gatherings, "she listened humbly to each one about what she had to suggest. . . . The sisters left edified, touched, convinced that Mother de Vinols was making the wisest decisions for the good of the community, and especially for the spiritual progress of the sisters."[136]

At the end of her first three-year term, Sister Saint-Charles asked insistently to be relieved of her duties because of her faults during the time she was superior and her inability to carry out this role. Despite her fears, she placed herself entirely at the service of God's will.[137] At the end of her second term, she again pleaded in vain with her sisters and ecclesiastical superiors to be relieved of this burden. She continued as superior for almost twenty-five years, until 1771. During her second term she carried out a project that had been close to her heart for a long time: the sisters' chapel was small and very poor; they needed to build a church beside the house. When she first suggested this idea to the sisters, the treasurer ridiculed it as impossible because the community had no money. A second time, Mother de Vinols spoke with such assurance, resting solely on her confidence in Providence, that her opinion carried the day. Providence did not disappoint her. With some loans and gifts, the community soon had a new church.[138]

One of Mother de Vinols' principal apostolic activities was giving eight-day retreats, something she had started shortly after her profession.[139] As superior she continued to give yearly retreats to her sisters. The retreat began on the Feast of the Ascension, as stipulated in the constitutions. Mother Saint-Charles was often ill prior to the beginning of a retreat, but her good health returned as soon as she began. In her desire to lead them to the highest perfection, she preached to the sisters renunciation of self and of all things that encumbered their hearts. She also gave retreats to young women and spoke to them about the need, from time to time, to reflect on their interior life, on Christian virtues, and the particular dangers of youth. She got them to make a general confession. Many people came to hear her, including priests, when she gave her conferences in public. She would ordinarily climb into the pulpit in order to be heard by a crowd that was often so numerous that the church could hardly contain everyone. At these times, the ecclesiastical authorities attested publicly to their esteem for her, allowing her to have Benediction of the Blessed Sacrament in the sisters' church every day. Usually this special favor was granted only when a priest gave the retreat, never to the superior of a small community.

Mother de Vinols did not confine her her zeal to Craponne. Several country houses of the congregation, where the *agrégées* sisters were unable to
make fruitful retreats without someone to direct them, asked her to come and
help them. It caused her pain that anyone would think her capable of doing
so, but she responded to the requests, with permission from her ecclesiastical
superior, in the hope that these sisters would draw some good from it. In this
way, the communities of Saint-Just, Beaune, Saint-Hilaire-de-Rosier,
Beauzac, Saint-Maurice-de-Roche, Saint-Julien-d'Ance, and several other
houses of the congregation benefited more than once from her zeal.[140]

Mother de Vinols was attentive not only to the spiritual needs of the sisters,
but also to their corporal necessities and to all the wants of the poor. To respond to the latter, she tried to cultivate the charitable works done by her
community. In order to put them on a more stable basis, the inhabitants of
Craponne petitioned Louis XV in 1776 for letters patent on behalf of the Sisters of St. Joseph:

> [The] demoiselles, daughters associated under the name of St. Joseph . . . are
> wholly devoted to the public good . . . [they] instruct and educate nearly all the
> youth of this community [Craponne] and of the surrounding places. Committed
> voluntarily by their vocation to visit the sick and the hospitals, they never cease
> to perform this human and Christian charity . . . and [they] secure resources for
> the material relief of others, abandoned and disgraced in their destitution. . . .
> They make it a duty to shelter in their house many poor orphan girls whom they
> raise and care for in health and in sickness . . . finally, it cannot be concealed
> that the establishment of these *demoiselles* forms a veritable workshop of lace;
> they continually supervise about two hundred fifty girls, and often more than
> three hundred, of every age and every condition, taking pains to enable them to
> work. It is they who train and teach the young girls in this work, who are thereby
> in a position to help support their families, and when they finish there, they have
> better prospects for marriage. And without the help of lace, what would become
> of this region?[141]

It was actually in the best interests of the people of Craponne "that the establishment of the said *demoiselles,* associated daughters, endure and be secured
in a solid and stable manner." To avoid its distruction by "a mischief-making
mind . . . [a] danger which would be the total ruin of this region" the authors
begged the "Lord Bishop and *Monsieur* the Viscount de Polignac" to take an
interest in their request and to intercede with the king, "their beloved Louis
XV." Even if this letter embellishes the sisters' contribution for the purpose at
hand and exaggerates the dangers of their disappearance, it is clear that the
sisters had a great influence on the education of the women and the life in the
region. The extent of the service done had its importance, but for Mother de
Vinols, the manner of giving it was at least as important as the service itself.

When she could, she did these works herself. She had a preference for the *pauvres honteux,* giving them all the help possible, and consoling them when she could not relieve them materially. It was especially painful for her to see afflicted people whom she could not help.[142]

Several times Mother Saint-Charles was called upon to step in to bring peace where persons or communities were divided. On one occasion she was called upon by a community of the congregation (the name is not indicated) which had just elected a young superior who was not accepted by several members of the community. They refused to recognize and obey her. This resistance resulted in an improbable scenario involving three distinct parties. The local priest had tried to resolve the conflict in vain. Then the bishop had sent a delegate, Abbé Delolme, priest of Retournac and dean, to try to calm things down, but he had no success. He suggested to everyone that they submit the conflict to Mother de Vinols. The sisters agreed and promised to follow her judgment. Mother de Vinols came, not without praying ahead of time. She began by listening to each sister individually in order to understand the different points of view. Mother de Vinols also heard the new superior, rightfully elected, and asked her to submit her resignation voluntarily. She did so very willingly. Then Mother de Vinols had the community undertake a new election in the presence of the pastor and the young ex-superior. She allowed the sisters complete freedom of choice. She only exhorted them to ask for and to follow the guidance of the Holy Spirit, letting go of their prejudices. The sisters agreed to enter into these dispositions, something unbelievable a short time before. The election took place. The same sister was elected superior by the unanimous consent of all the sisters. The first sister to vote for her was the very one who had most opposed her. Peace was restored to the community. Shortly before her death, Mother de Vinols was again engaged in a reconciliation, this time between a father and son, each driven by murderous rage toward the other. Although it involved great suffering, she succeeded in helping them to conquer their hatred and to allow room for love and forgiveness.[143]

On June 6, 1771, Mother de Vinols was finally released from her duties as superior at her own request. She was named mistress of novices. "She herself became a novice once more," her biographer writes.[144] Precisely what he meant by this expression is difficult to determine. After twenty-four years in a position of authority, Sister Saint-Charles very likely felt the need for a kind of re-apprenticeship, like a novice, in order to find a different place within the community. At this time she seems to have suffered from scruples, especially about asking "permissions." It is hard to say whether that was to some extent a way of controlling the new superior, or if it was simply the author, sometimes tainted with Jansenism, who emphasized this characteristic. Becoming a novice again can also echo the words of the Gospel: "Unless you become like little children, you shall not enter the Kingdom of Heaven" (Mt 18:3). Charlotte de Vinols was actually very close to her own entry into the Kingdom. On January 13, 1775, she died (in the language of the times) in the odor of sanctity.

LIFE IN COMMUNITIES AND THE CONSTITUTIONS: MUTUAL CLARIFICATION

The events conveyed in the history of the three houses of Vienne, Lyon, and Craponne illustrate diversity in the exercise of authority, whether the situation involved successive superiors within one house, as at Vienne, the entire life of a community, as at Lyon, or the example of one woman as superior over a long period of time, like Craponne. In every type of house, different authorities sometimes joined forces and sometimes opposed one another. These include external authorities: those of bishops, pastors, administrators of hospitals, or notables of the parish, and internal authorities described in the constitutions: the superior, the community itself, and the spiritual reality of the congregation as a whole. The history of the three communities considered also illustrates different approaches to living out the constitutions. The interpretive challenge in these stories is to read the degree of coherence evident between the theoretical principles and the lived reality and to identify the main emphases that were retained and valued. Having seen the different authorities to which the superiors and the communities were subject, we examine first how and from whom superiors actually received their authority and what real freedom they commanded; then, how they used their authority within the community and in the surrounding world; and finally, how the congregation as a whole supported and regulated the exercise of power on the part of the superior.

The Appointment of the Superior

The ambiguity in the 1694 Constitutions regarding both the method of appointing or electing a superior and the authority who granted this power caused tension in certain communities, especially those in hospitals. The source of tension in these communites was the alternate authority exercised over the sisters by the administrators. The textual ambiguity concerns the designation of superior by the authority of the bishop or that of the community. As explained above, the bishop could "on his own authority appoint the superiors . . . or indeed he may have them elected by the chapter of the sisters."[145] The text leaves no ambiguity, however, about the administrators' lack of authority, either for the appointment of the superior or for any issue dealing with the spiritual guidance of the community.

Marguerite Burdier had recognized the threat of ambiguous authority in Vienne. To avoid it, she framed several proposals, making perfectly explicit the different authorities and to whom they belong. In their work at the hospital, the sisters were completely under the authoirty "of the *bureau* and of *Monsieur* the mayor-administrator," and they had to "give them an account of their administration of the temporalities" whenever they were asked. On the spiritual level the sisters had only one "sole and legitimate superior . . . who is His Excellency the Archbishop of Vienne" or his delegate. Anne Félix, Mother Burdier's successor, used the same language: "On the first of March, 1700, His Excellency the Archbishop appointed me superior of the Sisters of St. Joseph and the members of the *bureau* appointed me director." She referred neither to an election nor to consultation with the community before her appointment by the archbishop, probably because the matter was arranged between the archbishop and the sisters. Although the same person exercised the dual function of superior and director, the duties of each role involved very different types of responsibillity. Anne Félix did not confuse them, but it was useful to formulate the distinction.

In Lyon, even though the same distinctions were recorded in the contract of December 22, 1696, between the the administrators of the Maison des Recluses and the Sisters of St. Joseph, these men did not consider it an abuse of power to accept or reject novices without consulting the community. In the appointment of a superior, they feared that the sisters wanted to make use of the right, ensured by their constitutions, to make a recommendation to the archbishop. The administrators may have been influenced in their attitude toward the Sisters of St. Joseph because they were also in charge of the sisters of the Hôtel-Dieu of Lyon, whom they governed as they pleased in regard to their service, because at this point, they had neither religious commitment nor constitutions. Before the Sisters of St. Joseph arrived in Lyon, Mother Burdier had already noted this difference in a letter already cited, ". . . we can in no way follow the example of that of Lyon which you point out to me, for it is absolutely under the authority of the *messires* [rectors], and we are like religious outside the cloister." In other words, we are not completely under the authority of the rectors. It is also possible that the separation of the Lyon community from Vienne around 1729 made the Lyon sisters more dependent upon the administrators of the Hôtel-Dieu. These men did not dispute the right of the archbishop to appoint the superior; they only questioned the right of the sisters to propose as superior a candidate of their choice.

At Craponne and generally in all the houses except the smallest, which were at least more autonomous than the hospitals in regard to the sisters' residence, the superior was always chosen by election in the presence of the bishop or his representative (the *curé*, a dean, or someone else). The register of the acts of chapter of the community of Craponne mentions that Charlotte de Vinols was elected April 20, 1747, as superior of the Sisters of St. Joseph, "and as assistant, Sister de St Joseph Porrat, who [pl] humbly accepted the said duties, confident of receiving from the Lord the graces to accomplish them."[146] The election was presided over by "*Messire* Etienne Delolme, *curé* of Retournac and dean of St. Paulien, conducting the election," and "in the presence of *Messire* Jean-Baptiste Parrel, *prêtre sociétaire* of the said town and director of this community." In this instance, the clerical presider is there as witness to the election and acknowledges it in the name of the church. The community itself chooses the superior and presents her to the witness. In other cases, the way in which the act of chapter is transcribed puts more emphasis on the role of the confirmation provided by the priest than on the choice made by the community. The *curé* (who made the entry) may have done this at times as a way of diminishing the community's authority. Aside from a crisis situation, however, there is no record of a case where a *curé* alone would have decided the appointment of the superior.

At Bas-en-Basset, the register of the acts of chapter begins in 1740 with an entry by "Jean Page, priest, Bachelor in Theology, *curé* of the parish church of Bas and Archpriest of Monistrol, superior in this district of all communities of the Sisters of St. Joseph." Father Page records giving the habit to Isabeau Goudonnier and Anne Jouve "after having examined them," without any mention of consulting the community, as if they were admitted on his sole authority.[147] Three years later, however, the act of chapter giving the habit, still recorded in his handwriting, mentions "the consent of Sister de St Joseph, superior" and two other sisters of the community. Farther on in the book, Father Page noted that a candidate was "received with a unanimous vote of the full chapter." The priest appears to have learned his appropriate role in regard to the community. On July 3, 1759, he conducted "the election of the superior . . . [during which] Sister Catherine was elected with a plurality of votes." He was content to "confirm the above- named . . . with the authority of His Excellency the Bishop."

In small rural communities, which were by far the most numerous, elections took place in the presence of the *curé* or another ecclesiastic delegated by the bishop, with a solemnity relative to the importance of the community. At Saint-Félicien in 1730:

> Sister Chometier, superior, hoping to be relieved of the burden she had carried for several consecutive years . . . all the sisters voted that Sister de St. Félicien take the position of assistant, which she accepted, and that Sister St. Augustin take charge of the financial management of the house, which she also accepted,

and these two were very satisfied, and all the other sisters as well, that the superior be relieved of the many cares and afflictions she had known previously.[148]

With this arrangement, Sister Chometier was able to remain superior until her
death on April 9, 1756, leaving "great examples of every kind of virtue."
Competition for power, apparently, was not an issue at Saint-Félicien.

The act of chapter recording the election of the superior quite often mentions other officers, at least the assistant and treasurer, depending on the size
of the community. These nominations were made by election on the suggestion of the superior, as specified in the constitutions.[149] At Saint-Jean-de-Bonnefonds, near Saint-Etienne, on March 11, 1724, "six *sœurs agrégées* of the
Congregation of St. Joseph" realized, outside the normal time for the election,
it seems, that the superior was "responsible for all the duties of the house."[150]
To alleviate her work, they elected officers:

> Sister Marie Joseph as mistress of novices, Sr. Jeanne-Marie Gilibert de
> Longeron as treasurer of the house, and Sr. Marie-Thérèse as Sacristan. They
> will take turns assuming the duties of the portress and cook; and when there is
> need to fill in when one is missing, Sr. Isabot will be available to help there.

The *curé* presided at this election. He noted that "the different offices were
appointed, each in particular, according to the rules of their constitutions, after having voted for each one separately." The document closes with a reminder that the sisters "are assembled in a chapter to conserve and maintain
union and peace among themselves, having only one heart and one spirit, and
all for the glory of God."

In the beginning the Sisters of St. Joseph sometimes had to assert their
rights with administrators, as with pastors, in order to be respected for what
they really were as defined in their constitutions, or, in the words of Mother
Burdier, "nuns . . . outside the cloister." They understood well how to live that
reality, even if they did not have the appearance of doing so.

Superiors and Sisters in the Community

It is not easy to find traces of how superiors carried out their primary duty of
supporting the spiritual life of their communities. In Vienne Mother Burdier
asked the administrators that the sisters "have in the hospital some apartment
of their own to perform the exercises of their Rules," because these exercises
"can only be done well in places a little apart." This detail implies that until
1686, the sisters had lived with the other people in the hospital. It also shows
that the administrators tended to assimilate them, their works and their whole
way of being, to other hospital personnel. Mother Burdier had to settle these

issues. She did the same with the reception of novices. The administrators had to be satisfied to "receive the money or belongings" brought by the novice. The sisters alone retained the right to "test her vocation, give her the habit . . . if His Excellency the Archbishop gives permission for it." Hospital administrators had nothing to do with discerning vocations. Mother Burdier made it understood simply and clearly, in a positive collaboration. After Mother Burdier's term, things were not always the same. As the Vienne community began to turn little by little to "the regularity of cloistered daughters," a certain arrogance crept in that did not facilitate a working relationship with the hospital administrators.

At Lyon the administrators were "extremely satisfied with the piety, zeal, and good management of the sisters," but we know nothing of how the sisters sustained this piety and zeal in the community. In Craponne, by contrast, it is possible to see how Mother de Vinols was solicitous for the spiritual direction of each sister, respectful of each one's spiritual path, refusing to impose on another what was right for her. Soon after her profession, she had understood the apostolic benefit of spiritual retreats and how, in promoting them for the sisters and others, "the people would draw more benefit from the community." She tried in that way to put into practice what the constitutions said about annual retreats: the sisters "will take their meditations, readings, and the other exercises of their retreat, either from some very spiritual director or from their [sister] superior."[151] Undoubtedly, few sisters of St. Joseph ever exercised this charism as fully as Mother de Vinols, who organized retreats not only for the community of Craponne, but also for the communities in her district and for the men and women who benefited from the sisters' service.

In attending to the spiritual needs in the communities, the superior had the help of the spiritual father or ecclesiastical superior, and the confessor or director of the community. The register of the Religious of St. Joseph of Vienne shows, that at first, their confessors were Carmelites and, at the beginning of the eighteenth century, Augustinians, followed by Dominicans, and after that, "the Reverend Jesuit Fathers from 1719 or 1720 until the present" (around 1773).[152] Houses in smaller towns or villages did not have such a wide choice. Through the sisters' request or the bishop's zeal, however, every community had the possibility of benefiting in a real way from the support of the confessor and the ecclesiastical superior. The act of chapter for the election of Mother de Vinols, for example, mentions both: "*Messire* Etienne Delolme, *curé* of Retournac and dean of St Paulien conducting the election of the superior . . . in the presence of *Messire* Jean-Baptiste Parrel, *prêtre sociétaire* of the said town and director of this community." At Bas-en-Basset, following the election of the superior on July 3, 1759, presided by the *curé*, Jean Page, assisted by "*Monsieur* Favier *théologal* from Bas," the former gave some "points to observe for the good order of the Community: 1, Each sister will comment on the reading during her week, which each takes; the superior will begin the series of weeks, with each following according to her rank."[153] The points stop there in the book. There is no "second." At Boisset (Haute-Loire) in 1664, the *curé*, Vital Bodet, gathered seven women together. They had been "fully instructed and well trained for four years and have practiced to the best of their ability the said rules under the direction of *Monsieur* Vital Bodet, their spiritual superior." The country sisters of humble origin seem generally to have received spiritual support equal to that available to sisters of large houses in the towns. The pastors who requested the Sisters of St. Joseph were often zealous, active, and desirous for the good of their parish. The risk of tyranny from these pastors was no greater than it was from the administrators of hospital communities.

There remained the risk, nonetheless, of pressure on the superior or the community from either pastors or hospital administrators to accept women from their families or the families of patrons as novices in exchange for gifts and inheritances. In Vienne, for example, *Demoiselle* Antony exercised such influence with disastrous results. In the smaller rural houses, there are cases of pastors who donated gifts or wrote their will in favor of the community on condition that they accept a niece or relative. Certain communities appear to have agreed to such demands. On February 24, 1697, the will of Jean Farissier, a dealer in small wares in Saint-Romain-Lachalm, constituted the Sisters of St. Joseph, "ribbon makers of the said St. Romain," as his beneficiaries "with the obligation to provide food and keep for Marguerite and Marie Farissier, his nieces, who will be held to work for the profit of said beneficiaries to the best of their ability."[154] Were the girls to marry, the testator "severs and revokes the said food and keep" he promised them, but he wanted "other relatives to be received in their place." The two nieces were admitted to the community in 1695 and 1704. They do not appear to have left in subsequent years. Some communities fixed time limits to this type of contract; others refused altogether to agree to such bargaining. Communities could suffer either from accepting or refusing this type of arrangement. Often, however, the houses involved were small, and the harm rarely extended beyond the limits of the parish. In general, the communities of St. Joseph did not give in to this sort of pressure. With the help of their pastors and the example of neighboring communities, they preferred to receive good subjects rather than material advantages at the expense of the true well-being of the community.

Apostolic tasks and services were usually defined and limited in those establishments with clearly specific services: hospitals, orphanages, houses of refuge, or the Maison Forcée des Recluses in Lyon. With her sisters, the superior took responsibility for directing these services, without complete freedom to choose or modify them. An exception was the hospital at Vienne. Mother Burdier added other works: the Maison de Providence for fallen women and *petites écoles* for girls. In Lyon, by contrast, the administrators seem to have confined the sisters with the recluses; there is no evidence that the superior was able to expand the activities of that community beyond the Maison des Recluses. At the same time, in Craponne the spiritual leadership given the community by Mother de Vinols was manifest in its apostolic vitality. It included the education of girls, lodging and care for orphans, the organization of workshops for lace, visiting the sick, giving alms to the *pauvres honteux*, and helping as needed in the hospital.[155] In the houses of St. Joseph, according to the regions and needs of the population, there was generally a rather large diversity of works: preparing ordinary medications; more rarely, as in Grenoble, working as a surgeon; upkeep of churches almost everywhere; and instruction of new converts in Protestant regions such as Tence, Le Cheylard, or Gap. The superior certainly played a role in the choice and breadth of charitable and apostolic activities, and she influenced the way these services were carried out. Her actions are remarked even more when things turned out badly in a community. In 1685 in Sauxillanges, near Issoire, war broke out between the sisters and the hospital administrators. The superior, Marie Faure, led the opposition with the active collaboration of two other sisters. When she died in 1690, the two others capitulated.[156] In some rural houses where the sisters were very close to the people—Chomelix (Haute Loire), for instance—it was emphasized that one of the benefits received from the sisters was "the good example that they constantly give to the public."[157] This sort of remark is not uncommon in the archives of communities of St. Joseph. It witnesses to the truth that people could see the sisters living in their midst, and this presence was often in itself constructive and apostolic.

This rapid glance at the apostolic works of the sisters suggests that the dispersion of communities in both rural and urban areas, as well as the spirit of initiative on the part of the superiors and sisters, enabled the communities to sustain a universal apostolic openness and availability in the places where they were established. Even after the publication of the 1694 Constitutions, which limited the scope of their work, the sisters continued to take on "all the works of mercy, both spiritual and corporal," of which women of their times were capable.

The Authority of the Congregational Body

Although the 1694 Constitutions emphasized the sanctity and the perfection of the sisters, envisaged above all in spiritual exercises and life within the houses, that did not prevent the Sisters of St. Joseph from giving themselves to all kinds of apostolic and charitable services, both within and outside the house. By the time the constitutions were printed at the end of the seventeenth century, ways of operating had already taken shape in the communities; patterns were formed. Houses where the sisters were numerous in the country or in towns tended to have a more regular life, in the twofold sense of regulation of time and fidelity to the rules for the sake of order. Such regularity in the house, however, did not always mean that the sisters had fewer external activities with their neighbor. When Mother de Vinols was elected superior at Craponne, there were eight sisters in the community. Ten years later, they numbered ten. Despite this rather significant number, it was obvious how much the sisters were present to the needs of those around them, largely because of the community's authentic spiritual life. Small communities could not observe the same sort of regularity. Although the distinction was clearly made between the congregation properly speaking and the communities of *sœurs agrégées,* these differences in operation seemed to be taken for granted without creating problems. The 1694 Constitutions, in blending a diversity of texts, allowed for customs already in existence to continue. They permitted diversity and flexibility both in the life of the house and in external activities, on individual as well as community levels. The constitutions were a stable point of reference recognized by all the sisters. When the sisters of Vienne wanted to turn their house into a monastery, they had to modify the constitutions. Although not entirely faithful to the original intent of Father Médaille, the 1694 Constitutions served in certain ways to secure the vocation of the Sisters of St. Joseph.

When the community at Vienne deviated from this vocation, becoming a monastery under fraudulent circumstances, the congregation as a whole met it with universal resistance. The first to react to the proceedings of the sisters at Vienne had been the administrators of the hospitals similar to Vienne that also employed Sisters of St. Joseph. Between 1727 and 1729, the administrators of the Maison des Recluses in Lyon and the Maison de Refuge in Clermont severed the relationship of these communities with their founding house at Vienne. The communities as well dissociated themselves from Vienne. By the time of the French Revolution, a list "of the former religious of the Congregation of St. Joseph of Vienne currently employed outside," dated October 26, 1792, names only five houses that had sisters from Vienne: the hospital at Annonay, the hospital of the Providence and the house of the Propagation of the Faith in Grenoble, the hospital at Digne in Provence, and the house of Incurables in Lyon.[158] Some communities may have broken away from their parent community of Vienne because of the revolution effected in that house. Others, however, had acquired their independence well before that. No other community is known that attempted to follow the example of Vienne. The congregation as a whole acted as a standard and a source of regulation. It maintained a level of coherence between the definition of the vocation of St. Joseph in the texts and how it was carried out in life.

Who, in the end, governed the communities of St. Joseph? In the short term and depending on the situation, it may have been the bishop, the pastor, the hospital administrators or parish dignitaries, the sister superior of the community, or even some influential members. Whatever the power plays, the juridical authority over the community remained unequivocally with the bishop, and the spiritual authority, most important and day-to-day, rested with the sister superior. In the long run, however, it is evident that the body as a whole, in its desire to make the spirit of the constitutions live, was in reality the internal organ of governance.

NOTES

1. *CV* 1694, 151 ff.
2. *CSJ* 1970, 164, no. 284.
3. Material in this section is from *CV* 1694, part 4, chap. 1: "Des règles de la Prieure" 152-58, nos. 3, 4, 6, and 8.
4. Ibid., part 3, chap. 5: "Du vœu de l'obéissance," 123 ff.
5. Ibid., 127.
6. Ibid., part 3, chap. 6: "Du vœu de la chasteté," 132-34.
7. Ibid., chap. 7: "Du vœu de la pauvreté," 135-47.
8. Ibid., part 1, chap. 6: "Des Supérieurs de la Congrégation," 24.
9. *CSJ*, 1970, 267, no. 603.
10. Ibid., part 6, chap. 12 : "Du moyen d'éviter la contrainte de la conscience des Sœurs," 353.
11. Ibid., part 4, chap. 1, "Des règles de la Prieure," 153.
12. Ibid, part 4, chap. 2, "Des règles de l'Assistante," 167; and part 4, chap. 3, "Des règles de la Coadjuratrice qui sera la maitresse des novices," 174.
13. Ibid., part 4, chap. 4, "Des règles de l'Econome," 185.
14. Ibid., part 4, chap. 7, "Des règles de l'Intendante des Pauvres," 203.
15. Ibid., part 4, chap. 8, "Des règles de la Directrice de la Miséricorde," 208.
16. Ibid., part 2, chap. 3, "Des services que les Sœurs doivent rendre au prochain," 62.
17. Ibid., part 4, chap. 9, "Des règles de la Portière," 216.
18. Ibid., part 6, chap. 6, "Des conférences," 318.
19. Ibid., part 4, chap. 6, "Des règles des Conseillères," 198.
20. Ibid., part 4, chap. 13, "Des règles de la Prieure,"159, no. 12.
21. Ibid., part 4, chap. 5, "Des règles de l'Admonitrice," 194.
22. Ibid., part 1, chap. 8, "Des sœurs Agrégées," 34 ff.

23. Ibid., part 4, chap. 12, "De l'élection de la supérieure," 245.

24. Ibid., part 6, chap. 5, "Des moyens pour éviter la négligence de la Supérieure, à veiller et à corriger les Sœurs," 312ff.

25. Ibid., part 6, chap. 5, "Des moyens pour éviter la négligence de la Supérieure."

26. Ibid., part 6, chap. 4, "Des moyens d'empêcher aux supérieures le mauvais usage de leur autorité," 306 ff.

27. Ibid., 308.

28. Ibid., 311.

29. Ibid., part 4, chap. 11: "De la Nomination des Officières," 226.

30. Ibid., part 4, chap. 12: "De l'Election de la Supérieure," 230.

31. *TP* 1981, CP, 79-82, nos. 378-96.

32. *CV* 1694, part 4 chap. 1: "Des règles de la Prieure," 161.

33. Ibid., part 4 chap. 1: "Des règles de la Prieure," 161-62.

34. Ibid.

35. Ibid., part 6, chap. 1: "Du moyen pour ne recevoir que de bons sujets dans la Congrégation," 296.

36. Ibid., part 3, chap. 3: "Du Novitiat et de l'éducation des Novices," 105-106.

37. Ibid., part 6, chap. 13: "De l'obligation que les Sœurs ont de sçavoir et d'observer leurs Constitutions," 368.

38. Ibid., part 1, Chap. 6: "Des Supérieurs de la Congrégation," 25.

39. Ibid., part 6, chap. 8: "Des moyens pour éviter le défaut et l'excès des biens," 333.

40. Ibid., 334.

41. Ibid., part 6, chap. 8: "Des moyens pour éviter le défaut et l'excès des biens"; and part 1, chap. 7: "Du père spirituel," 29.

42. *TP* 1981, R, 106, no. 8.

43. *CV* 1694, part 4, chap. 13: "Règles communes à toutes les Sœurs," 259.

44. Ibid., part 5, introduction, 261.

45. Ibid., part 6, chap. 13: "De l'obligation que les Sœurs ont de sçavoir et d'observer leurs Constitutions," 359.

46. Ibid., "Approbation et Confirmation des Constitutions des Sœurs de St Joseph par Monseigneur l'Archevêque de Vienne," 20 november 1693.

47. Ibid., part 4, 157-58.

48. Ibid., part 4, chap. 1: "Des Règles de la Prieure," 150.

49. Ibid., part 1, chap. 6: "Des Supérieurs de la Congrégation," 25.

50. Ibid., part 1, chap. 7: "Du Père Spiritual," 28.

51. *TP* 1981: "Lettre Eucharistique" 5, no. 7.

52. BM Grenoble, R 8372, Registre des religieuses de Saint-Joseph de la ville de Vienne, a commencer en l'année mil-six-cent-soixante-huit, 1.

53. BM Grenoble, R 8372, Registre des religieuses de Saint-Joseph, Table alphabétique des Matières, fol. 13r.

54. AD Hautes-Alpes, 3 H suppl. 278, Hôpital de Gap, 531.

55. BM Grenoble, R 8372, Registre des religieuses de Saint-Joseph, fol. 8.

56. Ibid., fols. 30 ff.

57. Ibid., fols. 55 ff.

58. AM Vienne, Hôtel-Dieu, G 4, 1710-1783, "Mémoires dressées sur plusieurs délibérations verballes du Bureau de l'Hôtel Dieu de la ville de Vienne, remis aud. Bureau le 5 septbre 1723," fols. 8-12.

59. BM Grenoble, R 8372, Registre des religieuses de Saint-Joseph, Table alphabétique des Matières, fol. 6v.

60. AM Vienne, Hôtel-Dieu, G 4, 1710-1783, Relevé des Délibérations du Bureau de l'Hôtel-Dieu concernant la maison de Providence, 1667-1732, 2.

61. BM Vienne, GG 42, État Civil de l'Hôpital, 1680-1733, 76.

62. AM Vienne, G 4, Relevé des Délibérations du Bureau de l'Hôtel-Dieu concernant la Maison de Providence, 1667-1732, 4.

63. AM Vienne, G 1, 1668-1789, no.1, 15 pp.

64. AM Vienne, Hôtel-Dieu, G 4, 1710-1783, "Mémoires dressées sur plusieurs délibérations verballes du Bureau de l'Hoteldieu de la ville de Vienne," 5 septembre 1723, fol. 16.

65. AM Vienne, Hôtel-Dieu, G 4, 1710-1783, Relevé des Délibérations du Bureau de l'Hôtel-Dieu concernant la Maison de Providence, 1667-1732.

66. BM Grenoble, R 8372, Registre des religieuses de Saint-Joseph, fol. 98.

67. Ibid., fol. 105.

68. BM Vienne, Hôtel-Dieu, B 1389, Mémoires de la sœur Jeanne Burdier, économe de l'Hôtel-Dieu de Vienne, 1680-1692, extracts transcribed by Jean Lecutiez, 147-53.

69. BM Grenoble, R 8272, Registre des Religieuses de Saint-Joseph, donation de la Mère Jeanne Burdier, 14 oct. 1690, fols. 22-25.

70. BM Vienne, Hôtel-Dieu, B 1389, Mémoires de la sœur Jeanne Burdier, économe de l'Hôtel-Dieu de Vienne, 1680-1692, extracts, 95-96. The reference is to the sisters of the Hôtel-Dieu of Lyon.

71. *TP* 1981, AR, 133, no. 1; and *CV* 1694, part 1, chap. 8: "Des sœurs agrégées," 34-35.

72. AD Isère, 21 H 1, Registre des professions de la communauté de Vienne, 1683-1792.

73. Ibid., 3.

74. AD Hautes-Alpes, 3 H suppl. 278, Hôpital de Gap, 535.

75. AM Vienne, E 334, "Plusieurs mémoires tant de la sœur Burdier . . . que de la sœur Félix," large notebook containing scattered notes without pagination.

76. Ibid.

77. BM Grenoble, R 8272, Registre des Religieuses de St Joseph, fol. 34.

78. *CV* 1694, part 6, chap. 1: "Du moyen de ne recevoir que de bons sujets dans la Congrégation," 293 ff.

79. AD Isère, 21 H, Registre des professions de la Communauté de Vienne, 1683-1792, fols. 3-4.

80. Ibid., fols. 4-6.

81. Ibid., 1683-1792, fol. 7.

82. Ibid., Constitution de pension pour la réception de Demoiselle Françoise de Vincent de Rambion, 14 décembre 1689.

83. AM Vienne, E 59, Registre des Délibérations de l'Hôtel-Dieu, 1691-1699 (no pagination), 7 décembre 1699.

84. AM Vienne, E 59, Registre des Délibérations de l'Hôtel-Dieu, 1700-1709, 6 novembre 1701.

85. Ibid., 24 mai 1706.

86. AM Vienne, G 4, 1710-1783, Relevé des Délibérations de l'Hôtel-Dieu concernant la Maison de Providence, 1667-1732.

87. AM Vienne, E 62, Registre des Délibérations du Bureau de l'Hôtel-Dieu, 1713-1721, 29 avril 1714.

88. Denis de Saint-Marthe, and Barthélemy Hauréau, eds. *Gallia Christiana in provincias ecclesiasticas distributa*, vol. 15, *Ecclesia Viennensis* (Paris: Ex Typographia Regia, 1716-1865), 132.

89. Louis de Rouvroy, duc de Saint-Simon, *Mémoires*, Bibliothèque de La Pléiade (Paris: Éditions Gallimard, 1953), chap. 51, 723-24.

90. *Gallia Christiana*, 16:132.

91. AM Vienne, Hôtel-Dieu, G 4, 1710-1783, "Mémoires dressées sur plusieurs délibérations verballes du Bureau de l'Hoteldieu de la Ville de Vienne," 5 septembre 1723, fol. 16.

92. The Vienne archives, at least those classified, contain very little information on the conflicts between Bishop de la Tour d'Auvergne and the administrators of the Hôtel-Dieu in Vienne, but the reality of conflicts between sisters and administrators is nonetheless perceptible.

93. AD Isère, 21 H 1, Registre des Professions de la communauté de Vienne, 1683-1792. Mother de Bontoux's signature appeared for the first time on February 12, 1720, for the profession of Claudine Jacquin, 9.

94. AM Vienne, G1, Relevé des délibérations du Bureau de l'Hôtel-Dieu, 1667-1732, 5-6.

95. AD Isère, 21 H 1, Registre des Professions de la communauté de Vienne, 1683-1792, 2.

96. Ibid., 10.

97. BM Grenoble, R 8372, Registre des Religieuses de St Joseph, 103.

98. Ibid., 107.

99. AM Vienne, Hôtel-Dieu, G 4, Lettre de la sœur Roman, économe, au Bureau de l'Hôtel-Dieu.

100. AM Vienne, Hôtel-Dieu, E 64, Registre des Délibérations de l'Hôtel-Dieu, 1727-1730, 13 décembre 1728.

101. *Règles et Constitutions pour la Congrégation des Sœurs de Saint-Joseph*, à Vienne, chez Laurens Cruzi, 1693; see Supporting Documents, 13.

102. Ibid., 7.

103. *CV 1694*, 158.

104. AD Isère, 21 H 1, Registre des Professions de la communauté de Vienne, 29 mai 1732, 13.

105. BM Grenoble, R 8372, Registre des Religieuses de Saint-Joseph, Table alphabétique des Matières, fol. 12v.

106. BM Grenoble, R 8372, Registre des Religieuses de Saint-Joseph, fol. 107.

107. AM Vienne, Hôtel-Dieu, G 4, Mémoire pour les Dames Religieuses de Saint-Joseph de la Maison de Providence de Vienne, 19 avril 1780, 22, marginal notes.

108. [Battut, Mère Augustine], *Origine et développement de la Congrégation de Saint-Joseph du Bon Pasteur* (Clermont-Ferrand: Imp. de Vve Petit, 1879), 85; and AMM Sœurs de Saint-Joseph de Saint-Vallier.

109. AM Vienne, Hôtel-Dieu, G 4, Relevé de plusieurs délibérations du Bureau exposant des faits de révolte des sœurs . . . 21 février 1754 à 15 décembre 1754.

110. AM Vienne, Hôtel-Dieu, G 4, Mémoire pour les Dames Religieuses de Saint-Joseph de la Maison de Providence de Vienne, 19 avril 1780, 23-24, 26.

111. AM Vienne, Hôtel-Dieu, G 4, Copie des Lettres Patentes. Marginal notes are in another hand.

112. AM Vienne, Hôtel-Dieu, G 4, Mémoire pour les Dames Religieuses de Saint-Joseph de la Maison de Providence de Vienne, 19 avril 1780, 27.

113. AD Rhône, 44 H 150, no. 42, Livre de l'Assemblée de la Maison Forcée, 29 Aoust 1686.

114. AD Rhône, 50 H 115, Registre des Délibérations de la Compagnie du Saint Sacrement, 1682-1690.

115. AD Rhône, 50 H 116, 1694-1699.

116. AD Rhône, 44 H 143, no. 27.

117. *CV* 1694, part 1, chap. 6: "Des Supérieurs de la Congrégation," 25.

118. AD Rhône, 44 H, liasse 143, no. 4.

119. AD Rhône, 44 H, liasse 142, Registre, Cartulaire des Titres de la Communauté, 42.

120. For a description of this church and the locality of the Maison des Recluses in Lyon, see A. Poidebard, "L'Église Saint-François de Sales, à Lyon," *Bulletin historique du Diocèse de Lyon* 4 (1903): 57-63. –Trans.

121. AD Rhône, H, liasse 142, Registre, Cartulaire des Titres de la Communauté, 44.

122. Vacher, M.-Th., "Histoire des Constitutions imprimées des sœurs de Saint-Joseph, de 1694 jusqu'au milieu du XIXe siècle," *Bulletin de la Fédération Française des Sœurs de Saint-Joseph*, no. 41 (1985).

123. *Constitutions pour la petite Congrégation des Sœurs de Saint-Joseph*, à Lyon, chez André Laurens, MDCCXXX, "A Monseigneur."

124. AD Rhône, 44 H 142, Registre, Cartulaire des Titres de la Communauté, 109.

125. AD Rhône, 44 H 141, Inventaire des Titres et papiers de la Maison des Recluses no. 4, fol. 10r, Sœurs de Saint-Joseph.

126. Ibid., fol. 10v.

127. The italicized phrase is underlined in the manuscript.

128. AD Rhône, 44 H 141, Inventaire des Titres et papiers de la Maison des Recluses no. 4, fol. 10v.

129. AD Rhône, 44 H 142, Registre, Cartulaire des Titres de la Communauté, 110.

130. BM Lyon, 353 321, *Légende surdorée ou supplément au martyrologe de Lyon*, anonyme, 1790. [The title plays on the work known in French as *La Légende*

dorée (The Golden Legend, Legenda aurea), a popular compilation of lives of saints and martyrs written by Jacobus de Voragine between 1261 and 1266. –Trans.]

131. BM Lyon, Fonds Coste, MS 357, Mémoire pour la maison des Recluses de Lyon, n.d.

132. BMU Clermont-Ferrand, Fonds Paul Leblanc, MS 850, fol. 36 ff, Contrat d'Association de Louise Dupoux et Jeanne-Marie Porrat Delolme.

133. AMM Le Puy, Communauté de Craponne, Abbé Clavel, "La Vie de la Vénérable Mère de Vinols," MS, 60 pp. bound, large format. The manuscript indicates merely "abbé Clavel." He may have been the vicar of Craponne or his brother, a Vincentian, both of whom were killed during the Revolution. [Antoine Clavel, former vicar of Craponne, was condemned and executed with his brother, Jean-Baptiste Clavel, and his brother's wife, Catherine Boutin, at Le Puy, June 20, 1794, Aimé Guillon, *Les martyrs de la foi pendant la révolution française*, 4 vols. (Paris: Mathiot, 1821), 2: 436-37. –Trans.]

134. AMM Le Puy, MS Abbé Clavel, La Vie de la Vénérable Mère de Vinols, 20-21.

135. Ibid., 26.

136. Ibid., 30 and 39.

137. Ibid., 30 and 39.

138. Ibid., 31.

139. Ibid., 18, 39, 40, 41.

140. Ibid., 41.

141. BMU Clermont-Ferrand, Fonds Paul Leblanc, no. 850, MS 131, Délibération des habitants de Craponne pour une demande de Lettres Patentes en faveur des filles associées sous le vocable de Saint-Joseph; see Supporting Documents, 17.

142. AMM Le Puy, MS Abbé Clavel, La Vie de la Vénérable Mère de Vinols, 26.

143. Ibid., 55.

144. Ibid., 48.

145. *CV* 1694, part 4, chap. 11: "De la nomination des Officières," 226.

146. AMM Le Puy, Communauté de Craponne, Registre des Actes Capitulaires 1723-1857.

147. AMM Le Puy, Communauté de Bas-en-Basset, "Livre des receptions comme des professions des Sœurs de la Congregaõn de Sᵗ Joseph établie dans le bourg de Bas, fait ce 5ᵉ juillet 1740" (book ends July 30, 1875).

148. AMM Aubenas, Communauté de Saint-Félicien, "Livre de Létablissement des Sœurs de Sᵗ Joseph a Sᵗ Félicien l'an mil sept cents trois" (last date: March 1799).

149. *CV* 1694, part 4, chap. 12: "De l'élection de la Supérieure," 230.

150. AMM Lyon, manuscript book of the Constitutions preserved in Lyon (MS L). At the end of the book is a list of the acts of chapter for the community of Saint-Jean-de-Bonnefonds, 199 ff.

151. *CV* 1694, part 5, chap. 1: "Des exercices de l'année," 266.

152. BM Grenoble, R 8372, Registre des Religieuses de Saint-Joseph, Table alphabétique des Matières (lettre Z).

153. AMM Le Puy, connunauté de Bas-en-Basset, livre des réceptions.

154. AMM Le Puy, Communauté de Saint-Romain-Lachalm, Testament de Jean Farissier, le 24 février 1697.

155. BMU Clermont-Ferrand, Fonds Paul Leblanc, no. 850, MS 131, Délibération des habitants de la ville de Craponne, etc. See Supporting Documents, 17.

156. Auguste Achard, "L'hospice de Sauxillanges (1664-1904)." *Revue d'Auvergne* 21 (1904): 29-46, 128-32, 188-208, 285-92.

157. AMM Le Puy, Communauté de Chomelix, Délibération des habitants pour la demande de Lettres Patentes royales, 13 août 1684.

158. AD Isère, 21 H 1, Sœurs de Saint-Joseph de Vienne.

Chapter Six

Structures of Daily Life

The Sisters of St. Joseph during the ancien régime adopted structures of life consonant with their vocation and with their social milieu. At the end of the Eucharistic letter, having expressed through a symbolic comparison with the Eucharist everything that made up the life of the Little Design, Father Médaille briefly mentions four points, or structures, that anchored or incarnated the sisters' vocation in the world. These were *le vivre*, or standard of living, and more specifically, food; *le vêtir*, the sisters' dress; *les maisons*, or types of lodging; and *les emplois*, which covered simultaneously the sisters' work, their choice of services, and how they carried them out.[1] To say anything of significance about the sisters' standard of living (*le vivre*) would require another complete study of their dowries, the communities' financial records, contracts for putting goods in common, the sisters' work, their wills, and the economic situation in the various places where the houses were located. Rather than attempting that considerable project, this chapter focuses on three aspects of the sisters' life: their dress, their houses (both things that assumed particular importance in the wider society of the time), and the issue of prayer and work in daily life.

THE SISTERS' DRESS

During the second half of the seventeenth century, when the Sisters of St. Joseph were being established, all of France lived, as it were, in a tableau. The court of Louis XIV provided the model, which was mirrored down to the smallest group in the tiniest village. In this universal tableau, dress served as a point of reference, expressing the structure of society in everyday life. In

their study of ancien régime culture, Goubert and Roche remark that "Dress
is at the heart of a system of apprenticeship in the society of appearances; it
is dress that teaches social disparity and reinforces its image. Any change of
dress, even from a young age, marks an entrance into another world."[2] This
was true for women. Clothing marked the stages of life—young girl, married
woman, or widow. There were, similarly, precise and well-known standards
for military attire, dress at court, or clothing appropriate to different social
classes. Distinctive marks signaled various occupations. Men and women
who worked in hospitals wore clothing characteristic of their role. This was
the case with the *donnades,* pious women committed to charitable service in
the hospitals. On September 6, 1654, the administrators of the Hôtel-Dieu of
Le Puy had a serious discussion concerning

> the form of headdress they wanted to give to the *donnades* . . . the *messieurs* of
> the chapter found it appropriate to give them nothing other than a simple head-
> dress of light taffeta like that worn by the *tourières* of religious houses in this
> city, as . . . easier to put on quickly, less expensive, and much more modest.[3]

The members of the Chapter also "found it appropriate to give the said *donnades* a small silver cross . . . for them to wear around their neck so that they
might be recognized when they walked through the city." It seemed natural to
these men, as to everyone, that the *donnades* wear a small sign in order to be
recognized for what they were—women given to charitable service.

The Sisters' Dress According to Father Médaille

Around the same time, shortly before 1650, when Father Médaille wrote the
Règlement for the first Sisters of St. Joseph, he dedicated only two lines to
this aspect of their life: "Their food and clothing will consist of a fitting sustenance (*un honneste entretien*), appropriate, in religious moderation, to their
social class and to the background from which they come."[4] He said nothing
specific about their dress. The founder placed the accent entirely on moderation and religious simplicity, and what was appropriate to the social condition
of each sister. These characteristics seem to apply, moreover, to the standard
of living in general ("a fitting sustenance") rather than merely to the type of
dress. What is striking in Father Médaille's comments about the sisters' clothing and their life as a whole is precisely their conformity to what was done by
women of the same social circumstances, and, as a result, the absence of any
distinctive sign.

The first reference to dress in the original Constitutions, written several
years after the Règlements, occurs in the first chapter, following an explanation of the diversity of social conditions within the new congregation. Despite

this differentiation in social status, Father Médaille states, "the same Institute [that is, the same collection of rules] will serve, nevertheless, for everyone," with certain differences "in regard to food, clothing, the time spent in prayer and daily occupations."[5] The need to take into account the diversity of circumstances again precludes uniformity. Later in the same chapter Médaille says simply, "Their attire will be like that of respectable widows, with a veil covering the upper part of the face."[6] The first Constitutions provide no further information about the dress of Sisters of St. Joseph. Undoubtedly familiar with the garb for widows of their social class, the sisters would have needed no further details. What is said remains broad, with no precise description, and without any reference to a religious habit.

Ten years later, during a crisis caused around 1660 by the rapid increase in the number of houses and their variety, Father Médaille and Bishop de Maupas were summoned to step in and establish a degree of order. In his Avis et Règlements, Father Médaille spoke very little of the sisters' dress—a total of seven lines in four pages—but gave much greater importance to recommendations for spiritual formation. He conducted a kind of spiritual re-centering in order to clarify the apostolic meaning of the diversity of external forms in the sisters' life.

In his conference to the sisters of Le Puy in 1661, Bishop de Maupas provided greater detail about the dress of the town sisters, that of the country sisters or *agrégées*, and the attire worn by servants working with the Sisters of St. Joseph in houses of the hospital type. He no longer spoke about a diversity of social circumstances, but only (which amounts to the same thing) of the differences between the style of dress worn in the towns and country apparel. Because clothing in the towns was generally more refined than in the country, sisters in the villages were to wear "garments and linen of coarser material " than did the city sisters.[7] The dress described by Bishop de Maupas, nevertheless, was still that of "respectable widows," which meant it was simple in style. The bishop specified "that the bodice of their dress [will be] without a waist," implying that it would be neither form-fitting nor furnished with stays. The sleeves were not to be too large because larger sleeves frequently typified monastic garb. The town sisters could wear a sleeve ornament called the *haut de manche*, but the *agrégées* in the villages "will put there [on the sleeves] nothing . . . except the fabric of the dress." The skirt was not to touch the ground because a train signified the superior social status of the woman wearing it. Sisters in the towns were to wear a headdress of white linen under one of black taffeta. The village sisters, like other women in this milieu, wore a single head covering of white linen. All members wore "a simple scarf" covering the neck with a crucifix hung around the neck. They also had a rosary on the cincture. Finally, the band, the distinctive sign of a widow, was to be worn "by both groups . . . to the middle of the forehead."

The dress described by Bishop de Maupas was not a religious habit. Except for the band, which was not exclusively monastic, the other components had nothing in common with the religious garb of the time. Nuns always wore long veils, a guimpe hiding the neck, a scapular, large sleeves, and skirts that touched the ground and had to be pinned up for work. None of these appeared in the dress of the Sisters of St. Joseph, because they were not nuns. The 1694 Constitutions give the same description as Bishop de Maupas had for the sisters' dress, except that the black silk headdress worn "always in their houses" had taken on the shape of "a small veil." When the sisters went out, they wore "another head covering of black taffeta, the size of that worn by respectable widows. They will wear this large head covering tied under the chin."[8] This modification of the sisters' habit reflected the evolution of widows' dress. When going out of their houses, widows had begun to wear a larger head covering fastened under the chin, and Sisters of St. Joseph adopted the contemporary change. That they quite naturally followed this development in style shows that the way of dressing had not yet become calcified. The *agrégées* sisters in rural areas "dressed in the same manner as the sisters of the Congregation" except for the headdress: they "will wear, both inside and outside their house, only a simple coif of white cambric; they will never wear them in black."[9] Because forms of dress in rural areas did not change so quickly as in towns, the *agrégées* sisters, like other country women, continued to wear the same headdress as in 1661. All Sisters of St. Joseph, whether "of the congregation" or simply *agrégées*, adopted a common sign: "a bronze crucifix on black wood, which will be fastened around their neck, and will hang in front of the breast."[10] For the *sœurs agrégées*, this crucifix "will be slightly smaller than that of the sisters of the congregation." Fifty years after their foundation, only the wearing of this crucifix distinguished the dress of Sisters of St. Joseph from that of the widows of their day.

Paintings from the period, particularly those of Jean-Baptiste Chardin (1699-1779), give an idea of the sisters' dress. His most famous paintings, such as *Le Benedicite* or *La fille de cuisine*, portray women wearing white caps with the flaps, or lappets, pinned up for housework. In *Le négligé*, also known as *La toilette du matin*, a young woman is dressed to go out. She is wearing a large dark headdress on top of a white cap whose unpinned lappets are visible, framing her face. The larger head covering, called a *capeline* (hood), falls onto her shoulders. All these details confirm, if there is still any need, that the Sisters of St. Joseph did not wear religious garb. If sisters wanted to leave the congregation, "their band and the crucifix" were removed.[11] Leaving was not a matter of changing their dress.

The Meaning of Taking the Habit

Although the dress of the Sisters of St. Joseph was not a religious habit, the communities' registers and acts of chapter all contain the "reception of the sisters," which was marked by taking the habit. It must have been considered important. Some registers or notebooks even provide lists of receptions or taking the habit without any indication of professions for the same sisters. Only after a number of years that could vary a great deal—sometimes more than a century—did the mention of profession begin to appear in these notebooks, following each reception of the habit and the period of novitiate. The records of three communities, all in the diocese of Le Puy at the time of their foundation, are typical. The register for the community of Marlhes, established by Father Médaille in 1651, records the community's first profession, that of Thérèse Champagnat and Anne-Marie Ravel, on September 29, 1777.[12] At Saint-Romain-Lachalm, founded in 1652, the profession of Françoise Vialeton, the first in the book, appears on September 8, 1727 and indicates that she completed two years of novitiate.[13] The first profession recorded for Riotord, founded in 1659, occurred in 1706.[14] Following a list of receptions, the register for Izieux in the Lyon diocese, where the congregation "began its establishment . . . on the day of Saint Martin in the year 1672," mentions the first profession only on February 27, 1734. Other registers reveal that the first acts of profession are those of women who had taken the habit at some point in the near or distant past. At Jonzieux, in the Le Puy diocese at the time the house was established in 1660, four sisters made their profession on August 15, 1713. Their personal reception of the habit had occurred thirty-six, twenty-four, nineteen, and three years previously.[15] With the passage of time, the registers mention professions more and more regularly, a year or two after reception.

The absence of a record of profession in the register does not always mean that one did not take place. Professions are often cited elsewhere, in particular, in the contract for the common possession of goods. In Saint-Romain-Lachalm the act of association for each sister refers to the profession that would be made after the novitiate, sometimes with a promise of additional dowry. In those houses where only the reception is recorded over a period of time, acts of placing possessions in common, acts of entrance, or acts of association almost always coincide with taking the habit. At that time the candidate explained before a notary her motives for entering the Sisters of St. Joseph and specified the material arrangements for her admission. Taking the habit in that case assumed an important significance, more important for the sisters, the community, and the families than the profession, because it was associated with a juridical action done before a notary.

In other communities, however, the profession of vows after reception and a novitiate of variable duration was regular practice from the beginning. These houses were usually in towns and larger villages and had sometimes been granted letters patent. The house of Satillieu (Ardèche) was established under the authority of Henry de Villars, Archbishop of Vienne, on December 6, 1661. The archives of this community possess loose pages from a notebook, now lost, indicating that Madeleine Courbis professed her vows in 1662, that three other sisters made vows in 1665, and that receptions and professions occurred regularly until 1721, where the pages leave off. In the records of Saint-Félicien, founded in 1703, and Craponne, founded in 1723, professions follow receptions rather regularly from the beginning. In Vienne, founded in 1668, the register, which begins only in 1681, notes receptions and professions very regularly. In these houses, profession had a different significance and received special recognition. They nonetheless continued cataloging receptions of the habit, which remained important events. What importance and what meaning were attributed to taking the habit need to be understood, because, even if the habit was that of widows and not of religious, it was a change of dress.

The first indication of the dress, or habit, of widows appears in the primitive Constitutions shortly after 1650. Just what took place when women received the habit? It was often done in their own *pays*, the place where they were born and would ordinarily spend their lives. When Father Médaille gave the habit at Saint-Romain-Lachalm in 1652 to Jeanne Périlhon and Marguerite Montchouvet, both twenty-eight years old, they were establishing a house of St. Joseph in their home town.[16] At Estivareilles (Loire) in 1708, as at Saint-Romain-Lachalm and many other small houses, the postulants remained in their place of origin. Taking the habit occurred in the sisters' chapel, if they had one, in their oratory, or in a nearby chapel. Otherwise, and generally for houses enjoying a more official establishment, it could take place in church. At Saint-Paulien, for example, on October 30, 1701, Isabeau Delolme, who wished "to devote herself to the instruction of the youth" of her sex, took the habit in a ceremony "during high Mass in the parish church."[17]

Depending on the situation, the ceremony of the *prise d'habit* was public or not. In no case did it give the impression of being secret. In any event, these women were known by their fellow citizens, and everyone could observe the transformation. From one day to the next, by changing their dress with the approval of ecclesiastical authority, they changed their social status. Attired as widows, they could then go out in public, preferably in pairs, to be at the service of the poor or the sick without any impropriety. They could, in addition, receive all sorts of people in their home—men, women, and the girls to be taught—without flouting rules of decorum. Célimène in Molière's *Misanthrope* used the increased freedom of life and action allowed a widow in order to receive her suitors. Father Médaille was going to use it to offer the Sisters of St. Joseph complete apostolic freedom. Their dress was not synonymous with enclosure. On the contrary, for women it symbolized openness to the world. Once they received the habit, and often earlier, the sisters no longer lived with their parents. For the people of their village as for themselves, this change of dress meant a change, a separation, in regard to their former life.

The new clothing the sisters adopted was, nevertheless, borrowed from their own milieu. Because so many men died in seventeenth-century warfare, widow's garb was often the most common form of dress for women. Even if the sisters added a special cross on the breast, other women in their villages wore the same clothing. By taking this form of dress, the sisters affirmed in a particular way that they really belonged to their place of birth and social milieu. At the same time, they wore this costume in a new way, because with it they had chosen a particular way of life. According to Father Médaille, the "food and clothing" of the sisters was to consist of "a fitting sustenance," that is, appropriate to their circumstances.[18] Their way of life and style of dress bespoke a way of being simultaneously present in the world and effecting a certain break with the ways of the world by deliberately adopting something that was simple, ordinary. A passage from the Jesuit Constitutions expresses a similar approach: "For sound reasons and with attention always paid to the greater service of God, in regard to what is exterior the manner of living is ordinary."[19] It is increasingly clear that the insistence on taking the habit among Sisters of St. Joseph did not have a monastic significance, but rather one that was entirely apostolic.

From the juridical point of view, most of the small country houses had no well-defined status. The vows made by the sisters were simple vows of private devotion, a commitment having no official standing. It was preferable for that reason that the acts subscribed to in the presence of the notary be connected with a public event known to everyone, such as taking the habit, since this event was accompanied by a change of social status for the sisters. Over time, even in the small houses that existed only through their attachment to a larger, "recognized" house, and even when it was the vow of stability taken by the *agrégées* sisters, the profession little by little took on legitimacy. From the second half of the eighteenth century until the Revolution, the acts of chapter in all houses mention both taking the habit and profession. In the meantime, the meaning of taking the habit had already begun to shift.

After the 1694 Constitutions: Dress in the Eighteenth Century

The description of dress in the 1694 Constitutions mentioned above is similar to that in the manuscripts: the primitive Constitutions, Avis et Règlements, and the Conference of Bishop de Maupas. By 1694, however, circumstances surrounding the reception of the habit had changed. In the original texts, there is no suggestion of two kinds of reception, one for sisters of the congregation properly speaking and another for the *sœurs agrégées*. Nevertheless, Bishop de Maupas' statement in his conference of 1661, that "the sisters in the villages [the *agrégées*] can receive the daughters" and give them the habit "without the presence of the [ecclesiastical] superior or the [sister] superior for the district being necessary," implies that the ecclesiastical superior was ordinarily present at the reception of sisters belonging to the main houses.[20] We know in fact that Bishop de Maupas came to give the habit to the sisters of Le Puy (1650) and Tence, and Father Médaille, to those in the small houses at Dunières, Marlhes, and Saint-Romain-Lachalm in the Le Puy diocese, and later, at Arlanc and Sauxillanges in the diocese of Clermont. There is no textual evidence from that period confirming these different ways of giving the habit. They are quite explicit, however, in the 1694 Constitutions. When a postulant for the congregation was admitted to receive the habit, after having been "examined by His Excellency the Bishop, or by the spiritual father," or their delegate, "one of them will give her the habit with the usual ceremonies."[21] For the reception of an *agrégée* sister, after the necessary examination, the postulant would "take the habit of the *agrégée* sister from the hands of the [sister] superior without ceremony in front of the oratory of their room."[22] These two ways of taking the habit clearly reflect the difference in status of each type of community. They certainly expressed the reality of life for Sisters of St. Joseph at the time. They may also have carried the seeds of the evolution in each type of community during the ancien régime.

The more official recognition conferred on the principal communities by the church entailed the risk of sacralizing the forms of life recognized by authority and also of strengthening these communities' conventual tendencies. The most obvious example of such a development is the house of Vienne, which became a monastery in 1730, having changed the habit of the Sisters of St. Joseph from attire enabling universal presence to one of separation from the world. At the same time, other communities felt the need to express the interior regularity of their life by exterior signs that were more conventual. The house in Clermont kept the habit received from Vienne in 1725, with its skirt with a train and its more monastic style. In Satillieu, on September 18, 1774, the sisters requested permission of the archbishop of Vienne to wear the guimpe. They reported that they "have a small collar that is not fastened in any way, which, in caring for the sick, is liable to inconveniences and improprieties." They begged the archbishop to "allow them to dress like all the Sisters of St. Joseph of the Le Puy diocese, and those of the city of Vienne . . . of Annonay, of the parish of Saint-Sauveur."[23] Three days later, on September 21, they were authorized "to take the guimpe and to fasten it in a way which would prevent any scandal." According to this request, the Sisters of St. Joseph in the diocese of Le Puy, at least in the larger houses, were already wearing the guimpe (an element of the religious habit) in place of the white linen scarf.

There are clues, at least in some communities, about the costume of the *sœurs agrégées* during the eighteenth century. At Dunières the act of entrance into religious life, concluded in the presence of the notary on May 23, 1722, by which Marie Mousnier joined the community, noted as part of her dowry, "a dress of black serge in keeping with her social status."[24] Three other acts of entrance for this house (dated 1712, 1716, and 1720) included, after details of the dowry, the funeral rites promised for each of the three involved. Each woman asked the community "to have her funeral honors done according to her social status and what her means could provide," or, in another case, "according to her rank and social status." At Saint-Victor-Malescours, another house of *agrégées*, two acts of entrance refer to clothing appropriate for the social condition of the new sisters: on December 28, 1727, Jeanne Ferraton brought as part of her dowry "a dress in keeping with her social status," and Claudine Lacombe, on May 28, 1733, presented a dowry including "two dresses in keeping with her condition of birth and social status."[25] At Saint-Romain-Lachalm, Françoise Vialeton asked in her will, dated April 8, 1758, that the community "provide her funeral honors in keeping with her social status and the custom of the assembly."[26] These examples imply that at least in some communities of *agrégées,* the sisters continued to dress like the women of their milieu and social status.

Registers containing the receptions of *sœurs agrégées* proffer no details about the habit. The Saint-Pierre-Duchamp register makes reference simply to "our holy habit," and that of Vanosc records only that the sisters received "the habit of the *agrégées* Daughters of St. Joseph." By the end of the eighteenth century, it appears that in a number of *agrégées* houses, "the habit of the *agrégées* Daughters of St. Joseph" tended to become less a costume consistent with their social position than one in keeping with the life of the community. In a manner less formal than it was for sisters in the principal houses, taking the habit among the *agregées*, most often in their own house, retained its character of personal separation from the sister's previous life and, at the same time, of her continued belonging to her original milieu. The subject of the habit introduces once again a hint of divergence in ways of living the vocation of St. Joseph, that sense of a problem in connecting the inside and the outside, the "convent" and service, contemplation and action.

THE SISTERS' RESIDENCE

Under the ancien régime housing as well as dress identified the person and family, not only, as today, in regard to financial status, but also in terms of social rank and respectability. It would be interesting to study houses of Sisters of St. Joseph from this perspective. Very few pictorial documents have survived about the buildings that housed the Sisters of St. Joseph during the seventeenth and eighteenth centuries. Some houses still exist. They are either the most beautiful—which were often gifts—or the sturdiest, or those that escaped demolition in the process of urban planning. Given its limits, this study will not focus on architectural aspects of the houses or attempt to reconstruct their interiors by searching account books, dowries, or inventories compiled during the Revolution to determine what furniture, utensils and other objects composed it. Rather, after examining what the normative texts (the Règlements and the Constitutions) say about houses, it will try to see what real choices Sisters of St. Joseph made concerning their housing and to understand how the houses supported the life of the communities.

Types of Dwelling Described in the Texts

The Règlements Manuscripts

Father Médaille states in the Règlements that the sisters "will try to have a small house which may become permanent," where there would be at least three and no more than six sisters.[27] It was appropriate for these "single women and widows . . . who wish to live chastely in the world"[28] to try "to have a small house," and that it should be stable enough to last, both materially and spiritually. If there were many candidates, they "may set up various small houses, all dependent on a single [sister] superior." They would nevertheless have "a superior in their house . . . [and] officers . . . as necessary."[29] The sisters were to keep "a kind of enclosure in their house, which will never be open to men, and will leave the house only to go to church . . . [and for the] works of charity."[30] Their enclosure simply reflected contemporary rules of propriety in rural areas. A moral prohibition forbade men to enter a rural house where women were alone, in contrast with urban situations, where there was often a great lack of privacy.[31] As nothing is said about the rest of the sisters' way of life, they must have continued to follow the customs of their environment, but with individual practices specified: "to go to church," and to visit "the sick, hospitals, and prisons, and other works of charity."

The Original Constitutions

The original Constitutions state that the sisters live "in the same house, in the manner of religious, few in number."[32] This house is

> ordinarily an apartment in a hospital or an orphanage. It will have several sections: an enclosure for [the sisters] . . . another to which they can go out to accommodate the *dames* and *demoiselles* who will want . . . to be instructed in virtue; and in the second apartment, they might arrange several rooms and bedrooms for the various assemblies of mercy, as well as for orphan girls who can be lodged there and trained for work, and to confine fallen women in need of help.[33]

As for the *agrégées* sisters, "as far as possible, they will live in the same house, only two or three together" and follow the same exercises as the other sisters.

The primitive Constitutions indicate two types of lodging. The first is housing for the sisters who work in a hospital or another house for the poor. In principle, these sisters have their own apartment, subdivided into "several sections," including a cloistered area for themselves and another, which can also be divided into smaller sections, for receiving lay persons in response to the demands of charity, both spiritual and corporal. The second type is housing for the *agrégées* sisters. As far as possible, they live in groups of "two or three together" in the same house. Apparently that sort of lodging was not always feasible. The Constitutions' description of the second kind of housing repeats what had already been proposed in the Règlements.

According to the original Constitutions, it seems the sisters rarely lived in a separate home, but rather in a section of a hospital establishment. This house usually did not belong to them. There was a good deal of circulation in the house: from the sisters' apartments to those reserved for hospitality or service, and from inside the house to the outside. There is no question of Francis de Sales' infinite precautions for the Visitation or Jeanne de Lestonnac's for the Company of Mary Our Lady. Fifty years earlier it had been necessary to provide for movement in and out of the house by setting up rules to cover propriety and adherence to the imperatives of the Council of Trent. Within fifty years, the standards for decorum had evolved, and as far as enclosure was concerned, the Sisters of St. Joseph were not nuns. Although the strict rules of enclosure dictated by the Council of Trent did not relate to them in their detailed rules of application, they did, very much so, in regard to their meaning of a break with the world. For this reason, in addition to the place for hospitality, they had a place of enclosure, in the sense of a place of retreat where they could perform their spiritual exercises more easily. For Father

Médaille, the sisters' house was similar to a tabernacle: what was lived within sent them outside "to the holy exercise of the advancement of the glory of God."[34]

The house for the sisters of the congregation, like that of the *agrégées* sisters, had an apostolic openness. No description is given of these houses because no structure was indispensable to them, not even a chapel. The sisters could have their own oratory and, for worship, share the life of the parish community. Any house could be suitable, provided that it was able to be adapted, according to the situations and the needs, for the ordinary life of the sisters and the apostolic service of the neighbor.

The Constitutions of Vienne (1694)

The Constitutions of Vienne contain guidelines similar to those of the original documents with some minor differences: sisters' housing in hospitals seems no longer the norm. The sisters' house is presented as autonomous, yet still divided into several apartments.[35] If possible, "there will be . . . a particular apartment for a dormitory" in which each sister will have her own room or at least her own bed "in so far as that is possible." This dormitory with individual cells is a mode of conventual life. For example, it was recommended for the Visitation nuns: "As far as possible, the sisters will each have her own small room, and at least they will sleep alone, each to her own bed."[36] Other apartments in a house of Sisters of St. Joseph, if they had them and it was possible, were used for those who wished to make a retreat among the sisters and also for Assemblies of Mercy. Finally, the text speaks of the sisters who were "established in hospitals . . . houses of orphans or of penitents." These lodgings seem to have become the most poorly apportioned, since they were to house themselves there "however they could." They were, nevertheless, to try to have "a separate apartment, to sleep in . . . and to make their [spiritual] exercises." The Rules for the Portress state that in "hospitals and other houses for the poor," the housing for the sisters "cannot be so regular."[37] An enclosure might exist between the inside and outside of the house, but this separation was undoubtedly much more difficult to observe within the building. Therefore, the portress was to be all the more attentive to the persons entering and leaving and to all that went on in the house.

The redactor of the 1694 Constitutions seems to have been in something of a quandary in drawing up the chapter on housing. After recalling the general principle from the original Constitutions that "the Sisters shall not observe a strict enclosure" because they "must be dedicated to the service of the neighbor," the text presents three suggestions, or rather three preferences, concerning the sisters' lodging, in particular about their bed, the apartments used for the spiritual and corporal works of mercy, and the housing of sisters in hospitals. There is an impression that what is presented here, although desirable ("if it is possible") is not what usually occurred in all the sisters' houses. The text takes this into account by suggesting the ideal but allowing leeway for the possible.

The chapter on the *agrégées* sisters merely mentions their house, without saying anything more. The same chapter refers several times to the community of the *agrégées*. It is not clear whether the terms "house" and "community" completely overlap. The community of *sœurs agrégées* may have existed in the community of inhabitants that formed the parish without all of them living together in the house of the *agrégées*.

Like the previous texts, the 1694 Constitutions do not describe the houses of the Sisters of St. Joseph as monasteries. In 1694 as in 1650, the same conditions are required for a house compatible with the sisters' vocation: a minimum of enclosure along with apostolic proximity to the neighbor.

The Sisters' Lodgings and Life in the Communities

A comparison of the houses of Sisters of St. Joseph in the seventeenth and those of the eighteenth centuries would evidence great differences in size and architecture, generally connected with geographical diversity. Most houses of the Sisters of St. Joseph, however, were located in the country, in rural areas of the Massif-Central, so some grasp of the peasant housing at this period is necessary to understanding the sisters' habitation. The peasant house was not simply a building to lodge the family group. It also housed everything that pertained to the family: storerooms for food, tools, harvested crops, and animals.[38] The word "house" referred to all the private belongings the family possessed. Nevertheless, study of the dwelling in its material aspects cannot be separated from consideration of the related persons who lived together there. Documents coming from early houses of Sisters of St. Joseph demonstrate effectively how much the buildings where they lived were related to their life. In general, the sisters moved into lodgings that they thought compatible with the apostolic and charitable works they wanted or had been requested to do. In the latter case, if it were a hospital, they accepted the lodging provided them by the administrators in a section of the house. The situation of the Sisters of St. Joseph regarding both lodging and work in the hospital houses can provide grounding for the subsequent examination of other varieties of their housing and settings.

The Hospital Houses

The first community established in Le Puy in 1650 and authorized by Bishop de Maupas was at the Hôpital des Orphelines in the Montferrand quarter. We have no information about the sisters' lodging there. Manuscript constitutions of the same period probably describe either how the sisters lived or what they were trying to organize: "Various sections: one, an enclosure for them . . . another to which they can go out to accommodate *dames* and *demoiselles* who will want . . . to be instructed in virtue." In the latter space, they could use "several rooms and bedrooms for . . . teaching the orphan girls to work." The administrators in many other hospitals provided housing for the Sisters of St. Joseph within the workplace, as they did for the *donnades* and other groups of women in hospitals. The contract "between the *Dames directrices* of the Hôpital de la Providence and the Daughters of St. Joseph" in Grenoble on December 17, 1694, noted that the directresses "promise . . . to provide in the said Hôpital de la Providence a private room in which [the sisters] will each have a bed with the furnishings they will need."[39] The contract for the house of the Bon-Pasteur in Clermont specified that the "administrators will provide each of the said sisters with a room or bed and the furnishings, and common linen."[40] Other larger hospitals, such as the Maison des Recluses in Lyon or the hospital at St. Vallier, signed similar contracts with the Sisters of St. Joseph.

Sometimes the sisters in smaller houses worked at the hospital without any specific contract. A report of 1724 describes the hospital of Bourg-Argental in the Forez, near Vienne:

> There are ordinarily eight sick poor or elderly (having only that number of beds). . . . The house is directed by five or six *filles dévotes* associated under the name of Sisters of St. Joseph, but without vows or contract with the Hôtel-Dieu, living on their own goods and with no remuneration other than their simple lodging which they have in the house.[41]

Having a contract, however, did not guarantee that its terms would be kept. In Vienne the rectors of the hospital did not fulfill their part of the bargain to give the sisters lodging separate from that of the poor. Mother Burdier and her sisters had to petition a second time that "without inconveniencing the quarters of the poor, they might have in the hospital some apartment of their own to perform the exercises of their Rules."[42] As needs changed, contracts and conditions of lodging evolved. At the hospital in Gap, a contract signed on September 17, 1671, stated that "the said sisters will have an apartment in the said hospital that is appropriate to their way of life."[43] By the following year, however, there was already mention of the purchase of "a small house that is attached to the said hospital, on the west side . . . to create several rooms to lodge the religious and put the furnishings from the said hospital." Because the administrators made this decision, it was they who assumed the financial burden. The transit of troops and epidemics made work in the hospital at Gap particularly heavy, and the sisters needed housing that would enable them to have enough privacy to recover from the serious fatigue it entailed. In Vienne Mother Burdier bought a house at the end of the seventeenth century, with permission from the archbishop and administrators, to be used by the penitent women and sisters. This house became the property of the community and, later, the "monastery" of the Sisters of St. Joseph of Vienne. As far as we know, the sisters did not become owners of separate housing at the Maison des Recluses in Lyon or the Bon-Pasteur in Clermont. For the entire time up to the Revolution, they lived in the institutions where they worked. It would be interesting to have an idea of how much space the sisters occupied in a hospital in comparison with the inmates. Unfortunately, no diagrams have survived. When the Refuge in Clermont was sold as property of the state, the assessor noted that the building was "of good construction and very beautiful architecture."[44] If this new building, put up between 1767 and 1770 and larger than the previous one, permitted inclusion of a boarding school, then it certainly could offer sizeable accommodation for the sisters and for the penitents, the primary purpose for the construction.

None of this detail yields any information about the conditions of life for the sisters within their houses. The growing number of sisters employed in hospitals by administrators may signify that their works were evolving, and consequently, their living conditions. There were originally six sisters for forty residents at the orphanage in Le Puy.[45] In 1790 the Revolutionary inventories reported "fifteen sisters, one lay sister and one servant," and only "fifteen poor little orphans."[46] By then, and for a long time, the sisters had become the owners of the houses where the orphans lived at Montferrand and acquired in addition several other properties and domains. Such good management allowed them to provide needed renovations for the hospital.

The Maison des Recluses in Lyon was also enlarged. In 1696, only three sisters signed the contract with the directors. By 1757 there were ten sisters; in 1766 and 1773, nine; and in 1784, twelve.[47] Since 1730 this community had been independent of Vienne and had operated its own novitiate, for which the rectors would have had to provide housing. From then on, the number of sisters at the service of the interned women could grow more freely. Records of the *Maison forcée* always mention, along with the sisters, a "*tourière* and servant," who belonged to the personnel of the house rather than to the religious community. The number of women confined also grew after 1730: by 1778 there were eighty, and plans were made to enlarge the house to accommodate up to 100 or 150.[48] This development indicates good administration on the part of the directors in a felicitous cooperation with the sisters. Because the administrators' satisfaction with the sisters' work at the Maison des Recluses is documented, it is reasonable to think, that besides enlarging the house, they also ameliorated the conditions of life and work for the community. Satisfaction did not mean equality. The new hospital rules, dated December 2, 1773, reiterate that the sisters "will conform themselves in everything to what the general good of the work will require under the inspection and orders of the *bureau*."[49]

Conditions were different at the Hôpital de la Providence in Grenoble. Four sisters were hired by contract in 1694 to "care for the poor of the said hospital."[50] Among them, "one will perform the surgery and the other run the pharmacy." Along with the sisters, the administrators hired as many servants as necessary to take care of the poor—rather than the sick—but the number of sisters remained set at four. In 1764 there were six servants with the four sisters; in 1782, there were thirteen.[51] The contract with the hospital stipulating four sisters had been signed by Jeanne Burdier in the name of the sisters of St. Joseph of Vienne. The House of Grenoble did not have a novitiate and continued under the authority of the Vienne community until the Revolution. Both parties maintained the terms of the contract: Vienne sent four sisters who would occupy the same positions, and the hospital continued to provide the sisters "a private room" with "a bed" and furnishings.

The Bon-Pasteur in Clermont illustrates yet another arrangement. Like the sisters at Grenoble, those who arrived in Clermont in 1723 came from Vienne. In 1729, however, the community of Clermont broke its ties with its house of origin. Armed with the permission of Bishop Massillon and the administrators, it opened its own novitiate. According to the contract signed by three sisters in 1725, they had been asked for "in order to direct, govern, and administer the said house of the Refuge under the authority and direction of their Excellencies the Bishops of Clermont."[52] The sisters reported to the bishops about management of the house. The contract says nothing precise about housing, except that the sisters would have a room or a bed and furnishings. The provisions made for the sisters at Clermont allowed them much greater freedom than the community at the Maison des Recluses in Lyon, which pursued similar charitable activities. This freedom may have been the reason why it seems the sisters at the Bon-Pasteur of Clermont never purchased another house for themselves. They were satisfied to live in the Refuge, but under conditions where they could use the freedom given them to open the house to the exterior by taking in orphans and creating workrooms, free classes, and even a boarding school. On the eve of the Revolution the sisters' lodgings had certainly been considerably enlarged, since the list prepared for the revolutionaries on April 17, 1792, includes nineteen sisters and one *agrégée*.[53]

This brief overview of some of the larger hospitals where Sisters of St. Joseph worked reveals a diversity related to various situations, needs, customs, and persons. We still know nothing specific about the sisters' living quarters and how they lived in them. Nothing unique to the Sisters of St. Joseph emerges from the various houses and their ways of life. Part of the distinctive style of the Congregation of St. Joseph appears to be precisely the sisters' capacity for working with others, for taking situations as they are. The sisters' lodging in the hospital houses had so little importance from the point of view of the administrators that they hardly mention it. Its unimportance accentuates that the sisters' housing, in the hospital establishments as in the small outlying houses, was first and foremost a means to apostolic presence. Even though we do not know exactly how they lived community in the different types of hospitals, it is obvious, as much in reality as in the texts, that the sisters' housing was nothing like a monastery.

The Small Country Houses

Apart from the very distinctive hospital establishments where the sisters lived in what might be called functional housing, it is challenging to find categories for classifying all the other buildings. A way to begin is simply to study what happened in regard to housing at the foundation of the humblest communities of St. Joseph, those established in the country.

The papers of the earliest small communities seldom mention the house where the first sisters gathered together. Sometimes they refer to rooms rented by the sisters in order to live together and carry out their "spiritual exercises." This was the case for Riotord (Haute-Loire), founded in 1659, and Vanosc (Ardèche), in 1675. How long the sisters rented their housing depended upon their number, works, and resources. At Izieux, near Saint-Etienne (Loire), the first three sisters began to live together in 1672 and "lived as renters for about eight years."[54] At Saint-Genest-l'Erpt, also near Saint-Etienne, a house of St. Joseph was established in 1680.[55] The sisters there "rented until 1723," or more than forty years. On September 29 of that year, "they made the acquisition of a house with a garden" using "their savings" and the modest dowries they had brought. In other cases, any mention of lodging came only some years after the date of foundation. At Saint-Jeures, Le Puy diocese, where the community was established in 1657, "*Messire* François Gervais, priest and *curé* of Saint Jeures," donated to the sisters "a house to live in" on August 5, 1661. Where they lived between 1657 and 1661 remains unknown. In Jonzieux, formerly in the Le Puy diocese, three women had come together in 1660 to constitute "a group of daughters of the congregation of St. Joseph [whose] rules and statutes they have observed."[56] These women did not make their first commitment until February 1, 1664, however, "because the house of the said daughters was not completely settled and they had no assured lodging." By 1664, their lodging must have been secured. At the time they made their profession, their relatives—two brothers and a father, all three of them farmers—guaranteed the dowry before the notary.

There is no word about housing in the records of Saint-Romain-Lachalm, one of the earliest small communities of St. Joseph, which record that Father Médaille gave the habit to Jeanne Perrilhon and Marguerite Monchouvet on October 15, 1652. [57] The purchase of lodging does not appear until December 6, 1659, when Jeanne Périlhon, the first superior, and Louise Brunet bought a house "composed of two rooms and roofed with tiles." Many other examples of the same type occur in the documents, all of them demonstrating that to live the vocation of St. Joseph in this way, the simplest house sufficed, and it was acquired as soon as possible. In some rarer cases, the house was provided from the beginning by a pastor, the family of a sister, or a generous benefactor, but it was never a very large house. The Règlements stated in fact, "the sisters will try to have a small house." If they do not have one in the beginning, they "will try" to acquire one. Their houses were comparable in every way to other houses in the area. As the number of sisters increased, the house had to be enlarged or another acquired. At Saint-Julien-Vocance, (Ardèche), the Sisters of St. Joseph were established around 1654 or 1655.[58] By 1726, their number had grown, and also their work. The house was too small and the superior, Catherine Giraud, explained their difficulty:

> they have trouble turning around in their house or setting up their looms to make ribbon there or even, in the winter, finding a place for the children whom the parish sends them to teach. There is no space even to make a cellar to store chestnuts, potatoes, beets, and other things; and even when they have something, the harshness of the winter spoils it all for them. [She therefore] begged and supplicated the said *Messire* Perret [the parish priest] to give them a corner of his garden . . . in order to construct a cellar and, above that, a room to put some beds and a pair of looms for making their ribbons.[59]

With the consent of the parishioners, the agreement was concluded before the notary by *Messire* Pierre Perret for the symbolic price of ten *sous* yearly plus thirty *sous* "for rights of entry." The house of the sisters adjoined the pastor's garden. It was also close to the church, because they had no chapel. It was common for all the small houses like Saint-Julien to be established near a church because they were without chapels.

In some aspects, these small communities set up in ordinary housing were similar to those in large hospital-based houses. They, too, began often without a house that belonged to them. The sisters' housing, whether large or small, was always incidental to what went on within. Although in a way different from that of the hospital sisters, those in these small country houses were also able to be very present to their milieu for all kinds of apostolic service.

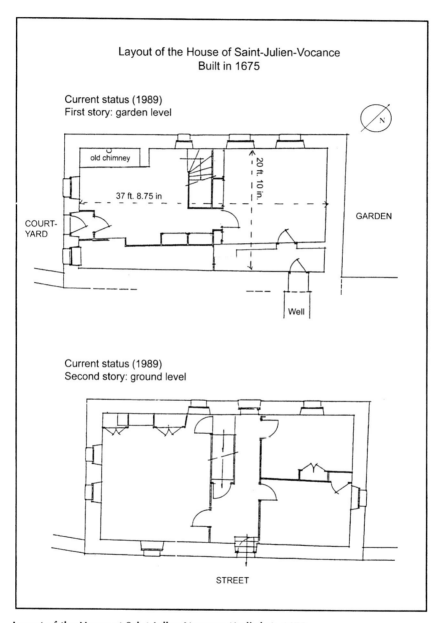

Layout of the House at Saint-Julien-Vocance (Ardèche), 1675

The "Houses of Our Principal Daughters"

At the beginning of the eighteenth century, between the larger hospital houses (where the Sisters of St. Joseph were not necessarily numerous) and the small lodgings of the *agrégées* sisters, there was a gamut of other houses, as diverse in their size as in their works. In the Eucharistic Letter, Father Médaille refers to the "houses of our principal daughters," that is, houses or communities of the sisters properly speaking of the congregation. By definition, these principal houses were different from those of the *agrégées*, but, like the orphanage in Le Puy, they could be established and exist within the walls of a hospital. Telling the two types of houses apart is not entirely simple. Every house not specifically designated in the documents as one of *agrégées* was not necessarily a house "of our principal daughters." In many cases there is not enough precise information to be able to place a house in one category or the other. These categories had evolved, moreover, by the time houses were established in the eighteenth century, and it is impossible to refer to them in the same way as those founded in the mid-seventeenth century. Nonetheless, among the larger houses, some can be identified that seem to have played the role of a "principal house" as Father Médaille described it in the Avis et Règlements, that is, a house responsible for several small communities.[60] What follows is a study of the texts to determine whether they reveal any relatively constant traits in regard to the housing of the principal sisters.

Le Puy and Vienne were quite obviously among the principal houses in the history of the Sisters of St. Joseph—the latter, at least for part of its history. Other larger houses that were certainly principal houses include Saint-Didier, Tence, Craponne, and Chomelix in the Le Puy diocese, Viverols in the Clermont diocese, and perhaps Langogne in the diocese of Mende. Some houses, either because of the aid they offered or the responsibility they accepted for smaller houses from time to time, belong to a middle level between the principal houses and those of the *agrégées*. Others played the role of principal house in relation to only one or two daughter-houses, not necessarily smaller, such as Clermont for Cusset (Allier), a house established in 1763 at the hospital of Cusset, and Champeix for Vensat (Puy-de-Dôme). Some houses of *sœurs agrégées* seem in time to have become principal houses. These established other communities of *agrégées* for which they eventually became responsible. Such was the case of Dunières, the first house of *agrégées* sisters, Vanosc in the Ardèche, and Boisset in the Le Puy diocese. Other houses, either in their construction or their way of operating, had the aura of principal houses, for example, Saint-Anthème in the Clermont diocese and Saint-Paulien in the Le Puy diocese. At the present stage of research, however, there is not enough information to substantiate this impression.

Unlike houses of *agrégées* sisters, communities of sisters of the congregation properly speaking were always established from the outset in a specific house, bought or donated in advance for that purpose. The entire first part of this study demonstrated, in the case of the Le Puy community, how the preparation of the orphan hospital preceded the assembly of the first sisters. The community of Saint-Didier bought "houses and gardens . . . by contract of September 2, 1655," the approximate year of its foundation.[61] In Tence, where the community began around 1653, the sisters lived in a house belonging to the Jesuits, who held the benefice of Tence and to whom they paid manorial dues.[62] At Craponne in 1723, the pastor and uncle of one of the first sisters, "*Messire* Caprais de Vinols, prior of the said Craponne," gave to the community by "gift . . . inter vivos . . . a house which he owns in his own right." The sisters could not dispose of this house except to exchange it "for another which they subsequently judge more suitable for their exercise of piety and for housing their community."[63] This contract of association was passed and signed the very day of the foundation of the community of Craponne, April 23, 1723.

Notes in the community file for Viverols (Clermont diocese) show that at the time of its foundation, August 18, 1696, the patrimony of the community consisted of the dowries of the first sisters and a donation granted by Jean Breul, *curé* of Viverols.[64] The following year, on August 23, 1697, the Marquise of Colombines made another donation to the community on the occasion of the profession of the first sisters. Although there are no details about the content of these dowries and donations, given the social status of the first sisters' families, which included a lawyer-notary and a merchant, they undoubtedly contained buildings to be used for lodging. At Saint-Paulien in the Le Puy diocese, in 1700 Isabeau Delolme, a single woman who had reached her majority and whose father and mother were deceased, pledged to establish a house of Sisters of St. Joseph. She took the habit on October 30, 1701.[65] At the same time, the *curé*, Anthoine Viannès, purchased a house for the sisters. Catherine Jouve joined Isabeau in 1702 and signed a contract of association with her. In the Forez at Saint-Anthème (Clermont diocese), the community was founded as early as 1663 by "noble Balthazar de Pierrefort La Roue."[66] He gave the sisters buildings and a garden plus an annual income of 175 *livres* and 15 *sous*, desiring nothing in recompense for his "good works of mercy" but "eternal beatitude."

Another general characteristic was that the houses of the sisters properly speaking were larger and better organized than those of the *agrégées* sisters. Few descriptions survive of the dwellings sisters had at the foundations of principal houses. In Le Puy, where the sisters lived at the Hôpital des Orphelines, the provisions made by Bishop de Maupas were a renovation of the

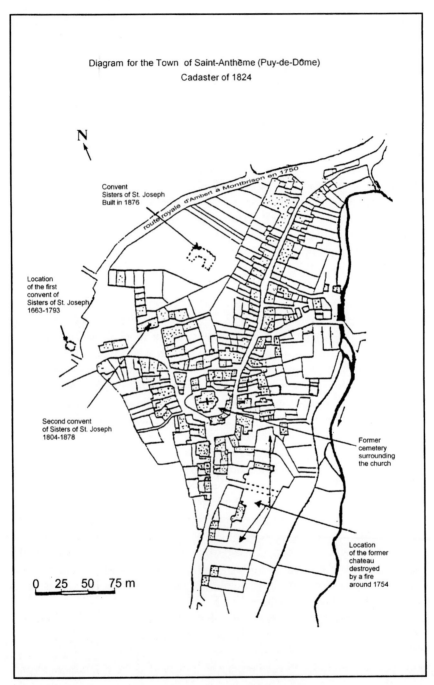

Diagram for the Town of Saint-Anthéme (Puy-de-Dôme)
Cadaster of 1824

N

Convent
Sisters of St. Joseph
Built in 1876

route royale d'Ambert a Montbrison en 1750

Location
of the first
convent of
Sisters of St. Joseph
1663-1793

Second convent
of Sisters of St. Joseph
1804-1878

Former
cemetery
surrounding
the church

Location
of the former
chateau
destroyed
by a fire
around 1754

0   25   50   75 m

Diagram of the Town of Saint-Antheme (Puy-de-Dôme), 1824

buildings and reorganization of the orphanage. One can imagine that the improvements occasioned a more specialized use of the rooms that facilitated both life and work. At Champeix in the Clermont diocese a house was purchased on May 12, 1731, for the community established there on August 6, 1729.[67] The house "was in the district of La Treille, composed of lower and upper rooms, an attic on top, two dovecotes, three small rented sheds, cellar, farmyard, granaries, barns, and other facilities." The house at Saint-Anthème donated by the Lord of Pierrefort La Roue had a chapel, kitchen, and refectory, along with two lower rooms, six upper rooms with cells, attics and storage, and a large garden. For a community just starting, this would have been a large house indeed.

Principal houses always had a chapel. If they did not have one when the community began, they soon acquired one, which explains why they were not always located near a church. At Craponne the sisters had a chapel from the beginning, but Mother de Vinols had a larger one built to accommodate an increased number of people for spiritual retreats. At Saint-Paulien the sisters had a chapel, and their house was situated "on the outskirts of the town of Saint-Paulien."[68] At Saint-Anthème the house was located on the edge of the built-up area, signifying that the principal sisters' houses were less integrated in the life of the village than those of the *agrégées*.[69]

A final characteristic of the beginnings of principal houses is that the contracts, conventions, authorizations, and other documents which gave official status to a community were obtained at the time of its foundation. It was important for the community to be situated and defined, not only in the eyes of those who expected services or a presence, as they did from the small houses of the *agrégées* sisters, but also in the eyes of the authorities who could recognize and support its existence. Although the sisters in the principal houses maintained within and outside their houses quite a number of the apostolic services of the *agrégées* sisters, they were better organized and enjoyed more resources, allowing them to expand these same services and to find the necessary social scope for the recognition, whether juridical, royal, or ecclesiastical, of the life of the Sisters of St. Joseph in these communities.

In conclusion, whether small houses of *agrégées* sisters, more prominent houses of principal sisters, or places reserved for sisters in the hospitals, there was no typical dwelling for Sisters of St. Joseph. For the small *agrégées* communities, the house itself displays no real importance. The style of housing for the *agrégées* sisters followed local custom and construction. As their works developed, the sisters would progressively enlarge their houses. Some small communities in service to a hospital could also be attached to a small house of *agrégées*: at Sauxillanges they were referred to as "secular daughters joined as a group in the Confraternity of St. Joseph."[70] Within the hospitals, whatever the services rendered, the sisters' lodging, separated only with difficulty from the rest of the house, often placed them in great proximity to the poor. Father Médaille had compared the principal houses "to tabernacles, always locked with a key, from which our sisters will leave only through obedience . . . only for the holy exercise of the advancement of the glory of God."[71] The frequent location of such houses at the edge of a town or village could indicate that the sisters maintained the aspect of retreat expressed in the comparison. The evolution of these houses and their works can demonstrate their apostolic openness as well.

DAILY LIFE: PRAYER AND WORK

The new institutes of nuns established in the first half of the seventeenth century to include charitable works (such as the Congregation of Mary Our Lady), had found it necessary to adapt the ordinary monastic schedules or forms of prayer in order to make room for care of the poor and sick, the education of girls, or other types of charity toward the neighbor. The daily life of the new orders was almost always modeled, with adaptations, on that of existing monasteries. Convents of the mendicant orders founded in the Middle Ages generally followed the daily framework of a Benedictine monastery, with differences that emphasized their own characteristics. In a similar pattern, the arrangement of daily exercises of the Visitation in the seventeenth century closely followed that proposed by Teresa of Avila in the Constitutions of 1567 for the reformed Carmelites.[72]

In the nearly parallel unfolding of the day for Carmelite and Visitation nuns, differences lay more in how their exercises were done than in their nature. Carmelites spent longer periods of time in silence and in their cells than the Visitation nuns. They also spent more time in mental prayer (two hours in Carmel and an hour and a half at the Visitation) and did a little more spiritual reading (an hour on the one hand, half an hour on the other). The Visitation nuns, however, finished their spiritual reading with a time for exchange, meant for communication and mutual spiritual support. Apart from services in the monastery carried out by the officers, each Carmelite worked in her cell. Work was presented as a means of livelihood, and also as an opportunity for disposing the mind for prayer. At the Visitation, each worked morning or afternoon "where she will think appropriate." After a mid-day recess, the Visitation nuns spent the work period between noon and two o'clock on their own in silence. Work was not regarded as a means of making a living—the sisters must have had sufficient dowries to live on—rather, as at Carmel, it was a means to free the mind through manual labor or physical exercise. In general the Visitation schedule offered more relaxation, recreation, mutual presence, and communication among the sisters than the schedule at Carmel, but this merely exemplified the vocation of the Visitation, which included, in a very particular way, the sisters' charity toward one another through spiritual, material, and corporal support, especially for those in poor health. Taken as a whole, the daily schedule of the Visitation is modeled on that of Carmel. The observable differences only highlight the unique aspects of each vocation.

The Daily Schedule in Texts of Sisters of St. Joseph

The schedule given in the various manuscripts of the Règlements shows at a glance that the framework of the daily life of the Sisters of St. Joseph recaptures the framework for the Visitation.[73] The Constitutions manuscripts present a more detailed schedule than those of the Règlements and they contain the same daily markers as the Visitation horarium.[74] Some similarities may be due to common references to local customs in the south of France. For example, dinner at 10 a.m. and supper at 6 p.m., whether at Carmel, the Visitation, or St. Joseph, could only be attributed to local custom. During the same period, the Daughters of the Cross and the Daughters of Charity of Vincent de Paul in Paris had dinner at noon or 11:45.[75] Such differences, insignificant in themselves, indicate the influence of local custom on the life of religious communities.

Much more indicative of a particular type of vocation is the form of prayer and the distribution of prayer and work throughout the day. In the manuscript Constitutions of the Sisters of St. Joseph, as in those of the Visitation and many other monastic or apostolic institutes, there were two periods for meditation: the first, upon rising in the morning (half an hour for St. Joseph, an hour for the Visitation); and the second in the afternoon, after the various activities of the day (half an hour in each case). In the St. Joseph schedule, vocal prayer figures strongly throughout the day: the Angelus, Little Office of the Holy Spirit, various litanies, *De Profundis*, the rosary, and prayers for benefactors or those who are dying. Their placement during the day (morning, noon, four o'clock, and evening) indicates that they replaced the hours of the Office sung by nuns in choir. Several manuscripts note that the Sisters of St. Joseph attended "only one Mass" each day. This probably means that these houses had a chapel where several Masses took place daily. Some sisters may have been enticed to spend too much time there, perhaps out of a mistaken devotion or the temptation to laziness. There must have been reasons for specifying attendance at one Mass. In fact, the devotion of the Sisters of St. Joseph should, by definition, be shown as much in work and service as in prayer.

Work actually took up a very large part of the day. The sisters began manual work in the morning after prayer, when they gathered around seven

DAILY SCHEDULE

SISTERS OF ST. JOSEPH

VISITATION

Summer schedule
(one hour later than in winter)

-Rising	
-mediation (1 hour)	5 h 30
-prime (recited)	6 h
-pysical excercise and various charges	7 h
-Terce and Sext	8 h
- Mass and Nones	
-Examen	
-"Work," each one where she wishes	
-Dinner in silence with spiritual reading	10 h
-Recreation until noon	
-Work, in silence and alone	12 h
-Siesta (1/2 hour) if they wish	1 h

Constitutions manuscripts (B, G, S)¹

5 h	-Rising followed by vocal prayer
	-meditation (1/2 hour)
	-Office of the Holy Spirit and other vocal prayers
	(fix one's room, charges, prepare dinner: Ms A and L)
	-Manual work while giving an account of the meditation
8 h	-Mass ("only one Mass")
	-Work
10 h	-Examen *("and their particular examen": Ms L)*
	-Dinner, silence and spiritual reading
	-Recreation (1 hour) with the freedom to work or not
12 h	-Angelus, De profundis, litany of Our Lady, then work in silence
1 h	-Spiritual reading (1/4 hour) while all work, followed by a discussion about the reading

Reglements manuscripts

4 h	-Rising
	-same
	-same Between rising and the examen at ten o'clock, no precise time is given for any exercise
	-same
	-same
	-same
	-Work
10 h	-Examen
	-Dinner, reading (for half the meal, followed by silence)
	-same
	-same
	-same + particular examen and silence
	-same

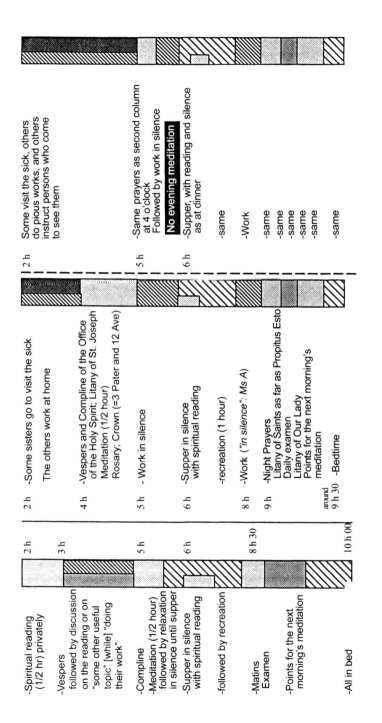

	Column 1		Column 2		Column 3
2 h	-Spiritual reading (1/2 hr) privately	2 h	-Some sisters go to visit the sick / The others work at home	2 h	Some visit the sick, others do pious works, and others instruct persons who come to see them
3 h	-Vespers followed by discussion on the reading or on "some other useful topic" [while] "doing their work"	4 h	-Vespers and Compline of the Office of the Holy Spirit; Litany of St. Joseph Meditation (1/2 hour) Rosary; Crown (=3 Pater and 12 Ave)		
5 h	-Compline	5 h	- Work in silence	5 h	-Same prayers as second column at 4 o'clock Followed by work in silence **No evening meditation**
6 h	-Meditation (1/2 hour) followed by relaxation in silence until supper	6 h	-Supper in silence with spiritual reading	6 h	-Supper, with reading and silence as at dinner
	-Supper in silence with spiritual reading		-recreation (1 hour)		-same
	-followed by recreation	8 h	-Work ("in silence": Ms A)		-Work
8 h 30	-Matins Examen	9 h	-Night Prayers Litany of Saints as far as Propitus Esto Daily examen Litany of Our Lady Points for the next morning's meditation		-same -same -same -same
	-Points for the next morning's meditation	around 9 h 30	-Bedtime		-same
10 h 00	-All in bed				-same

Legend:

Prayer   Formation   Work   Daily Living   External activities

Daily Schedule for Visitation Nuns and Sisters of St. Joseph

o'clock to discuss their meditation. They worked between Mass, which finished around nine o'clock, and the examen, which began at ten (in summer). Work continued from noon until one o'clock and during the time of spiritual reading and discussion. The sisters also worked in the afternoon, whether or not they went out for apostolic or charitable works, then from five until six in the evening, and finally from eight until nine o'clock, before the prayers that concluded the day. During their recreation after meals they had "freedom to work or not." Thus their workday totaled between seven and nine hours each day.

There were various types of work done for different purposes. In every case, work was done first of all to support the life of the community, as in Carmel, and to "provide from that for the needs of the poor."[76] Work also prevented boredom and idleness. In addition to utility, work supported and accompanied times for personal reflection, periods of silence, and spiritual sharing after the reading. In this case, it was simple work that did not absorb the mind. Certain handiwork could also contribute to relaxation during recreation time or could even be done when a sister was in the parlor. In addition, the sisters' work, inside the house or outside, necessarily included many aspects of charitable and apostolic service, since by their very vocation, they were to be at the service of every kind of neighbor. Several manuscripts of the Constitutions note that during the day, "some sisters will go out to visit the sick" between two and four in the afternoon, while others remain at home working. These manuscripts come from Le Puy, Gap, and Saint-Didier, orphanages or hospitals where the works of mercy were exercised inside the house. Visiting the sick outside the house only complemented and extended the principal activities of the house, and so only "some sisters" went out to visit the sick.

A comparison of the distribution of time in the manuscripts of the Constitutions and the Règlements shows that generally the schedule of the latter was more fluid. In the Règlements the morning includes the same exercises as in the Constitutions, but no precise information about time is given between rising (four o'clock in the summer) and the time for the meal at ten o'clock (preceded by the examen). There is not even a precise time given for Mass. The Règlements were intended for the *agrégées* communities in the country, and these had no chapel in their houses. The *agrégées* sisters attended Mass at their parish church. Since the time of Mass would vary from parish to parish, the times for morning exercises varied as well, and it was therefore impossible to establish a uniform schedule for all the houses of the *agrégées*.

The afternoon schedule for the *agrégées* as given in the Règlements differed somewhat from that of the principal sisters described in the Constitutions. According to the Règlements manuscripts for the *agrégées* houses, beginning at two o'clock "some will devote themselves to visiting the sick and other pious works; others will take care of instructing those persons who will come to see them."[77] They might also "teach catechism or give lessons to children;" however, all would "work as much as their spiritual exercises will allow." It seems they were all involved in apostolic work. At five o'clock only, not at four as in the Constitutions, the sisters came home and gathered to recite the same vocal prayers offered by the sisters of the principal houses: Vespers and Compline from the Office of the Holy Spirit, litanies of St. Joseph, and the rosary with its crown of three Our Fathers and twelve Hail Marys. The *agrégées* sisters did not, however, make the half hour of meditation scheduled for the principal sisters. After the rosary they worked in silence until supper at six. The day ended identically in both types of communities. Supper (like dinner) was accompanied by reading and silence. It was followed by an hour of recreation until eight o'clock, then another hour of work from eight until nine o'clock. The day ended with the recitation of the Litany of the Saints, the examen for the day, and reading of the points for meditation for the following morning.

The differences in schedule between the *agrégées* sisters and principal sisters raise the following questions: Were the *agrégées* sisters religious? If they gave less time to meditation and more time to service inside and outside, were they not similar to the *donnades* sisters of the hospitals? A study of the "Règlement for the *Donnade* sisters of the Hôtel-Dieu of Notre Dame du Puy" shows that their primary task was service of the sick: "The ordinary work of the *Donnade* Sisters consists in perpetual exercises of charity, and . . . charity indispensably demands an order."[78] There is a parallel between the organization of the works of charity in the Règlement of the *donnades* and the long periods set aside by the *agrégées* of St. Joseph for service to the neighbor. Later, article 15 of the same règlement states:

> The little Règlement only describes the distribution of hours of the day; the [*donnades*] sisters should make sure that none of those [times for prayer] should take precedence over service to the sick, and during the time ascribed to the said exercises, if need demand it, they should leave everything and go back to [the sick] to be with them as long as necessary.

Clearly, the raison d'être for the *donnades* was work with the sick. The times for prayer—meditation for half an hour, Mass, rosary, and spiritual reading— were organized as a support for their Christian life and their charitable works, in order to "inspire them with means to accomplish their task . . . according to God's will" (art. 2). Despite the similarities, it was not exactly the same for the *agrégées* Sisters of St. Joseph. According to the rule for the *donnades*, the exercises of piety, shorter than those of the *agrégées*, did not present the same quality of pursuit of profound Christian perfection for those who practice them. There is no mention of apostolic work or spiritual help for the sick. It seems that the *donnades* only responded to the corporal needs of the sick.

Their schedule and the well-defined aims it includes are very different from those of the *agrégées* of St. Joseph.

If not *donnades*, were the *agrégées* sisters closer to the *béates* or other women who were members of third orders in the Massif Central? The oldest religious orders, particularly mendicants—Carmelites, Dominicans, and Franciscans—had always gathered into their orbit groups of pious lay women, living the same spirituality and dedicated to charitable works. There was a Third Order of Mount Carmel at Saugues in the Haute-Loire and a Third Order of Saint Dominic at Langeac. In 1668 in Le Puy, slightly later than the founding of the Sisters of St. Joseph, Anne-Marie Martel founded the congregation of the "Demoiselles de l'Instruction" and a type of third order belonging to the congregation, the "Filles de l'Instruction." These groups of associated women, who in part formed the origins of the *béates* of the Velay, grew very rapidly. They played a crucial role in the evangelization of rural populations and in the education and instruction of young girls and women, not only in the Velay, but in the neighboring regions of southeastern France.[79]

The apostolic and charitable work of the Filles de l'Instruction and the *béates*, their way of being present to all, closely resembled certain educational activities and types of apostolic presence on the part of the *agrégées* of St. Joseph dispersed through the countryside. The *Vie de M. de Lantages*, which gives an account of the beginning of Filles de l'Instruction, contains a description of the daily life of these sisters: "They rose at a given hour and after prayer they devoted themselves to meditation for half an hour . . . followed by holy Mass. . . . Each action had its time: there was an hour for recreation, an hour for silence," times for instruction and work. With the young women whom they instructed, they "recited the rosary antiphonally."[80] These directions are too vague to allow anyone to know the exact spiritual core for the Filles de l'Instruction. By contrast a document printed at the beginning of the 19th century, the *Règle et conduite pour les Filles Associées de la Maison de l'Instruction de la ville du Puy*, indicates that there is a certain similarity both in life and action to the *agrégées* Sisters of St. Joseph. This evidence is not surprising, since passages of the *Règle et conduite* were borrowed from the Constitutions of the Sisters of St. Joseph. An example is the chapter in regard to the charity of the sisters among themselves, titled "Rules common to all the Filles de l'Instruction."[81]

A certain relationship cannot be denied between the *agrégées* Sisters of St. Joseph and the Filles de l'Instruction, at least in external forms of service, even if the Sisters of St. Joseph did not limit their apostolic activities to education "of young persons of their sex." In order to understand this kinship better, we must study more closely the nature of the commitment which joined the *agrégées* sisters to the vocation of St. Joseph. The problem is whether the *agrégées* sisters, like the Filles de l'Instruction in their connection with their congregation, simply collaborated in apostolic works based on the same spiritual orientation, like a third order, or if they really and wholly shared the same vocation as the principal sisters but lived it differently.

Neither Nuns Nor *Béates*

Although the framework for the daily life of the Visitation served as a basis to organize the day for Sisters of St. Joseph, the content inserted in this framework was quite unlike the life of Visitation nuns. For instance, chanting the Divine Office in choir was replaced by various vocal prayers on weekdays and by the Little Office of the Blessed Virgin on Sundays and holy days. The Sisters of St. Joseph devoted a little less time to mental prayer than the Visitation nuns, but many more hours to work. Above all, Sisters of St. Joseph had no monastic enclosure so they could do apostolic and charitable works for every kind of neighbor.

Variations in the manuscripts concerning both the exact allocation of hours of the day and the activities that filled them show clearly that each house of St. Joseph, large or small, adapted the prescriptions of the texts to its own needs. Each retained a level of autonomy in setting up its daily life. It is practically impossible, nevertheless, to grasp how the sisters actually brought together prayer and action in their daily organization in each house because there are not enough documents revealing the spiritual life of individuals or communities during this time. At most, through information about types of work and service, we can detect the degree of apostolic openness on the part of a given community, both inside and outside the house. One can retrieve certain facets about the allotment of time indirectly through variations in the manuscripts of the Constitutions and Règlements. The 1694 Vienne Constitutions completely eliminated those variations, at least in theory, and the question remains whether the content of the Constitutions and the Reglements was actually applied, and in what way. We must examine the historic diversity of apostolic services once more to try to detect their impact on the daily life of the sisters.

In hospital houses that had a well-defined juridical status, in addition to the principal activities—services to penitents, orphans, the sick, and so forth—other activities were often added either within or outside the house. At Vienne in 1723, thanks to the generous endowment of *Demoiselle* Antony, six sisters worked at the Hôtel-Dieu, two others took care of "the instruction of the poor girls of Vienne and the surrounding places," and two other sisters were "living in the house of the penitent women . . . to direct them."[82] In these houses, managed ultimately by the administrators, eventual changes in the charitable works or employment of sisters in other services depended in part on the apostolic openness of the community, and above all of its superior, but also on the rapport between the sisters and their employers. At the Maison Forcée des Recluses in Lyon, sisters seemed to have devoted themselves exclusively to the purpose of the house without looking beyond it. If they expressed other desires, they were not recorded. Even though their number increased from three in 1696 to ten in 1757, we have no evidence of the administrators' allowing them to pursue other works of mercy.[83]

Within the community the activities called "manual work," equivalent to "the work" of the Visitation nuns, varied from region to region according to local custom. In Le Puy, Craponne, and in the Velay, the sisters taught lace making to the girls. In the Forez, most sisters in small houses were called "ribbon makers," because making ribbon was how they earned their living, and the technique of weaving ribbon was what they taught the young girls. At the hospital of Vienne, they sewed and span; early in the eighteenth century, there was also a "place for spinning the work in hemp and wool done by the poor for the people in town." At the Refuge in Clermont, "the work of the community consisted in sewing and embroidery with thread," which was done by both day students and penitent women.[84]

In houses where the sisters themselves directed and organized the work under the authority of the spiritual father or the pastor, they more easily undertook diverse occupations. A census of religious houses in the Clermont diocese in the mid-eighteenth century indicates that the community of Sisters of St. Joseph of Arlanc, a small town of the Livradois, was composed of ten sisters, of whom one provided help "for the Hospital of Arlanc . . . taking turns with the other sisters who are in their house next to the hospital."[85] The majority of other sisters were involved in the education of girls. At Craponne (Haute-Loire), where the primary works of the sisters also had to do with various types of education for girls and women, the request for royal letters patent in 1766 shows that the sisters "never refused their aid" to the hospital of the town; whenever "they thought they could be useful, they always went there with ardent zeal."[86] Many other houses could provide evidence showing that the principal activity of the community within the house did not exclude participating in other services outside. The papers of the house in Langogne, near Mende in Gévaudan, offer a helpful overview of how the eight sisters of the community there in 1745 gave great service, both within the house and outside.

> [They] are useful to the public: 1st Because they take care of the instruction of young girls, raising them in the love and fear of the Lord. 2nd They accept and provide for orphan girls gratis and give them the education necessary to their social status. 3rd They tirelessly visit prisoners, the sick, and the afflicted, consoling them by bringing them all back to God through their pious exhortations. 4th They are of very great help to families shamed by the charities which they obtain from pious persons, which they [the sisters] arrange to have given secretly into their hands. 5th Women or girls of ill repute are placed with them to put an end to their disorder.[87]

Despite this real diversity of services, nothing permits further insight into the effect of their apostolic work on the sisters' daily life in the house.

Historical evidence about apostolic openness in the communities of St. Joseph is perfectly in accord with the guidelines found in the manuscripts; it shows that the importance of work outside the house did not depend solely on the size of the community or its juridical status. Larger houses, which necessarily had more potential for external action, did not therefore have more apostolic freedom. Even so, the lay administration of a hospital did not always restrict the apostolic freedom of the sisters who worked there. Although it is true that the sisters in a larger house who were involved in institutional work directed by lay administrators tended to have lives more focused inside the house, this did not mean inside a cloister. The sisters could live there in close contact with the poor. On the other hand, a community, whether large or small, that was not tied to an institution could more easily modify its apostolic direction, and therefore its daily life, in response to local needs, the sisters' aptitudes, and the resources of the community. This type of generic information, however, does not help in distinguishing those aspects of life that were in fact most important to the sisters from others that simply took time. In many cases the work done by sisters in the smaller communities seems to place them more on the side of the *béates* than of the Visitation nuns. Under those circumstances, how could the Sisters of St. Joseph claim to live "in the manner of the most observant religious?"[88] How was the time spent in service of neighbor integrated into an authentic life consecrated to God? In other words, is there evidence in their life, as well as their texts, that the Sisters of St. Joseph drew as much spiritual profit from action and from every form of service as they did from prayer and contemplation?

Although more explicit documents on the spiritual life of the sisters do not exist, several necrologies providing details beyond simple mention of the death or the work done by the sister can reveal what was particularly valued by specific communities. The most interesting information comes from the register of professions of the house of Vienne, which includes the necrologies of a rather large number of sisters during the eighteenth century.[89] These were written towards the end of the century, after the community had become a monastery. It is not surprising to find singled out among the sisters' virtues, "the most exact regularity," or "zeal for wise and enlightened regularity," or "exactitude in the exercises of the rule." Such comments do not appear with the same insistence in the registers of other houses. The Vienne obituaries also refer to the gift of prayer in one sister or another. Sister Françoise Hervier was "very much given to vocal prayer which she often repeated aloud, as if she had been alone with God . . . she had no less attraction to mental [prayer]." Jeanne de Saint-Prié de Chateauneuf, "called Sister des Anges, had so much love for Jesus Christ in the Blessed Sacrament that in the last years of her life she was permitted daily communion." She said that "she considered herself more honored by the dignity of her habit than by the nobility of her house." For many years, "she gave beautiful witness . . . to her love for the poor." It is apparent that the problems the Vienne community had in understanding its own vocation did not prevent the sisters from becoming holy, even in the thick of these difficulties.

In addition to the extraordinary piety of certain sisters, the Vienne necrologies report other qualities as gifts from God for apostolic service—"dexterity in work," the gift of "educating the young," "zeal . . . to return to God souls who have gone astray," and "much piety, virtue, a kind heart combined with strength." Sister Françoise Bordin, it says, "was very fond of reading holy books. She owned the history of the Holy Bible and of Grenade [Louis of Grenada], from which she made very beautiful applications." The register of Vienne also records the human qualities of the sisters, their zeal in their charitable activities, and their assiduous presence in choir when they chanted the Office. In spite of all their claims, they were probably not so monastic as they would have had one believe. Present in choir, they continued in their own way to serve the neighbor.

Obituaries from other registers merely enumerate the sisters' virtues, especially charity, humility, and simplicity. At Saint-Amant-Roche-Savine and at Viverols in Livradois, the notices are much more stereotyped.[90] Very often, if not in every entry, the sister "became exemplary," and she did this "by the exact practice of the obligations of our holy institute." A frequently recurring theme was the community's edification: "by the practice of patience"; by patience and "resignation to the will of God in her illness"; and by the "singular patience with which she was animated through a tender and sincere love for the poor and sick." More personalized expressions occasionally appear amid the stereotypes. At the beginning of the nineteenth century two sisters from the house at Job related that Sister Madeleine Goutte, born in Job in 1760 and imprisoned in Clermont during the Revolution, had such great union with God during prayer that it made her insensible to everything that was happening around her. They said it was enough for them to look at her for an instant to become recollected as well. Sister Madeleine was equally remarkable for her love and practice of poverty and in her charity toward the destitute.[91] At Saint-Amant-Roche-Savine, Sister Marguerite Cartier also gave "exemplary edification . . . whether by a profound humility or the ardent love she had for the poor, or finally, by her fervor for holy and frequent communion." These brief annotations from the archives of several communities parallel what Abbé Clavel's biography portrays about Mother de Vinols in Craponne—that union with God sent her toward service of the sisters and her neighbor, and charitable and apostolic service turned her toward God.

Prayer and action cannot not be separated in the life of Sisters of St. Joseph as a whole any more than in their daily schedule. Prayer and action must interpenetrate and mutually validate each other by means of a sustained pedagogy of prayer and the spiritual life. All of the manuscripts designate such means. So, too, do the 1694 Constitutions of Vienne, which closely follow the daily schedule in the Constitutions manuscripts (MSS B, G, S). The first of these pedagogical means was reflection on the morning meditation: while doing manual work, the sisters were to give an account "with humility and candor, of the *sentiments*[92] God gave them during meditation."[93] This practice echoes the care required in the rules for the superior and the novice mistress in teaching the sisters "how to meditate well," this exercise being "very necessary to help all the sisters in the practice of what is most perfect . . . and in all their actions in life."[94] Spiritual reading, for the Sisters of St. Joseph as for Teresa of Avila and all spiritual authors, was considered a "sustenance for the soul . . . in some way as necessary as is food for the body," and it was important to profit from it.[95] All the St. Joseph manuscripts indicate that spiritual reading is always accompanied by time for reflection and discussion among the sisters, either on what they remember of the reading or on a related topic. This exchange, already practiced by the Visitation nuns, contributed toward the formation and mutual spiritual support of all the sisters, but still more, of those who could not read. Another daily means for apprenticeship in the spiritual life was the "examen of consciousness."[96] This tool for spiritual progress, known and practiced for several centuries before the Sisters of St. Joseph, was proposed to every Christian and to religious orders in particular. In the sixteenth century, Ignatius Loyola had given it a more precise form, used by the Jesuits and the members of their Marian congregations. All St. Joseph manuscripts, both the Constitutions and the Règlements, indicate that this daily examen took place at the end of the morning before the meal and at the end of the day before going to bed. The Règlement manuscripts speak of a "particular examen" that took place during noon prayers. It was a time when each sister would focus before God on a particular point in her personal life on which she chose to examine herself in order to progress. During this time of prayer each sister tried to understand what made her succeed and what for her was an obstacle.

In addition to this daily personal examen, once a week or bi-monthly, all the sisters of the community would confer together "on Sundays for half an hour on the state of their congregation and the works and actions which they ordinarily perform," especially their "works of zeal."[97] By this practice, they hoped to maintain the "good state of their congregation" and to identify the "faults that could slip in so that they might correct them." Other weekly, monthly, or annual exercises included confession, the *défi*, or challenge to virtue, the "protestations," times of recollection in preparation for holy days, and annual retreats. All of these were occasions to reflect upon their actual experience, and at the same time, to keep the vocation of St. Joseph always before their eyes in order to inspire in themselves the desire to tend toward it. The Règlement closes with "Exercises pertaining to the neighbor."[98] Just as they work toward their own sanctification, the sisters should take "care to give spiritual education and direction of life to all persons of their sex, according to their social status, age, and profession of life" while consulting "prudent and virtuous persons" about it. Working toward the sanctification of the neighbor was an integral part of the sisters' own program of sanctification.

The means of spiritual formation proposed by Father Médaille to the Sisters of St. Joseph were not their own. Nevertheless, the combination of these means and the way of suggesting them, in relation to the type of commitment made, shows that the Sisters of St. Joseph are neither Visitandines nor *béates*. Like the *béates*, they did a great deal of skilled work with their hands. For an understanding of their life, however, it is not the *béates* who form the model. Considering the time spent in service and apostolic work, the Sisters of St. Joseph again appear closer to the Jesuits. The activities listed in Chapter 4, Part 7, of the Constitutions of the Society of Jesus, discussing "Ways in which the houses and colleges can help their fellowmen," contain every type of work carried out by the Sisters of St. Joseph. "The first way" to help the neighbor, according to this chapter, is "good example . . . through the effort to edify by good deeds no less but rather more than by words, those with whom one deals." Secondly, "the neighbor is aided by desires in the presence of God Our Lord and by prayers for all the church . . . [and] for those for whose special benefit they . . . are working." Another means consists in "the teaching of Christian doctrine." Again, one can "be profitable to individuals by spiritual conversations, by counseling and exhorting to good works." Finally, the Jesuits

> will also occupy themselves in corporal works of mercy to the extent that the more important spiritual activities permit and their own energies allow. For example, they can help the sick, especially those in hospitals . . . and do what they can for the poor and for prisoners in jails, both by their personal work and by getting others to do it.[99]

Father Médaille did not retain what had to do with the Mass and the sacraments, ministries that were reserved for priests. All other ministries of the Society, however, could be carried out by the Sisters of St. Joseph: the ministry of presence and prayer, the ministry of the word under the form of teaching or counsel, the ministry of charitable service, to be shared with others and multiplied around oneself. This is also what the Eucharistic Letter says, where it recalls the ministry of the word exercised by "the sixteen apostles and evangelists," then "the service of mercy and charity in honor of the seven deacons," and finally, universal evangelization through the seventy-two disciples in all places and by every kind of means.

A comparison of the schedule for prayer and work in the daily life of the Sisters of St. Joseph with the Constitutions of the Society of Jesus reveals that Father Médaille organized the life of the *agrégées* sisters according to the model used for Jesuit scholastics and coadjutors. The exercises prescribed for them do not follow a precise timetable. They attend Mass daily, go to confession and communion weekly, examine their conscience twice daily, and add to that other devotional prayers.[100] In this section, personal prayer is not presented as uniform: "For those who do not have experience in spiritual things and desire to be helped in them, some points for meditation and prayer could be proposed to them in the way that seems best for persons of this kind" (no. 343). Others, for example certain brothers who do not know how to read, "will have in addition to the Mass their hour, during which they will recite the rosary or crown of our Lady, and they will likewise examine their consciences twice a day, or engage in some other prayers according to their devotion, as was said about the scholastics."(no. 344). The time and duration of mental prayer are not indicated, because they should organize their prayer "in the way that seems best." The lack of precision in the schedules contained in the Règlements of Sisters of St. Joseph probably means the same thing: they had to discover what suited them best. Another provision was given for the scholastics "after they have been approved," that is, after the period of their formation. On the one hand, they had to be watchful, that in giving themselves to study,

> they do not grow cool in their love . . . of religious life, so also during that time there will not be much place for mortifications and long prayers and meditations. For their devoting themselves to learning . . . with a pure intention of serving God . . . in a certain way requires the whole man.

To give themselves entirely to study out of obedience and for God, "will be not less but rather more pleasing to God Our Lord" (no. 340). This rule about studies can be applied in a parallel way for the *agrégées* sisters to their apostolic and charitable action toward every kind of neighbor. Apostolic urgency required that they give more time to the neighbor, even if it meant that they not meditate in the evening. That "will be not less but rather more pleasing to God Our Lord," provided they do it in obedience and use the means that will allow them to discern what makes them advance both in love for God and in love for the neighbor. For both Sisters of St. Joseph and Jesuits the superior and the spiritual director played a crucial role in this discernment.

The truth is, however, that the Constitutions printed in 1694 did not communicate the more flexible daily life of the *agrégées* sisters, but rather the more precise schedule from the Constitutions manuscripts, which to some degree reflected the daily schedule of the Visitation. In addition, the 1694 Constitutions gave less importance to the spiritual director than the manuscript constitutions. Without the necessary discernment provided regularly by the director and the superior, the sisters required a more stable organization of their daily life. Like other religious women living an apostolic life, the Sisters of St. Joseph accepted the means of their times to live out their vocation. The 1694 Constitutions probably did not hand on the daily schedule suggested for the *agrégées* sisters in the manuscripts because, by the end of the seventeenth century, the sisters themselves and their ecclesiastical superiors considered the omission of the half-hour prayer in the afternoon, not as the fruit of a choice made in discernment, but as a loss suffered on account of the importance of works. In the 1694 edition, the chapter on *agrégées* sisters, in place of a schedule, says "they will observe as far as they can all the rules prescribed in these Constitutions."[101] They were not required to recite certain vocal prayers, and ordinarily they received communion "only on Holy Days and Sundays." There is no mention of times for meditation. The entire chapter bears a tone of caution and constraint. The expression, "as far as they can," might also mean "in so far as they are capable of it." The institution of the *agrégées* Sisters of St. Joseph could not be recognized in its quite original uniqueness as religious life, contemplative in action. The apparent hiddenness of the *sœurs agrégées*, their real littleness, and the absence of external support, all contributed to make them look, little by little, like what they were not—a third order of the Congregation of St. Joseph.

NOTES

1. *TP* 1981, LE, 9, nos. 45-49.

2. Pierre Goubert, and Daniel Roche, *Culture et société*, vol. 2 of *Les Français et l'Ancien Régime* (Paris: A. Colin, 1984), 190.

3. AD Haute-Loire, Fonds de l'Hôtel-Dieu of Le Puy, 1 E 1, Registre de délibérations du bureau de l'Hôtel-Dieu, 1651-60, 78, fol. 42, 6 septembre 1654.

4. *TP* 1981, Règlement, 105, no. 6. The explanatory phrase, "with their social class and the background from which they come," appears only in the Vienne (Lyon, MS L) manuscript and must have been added by Marguerite Burdier.

5. *TP* 1981, CP, 18, no. 26.

6. Ibid., CP, 19, no. 34. Two manuscripts (of thirteen) contain later additions, borrowed from the Conference of Bishop de Maupas, 1661.

7. *TP* 1981, CM, 137, nos. 10-13.

8. *CV* 1694, part 1, chap. 4, "De l'Habit des Sœurs," 16-19.

9. Ibid., part 1, chap. 8: "Des Sœurs agrégées," 35.

10. Ibid., chap. 4, 18.

11. Ibid., part 1, chap. 2, 13.

12. AMM Lyon, Communauté de Marlhes, Registre, 6 octobre 1651-30 août 1900. [Sr. Thérèse Champignat was the aunt of St. Marcellin Champignat, a native of Marlhes, who founded the Congregation of Marist Teaching Brothers in 1817. –Trans.]

13. AMM Le Puy, Communauté de Saint-Romain-Lachalm, Registre, 15 octobre 1652-18 mars 1876.

14. AMM Lyon, Communauté de Riotord, small notebook of 4 loose pages, beginning undated, to 1776.

15. AMM Lyon, Communauté de Jonzieux, Actes de profession de Jeanne Tuilhier, Jeanne Bayle, Catherine Didier et Antoinette Didier, 15 août 1713.

16. AMM Le Puy, Communauté de Saint-Romain-Lachalm, Registre.

17. AMM Le Puy, Communauté de Saint-Paulien, Livre des filles de Saint-Joseph.

18. *TP* 1981, R, 105, no. 6.

19. *CSJ* 1970, The General Examen and Its Declarations, chap. 1, 80, no. 8.

20. *TP* 1981, CM, 137, no. 5.

21. *CV* 1694, part 3, chap. 1, 94.

22. Ibid., part 1, chap. 8, 36.

23. AMM Aubenas, Communauté de Satillieu, Permission de la guimpe accordée aux Sœurs de Saint-Joseph de Satillieu, en 1774.

24. AMM Le Puy, Communauté de Dunières.

25. AMM Le Puy, Communauté de Saint-Victor-Malescours.

26. AMM Le Puy, Communauté de Saint-Romain-Lachalm.

27. *TP* 1981, R, 105, no. 5.

28. Ibid., R, 105, no. 1.

29. Ibid., R, 105, no. 7.

30. Ibid., R, 106, no. 9.

31. Philippe Aries and Georges Duby, *Passions of the Renaissance*, vol. 3 of *A History of Private Life* trans. Arthur Goldhammer (Cambridge, Mass.: Belknap Press of Harvard University Press, 1989), 413.

32. *TP* 1981, CP, 17, no. 21.

33. Ibid., CP, 18, no. 29.

34. Ibid., LE, 9, no. 47.

35. *CV* 1694, part 1, chap. 3, 13.

36. François de, Sales, *Œuvres de Saint François de Sales Évêque de Genève et docteur de l'Église,* vol. 25, *Opuscules* (Annecy: Monastere de la Visitation, 1931), 72.

37. *CV* 1694, part 4, chap. 9, 222.

38. Ariès and Duby, 3:500.

39. AD Isère, 4 G 23, "Convention entre les Dames directrices de l'hopital de la Providence et les filles de Saint-Joseph," le 17 décembre 1694.

40. AD Puy de Dome, 90 H Fonds du Bon Pasteur de Clermont, 1 C 9, "Contrat d'Établissement de trois Religieuses de l'hopital de Vienne en la maison du Bon pasteur de Clermont-fd du 30 mai 1725."

41. AM Bourg-Argental, Archives de l'Hospice, A 2-I, "Mémoire concernant l'hôpital de la ville du Bourgargental, et sa situation par rapport à l'exécution de la déclaration du Roy, du 18e juillet 1724, concernant les mendiants."

42. BM Vienne, Hôtel-Dieu, B 1389, Mémoires de la sœur Jeanne Burdier, économe de l'Hôtel-Dieu de Vienne, 1680-92, extraits transcrits par Jean Lecutiez, Proposition des Sœurs de Sainct Joseph présentée à Monseigneur larchevesque et a Messieurs les recteurs de lhospital de Vienne, 8 décembre 1686, 147-153.

43. AD Hautes-Alpes, 3 H suppl. 278.

44. AD Puy-de-Dome, Q 1936, quoted by Pierre-François Aleil, "Le Refuge de Clermont, 1666-1792," *Bulletin Historique et Scientifique d'Auvergne* 86 (1973), 34.

45. AMM Le Puy, "Délibération des administrateurs de la Maison de la Charité des Filles orphelines de Saint-Joseph," 3 mars 1648.

46. AD Haute-Loire, 1Q 91, État des rentes des religieuses de Saint-Joseph du Puy et des orphelines, vers 1790.

47. AHC de Lyon, Boîte 394, La maison forcée des Recluses.

48. AHC de Lyon, Boîte 394, Mémoire sur la nécessité de l'œuvre des Recluses.

49. AD Rhône, 44 H 148, "Reglemens pour l'Administration de la Maison des Recluses, du 2e décembre 1773."

50. AD Isère, 4G 23, "Convention entre les Dames directrices de l'hopital de la Providence et les filles de Saint Joseph" 17 décembre 1694.

51. AD Isère, 4G 23, Lettre de M. de la Millière to M. l'Intendant de Grenoble, 25 mai 1782.

52. AD Puy-de-Dôme, 90 H, Fonds du Bon-Pasteur, 1C 9.

53. AD Puy-de-Dôme, L 2311, Maison du Bon-Pasteur de Clermont.

54. AMM Lyon, Communauté d'Izieux.

55. AMM Lyon, Communauté de Saint-Genest-l'Erpt.

56. AMM Lyon, Communauté de Jonzieux.

57. AMM Le Puy, Communauté de Saint-Romain-Lachalm.

58. AMM Aubenas, Communauté de Saint-Julien-Vocance. The approximate date of foundation comes from two other documents.

59. Ibid., "Albergement ou loyer perpétuel passé par Mre Pierre Perret, prieur et curé de St Julhien Vaucances, & honneste Sœur Catherine Giraud, Sœur de St Joseph dud. St Julhien . . . du 2 9bre 1726"; see Supporting Documents, 16.

60. *TP* 1981, AR, 133, no. 11.

61. AMM Le Puy, Communauté de Saint-Didier, "Copie des dons faits par le Seigneur de St Didier aux Sœurs de St Joseph de lad. ville."

62. AMM Le Puy, Communauté de Tence, "Les sœurs de Saint-Joseph doivent pour censive et laud au Pères Jésuites prieur de Tence. . . ."

63. BMU Clermont-Ferrand, Fonds Paul Leblanc, MS no. 850, fols. 36 ff, "Contrat d'Association des sœurs de Saint-Joseph de Craponne contenant donnation réciproque, le 23 avril 1723."

64. AMM Clermont, Communauté de Viverols, Notes de l'Abbé Adam, 1928.

65. AMM Le Puy, Communauté de Saint-Paulien, Établissement d'Isabeau Delolme, pour la fondation de l'école de Saint-Paulien.

66. René Clement,: "L'historique des premières écoles . . . à Saint-Anthème," in *Dix siècles d'histoire en Vallorgue* (Le Puy: Impr. Jeanne d'Arc, 1989), chap. 10, 79 ff. Clement presents the act of foundation for the community in 1663 by "noble Balthazar de Pierrefort La Roue, Seigneur de Saint-Anthème," document preserved in the archives of the Maison de la Roue, Milan (Italy).

67. AMM Clermont, Communauté de Champeix, "Vente d'une maison par Marc Sabbattier à Sr Thérèse Sappin, sup^{re} des filles de St Joseph establyes en ce lieu de Champeix . . . le 12 mai 1731."

68. AMM Le Puy, Communauté de Saint-Paulien, un registre: "Livre des filles de St Joseph, de la maison naissante d'icelles, dans les fauxbourgs de la ville de St Paulien."

69. See Fig. 6.2, Diagram of the Town of Saint-Anthème (Puy-de-Dôme) Based on the Cadaster of 1824, from René Clemet, *Dix siècles d'histoire en Vallorgue* (Le Puy: Imprimerie Jeanne-d'Arc, 1989), 79.

70. Auguste Achard, "L'hospice de Sauxillanges (1664-1904)," *Revue d'Auvergne* 21 (1904): 11.

71. *TP* 1981, LE, 9, no. 47.

72. François de Sales, "Règles et Constitutions, De l'employte du Jour," in *Œuvres* (Annecy : Monastery of the Visitation, 1931), 25:233; and Teresa, of Avila, *The Collected Works of St. Teresa of Avila* (Washington: Institute of Carmelite Studies, 1976-), 3: 319, 327.

73. A parallel synopsis appears in *TP* 1981, R, 102-103; see Fig. 6.3, Daily Schedule for Visitation Nuns and Sisters of St. Joseph.

74. The "distribution des heures du jour" from MS A; and "Règlement des Sœurs de Saint-Joseph pour les jours ouvriers" in MS S.

75. Archives nationales, section historique, MS L. 105, no. 77, "Règlement soumis par Madame de Villeneuve à Jean-François de Gondi, archevêque de Paris, et approuvé par ordonnance épiscopale, le 27 avril 1640."

76. *TP* 1981, CP, part 6, 86, no. 420.

77. Ibid., R, 112, no. 32.

78. AD Haute-Loire, Fonds de l'Hôtel-Dieu du Puy, 1E 19, a notebook of 11 pages, n.d., eighteenth c.

79. [Étienne-Michel Faillon], *Vie de Monsieur de Lantages, prêtre de Saint-Sulpice, premier supérieur du Séminaire de Notre-Dame du Puy* (Paris: Adrien Le Clère et Cie, 1830), 305-308, and 321-23.

80. *Vie de Monsieur de Lantages,* 296.

81. *Règle et conduite pour les Filles Associées de la Maison de l'Instruction de la ville du Puy* (Le Puy: P.B.F. Clet, 1834), 51 and 53; *T P*, CP, 62, no. 297; and *CV* 1694, part 2, chap. 4, 73-77.

82. AM Vienne, Hôtel-Dieu, G 4, 1710-1783, "Mémoires dressées sur plusieurs délibérations verballes du bureau de l'Hôtel-Dieu de la ville de Vienne," 5 septembre 1723.

83. AHC Lyon, Boîte 394, Titres de l'Établissement de la Maison des Recluses.

84. AMM Clermont, Communauté du Refuge de Clermont, État de la Maison du Refuge pour l'année 1772.

85. AD Puy-de-Dôme, IG, 1573, Religieuses de Saint-Joseph.

86. BMU Clermont, Fonds Paul Leblanc, no. 850, MS 131, Demande de Lettres Patentes pour la maison des sœurs de Saint-Joseph de Craponne.

87. AD Lozère, H. 375, "Établissement des Sœurs de Saint-Joseph dans la ville de Langogne."

88. *TP* 1981, CP, part 1, 20, no. 41.

89. AD Isère, 21 H, Registre des professions des sœurs de Saint-Joseph de Vienne.

90. AMM Clermont, Communauté de Saint-Amant-Roche-Savine et de Viverols.

91. AMM Clermont, Communauté de Job.

92. The meaning of *sentiment* in the seventeenth century included "the affections, the passions, and all the movements of the soul," *DAF* 1694, s.v. "sentiment." –Trans.

93. *TP* 1981, R, 108-109, no. 26.

94. Ibid., CP, 39, no. 134; and 48, no. 185.

95. Teresa of Avila, *The Collected Works of St. Teresa of Avila* (Washington: Institute of Carmelite Studies, 1976-), 3: 321.

96. "Examen of consciousness" is commonly used to designate a reflection primarily oriented toward discernment of God's action in one's life, rather than a moral examination of conscience, see James W. Skehan, SJ, *Place Me With Your Son: Ignatian Spirituality in Everyday Life*, 3rd ed. (Washington, DC: Georgetown University Press, 1991), 11. –Trans.

97. *TP* 1981, R, 117, MS L, no. 39; 118, no. 42; and 119, no. 41 (MSS B, G, and S).

98. Ibid., R, 128. Text does not appear in the Constitutions MSS A, B, G, H2, and S.

99. *CSJ* 1970, part 7, chap. 4: "Ways in which the houses and colleges can help their fellowmen," 281-83, nos. 637-38, 645, 648, and 650.

100. Ibid., part 4, chap. 4: "The care and welfare of the scholastics admitted," 118, no. 342.

101. *CV* 1694, part 1, chap. 8: "Des sœurs agrégées," 38.

Chapter Seven

Principal Houses and *Sœurs Agrégées*

The confrontation of normative texts and records of practical experience in the preceding chapters has yielded a better understanding of the spirituality of the Sisters of St. Joseph as well as the forms which their vocation assumed in time and space. A real grasp of their roots in the society that produced them would require a study of the politics of recruitment for the Sisters of St. Joseph in the regions where they existed. It is readily evident that *agrégées* sisters in the small rural houses were enlisted from the villages where their houses were established or from surrounding villages. The more important houses in towns, by contrast, give the impression of recruitment far beyond those towns. Although the social origin of the sisters varied, the middle classes of the bourgeoisie were dominant in the town houses, and the social level of sisters appears to have risen during the eighteenth century. A more thorough study of statistics, family structures, or the sisters' place in their families would be extremely long and complex. In line with the overall focus of this work, the present chapter simply tries to demonstrate how the differ-ent aspects of the vocation of St. Joseph were concretized and articulated in various situations. Through a presentation of different types of communities, it attempts to comprehend the regular relationship in the community between the life lived inside the house and that lived outside and between prayer and action. It addresses the simple, yet central issue: What were the various ways in which Sisters of St. Joseph could be "nuns" in the world?

A "PRINCIPAL HOUSE": THE BON-PASTEUR OF CLERMONT

Throughout the seventeenth century, in the Auvergne as in nearly all of France, hospital establishments expanded and multiplied. Some specialized

in a precise clientele of poor, sick, and beggars. Other houses, often those operated by communities of women religious, were organized to take in women
of ill-repute who were on their own without resources, women whom Father
Médaille called "fallen women in need."[1] Like all the other poor, sick, and
marginal, these women were confined. Houses of refuge and hospitals did not
allow those whom they cared for, housed, and fed, to go out until they were
trained for work and given religious instruction, so that they might "save their
souls."[2] There were two types of reformatories for such women. In addition
to the *maisons de Refuge*, intended for penitent girls and women responsive
to rehabilitation, there were also *maisons de Force*, with a more disciplinary
regimen for dissolute women who seemed less corrigible. Sometimes penitents came of their own accord. At others, they were turned in by a family
member or the police. Usually the inmates in the *maison Forcée*, referred to
as *recluses*, did not come willingly. Both penitents and *recluses* could also be
confined by royal authority in the form of a *lettre de cachet*, which was actually more discreet than other sentences and less degrading for the family.[3] The
lowliest father could resort to the king to ask his help in reforming a member
of his family. By the end of the seventeenth century, royal authority system-
atically encouraged houses of women religious to serve as *maisons de Refuge*
in return for regular payment.[4] Directors of these houses were eager to obtain
the services of these devoted workers who were advantageous from many
points of view.

The Refuge of Clermont: Establishment and History

The Maison du Refuge of Clermont was founded in 1666 when Father Médaille was still at the College of Clermont. A canon of the cathedral, *Monsieur
Claude Laborieux*, wanting to furnish "a place of retreat . . . for the correction
of the morals of women . . . gave his house with all its conveniences and ap-
purtenances."[5] Other persons of consequence contributed generous gifts toward the establishment of the house. Louis XIV granted it letters patent the
same year, registered with the Parlement of Paris on July 7, 1667. The house
was intended for women who had "fallen into sin," but who wished to "leave
it behind." The house also accepted those sent by "fathers or mothers . . . or
other close relatives" asking that they "be confined there" to "bring them
back to their duties," as well as "those who are conducted there by court order because of their prostitution, up to the number of twelve or more," insofar as charitable resources allowed. The letters patent listed services to be provided in the house of refuge, requiring that these women

> shall be fed, clothed, instructed in the fear of God, and shall learn all the arts and
> crafts suitable for earning their living, either sewing, embroidery, spinning or

other skills appropriate to their sex. . . . After staying in the said house for some time, having there learned virtue and completely abandoned vice . . . [they should] be placed by the Administrators . . . with Persons who will take care to maintain them in their good intentions.[6]

Women of exemplary life with adequate experience were to direct the house. At first there were three such women for twelve penitents; by 1685 there were six for thirty-one penitents.[7] In 1696, after problems arose between the voluntary penitents and the fallen women who had been remanded by police, the two groups of women were separated by creating within the framework of the Refuge a sort of *maison de Force,* called *Les Loges* (the cells), which remained distinct from "the interior" of the house. In addition to problems created by the penitents, there were those stirred up by the women in charge. Too few for the amount of work, they were also too numerous for the revenue of the house and would sometimes argue with one another, making it difficult to find a satisfactory solution for governing the house. The situation was aggravated by negligence on the part of the administrators, who too often failed to attend meetings of the *bureau* and to enforce the rules. The bishop was obliged to intervene.

After several attempts to improve this situation, the administrators decided to replace the women in charge with religious. With the consent of Jean-Baptiste Massillon, who had become bishop of Clermont, they appealed to the Sisters of St. Joseph at the Hôtel-Dieu in Vienne in Dauphiné. Two sisters, Marguerite Buisson and Marie-Anne Bourlier, came to Clermont in July of 1723, joined by a third, Marianne Grubis, in January of 1724. At the request of administrators of the Refuge, the Archbishop of Vienne, Henry Oswald de La Tour d'Auvergne, agreed to a contract of establishment between the three religious and the administrators' representatives. It was signed on May 30, 1725, at the house of the Bon-Pasteur. The administrators pledged to feed and support the three sisters and to take care of them in need. They would also give them each fifty *livres* annually. For their part, the sisters would

> have the responsibility to direct, govern, and administer the said house, to have those who will be confined there work and keep them occupied, and to give an account of their administration to the said *Sieurs* administrators. In spiritual matters, the said sisters will be subject in everything to the Lord Bishop of Clermont who will give them a priest, secular or religious, whom he will deem appropriate for their direction and confession.[8]

The links between the sisters at Clermont and the community in Vienne were broken rather quickly after 1727. Beginning in 1729, the sisters of the Refuge recruited their own novices without consultation with Vienne, obtaining only the agreement of the bishop of Clermont and the administrators of the house.

Meanwhile, the number of women accepted at the refuge increased. At the same time, the premises proved too small to accommodate all those remanded by the courts. It was necessary to enlarge the buildings and build a *maison de Force* next to the house for the penitents. The *intendant* (royal administrator) of the Auvergne, Bidé de La Granville, received from the Conseil d'État an agreement of financial support and "the sum of eight thousand *livres*" for the new construction.[9] Unfortunately, *Monsieur* Bidé "was assigned to Lille; his successor . . . *Monsieur* de Trudaine . . . on his arrival let himself be won over by the urgent solicitation of the *Messieurs* the administrators of the general hospital," who clamored to have the *maison de Force* and the anticipated annuities allocated to them. This maneuver was very detrimental to the Refuge and felt as an injustice by its administrators.

Unable to enlarge the house, the administrators transformed the existing buildings in order to expand the different operations. In 1749, the community of St. Joseph had nine members. Jeanne Assolent, the superior, proposed organizing a home visitation for those poor who were ashamed to beg publicly.[10] She also wished to accept children and young girls from poor families to give them instruction and education in order to prevent the disorders caused by vice and ignorance. The administrators accepted these proposals and took the necessary steps to adapt the house for the additional services. Once again, the increase of activities brought about the need to enlarge the house, due to the necessity of avoiding contact between the young boarders and the penitent women.

Plans were drawn, purchases considered. Almost immediately the administrators thought it preferable to transfer the Refuge to a larger site, situated closer to the outskirts of town. Royal authorization for the purchase of land, new construction, and sale of the old property was obtained. With the promise of royal financial help for the building as well as the subsequent support of the detained women, the construction, which was major, began in 1765. When the work was already well advanced, however, in 1767, *Monsieur* de Ballainvilliers, *intendant* of Auvergne, died of smallpox. His replacement, *Monsieur* de Monthyon, in no way shared his predecessor's views. He refused to pay for continuing the construction and simultaneously withdrew the promised financial support. The Refuge was in danger of disappearing—it was a moment of real anguish. The contractor, the *sieur* Duclos, who had almost completed the construction, had been practically unpaid. To meet the debt, the administrators considered selling two houses that belonged to the Refuge but were not judged indispensable to its operation. They obtained permission from the municipal magistrates and the officers of the *Sénéchaussée* of the Auvergne. Although this measure would cover current debt, the challenges of completing construction and maintaining the house in the future remained.

The superior, Mother Sainte-Agnès Labas, considered, upon reflection, that the twelve sisters of her community could instruct and train young women of high social rank. An exclusive boarding school would provide the Refuge with sufficient and regular income. The administrators again welcomed the suggestion. Its success was not assured, because there was already competition in the city for the same clientele. The Ursulines, Bernardines, and Benedictines already had boarding schools in Clermont. The administrators nevertheless put their faith in the sisters' proposal and gave them the means to realize their project. In the meantime, the sisters were announcing the imminent opening of this new boarding school throughout the province of Auvergne. In the new buildings, still unfinished, where the Refuge had already been installed in 1769-70, the young women of the *haute pension*, or elite boarding school, would have no contact with the penitents. Each boarder would pay eighteen *livres* per month. The families must have had confidence in the Sisters of St. Joseph at the Bon-Pasteur, because in 1772, three years after it opened, the school boasted twenty-seven boarders.[11] Income from the boarders amounted to 5,832 *livres* annually, which was enough to support the penitents. Of the latter, twenty out of twenty-six gave the house nothing but their work in exchange for room and board. Four of them paid eight *livres* per month; one, twelve; and the last, confined by *lettre de cachet*, brought in 300 *livres* annually. Again, thanks to the sisters, the Refuge was saved from the successive threats engendered by the unpredictability of royal administration.

An account of the revenues and duties of the community of religious at the Bon-Pasteur for the year 1772 reveals the different groups of persons then living in the house. They included "twelve professed religious under the rule of St. Joseph, who are not cloistered, make simple vows, and live under the authority of His Excellency the Bishop . . . they have letters patent. . . . There are no lay sisters." By the end of the year, the community also had "two postulants." There was also a group of "women retired from the world living in the Community of the Bon-Pasteur." They were "two ladies and a servant" and "eight persons who are insane," confined by *lettre de cachet*. The house had twenty-seven "young boarders of the *haute pension*" and twelve "young boarders at the *petite pension*" (a group of orphan girls). Last of all, the group that gave the house its raison d'être, were "the penitent women [whose] number in an average year is twenty-six." Mentioned among the servants of the house were "three girls" who received wages and "another girl to serve the young boarders," who contented herself with "the gratuities that she received." These four girls probably lived in the house, whereas the gardener and vintner certainly lived outside. In 1772, the number of people living in this house totaled approximately one hundred. The number of inhabitants and the variety of charitable and educational services provided show that this was a considerable establishment. A customs book written in 1775 illustrates how

the sisters' life centered around the works of the house, above all care for the
penitent women.

The Customs Book of 1775

After the serious problems it had passed through, by the early 1770s the house
of the Bon-Pasteur recovered equilibrium. It had been necessary to dismiss
several penitents when the house was on the point of closing. Their number
had not yet reached its potential maximum, but the numbers were growing.
The house took up again on a new basis with a different system, since in addition to the retired ladies and the *petite pension* for orphans, there were also
residents "of the *haute pension*." The altered situation required changing the
schedule and drawing up a new customs book, which was composed in
1775.[12]

This small notebook, kept in the Clermont Motherhouse, states that it "includes the customs of the house of the Bon-Pasteur which, without changing
the rules of the said house or those of the religious, were modified only in regard to time, and that for good order and a greater good." The notebook is divided into four parts. "The first part deals with what is observed yearly, the
second contains the usages of each month, the third, for each week, and the
fourth, for each day." The revision sought to harmonize the rules practiced at
the Bon-Pasteur with those of the sisters, so that everything might take place
in an orderly way, while respecting both the life of the religious and that of
the penitents.

As usual in such documents from hospitals of the seventeenth and eighteenth centuries, the schedule in the Bon-Pasteur customs book contains numerous exercises of piety. First, the penitents perform all the exercises of the
sisters: vocal prayers, morning and evening meditation, Mass, the Office of
the Holy Spirit and the Office of the Blessed Virgin, examen, rosary, reading,
etc. Further, a reminder of the presence of God each hour took the shape for
them of short biblical verses in Latin, sung by all, and repeated each time in
French by one person. At 9:00 a.m., they sang *Ne derelinquas* and *Gloria Patri*. At 11:00 a.m. before the examen, they prayed the *Averte faciem*, then the
Veni Sancte, and the prayer to the Holy Spirit. At 3:00 p.m., they recalled the
death of Christ by singing the *O Crux Ave* on their knees with arms extended.
At 6:00 p.m., after the various times for vespers, meditation, rosary, and other
prayers, they chanted the versicle *Ne projicias me* with the *Gloria Patri*. At
8:00 p.m. they ended recreation by singing *Maria Mater gratiae*. All these
prayers, with the exception of Mass, which took place "in the choir," were
said in "the room," the place where the penitents spent most of their life and
where it seems the sisters also came for prayer.

In 1775, the new house for the Refuge did not yet have a chapel; its construction began only after 1777, when the house received an anonymous gift of 1,200 *livres* for a basement and a place for making wine over which they decided to build a chapel.[13] In 1775, the choir mentioned in the customs book was simply a room where an altar had been placed. The room where the penitents usually stayed was where all work took place. It consisted mainly "in sewing and embroidery with thread." Prayer and work formed the background for the penitents' life. In the morning, according to the 1775 customary, "everyone"—sisters and penitents—"goes to the room" for prayer. They "kneel for meditation." Following that and "after the first reading," during the vocal prayers that follow, "the penitents will take up their work and each one will stay in her place until . . . the reading of the Gospel which will be heard standing . . . then the four little hours of the Office will be said, during which the penitent women will work." Although the penitents were present for the sisters' prayers, which were said in their room, it seems that they did not necessarily participate in all the prayers since they are seen working during that time. The women took up their work again "after breakfast was served . . . in the room" and "they [begin] to work until dinner," actually, until the examen preceding dinner, for which the bell was rung at eleven o'clock. Then, "after a half-hour of recreation, they [recommenced] work." Nothing is said about how the work was divided from recreation until bedtime, but work probably accompanied the penitents' afternoon as it had the morning. The rules for the penitents harmonized with the sisters' schedule, where work occupied the entire afternoon unless they were at prayer or occupied in the service of other persons.

The customs book also suggests activities throughout the penitents' day, which, directed toward Christian life, were also a means of formation. Reading was the primary instrument of this formation. Meals, taken in silence, featured reading. In the morning during breakfast the life of the saint of the day was read; at dinner and supper, some other type of spiritual reading. At nine-thirty in the morning the penitents chanted the commandments of God and the Church, followed by a reading and "fifteen minutes of silence, [after which] the eldest sister will have an account given of the reading." Following recreation there was another reading at one-thirty in the afternoon, preceded by the singing of *Veni Creator* and followed, as in the morning, by fifteen minutes of silence, after which "someone will give an account of it." This was the same pedagogy proposed for the Sisters of St. Joseph, who had a short discussion after their own reading to help them draw more benefit from it. It appears that a number of sisters worked with the penitent women, since the eldest of them was responsible for having an account given of the reading. On Sundays and holy days more time was set aside for this formation: "A religious (each in her turn) will teach the catechism, which she will explain after having all the penitents recite a chapter of it." The catechism lesson probably occurred in the afternoon, because in the morning following the usual 9:30 reading, there is mention of a recitation of the Gospel by "the one responsible for it," and afterwards, "someone will give an instruction on this subject." As an aid to understanding the Latin texts chanted by the penitents, we have already seen that one of them had to repeat in French all the verses sung in Latin. Every penitent woman assumed this role "according to her seniority, and for a whole week." The same person recited "the morning and evening prayers, and those of the examen" for the entire community of sisters and penitents. During that week she also "announced the mysteries of the rosary."

Meals and recreation were the more pleasant occupations of the day. They could be counted among those rare times when the community of religious as a whole was separated from the penitent women. When the six bells sounded for the sisters' dinner, the penitents went to the refectory where the "religious on duty" came to serve them, after which, the book of customs states, she "will do the reading, which shall be listened to with attention, keeping silence until grace." Each religious "by seniority, and each her week" took her turn on duty with the "girls in the refectory and in the room during recreation." The sisters must have been much in need of some moments of relaxation after having spent a large part of their day with this restless group of girls and women, more or less balanced, who must have resented the restrictions placed on them. At the end of the day, aside from the prescription of silence after night prayer, nothing is said about going to bed. The sisters must have been on duty by turns, as they were at mealtimes.

The 1775 customs book makes little reference to groups other than the penitents living in the Bon-Pasteur. The girls of the boarding school are barely mentioned. Regarding the schedule for meals, the customs book refers to the "boarders' dinner," and notes that in the evening, a bell is rung for "the boarders' supper." They appear one other time, in the yearly exercises, in reference to the procession during Rogation Days. "After coming out from Mass" the sisters and residents left in procession, "singing the litanies of the Saints," while the penitents remained in choir with a sister, reciting the same litany. The penitents would then go "to the room, where they will begin their work." The nearly total invisibility of these students in the customs book demonstrates the reality of what had been firmly assured when the boarding school was established: no contact between the penitents and the young boarders. These two groups had only a glimpse of one another in the choir and probably entered by separate doors. There is not the slightest allusion in the customs book to the women living there, including those who were insane. The financial accounts show the revenue they brought in, but no other document gives information about their dealings with the Sisters of St. Joseph within the house. This silence also confirms that the house remained, above all, the Maison du Refuge. Although the customs book illuminates only the relations of the sisters with the penitents, what it reveals, in light of other data, can be indicative of how the Sisters of St. Joseph lived out their vocation within this important house.

Most aspects of the penitents' life outlined in the customs book for the Refuge were not original. Many rules for institutions of that period mention some form of prayer every hour, work throughout the day, and spiritual reading during meals. The schedule, whether for the Bon-Pasteur in Lyon, the Maison des Recluses in the came city, the Hospital of Tarbes, or the "Rules for children" (for the education of girls) included in the Constitutions of the Monastery of Port-Royal, are very similar.[14] There are some differences of emphasis, however. The rule for the hospital at Tarbes was naturally less adamant about silence. At the Bon-Pasteur in Lyon the Rule for the community was quite meticulous, but the sisters were very present to their penitents. At Port-Royal, as one might expect, the "Rules for the children" were imbued with strict asceticism. At the Lyon Maison des Recluses, the sisters—also Sisters of St. Joseph—appear to have been less present to the confined women. The Rule given by the archbishop noted that when the recluses were sick, they had "one of the sisters notified to help them." The sisters were therefore not close to the women on a daily basis. Of course, this institution was a *maison de force*, not a house of penitents.

On the contrary, the continuous presence of the sisters to penitents in the Refuge at Clermont is one of the most striking aspects found in the customs book. The house was organized in such a way that the women and sisters shared one another's lives. Constant presence served the immediate purpose of supervision, as a 1760 report makes clear, "[The] religious are eight in number, and this number is necessary given that almost all the women confined in this house must be kept in view to prevent the effects of their malice and the excesses to which they could be driven in order to escape."[15] The same report reiterates the purpose of the foundation, as expressed in the royal letters patent: that the women learn "virtue, [abandon] vice completely, and be placed in good situations." The account adds farther on that it "has been seen that several [penitents] die at an advanced age, after showing signs of sincere penitence and having been examples of virtue there." This suggests a second reason for the sisters' presence: to encourage and support the penitents' efforts toward conversion. In an article on the history of the refuge of Clermont, Pierre François Aleil emphasizes that the sisters' support helped the women gradually to become more self-aware and take responsibility for their actions.[16] On February, 4, 1752, Anne Bernard, 22 years old, claimed that she was pregnant by a merchant in Lyon. On October 5 of the same year, however, she wrote the following statement: "I confess to have given the name of Nanette Bernard, which is false. My name is Jeanne Compagniat; I am guilty of doing so out of no evil purpose, but to protect myself. I hope that M. Duboucher will indeed exercise charity toward me. Written by me, Jeanne Compagniat, penitent at the Bon-Pasteur, in the presence of the mother superior and her assistant."

Jeanne Assolent was the superior in 1752. She was the same sister who in 1749 had proposed a form of preventive service for young girls in poor families. Together with the sisters of the community, she was in a position to help Jeanne Compagniat take responsibility for herself. Moreover, as Jeanne was on the verge of giving birth, it may have been a way for her to bring *Sieur* Duboucher to account, so that he too could also take responsibility for his actions. Such an example appears to be rare, however. The register where this penitent composed and signed her own declaration contains only three signed entries out of eighty-four. It is evident, nevertheless, that in accompanying the penitents the sisters did not restrict themselves to the devotional level, but entered the realm of real life.

Responsibility for organizing the exercises of piety, which took up a large part of the day and was therefore one of the main purposes of the customary, seems to have rested almost entirely with the sisters. There is no mention of the involvement of a confessor or a chaplain, although the letters patent explicitly designate a "Priest for administering the Sacraments to the said women and girls." Apart from daily Mass and Benediction of the Blessed Sacrament on certain Sundays and feast days, the customs book does not speak of the priest's participation in the life of the house, since it indicates only the sisters' responsibilities. During retreat, between Ascension Day and Pentecost, the penitents went to the choir at four o'-clock to hear a sermon given by the chaplain or another preacher. But all instructions to the penitents, on Sundays and on the eves of holy days, were provided by the sisters. They must, in that case, have had a spiritual formation adequate to such a task. It does not appear that the women were pressured into receiving the sacraments, as sometimes happened in other places in order to bring about conversions that were to some degree forced. It is known, however, that on their arrival at the house the women were frequently put to the test first in the *Loges*, or in the prison cells of the *Maison de Force*.[17] During that period, "the penitents were urged to confess" in order to be admitted to the main part of the house, where life was less severe. It is difficult to know exactly what took place, because the customs book does not say everything, and practice was often quite different from the rules.

THE REFUGE AT THE END OF THE EIGHTEENTH CENTURY

Almost from the time they arrived at the Refuge of Clermont, the Sisters of St. Joseph were faced with the important question of what type of penitent the house should admit. The letters patent of 1666 specified, that whether women came on their own, were brought by a close relative, or ordered there by the court, they should be open to a change of life, capable of receiving instruction and learning a trade, and following their stay, of regaining their place in society. According to the records, around 1728, "*Monsieur* the Lieutenant General . . . had one woman sent there who had been sentenced in perpetuity."[18] The administrators refused her, clarifying to the *intendant*, then *Monsieur* Bidet de la Granville, that the Refuge did not accept this sort of woman, and that it would be necessary "to obtain from his Majesty the creation of a *maison de Force.*" The decision was made and the finances provided, but the *maison de Force* never came about. The *loges* and prison remained in place. The incorrigible women were kept separate—at least in principle—from the penitents of good will. The sisters remained in charge of the penitents inside the house, and according to the letters patent, the administrators were to handle "the external management" and "complete control of the goods."[19]

Distinction between the categories of penitents, insisted upon by both sisters and administrators, meant that the measures of reform employed inside the house did not have the severely disciplinary character of those in the *Loges* of the Bon-Pasteur and other Maisons de Force. The windows, of course, had to be "barred and strong" and the doors carefully locked. These methods characterized the mentality of the times. But the sisters' reports do not mention "iron chains" or "pairs of handcuffs" and other instruments of penance, as the administrators' accounting books do. Such devices might have been restricted—though this is not certain—to the women confined outside in the *Loges*. At that time the refuge of Riom, run by the Ladies of Mercy, used more repressive correctional methods, such as "chains on the feet and hands," "penitential robes," the "*prie-dieu* for punishment . . . with its accessories," stays of several months in the cells, and so forth.[20] Riom, however, was a judiciary town influenced by the Company of the Blessed Sacrament, where repression was directed mainly at sins of the flesh in an attempt to impose morality by force. The transfer of a penitent from Clermont to the refuge in Riom was a severe punishment. By contrast, change from the Refuge of Riom to the one in Clermont, if not a reward, was at least a sign of progress. The Sisters of St. Joseph in Clermont probably used some form of corporal punishment, done routinely at that time, but they also used positive reinforcement and encouragement.

In 1761, Sister Sainte-Agnès Labas, now the superior, proposed the creation of ranks that the penitents could reach successively, depending on their progress and a favorable report from all the sisters.[21] The innovation proved a great stimulus toward competition and improvement. Some women, however, fought all discipline and aimed at one thing only: escape. Records of the Bon-Pasteur of Clermont mention several runaways. On the word of some reports, the sisters seem at times to have promoted the escape of penitents who were little interested in reform, especially if they did not contribute toward covering their costs. That implication is clear in a letter sent by a sub-delegate to the *intendant* concerning a woman who was perfectly unbearable: "The *dames directrices* of the Refuge no longer want to keep her for so little board . . . they will allow her to run away, not wanting to be obliged to keep her for life."[22] Even civil authorities did not respond to all requests for detention from the relatives of those in question, from clergy, or others. When a *curé* asked the police to take a certain single woman and her male companion by surprise in 1756, the *intendant* of Auvergne responded: "Take care not to have this girl arrested. . . . Those who serve the Lord should use the means only of gentleness and admonition."[23]

The account already cited, of the resources and expenses during 1772 for the women interned by *lettres de cachet*, mentions among the "ladies sequestered in the Community of the Bon-Pasteur . . . eight persons who are insane," and two women with a servant. All seem to belong to a higher social class, because four paid 400 *livres* per year for board and lodging, three paid 300 *livres*, and three others, 280, 200, and 192 *livres*. Little information has survived about this group of inmates, who were probably difficult to handle because of their mental illness. The superior of the Bon-Pasteur at the time, Marguerite Buisson, wrote to the *intendant* on June 26, 1744, to complain about one of these women and the "bizarre predicaments she puts us and the entire house in, by her madness." With her is "a girl who never leaves her and to whom one has to be very indulgent lest she lose heart."[24]

Unbalanced women were not the only ones confined by *lettres de cachet*. In 1772, a penitent was ordered to the Refuge by *lettre de cachet,* and in 1782, Sister Clair Philibert de la Motte, an Ursuline nun of Tours, arrived in the same way. The following year a letter from the Bon-Pasteur, addressed to the bishop of Clermont on August 10, 1783, petitioned her release.[25] She had been ushered "into the convent of the Bon-Pasteur at Clermont in Auvergne . . . by order of the King, the eleventh of September 1782." Since that time, she was "held prisoner" because she had escaped "from the monastery of the Ursulines at Thiers in Auvergne, where she had made profession at the age of sixteen despite the revulsion, or rather horror, she felt toward the religious life. It was only despair, and not a libertine spirit, that made her scale the walls of her convent." The letter requested that she be allowed to go to her mother's house until she found a convent of her choice. The permission was given immediately, on August 18, 1783. Faced with such a diverse and difficult clientele, the sisters, particularly the superior, needed a penetrating understanding of circumstances to interact in a way that was discerning and beneficial to each of the persons involved. From this perspective, the thought of Mother Sainte-Agnès Labas at the time of the financial crisis in 1769 makes sense: she believed the sisters in her community capable of giving a good education to daughters of well-bred families because she realized that they had the training and experience necessary to open a boarding school.

Documents describing the set-up of the boarding school at the Bon-Pasteur before the Revolution, unfortunately, have not survived. Only a "Historical Memorandum of the Establishment of the House of the Refuge of the city of Clermont-Ferrand," written probably between 1785 and 1789, reports that "the boarding school authorized in the house of the Refuge . . . [has] grown considerably because of the good education that the young *demoiselles* receive there, without any communication with the penitent girls."[26] A member of the lower nobility living in Clermont, *Monsieur* Blan, who wanted "to procure the same advantage to young women from reputable families" but with fewer resources, established two scholarships for the free education of two girls in the boarding school. This endowment, "made on June 29, 1778," was accepted by the administrators and recorded in the register. Noted among the clauses containing the financial stipulations are some facts about the education these girls would receive:

> The work the recipients do will belong to them, and their parents will furnish the cloth and other things needed for their work. They will be taught the catechism of the diocese, reading, writing, and work skills; they will participate in all the types of education given in the house, both in piety and morals. They will be treated in everything like the boarders of the boarding school.

If this report is correct, the boarding school was completely successful. That success, according to the author of the *Mémoire*, encroached on the primary goal of the Refuge, which was intended first of all for penitent women and poor children. "It is desirable," he insisted, "that the Refuge be recalled to its original purpose." For this to occur, the administrators would have to find "the means to pay the debts so that the revenues might be sufficient for the food and lodging of the community, [putting it] in a position to help the poor families by resuming . . . the free education . . . of poor girls as they did before the move" to the new building. The anonymous author calls upon the royal administration to intervene so that the existence of the Refuge need not depend any longer on income from the boarding school, and that better care be taken of the poor. On the eve of the Revolution, he dreams, ironically, of restoring "gentleness in manners and blessed harmony in the family." What about the sisters? Without further information it is impossible to say whether they, too, desired to return to the education of poor girls, or whether they deserved the author's implied criticism, that they had become too much occupied with "good families" and not enough with others.

From the time of their arrival in Clermont the sisters appear to have established a good relationship with the various authorities to whom they reported. The Contract of Establishment ratified in May 1725 clearly defined their role. This agreement between the sisters and the Abbé de Champflour, vicar general of the bishop of Clermont and representative of the members of the *bureau* of the Refuge, clearly defined the sisters' role: "To direct, govern, and administer the said house of the Refuge under the authority and guidance of the Lord Bishop of Clermont."[27] They were also required

> to have those who will be confined there work and to keep them occupied, and to give an account of their administration to the said *Sieurs* administrators. In spiritual matters the said sisters will be subject in everything to the Lord Bishop of Clermont who will give them a priest, secular or religious, whom he will deem appropriate for their direction and confession.

Marguerite Buisson, one of the three sisters who signed the agreement and would be the first superior, was a veteran of such contracts. She had been sent as "the first one to the establishment of [the house of] the recluses in Lyon on September 19, 1692," in preparation for the arrival of a community of Sisters of St. Joseph there in 1696.[28] Her obituary notes that "She was a sister capable of maintaining and undertaking good works." The administrators actually expressed their satisfaction at the end of a two-year trial period, even before having signed the contract. Under her impetus, the Refuge was organized and it grew. After Marguerite Buisson's death in 1749, Mother Jeanne Assolent succeeded her as superior. She opened the house to external works by organizing outreach to those poor who were ashamed to beg. With the agreement of *Monsieur* de Champflour and the administrators, Jeanne Assolent also initiated free classes for children from different quarters of the city. In 1760, she was replaced by Sister Sainte-Agnès Labas, "a woman of great intelligence and judgment, full of tact, and insight," who faced the grave financial difficulties occasioned by moving the Refuge to another part of town.[29] Her ingenuity and courage saved the house by proposing and creating the boarding school. At the time of the Revolution, the house had been governed since 1787 by a young superior, Sister Marie de Jésus Charren, "a woman remarkable for her virtues and talents."[30]

For three quarters of a century, from the arrival of the community at the Refuge until the Revolution, there were never any real problems between the Sisters of St. Joseph and the administrators. When they brought the sisters to the Refuge, the administrators had asked only one thing: to be relieved of the worries caused by the instability or incompetence of the women in charge. As a result, they were all the more welcoming of Marguerite Buisson and her companions. Nothing suggests that the administrators ever interfered in the internal affairs of the house. That did not prevent them from criticizing the sisters when they considered it necessary. In June 1761, just after Sister Saint-Agnès Labas became superior of the community, the *bureau* reproached the sisters for making too many trips, for welcoming too many persons from the outside, especially on market day, and also for "often dismissing penitents confined in their house capriciously."[31] These criticisms, however, were short-lived. Perhaps the new superior had needed time to adjust to her duties and gain the confidence of the sisters before exercising a constructive influence.

The most important link between the sisters and the different levels of operation of the Refuge was ordinarily assured by a vicar general of the bishop. *Monsieur* Jean-Batiste de Champflour, vicar-general of Bishop Massillon, signed the contract made with the sisters in 1723 by virtue of his status as administrator of the Refuge. He also served as spiritual father, or the ecclesiastical delegate representing the bishop, for the community. The sisters consulted him quite spontaneously when there was a decision to be made. For example, when Mother Jeanne Assolent decided to organize what could be called a preventive service among the poor, she revealed it to *Monsieur* de Champflour, who persuaded the administrators to make the renovations required for creating free classes.[32] Mother Saint-Agnès Labas communicated her proposal for opening a boarding school to Champflour's successor, *Monsieur* de Féligond, asking him to discuss it with the administrators, who accepted it. The sisters needed the authorization of both administrators and vicar-general to admit new women to the refuge. In 1728, the *intendant* Bidé de La Granville asked the administrators to accept three young women from Ambert. On his part, *Monsieur* de Champflour gave his authorization to the superior, Marguerite Buisson, to accept them.[33] Recognition is due to the bishops of Clermont and their vicars general for doing everything in their power to support the life of the Refuge, for respecting and making respected the responsibilities of each person, and allowing the sisters a good bit of initiative.

Beyond the Texts, Fidelity to the Spirit

The first Sisters of St. Joseph in Clermont brought in their baggage, or received shortly after, the modified Constitutions for the house of Vienne, falsely dated 1693. These Constitutions were oriented toward "the regularity of cloistered Daughters."[34] These first sisters wore the habit described in these Constitutions: pleated dress, long sleeves that covered the hands, skirt "with a tapered train," a large veil "all made of black wool," a "round guimpe," and buckled shoes.[35] This habit more closely resembled that of nuns of the time than the dress of widows worn by other Sisters of St. Joseph. They could well have followed the monastic tendencies manifest at Vienne, which developed rapidly after 1730. As mentioned above, however, the house of Clermont broke its ties with Vienne in 1727, at the moment when the house of Vienne received royal letters patent, thanks to the power of its archbishop. The bishop of Clermont and the administrators of the Refuge made the same decision, at the same time, as the rectors and archbishop of Lyon, who separated the Maison des Recluses from Vienne. In order to avoid repercussions in their own institutions, they must have thought it preferable not to become implicated in the problems at Vienne.

The history of the house of Clermont shows that the sisters did not follow the direction taken by the Vienne community. They kept the habit and the Constitutions, said to be of 1693, but the way of life they handed on had been received by Marguerite Buisson from Mother Jeanne Burdier. Sister Marguerite had lived in Vienne with Mother Burdier for ten years. Upon Mother Burdier's death in 1700, she had been sent to various houses before arriving at Clermont in 1723. As the first superior of the refuge, she does not appear to have cloistered her community with the penitents, and even less, any of her successors. Given their principal work, it is likely that the sisters did not leave the house much. Their daily contact with the penitents, however, and later with the boarders and other residents of the house, meant that the world was with them inside the house. Because of the penitents, doors were carefully locked and there was a grille in the choir of the chapel. Nevertheless, this did not transform the sisters' community into a monastery.[36] Certain documents refer to a *tourière*, but she does not appear on the list of sisters of the community. There had been a *tourière* in the Refuge previously, when the house was governed by lay women. In this type of institution, it was common to have a person who assured relations between the exterior and the interior of the house. Toward the end of the eighteenth century, in the 1772 inventory of income and expenses, the sisters defined themselves as "not cloistered," making simple vows, living "the rule of St. Joseph . . . under the authority of his Excellency the bishop." They also added that they had "no lay sisters." At Clermont, just as in Vienne, ecclesiastical superiors played a major role in the evolution of the house. For Vienne, we have seen how this influence coalesced with the inclinations of the sisters themselves toward the creation of a monastery. In Clermont, the sisters were extremely fortunate that the vicars

general delegated by the bishops were not Jansenists.[37] They appear to have
been an open and positive influence for the community, allowing it the freedom to find for itself its own way of life consecrated to God in service of the
neighbor.

Was Clermont a "principal house," in the sense meant by Father Médaille?
The Refuge, and more generally, the house of the Sisters of St. Joseph of the
Bon-Pasteur, with all its apostolic activities, was an important one. It does not
seem to have aggregated or established secondary houses around it with the
responsibility of oversight. In 1763, the administrators of the Hospital of Cusset, near Vichy, asked the bishop of Clermont and the administrators of the
Refuge for a few Sisters of St. Joseph to manage their hospital. The sisters of
Cusset, however, remained dependent on the sisters of Clermont for only a
few years. The administrators of each house—and perhaps the sisters themselves—preferred that each community keep its autonomy. Other small
houses of Sisters of St. Joseph founded in the diocese do not appear to have
been dependencies of the community at the Refuge.

At the end of the eighteenth century, this house of the Sisters of St. Joseph
enjoyed full prosperity. Revolutionary records of 1792 list nineteen sisters
and one *agrégée*. Five were under thirty years of age, four were in their thir-
ties, and only one was over sixty. They generally came from families of the
bourgeoisie or the lower nobility. Recruitment came in part from students in
the boarding school. Their way of life was inspired by the 1694 Constitutions,
with a mixture of semi-conventual forms and apostolic availability. At that
time the house of Clermont had a wide scope, in terms of its diverse apostolic
services and rich human resources. The sisters' way of life, close to both penitents and boarders, made them, unquestionably, "nuns" in the world.

THE *SŒURS AGRÉGÉES*

From the establishment of the first houses of St. Joseph, Father Médaille referred in the earliest Constitutions to a group of sisters he called the "*sœurs
agrégées*."[38] Since this is a category almost unknown today, one has to ask
whether it really existed and if those in question were religious or only a third
order.

Evidence from the Constitutions

In the original Constitutions of Father Médaille, we read that the *agrégées* sisters did not form part of the "body of [the] new congregation," yet in "various places of the towns, and surrounding villages" they performed "the same

exercises" as the sisters. As far as possible, they lived in the same house, "only two or three together." In both towns and villages, they were attached "to [the] little congregation by the vow of stability," and observed "special rules." They could be unmarried women who "do not have sufficient means to enter a religious order . . . [or] great ladies who, by necessity or social status, remain in the world against their will." Ten years later, both the Avis et Règlements and the Conference of Bishop de Maupas evidence a greater difference between the sisters of the towns and the those of the country than between the *agrégées* and the principal sisters. It seems that the country sisters became assimilated to the *agrégées* sisters and the town sisters to the "body" of the congregation. This is also the distinction that appears in the 1694 Constitutions, where the *sœurs agrégées* are regarded as "Poor and peasant women in the villages." Gathered in "small communities of only three or four," they were under the authority "of the superior of the closest house of Sisters of St. Joseph."[39] Dressed almost "in the same way as the sisters of the Congregation," they, like the other sisters, made "three simple vows of poverty, chastity, and perpetual obedience, as long as they remain among the *sœurs agrégées*." The vow of stability is no longer mentioned, but the context of their commitment, "as long as they remain among the *sœurs agrégées*," describes the same reality. They no longer had their "special rules," as in the primitive Constitutions, but were to observe "as far as they are able, all the rules prescribed in these Constitutions." So many precise details in the text demonstrate that the *agrégées* sisters must have existed in sufficient number in the Congregation of St. Joseph at the end of the seventeenth century to warrant their own chapter in the Constitutions.

What were these communities of *sœurs agrégées*? The archives of several houses contain various documents (acts of chapter, contracts of association, wills, death notices from parish registers, bills of purchase or sale of goods, etc.) where expressions occur such as *sœurs agrégées, filles agrégées, sœurs ou Filles agrégées et associées sous le vocable de la Congrégation de St Joseph*, and others.[40] These expressions all connote a special status in regard to the individuals and the community. There are also indications of small communities around a larger house, reminiscent of the organization of districts. Toward the end of the seventeenth century districts were most often formed of smaller country houses grouped around a more important one located in a city or large market town. These smaller houses were often those of *sœurs agrégées*. The life of Mother Charlotte de Vinols, superior of the house of Craponne (Haute-Loire), reveals how she gave retreats, gathering together "several houses of the Congregation scattered in the countryside, where the *filles agrégées* [were not in a position to] make a fruitful retreat."[41] The present research has identified forty houses of *agrégées* sisters living in small country communities. There were certainly many more.

The Life and Works of the *Sœurs agrégées*

The sisters in the community of Boisset (Haute-Loire) are referred to as "*agrégées*" in a bill of sale dated May 24, 1664.[42] That same day they made an act of association before the notary, which in effect describes their life.[43] Gathered together by Vital Bodet, the parish *curé* they were seven women, who wanted "to live spiritually in the observance of the rules and statutes of the daughters of St. Joseph." In these matters they "had been fully instructed and well informed for four years." Under the direction of *Messire* Bodet, "their spiritual superior," they had "practiced to the best of their ability the said rules, consisting of very frequent reception of the sacraments, living in holy community, instructing the young, visiting the sick, looking after the poor of the parish, decorating the altars, and seeing to the care and cleaning of the church." They "promised both for themselves and for those who . . . will want to join [them] in order to live in community in the observance of the said rules, to apply themselves to doing good, as much as the resources of their house will permit." They sought to take "great care to attract the young in order to lead them to love and serve God." The provisions for holding their goods in common follow.

The same type of document is found for the establishment of the house of Saint-Just-Lès-Velay (now Saint-Just-Malmont, Haute-Loire), dated September 4, 1686, and "received by Charra, Notary." The formulation of the sisters' way of life and their occupations is almost identical to that of Boisset. They added that they received their rules from the "sisters of Saint-Victor-Malescours, *agrégées* to those of Saint-Didier." These rules they desired to observe perfectly.

A third document repeats, with some embellishments to help its cause, the content of the two previous contracts. It says that the sisters at Chomelix, having been in the town for twenty-two years, "are resolved to obtain Letters Patent from his Majesty for the continuation and authorization of their establishment." They therefore asked the community of inhabitants of Chomelix for a consultation approving their institution. This assembly took place after the High Mass on August 13, 1684.[44] The testimony of the leading citizens present suggests that it was probably the Sisters of St. Joseph themselves who, at least in part, wanted to assert the benefits of their presence. These benefits consisted in

the good example which they unceasingly give the public in the Christian instruction of small children, in the salutary education of young girls, in the edification and the charitable service which orphans and widows receive from them, in the perfect charity they exercise so assiduously toward the sick, visiting them, consoling them in Our Lord, and serving them with their hands and their goods; and in regard to the poor lacking what is necessary for survival, assisting them both corporally and spiritually, and through the perpetual exercise of a thousand other good works that make them respected by all as true religious of the Church of God, that render them perfect daughters of St. Joseph and thereby spread the good odor of Jesus Christ wherever they are.

On account of "the advantages from which they profited in the twenty-two years that the said Sisters of St. Joseph have been in their town" and all future benefits they hoped for, the inhabitants approved the steps taken by the sisters and joined them in asking for recognition of their establishment through royal letters patent.

There are striking similarities between these documents and the letters of authorization and confirmation from Bishop de Béthune, dated September 23, 1665. The bishop does not hesitate to say that the Sisters of St. Joseph, *agrégées* included, "are able to have no less of religious life than the cloistered nuns." The people of Chomelix said the same thing: they were "like true religious of the Church of God." The way of life and activities described at Boisset, Saint-Just, and Chomelix were very similar, reiterating what was said in the bishop's letters. These texts always note what Bishop de Béthune called "the great edification and good odor of their conversation." At Chomelix it was "the good example which they unceasingly give the public." The documents from Boisset and Saint-Just speak of the piety of their life—"very frequent reception of the sacraments [and] living in holy community." These descriptions, even if embellished, allow us to see that that the sisters' house was open to the world and that people could see their way of life. This proximity became an apostolic channel. The people recognized that the sisters' way of life—of which they were both witnesses and beneficiaries—built up, "edified," their own community.

At the same period, the letters patent granted by Louis XIV to the houses of Saint-Didier and Le Puy in January of 1674 begin precisely by pointing out "the good example and edification" given by "the associated daughters living in community under the title of the Congregation of St. Joseph established throughout the Diocese of Le Puy-en-Velay."[45] The mention of "the practice of Christian charity, of the works of mercy, spiritual and corporal" is made only later in the text. Similarly, the letters patent for the community at Tence in June of 1687 begin with the same formula, putting in first place "the good example and the edification" given by the Daughters of St. Joseph.[46] Such analogous references in the acts of establishment and the letters patent cannot have been the result of chance. They must reflect the quality of presence on the part of the Sisters of St. Joseph "established throughout the Diocese of Le Puy."

The earliest formulation praising the good example of the sisters appears in the act of association by the sisters belonging to the house of Boisset in 1664.

This formula may have already been in use by other communities. In 1665, the new Bishop of Le Puy, Armand de Béthune, confirmed and authorized the houses of St. Joseph after "having heard the said daughters . . . and having taken the advice of persons very highly regarded for their integrity and ability."[47] Thanks to his request, the house of Tence obtained letters patent in 1687. By that time, twenty years after coming to the diocese of Le Puy, he had been able to verify for himself what these "persons very highly regarded" had asserted. More than Bishop de Maupas, he perceived in the houses of the Sisters of St. Joseph what he expressed as "the effect of God's grace, which is visibly communicated to them and causes them to act."[48]

The formulation for the acts of establishment of houses must have been passed along, together with the Règlements, from community to community: the sisters of Saint-Just-Malmont received them from the sisters of Saint-Victor-Malescours, who got them from the sisters at Saint-Didier. The current existence of manuscript copies of the Règlements attests to such transmission. In his letters patent, Armand de Béthune made no distinction between the sisters of the congregation and the *agrégées* sisters. He did not allude to it. He said that he issued his confirmation of the congregation at the request of "the daughters of the Congregation established in our present city in the hospital of Saint Joseph and in that of Saint Didier, both in their name and [that] of all the others who are in other places of our diocese." Bishop de Béthune's authorization, in accordance with the sisters' request, was therefore approval for the whole of the congregation, in which there were women earning their living "by the work of their hands," others directing hospitals, and others who could "instruct young girls and married women," and so on—each taking part in her own way in the zeal of the entire congregation. The enumeration of activities, though not exhaustive, opens up the possibility of considering the sisters of the congregation and the *sœurs agrégées* under different categories.

Most *agrégées* sisters would certainly be among the women who earned a living from the work of their hands, especially all those designated as *dentelleuses* and *rubanières* (lace makers and ribbon makers). The work of their hands, however, was also a means of both service and education. In Dunières, a house of *sœurs agrégées*, Anne Deschaux, the first superior, declared in her will of October 23, 1675, that she gave fifty *livres* "for the room and board of the poor girls [of Dunières] to have them learn the principles of the faith and some appropriate skills."[49] She did not know how to sign the will, but she wanted to provide in her way for the care and education of the poor girls of her village. At Saint-Romain-Lachalm, like Dunières a house of *agrégées*, the sisters refer to themselves in wills from the middle of the eighteenth century as "ribbon maker of the Assembly of the Daughters established in the town and parish of Saint-Romain-Lachalm for the *petites écoles* and for instructing the youth."[50] Earning a living by the work of one's hands does not appear to be incompatible with the education of youth and other kinds of service to the neighbor. A vicar of Vanosc in 1763 wrote the history of "the community of the *filles agrégées* of St. Joseph in the town and parish of Vanosc," providing his own description of their life:

> I can say, to the glory of God . . . that since their Establishment in this parish, [the sisters] have always had the good odor of Jesus Christ. A part of the day is devoted to spiritual exercises, according to their Règlement and their Constitutions. Later, they reel silk, make ribbons, and teach the young girls. They visit the sick, rendering them all the services of which they are capable, [and] beg for those who are poor.[51]

They also took care of the church linens. In working with their hands to earn their living, the sisters were numbered among the lace-makers, makers of passementerie, and other weavers who were very numerous in the regions of the Velay and the Forez. The terms *filles rubanières, filles majeures rubanières*, and *filles dévotes rubanières* appear most frequently in legal documents for the purchase or sale of properties or in wills. The sisters may have become part of the corresponding trade associations, which would have given them a degree of social recognition within their own milieu. By their work, as by their dress, the sisters were still, and very much, full members of the local community of inhabitants. According to Father Médaille, "their little work" allowed them "to earn a living and . . . to provide for the poor in their necessity."[52] Such work did not prevent them from educating women and girls, caring for the sick, and serving the poor insofar as it was possible. In this way, as much through the edification of their life as through their daily work or various services to the neighbor, the sisters fulfilled the two aspects of their vocation—their own sanctification and the sanctification of the neighbor.

Community Life: Did the Sœurs Agrégées Live Together?

The original texts always present a community house for the *sœurs agrégées* as a hope, something to be aimed towards. "They will try to have a small house," according to the Règlements.[53] The original Constitutions ask the *agrégées* sisters to live together in small groups of two or three "when the circumstance permits." The 1694 Constitutions seem to emphasize the community of the *agrégées* sisters rather than their house: "With the Bishop's permission and advice of the spiritual Father, [the sisters] may adjoin (*agréger*) to their Congregation these types of poor daughters and establish them in the villages, as small communities of three or four only."[54] Before taking the habit, "they will remain for at least three months in the house of the *agrégées* sisters to be tested." After taking the habit, the Constitutions stipulate, "they shall make two years of novitiate," but without saying where. As far as possible, "in each community of the *agrégées*, there will be at least one who knows how to read." Should there be "any considerable abuse," in one of the *agrégées* houses, the spiritual father will determine with the superior of the district whether the sisters should be changed to another house. If any among them are found to be incorrigible, the spiritual father will put them "out of the community." It seems that the communities of *agrégées* were not always ideal!

To understand the community life of the *agrégées* sisters of the Congregation of St. Joseph, especially in light of their immersion in their own milieu, it is important to understand what was meant by the terms "house" and "community" in this region of France. Everywhere it was common to speak of people living in the same place—whether city, town, or parish—as the community of inhabitants. According to Furetière, the word *community* also referred to "several individuals who have placed their goods together, whether in order to do business or to live more peacefully, or indeed who possess or who have to share goods in common."[55] The term *house* referred primarily to the building where people lived together with all of the family's private goods. Still following Furtière, house is also said "of a convent, of a monastery." The head of an order "has a certain number of houses subject to him." In addition, house refers to "the household, the members of a family living in a house." The word *community* therefore has a broader, more juridical meaning, whereas the word *house* refers to the building as symbolic of a social structure, with a particular accepted meaning in reference to the life of religious. In Basse-Auvergne and several neighboring regions, the community as a partnership of goods took particular forms. In large familial communities, patriarchal in nature, associations were frequently formed by two or three individuals and their families who put their goods in common, often to cope with financial difficulty.[56] There were also legally formed "associations of pot and hearth" (*associations à pot et à feu*) by which two or more persons grouped their families together as one taxable household.[57] These different types of association did not necessarily mean close cohabitation. Each participating group would naturally try to find the form of living together that gave it control over its own space.

This historical information makes the recommendations for the *sœurs agrégées* found in the Règlements and the Constitutions more comprehensible. They were asked to establish community by placing their goods in common and to share the reality of their existence in small groups of two or three, as far as possible in the same house. There is no question that the *sœurs agrégées* placed their goods in common. The acts of entrance or the acts of association inscribed in all the registers—whether at the time of taking the habit or at profession—demonstrate the existence of community of goods among the *agrégés*. The form of the notarized acts recording the sisters' incorporation into the community was generally the same as comparable legal contracts made by other people in the same region. To cite one example, the eight women who formed an association on June 22, 1696, "all eight living the same pot and hearth (*mesme pot et feu*) in the town of Beurières" in Livradois, diocese of Clermont, ratified a contract making them mutual inheritors through a will: "the survivors [inheriting] from the first ones to die," according to the custom of the Auvergne.[58]

If the sharing of goods is uncontested, the sharing of daily life among the *sœurs agrégées* is obscure and more difficult to confirm, particularly whether they lived together in the same house. In Riotord (Haute-Loire) the notebook containing the register dating from the establishment of the house in 1659 reports that the founders, Gabrielle Riou and Jeanne Froment, "were the first to rent a room to do this."[59] To do what is not explained. The brief historical summary of the beginnings of the house at Vanosc in 1675 states that the first two sisters, Anne Bonnet and Anne Giraud, "rented various rooms where they performed their exercises" for several years, since they obtained "permanent lodging only in 1686."[60] At that time, and above all in mountainous areas, one room would suffice for two persons with their equipment for reeling the silk and making ribbon. In all likelihood, being only two women, if they paid rent, the room, or rooms, would have been used not only for their "exercises" of piety, but additionally at least for their work and all the services of mercy, and perhaps even for their lodging. Community registers report that sisters in other places "lived in rented space" but give no information about how they occupied these places.

Wills made by the sisters offer another source of information about housing. Two wills from the community of Boisset refer to the residence of the testators as their own house. On June 21, 1765, Claudine Mosnier bequeathed "her furniture . . . worth only about 95 *livres*, of no consequence." The will concluded with the formula, "made and ratified at the said Boisset, house and kitchen and residence of the said testator." It certainly seems that this woman was living in her own home. Jeanne Desnaves made her will eleven years later, on September 26, 1776, "in one of the rooms on the third floor of the house where the said testator was living, in front of her bed."[61] This house may have served as her personal residence, since her sole beneficiary, "also a single woman, a lace maker, living in the said place of Boisset," is not mentioned as living with her, whereas a bill of sale from two years previous in 1774 speaks of "single women . . . living together in the place of Boisset." One can infer from these documents that in the same place and at the same time, some Sisters of St. Joseph lived together and others, living in their own homes, were members of the same community.

The house at Saint-Genest-Malifaux was also a community of *agrégées* sisters.[62] On February 1, 1766, Jeanne Malescour, "a single woman and ribbon maker living in the town and parish of St. Genest de Malifaux," being ill, wrote her will. Her beneficiaries were two "single women living in the said St. Genest." It is not specified that they were living together or living with her. She "wished and asked that her said goods be equally divided" between her beneficiaries.[63] It appears that these three ribbon makers lived in three different houses. Another will, that of Flourie Bere, *sœur agrégée* of Saint-Julien-Vocance, was notarized on January 5, 1703. "Being indisposed . . . in her bed," she wrote her will in "the house where she lives."[64] Other wills were written "in the house of the said congregation," but this phrase does not necessarily signify that the sisters lived there.

Parish registers contain a few death certificates of Sisters of St. Joseph in Jonzieux. In 1671, "Françoise Grangier, Sister of St. Joseph of the said Jonzieux, previously bedridden by illness, during which time she received the sacraments . . . [died] in the house where she lived in the said place of Jonzieux."[65] At Saint-Romain-Lachalm, in the acts of entrance into religious life, each sister expressed her desire "to spend her life in the practice of virtue" with the other sisters and to "follow their rules." To this end, each sister spent a shorter or longer time of novitiate in the house of the Congregation. For one, it was "fifteen months," for another, "four years," and, for another, "some time," before taking the habit and being received into the Congregation. It is not clear whether they lived in the same house after the novitiate. In the end, the evidence is inconclusive: although some wills and necrologies explicitly indicate that the sisters involved lived together, when that indication is lacking, it cannot be deduced with certainty that the others lived separately.

Compared with all the documentation preserved in the archives of the Sisters of St. Joseph, data concerning the *sœurs agrégées* is minimal. There are many possible reasons for this lack of information. First, even if the *sœurs agrégées* were numerous, they appear to some extent on the fringe of the congregation. Details about their life were not deemed important enough to be recorded. Life in the houses of the principal sisters was inevitably regarded as more representative and of greater consequence. The specific information we find in the wills of one or another of the *sœurs agrégées* was recorded often because of her illness, forcing the notary to come to the sister's home, and the unusual circumstance was recorded in the will. Even the smallest clues found in the archives are nevertheless significant and impart an impression of diversity within the category of *agrégées* sisters. Some houses of St. Joseph defined themselves immediately as "community of *filles agrégées* of St. Joseph." The best example is the community of Vanosc, cited above. Over time, however, there is evidence of change in the communities of *agrégées* sisters in regard to their own status. At Boisset, for example, early references to the "*Sœurs agrégées* of the Congregation of St. Joseph" or the "*filles agrégées* under the patronage of St. Joseph" give way by the end of the seventeenth century to "*sœurs associées*" or "*sœurs agrégées et associées.*" This designation probably recovers two juridical modes of existence, and possibly two ways of living community—living together within the house and living separately. Toward the end of the eighteenth century, there were also some *agrégées* sisters in isolated situations. The list of sisters recorded by the revolutionaries in 1792 at the House of the Bon-Pasteur in Clermont mentions only one *agrégée*, Anne Guillaume, 50 years of age, who seems to have been connected to the community.[66] Throughout the eighteenth century, the *sœurs agrégées* of St. Joseph, like the principal sisters, certainly evolved in their way of life and probably in the understanding of their vocation.

If we try to get back into the thought and plan of Father Médaille, it seems that the fringe of the congregation made up by the *sœurs agrégées* would have been closely akin to the apostolic outposts of the Jesuit missionaries. Father Médaille was a missionary himself. According to the Society's Catalogues around 1636, a mission was "a pied-à-terre in a town . . . which houses two or three Jesuits for part of or for an entire year, with or without a superior on site."[67] Such a mission always remained subject to a college nearby. In the mountain areas, for instance in the Cévennes, there were sometimes twelve to fifteen of these missions under one superior, who remained in one of the more accessible centers of the region.[68] In creating the *sœurs agrégées* and grouping their small houses around the more important ones constituting the districts, Father Médaille transposed the Jesuit networks of missionary outreach to women of his time, to the humblest of the sisters of the Congregation of St. Joseph.

Were the *Sœurs Agrégées* Religious?

According to the Council of Trent, no Sister of St. Joseph was a religious. From a canonical point of view, their status was clear. In town or country, *sœurs agrégées* or sisters of the congregation strictly speaking, they all knew very well that without strict enclosure, without solemn vows or Divine Office in choir, they were simply *filles séculières*, living "in the same house, in the manner of religious," without really being nuns. Within their status as *filles séculières*, there were additional distinctions between the principal sisters of the Congregation and the *agrégées* sisters. The two major differences between these categories in the original Constitutions had to do with their living together or not, and with their type of commitment, either by simple vows or by the vow of stability. According to the Constitutions the principal sisters of the Congregation were to lead the life of the "most regular religious," in other words, of nuns who had a recognized rule, like the Benedictines or the Poor Clares.[69] They were bound by simple vows and lived together in the same house. Although the *sœeurs agrégées* were included under the same rule, they were not subject to strict rules of life in the same house. Their commitment consisted in the vow of stability, binding them to the Congregation.

The meaning of the vow of stability, and why Father Médaille asked it of the *agrégées,* had several precursors. The notion of monastic stability comes from the rule of St. Benedict. It carried the very strong meaning that the commitment to God is total, definitive, and irreversible, and it is lived in permanent presence to a specific community, whether monastic or simply Christian. If a religious left the community for whatever reason, he or she, by that very fact, was released from his or her vow.[70] In the original constitutions, Father Médaille specifies that through the vow of stability, the *sœurs agrégées* of St. Joseph were "attached to the Congregation," signifying that there was a mutual commitment between the *agrégées* and the Congregation. The "protestation for the Sisters of St. Joseph," found in two Règlements manuscripts (Apinac and manuscript C, which comes from Dunières), contains what appears to be a formula for the vow of stability made by the *sœurs agrégées.*[71] According to this formula, the sister commits herself to "enter . . . the dear Congregation of the Daughters of St. Joseph with resolution never to leave it and to live there according to the Règlements of the said Congregation." This formula is inspired directly by the earliest expressions of commitment for the spiritual coadjutors in the Society of Jesus.[72] The central element, in the formula suggested by Fr. Médaille as in that proposed by St. Ignatius, is integration of the member into the body of the Congregation. On her part, the *agrégée* sister realized this integration by living in accordance with the Règlements, particularly through a life of poverty, chastity, and obedience. The Congregation, however, which had the power to secure the bond of commitment, had also the power to undo it. The Constitutions of the Society of Jesus expressed the same reality in regard to the vows of the coadjutor:

> The reference to the bulls and the Constitutions makes clear that the coadjutors take these vows with a tacit condition in regard to the perpetuity. This condition is: if the Society will desire to retain them. For although they on their own side bind themselves perpetually for their devotion and stability, the Society remains free to dismiss them . . . and in that case they are entirely freed from their vows.[73]

The vow of stability proposed by Father Médaille is of the same type.

We cannot say how long the *agrégées* Sisters of St. Joseph used the formula of the vow of stability. In the Avis et Règlements, Fr. Médaille tells the country sisters that they "will make three vows of poverty, chastity, and obedience for as long as they live in the congregation, vows to which they are no way bound if they happen to leave it, even if they wish to leave it by their own will."[74] Ten years after the foundation, Father Médaille repeated and explained to the *sœurs agrégés* several points of varying importance on how to live their vocation. He offered clarifications in particular about the vow of stability, relating it to poverty, chastity, and obedience. That does not necessarily mean that the formula for the vow of stability was no longer used at that point. The chapter on the *sœurs agrégées* in the 1694 Constitutions, however, makes no mention of the vow of stability. It says simply, repeating the formula from the Avis et Règlements, that the sisters will take the "three simple vows of poverty, chastity and perpetual obedience as long as they remain among the *sœurs agrégées*." Should they leave the community, either on their own or through dismissal, they are "absolutely free . . . without other dispensation."[75] This explanation, given by Fr. Médaille and repeated almost literally in the 1694 Constitutions, presents the content of the commitment of the *sœur agrégée* as identical to the vow of stability: it consists of living the three vows and it is perpetual, although on condition of remaining "among the *sœurs agrégées*." The formulation of 1694, nevertheless, shifts the emphasis, stressing the personal commitment of the vows more than integration into the social body. In pronouncing the vow of stability, each sister expressed both the total gift of herself to God and incorporation into the life of the entire congregational body. That was undoubtedly necessary, given the marginal status of the *sœurs agrégées*. The formulation of 1694, which became official, risked diminishing both their marginality—the *agrégées* made the same vows as the other sisters—and their true integration: they could leave the congregation without any dispensation.

A search of the registers of receptions and professions in the communities of *agrégées* yields some interesting traces of the vow of stability. Recall that they frequently show a lapse of time, whether short or long, between the entries for taking the habit and for profession. In fact, there is always a record of taking the habit, not necessarily followed by one for making profession. The absence of records of professions in the registers—whether for principal sisters or *agrégées* sisters—may be attributed to the fact that their vows as *filles séculières* had no legal status. In the case of the *sœurs agrégées* the absence of profession in the registers may also mean that the vow of stability was not necessarily considered as a true profession made explicit in the three vows. Marie Blanc ratified her dowry contract in 1662 before the notary in Dunières because she was "about to make general profession."[76] In Riotord, established in 1659, the first profession is dated December 8, 1723, and formulated in an all-inclusive way: "I the undersigned . . . made profession." All subsequent professions at Riotord are recorded in the same manner. In the register for the house of Saint-Félicien (Ardèche), established in 1703, the formula is brief and does not change until the Revolution: "each sister has made profession in our house." The register for the community of Izieux (Loire) contains a similarly nonspecific formula.

This type of comprehensive formulation of commitment, which does not occur for the principal sisters, reflects the vow of stability from the earliest days. This "protestation" was certainly used by the *sœurs agrégées* of St. Joseph, yet not in a systematic manner in every house. There is no mention of profession at the beginning of the register for Saint-Romain-Lachalm, one of the oldest houses of *agrégées*, dating to 1652. When it appeared for the first time in 1723 with the profession of Françoise Vialeton, the vow formula explicitly mentioned the three usual vows. Why one formula was chosen over another is not explained. The first mention of a profession in the register of Izieux occurs following a change of pastor. In 1732, after the reception of Françoise Matricon, we read: "Here ends the reign of *Monsieur* Ciber, *Curé*."[77] In 1734, his successor, Father Durdilly, signed the "profession in my hands" of Sister Marie-Anne. The formula changed again in 1759, with the advent of *Monsieur* Flachat, his successor. The "reign" of these successive pastors probably influenced the sisters' choice, not of formulas alone, but also of how to live the reality they expressed. By itself, however, this does not explain everything. One has to ask as well about the level of awareness possessed by the *agrégées* sisters themselves in regard to their vocation.

Whether people were aware of the type of commitment made by the *sœurs agrégées* is unclear. Everyone knew about the commitment of the principal sisters of the Congregation, since their profession of simple, perpetual vows usually took place during the high Mass in the parish church. By contrast, the *agrégées* sisters made profession in their oratory or chapel, if they had one, in the hands of their pastor or the spiritual father of their community in the presence of the other sisters. Before the middle of the eighteenth century it seems that lay persons, although knowing the *agrégées'* commitment from seeing their way of life, were not admitted to the ceremony. Little by little the profession of the *sœurs agrégées* took on the more standard forms used by the principal sisters. The register of the acts of chapter for the community at Izieux mentions the presence of relatives for the first time at the profession of Sister Antoinette Badoil on January 24, 1763.[78] On that same day, Françoise Fournel's relatives were also there for her reception of the habit, and this practice continued until the Revolution. At Vanosc, starting in 1767, the profession of the "*filles agrégées* of St. Joseph" took place "in the parish church of Notre Dame de Vanosc," but the habit was always given "in our house of Vanosc." During the eighteenth century, in a number of houses and with some variations, the differences between the professions of principal sisters and *agrégées* sisters gradually diminished. The private devotional vow of the *sœurs agrégées*, whether a vow of stability or profession of three simple vows—recognized by the bishops from the beginning of the St. Joseph houses—took its rightful place in the parishes and local churches.

Things were quite different when it came to royal legislation. The more widespread houses of St. Joseph became, whether of principal sisters or of *agrégées*, and the more numerous the sisters in each house, the more legal pressure was brought to bear on these unrecognized communities of *filles séculières* to make sure they did not evade the tax collectors. Records testify to various interventions on the part of pastors and notables to shield them in this matter. On August 25, 1713, the *curé* of Apinac (Loire) certified that the four sisters of St. Joseph "residing in [his] parish . . . joined together to buy a corner of a barn or stable [?], and work together there in order for each one to earn their [*sic*] living by making lace." They "form neither a body, nor an associated community, nor confraternity, but only live piously, having made no vows which could prevent them from marrying or disposing of what each one of them might have." This certificate is signed by *Monsieur* Favier, *curé* and doctor in theology.[79] The priest knew what he was talking about: juridically, it was correct to say that the sisters of Apinac "form neither a body nor a community" and therefore had neither the advantages nor the obligations of such groups. It was also correct, that before the law, the vows they took, not being solemn, did not prevent them from marrying or disposing of their possessions. In 1714 the pastor of Bas-en-Basset also requested that the Sisters of St. Joseph be exonerated from paying taxes. "These are poor peasants, neither veiled nor cloistered, who have taken no vow."[80] The *sœurs agrégées* themselves, particularly at the time of the Revolution, would use this legal ambiguity to affirm, that not being religious, they did not come under the force of the law and could therefore retain their properties.

House registers, and not only those of *sœurs agrégées*, confirm the reality of the sisters' freedom to leave the community. They also record how things happened in these rather sensitive circumstances. At Arlanc (Puy-de-Dôme), for example, on October 9, 1681, Sister Claude Passelaygue wished to leave the Congregation of St. Joseph. She explained "the reasons and motives [for her] change of state" before her pastor, assisted by two witnesses "to help the said sister" so that she might more easily obtain the authorization.[81] In 1751, Sister Thérèse, who had been in the house of Saint-Félicien for about 30 years, chose to leave the Congregation. She asked to be refunded her dowry "of 700 *livres*, which was counted out to her, and she was released from the society by the permission of *Monseigneur* de Saléon, Archbishop of Vienne." Jeanne Théoleyre, of the community at Apinac, requested the dispensation of her vows on February 7, 1763 to go and care for her parents who were elderly and ill. She received the dispensation. She recognized, however, that according to the contract of association made at her entrance, the expenses she had incurred for her living during her years in the congregation far exceeded the value of her work and begged the superior to accept in compensation 150 *livres* deposited as partial payment on her dowry. Anne Ganiayre, the superior, freed the sister from her obligations toward the house, being satisfied with the 150 *livres*, and returned to Jeanne the effects she had brought upon entering the community. Perhaps not all sisters left in such humane and peaceful circumstances, but the very fact of their leaving demonstrates the genuine freedom of their commitment. The percentage of sisters leaving *agrégées* houses overall appears quite low. The freedom allowed the *agrégées* sisters in their commitment and in their life does not appear to have make them any less stable.

Some *agrégées* sisters moved from one house to another, either because they wanted to or because an ecclesiastical authority had requested it. Their mobility, however, was not a sign of instability. At Saint-Julien-Vocance, founded by Dunières in 1655, Marye Mazet wished to "fulfill the promise she made to God to enter the Congregation of *Monseigneur* St. Joseph, as she already had about ten years ago." At that time she was at Dunières, "in the house of the said congregation," and she had "been instated by the worthy daughter Suzanne Deschaux, superior" of the Congregation of Dunières. Now, in 1664, she wished "to continue her vow of devotion in the house where they are in the said place of Saint-Julien-Vocance. Further, "to improve her circumstances," she constituted a dowry for the benefit of the congregation.[82] This change does not appear to have been the result of instability, for Marye Mazet became superior of the house of Saint-Julien-Vocance and died there.

From the beginning, it seems, there was difficulty in setting up communities of *sœurs agrégées*. During the first years of the house at Marlhes, before 1664, Agathe Charroin had to be called from Dunières to take charge of the small community. Around 1705, Catherine Giraud, of Vanosc, was asked to become the superior of the *sœurs agrégées* in Saint-Julien-Vocance, as the house was then—according to the register at Vanosc—on the verge of falling apart. More information would be necessary to determine the real meaning of these problems. They may have resulted from the people involved, the novelty of this form of life, or the incomprehension of those around them. With time and with mutual support among the communities, the crises were overcome, and the *sœurs agrégées* became very numerous.

This overview of the life and commitment of the *sœurs agrégées* helps in understanding their place among the various categories of women consecrated to God. They were not the same as the Filles du Travail and de l'Union at Rodez, or the third orders and other confraternities of devout women. Like these various groups, the *sœurs agrégées* lived in contact with their own social milieu in a solicitude marked by apostolic and charitable presence. In regard to commitment, the members of confraternities, the Filles du Travail, and women in the third orders made promises that bound them to serve the poor or to live a Christian life together within a certain spiritual tradition. The commitment of the *agrégées* sisters was different. It consisted in the preferential choice, absolute and definitive, to live in the following of Christ, even though the actual realization of this choice was subordinate to the mutual commitment of the whole body—community or congregation—and of the members. This choice gave meaning to their apostolic and charitable work. The *sœurs agrégées* were not a third order of the Sisters of St. Joseph, although they appeared even less like religious in the monastic sense of the word than the sisters who formed the body of the congregation. Not only did they lack strict enclosure, but they did not always live under the same roof, and, as Father Médaille wrote, "contact with the world . . . must be ordinary for them according to their Constitutions."[83] Their apostolic dispersion in the world made them similar to the Jesuits, and their form of religious commitment was like that of the spiritual and temporal coadjutors of the Society of Jesus. Were they religious? To Fr. Médaille, there was no doubt that the *sœurs agrégées* of St. Joseph were truly religious. In terms of their commitment, they made a preferential choice to follow Christ, as did nuns. Fr. Médaille knew that in the bull *Ascendente Domino* of May 25, 1584, Pope Gregory XIII had recognized that the simple perpetual vows of Jesuit scholastics and coadjutors granted them religious status, on a par with the members of other orders. Therefore, the Sisters of St. Joseph, and particularly the *sœurs agrégées*, who in their own manner followed the same way of life, were also fundamentally religious. Their institute was a religious institute in the actual sense of the word. It was simply not cloistered. Both the principal sisters and the *sœurs agrégées* were, as Father Médaille had imagined them, nuns without cloister.

The Evolution of Houses and Districts among the *Sœurs agrégées*

Marked growth characterized all houses of St. Joseph throughout the eighteenth century, above all during the second half, and particularly in houses of the *sœurs agrégées*. The number of sisters in those houses could grow more easily than in the hospitals, where the administrators regulated the number of sisters needed by the institution. The sisters who made up houses of *agrégées* became more capable of responsibility for themselves, and the mode of dependence on the principal houses of their district changed. In Fr. Médaille's time, according to the Avis et Règlements, districts were composed of several smaller country houses grouped around one major house in a city or larger town. Sisters living in the larger houses were those whom Father Médaille called "our principal daughters," or the sisters properly speaking, and the others were the *sœurs agrégées*.[84]

At the beginning of the eighteenth century, and in certain cases as early as the late seventeenth century, the structure of the districts changed. The manuscript of the "Principal Obligations of the Sisters of St. Joseph," dated at the beginning of the eighteenth century, refers to districts of city houses and districts of country houses.[85] The former were to model themselves after the house of Le Puy and the latter, after that of Dunières, because these two houses were "the first of the Institute." Later, houses of *agrégées* sisters in the country founded other houses of *agrégées*. The Vanosc house founded a new community in the neighboring parish of Ville (Villevocance) in 1723. Then, in 1732 it established the community of *agrégées* Sisters of Saint-Joseph at Quintenas, and around 1750, another community of *agrégées* in Saint-Alban d'Ay. These three houses, like Vanosc, were in the Vienne diocese. With the organization of city houses into districts, houses of *sœurs agrégées* also appear to develop in the towns. In the late seventeenth and early eighteenth centuries the Vienne house served as principal house to secondary communities that it had established at Saint-Félicien, Annonay, Grenoble, Lyon, Saint-Vallier, and several other houses. In 1744 a house of St. Joseph was established at Riverie in the Lyon diocese. The archbishop noted in his approbation that this new community should find a house that was more important and nearby on which it wished to depend.[86] He referred to the district structure, but it is not clear whether Riverie was a house of *sœurs agrégées*. The structure of districts no longer matched the categories of *"filles agrégées"* and "Sisters of St. Joseph" described in the early documents.

Despite changes that occurred in the organization of districts and houses of *agrégées*, the congregation continued to express its awareness of itself as a body in many ways. The Constitutions printed in Vienne in 1694 had indicated, that at the time of a sister's death, the superior should be "careful to inform all the houses of the congregation in every diocese" so that in each house "the superior have the community pray for the deceased sisters."[87] Such communications actually took place, not only for deaths, but also for other news, as exemplified by two surviving lists. The first, kept in Satillieu (Ardèche) and written in the nineteenth century, certainly reproduces an older list of houses, enlarged by the addition of new ones. The second, entered in the register of Saint-Paulien (Haute-Loire), dates from the second half of the eighteenth century. In this "Catalogue of the communities of St. Joseph and outline of their addresses," all houses are given the same status: there is no difference between the houses of *sœurs agrégées* and others. Together, all of them make up the Congregation of the Sisters of St. Joseph.

NOTES

1. *TP* 1981, CP, 18, no. 29.
2. Jean Pierre Gutton, *La Société et les pauvres. L'exemple de la généralité de Lyon, 1534-1789* (Paris: Société d'édition "Les Belles Lettres," 1970), 295 ff.
3. Claude Quetel, *De par le Roy, Essai sur les lettres de cachet* (Toulouse: Privat, 1981), 134.
4. Quetel, 134.
5. AMM Clermont, "Mémoire historique de l'Établissement de la maison du Refuge de la ville de Clermont-Ferrand," large manuscript book, copy from end of eighteenth century, not paginated.
6. AMM Clermont, "Lettres Patentes portant Établissement d'une Maison de Filles Pénitentes, en la ville de Clermont en Auvergne, appelée Le Refuge ou du Bon Pasteur," June 1666, registered with the Parlement of Paris, July 7, 1667.
7. Pierre-François Aleil, "Le Refuge de Clermont, 1666-1792," *Bulletin Historique et Scientifique d'Auvergne* 86 (1973): 19.
8. AD Puy-de-Dôme, 1 C 9, "Contrat d'Établissement de trois religieuses de l'Hôpital de Vienne, en la maison du Bon-Pasteur de Clermont, du 30 May 1725."
9. AMM Clermont, "Mémoire pour ce qui concerne la Maison du Bon Pasteur," n.d., ca. 1730.
10. AMM Clermont, [Mère Augustine Battut], *Origine et développement de la Congrégation de Saint-Joseph du Bon-Pasteur* (Clermont-Ferrand: Impr. Vve Petit, 1879), 87.
11. AMM Clermont, Maison du Refuge, État pour l'année 1772.
12. AMM Clermont, Communauté du Refuge, Bon Pasteur de Clermont, Coutumier de la maison du Bon Pasteur, rédigé en 1775, small notebook (11 x 17 cm) of twenty pages, not paginated, unquestionably later than the date of redaction.
13. *Origine et développement de la Congrégation de Saint-Joseph du Bon Pasteur,* 98.
14. AD Rhône, 44 H 7, Bon-Pasteur, Registre: Règles de la communauté, 1689; and 44 H 11, Cahier: Règles qui s'observent dans la maison du Bon-Pasteur, 1748-1750; "Règlement de Monseigneur l'archevêque de lion, du 8e avril 1705" [for the maison des Recluses], in Georges Guigue, *Les papiers des dévots de Lyon* (Lyon: Blot, 1922), 201; "Règlement rédigé en 1693, pour l'Hospital des pauvres enferméz de la ville de Tarbe," described in Gutton, *La société et les pauvres,* 180; and René Taveneaux, *La vie quotidienne des Jansénistes* (Paris: Hachette, 1973), 72.
15. AMM Clermont, Communauté du Refuge, "Mémoire concernant l'établissement de la maison du refuge, dite du Bon-Pasteur de la ville de Clermont-Fd . . . fait pour etre envoyé au Conseil de sa Majesté," n.d., ca. 1760.
16. Aleil, 58; and AD Puy-de-Dôme, CL 1053 B.
17. Aleil, 53.
18. AMM Clermont, Maison du Refuge, Mémoire pour ce qui concerne la Maison du Bon Pasteur.
19. AMM Clermont, "Lettres Patentes portant Etablissement d'un Maison de Filles Pénitentes, en la ville de Clermont," juin 1666.

20. AM Riom, GG 145, a register, 1690-1714.

21. *Origine et développement . . . du Bon Pasteur*, 90.

22. Aleil, 60; and AD Puy-de-Dôme, C 1707.

23. Aleil, 46.

24. Aleil, 60; and AD Puy-de-Dôme, C 1705.

25. AD Puy-de-Dôme, 1G 1579.

26. AD Puy-de-Dôme, H, Bon-Pasteur, liasse 10, Leather-bound register, "Mémoire historique contenant inventaire de l'établissement de la maison du Refuge de la ville de Clermont," n.d.; and AMM Clermont, a register, likewise with leather binding, containing a nineteenth-century copy of the "Mémoire historique," not paginated.

27. AD Puy-de-Dôme, H, Fonds du Bon-Pasteur, 1C 9, "Contrat d'établissement de trois Religieuses de l'hopital de Vienne, en la maison du Bon pasteur de Clermont-Fd du 30 may 1725."

28. AD Isère, 21H, Registre des professions des Sœurs de Saint-Joseph de Vienne, fol. 2.

29. *Origine et développement . . . du Bon Pasteur,* 89.

30. Ibid., 111.

31. Aleil, 26.

32. *Origine et développement . . . du Bon Pasteur,* 88.

33. Aleil, 39.

34. *CV* 1693 A, part 1, chap. 1: "De l'origine et du Nom de cette Congrégation," 2.

35. *CV* 1693 A, chap. 4: "De l'habit des sœurs," 7.

36. AMM Clermont, Communauté du Refuge, Coutumier rédigé en 1775.

37. Abel Poitrineau, *Le diocèse de Clermont* (Paris: Beauchesne, 1979), 181.

38. *TP* 1981, CP, part 1, 18-19, nos. 30-33.

39. *CV* 1694, part 1, chap. 7: "Des sœurs agrégées," 33-42.

40. AMM Le Puy, Communauté de Saint-Julien d'Ance, Testament mutuel, 4 oct. 1723.

41. AMM Le Puy, Commmunauté de Craponne, "La vie de la Vénérable Mère de Vinols (1702-1775)," par l'Abbé Clavel, manuscript from the end of the eighteenth century.

42. AMM Le Puy, Communauté de Boisset, "Vente par George Brun . . . aux sœurs . . . agrégées dans la maison de St Joseph aud. Boisset," le 24 mai 1664.

43. AMM Le Puy, Communauté de Boisset, Minutes de Bouchet, notaire royal, copy of the notarized act found at end of the notebook in the Règlement MS of Boisset.

44. AD Haute-Loire, 30 H, Délibération de la communauté des habitants de Chomelix approuvant l'établissement des religieuses, le 13 août 1684.

45. AMM Le Puy, Copie des Lettres Patentes de Louis XIV pour les sœurs de Saint-Joseph du Puy et de Saint-Didier, janvier 1674; see Supporting Documents, 10.

46. AMM Le Puy, "Lettres Patentes d'establissement d'une communuaté des filhes de la Congregaõn de Saint-Joseph en la ville de Tance," juin 1687.

47. See Supporting Documents, 9.

48. Ibid.

49. AMM Le Puy, Communauté de Dunières. The designation as a house of *sœurs agrégees* occurs in several acts of entrance: June 20, 1716 ("avec les autres y agrégées"), May 23, 1722, and December 16, 1730.

50. AMM Le Puy, Communauté de Saint-Romain-Lachalm. Many documents in this dossier refer to "the *sœurs agrégées* of Saint-Romain."

51. AMM Aubenas, "Memoire abregé de l'Établissement et des progrès de la communauté des filles aggrégées de St Joseph dans le bourg et parroisse de Vanosc," 1763.

52. *TP* 1981, CP, part 6, 86, no. 420.

53. Ibid., R, 105, no. 5.

54. *CV* 1694, part 1, chap. 8: "Des sœurs agrégées," 34.

55. Antoine Furetière, *Le Dictionnaire universel*, 3 vols., À La Haye et à Rotterdam, Chez A. et R. Leers, 1690, s.v. "communauté."

56. Abel Poitrineau, *La vie rurale en Basse-Auvergne, au XVIIIe siècle, 1726-1789*, 2 vols. (Paris: Presses universitaires de France, 1965), 1:597.

57. Poitrineau, 1:596.

58. AMM Clermont, Communauté de Beurrières, "Expédition d'acte d'association passée entre Anthoinette Maistre, Catherine et Jeanne Mosneyron et autres," 22 juin 1696.

59. AMM Le Puy, Communauté de Riotord, "Registre du nom des soeurs de St Joseph reçues dans la Congregation de Riotor." This includes a list of names of sisters, with no other date than 1659, followed by a list of receptions and professions from 1706 to 1776.

60. AMM Aubenas, Communauté de Vanosc, "Mémoire abrégé de l'Établissement et des progrès de la communauté des filles aggregées de St Joseph dans le bourg et parroisse de Vanosc," 1675 à 1943.

61. AMM Le Puy, Communauté de Boisset, testament de Claudine Mosnier, le 21 juin 1765; testament de Jeanne Desnaves, le 26 septembre 1776.

62. AMM Lyon, Communauté de Saint-Genest-Malifaux, Acte d'Ingrès d'Antoinette Verney, 11 juillet 1729. The sisters of Saint-Genest, "filles agrégées a laditte Congregation" accepted the candidate.

63. Ibid., Testament de Jeanne Malescour, le 1er février 1766.

64. AMM Aubenas, Communauté de Saint-Julien-Vocance, Testament de Flourie Bere, 15 janvier 1705.

65. AM Jonzieux, registres paroissiaux, 1671.

66. AD Puy-de-Dôme, L 2311, Maison du Bon-Pasteur de Clermont, Nom et âge des Dames religieuses qui la composent, 17 avril 1792.

67. Adrien Demoustier, *Les catalogues du personnel de la province de Lyon en 1567, 1606 et 1636* (Rome: Archivum historicum societatis Jesu, 1974), 34.

68. Pierre Delattre, *Les établissements des jésuites en France depuis quatre siècles,* 5 vols. (Enghien: Institut Supérieur de Théologie, 1940-1957), 1:xii.

69. "des . . . religieuses les mieux réglées," *TP*, CP, 20, no. 41

70. Raoul Naz, ed., *Dictionnaire de Droit Canonique*, 7 vols. (Paris, 1965), 7: col. 1078.

71. *TP* 1981, Protestation pour les sœurs de Saint-Joseph, 272; On the inside cover of manuscript C, one can read: "Ce livre apartien o sœur de Saint-Julien." The community indicated is almost certainly that of Saint-Julien-Vocance, established in 1655 by the house of Dunières. This manuscript of the Règlement is the oldest of this type (ca. 1670), and may come from Dunières or be a copy of a manuscript at Dunières.

72. *Constitutions de la Compagnie de Jésus*, ed. François Courel and François Roustang (Paris: Desclée De Brouwer, 1967) 2:79 and 223 (Commentary on part 5, "L'incorporation dans la Compagnie").

73. *CSJ* 1970, part 5, chap. 4, 241, no. 536.

74. *TP* 1981, AR, 131, no. 2.

75. *CV* 1694, part 1, chap. 8: "Des Sœurs agrégées," 38.

76. AMM Le Puy, Communauté de Dunières, Contrat de dot fait par Marie Blanc, le 10 février 1662.

77. AMM Lyon, Communauté d'Izieux (Loire), Registre des actes capitulaires, 1672-1902, 7 and 15.

78. Ibid., 17.

79. AMM Lyon, Communauté d'Apinac, Certificate noted down on a small loose sheet.

80. AMM Le Puy, Communauté de Bas-en-Basset.

81. AD Puy-de-Dôme, 1 G 1573, Religieuses de Saint-Joseph, Arlanc, nos. 1-2.

82. AMM Aubenas, Communauté de Saint-Julien-Vocance, "Acte de devotion de la Congregaõn de Monseigneur St Joseph faict par honneste Marye Mazet," 5 août 1664. See Supporting Documents, no. 15.

83. TP 1981, R, 106, no. 19.

84. Ibid., LE, 9, no. 47.

85. AMM Clermont, "Obligations principales des sœurs de Saint-Joseph," beginning of eighteenth c.; and *TP* 1981, 278-85.

86. AMM Lyon, Communauté de Riverie.

87. *CV* 1694, part 2, chap. 6: "De la Charité qu'il faut faire aux Sœurs après leur mort," 86.

Conclusion to Part II:
Father Médaille's Legacy

The principal goal of this research was to establish the history of the origins of the Congregation of St. Joseph in order to gain an enriched understanding of the connection between the spiritual dynamic that brought it into being and the historical forms it eventually assumed. The landscape of religious life for women during the seventeenth century was shaped by the Council of Trent and framed to some extent by royal legislation. In adjusting to those parameters, numerous new institutes had to give priority either to charitable and apostolic activities or to consecration to God. The founding texts of the Sisters of St. Joseph show that they fit into neither group. From the beginning, they knew that they were called to live both of these realities. Understanding how they did so required research into the circumstances that accompanied their foundation.

Apart from reliable facts about Jean-Pierre Médaille and Henry de Maupas, some discovered quite recently, many others remained unknown or inadequately substantiated until now. For the first time it has been possible to cast some light on the group of women who composed the first community of Sisters of St. Joseph at Le Puy. Although other research remains to be done, this little group can begin to take new shape and life. The few pieces of information about Marguerite de Saint-Laurens and Lucrèce de la Planche confirm their existence and explain a little about their involvement in the foundation. Father Nepper had already noted Father Médaille's connections with the Company of the Blessed Sacrament, but not the points of convergence between the first Sisters of St. Joseph and the Ladies' branch of the Company.[1] A more detailed study of pertinent documents, primarily the "Statute and Rules of the Company of Ladies," as well as their comparison with certain texts of Father Médaille, the Règlements in particular, has revealed interesting similarities. To this point, no exploration had been made of the Jesuits'

Marian Congregations to find if they held any clues to the origins of the Sisters of St. Joseph, or more accurately, to their collaborators. Weighing the early normative texts against the historical data currently available allows us, furthermore, to affirm that there were not two successive foundations of St. Joseph, one that failed and another that succeeded. The first houses of Sisters of St. Joseph governed by the Règlements clearly belonged to the congregation begun by Father Médaille around 1646 and authorized by Bishop de Maupas in 1650. There were not two foundations of the Congregation of St. Joseph, but rather one congregation in an extended process of development.

The first houses of St. Joseph came into being on the frontiers of the Velay and the Forez. No evidence confirms Father Nepper's hypothesis about the first foundation at Saint-Flour. Beginning with the foundation of the small house of Dunières in 1649, all the early houses of St. Joseph, apart from those of Le Puy and Tence, were located at the conjunction of the three former dioceses of Le Puy, Lyon, and Vienne. Father Médaille provided the spiritual genesis of the community, but its juridical origins trace to Bishop de Maupas, whose authorization gave it the possibility of existing as a new community. Henry de Maupas' membership in the Company of the Blessed Sacrament most likely influenced his consent to founding the congregation, as did undoubtedly his esteem for the Jesuits, and more specifically, for Father Médaille. The Congregation of St. Joseph owes its canonical existence, after Henry de Maupas, to his successor, Bishop Armand de Béthune who, perhaps more than Maupas, seems to have understood this type of vocation.

The Heritage

The first texts Father Médaille wrote for the Sisters of St. Joseph concern, although in different ways, the entire ensemble of houses and communities that came about as a result of his project. These texts, alive with Ignatian spirituality, define the consecrated apostolic life of the Sisters of St. Joseph. They also describe the sisters' various ways of life. From that aspect, the Règlement is addressed primarily to the *sœurs agrégées* and the Constitutions to the sisters properly speaking. They are not mutually exclusive, however, because the manuscripts of the Règlements also contain the principal chapters of the Constitutions, and the latter incorporated the "distribution of time for the Sisters of St. Joseph" from the Règlements. The hundred Maxims of the Little Institute, a summary of the spirituality of the Sisters of St. Joseph, are directed to all the sisters without distinction. The Little Directory, later added to the Constitutions, was not the work of Father Médaille. Finally, the Eucharistic Letter, the last—and not the first—of the spiritual texts Father Médaille wrote for the Sisters of St. Joseph, was very probably addressed to Marguerite Burdier, then superior of the community of Tence, around 1660.[2] In a prophetic manner this letter describes the vocation of the Sisters of St. Joseph as it was at that time, but also as Father Médaille envisioned it in the future.

In 1660 Father Médaille could already see the first developments of his comprehensive plan. In its totality, the Little Design included three categories: the Daughters of St. Joseph, the *sœurs agrégées*, and the *associées*. The first category, that of the Daughters of St. Joseph, is obviously the best known, but not necessarily the most significant—at least not by itself. The role of the principal sisters can be understood only in relationship to the *agrégées*; together both groups define the project. These two categories existed through one another and with one another. New information about the *sœurs agrégées* demonstrates the originality and authenticity of their form of consecrated apostolic life in the world. The third category, that of the *associées*, is more difficult to identify. This word is not always used clearly in the texts. Sometimes it designates the sisters, sometimes other persons. The foundational texts, moreover, contain only a few passages about the *associées*. Father Médaille does not mention them in the description of the congregation in the first chapter of the Constitutions because they do not belong to it. They were pious laywomen working with the Ladies of Mercy, but partly distinct from them.[3] In addition to their general meetings with the Ladies of Mercy to organize their work, the *associées* had special meetings with the sister who was "Directress of Mercy" for spiritual direction, in order to move toward "the perfection which is in keeping with their state of life." In addition to assuming responsibility for charitable activities, the *associées* were invited in these meetings to partake in a particular attitude of heart. They shared the same basic orientation as the two categories of sisters who made up the Little Design: all are called to seek "their salvation and perfection" in the whole of their life and in the works of mercy "for the salvation and perfection of the neighbor" and for the greater glory of God. With the Directress of Mercy, who became their spiritual guide, the *associées* reflected on their ways of living and acting, personally and as a group; they discerned and deepened them, according to each one's motivation. The influence of the Jesuit Marian Congregations is once more evident. Father Médaille adapted the way they operated so that the Sisters of St. Joseph could play a role with the laywomen who worked with them analogous to that of the Jesuit priests who were prefects of the Congregations.

In the seventeenth century many other religious institutes, if not all, whether new or older, consisted of two or three categories. For example, the Congregation of the Sisters Hospitallers of St. Joseph, founded at La Flèche in 1636, was composed of the sisters properly speaking, of domestic sisters for the most arduous works, and lastly, the "*associées* and boarders." The Visitation Nuns comprised choir sisters, domestic sisters, and turn sisters.

Among the Filles de l'Enfance established at Toulouse by Jeanne Julliard, Dame de Mondonville, in the second half of the seventeenth century, there were also three types of sisters: "The first are the nobility, the second are daughters of lower status, the third are maids and women servants." It is apparent that the differences in categories could take on very different meanings, according to the case. The three categories of women mentioned by Father Médaille express jointly the totality of his plan, which was focused entirely on mission. The *associées*, who naturally live in the world, can help to bring "families . . . and all kinds of persons . . . to the cherished virtues of the Gospel."[4] By their life in the world, the *sœurs agrégées* seem to have been a hinge between the principal sisters and the *associées*, since they had made a commitment like the sisters and at the same time lived in an ordinary manner in the world. Houses of the principal sisters seem to have been reference points—not as more conventual houses, but as communities that animated and sustained the whole of the plan. Sisters of the principal houses organized the Confraternities of Mercy and provided spiritual direction for the *associées*. The superiors of these houses were responsible, at least in the beginning, for the life and spiritual support of the small houses of the *sœurs agrégées*.

Father Médaille must have formed a high opinion about the ability of the women of his time. Whether they were numerous "poor and peasant daughters" or women of a higher social status, he believed them capable of living in their own way the same vocation he had in the Society of Jesus. For them and with them he invented a transposition of Jesuit forms of life that took account of their situation as women, with the social limits that included, and also recognized their various levels of education. The rules he gave them simplified the texts of the Jesuit *Constitutions* but retained all of their spirit. This spirit was explicitly transmitted in particular by the structure of the entire body and by the rules for officers. It was summarized, concentrated, in the vow formula, where Father Médaille expressed what belonged uniquely to the Sisters of St. Joseph: the profound littleness and humility of their life before God and before their brothers and sisters, together with a universal charity, lived on the ground, in the field, but open to the whole world.

Mutations of the Heritage

The difficulty of understanding and accepting the forms of life proposed to the first Sisters of St. Joseph by Father Médaille appeared almost from the beginning, since we find evidence of it before 1660 in the Little Directory with its reference to the recitation of the Divine Office. The *Constitutions* printed at Vienne in 1694 imply that the sisters, and perhaps those around them, were looking for more conventual forms of life. To put this in place, the redactor borrowed patterns from the constitutions of the first Visitation, which are reproduced in form but not in spirit. Besides these interpolations, changes that were apparently minimal transformed the entire atmosphere of the constitutions written by Father Médaille. In many aspects they became stricter and more regimented. The main emphasis shifted imperceptibly to life within the house; apostolic presence and action in the world became an aspect added onto rather than integrated into life consecrated to God.

The principal reasons behind these changes were the consistent pull of the cloister and the sisters' lack of adequate formation in an essentially Ignatian ideal. Some communities, significant because of the number of sisters or their social status, were attracted toward more monastic forms of religious life. The most notable example was obviously Vienne. Temptations toward the cloister, whether they arose within the community or were imposed by external pressure, persisted to a greater or lesser degree throughout the eighteenth century. During the fifty years following the foundation, the Sisters of St. Joseph also lacked the means of spiritual direction to help them understand the vocation that Father Médaille had outlined. The first houses were most often established in parishes where Jesuits held title to the benefice. Afterwards, with permission from the bishops, houses were founded everywhere pastors asked for them. Despite good will and their desire to support the sisters' spiritual life, pastors and other ecclesiastics were not always able to comprehend how an authentic consecrated life could be lived right in the middle of the world. Compared to what Father Médaille had proposed in the original constitutions, the *Constitutions* of 1694 reduce the importance of forming each sister to personal responsibility for her own spiritual life. This change risked turning from constructing a vertebral column in individuals and in the congregation to buttressing a lifestyle. In fact, that is what happened in the 1694 *Constitutions* and consequently, most likely in a good number of communities. The result was that the interior life became measured by the number of times for prayer and their length rather than by its spiritual quality and the sound correlation of prayer and action.

This shift of accent at the end of the seventeenth century opened a kind of fissure between the types of communities of Sisters of St. Joseph corresponding to the dichotomy between prayer and action, and linked to a dichotomy between the interior and the exterior of the house. Seen in this light, the *sœurs agrégées* typified the focus that was most immediately apostolic and directed toward the exterior. That of the principal sisters seemed more contemplative because it was more turned inward on the life of the house. Fascination with the cloister at this period produced a tendency to put greater value on what

happened within the house. By contrast, everything directed toward the outside was more or less consciously devalued. The organization of the 1694
Constitutions betrays this attitude in the place it assigns to the chapter on the
sœurs agrégées. It is tacked on at the very end of the description of the congregation, after the presentation of the principal sisters, the vows, enclosure,
dress, prayers, ecclesiastical superiors, and the spiritual father.[5] The *agrégées*
do not fit; they are like a voice singing off key in the choir. In the Constitutions written by Father Médaille, however, they are integrated into the first
part, immediately after the description of the principal sisters and their lodging.[6] In order to articulate the reality of the vocation of St. Joseph, since neither group by itself adequately embodied it, they should have appeared together. The *Constitutions* of 1694, however, present a Congregation of St.
Joseph composed of two distinct elements—each representing a specific tendency of the congregation—running on two more or less parallel tracks. Despite this failure, a certain inner coherence of the whole remained. Even if
there was considerable duality, there was no absolute separation, either of the
groups or the values they represented. Over time the differences between the
way of life of the *sœurs agrégées* and that of the principal sisters of the congregation lessened. The latter increasingly took first place and little by little
carried the *agrégées* along in their wake.

   The shift of emphasis in the 1694 *Constitutions* gradually produced an evolution in the way that communities related exterior charitable and apostolic
works to what went on inside the house. At first, if sisters worked in hospitals and other institutions for the poor, they lived there as well. During the
eighteenth century, as we have seen, they tended to live in houses separate
from those institutions. From a twentieth-century perspective, it might seem
that the sisters working in the hospital-based houses of all kinds lived a more
conventual life than the others, since they lived and worked under the same
roof. The laws confining beggars and fallen girls and women also confined
sisters who worked with the poor and the sick in a way that would seem to
have made their life more monastic. This was not the case. The rules for the
portress in the 1694 *Constitutions*, for example, say she must watch particularly over the comings in and goings out.[7] Sisters were much more in contact
with all kinds of people in hospitals than when they lived in their own houses.
Even in their own houses, their life was not monastic. Women of middle or
underprivileged classes who were the contemporaries of the sisters spent
most of their lives in the house. The man lived outside, the woman by the
hearth. Her principal work was domestic.[8] For the sisters, as for all women,
the house was their privileged place of life and evangelization. This is the
main reason why Father Médaille spoke in the Eucharistic Letter of the community and the house in terms of apostolic consecration.[9] Nevertheless, the

forms of life he described, and also those revealed in this history, are not conventual forms. The sisters' need for times and places where they could be apart was entirely real and completely in line with their vocation. It is not surprising, that like Mother Jeanne Burdier at Vienne, they allowed themselves a way to respond to that need by installing themselves in their own house.

Another aspect of the evolution in the relationship of the internal to the external was a gradual tendency to bring various activities and charitable services inside the house. At Craponne the request for royal letters patent in 1766 says the Sisters of St. Joseph have "made it their responsibility to shelter in their houses . . . poor orphan girls." The sisters' house, according to the petition, had become the "hospital" for the orphan girls, to the "great relief" of the town hospital. Letters patent of Louis XVI for Satillieu in 1776 mention the education of all the youth of the region as provided by the sisters in their own home. The few letters patent extant from the second half of the eighteenth century acknowledge above all the services rendered within the house and without. They no longer mention the edification given by the community. Although there is often reference to the virtues of the sisters and to their dedication, there is no longer the same sense of closeness to the people.

For Sisters of St. Joseph, as for any Christian, there were various ways of responding to the poor and of proclaiming the Gospel with their whole life. The question is whether the forms of life, that by the end of the eighteenth century had become closer to the monastic model, were consistent with the vision of Father Médaille, and whether the sisters were more "religious" on account of that. Juridically, they were no more nuns than in Father Médaille's day. Nuns or not, they were less and less in the world.

Rediscovering the Heritage

Following the Revolution, Sisters of St. Joseph reconstituted many of their communities by gathering former sisters together or receiving new members. Naturally they tried to collect the riches of their vocation as Sisters of St. Joseph and to reassemble the treasures of their heritage. The forms taken by these new communities reveal what the sisters considered most important, what they wanted to revive and put back into practice. Although the general shape of these communities was determined by Napoleonic law, requiring them to accept the administrative structure of congregations with a centralized authority over a considerable number of houses, on closer inspection interesting patterns appear.

In 1816, Mother Saint-Jean Fontbonne established a central house for the Sisters of St. Joseph in Lyon. Beginning in 1807 she had opened several communities at Saint-Étienne in the Lyon diocese and elsewhere. A register entitled "List of the Houses of St. Joseph of the diocese of Lyon" begun in 1807 reveals the methods she used to organize the communities.[10] At that period numbers were increasing with lightning speed. Beginning in the year 1821, but above all in 1822 and 1823, Mother Saint-Jean created or re-created a great number of small houses composed of two or three sisters. Most often the community included only two. The "List of Houses," after indicating the place, presents such communities as: "Sister N___, *née* M___, superior, with Sister X___, *née* Y___." During 1822 alone, eighteen small communities were founded: twelve with two sisters and six with three. Mother Saint-Jean reproduced the kind of structure she knew before the Revolution, that is, small houses of *sœurs agrégées* attached to a more important house. They were not *sœurs agrégées*, however, or communities of *agrégées*. The sisters all seem to have been viewed as Sisters of St. Joseph. Nevertheless, their way of life could have been very close to that of the *sœurs agrégées* of Fr Médaille's time, considering their apostolic works and the smallness of their communities, which placed them in very close contact with their neighborhood.

A different resurgence of the *sœurs agrégées* occurred in the Ardèche in the commune of Les Vans. A house of Sisters of St. Joseph was established there after the Revolution, and some pious single women wanted to be connected with the community as *sœurs agrégées*, or country sisters, to teach the young girls of the countryside and to care for the sick. The bishop asked the superior of the house to draw up the necessary rules for these women. The resulting *Règlement pour les Sœurs Rurales de la Communauté de Saint-Joseph des Vans* was printed at Lyon in 1852.[11] The people of the area probably retained a keen memory of the former *sœurs agrégées*. Several *agrégées* in the Ardèche from the houses of Vanosc and Saint-Julien-Vocance had been guillotined during the Revolution. The group of pious women and the superior at Les Vans apparently wanted to revive this branch—simultaneously esteemed and diminished—of the Sisters of St. Joseph. The *sœurs agrégées* described in the new *Règlement* little resembled the *agrégées* of Father Médaille, however. They were *filles dévotes*, "capable of instructing the youth," committed to the congregation by promises made to the superior general. Identified primarily by their charitable works, they were more closely related to the Filles de l'Instruction of Le Puy or to the *Régentes* in the Filles du Travail and de l'Union at Rodez than to the *agrégées* of Father Médaille.

Difficulty with integrating the forms of an apostolic vocation into the sisters' consecrated life continued through the nineteenth and early twentieth centuries. Sisters could not imagine that life in the communities of Father Médaille's day was different from what they had known and received. For them, fidelity consisted in accepting and developing the way of life passed on to them. That is the reason for the multiplication during that era of enormous motherhouses with extremely conventual ways of life. The motherhouse was often presented as a model to novices, novices who might then go on to spend their religious apostolic life in tiny country houses. The duality between apostolic activity and consecrated life did not disappear. During the same period the growth of charitable and apostolic institutions taken on by the sisters contributed toward defining the Congregations of St. Joseph by their social purpose.[12] This movement was obviously initiated in general in the pre-Revolutionary communities of St. Joseph. It would continue on the whole until Vatican II.

In the time since Vatican II, it has become possible to rediscover and reconstitute the complete heritage of Father Médaille. Over the centuries, external conditions, especially in psycho-sociological and juridical realms, limited the full realization of his insight. Changes now experienced on multiple levels—not least in historical understanding—have put all the cards back in our hands. For Sisters of St. Joseph, this provides the prospect of discovering, through the life lived by women of their own time, genuine forms of fidelity to their vocation.

NOTES

1. Marius Nepper, SJ, *Origins: The Sisters of St. Joseph*, trans. commissioned by the Federation of the Sisters of St. Joseph, USA [Erie: Villa Maria College, 1975], 10-11.

2. The author's research following the publication of the French edition has led her to consider it possible that the first part of the Eucharistic Letter may have been written in the first days of the Institute, and the latter part, which describes the different houses, around 1660.—Trans.

3. *TP* 1981, CP, 26, no. 84; 28, no. 93; 59, no.274; and 60, nos. 276-79.

4. Ibid., CP, 22, no. 46.

5. *CV* 1694, part 1, chap. 8, 33 ff.

6. *TP* 1981, CP, part 1, 18-19, nos. 30-33.

7. *CV* 1694, part 4.

8. Philippe Aries and Georges Duby, *Passions of the Renaissance*, vol. 3 of *A History of Private Life* (Cambridge, Mass.: Belknap Press of Harvard University Press, 1989), 407.

9. *TP* 1981, LE, 9, nos. 38 and 47.

10. AMM Lyon, État des Maisons de Saint-Joseph du diocèse de Lyon, Registre, 14 août 1807-1824.

11. AMM Aubenas, Communauté de Vans, *Règlement pur les Sœurs Rurales de la Communauté de Saint-Joseph de Vans*.

12. Claude Langois, *Le Catholicisme au féminin: les congrégations françaises à supérieure générale au XIXe siècle* (Paris: Cerf, 1984), 67.

Supporting Documents

1
BAPTISMAL RECORD OF FATHER JEAN-PIERRE MÉDAILLE

AD Aude, Carcassone, Paroisse Saint-Michel, Baptêms, 1610

Jean Pierre Médaille   October 1610
On the tenth of October Jean Pierre was baptized, son of Jean Medalle [*sic*],
king's counsel (*avocat*); mother, Phelippe d'Estevenel; godfather, *Monsieur Maître* Pierre de Moulhet, judge; godmother, Jeanne d'Estevenel.

2
DEATHS OF THE FIRST SISTERS OF ST. JOSEPH

AM Le Puy, E 67, Registre Mariages et mortuaires de l'Église paroissiale Saint-Georges, 15 November 1645–29 December 1683, fol. 35 v.
May 1683
The year and month above and the twenty-third day, Sister Françoise Heyraud [*sic*], superior of the house of St. Joseph of Le Puy, deceased the previous day at the said house of Saint Joseph at the rue de Monferrant [*sic*] at the age of about seventy-two years, having received all the sacraments, was buried inside the church in the chapel of St. Magdalene. [Those who] assisted in taking the body to the tomb: Bartélemy Arnaud, illiterate, and Antoine Layre, acolyte, undersigned. JULIEN LEYRE vicar
AM Le Puy, E 68, Paroisse Saint-Agrève-Saint-Georges, Registre Mariages et mortuaries, 1684-1700, fol. 47
1685, January

On the twenty-fifth day of the year and month above Sister Anne Brun, Sister of Saint Joseph, deceased the previous day at their house of Saint Joseph in the rue de Montferrand at about fifty years of age, having received all the sacraments, and being the said sister superior of the said House of St. Joseph, was buried inside the church. Antoine Largier, *Maître* Sifferant, and Mathieu Couvon, paid laborer, both from Le Puy, assisted in taking the body to the tomb and have signed.

Same register, for the year 1694, fol. 67.

In the year 1694 and the 7th of September Anne Chalayer, Sister of St Joseph, about 90 years of age, was buried in the Chapel of St. Joseph having died the preceding day at St. Joseph. Those who assisted in taking the body to the tomb were my [?] Gabriel Devalery, priest, and Jean . . . and Jean, deacon, Jean Irail, ecclesiastics from the seminary. Undersigned

De Valery, priest

[The decennial records of the parish Saint Georges/Saint Agrève refer to "Chalaÿer Anne sister of the third order"].

    Baptism and death of Marguerite Burdier (alias Sister Jeanne)

AM paroisse Saint-Julien-Molin-Molette (Loire)

Premier registre, 1614-1693, acte de Baptême.

The year 1626. Today [October 23, from another baptism recorded the same day], Marguerite was baptized, daughter of Guy Burdier and of Marg . . . [?] de Plauder; present, godfather, Jehan Baroigne and godmother, Marguerite Jullin [or Jullier?].

BM Vienne (Isère), GG 42, Etat-civil de l'Hôpital, Registre 1680-1733, fol.75v: Acte de decès.

Sister Jeanne Burdier of the Congregation of St Joseph, superior of these daughters of the said Congregation of the Hôtel-Dieu of Vienne, died in the said Hôtel-Dieu the twelfth of February in the year 1700 after having received her sacraments.

J. Thome

3
LETTER OF ANNE FELIX ANNOUNCING
THE DEATH OF MARGUERITE BURDIER

Archives of the Sisters of St. Joseph, Saint-Vallier: Copy of the letter kept without further identification.

Vienne, this 13 February 1700

My very dear Sisters,

I am obliged to send you word of the death of our much honored Mother Jeanne Beurdier [*sic*] who died the 12th of this month at two hours after midnight, having been ill and stricken by fever and extraordinary suffering for about six months, after several years of very poor health. Throughout her afflictions and her illness she always gave examples and visible signs of patience and of a perfect submission to the most holy will of God. She died in these sentiments as well, because before entering into her agony, the last words she said to her confessor were these, "By the grace of God my soul is very much at peace, because I no longer want anything but what God wants; if he wants me to suffer longer, I want it, and if he wants me to die, I want that too with all my heart." During her illness she received Viaticum several times and Extreme Unction twice, always with great sentiments of piety. And since she had been one of the first who established the Congregation of the Sisters of St Joseph, she always loved her state of life so much that she lived it in an exemplary way and worked unremittingly for the growth of her congregation through the large number of houses that she established in the neighboring provinces. Before she died she urged the sisters of her congregation very particularly to love their vocation and to work with all their strength to maintain it for the glory of God, for their own perfection, and for the service of the neighbor. From this you see, my dear sisters, that the charity and gratitude which we owe her obliges us to pray for her as our constitutions direct us, which is what I commend to you with all my heart on behalf of our entire community, which sends you its very humble respects, begging you also to unite your prayers to ours in asking God to imitate the virtues of which this good mother gave us the example, particularly her love and her perseverance in our vocation. I am, with much affection in our Lord.

[Line added in another hand:] This is the testimony of the Reverend Father Baltazard, her long-time director.

> Your very humble and very
> obedient servant
> Sister Anne Felix superior of the Sisters
> of St Joseph of Vienne

4
DEATH AND BURIAL OF LUCRÈCE DE LA PLANCHE AND OF HER HUSBAND, DANIEL DU RANCQ DE JOUX

AD Haute-Loire, E Dépot 11, 2, Registre d'État-Civil de Tence, Sépultures, 1623-1672

Demoiselle Lucrèce de La Planche, wife of *Monsieur* de Joux, having received all the sacraments, died on the twenty-second of November in the year one thousand six hundred fifty-three and was buried in her tomb in the church of Tence.

Noble Daniel du Ranq *Seigneur* de Joux, having made a profession of faith and received extreme unction, not being able to receive the sacrament of the Eucharist because of his illness, died the seventeenth of December in the year one thousand six hundred fifty-three and was buried in his tomb in the church of Tence according to his request.

5
DOCUMENTS REGARDING FATHER MÉDAILLE
ARCHIVES OF THE SOCIETY OF JESUS, ROME

Letters of Father General Vincent Caraffa (Tolos. 2^{II}, 241),
(Archives of the Society of Jesus, Rome)

to Father Degieu, Rector of the college of Saint Flour, 8 March 1647:

P. Medailleus [sic] mulierum coetui praescribere regulas nisi Provinciali approbante non debuit.	Father Médaille ought not to have prescribed rules for an association of women without the approval of the provincial.

to Father Jean-Pierre Médaille, at Saint Flour, 8 March 1647 (Tolos. 2^{II}, 241 v):

. . . de coetu pio feminarum cui se narrat initium dedisse non possum aliud respondere nisi absque provincialis approbatione id instituendum non fuisse, multo minus leges nisi eo probante ipsis prescribendas, cum utrumque posit multis sermonibus quaerelis, fortassis etiam periculis esse obnoxium. Curabit itaque R.V. de re tota ut a Provinciali plenius docear ut si sit ad Dei gloriam quanto tutius, tanto utilius peragatur.	In regard to the pious association of women which you report you have founded, I can only reply that it should not have been begun without the approval of the provincial. Much less should rules have been prescribed for them unless he approved, since both could be liable to many rumors, complaints, perhaps even dangers. And so Your Reverence is to take care that I am informed more fully about this entire matter through the provincial, so that if this be for the glory of God, it may be more beneficial for having been accomplished more safely.

to Father Médaille, at Saint-flour, 15 April 1648 (Tolos. 2^{II}, 260):

. . . vestras nimis seras accepi litteras et quod Ram Vam spectat, ne quidem sat plenas, nihil enim vetabat quominus de re domestica scriberet, quantum vis monitum Rev. Vest. Pater Assistens appulisset; in aliis gaudeo nihil animadversum quod mea	. . . I received your letter too late, and regarding what concerns Your Reverence, it was not complete enough. There was nothing to prevent your writing about affairs in the house, however strong an admonition Father Assistant had imposed

sollicitudine egeret. Saluto P. Baillandum.

on Your Reverence. For the rest, I am happy that nothing has been noticed that would demand my attention. Greetings to Fr. Bailland.

to Father Pierre Degieu, at Saint Flour, 25 June 1648 (Tolos. 2[II], 260):
. . . saluto Patrem Medaille.

. . . greetings to Father Médaille.

Minutes of Father General Piccolomini (Tolos. Tolos. 2[II], 297 r. and v.):
to Father Ignace Gras, at Le Puy, 20 February 1651:
. . . caetera nobis esse prospera necesse est cum habuerit Ra. Va. quod me monendum putaret de nova illa institutione ["congregationis" has been erased] faeminarum quam habet in mente P. Petrus Medaille, rem Provinciali commendabo.

. . . everything else must be in our favor, since Your Reverence thought that I should be warned in regard to that new institute ["congregation" has been erased] of women which Father Peter Médaille has in mind. I shall refer the matter to the provincial.

to Father Gabriel Garreau, Rector of the College of Le Puy, 20 February 1651:
. . . de consilio Patris Petri Medaille ad Provincialem scribo . . . elogium vero Patris Fr. Regis Societati[s] Martyrologio inferendum curabo.

. . . I am writing to the provincial about Father Peter Médaille's plan. I shall certainly take care that the eulogy of Father Fr[ancis] Regis is put into the Martyrology of the Society.

to Father Antoine Savignac, Provincial of Toulouse, 20 February 1651:
Anicii dicunt Patrem Petrum Medaille mira moliri pro instituendo nescio quo femineo coetu, Scire cupio, quale sit istud consilium et a quo facultatem habuerit hisce rebus se immiscendi, quae non admodum Instituto nostro conveniunt.

Those [the Jesuits] at Le Puy say that Father Peter Médaille is launching an extraordinary undertaking to establish some type of association of women. I want to know the nature of his plan and from whom he obtained permission to get involved in these matters which are not at all in accord with our Institute.

Necrology of Father Médaille (Tolos 23, Tolos Aquit. Necrologia, fol. 168v.):
P. Joannes-Petrus Medaille, Carcassonensis, professus 4 votorum, obiit Billomi. 1669, aetat. 59, Soc. 43.
Magnam vitae partem in provinciae missionibus insumpsit tanta cum zeli et sanctitatis laude ut sanctus et Apostolus passim vocaretur, nec fama fructus fuere minores in omni laborum apostolicorum genere, ita ut divitibus aeque ac pauperibus sed Episcopis in primis in quorum diaecesibus laboravit aceptissimus semper fuerit.

F[ather] Jean-Pierre Médaille of Carcassonne, professed of four vows, died at Billom, 1669, at the age of fifty-nine. He had been in the Society for forty-three years. The greater part of his life was spent in the missions of the [Toulouse] province with such zeal and so great a reputation for holiness that here and there he was called saint and Apostle. Nor were the fruits of his apostolic labors of every kind less than his reputation, so much so that he was always highly esteemed by rich and poor alike, but especially by the bishops in whose dioceses he labored.

6

"RECOLLECTION OF A GREAT MIRACLE
THAT OCCURRED AT ST. JOSEPH"

Archives privées de monsieur Ch. Bayon de la Tour, Le Puy

I, the undersigned Gabriel Lanthenas, merchant of the present city of Le Puy, was present at what happened in the following, on the fifteenth day of the month of October one thousand six hundred fifty-four.

The *messieurs* the magistrates of the *sénéschal*, the officers of the communal court, and the consuls being assembled in the chamber of *monsieur* the *juge-mage* for some business I had with he community of the present city of Le Puy, a leader of one of the most important of these three bodies made a long address to the company, saying among other things, that the excessive number of convents of women religious that the community has permitted to be established in this city would be the entire ruin of this city and would cause a shortage of food, and several other arguments in order to effect his plan, which the devil had placed in his mind. After that he began to say that with impunity, on their own authority, without having asked permission from the community of the city or having observed any of what should be observed in order to establish a convent of nuns in a city, and to the great detriment of the Hôpital des Orphelines, a convent of nuns who are outsiders was established in the house and hospital of the orphan girls, without having asked any permission or the consent of anyone. And there were several other arguments for carrying out his plan, to which the entire assembly agreed. At the same time, because these daughters were established by their own authority in the hospital for the orphan girls of this city without any permission, it was decided that they should be driven from this house and out of the city and banned from returning to it, and specifically to this house of orphan girls or anywhere else in the said city, with very express prohibition for the mistress of orphan girls to receive them under pain of having the blame laid on her. And in order to implement this decision they deputized two persons from each of the three groups—among them, the one who had put the flea in the ear of all the others—who departed at once with great zeal to carry out their mission.

Seeing these doings, I, who have a special affection for these holy daughters, having known particularly the great sanctity of the person who founded this institution, of whom I will speak later, I followed these *messieurs* to try to take these good souls and give them shelter in my home.

When these *messieurs* entered the door of the lower courtyard, they asked to see the mistress of the orphan girls and began to accost her rudely. Meanwhile, I went to the room of these holy souls who were making ribbon to warn them about the intentions of these *messieurs* and to offer them my home. There, addressing the superior, I said to her: "Alas! My good sister, do not be alarmed; they are coming to throw you out of here. But you will not be in need of a house, because God has given me one large enough to shelter you." The superior said to me in response: "Ah, Sir, if that is so, then it is an act of Providence that should cause us not to be alarmed, but to adore." At that moment, these *messieurs* came in, but God so changed the mind of everyone by his Providence that their entire behavior and conversation were nothing other than a proper and very civil visit, as if they had been sent to call on them on behalf of the community, and they left in the same manner. Oh! How embarrassed I was to have told these good daughters something that was not presented to them at all, but quite the opposite: every kind of civility and esteem on their [the men's] part toward them. I followed these *messieurs* to see what report they would give of their commission; but instead of giving a report, they separated and each returned to his own home without saying a word on the subject of their deputation or why they had gone there. You have to believe that I was quite astonished to see such a great change and in so many persons, having seen them so feverish to carry out their commission, and particularly the author of this exploit. God be praised.

This holy daughter who made this holy foundation is called Sister Margot de St. Laurans; she is from Chaudes-Aigues in Gévaudan. She founded this institution in the year 1650 with the Reverend Father Medalhe [*sic*], a Jesuit, who was her director. She followed him in his missions. She did not remain long with these religious after establishing them. After that, she made many sojourns in Saint-Flour during the time of the last bishop because he persecuted her strangely. After his death[1] she became a recluse near a parish five leagues from Saint-Flour, where she knew a *curé* who is a great servant of God, and lives in a cave of a rock. All this good *curé* can do is to make her accept a little straw under her. This same *curé* takes care to have some bread and water brought to her. She writes incessantly, I believe, about the duties of ecclesiastics. When she was in this city, she predicted to us in writing, which she left in the hands of the testator, *Monsieur* Bernard, the great disorders which have come upon us and have taken this good bishop, *Monseigneur* de Maupas, away from us.

When I recounted this event to a great servant of God, he told me it was a greater miracle than having raised a dead person who had been in the ground for fifteen days.

I certify the above to be true; in testimony whereof I sign

Lanthenas

7
LETTERS OF APPOINTMENT GIVEN BY
MONSEIGNEUR HENRI DE MAUPAS DU TOUR, BISHOP
OF LE PUY, IN FAVOR OF THE DAUGHTERS OF THE
CONGREGATION OF SAINT-JOSEPH OF LE PUY
CONCERNING THEIR ESTABLISHMENT, 10 MARCH 1651

AD Haute Loire, 12 h 1.

Letters of Appointment . . .10 March 1651

We, Henry de Maupas du Tour, Bishop and Lord of Le Puy, Count of Velay, Immediate Suffragan of His Holiness, Abbot of Saint-Denis of Rheims, Counselor of the King in his Councils and First Chaplain to the Queen Regent, desirous of advancing the glory of God and the salvation of souls and the service of

**Constitutions
1693 A: some Dames and Demoiselles*

charity in our diocese, having learned that *several good widows and single women, wishing to devote themselves to the laudable works of charity, both for the service of the principal hospital and the sick poor of our city and for the education and guidance of the orphan girls of our Hospital of Montferrand, and that to be able to attend with more adequate time to the said works, they desired, with our consent and by our approbation, to form a

**Constitutions 1693 A, adds: in perfect observance of the rule in the manner of enclosed sisters,

society and congregation where, living in community,** it would be permissible for them without any hindrance to devote themselves to the said services, we considered this design so admirable that we have embraced it with great affection. We have permitted and do permit the said widows and single women to establish their congregation under the name and title of Daughters of Saint Joseph, and to come together and live in community in one or several houses as it will be necessary for them better to spread the fruit of their charity, and to be able to multiply their said houses in all the places of our diocese

where we will judge it appropriate. And so
that all things be done with greater order to
make the said new congregation prosper,
we have drawn up and given rules
(règlements) to the aforesaid single women
and widows, which they shall observe
exactly for the greater glory of God and the
edification of the neighbor as they have
begun to keep them at the aforesaid
Hospital of Montferrand. We henceforward
take the said widows and single women
and their congregations, present and to
come, under our protection and command
our vicars and officials to see to it that their
praiseworthy enterprise may never cease to
obtain new growth and that no one come
to trouble the said widows and single
women, to whom we give our blessing
from the whole extent of our affection, and
we ask, with the same affection, the
blessing of God the Father, Son, and Holy
Spirit. At Le Puy, this tenth day of March,
one thousand six hundred fifty-one.

Henry B. of Le Puy, Count of Velay
By my said Lord
GERARDIN

8
"PERMISSION GIVEN TO THE DAUGHTERS OF ST. JOSEPH BY THE LORD DE MAUPAS, BISHOP OF LE PUY REGARDING THEIR ESTABLISHMENT"

13 December 1651

The year one thousand six hundred fifty-one and the thirteenth day of the month of December before noon, before me, royal notary of the city of Le Puy, undersigned and witnessing, those named below, appearing in their persons: Françoise Eyraud, native of the place of Saint-Privat, diocese of Le Puy; Clauda Chastel, widow of the late Guilhaume Mazaudier of the town of Langogne, diocese of Mende; Marguerite Burdier, native of Saint-Julien-en-Forez; Anna Chaleyer, from the place of Saint-Genest-Malifaux, diocese of Lyon; Anna Vey, from Saint-Jeure; and Anna Brun, from Saint-Victor, diocese of Le Puy, all at this time inhabitants of the present city of Le Puy, who, knowing that His Excellency the Bishop of the said Le Puy gave permission to some widows and single women to to consecrate themselves to the works of charity both for the service of the principal hospital and of the sick poor of our city and for the education and direction of the orphan girls of our hospital of Montferrand, also in the present city, and for these ends and live in community in one or several houses as it will be necessary for them better to spread the fruit of their charity, and, [illegible] as is contained in the said act of permission inserted hereafter verbatim

We, Henry de Maupas du Tour . . . [There follows the text of the Letters patent of Bishop de Maupas dated March 10, 1651]

Of their own accord and free will form an association in order to devote and dedicate themselves to the education, care, and instruction of the orphan girls of the said Hospital of Montferrand of the present city, and to these ends have promised and do promise by these present acts to live together on the grounds of the said hospital and to live in community, to keep and observe the rules which were prescribed by the said Lord Bishop for this purpose; and for their livelihood, food, and upkeep, to employ every kind of work and skill, and to consign to their said community each and every one of their goods, rights, and legal claims that belong to them and that might come to them hereafter in any way and manner whatever. And the said Clauda Chastel, widow of the said deceased Guilhaume Mazaudier of the town of Langogne, promised expressly to bring the sum of eight hundred *livres*, forming part of the sum of one thousand seventy-two *livres* owed to her by contractual indebtedness in her favor by Guilhaume Grioulle, merchant of the said city of Langogne, her brother-in-law, received through *Maître* Yssartel, notary, on the eighth of April, one thousand six hundred forty-nine, bearing the cancellation of a pending debt also made in her favor by the said Grioulle: the same sum of one thousand seventy-two *livres*, received also [through] Yssartel, notary, on the seventeenth of June one thousand six hundred forty-seven, subject to the reserve on this first indebtedness. That is: the said Clauda Chastel reserved by authorization of the other aforesaid appearers the surplus of the said debt which is the sum of two hundred seventy-two *livres* to dispose of according to her pleasure and as she wishes; and the said Anna Vey also promised expressly to bring the sum of five hundred *livres* which [she] said Jacques Vey, her father, had promised her to pay in the event that she join the said association and community; the present contract and agreement having been passed subject to the consent of the said Lord Bishop, who will be entreated, for the greater validity of the present contract of association, kindly to approve and authorize it and to give to the aforesaid appearers His Holy Benediction. And as it is stated above, the said appearers promised, swore, to expect to keep and not to contravene thereto by means of an oath taken by them on God's holy gospels under obligation of all and each of their goods, present and future, which [they] have submitted to the courts and conditions of *Monsieur* the *Sénéschal* of Le Puy and to all others of the present kingdom, and each of them renounces every right and faculty contrary to the above. Done and decreed at Le Puy in the hospital of the said Montferrand in the presence of *Monsieur Maître* Maurice Dasquemye, priest and canon in the cathedral church of Notre Dame du Puy; *Monsieur Mâitre* Pierre Leblanc, also priest and canon in the said church; *Monsieur* Armand Beaumont and Jean Beraud, present. Undersigned with the said Cl[auda] Chastel, the others unable to sign as required, and me, royal apostolic notary, undersigned, accepting. [singed] Fr. Arcis, notary, C. Chastel, M. Dasquemye present, Leblanc present, Beraud present, nous present, A. Beaumont. Thus it is signed in the original.

We, Henry de Maupas du Tour, Bishop and Lord of Le Puy, Count of Velay, Immediate Suffragan of His Holiness, Abbot of Saint Denis of Rheims, Counselor of the King in his Councils, and First Chaplain of the Queen regent, having seen the above contract of association made and passed by the said Françoise Eyraud, Clauda Chastel, Marguerite Burdier, Anna Chaleyer, Anna Vey and Anna Brun for the education, care, and instruction of the said orphan girls of our hospital of Montferrand, recognizing their zeal, dedication, and charity, have approved and authorized the said contract, willing that it take effect [and that] no one be able to hinder them in any way. Done at Le Puy in our episcopal palace this thirteenth of the said month of December in the said year one thousand six hundred fifty-one. Henry B[ishop] of Le Puy, Count of Vellay. Thus it is in the original.

Extracts taken from their originals by me, Royal Apostolic Notary, received in the presence of comparisons [to the original] at the said request of the said associated women

Arcis, notary App. [Apostolic]

9

AUTHORIZATION AND CONFIRMATION
OF BISHOP DE BÉTHUNE

AD Haute-Loire, 12 H 1.

Authorization and Confirmation of Bishop de Béthune

> Bishop of Le Puy, 23 September 1665
> Armand de Béthune, Bishop and Lord of Le
> Puy, Count of Velay, Immediate Suffragan of
> the Holy See, Abbot of Notre Dame de la

Vernuse, Counselor to the King in all his councils, to all to whom it concerns, greetings in our Lord. In the intense desire we have to see the spirit of true Christianity reign under our governance and knowing how God is very often pleased to enkindle the flames of his holy love abundantly in the female sex to make them the instrument of the greatest devotion, and having learned of the zeal which the congregation of widows and single women established in our present city of Le Puy and in

The lines between the slashes are suppressed in the 1693A edition of the Constitutions.

other places of our diocese for about fifteen years has demonstrated: to receive into their society those of their sex who, for lack of means cannot enter the monasteries, can have no less of religious life than the cloistered nuns; to live together in the manner of a [legal] community; to instruct young girls and married women as well as others who are heads or other members of families of the world; to help the sick by their service or by their means, which they bring with them or are earning by the work of their hands in the congregation where they are; to visit, serve,

*Addition in 1693 A :
where they will / direct the hospitals

and* / direct the hospitals entrusted to them when the occasion requires it; and several other works of mercy which they practice; in addition to the great edification and the good odor of their conversation, which they have spread far and wide and which has caused them to be invited into several other dioceses to exercise their charity there. This makes us hope for ours a greater growth of their fervor that seems to increase each day through the effect of God's grace, which is visibly communicated to them and causes them to act so faithfully that we expect them to advance even farther their praiseworthy design under the protection of the glorious Saint Joseph, whom their congregation has taken for patron. WE FOR THESE REASONS, at the very humble supplication of the daughters of the congregation established in our present city in the hospital of Saint Joseph and in that of Saint Didier, both in their name and [that] of all the others who are in other places of our diocese in the said congregation, for whom the said daughters of the hospital of Saint Joseps [*sic*] and those of Saint-Didier have asked of us the confirmation of their said congregation and of their rules,

Having seen the statutes, constitutions, and rules of the said congregation and the authorization, confirmation and approbation given to them by BISHOP HENRY DE MAUPAS, our predecessor, on the tenth of March one thousand six hundred fifty-one; having heard the said daughters on the matter of their activities and having taken the advice of persons very highly regarded for their integrity and ability, we have, insofar as there is again need for our authority, accepted, confirmed, and approved, do accept and do approve the said congregation established in our present city, that of Saint-Didier, and other places of our diocese, with authorization to the said daughters who compose the groups of the said congregation to exercise there the works of mercy and charity, spiritual and corporal, which they make profession of practicing according to their rules and constitutions, which we have also approved and confirmed in all their principal points.

Desiring that they have the benefit in all the said places of all the favors, privileges, and advantages that are accorded by right to the congregations that are instituted for the exercise of religion and the practice of the works of piety and of mercy: GIVING ORDINANCE IN WRITING to our promoter to see to it and to take care that the said congregation not be impeded or troubled in its functions and works, and toward these ends, with authority, if need be, even to invoke the secular arm. In testimony whereof we have signed the presents and had them sealed with our Seal: given at Le Puy in our episcopal palace the twenty-third day of the month of September of the year one thousand six hundred sixty-five.

Armand de Bethune
Bishop of Le Puy and Count of Velay
By order of the said Lord
Dhugla, Secretary

10
LETTERS PATENT OF LOUIS XIV
FOR THE HOUSES OF LE PUY AND OF SAINT-DIDIER

AMM Le Puy: Copy of the Letters Patents of the Sisters of St. Joseph of Saint-Didier to Serve for Those of Saint-Ségolène. MS in-fol, 8 pp.

LOUIS, by the grace of God King of France and of Navarre, to all present and to come, greetings.

The good example and edification which the associated daughters living in community under the title of the Congregation of the Daughters of St. Joseph established throughout the Diocese of Le Puy-en-Velay have given to the public and continue daily in the practice of Christian Charity, of the works of mercy, spiritual and corporal, for instructing young girls, raising orphans, visiting hospitals and the sick as well as poor families who are very numerous in the small villages where they ordinarily lack necessities. And, since the practice of this commnunal life cannot be subject to enclosure because it would be incompatible with its functions, the late Lord de Maupas du Tour, Bishop of Le Puy, was persuaded to accord them permission for their establishment in the towns of Le Puy and of Saint-Didier and other places in the extent of his diocese by his ordinance of tenth March one thousand six hundred fifty-one, which permission has since been confirmed by the Lord de Béthune, current bishop of the said diocese of Le Puy, by his ordinance of thirtieth September one thousand six hundred sixty-five. As also the said permissions have been requested and approved by the officers, consuls, and inhabitants of these places in consideration of the good example and utility which the public derive from them, as is evident from their certificates and attestations attached here under our counterseal, and inasmuch as up to the present the petitioners have not obtained our letters patent that would be expedient for them in making their establishments, fearing to be disturbed in the future by our officers for lack of the said letters, they have humbly petitioned us to grant them our letters of confirmation of their establishment on account of this necessity

IN CONSIDERATION OF THE ABOVE

inasmuch as the said establishment was made only for a good and praiseworthy design for the greater glory of God and for the public, particularly of the inhabitants of the said towns of Le Puy and of Saint-Didier, wishing to deal favorably with them and to give them more opportunity to devote themselves to the divine service, to the prayers which they make daily to God for us and for the prosperity of our state, to the instruction of young girls, to raising orphans, and visiting hospitals and the sick

We have, by our special favor, full power, and royal authority approved, confirmed, and authorized, and, by these presents signed by our hand, do approve, confirm, and authorize the establishments of the aforesaid daughters of the Congregation of St. Joseph of the said towns of Le Puy and of Saint-Didier in Velay in the diocese of Le Puy, for them and those who will succeed them, to live there according to their rule and constitutions and the jurisdiction of the Ordinary. Those whom we have taken under our protection and safeguard we declare capable of accepting all the gifts, legacies of goods movable as well as immovable, which have been or may be given or bequeathed to them through donations *inter vivos* or by reason of death, made in their favor or otherwise. To this effect, we direct our officers not to disturb them or investigate them unless, in virtue of these presents, they might claim any amortization other than on buildings and places on which their oratories or chapels, houses, and gardens are built; these we have amortized and do amortize as dedicated and consecrated to God in order that they and those who follow them might enjoy the said houses free and clear, without which they would be obliged to turn them over, [or?] to deliver to us an *homme vivant et mourant*; nor [are they obliged] to pay to us and to our successors as King any taxes, indemnities, or other rights whatever, of which we have exempted and do exempt them, to whatever sums they might amount. We have given and do give it to them as gift, with the injunction to pay the indemnities, rights, and obligations due to others than us, and to pray God for our health and prosperity and for our State.

We give this as ordinance in writing to our beloved and loyal counselors, the persons holding our court of the Parlement of Toulouse, the *Sénéchal* of Le Puy or his Lieutenant, and other judges and officers to which it will appertain, that they have the presents registered and that the said petitioners and those who will succeed them in the said houses enjoy and use what is contained in them fully, peacefully and perpetually;

Ceasing and making cease all disputes and impediments to the contrary. For such is our pleasure, and in order that this might be something firm and stable forever, we have had our seal affixed to these said presents.

Given at Saint-Germain–en-Laye in the month of January in the year of grace one thousand six hundred seventy-four and the thirty-first of our reign.

LOUIS

for the King: Phelipeaux

The Court has ordained and does ordain that the said letters patent will be recorded in its registers in order that the said Religious of St. Joseph of the said towns of Le Puy and of Saint-Didier might enjoy their effect and contents according to their form and terms. Declared at Toulouse in Parlement the seventh of April one thousand six hundred seventy-four.

De Malenson
Verified: Fornairon
Monsr de Catelan, reporter

The year one thousand six hundred seventy-four and the fourth day of the month of July, the aforesaid acts were recorded in the Registers of the Jurisdiction of Le Puy according to the ordinance of the said day.

Trevys, *greffier*

11

TWO UNPUBLISHED MANUSCRIPT DOCUMENTS FOLLOWED BY THE COPY OF A LETTER OF FATHER MÉDAILLE

AMM Le Puy

THE REVEREND FATHER

Maidaille [*sic*] recommended to us with great insistence never to receive candidates who are not truly called by God and who do not have a good temperament; those who are found not to have the aptitude and the talent for the little congregation should never be accepted for profession because the principal cause of laxity in religious life comes from admitting persons whom God does not call; not only do they fail to keep the rules, they prevent others from keeping them.

It should be explained to the candidates:

1st) that they must leave the world, that is to say, die to the world and its maxims, vanities, riches, pleasures, disordered love of relatives, and all earthly friendships, especially between persons of the opposite sex;

2nd) that they must die to their own judgment, to their own will and to all their self-love; in a word, they should have a horror for all that the world loves, and on the contrary, love what the world abhors;

3rd) that if they do not want to live in charity, poverty, simplicity, obedience, modesty, and work proper to the institute of the Daughters of St. Joseph, they should not commit themselves to it. The mistresses of novices should be prudent and given to prayer and awareness of the presence of God; they should take very particular care to understand the rules of the institute well and to teach them correctly to the novices.

They [the novices] should be instructed in the manner of performing the ordinary and extraordinary actions of the congregation properly, and above all, how to receive the sacraments well and how to make meditation (*oraison*) and the practice of the holy presence of God; that they be required to give an account each day of the progress they are making in prayer and of the methods they use in the subject of their meditation, as well as the benefit they derive from it. They should be taught how they ought to act in times of consolation and in times of dryness in prayer, and in all things to detach themselves from their own will.

They should be taught do and to practice with perfect faithfulness the rules and particular instructions for their duties.

They should be made to understand the least faults against them as very considerable shortcomings, since on that depends all the good order and all the success of their congregation, which will begin to decline when small faults are neglected, even if they are not sins but only a failure to estimate the importance of their observance.

They should be encouraged toward obedience, modesty, silence, and charity, which are the infallible signs of good order in religious life, which is certainly disordered when it is lacking in prompt obedience and charity, and silence is not kept during the stated hours, and the sisters live there without restraint.

They should be taught that it is necessary to conquer self, and that if they do not overcome themselves, they show that they are little suited to live in the institute of the said congregation; that if they do not correct themselves they will have to be dismissed.

They should be taught in addition to be candid and sincere in opening their interior life to the superiors and mistresses of novices, and if they have a spirit that is closed, hidden, and concealed, they must not be admitted to profession unless they correct themselves; in regard to this issue, they should be required to give an account of their conscience at the time prescribed by the rule without fail.

No fault contrary to charity should be tolerated; they should be given penances frequently, even for non-culpable faults; the most disagreeable things and tasks in the house should be given them.

The mistresses should not be negligent in anything, because their task is to nurture the souls in which God establishes his dwelling; she should govern them with tenderness and love, not being shocked at their faults; she should mortify each one according to the capacity of her spirit. The mistresses should often pray for them, give them good example, and love them tenderly in Jesus Christ and devote themselves seriously to their formation and to the sanctification proper to their institute, to moderate the excesses of the fervent and to encourage the tepid and lax to virtue.

VARIOUS SIGNS OF A TRULY REGULAR
ORDER OR CONGREGATION

1st When the novitiate is made with exactitude, that is to say, when the novices are formed in the spirit of [a] religious order or congregation by a sure and virtuous mistress; and when they are kept secluded during the time of the novitiate, as far as possible away from contact with the world, working to correct their faults and to know themselves well and mortify themselves with discretion; finally, to be instructed to do all the ordinary and extraordinary actions of the order or congregation well and to despise the world in order to attach themselves solely to the love of Jesus Christ and their rule. All the good order of a regular community depends entirely on the good formation of the novices and of their fervor.

2nd When the superiors act with simplicity, humility, and charity, applying themselves seriously to see that the rule and prescribed way of life of the community are kept well, and particularly to make a point of maintaining peace and union among the sisters; when they do not act out of passion, and when they have no particular friendship; when they act not out of human respect but only by the lights of grace, of religious life, or the counsel of wise persons; finally, when they love their subjects purely in our Lord without excepting anyone, [and are] zealous, mortified, exemplary, charitable toward the sisters, and very united with God from the heart, from whom they should draw all the lights necessary to govern and sanctify their house well. Finally, at the hour of death, they must render a very exact account to God of the good or bad order of the house which they govern.

3rd When the subjects are attracted [?] to the observance of the rule and a tender affection for their vocation; when they respect the superior and the subaltern officers who are like the person of Jesus Christ; when they never murmur against anyone, not even against the officers; when they live in a perfect union, bearing with each other and loving each other cordially; when they love silence and despise gossip and curiosity; when they love the good of the community and prefer it to their own interests and little conveniences and keep confidential what happens in the house, which can, however little it be, disedify outsiders and diminish the esteem which they might have for the good standing of the congregation; finally, when in all their conversation, they show themselves truly and without affectation gentle, humble, modest, and recollected.

4th When the sisters go punctually to exercises at the sound of the bell, and when they carry them out with exactitude; when those on whom good order depends are the most regular and exhibit good order in everything; when silence is well kept outside the times when it is permitted to recreate in appropriate conversation.

When the house is kept very neat and clean and particularly the chapel, the sacristy, the furniture and decoration of the church, and above all what concerns appropriate surroundings for the Blessed Sacrament.

When the sisters in conversation seem completely detached from the curiosities of the world and only desirous of advancing the neighbor in virtue;

when they avoid a clamorous voice [and] immoderate laughter, especially in places where they can be heard by seculars.

When they walk with modesty and without making a loud noise throughout the house, not speaking in a tone of voice that is too loud, especially in the choir and the vicinity of their chapel, and in the refectory or dormitory.

When they keep profound silence from the supper recreation until the following morning after the meditation, not speaking during this time except about necessary things and in a low voice.

5th When the sisters have a cheerful disposition among themselves and in conversation among seculars [and] at the same time a religious reserve, because this cheerfulness is a sign of the interior peace of their soul and of the esteem which they have for their vocation in which they live so happily.

When no sister has anything on her own initiative, without the knowledge of the superior and independently from her, but rather all things are in common in order to be distributed to the sisters according to their need. Finally, when no secret friendship or particular prerogative appears in the conduct of the sisters, above all that of the officers, nor any attachment to clothing, furniture, and superfluous conversation, gestures, and manners of speech that echo vanity or self-love, opposed to religious simplicity and sincerity.

6th When the Sisters are devoted to work and abhor laziness; when they contribute their work towards the good of the community and not to securing for themselves a collection of little, rather useless pieces of handiwork to use as presents in order to attract the friendship of relatives or outsiders to themselves; when the reading of novels or similar books is completely banished from the community, for this sort of reading indubitably leads to the loss of devotion and very often of a sense of decency.

When no sister is valued just for her birth or her natural gifts but only for virtue; when the sisters nave no disordered attachment to any kind of director; when the sick are well cared for and assisted according to the means of the community.

When conversations in the parlor are well ordered and the listeners are always present when [the sisters] confer with persons from outside, and the discourse and behavior are completely edifying; the sisters should be carefully on their guard and even avoid [?] too long and too frequent conversations with male religious and ecclesiastical persons, who begin their discourse in the spirit and end ordinarily in the flesh; one cannot say how much these conversations have harmed and continue to harm the sisters consecrated to God and the good odor of their house.

Finally, when uniformity is truly kept in all the houses of the same congregation in respect to the rules, observances and customs, general and particular, and everything is adhered to exactly everywhere, without any deviation.

All the things above are infallible signs of the good condition of a religious order or devout congregation.

COPY OF THE LETTER OF THE REVEREND FATHER MÉDAILLE
WRITTEN TO THE SISTERS OF SAINT JOSEPH OF LE PUY

My very dear sisters, I should wish, if your superiors approve, that each of your houses have a copy of this text and that it be read from time to time, either at chapter when you have it or in the refectory during meals. The desire I have for the perfection of your congregation has led me to take the liberty to send you this reminder. I commend myself to your holy prayers and am in our Lord.

Your very humble and very obedient servant
Jean Pierre Medaille of the Society of Jesus

12

APPROBATION AND CONFIRMATION OF THE CONSTITUTIONS OF THE SISTERS OF SAINT JOSEPH BY HIS EXCELLENCY THE ARCHBISHOP OF VIENNE WITH HIS DECREE FOR PRINTING THEM

HENRI DE VILLARS, Archbishop and Count of Vienne, having seen and examined the rules and the conduct of the Sisters of the Congregation of St. Joseph, whom we established twenty-five years ago in the hospital of this city to serve the sick poor there, we have been convinced by experience that all the rules and practices of piety contained in their Constitutions are completely holy and very appropriate for sanctifying all the souls who observe them, and further, very advantageous for the salvation and the service of the neighbor, particularly of the sick poor. And because the said Constitutions have existed only as manuscripts up to the present, we have judged it necessary to have them printed, so that all the sisters who compose the said Congregation might more easily know their rules and practice them more exactly. For this reason, having had them examined again and put in better order, we have approved them, ordering all the sisters of St. Joseph who are in our diocese to observe them exactly, and afterwards we permitted sieur Laurent Cruzi, master printer and book vendor of this city, to print them.

Given at Vienne, in our Archepiscopal Palace, 20 November 1693.

HENRY, Archbishop of Vienne.

PERMISSION

We permit *sieur* Laurent Cruzi, Master Printer and Book Vendor, to print the book entitled "The Constitutions and Rules of the Daughters [1693 A: Sisters] of St. Joseph." Done this 24 November 1693 [1693 A: 23 November 1693].

Let it be done according to the terms of the King's Procurator. This 25 November 1693.

DE MARTEL vib

13

CONSTITUTIONS FOR THE LITTLE CONGREGATION OF THE SISTERS OF SAINT JOSEPH ESTABLISHED AT LE-PUY-EN-VELAY BY MONSEIGNEUR DE MAUPAS, BISHOP OF LE PUY PREFACE: EDITIONS OF 1693A AND 1694 COMPARED

Ed. 1694 (and 1693 B) | Ed. 1693 A

The Little Congregation of the Sisters or the Daughters of Saint Joseph had its origins in the city of Le Puy-en-Velay, where it was established by His Excellency, the Most Illustrious and Most Reverend Henry de Maupas, Bishop of the said city, because of the plan inspired in him by the Reverend Father Jean-Pierre Médaille, great missionary of the Society of Jesus, who spent his life fruitfully in giving missions, not only in the diocese of Le Puy, but also in those of Clermont, Saint-Flour, Rodez and Vienne.

The Congregation of Sisters of Saint Joseph had its origin in the city of Le Puy-en-Velay, where it was established by His Excellency, the Most Illustrious and Most Reverend Henry de Maupas, Bishop of the said city, because of a plan inspired in him by the Reverend Father Jean-Pierre Médaille, great missionary of the Society of Jesus, who spent his life fruitfully in giving missions, not only in the diocese of Le Puy, but also in those of Clermont, Saint Flour, Rodez and Vienne.

This good Father, having had such great zeal that he was inspired by the divine spirit to communicate his design and his undertaking to His Excellency the Bishop of Le Puy, who wanted to fill the place which the Sisters of the Visitation had just vacated by their enclosure, and because the neighbor could not do without the works of charity which they performed, and as these provided great succor, it was necessary to establish another congregation in their place,

This good father having met in the course of his missions several pious widows and single women who, not wanting to marry, planned to leave the world to devote

and because he had met in the course of his missions several pious widows and single women who, not wanting to marry, planned to leave the world to devote

themselves to the service of God and to
their salvation

themselves to the service of the Lord and
to their salvation, and that being so, it
would not be difficult for him to establish
a congregation. This great prelate
accepted the proposal,

and could not enter the monasteries for
lack of sufficient means, decided to
propose to some bishop the establishment
of a congregation that these devout
widows and single women could enter to
work for their salvation and to devote
themselves to all the exercises of which
they were capable for the service of the
neighbor.
For this reason he appealed to the said
Lord de Maupas, Bishop of Le Puy, and
from what he knew of the sublime
virtue and extraordinary zeal of this great
prelate for the glory of God and the
salvation of the neighbor, he firmly
believed that he would not reject the
proposal he wished to make. Indeed, as
soon as he had done so, His Excellency
approved it and found it so advantageous
for the increase of the service of God and
of the neighbor

that he had the daughters called to Le Puy
whom the said Father had found disposed
to leaving the world and to the service
of God.

and immediately His Excellency had the
widows and single women called to Le
Puy whom the said Father had found
disposed to leaving the world and to the
service of the Lord;

When they arrived in Le Puy, all of them
stayed several months with a very virtuous
demoiselle named Lucrèce de la Planche,
wife of *Monsieur* de Joux, nobleman of
Tence, who was then living at Le Puy. Not
only did this pious *demoiselle* contribute
everything in her power to the
establishment of these daughters, but she
also worked until her death with an
extraordinary zeal and charity for the
advancement of their congregation.

when they arrived in Le Puy, all of them
stayed for several months with a very
virtuous *Dame* named Lucrèce de la
Planche, wife of *Monsieur* de Joux,
nobleman of Tence, who was then living
at Le Puy. Not only did this pious *Dame*
contribute everything in her power to the
establishment of these *Demoiselles*, but
she also worked until her death with an
extraordinary zeal and charity for the
advancement of their congregation.

Finally, everything having been prepared
by the said Lord Bishop for carrying out
such a pious design, His Excellency

Finally, everything having been prepared
by the said Lord Bishop of Le Puy for
carrying out such a pious design, His

assembled all these Daughters in the Hôpital des Orphelines of Le Puy and confided its direction to them and [*sic*] the fifteenth day of the month of October, feast of Saint Theresa, in the year one thousand six hundred fifty. This illustrious prelate gave them an exhortation, completely filled with the unction of the Spirit of God, by which he stirred all these new sisters to the most pure love of God and to the most perfect charity toward the neighbor; and at the end he gave them his blessing with extraordinary signs of cordial affection and paternal kindness toward their congregation. He then placed them under the protection of the glorious Saint Joseph and ordained that their congregation should be called the Congregation of the Sisters or of the Daughters of Saint Joseph; he gave them rules [*Règles*] for their guidance and prescribed a form of habit for them; and finally he confirmed the establishment of the said congregation and the rules [*Règlements*] which he had given them by his letters patent of the tenth of March one thousand six hundred fifty-one, which are inserted hereafter, and throughout his entire life, he always had a great benevolence and such great care for the progress of the congregation that he made several foundations of it in his diocese

After his death, His Excellency Armand de Béthune became bishop of Le Puy, who, having been convinced by experience and by evident proofs of the considerable services which the sisters of this congregation rendered to God and to the neighbor in his diocese, he confirmed it anew and approved the Constitutions and the Rules which the sisters had observed since their foundation by the letters patent, inserted hereafter, dated the twenty-third of September one thousand six hundred sixty-five.

The most Christian King, Louis the Great, also confirmed by his letters patent the

Excellency assembled all these *Demoiselles* in the Hôpital des Orphelines of Le Puy and confided its direction to them on the fifteenth day of the month of October, feast of Saint Theresa, in the year one thousand six hundred fifty. This illustrious prelate prescribed their form of habit and gave it to them himself, giving them an exhortation completely filled with the unction of the Spirit of God, by which he stirred all the new sisters to the most pure love of God, and to the most perfect charity toward the neighbor; and at the end he gave them his blessing with extraordinary signs of cordial affection and paternal kindness toward their congregation. He then placed them under the protection of the Glorious Saint Joseph and ordained that their Congregation should be called the Congregation of the Hospitaller Sisters of Saint Joseph; he gave them rules for their guidance and finally he confirmed the establishment which he had given them by his letters patent of the tenth of March 1651, which are inserted hereafter, and throughout his entire life he always had a great benevolence, and such great care for the progress of the congregation that he made several foundations of it in his diocese.

After his death, His Excellency Armand de Betune became bishop of Le Puy, who, having been convinced by experience and by evident proofs of the considerable services which the sisters of this congregation rendered to God and to the neighbor in his diocese, he confirmed it anew and approved the Constitutions and the Rules which the sisters had observed since their foundation by the letters patent inserted hereafter, dated 23 September 1665.

The most Christian King, Louis the Great, also confirmed by his letters patent the first establishments of the sisters of this congregation, in the towns of Le Puy, of St Didier, and in several other places of the Velay.

Since that time God has protected this little congregation so well that by his holy grace it has extended to the dioceses of Clermont, Vienne, Lyon, Grenoble, Embrun, Gap, Sisteron, Viviers, Usez, and several others. The number of sisters has also increased so much, that in order to give them the means for each one in particular to know her Rules well and to observe them very exactly, it has been absolutely necessary to have the Consitutions of the Congregation printed, which until the present have existed only as manuscripts; and for this reason, they have been reviewed and put in better order through the solicitude of His Excellency Henry de Villars, Archbishop of Vienne, who then gave permission to print them.

first establishments of the sisters of this congregation in the towns of Le Puy, of Saint Didier, and in several other places of the Velay.

Since that time God has protected this congregation so well that by his holy grace it has extended to the dioceses of Clermont, Vienne, Lyon, Grenoble, Embrun, Gap, Sisteron, Viviers, Usez, and several others. The number of sisters has also increased so much, that in order to give them the means for each one in particular to know her Rules well and to observe them very exactly, it has been absolutely necessary to have the Constitutions of the Congregation printed, which until the present have existed only in manuscript, and for this reason, they have been received and put in better order through the solicitude of His Excellency Henry de Villars, Archbishop of Vienne, who then gave permission to print them.

14
FORMULA OF VOWS FOR THE SISTERS OF ST. JOSEPH (CONSTITUTIONS OF VIENNE, 1694) AND FORMULA OF VOWS FOR THE SCHOLASTICS IN THE CONSTITUTIONS OF THE SOCIETY OF JESUS

Sisters of St. Joseph

My God, almighty and eternal,

I N.............,

Your most unworthy daughter and servant, desirous of living entirely for you and of depending absolutely on the help of your grace,

In the presence of Jesus Christ your Son,[1] and of the glorious Virgin Mary, of our Patriarch Saint Joseph,

Scholastics of the Society of Jesus

Almighty and eternal God,

I N.............,

Although altogether most unworthy in Your divine sight, yet relying on Your infinite goodness and mercy and moved with a desire of serving You,

in the presence of the most Holy Virgin Mary

and of the whole heavenly court,
vow to your divine Majesty perpetual
poverty, chastity and obedience in the
dear Congregation of the Sisters of Saint
Joseph, and this in your hands, *Monsieur*,
who hold the place of His Excellency our
bishop and very honored superior,

And I promise, according to the rules of
the said Congregation,

to profess, with your grace, the most
profound humility in all things and the
most cordial charity toward the neighbor,
whom I desire to serve by the exercise of
all the works of mercy, both spiritual and
corporal, done by our little Institute.

My God, receive this offering in an odor
of sweetness. Amen.

and Your whole heavenly court,
vow to Your Divine Majesty perpetual
poverty, chastity, and obedience in the
Society of Jesus;

and I promise that I shall enter that same
Society in order to lead my entire life in
it, understanding all things according to
its Constitutions.

*and, in conformity with it [obedience], [I
promise] special care for the instruction
of children, according to the manner of
living contained in the apostolic letters of
the Society of Jesus and in its
Constitutions. I further promise a special
obedience to the sovereign pontiff in
regard to the missions, according to the
same apostolic letters and the
Constitutions.[2]*

Therefore I suppliantly beg Your Immense
Goodness and Clemency, through the
blood of Jesus Christ, to deign to receive
this holocaust in an odor of sweetness.

1. In the original manuscripts the formula of vows begins with "Lord Jesus, all powerful
and eternal." Therefore, in the following text, it reads only "In the presence of the
glorious Virgin Mary."
2. The added paragraph (in italics) is taken from the formula of profession for the Jesuits
who profess four vows.

15
"ACT OF DEVOTION OF THE CONGREGATION OF MY LORD ST. JOSEPH MADE BY THE WORTHY MARYE MAZET ON 5 AUGUST 1664"

AMM Aubenas, Community of Saint-Julien-Vocance.

The year one thousand six hundred sixty-four the fifth day of the month of
August before noon, appearing in person, the worthy daughter Marye Mazet,
daughter of the deceased Jehan Mazet and Catherine Tynal of the place of the
Laubiers [?], parish of Saint-Julien-Vocance, who, moved by devotion and

desiring to fulfill the promise she made to God to enter the Congregation of My Lord St. Joseph, as she has already done about ten years ago in the place of Dunières in the house of the said congregation established by the worthy daughter Suzanne Deschaux, superior of the said congregation of the said Dunières; and in order to fulfill and continue her vow of devotion in the house where they are in the said place of Saint-Julien-Vocance, to improve her cir-. cumstances, she constitutes [as dowry] for herself the sum of one hundred twenty *livres* and a blanket and two sheets, which she has promised to place at the disposal of the said house of the congregation with her other sisters; namely [?], the sum of thirty *livres* due her by Jehan Mazet, her brother from Laubiers [?] and all the rest she has at her disposal, which she promises to use to the profit of the said Congregation of St. Joseph and to continue her vow of devotion and promised it accordingly on the holy gospel of God, concerning which [she] requested a notarized act from me, notary, which I granted to her. Done at the said Saint-Julien, house of the worthy Jehan Tynal where the said sisters live, and the present appearers: *Messire* Jehan Villard, priest and vicar of the said Saint-Julien, undersigned; [illegible] and Pierre Montaignon, son of Barthelami du [illegible], who and the said Mazet, having been asked, do not know how to sign, and I, Jacques [illegible] royal notary, undersigned, handing over [illegible] to the said Mazet at her request.

16
"RIGHT OF PERPETUAL RENT GRANTED BY M^{RE} PERRET, PRIOR AND PASTOR OF SAINT-JULIEN-VOCANCE TO THE WORTHY SISTER CATHERINE GIRAUD, SISTER OF ST. JOSEPH OF THE SAID SAINT-JULIEN FOR 10 S. OF PAYMENT FOR ANNUITY AND 30 S. RIGHTS OF ENTRY ON THE 2ND NOVEMBER 1726. FOR THE SAID GIRAUD"

AMM Aubenas, Community of Saint-Julien-Vocance.
The year one thousand seven hundred twenty-six and the second day of the month of November, before noon, in the presence of the royal notary of finances, receiving, undersigned, and the witnesses named below, appeared the worthy Sister Catherine Giraud, superior of the Sisters of the Congregation of Saint Joseph established in the place and parish of Saint-Julien-Vocance, who had indicated to *Messire* Pierre Perret, prior and *curé* of the said Saint-Julien, that their house is too small, and also that they cannot admit any more sisters than there are at present; that they have trouble turning around in their house or setting up their looms to make ribbon there, or even finding a place for the children whom the parish sends them to teach in the winter. There is no space

even to make a cellar to store chestnuts, potatoes, beets, and other things; and even when they have something, the harshness of the winter spoils it all for them; and on account of that, the said Giraud, both in her own name and [that] of the other sisters, begged and supplicated the said *Messire* Perret to give them a corner of his garden joining their house on the east side as lodging and on condition of annual payment, in order to construct a cellar and, above that, a room to put some beds and a pair of looms for making their ribbons, having no other place to make the said cellar or room but this; seeing that their house is too cramped, and there is not enough space to repair it, and that it would not inconvenience his garden too much, seeing that it is fairly large and spacious, and even that there is a lot of land to enlarge it on the north side. All that [was] explained to the said *Messire* Perret. The latter told them and answered all their assertions, that all the things stated by the said Giraud were true, but that the said garden and the adjacent ground belong to him only as *curé* of the said parish of the said Saint-Julien, and that the inhabitants of the said parish would be opposed to it if he gave it to them without their consent. And the said *Messire* Perret, to improve their circumstances, and [in response] to her said supplication, and by reason of the consent of *Sieur* Floury Pourchas, bourgeois from the place of La Chanal, Pierre Chomeil and Jean Desmartins, his brother-in-law, from the place Duchampt [*sic*], Floury Archier of Saint-Julien, *Sieur* Allexandre Teyssyer, surgeon, Claude Despinasse from Malescot, Jean Vinal from Vinal, Jean Desgrand from the place of [illegible], and other inhabitants of the said parish here assembled, and subject to the good pleasure of the Archbishop of Vienne, has, by his own accord and free will, by authority of the consent of the aforesaid inhabitants of the said parish named above, both in their names and those of the other inhabitants of the said parish, sold and allocated for lodging by title of *censive* or perpetual rent to the said Sister Giraud, here present and accepting, and through her to the other future sisters. To wit: two *toizes* and a half in width of the said garden and six *toizes* at the lower level that faces on the east.[2] Garden remaining to the said *M^re* Perret: south, the road leading from Saint-Julien to Villard; west, house and garden of the said sister; north, land of the said *M^re* Perret, dependency of the said parish; everything following the boundaries established there with its other borders, with authorization to the said sisters to do what will be suitable for them in order to build and to expand their former garden on the east side, and this on condition of the annual and perpetual payment of the sum of ten *sous* for each year, which the said *M^re* Perret and the said inhabitants have declared to be the fair value of the aforesaid corner of the garden, with [the] donation of any more value, whatever it might be, to the said sisters, both in the present and for the future; that the said Sisters Giraud and her successors promised to pay to the said *M^re* Perret and his successers each year on each feast of St. John Baptist, beginning with the next and continuing thus year after year, and at each aforesaid feast of St. John Baptist paying the said *M^(re)* Perret. The aforesaid corner of garden [is] free and exempt from all charges of sale and taxes, both in the past and for the future, and neither the said *M^(re)* Perret nor [his] successors can forcibly evict the said Sister Giraud or her successors from the said corner of garden, excepting only for the aforesaid payment of ten *sous*; in the same way, the said sisters cannot abandon it without having paid the said rent and arrears, if there be any, for the said payment. And for the validity of the present acts, the said Sister Giraud immediately handed over to *M^(re)* Perret the sum of thirty *sous* for rights of entry, in full view of me, notary and witness to the said *M^(re)* Perret. [He] exonerated and does exonerate the said Sister Giraud from the aforesaid sum of thirty *sous*, according to the contract not to ask for [it] under pain of [incurring] all expenses. The said *M^(re)* Perret, divesting himself of the aforesaid land or corner of garden under the terms of divestiture, investiture, possession, [and] dispossession, constituted [her] administrator and beneficiary, beginning today, in order to take possession as the said Giraud will see fit, with all other terms required and necessary by law in this regard, by contract explicitly agreed and ratified between the said *M^(re)* Perret and the said Sister Giraud, that she will be responsible for paying the daily wages [for workers] required to build a wall at the bottom of the garden that remains to the said *M^(re)* Perret, to enlarge it in recompense for what [he] has given, and the said *M^(re)* Perret will feed the said masons; and thus the said parties concluded it under testimony, oath, submission, obligation, renunciation, [and] dues. Done and passed at the said place of Saint-Julien, at the house of the *curé* in the presence of *S^r* Jean Percie, son of me, said notary, and *S^r* Claude Lacoste, son of *S^r* Jacques, bourgeois of the said Saint-Julien, undersigned with the said *M^(re)* Perret and contracting parties of the deliberation; the others, with the said Sisters [*sic*] Giraud, do not know how to sign as asked and required. . . .

PERCIE notary

17
DELIBERATION OF THE INHABITANTS OF THE TOWN OF CRAPONNE TO REQUEST ROYAL LETTERS PATENT IN FAVOR OF THE DAUGHTERS ASSOCIATED UNDER THE NAME OF ST. JOSEPH, 25 MAY 1766

BMU Clermont-Ferrand, Fonds Paul Leblanc no. 850, MS 131.
Today, the twenty-fifth of May, one thousand seven hundred sixty-six, around the hour of two in the afternoon, the community assembled before us,

Loüis Parrel, Lord of Viraguet, *avocat* in parlement, seneschal and judge, civil, criminal, and disciplinary of this town and jurisdiction of Craponne, was represented by *Monsieur Maître* Antoine Gallet, *Sieur* de Fraixe, *avocat* in parlement and first Consul of this town, who, acting for the public good, recognized, as every good citizen should recognize, the utility and the advantage, which not only this town, parish, and jurisdiction of this town, but also all the surrounding parishes have experienced since the establishment of [the] *demoiselles*, daughters associated under the title of St. Joseph in the neighborhood of the tower of Constant of this said town, which [establishment] dates to the year one thousand seven hundred twenty-three, since it is manifest that these *demoiselles* are wholly devoted to the public good in practicing many acts of virtue [and] they teach a countless number of young girls to practice them; it is they who instruct and educate nearly all the youth of this community and of the surrounding places; committed voluntarily by their vocation to visit the sick and the hospitals, they never cease to perform this human and Christian charity; they strengthen many in it through their piety, and their good counsel, and advice; and [they] secure resources for the material relief of others, abandoned and ashamed to beg in their destitution; their zeal and charity do not stop there; they take it upon themselves to shelter in their house many poor orphan girls whom they raise and care for in health and in sickness—and how many others whose virtue would be continually in danger without this blessed refuge?—and through that they provide a great relief for the hospital of this town, to which they have never refused their help; when they thought they could be useful, they always went there with ready zeal; and finally, since it cannot be concealed that the establishment of these *demoiselles* forms a veritable workshop of lace, they continually supervise about two hundred fifty girls, and often more than three hundred, of every age and every condition, taking pains to enable them to work; it is they who train and teach the young girls in this work, who are thereby in a position to help support their families, and when they finish there, they have better prospects for marriage. And without the help of lace, what would become of this region? The majority of inhabitants is absolutely unable to pay the taxes; they would live in grinding poverty, which would necessarily result in depopulation.

Concerning which, after thorough examination, the assembled community, having recognized the accuracy and the sincerity of this account, unanimously decided, being useful and even necessary, not only for this town, parish, and jurisdiction, but also for the surrounding region, that the establishment of the said *demoiselles,* associated daughters, endure and be secured in a solid and stable manner, for fear that in the future it should be destroyed by some mishap, or by the lack of understanding that can come about and which would require only a befuddled mind inimical to the public good, in order to prevent this danger which would be the total ruin of this region, to supplicate our illustrious Lord Bishop and *Monsieur* the Viscount de Polignac, lord of this town, to be pleased to take an interest and to procure letters patent from our king, the beloved Louis XV, in order to approve and authorize the establishment of the Congregation of St. Joseph and those who will succeed them in this said town of Craponne, to live there observing the statutes, constitutions, and jurisdictions of the Ordinary in conformity with the rules practiced by the associated daughters living in community under the title of Congregation of St. Joseph established in the city of Le Puy, of Saint-Didier, [and] of Tence, and that to this effect, the house where the said *demoiselless* associated daughters live be amortized, likewise their garden and properties, the whole of which contains about four *arpents*, measure of Paris, Diocese of Le Puy-en-Velay, Province of Languedoc. The original is signed: Depujol, prior and *curé*; Gallet, lawyer and first consul, Privat, priest, Martin, procurator of the public treasury, Privat, Saignard de Sasselange, Favier, Piessac, Daurier, Dufayt, lawyer, Pastel, priest, Porrat, Ducluset *fils*, Delolme, Gallet, notary, Carl, former *curé*, Vernadet, Baudin, Grand, priest and vicar, Dubouchet, Faucon, Porrat from Les Pradeaux, Poncet, Marcon, Breul, Grand, Bregnon, Monnier, Duroure, Parrel de Viraguet, La Chomette from Le Montel, Grand, Marcon, Monnier, vicaire, Privat *fils*, Olier, priest, Privat, priest, Boulle, priest, Boulle, priest, Boulle, [a blank] Gard, [a blank], Derroddes, Torrillon, Delord, Delaigue, Girard, Danatte, Clavel, priest.

NOTES

1. Bishop Jacques de Montrouge, who died in 1664. Lanthenas therefore wrote his "Memoir" after 1664.

2. Although local units could vary, the *toize* (toise) of Saint-Julien-Vocance was equal to the royal *toise*, or 1.949 m, about 6.4 ft., Pierre Charbonnier, *Les anciennes mesures locales du Massif central d'après les tables de conversion* (Clermont-Ferrand: Institut d'études du Massif central, 1990), 44. –Trans.

Appendix 1

The Original Documents of the Sisters of St. Joseph Presented in Two Tables

The manuscripts of the original texts of the sisters of St. Joseph are kept in the Motherhouses of Le Puy, Lyon, and Clermont.

From their content and their structure, it is possible to separate them into two categories which are identified here as "MS Constitutions" and "MS Règlements."

The *Constitutions Manuscripts*, of which there are now six, always begin with the text of the Constitutions, given in full, and followed nearly always by the formula of Vows and some Maxims of Fr. Médaille.

The *Règlements Manuscripts*, of which there are now seven, all begin with the text of the Règlements. They all have the same content, in nearly the same order.

The following tables, taken from the work *Sœurs de Saint Joseph, Textes Primitifs* published at Clermont-Ferrand in 1981, present the content of these different manuscripts in a synoptic fashion.

"Constitutions" Manuscripts (Content and Structure)

St DIDIER	A (le Puy)	LYON	GAP	B	St HILAIRE - 2
Date of Manuscript: 1660-1665	Date of Manuscript: ca. 1690	Date of Manuscript: 1670-1690	Date of Manuscript: 1671	Date of manuscript: 1700-1750	Date of Manuscript: ca. 1750
Constitutions (six parts)	Constitutions (six parts)	Constitutions (six parts)	Constitutions (six parts)	Constitutions (six parts)	Constitutions (four parts) + the 5th toward end of Ms.
1st part: (mention of the Visitation)	1st part: (Beginning missing) (mention of the Visitation)				
1st, 2nd, and 3rd parts: developed	1st, 2nd, and 3rd parts: developed	1st, 2nd, and 3rd parts: developed	1st, 2nd, and 3rd parts: developed	1st, 2nd, and 3rd parts: developed	1st, 2nd, and 3rd parts: shorter (text often different)
4th part: The Superior and Officers 1 - The superior 2 - The coadjutrix 3 - The spiritual coadjutrix = mistress of novices 4 - The treasurer 5 - The sr. in charge of supplies 6 - The cook 7 - The councilors 8 - The directress 9 - The portress 10 - The directress of the Confraternity of Mercy + All the sisters	4th part: The Superior and Officers 1 - The superior 2 - The vicar, or assistant 3 - The spiritual coadjutrix = mistress of novices 4 - The treasurer 5 - The sr. in charge of supplies 6 - The cook 7 - Other officers 8 - The infirmarian 9 - The admonitrix 10 - The councilors 11 - The directress of the poor 12 - The directress of the Confraternity of Mercy 13 - The portress 14 - Other officers + Advice for all the sisters	4th part: The Superior and Officers (similar to Saint-Didier)	4th part: The Superior and Officers (similar to Saint-Didier)	4th part: The Superior and Officers (similar to Saint-Didier)	4th part: The Superior and Officers 1 - The superior 2 - The assistant 3 - The mistress of novices 4 - The admonitrix 5 - The Directress of the poor + Rules common to all the sisters + Other Rules (= extracts from Avis et Reglements and from the Conference of Bishop de Maupas) - At the Assembly, what should be said
5th part: developed Year, month, week, day (Visitation) (end of this part missing) + Distribution of hours of the day (cf. Réglements) 5th part: (2nd) [Little Directory shorter]	5th part: developed (as in St D.) Year, month, week, day (Visitation) + Distribution of hours of the day (cf. Réglements) 5th part: (2nd) [Little Directory]	5th part = [Little Directory]	- Distribution of time for the Sisters of St. Joseph (day, week, month, year cf. Réglements) Protestations (each month) 5th part = [Little Directory]	- Distribution of time for the Sisters of St. Joseph (day, week, month, year cf. Réglements) Protestations (each month) 5th part = [Little Directory]	Various Paragraphs: - The bishop, legitimate superior and the pastor, spiritual father - Dispensation from the vows - How to make their will - About receptions - About vows
6th part: (Beginning missing, pages removed) Protestations (each month) Formula of vows	6th part: (entire) (End of the manuscript)	6th part: (entire) Protestations (each month) Formula of vows mention of the Archbishop	6th part: (entire)	6th part: (entire)	

Maxims of the Little Institute	Maxims of the Little Institute	Maxims of the Little Institute	Maxims of the Little Institute	Maxims of the Little Institute
(absent, although indicated as "written down hereafter," in the 3rd part of the constitutions) [Little Directory] -Reglements of the sisters of St. Joseph for working days (without a general introduction)	[EUCHARISTIC LETTER] Summary of the constitutions (mention of the Archbishop) -Reglements of the Daughters of St. Joseph associated in honor of... (general introduction, then year, month, week, day)	Protestations (each month) Formula of vows -Avis et Réglements	-Avis et Réglements Protestations (each month) Formula of vows +ritual introduction	Protestations (each month) Protestations (every 3 mos.) Formula of vows Promise "Glorious Virgin Mary" at reception of the habit Formula of vows -Blessing of habits and reception of the habit
- Some Advice for the Congregations of St. Joseph, Given by "our reverend Father Medaille." "(...nos révérand Père Médaille)	- To three souls associated - Little réglement... somewhat similar to the preceding - General advice for all the sisters		-Avis et Réglements (2nd) (same)	5th part: = [Little Directory] - General réglement for all days, weeks, months, years.
- the 21st [12] day of May 1661 Bishop de Maupas	- Formula for the reception of the Daughters of St. Joseph (= taking the habit) (does not include the prayer "Glorious Virgin Mary") - Rules for the country Sisters agrégées to St. Joseph" (= extracts from Avis et Réglements Conference of Bishop de Maupas and the Réglements)	- Ceremony of taking the habit	- Rules for the Agrégées Sisters of St. Joseph (= Réglements: day, week, month, year)	- Manner of receiving the profession of the Sisters of the Congregation of St. Joseph - About conferences (+ the chapter of faults)
	- General and particular advice for all the sisters - Acts of profession for the sisters - Table of contents		- For the deceased	

"Réglements" Manuscripts: Content and Structure

APINAC	BAS	BOISSET	C	D	MONTFERRAND	St HILAIRE – 1
Date of Manuscript: ca. 1700 beginning 18th c.	Date of Manuscript: end 17th c. beginning 18th c.	Date of Manuscript: 1680-1700	Date of Manuscript: 1670-1680	Date of Manuscript: ca. 1730 — Little Directory	Date of Manuscript: 1680-1700	Date of Manuscript: end 17th c. beginning 18th c.
Réglements (day, week, month, year) + general introduction	Réglements (day, week, month, year) + general introduction	Réglements (day, week, month, year) + general introduction	Réglements (day, week, month, year) + general introduction	Réglements (day, week, month, year) + general introduction	Réglements (day, week, month, year) + general introduction	Réglements (day, week, month, year) + general introduction
Avis et Réglements	Avis et Réglements	Avis et Réglements / Avis et Réglements (2nd) (beginning as above, then different) -Destruction of the Cmty: 9 or 10 abuses -Sustenance of the Cmty: 9 or 10 means	Avis et Réglements	Avis et Réglements	Avis et Réglements	Avis et Réglements / Avis et Réglements (2nd) (= only 4 paragraphs from the beginning)
Conf. of Bishop. De Maupas 12 May 1661	Conf. of Bishop. De Maupas 12 May 1661	Conf. of Bishop. De Maupas 12 May 1661	Conf. of Bishop. De Maupas 12 May 1661	Conf. of Bishop. De Maupas 12 May 1661	Conf. of Bishop. De Maupas 12 May 1661	Conf. of Bishop. De Maupas 12 May 1661
At the Assembly, what should be said	At the Assembly, what should be said	At the Assembly, what should be said	At the Assembly, what should be said			At the Assembly, what should be said
Little Directory	Little Directory	Little Directory	Little Directory			Little Directory

Constitutions (3 parts)	Constitutions (3 parts)	Constitutions (3 parts)	Constitutions (3 parts)	Constitutions (3 parts)	Constitutions (3 parts)	Constitutions (3 parts)
Protestations (every 3 mos.)	Protestations (each month)	Protestations (every 3 mos.)	Protestations (each month)	Protestations (each month)	Protestations (each month)	Protestations (each month)
Promise taking the habit "Glorious Virgin Mary"		Promise taking the habit "Glorious Virgin Mary"				
Vow formula	Vow formula	Vow formula	Vow formula	Vow formula	Vow formula	
		Blessing of Habits				
		Protestation for the Sisters of St. Joseph = promise of stability in the Congregation				
Blessing of Habits						
Maxims of the Little Institute	Maxims of the Little Institute	Maxims of the Little Institute	Maxims of the Little Institute	Maxims of the Little Institute	Maxims of the Little Institute	Maxims of the Little Institute
(only 14)						
Promise taking the habit "Glorious Virgin Mary"	Promise taking the habit "Glorious Virgin Mary"					
			Little Directory			
				Reglement for the little Congregation of St. Joseph		
				-Some Officers -Direction of the Confraternity -Protestation or profession (= prayer "Glorious Virgin Mary")		
-Rite of profession						
-Consecration to the S.H. with renewal of vows						
-Chapter of faults						

Appendix 2

Data Concerning Father Jean-Pierre Médaille from the Triennial Catalogues Archives of the Society of Jesus, Rome

From its origins the Society of Jesus has kept catalogues containing the names of all the members of the Society by geographic provinces with some information on each one. The triennial catalogues collect particular information every three years. A first triennial catalogue, the *catalogus primus*, gives general information about each member: age, health, studies, ministries, etc. A second triennial catalogue, the *catalogus secundus*, reports more precise and more confidential information on the qualities, experience, and aptitudes of each Jesuit.

In 1983 Sister Pierangela Pesce, a Sister of St. Joseph of Cuneo, Italy, completed an inventory of the information about Fr. Jean-Pierre Médaille contained in the triennial catalogues of the Toulouse Province. Based on Sister Pesce's inventory, the following tables present all the data found in these catalogues regarding Father Médaille from his entry into the Society of Jesus until his death.

"CATALOGUS PRIMUS"

N° indi cat.	Nomen et cognomen	Patria	Actas	Vires	Tempus Societatis	Tempus studiorum	Ministeria quae exercuit	Gradus in litteris	An Professus an coadjutor formatus
Catalogus novitiorum tol.[i] Nov.[tus] (Tolos. 5, 180)									
1626 1627 19	Joan. Petrus Médaille	Carcasso- nensis	6 octob. 1610	firmae sed exiles	15 sept. 1626	Rhaet. 1			
Catalogus domus Probationis Tolosanae, ANNI MDCXXVIII (Tolos. 9, 226 r)									
1627 1629 18	Joan. Pet. Médaille	Carcas- sonnen- sis	6 octo- bris 1610	Exiles	15 sept. 1626	Rhaet. 1 an 1			Novitius
Catalogus primus colegii Carcassonensis (Tolos. 9)									
1633	Nomen est in indice (cf. Tolos. 9, 227 r) sed non invenitur in corpore : aegrotus ? (cf. Tolos. 9, 265 v)								
Ex "Catalogus primus Collegii Tolosani Anni M.D.C. XXXVI" (Tolos. 9, 287 r)									
Toulouse 1636 26	Joan. Petr. Médaille	Carcas- somnen- sis	1610 6 octob.	Debiles	16 sept. 1626	In Societ. Reth. an 1 Philos. 3 Theol. 1 et adhuc stu- det	Docuit. Gram. an.2		

"CATALOGUS SECUNDUS"

	Mortificatio	N° Indicat.	Ingenium	Judicium	Prudentia	Experientia rerum	Profectus in literis	Naturalis complexio	Ad quae Societatis ministeria talentum habeat
			Catalogus novitiorum tol. Nov.[tus]						
1626 1627	Magna et eximia		Eximium						
			Catalogus domus Probationis Tolosanae , ANNI MDCXXVIII						
1627- 1629	Eximia		Eximium						
(Tolos. 9)			Catalogus secundus colegii Carcassonensis						
1633					D E E S T				
			Catalogus secundus Collegii Tolosani Anni M.D.C.XXXVI						
1636					D E E S T				

	N° indicat.	Nomen et cognomen	Patria	Aetas	Vires	Tempus Societatis	Tempus studiorum	Ministeria quae exercuit	Gradus in litteris	An Professus an coadjutor formatus
(Tolos 9, 349 r)			Ex "Catalogus primus Collegii Auriliacensis ANNI M.D.C. XXXIX"							
Auril-lac 1639	9	P. Joannes Médaille	Carcas-sonnen-sis	natus 6 octob. an. 1610.	Infirmes	Ingressus Societat. 15 sept. an. 1626	In Soc. Stud Reth. an. 1 Philos. 3 Theol. 2	Docuit Gram. An. 2		
1642		Catalogus primus			DEEST					
(Tolos. 10¹, 36 r)			Ex "Catalogus primus Collegii Sanflorani Anni M.D.C. XLV"							
St-Flour 1645	4	P. Joan. Petr. Médaille	Carcas-sonnen-sis	an. 35	Infirmae	an. 18	Reth. an. 1 Phil. 3 Theol. 2	Docuit gram. an. 2 praef. stud an. 1 minister an. 5		Professus 4 votorum 11 oct. an. 1643
(Tolos. 10¹, 139 r)			Ex "Catalogus primus Collegii Sanflorani Anni M.D.C. XLVIII"							
St-Flour 1649	6	P. Joannes Petrus Médaille	Carcas-sonas [sic] in Occitania	6 octobris 1610	Infirmae	15 Septembr. 1626	In Rhetor. an. 1, in philoso-phia 2, in Theologia 2	Docuit gra-maticam 2 annos minister 5 an. pro-curator 2 an	praefectus 1 an mission. 6 menses	Profes-4 vo-torum 11 oct. 1643

	N° indi cat.	Ingenium	Judicium	Prudentia	Experien tia rerum	Profectus in literis	Naturalis complexio	Ad quae Societatis ministeria talentum habeat
	Ex "Catalogus secundus Collegii Auriliacensis ANNI M.D.C. XXXIX"							
1639				D E E S T				
Catalogus secundus								
1642				D E E S T				
(Tolos 10¹, 95)	Ex "Catalogus secundus Collegii Sanflorani Anni M.D.C. XXXXV"							
1645	4	Eximium	Optimum	magna et omnino religiosa	rerum spiritualium haud mediocris	summus in philosophicis praesertim et theologicis	biliosa et temperatissima	magnum talentum ad instruendas et regendas animas
(Tolos. 10¹, 179 v)	Ex "Catalogus secundus Collegii Sanflorani Anni M.D.C.XLVI.II"							
1649	6	Sublime		nimius credulus et ob id peccat contra prudentiam	non ita attendit	in superioribus et inferioribus eximius si liceat per valetudinem	constat humor melancholicus et biliosus	natus ad missiones

	N° indicat.	Nomen et cognomen	Patria	Aetas	Vires	Tempus Societatis	Tempus studiorum	Ministeria quae exercuit	Gradus in litteris	An Professus an coadjutor formatus
(Tolos. 10^{I}, 215 r)		Ex "Catalogus primus Collegii Auriliacensis Anni M.D.C.L.I"								
Aurillac 1651	7	P. Joan. Petrus Médaille	Carcas sonensis	6ᵉ oct. 1609 [sic]	Mediocres	15 sept. 1626	Rhet. 1 Philos. 3 Thgia. 2	Docuit gram. 2, praefectus stud. 1 conc. 2 Mission. 2 Minister 6 Procurator 3		Professus 4 votorum oct. 1643
(Tolos. 10^{II}, 297 r)		Ex "Catalogus primus Collegii Monferrandensis Anni M.D.C.L.V"								
Mont-ferrand 1655	6	P. Joannes Petrus Médaille	Occitanus.	1610 10 [sic] oct.	mediocres	1626 15 sept.	Philos. 3 an. Theol. 4 [sic]	Grammat. an. 3 coetera concionatur		Professus 4 votorum 1643 11 oct.
(Tolos. 10^{II}, 382 r)		Ex "Catalogus primus Collegii Monferrandensis Anni M.D.C.LVIII"								
Mont-ferrand 1658	7	P. Joan. Petr. Médaille	Carcas-sonnensis in occitania	natus 6 oct. 1610	Infirmae	15 sept. 1626	Rhet. 1 an. Phi. 3 an. Thgia. 2 in societate	Docuit gram. 2 an. fuit Praef. 2 Minister 6 Mission. 6 Concion.6		Professus 4 votorum 11 oct. 1643

N° indicat.	Ingenium	Judicium	Prudentia	Experientia rerum	Profectus in literis	Naturalis complexio	Ad quae Societatis ministeria talentum habeat
Ex "Catalogus secundus Collegii Auriliacensis Anni M.D.C.L.I." (Tolos. 10[I], 253 r)							
1651	*Eximium*	*Magnum*	*Magna sed videtur parum limitata*	*Non mediocris*	*Non mediocris in omnibus*	*Phlegmatica videtur*	*magnum ad omnes Soc[is] functiones*
Ex "Catalogus secundus Collegii Monferrandensis Anni M.D.C.L.V." (Tolos. 10[II], 337 r)							
1655	*Acutum*	*Bonum*	*Mediocris*	*Mediocris*	*Magnus*	*Melancholica*	*ad confessiones audiendas ad habendas cohortationes ad missionnes*
Ex "Catalogus secundus Collegii Monferrandensis Anni M.D.C.L.VIII" (Tolos. 10[II], 424 r)							
1658	*Acutum*	*Bonum*	*Mediocris*	*Magna rerum extern. et domesticarum*	*Magnus in humanoribus et philosophicis*	*Melanchol.*	*Ad literas humanores conciones missiones res spirituales*

	N° indicat.	Nomen et cognomen	Patria	Aetas	Vires	Tempus Societatis	Tempus studiorum	Ministeria quae exercuit	Gradus in litteris	An Professus an coadjutor forrmatus
(Tolos. 10^II, 484 r)		Ex "Catalogus primus Collegii Monferrandensis Anni M.D.C.L.X"								
Mont-ferrand 1660	5	P. Joannes Petrus Médaille	Carcasson. in occitania	6 oct. 1610	Infirmae	15 sept. 1626	Rhet. 1 an Phi 3 an Thgia. 2 in Societate	Gram. 2 an. fuit praef. 2 an. min. 6 an. mission. 8 concion. 6		Professus 4 votorum 11 oct. 1643
(Tolos 11, 38 r)		Ex "Catalogus primus Collegii Claromonferrandensis Anni M.D.C.L.XV"								
Clermont 1665	4	P. Joan. Petr. Médaille	Carcas-sonen-sis in occi-tania	6 oct 1610	Infirmae	15 sept. 1626	Rhetor. an. 1 Phia 3 Thgia 2 in Soc.te	Gram. 2 an. fuit praefectus 2 an. minister 6 concion. 6 mission. 13		Professus 4 votorum 5 Martii 1645 [sic]
(Tolos. 11, 85 r)		Ex "Catalogus primus collegii Claromontani Anni M.D.C. L. XIX"								
Clermont 1669	4	P. Joan. Petr. Médaille	Carcas-sonnen-sis	1607 [sic] 6 oct.	Infirmae	1626 15 sept.	in Soc. Rh. 1. Phi 3. Theol. 2	Gram. 3 minister 6 concion. et mission. 18 concion. in nostro templo 2		4 Vot. 1643 11 oct

	N° Indi cat.	Ingenium	Judicium	Prudentia	Experien- tia rerum	Profectus in literis	Naturalis complexio	Ad quae Societatis mi- nisteria talen- tum habeat
(Tolos. 10^II, 529 r) Ex "Catalogus secundus Collegii Monferrandensis Anni M.D.C.L.X"								
1660	5	Bonum	non firmum	Simplicior	Magna missiorum	Magnus	pituitosa	ad res litte- rarias ad conciones ad missiones ad confessiones audiendas
Catalogus secundus Collegii Claromonferrandensis Anni M.D.C.L.XV				DEEST				
1665								
(Tolos. 11, 134 r) Ex "Catalogus secundus Collegii Claromontani Anni M.D.C.L.XIX"								
1669	4	Bonum	Bonum	mediocris	magna missionum	magnus	Melancholi -ca.	ad missiones et confession. audiendas

Appendix 3

Remarks on the Manuscript from the House of Le Puy (Ms A, ca. 1690)

Manuscript A from the house of Le Puy is a notebook of 180 pages, one of the shortest manuscripts containing the first Constitutions of the Sisters of St. Joseph. Dated by archivists to the end of the seventeenth century and baptized "manuscript A" by Abbé Achard, it contains only the text of the Constitutions with the Little Directory included as the fifth part. It does not include an entire copy of the Constitutions, since some pages are missing at the beginning, deleting part of the first chapter, and pages are missing at the end as well, before the end of the sixth and last part.[1] The first chapters show dependence on the older Saint-Didier manuscript, with frequently similar variations in wording. Like the Saint-Didier manuscript, MS A adds a comparison at the end of the first chapter of the Sisters of St. Joseph to the "Holy Daughters of the Visitation." Its dependence on the Saint-Didier MS is also evident in its omission of passages crossed out there, for example, regarding "the instruction of girls."[2] By contrast, it departs visibly from the Saint-Didier MS in the final three parts, dealing with forms of life, and in the tenor of vocabulary. MS A is the only one to incorporate all of the following: a fifth part including "in brief the particular guidance of the daughters of St. Joseph" (as in the Saint-Didier MS), followed by a "distribution of the hours of the day" (as in the Règlement manuscripts), and the Little Directory (as in the MSS of Lyon, Gap, and B).

A study of this manuscript reveals that it was used by the community at Le Puy. It governs a rather large house, with more than thirteen officers listed.[3] It had a chapel.[4] To the widows and single women who come into the house, the sisters teach lace-making, typical in the region of Le Puy.[5] The sisters' principal activity apparently concerns orphan girls and the instruction of girls, because they teach classes.[6] At the end of the seventeenth century all these details taken together applied only to the house of Le Puy. The only other house in the diocese of Le Puy that could have had some prominence at this time was Tence. If MS A were used there, it would have had to mention the *nouvelles converties*, who are referred to in the royal letters patents just granted to the community of Tence in 1687. MS A unquestionably belonged to the house at Le Puy.

The witness it gives to a conventualizing and somewhat Jansenistic development in the community makes this manuscript of particular interest. MS A suppresses several paragraphs that discuss apostolic and charitable works outside the house. It omits the special assemblies of the Ladies of Mercy, divided according to their age and social condition, for spiritual direction.[7] It also omits dividing the city into quarters to remedy disorders, suggesting that the sisters did not often go out.[8] The place of the superior and her role have been modified. The description of her responsibility for the quality of the sisters' spiritual life makes one wonder what kind of freedom was left to them and where the mistress of novices fit in.[9] Unlike the other manuscripts, it does not speak of "confidence, cordiality and great hope in the guidance of God through the mistress" of novices, but only of "confidence in the ecclesiastical and sister superiors."[10] MS A also eliminates from the list of things that have caused great harm to congregations of women: "too great a constraint of the daughters who . . . [lack] the freedom to unburden their conscience . . . [being] obliged to depend on certain spiritual fathers."[11] In light of these omissions, it may be no accident that the last pages of the manuscript have been taken out, since they deal precisely with remedies to possible abuses that might occur relative to freedom of conscience, meeting with seculars, the spiritual direction of the Ladies of Mercy, and prudence in accepting sisters. Another exclusion appears to imply a desire to allow the sister superior's power free reign: in connection with the election there is no mention of the qualities of the superior. Although it indicates the first two conditions for validity (being thirty years of age and twelve, in religious life), MS A preserves neither the natural qualities of health, human maturity, and wisdom and prudence in conducting business, nor the spiritual gifts such as union with God, zeal for the glory of God and the advancement of the community, charity for the neighbor, and the spirit of the most profound humility described in the other manuscripts.[12] Succeeding paragraphs in the same chapter confirm this suspicion. The superior does not take the advice of her councilors in matters of importance, but merely that of the community officers and the spiritual director.[13] Although MS A maintains the function of the admonitrix, it makes no mention of her annual exercise of this role in order to prevent "too great a freedom and authority in the superior."[14] Rules for the assistant, the superior's right arm, evidence the same accent on authority. Even though they recommend that she fill "the office and duty of a gentle and charitable mother toward all the persons in the house," some passages unique to MS A seem like surveillance. She should "be everywhere the sisters are assembled to keep them respectful and observant of the Rule."[15] In the house she will "note the faults and failures that are committed there, particularly in matters concerning obedience, prayer, modesty, and silence, in order to let the superior know about them."[16] The latter should remind herself, moreover, "that her principal duty is to make regular observance flourish in everything."[17]

In regard to the sisters' spiritual life, MS A, like the others, certainly intends to propose all the demands of great virtue. The way it does so, seeming to put the accent on personal effort more than on the grace of God, appears most clearly in the chapter on the "rules for the spiritual assistant who will be mistress of novices."[18] All the manuscripts say that the mistress of novices should rouse them "insofar as possible, by the favor of divine grace, to desire and pursue the greatest holiness," but MS A suppresses "by the favor of divine grace."[19] In her attentive correction of the "character of each of the Sisters," the mistress endeavors to guide toward the "perfection of the pure love of God everything that might be useful and serve as an instrument of grace."[20] MS A simply says, "to correct the evil that may be in them." It does not allow that one's nature can also serve as an instrument of grace. MS A does not preserve the suggestion that the mistress, in order to help the sisters at the beginning of the novitiate, can propose to them "examples of their predecessors and other motivations to the great virtue."[21] In contrast it states that the mistress of novices can give "the sisters in the novitiate, with permission of the superior, some penances which they can perform individually," in proportion to each one's strength.[22]

Numerous passages expressing the same spirit exist in other chapters on the treasurer, the councilors, or the portress. The point is not to make a thorough study, but to identify modifications of vocabulary that seem significant. MS A very frequently censors words or phrases expressing felt response. The tears that accompany the superior's prayers for her sisters disappear.[23] Pleasure, too, disappears. The sisters "hear and practice" the spiritual Maxims, but they do not "savor" them, as in the other manuscripts.[24] The treasurer is not invited to love poverty "with great tenderness."[25] Adverbs or adjectives expressing a superlative are also taken out, such as extraordinarily, enormously, or even "great" (peace and gentleness). These changes match the evolution of mindset at the end of the seventeenth century, but they do not occur in the other manuscripts.

Conversely, to its credit, MS A leaves out or modifies certain passages that appear as unnecessary explanations or simply redundant in form. In regard to humility, for example, the first chapter of the Constitutions (no. 64) in all the other manuscripts asks the sisters to make "everywhere profession of the most humble, profound and true humility." MS A requires them only to make "profession of the most profound humility known to them." The last paragraph of the Summary of the end (no. 112) says the sisters should make "profession . . . of a very perfect charity and mercy, according to God and the orders of their little Institute, toward every kind of neighbor." MS A does not find it necessary to point out that this charity and mercy should be "according to God and the orders of their little Institute," no doubt because that goes without saying. Certain omissions shorten the text. For example, most manuscripts direct that superiors not accept in the congregation persons "of an extraordinarily violent disposition, flighty and inconstant, or extraordinarily vain, or slow and lazy, or insensible and cool to the things of God." MS A simplifies this description. The congregation should not admit persons "with a violent disposition, flighty, inconstant, or extraordinarily vain and lazy, and insensible to the things of God." The simplification sometimes indicates a better level of intellectual formation. For example, MS A suppresses the model proposed for the examen of conscience in the Little Directory, probably because it was considered unnecessary. The sisters should know how to recognize their faults and formulate them by themselves. In the same way, in the chapter "On the Divine Office," the suppression of passages in paragraphs 45 and 47 gives more gravity to the text and allows more freedom of heart and mind to direct prayer interiorly according to one's own inspiration. Finally, although the Little Directory in this manuscript excises terms with an affective hue such as "gentleness" (of your devotion), "a loving" (recollection), etc., as in the rest of the Constitutions, certain additions deserve notice. They concern the name of St. Joseph, with appellations like " our glorious Father" and "the glorious St. Joseph" added six or seven times more than in the other manuscripts. Who could doubt that St. Joseph, thought of and invoked as "our good Father," did not watch over the community's progress!

MS A and the Saint-Didier manuscript are the two that mention the Visitation as a model for Sisters of St. Joseph: "they will try to mold themselves on the customs, the spirit and the of life of the holy Daughters of the Visitation."[26] Everything we have just said concerning MS A seems to show that the referent sought in the Visitation aims more at the customs and the "regular" way of life of the Visitation than the spirit of its founder. That suggests that the paragraph in reference to the Visitation could have been added in 1674, when the communities of Le Puy and Saint-Didier requested royal letters patent, since the other manuscripts do not mention it. As a way of putting themselves in a better light in the eyes of Louis XIV, a reference to the Visitation was politically sound. Other congregations had done that before the Sisters of St. Joseph. That insinuation could help—if not to give a modicum of luster to the very little congregation of Father Médaille—at least to allow it to obtain a degree of legal recognition, in the manner of the orders or congregations "of the most regular religious."[27]

NOTES

1. Manuscript A begins only at paragraph no. 30 of Chapter 1 of the Constitutions, *TP* 1981, CP, 18 and ends with no. 427 of Part Six, CP, 87.

2. *TP* 1981, CP, 28, no. 19.

3. See the table of the Constitutions MSS, Appendix 1.

4. *TP* 1981, CP 72, no. 346.

5. Ibid., CP 30, no. 104, marginal variant.

6. Ibid., , CP 28, no. 91 (3); 57, no. 258; re. classes: 72, no. 347, marginal variant.

7. Ibid., CP, 28, nos. 93-94.

8. Ibid., CP, 29, nos. 96 and 99.

9. Ibid., CP, 41, nos. 148-50.

10. Ibid., CP, 48, no. 184.

11. Ibid., CP, 78, no. 374.

12. Ibid., CP, 83, nos. 402-410.

13. Ibid., CP, no. 412.

14. Ibid., CP, 84, no. 414.

15. Ibid., CP, 43, nos. 157, §2 and 158, §3.

16. Ibid., CP, 44, no. 162, §7.

17. Ibid., CP, 41, no. 146, marginal variant.

18. Ibid., CP, 46-48, nos. 171-89.

19. Ibid., CP, 46, no. 173.

20. Ibid., CP, 46, no. 175.

21. Ibid., CP, 47, no. 178.

22. Ibid., CP, 48, 189, marginal variant.

23. Ibid., CP, 38, no. 132.

24. Ibid., CP, 48, no. 183.

25. Ibid., CP, 51, no. 208.

26. Ibid., CP, 20, no. 41 (1).

27. "enla maniére des . . . religieuses les mieux réglées," Ibid., CP, 20, no. 41.

Appendix 4

Traces of Father Médaille's Eucharistic Letter at Riotord (Haute-Loire)

The archives of the community of Sisters of St. Joseph at Riotord contain a small notebook, dated 1870 on the first page, in which Father Freycenon, then ecclesiastical superior of the community, introduces the Eucharistic Letter to the sisters. He discovered this document among the community's old papers, and thinking its content worthy of reflection, he gave the community some explanation and commentary on it. The notebook contains notations of long passages from the Letter as well as the very appreciative interpretations Father Freycenon gave to the sisters. He clearly did not understand the second part of the Letter, particularly the parts with symbolic numeration: "the sixteen apostles and evangelists . . . the seven deacons," etc. He arranged this second part in his own way, adding some paragraphs from Father Médaille's "Avis et Règlements." It is therefore likely that the original document also contained the Avis et Règlements.

These traces of the Eucharistic Letter at Riotord antedate its partial publication in 1878 by the Abbé Rivaux in his *Vie de la Révérende Mère du Sacré-Cœur*, second superior general of the Sisters of St. Joseph of Lyon. Could Father Freycenon have had the original in hand? In the same notebook, the sister superior of the community recorded that he took the document away and did not return it. She is not alone in voicing her regret.

Appendix 5

Approximate List of the Communities of St. Joseph Established between 1649 and 1789 Arranged According to Former Dioceses

DATE[1]	LE PUY	LYON	CLERMONT	VIENNE	OTHER
1649	Dunières				
1650	*Le Puy*				
1651	Marlhes				
1652	Saint-Roman-Lachalm				
1653	Tence				
pre 1655	St-Didier-en-Velay				
ca. 1655				Bourg-Argental	
1655	Aurec	Le Chambon		Saint-Julien-Vocance	
1657	Yssingeaux				
	St-Jeures-de-Bonas				
	Saint-Victor-Malescours				
1659	Riotord				
1660	Boisset				
	Montregard				
	Lapte				
	Saint-Georges-l'Agricol				
	Jonzieux				
(1660)					Le Cheylard (Dse Viviers)
ca. 1660		Saint-Jean-de-Bonnefont			
1661				Satillieu	
ca. 1661			Arlanc		
pre 1662	Monistrol-sur-Loire				
1662	Chomélix	Saint-Marcellin		Vocance	
1663					Langogne (Dse Mende)
1664	Grazac				
1665		Saint-Genest-Malifaux	Sauxillanges		

1. This inventory is approximate in regard to the houses listed: other houses certainly existed, which are now unknown. It is also approximate in regard to dates of foundation, at least for some of them, as indicated in the table.

DATE	LE PUY	LYON	CLERMONT	VIENNE	OTHER
1668				Vienne	
1669	Saint-Just-Chomélix[2]		Dore-l'Eglise		
1669			Death of Fr. *Médaille* at *Billom*		
ca. 1670					St-André-des-Effangeas[3] (Dse Viviers)
1671	Beaune-sur-Arzon				
	Le Pontempeyrat			Annonay (date?)	Gap
1672		Izieux			
1673	Beauzac				
pre 1674	Usson			Saint-Julien-Molin-Molette	
1674			Marsac		
			Beurrières		
1675				Vanosc	
1677				St-Saveur-en-Rüe	
1679			Saint-Anthème		
1680		St- Genest-l'Erpt (or 1660?)			Saint-Prix (Dse Valence)
pre 1681				Condrieu	
pre 1682	Sainte-Sigolène				
1682	St-Julien d'Ance				
1683				Saint-Vallier	
pre 1684					Aubenas (Dse Viviers)
1685		Saint-Romain-les-Atheux			
pre 1686					Manosque (Dse Sisteron)
1686		St-Just-Malamont			
pre 1687	Saint-Hilaire				
pre 1687	Bas-en-Basset				
1687		Saint-Héand			

2. Current name: Bellevue-la-Montagne.
3. Current name: Saint-André-en-Vivarais.

DATE	LE PUY	LYON	CLERMONT	VIENNE	OTHER
pre 1688					Sisteron
1689	St-Pierre-Duchamp				
1690				Bourgoin	
pre 1691	Apinac		Plauzat		
1693					Bagnol-sur-Cèze (Dse Uzès)
1694	St-Préjet d'Allier				
1696		Lyon	Viverols		
	Saint-Maurice-de-Roche (date ?)				
1697		St-Paul-en-Jarrez			
1698	Saint-André-en-Chalencon				
1700	Saint-Paulien	Saint-Martin-Aqualieu[4]		Saint-Trivier-en-Bresse	
1701		Saint-Romain-en-Jarrez			
1703				Saint-Félicien	
1705	La Chapelle d'Aurec				
1707			La Chapelle en La Faye		Avignon (Comtat Venaissin)
1708	Estivareilles	St-Rambert-en-Forez[5] (date?)			Embrun Die
pre 1709		Rochetaillée			
pre 1712			Saint-Bonnet-le Chastel		
1712				La Louvesc	
1715	Saint-Ferréol-d'Auroure Félines				
1716					Marseille
1717	Vernassal				

4. Current name: Saint-Martin-de-Coailleux.
5. Current name: Saint-Rambert-sur-Loire.

DATE	LE PUY	LYON	CLERMONT	VIENNE	OTHER
1719		Saint-Bonnet-le-Château			
1720			Juillanges		
post 1720					Apt
1722					Blesle(Dse Saint-Flour)
1723	Craponne		Clermont	Ville[6]	
1725	Sauvessanges	La Fouillouse			Chanéac (Dse Viviers)
pre 1726		Saint-Christo-en-Jarrez			
1727			Issoire		
pre 1729					Privas (Dse Viviers)
1729		Chevrières	Champeix		
1730					Chalancon (Dse Viviers)
ca. 1732	Saint-Vincent	Saint-Rambert-en Jarrez			
1732				Quintenas	
1734					Saint-Peray (Dse Valence) Carpentras
pre 1737			Vollore		
1737			Valcivières		
1738		Saint-Germain-Laval			
1739	Saint-Front	Bouthéon-en-Forez			
1742			Job		
			Besse		
1744		Riverie			
post 1745					Mende
ca. 1750				Saint-Alban d'Ay	
1750	Saint-Maurice-de-Lignon				

6. Current name: Villevocance

DATE	LE PUY	LYON	CLERMONT	VIENNE	OTHER
1754	Saint-Geneys près Saint Paulien				
1755	Saint-Julien-Molhesabate		Vensat		
1756			Saint-Amant-Roche-Savine	Luppé	Ribiers (Dse Gap)
pre 1757		Saint-Andéol-le-Château			
1757		La Valla			
		Firminy			
1759		Saint-Romain-sous-Urphé			
1760	Saint-Pal-de-Mons				
	Retournac				
1763			Cusset		
1764		Villars			
1775					Digne
1779	Araules				
ca. 1780				Crest	
1783		Saint-Chamond			
1784			Saint-Jean d'Aubrigoux		
1785				Tain	
1786	Raucoules		La Roche Blanche		
			La Chaulme		
pre 1789		Saint-Julien-en-Jarez	Olliergues		
			Médeyrolles		
			Saint-Just-de-Baffie		

Glossary

agrégée (*agrégé, -ée*). Associated to a body or society, with the same prerogatives as those who are members. The *sœurs agrégées* of St. Joseph were members of the congregation through their association with the body of the congregation (*corps congrégation*), formed by sisters in the principal houses.

anéantissement. State of being reduced to nothing, or to little; figuratively, to be humbled or to humble oneself in the extreme: "St. Paul says that the Lord made himself nothing (*s'est aneanti luy-même*) in becoming human and in taking the form of a slave" (*FDU* 1690, s.v. "anéantir," citing Phil. 2:7). The phrase is often translated as "emptied himself."

arpent. Measure of land equal to 10 *perches*, varying locally and according to use. Based on the *perche de Paris* (18 *pieds*): the linear *arpent* was approximately 58.47 m or 192 ft.; the square *arpent* was about .84 acre.

augment. Legal term (*augment de dot*), indicating what the husband gives to his wife in the marriage contract.

avocat. Lawyer of highest rank in the judicial hierarchy, roughly equivalent to an English barrister. In court he interpreted the law and the way it should be applied in a given case.

baillage. See *sénéchaussée*.

béate(s). Lay teachers formed by the Demoiselles de l'Instruction of Le Puy in the seventeenth century to teach religion, basic reading, and lace-making to women and girls in the villages and hamlets of the Velay.

bourgeois. Primary meaning at this time was a citizen or inhabitant of a city; also, wealthier members of the third estate; or, used to distinguish a commoner from the nobility.

bureau. Place where the community of inhabitants dealt with official affairs, e.g., the *Bureau de l'hôtel-Dieu*, the *Bureau des pauvres*; also could indicate the persons who worked there.

capitoul. See *consul*.

censive et laud. See manorial dues.

civilités. Collections of rules for proper way of living and conversing; courtesy.

consul. Chief municipal officer elected by the *bourgeois* in certain towns in the south of France, including Le Puy. In Toulouse they were referred to as *capitouls*.

constitutions. Rules or statutes of a particular religious order or congregation. The traditional plural form reflects Latin usage (*constitutiones*), meaning a collection of laws or decrees.

dame. Title originally given to women of noble extraction and gradually applied to those of an elevated social status, noble or bourgeois; given to some nuns in abbeys or cannonnesses.

demoiselle. Title originally reserved to daughters of nobles, by the late 1600s, given to one born of parents of a distinguished social class, either noble or bourgeois, unmarried or married.

élection. Division of a *généralité* that served as the basic unit for purposes of taxation.

fabrique. All material belongings of a parish church; also, the group responsible for them.

fille. Appellation applied universally to the state of an unmarried woman; also used of women consecrated to God, e.g., Filles de la Charité, Filles de Saint-Joseph.

fondateur. Benefactor who established a church or monastery and endowed it with fixed revenue.

géneralité. Basic administrative unit of ancien régime France governed by royally appointed *intendants* of justice, police, and finance.

gens de robe. Those involved in legal professions.

greffier. Officer in charge of official records including minutes, as well as judicial declarations and decisions.

haut de manche. Insignia worn on the upper part of the sleeve denoting rank or occupation.

homme vivant et mourant. A real person, appointed as the fictional proprietor of property held in mortmain by a moral person (church, hospital, etc.), on whose death the actual owner would pay rights of succession in order to keep the property.

hôpital (*hospital*). A charitable institution founded to accommodate the poor, the sick, vagrants, and others in need and to provide them with food and lodging.

hôpital des orphelines. "Hospital" for orphan girls, or girls' orphanage.

hôpital général. Institution chiefly for the poor and vagrants, founded in increasing numbers under the ancien régime.

hôtel-Dieu. Hospital for the destitute sick, originally administered by the church.

hospice. Small house serving as a pied-à-terre for religious of a specific order when traveling.

hospitalier, -ière. Person who provided lodging, food, and care for the poor or for travelers.

juge-mage. Officer who assumed the judicial functions of the *sénéchausée* in the south of France; in the absence of the *sénéschal*, he served as deputy.

lettres de cachet. *Lettres closes*, in contrast to *lettres patentes*: letters from the king folded and sealed, addressed to private persons about matters specifically concerning them.

livre. Unit of account worth twenty *sous* (or *sols*), each worth 12 *deniers*.

lods et ventes. Fee charged by the *seigneur* when a *censive* was sold; usually one-twelfth of the selling price. See "manorial dues."

maison de refuge (refuge). Institution where women were placed "to remove them from licentiousness," either voluntarily or through coercion by the courts or *letters de cachet.* A *refuge* was more directed toward reform than a *maison forcée* and its regime less severe.

maison forcée (maison de force). A hospital-prison for confining persons considered aberrant; often women confined by their families or the law for some type of misbehavior or prostitutes showing little inclination toward reform.

maître. Title given to any graduate in Roman and canon law, to magistrates and other *gens de robe*; often used in other contexts as a mere expression of respect.

manorial dues. Annual payment due a *seigneur*, mainly the *cens*, the essential mark of commoner land, entailing the obligation to pay all the other dues: *lods [laud] et ventes*, etc.

marguiller. One of the persons in charge of the material aspects, or *fabrique*, of a parish or confraternity. See *fabrique*.

measure. Before the legal introduction of the metric system in 1795 (and long after in practice), units could vary from place to place, hence expressions like "measure of Saint-Didier."

messire. Honorific given to ordinary secular priests.

monsieur. Title given to someone of a higher rank, or addressed in speech or writing.

nouvelles converties. Recent converts; here, Huguenot girls or women converted to Catholicism.

parlement. Chief judicial body under the ancien régime, a court of appeal, which also authenticated and registered edicts, declarations, and ordinances of the king.

pauvres honteux. Impoverished persons ashamed on account of their social status to beg.

perdues. Women who had "lost" (*perdu*) their honor through sexual misdeeds.

petites écoles. Elementary schools for poor children, providing instruction in religion and handiwork, sometimes rudimentary reading, and less frequently, writing.

prêtre sociétaire. Priests, originally established chiefly to say masses for the dead, who at this period usually lived with their families or in the parish, taking part in its life but not in charge.

procureur. Legal representative of litigants who prepared briefs and negotiated settlements, subordinate to the *avocat*; proxy.

procureur d'offices. Agent or solicitor to take care of the business of an organization.

reclus, -use. Hermit; also applied to "women of evil life . . . confined in a convent or in a permanent prison" (*FDU* 1690, s.v. "reclurre").

seigneur. Owner of a property, usually a feudal estate, entailing authority over subjects.

sieur. Honorific used ordinarily in legal terminology or toward a *seigneur*.

self-emptying. See *anéantissement*.

sénéchaussée. Basic traditional administrative division, generally called *baillaige* in the north and *sénéchaussée* in the south. The office of *bailli* or *sénéschal* was a royal appointment.

théologal. Canon assigned to teach theology and to preach.

toise (*toize*). Liner measure with local variants; the *toise* of Paris was about 1.949 m
   or 6.394 ft.

tourière. Turn sister, a lay servant or nun outside the enclosure in women's monasteries who passed anything brought to the monastery through the turn.

works of mercy. Forms of charitable assistance whose traditional enumeration is
   rooted in Mt 25:31-46.

Bibliography

This list of works is not exhaustive. It contains only the works that contributed toward focusing or furthering the research.[1]

MANUSCRIPT SOURCES[2]

AD Hautes-Alpes

3 H suppl. 278 Hôpital de Gap, "Conventions faites entre Reverende Mère Jeanne Burdier, supérieure des filles de St Joseph de la ville de Vienne . . . et les sieurs Consulz de la ville de Gap . . . le 17 septembre 1671."

AD Haute-Garonne

1 E 973 "Mémoire de la distribution des bouillons des pauvres malades," s.l., n.d.

AD Isère

4 G 23 "Convention entre les directrices de l'hospital de la Providence, à Grenoble, et la Supérieure des Filles de St Joseph de Vienne, 17 décembre 1694."

4 G 23 "Lettre de M. de la Millière à M[r] l'Intendant de Grenoble, le 25 mai 1782."

21 H 1 Registre de professions des sœurs de Saint-Joseph de Vienne, 1681-1792.

21 H 1 "Constitution de pension pour la réception de Demoiselle Françoise de Vincent de Rambion," 14 décembre 1689.

2 J 147 Bordier, Paul-Henri. "La Congrégation du Saint-Sacrement de Grenoble, 1652-1666." Maîtrise de Lettres. Grenoble, 1970.

R 5765 Registre des délibératons de la Compagnie du Saint-Sacrement de Grenoble, du 28 novembre 1652 au 8 avril 1666, in-fol., 290 ff.

AD Loire

Série B, carton 130 Baillage de Bourg-Argental, no. 37, Convention entre les R.P. Jésuites de Saint Sauveur et les S^{rs} cloistriers, 5 juin 1653.

1 J 70 Dispense du droit d'amortissement accordée aux Sœurs de la Congrégation de Saint-Joseph du Chambon, 28 mars 1742

1 J 136 "Recognoissance de la cure de Riotord a M^{rs} les Jésuites."

AD Haute-Loire

3 E 224, 9 Arcis N^e, 1651-53, fol. 571 ff Donation de Clauda Chastel à sa sœur Marie Chastel . . . à Langogne, 14 janvier 1653.

6 E 246, 1 Registres paroissiaux Saint-Privat d'Allier.

E-Dépôt, 11^2 Tence, registre S, 1623-92, Sépultures de Lucrèce de La Planche et de Daniel Du Rancq de Joux.

12 H (Filles de Saint-Joseph, Hôpital de Montferrand, 1651-92)

12 H 1 Lettres de provisions données par Mgr Henri de Maupas . . . en faveur des filles de la Congrégation de Saint-Joseph du Puy, 10 mars 1651.

12 H 1 Lettres Patentes de Mgr Armand de Béthune, 23 septembre 1665.

12 H 2 "Permission donnée aux Filles de St-Joseph par le Seigneur de Maupas, Evêque du Puy, touchant leur établissement. Contrat passé devant Me Arcis, N^{re} roial appostolique, 13 décembre 1651.

Sous-série H suppl (Fonds de l'Hôtel-Dieu du Puy)

H suppl H.D. 8 A1 Comptes d'Etienne Treveys, 7 avril 1646-mars 1648.

H suppl H.D. 8 A2 Délibératon du Conseil d'Administration de l'Hôpital de Montferrand, 3 mars 1648.

H suppl H.D. 1 B 38 Transaction passée entre Pierre Eyraud et l'Hôtel-Dieu du Puy. 22 septembre 1641.

H suppl H.D. 1 B 455 Papiers famille Eyraud, 1692.

H suppl H.D. 1 B 92 Papiers famille Eyraud.

H suppl H.D. 1 E 1 Registre des délibérations du bureau de l'H.D. 1651-60.

H suppl H.D. 1 E 19 Règlement pur les sœurs donades de l'H.D., s.d., XVIIIe s.

J 237/149 Curés de Marlhes, copie d'un extrait du "Livre terrier du S^r prieur de Saint-Martin de Dunyère."

J 237/149 Marlhes, chronique du Dimanche, 1905.

J 237/166 Famille du Rancq de Joux.

J 237/213 Transaction à l'amiable du 23 mai 1640 entre l'évêque du Puy, le Seigneur de Joux et les jésuites, à Tence.

1 Q 91 État des rentes des religieuses de Saint-Joseph du Puy et des orphelines, vers 1790.

AD Lozère

3E 4391 Issartel, 1647-49.

F 351 "Mariage de Pierre de Chateauneuf et de demoiselle Benoite Richard, 29 octobre 1661."

H 357 "Établissement des Sœurs de St Joseph de la ville de Langogne, le 4 août 1663."

AD Puy-de-Dôme

1G 1573, nos. 1 et 2: Religieuses de Saint-Joseph à Arlanc.

1G 1579 Ursulines de Thiers.

90 H, 1C9 "Contrat d'Etablissement de trois religieuses de l'hopital de Vienne, en la maison du Bon-Pasteur de Clermont-F^d, du 30 may 1725. "

90 H, 1C9 Extrait du registre des délibérations de la Maison du Refuge de Clermont, du 1er May 1725.

90 H, 10 "Mémoire historique conttenant inventaire de l'établissement de la maison du Refuge de la ville de Clermont," registre reliure cuir, s.d.

L 2311 État de la maison du Bon-Pasteur, le 17 avril 1792.

AD Rhône

D 144 "Union des prieurés St Martin de Dunières et Ste Marie de Tence au collège de la Trinité à Lyon," (1496-1581).

D 175 Prieuré de Tence, cure de Saint-Jeures-de-Bonas (1462-1611).

D 193 Prieuré de Dunières, cure de Saint-Romain-Lachalm (1669-1747).

D 194 Prieuré de Dunières, cure de Saint-Victor-Malescours (1483-1667).

1 G 52 Visites pastorales de Mgr Camille de Neuville, 1656.

44 H 7 Registre: "Règles de la Communauté du Bon-Pasteur de Lyon," 1689.

44 H 11 Cahier: "Règles qui s'observent dans la maison du Bon-Pasteur," 1748-1750.

44 H 141 Inventaire des Titres et papiers de la maison des Recluses, no. 4, fol. 10 r., Sœurs de Saint-Joseph.

44 H 142 Registre, "Cartulaire des Titres de la Communauté, 1729."

44 H 143 (no. 4) Convention des directeurs de la maison des Recluses avec trois sœurs de Saint-Joseph, 22 décembre 1696.

44 H 150 (no. 42) "Livre de l'Assemblée de la Maison Forcée," du 29 août 1686 à 1698.

50 H 115 Registre des délibérations de la Compagnie du Saint-Sacrement, Lyon, 1682-90.

50 H 116 Registre des délibérations de la Compagnie du Saint-Sacrement, Lyon, 1694-99.

AD Vaucluse

H 44 (no. 6) "Livre des Contrats depuis 1620," 402 pp., fols. 40 v. à 44 r.

AM Bourg-Argental

Archives de l'Hospice, A 2-I "Mémoire concernant l'hôpital de la ville du Bourgargental . . . du 18e Juillet 1724."

AM Le Puy

Série BB 2 Livre des Conseils de la maison consulaire de la ville du Puy, 1er Xbre 1639 au 8 8bre 1652, registre, 267 fols.

E 67 Livre des mariages et mortuaires de l'Église paroissiale Saint-Georges-du-Puy, 15 novbre 1654 – 29 décbre 1683.

E 68 Livre des mariages et mortuaires, de 1684 à 1700, Paroisse Saint-Agrève-Saint-Georges.

AM Lyon

H.C. Lyon, E H-D 44 "Mandats 1664-67."

H.C. Lyon, E H-D 45 "Mandats 1667-71."

H.C. Lyon, H 248 "Formulaire pour la Prise d'habit des nouveaux Frères et Sœurs, dans l'Eglise du Grand-Hôtel-Dieu de la ville de Lyon, par M. Prin, prêtre œconome. A Lyon, mille-sept-cent-soixante-deux."

H.D. Lyon Délibération du 19 avril 1598.

AM Riom

GG 145 Maison du Bon-Pasteur, Registre 1690 à 1714.

AM Saint-Jean-de-Bonnefonds

Registres paroissiaux, 1666, 1668, 1692, 1694, 1697, 1709, sépultures des sœurs de Saint-Joseph.

AM Saint-Julien-Molin-Molette

Registres paroissiaux, 1er registre: 1614-93, Baptême de Marguerite Burdier, 1626.

AM Vienne

E [Fonds d l'Hôtel-Dieu] 59 Registre des délibérations de l'Hôtel-Dieu, 1691-99 (sans pagination).

E 60 Registre des délibérations de l'Hôtel-Dieu, 1700-09.

E 62 Registre des délibérations du Bureau de l'Hotel-Dieu, 1713-21.

E 64 Registre des délibérations de l'Hôtel-Dieu, 1727-30.

E 334 "Plusieurs mémoires, tant de la feue Sœur Burdier Econome de l'Hôtel-Dieu que de la Sœur Félix,"1698-1701, gros cahier sans pagination.

G1 (1668-1789), no. 1 "Mémoire des Sœurs de saint-Joseph présenté en 1714," 15 pp.

G1 (1668-1789), no. 3 "Copie des Lettres Patentes (obreptices et subreptices) obtenues du Roy par les Filles de Saint-Joseph, servantes à l'hôptial de Vienne et maison de Providence," 1727.

G1 (1668-1789), no. 4 Mémoire concernant la juridiction de l'Hôpital sur la Maison de Providence (rédigé en 1773, première date dans le manuscrit: 1686).,

G4 no. 1 "Mémoire pour les Dames religieuses de Saint-Joseph de la Maison de Providence de Vienne, 19 avril 1780," 44 pp.

G4 no. 2 1710-83, Relevé des Délibérations du Bureau de l'Hôtel-Dieu concernant la Maison de Providence, 1667 à 1732.

G4 no. 3 Relevé de plusieurs délibérations du Bureau exposant des faits de révolte des sœurs . . . 21 février 1753 à 15 Déc^bre 1754.

G4 no. 4 Lettre de la sœur Roman, économe, au Bureau de l'H.D., 19 juin 1728.

H 75 Papiers de la Mère Burdier.

ARCHIVES OF THE SISTERS OF ST. JOSEPH

AMM Aubenas

Communauté de:

Satillieu, "Confirmation de l'établissement des sœurs de Saint-Joseph à Satillieu par Mgr Henry de Villars, archevêque de Vienne," le 6 décembre 1661.

Satillieu, Permission de la guimpe accordée aux sœurs de Saint-Joseph de Satillieu, 21 septembre 1774.

Saint-Félicien, "Livre de l'établissement des Sœurs de St Joseph a St Félicien l'an mil sept cents trois" (dernière date du livre: mars 1799).

Saint-Julien-Vocance, "Albergement ou Loyer perpetuel passé par M^re pierre Perret, prieur et cure de St Julhien Vaucances a honneste sœur Catherine Giraud sœur de St Joseph . . . du 2e nov^bre 1726."

Saint-Julien-Vocance, Testament de Flourie Bere, 15 janvier 1705.

Saint-Julien-Vocance, "Vœu de devotion . . . faict, par honneste Marye Mazet, du 5e Août 1664."

Vanosc, "Mémoire abrégé de l'Établissement et des progrès de la Communauté des filles agrégées de St Joseph . . . de Vanosc" (1675-1879), gros registre commencé en 1763.

AMM Clermont

Un manuscrit du Règlement, dit "de Montferrand," fin du XVIIe siècle.

"Obligations principales des Sœurs de Saint-Joseph," s.d., début XVIIIe siècle.

Correspondance de Mère Ste Agathe Dupuy de la Grand'Rive avec le P. Rivière, SJ, concernant Jean-Pierre Médaille et ses deux frères, 1899-1913.

Communauté de/du:

Beurrières, "Expédition d'acte d'association passée entre Anthoinette Maistre, Catherine et Jeanne Mosneyron et autres, le 22 juin 1696."

Champeix, "Vente d'une maison par Marc Sabattier à Sr Thérèse Sappin, sup^re des filles de St Joseph establyes en ce lieu de Champeix," le 12 mai 1731.

Refuge de Clermont, "Lettres patentes portant etablissement d'une Maison de Filles Pénitentes en la ville de Clermont en Auvergne, appelée Le Refuge ou du Bon-Pasteur, juin 1666," enregistrées au Parlement de Paris le 7 juillet 1667.

Refuge de Clermont, Mémoire pour ce qui concerne la Maison du Bon-Pasteur, s.d., vers 1730.

Refuge de Clermont, "Coutumier de la Maison du Bon-Pasteur, rédigé en 1775," petit carnet non paginé.

Refuge de Clermont, Mémoire concernant l'établissement de la maison du Refuge, dite du Bon-Pasteur de la ville de Clermont . . . fait pour être envoyé au Conseil de sa Majesté, s.d., vers 1760.

Refuge de Clermont, "État de la maison du Refuge tel qu'il fut trouvé le 30 Aoust 1753."

Refuge de Clermont, État concernant l'année 1772, destiné au Cardinal de Luynes, chef du bureau des pauvres.

Sauxillanges, Délibération des habitants de Sauxillanges pour l'établissement des Sœurs de Saint-Joseph, le 14 décembre 1664. (Dans les copies de signatures, celle du P. Médaille.)

Viverols, Établissement de la communauté, le 19 août 1696.

AMM Le Puy

Communauté de:

Bas-en-Basset, Un manuscrit du Règlement ([fin XVIIe-début XVIIIe siècle).

Bas-en-Basset, Demande d'exonération de taxes, 1714.

Bas-en-Basset, "Livre des réceptions comme des professions des Sœurs de la Congrégation de St Joseph . . . ce 5e juillet 1740."

Boisset, Un manuscrit du Règlement (fin XVIIe siècle).

Boisset, Acte d'association de sept sœurs, le 24 mai 1664, Minutes de Bouchet, copie dans le MS Règlement de Boisset.

Boisset, Testament de Claudine Mosnier, le 21 juin 1765.

Boisset, Testament de Jeanne Desnaves, le 26 septembre 1776.

Chomelix, Délibération des habitants pour la demande de Lettres Patentes, 13 août 1684.

Craponne, Registre des Actes capitulaires, 1723-1857

Craponne, "La Vie de la Vénérable Mère de Vinols," par l'Abbé Clavel, MS 60 pp. relié, grand format.

Dunières, "Constitution de dot, a soy faite par sœur Anne Deschaux, et par Marie Blanc," 10 février 1662.

Marlhes, Registre de prises d'habit et professions, 6 octobre 1651 au 30 août 1900.

Montferrand, au Puy, Lettres Patentes de Louis XIV, pour les maisons du Puy et de Saint-Didier, septembre 1674.

Montferrand, au Puy, Manuscrite des Constitutions de la communauté du Puy (MS A, fin XVIIe).

Montferrand, au Puy, "Le Reverend Pere Maidaille nous a recommendé, " suivi de "Diverses marques d'une religion ou congregation bien réglée" et d'une "Copie de la lettre du R^d Père Médaille," deux doubles feuilles manuscrites reliées par un fil, s.d.

Montregard, "Quittance donnée à Honneste Claude Ferraton, supérieure des sœurs de Saint Joseph," le 4 mai 1666.

Riotord, Petit cahier-registre, deux doubles feuilles non attachées, 1659 à 1776.

Riotord, Cahier Abbé Freycenon, contenant une copie de la Lettre Eucharistique du P. Médaille avec des commentaires, 1870.

Saint-Just-Malamont, "Établissement des Sœurs de Saint-Joseph, 4 septembre 1686, reçu Charra, N^e."

Saint-Didier, Lettre du P. Médaille à la sœur Fayolle, supérieure de Saint-Didier.

Saint-Didier, Copie des dons faits par le marquis de Nerestang, Seigneur de Saint-Didier aux Sœurs de Saint-Joseph de lad. ville, 12 septembre 1674.

Saint-Didier, Manuscrit des Constitutions, de la communauté de Saint-Didier (vers 1660-65).

Saint-Paulien, "Livre des filles de St Joseph de la maison naissante d'icelle" (1700-1850).

Saint-Pierre-Duchamp, Prises d'habit et professions des sœurs agrégées (1709-1907), registre.

Saint-Romain-Lachalm, Établissement de la Communauté, contrat reçu Chapuis, le 15 octobre 1652.

Saint-Romain-Lachalm, Registre des prises d'habit et professions (1652-1876).

Saint-Romain-Lachalm, Testament de Jean Farissier, le 24 février 1697.

Saint-Victor-Malescours, Registre des réceptions et professions (1657-1852).

Tence, "Les sœurs de Saint-Joseph doivent pour censive et laud au Pères Jésuites prieur de Tence."

Tence, Copie des Lettres patentes: Arch. Parlement de Toulouse, registre no. 26, juin 1687 et mars 1690, fol. 244 ff.

Yssingeaux, "Catalogue des Sœurs défuntes de la maison de St Joseph d'Yssingeaux puis l'année 1657," jusqu'en 1897.

AMM Lyon

Manuscrit des Constitutions (Lettre Eucharistique)

Communauté de/du:

Apinac, Manuscrit du Règlement, 1691.

Apinac, Attestation du Curé d'Apinac: les filles assemblées "ne font point un corps ne communauté," 25 août 1713.

Bourg-Argental, Demande d'approbation à l'archevêque de Vienne, le 6 mai 1675.

Izieux, Registre des Actes capitulaires et livre de comptes, du 11 novembre 1672 à 1949.

Jonzieux, Acte de profession de Louise Didier, Anne Brunon et Angélique Bayle, le 1er février 1664.

Jonzieux, Actes de profession de Jeanne Tuilhier, Jeanne Bayle, Catherine Didier et Antoinette Didier, 15 août 1713.

Le Chambon, Bref historique, dans un petit cahier, fin du XIXe s.

Le Chambon, "Registre Des sœurs qui ont decede Dans notre maison Depuis les premier" (liste des sœurs depuis le début de la communauté–date non indiquée, notices
nécrologiques depuis 1757).

Riverie, Autorisation de l'archevêque de Lyon, le Cardinal de Tencin, le 15 avril
1744.

Saint-Genest-l'Erpt, Acte d'Ingrès d'Antoinette Verney, le 11 juillet 1729.

Saint-Genest-l'Erpt, Testament de Jeanne Malescour, le 1er février 1766.

Saint-Hilaire, Un Manuscrit du Règlement, fin du XVIIe s. ou début XVIIIe s.

Saint-Hilaire, Un Manuscrit des Constitutions, milieu XVIIIe s.

Saint-Jean-de-Bonnefonds, Actes capitulaires des sœurs agrégées de Saint-Joseph
établies à Saint-Jean-de-Bonnefonds, du 28 mai 1719 au 11 janvier 1790 (à la fin
du manuscrit des Constitutions conservé à Lyon).

Saint-Jean-de-Bonnefonds, Un registre "Etat des Maisons de Saint-Joseph du diocèse
de Lyon," 14 août 1807-1824.

AMM Saint-Vallier

"Acte d'Assemblée portant Fondation de la communauté de l'Hôpital, le 1er janvier
1683."

Archivum romanum Societatis Iesu

Tolosanae Catalogi Breves 1609-47 / 1651-80 / 1587-1642 / 1645-51 / 1655-60 /
1665-75.

Tolosanae Catalogi Triennales 1587-1642 / 1645-51 / 1655-60 / 1665-75

Tolosanae Aquit. Camp. Necrologia: 1593-1696.

Tolosan. Epist. General: 1636-46 / 1646-56.

Assistentia Galliae, Epistolae General. de promovendis: 1610-1754.

Arch. Bayon De La Tour (Ch.)

"Mémoyre d'un grand miracle arrivé à saint-Joseph le 15 octobre 1654."

Arch. Charpin-Feugerolles (Comte de)

Notice sur le Château de Feugerolles, Lyon 1878 (Informations et document sur
l'établissement des sœurs de Saint-Joseph du Chambon, 125-31).

Arch. Sœurs Hospitalières de Saint-Joseph de la Flèche

"Constitutions de la communauté des Filles de Saint-Joseph établies dans l'Hôtel-
Dieu de La Flèche, en honneur de la sainte Famille de Notre-Seigneur, 20 octobre
1643."

Arch. Sœurs de Saint-François de Sales, dites de l'Union, à Rodez

MS Règlements de Pomayrols, de Rodez, et de Chirac.

Arch. des Filles de la Croix de Paris

Directoires de Me Abelly.

BN

MS Fr. 20636, G. 2782 Fonds Henri de Maupas.

Bibliothèque Mazarine

MS 3333, Constitutions de la Congrégation des Sœurs de La Croix, 196 pp., milieu XVIIᵉ s.

BMU Clermont-Ferrand

Fonds Paul Leblanc, no. 850, Documents sur les Associations des filles de Saint-Joseph, en Velay, de 1663 jusqu'après la Révolution
Fonds Paul Leblanc, no. 850, MS 131 Délibération des habitants de Craponne pour une demande de Lettres Patentes en faveur des filles associées sous le vocable de Saint-Joseph, 25 mai 1766 / Contrat d'Association de Louise Dupoux et Jeanne-Marie Porrat-Delolme, 22 mai 1723 / Retrait d'Anne Guilhomont du contrat d'association, le 8 août 1760.
Fonds Paul Leblanc, no. 850, MS 606 Recueil de pièces relatives au Collège de Clermont, fol. 71. Arrivée des Jésuites à Clermont, en 1662. Copie du récit du P. Soubrany, procureur au collège de Montferrand.

BM Grenoble

R 8372 "Registre des religieuses de St Joseph de la ville de Vienne, a commencer en l'année mil-six-cent-soixante-huit," MS in-fol., 207 pp.

BM Lyon

353 321 "Légende surdorée ou supplément au Martyrologe de Lyon," anonyme, 1790.
MS 357 "Mémoire pour la maison des Recluses de Lyon," s.d.

BM Saint-Étienne

MS 115, pièce 5 Vente de propriétés sises sur le mandement de Feugerolles, passée par "Sœur Jeanne Deville et Mathie Badinand de la Congrégation de Sainct-Joseph . . . 15ᵉ Février 1659."

BM Vienne

GG 42 État-Civil de l'Hôpital 1680-1733, décès de Marguerite Burdier, 12 février 1700.
GG 48, no. 28 Délibération concernant la Providence, du 7ᵉ et 10ᵉ juillet 1659.
B 1389 Mémoires de la sœur Jeanne Burdier, économe de l'Hôtel-Dieu de Vienne, 1680-92, extraits transcrits par Jean Lecutiez.

OLDER PRINTED SOURCES

Compagnie de Marie Notre-Dame. "Abrégé ou forme de l'Institut des Filles Religieuses de la glorieuse Vierge Marie Notre-Dame . . . le 7ᵉ jour du mois de mars 1606."

Constitutions et Règles de l'Ordre des Religieuses de Notre-Dame. Bordeaux, 1638.

Constitutions pour la petite Congrégation des Sœurs de Saint Joseph establie au Puy en vellay , par Monseigneur de Maupas, évêque du Puy, à Vienne, chez Laurens Cruzi, première édition, 1694.

Constitutions pour la petite Congrégation des sœurs de Saint-Joseph, approuvées par Mᵍʳ Camille de Neuville de Villeroy, archevêque de Lyon, à Lyon, chez André Laurens, 1730.

Crasset, Jean, SJ. *Des Congrégations de Notre-Dame, érigées dans les maisons des Pères de la Compagnie de Jésus,* à Paris, chez Urbain Coutelier, 1694.

Durand de Maillane, M. *Dictionnaire de droit caninique, et de pratique bénéficiale.* 2ⁿᵈ rev. ed. 4 vols. A Lyon, Chez Benoit Duplain, 1770.

Furetière, Antoine. *Dictionnaire universel, contenant generalement tous les mots francois tant vieux que modernes, & les termes de toutes les sciences et des arts.* 3 vols. La Haye: Arnout & Renier Leers, 1690.

Hélyot, Pierre, and Maximilien Bullot. *Histoire des ordres monastiques, religieux et militaires, et des congregations seculieres de l'un & de l'autre sexe, qui ont esté establies jusqu'à present.* 8 vols. Paris: J.B. Coignard, 1714.

Magnum bullarium Romanum, a Beato Leone Magno usque ad S.D.N. Benedictum XIII. Vol. 2 : *A Pio IV, ad Innocentium IX* . Luxemburgi: Sumptibus Andreae Chevalier; Henrici-Alberti Gosse & Soc, 1742.

Maupas Du Tour , Henry Cauchon de. *La Vie du venerable serviteur de Dieu François de Sales, Evesque et Prince de Geneve, fondateur des Religieuses de la Visitation de Sainte Marie.* A Paris: Chez Jacques Langlois et Emmanuel Langlois, 1657.

Maximes de perfection pour les âmes qui aspirent à la Haute Vertu: revue et augmentée de l'Exercice pour se dénuer de soi-même, se revêtir de Jésus-Christ. Par un Serviteur de Dieu très éclairé dans la Vie intérieure L.R.P.M.D.L.C.D.J., à Clermont, imprimerie Nicolas Jacquard, 1672.

Poullin de Lumina, Étienne Joseph. *Histoire de l'église de Lyon.* Lyon: J.L. Berthoud, 1770.

Pratique de dévotion et des vertus chrétiens suivant les Règles des Congrégations de Notre Dame, à Lyon, chez Jean-Baptiste De Ville, 1689.

Recueil des actes, titres et mémoires concernant les affaires du clergé de France. Paris: Chez G. Desprez [etc., etc.], 1768-71.

Règlement pour les sœurs rurales de la Communauté de Saint-Joseph des Vans. Lyon: 1852.

Règles de la Compagnie de Iésvs, à Paris, Chez Iean Fouët, 1620.

Règles et constitutions pour la Congrégation des sœurs de Saint Joseph establie au Puy en vellay, par Monseigneur de Maupas, évêque du Puy, à Vienne, chez Laurens Cruzi, première édition, 1693.

Rousseaud de La Combe, Guy du. *Recueil de jurisprudence canonique et bénéficiale, par ordre alphabetique*. Paris: Chez Samson, 1771.

Sœurs de Saint-Charles, *Nos Textes Fondateurs*, Règles de la Compagnie des Vierges et Chastes Veuves. Lyon, 1632. Reprint, Le Puy: Sœurs de Saint-Charles, 1984.

Sales, François de, Saint. "Entretien XIX: Sur les vertus de saint Joseph." In *Les œuvres de Sainct François de Sales, revues et très exactement corrigées sur les premiers et plus fidèles exemplaires* . . . . 11 vols. A Paris, chez Frederic Leonard, 1669-73.

PUBLISHED SOURCES

Books

Allier, Raoul Scipion Philippe. *La cabale des dévots, 1627-1666*. Paris: A. Colin, 1902.

———. *La Compagnie du Très-Saint-Sacrement de l'autel à Marseille, une société secrète au XVIIe siècle: documents publiés*. Paris: H. Champion, 1909.

———. *Une société secrète au XVIIe siècle: La Compagnie du Très-Saint-Sacrement de l'autel à Toulouse, une esquisse de son histoire*. Paris: Champion, 1914.

Ariès, Philippe, and Georges Duby. *De la Renaissance aux Lumières*. Vol. 3 of *Histoire de la vie privée*. Paris: Seuil, 1986. Translated by Arthur Goldhammer as *Passions of the Renaissance*. Vol. 3 of *A History of Private Life*. Cambridge, Mass.: Belknap Press of Harvard University Press, 1989.

Auguste, Alphonse, ed. *La Compagnie du Saint Sacrement à Toulouse, notes et documents*. Edited by Alphonse Auguste. Paris: A. Picard, 1913.

Aulanier, Hugues. *Moi, Hugues Aulanier journal de l'abbé Aulanier, curé de Brignon 1638-1691*. Edited by Sylvère Heuzé, Yves Soulingeas, and Martin de Framond. Documents et études historiques, 3. 6 vols. Saint-Vidal: Éditions de la Borne, 1987-2005.

[Battut, Mère Augustine]. *Origine et développement de la Congrégation de Saint-Joseph du Bon Pasteur*. Clermont-Ferrand: Imp. de Vve Petit, 1879.

Bertrand, Camille. *Monsieur de la Dauversière: Fondateur de Montréal et des Religieuses hospitalières de S-Joseph, 1597-1659*. Montréal: Les frères des écoles chrétiennes, 1947.

Blet, Pierre, SJ. *Le clergé de France et la monarchie: Étude sur les Assemblées générales du clergé de 1615 à 1666*. 2 vols. Rome, Librairie éditrice de l'Université grégorienne, 1959.

Bois, Albert. *Les Sœurs de Saint-Joseph, les Filles du petit dessein, de 1648 à 1949*. Lyon: Éditions et imprimeries du Sud-Est, 1950.

Boudon-Lashermes, Albert. *La Sénéchaussée présidiale du Puy*. Valence: Typographie et lithographie C. Legrand, 1908.

Boudon-Lashermes, Albert, and Gaston de Jourda de Vaux. *Le Vieux Puy*. 1: *Vieux logis et vieilles familles*. Saint-Étienne: Théolier, 1911.

――――. *Le vieux Puy.* 2: *La vie d'autrefois au Puy-en-Velay.* Saint-Étienne : Théolier, 1912.

Brioude, Mme [Marie]. *Recherches historiques sur une partie du Velay, principalement la ville et la paroisse de Tence.* Le Puy: Prades-Freydier, 1901.

Chanal, André. *Le Puy, ville sainte et ville d'art.* Le Puy [etc.]: Mappus, 1957.

Charrié, Pierre. *Dictionnaire topographique du département de l'Ardèche.* Paris: Guénégaud, 1979.

Chartier, Roger, Dominique Julia, and Marie-Madeleine Compère. *L'éducation en France du XVIe au XVIIIe siècle.* Paris: Société d'édition d'enseignement supérieur, 1976.

Chassaing, Augustin, and Antoine Jacotin. *Dictionnaire topographique du département de la Haute-Loire, comprenant les noms de lieu anciens et modernes.* Paris: Imprimerie nationale, 1907.

Châtellier, Louis. *L'Europe des dévots.* [Paris]: Flammarion, 1987. Translated by Jean Birrell as *The Europe of the Devout: The Catholic Reformation and the Formation of a New Society.* Cambridge [England] and New York: Cambridge University Press, 1989.

Chausse, Vital. *Saint-Didier-en-Velay [actualités, histoire, tradition].* Saint-Étienne: Impr. industrielle, 1948.

Chevalier, Cyr Ulysse Joseph. *Notice chronologico-historique sur les archevêques de Vienne d'après des documents paléographiques inédits.* Extrait de la Revue du Dauphiné et du Vivarais. No. de Mai-Juin 1879. Vienne: E. J. Savigné, 1879.

Clémet, René. *Dix siècles d'histoire en Vallorgue.* Le Puy: Imprimerie Jeanne-d'Arc, 1989.

Cognet, Louis. *La spiritualité moderne.* Vol. 1, *L'essor: 1500-1650.* Paris: Aubier, 1966.

Colly, Hippolyte. *Yssingeaux: Ses couvents, chapelles, confréries et dévotions dans le passé et le présent.* 1893. Monographies des villes et villages de France. Reprint, Paris: Res Universis, 1993.

Colombe du Saint Esprit. *Mémoires de la mère Micolon 1592-1659: recueil de la vie de la mère Antoinette Micolon, dite sœur Colombe du Saint Esprit.* Edited by Henri Pourrat. Clermont-Ferrand: La Francaise d'édition et d'impr, 1981. Translated by Linda Lierheimer as *The Life of Antoinette Micolon.* Reformation texts with translation (1350-1650), 4. Milwaukee: Marquette University Press, 2004.

Constitutions de la compagnie de Jésus. 2 vols. Translated by François Courel, SJ. Paris: Desclée, De Brouwer, 1967.

Constitutions of the Society of Jesus. Translated by George E. Ganss, SJ. St. Louis: Institute of Jesuit Sources, 1970.

Couanier de Launay, Etienne-Louis. *Histoire des religieuses hospitalières de Saint-Joseph (France et Canada).* 2 vols. Paris: V. Palmé, 1887.

Concilium Tridentinum Diariorum, actorum, epistularum, tractatuum nova collectio. 13 vols. Vol. 9, *Actorum pars sexta: Complectens acta post sessionem sextam (XXII) usque ad finem Concilii (17. Sept. 1562-4. Dec. 1563),* Collegit, edidit, illustravit S. Ehses. Freiburgi Brisgoviae: Herder, 1901.

Croze, Auguste. *Les Sœurs hospitalières des hospices civils de Lyon*. Lyon: M. Audin, 1933.

Delattre, Pierre. *Les établissements des jésuites en France depuis quatre siècles répertoire topo-bibliographique*. 5 vols. Enghien (Belgique): Institut supérieur de théologie, 1949.

Delcambre, Étienne. *Une institution municipale languedocienne: Le consulat du Puy-en-Velay des origines à 1610*. Le Puy-en-Velay: Aux éditions de la Société académique du Puy, 1933.

Deloche, Maximin. *Un frère de Richelieu inconnu, chartreux, primat des Gaules, cardinal, ambassadeur: Documents inédits*. Paris: Desclée, de Brouwer & cie, 1935.

Demoustier, Adrien, SJ. "Étude de la Lettre Eucharistique du Père Médaille." Fédération française des Sœurs de Saint-Joseph, 1969.

———. *Les catalogues du personnel de la province de Lyon en 1567, 1606 et 1636*. Thèse de doctorat. Rome: Archivum historicum societatis Jesu, Ext., 1974.

Dufour, J. E. *Dictionnaire topographique du Forez et des paroisses du Lyonnais et du Beaujolais formant le département de la Loire*. Dictionnaires Topographiques de La France, 32. Mâcon: Impr. Protat frères, 1946.

Faillon, Étienne Michel. *Vie de Monsieur de Lantages, pretre de saint-Sulpice, premier supérieur du séminaire de Notre-Dame du Puy*. Paris: Imp. A. le Clère et Cie, 1830.

Flandrin, Jean Louis. *Familles: Parenté, maison, sexualité dans l'ancienne société*. Paris: Hachette, 1976. Translated by Richard Southern as *Families in Former Times: Kinship, Household, and Sexuality*. Cambridge: University Press, 1979.

Furetière, Antoine. *Dictionnaire universel*. 3 vols. À La Haye et à Rotterdam, Chez A. et R. Leers, 1690.

Gadille, Jacques. *Le Diocèse de Lyon*. Histoire des diocèses de France, 16. Paris: Beauchesne, 1983.

Goubert, Pierre. *La vie quotidienne des paysans français au XVIIe siècle*. Paris: Hachette, 1982. Translated by Ian Patterson as *The French Peasantry in the Seventeenth Century*. Cambridge, [Cambridgeshire] and New York: Cambridge University Press, 1986.

Goubert, Pierre. *Les Français et l'Ancien Régime*. 2 vols. Paris: A. Colin, 1984.

Gouit, F. *Une congrégation Salésienne: Les surs de Saint-Joseph du Puy-en-Velay, 1648-1915*. Le Puy: Impr. de l'Avenir de la Haute-Loire, 1930.

Guigue, Georges, ed. *Les papiers des Dévots de Lyon, recueil de textes sur la Compagnie secrète du Saint-Sacrement, ses statuts, ses annales, la liste de ses membres: 1630-1731: documents inédits publiés d'après les manuscrits originaux*. Lyon: Librairie ancienne Vve Blot, 1922.

Guitton, Georges. *Les Jésuites à Lyon sous Louis XIV et Louis XV: Activités, luttes, suppression (1640-1768)*. Lyon: Procure, 1953.

Gutton, Jean Pierre. *La société et les pauvres: l'exemple de la généralité de Lyon, 1534-1789*. Paris: Société d'édition "Les Belles Lettres," 1971.

———. *La sociabilité villageoise dans l'ancienne France: Solidarités et voisinages du XVIe au XVIIIe siècle*. Paris: Hachette, 1979.

————. *Villages du lyonnais: Sous la monarchie, XVIe-XVIIIe siècles*. Lyon: Presses universitaires de Lyon, 1978.

Guyot, Pierre Jean Jacques Guillaume. *Répertoire universel et raisonné de jurisprudence civile, criminelle, canonique et bénéficiale*. 63 vols. À Paris: chez Panckoucke, Dupuis, 1776-1783.

Hélyot, Pierre, and Maximilien Bullot. *Histoire des ordres religieux et militaires, ainsi que des Congrégations séculières de l'un et de l'autre sexe, qui ont été établies jusqu'a présent*. Paris: Louis, 1792.

Huguet, Edmond. *Dictionnaire de la langue française du seizième siècle*. 7 vols. Paris: E. Champion, 1925-1973.

Imbert, Jean, and Michel Mollat. *Histoire des hôpitaux en France*. Toulouse: Privat, 1982.

Jacmon, Antoine. *Mémoires d'Antoine Jacmon, bourgeois du Puy*. Edited by Augustin Chassaing. Recueil des chroniqueurs du Puy-en-Velay, 4. Le Puy-en-Velay: Marchessou, 1885.

Jourda de Vaux, Gaston de. *Le nobiliaire du Velay et de l'ancien Diocèse du Puy (noms féodaux)*. 7 vols. Le Puy: Impr. Peyriller, Rouchon & Gamon, 1924-31.

Isambert, M., Jourdan, and Decrusy. *Recueil général des anciennes lois françaises, depuis l'an 420 jusqu'à la révolution de 1789*. 29 vols. Paris: Berlin-Le-Prieur, 1821-33.

La Brière, Yves de. *Ce que fut la "Cabale des dévots," 1630-1660*. Paris: Bloud et cie, 1906.

La Tour-Varan, Jean Antoine de. *Chronique des châteaux et des abbayes: Études historiques sur la Forez*. 2 vols. in 1. Saint-Étienne: Montagny, 1854-57. Reprint, Marseille: Laffitte, 1976.

Langlois, Claude. *Le catholicisme au féminin: Les congrégations françaises à supérieure générale au XIXe siècle*. Paris: Cerf, 1984.

Latreille, André, Étienne Delaruelle, and Jean-Rémy Palanque. *Histoire du catholicisme en France*. 3 vols. Paris, Éditions Spes, 1957-62.

Ledóchowska, Teresa. *Angèle Merici et la compagnie de Ste-Ursule à la lumière des documents*. 2 vols. Rome, Ancora, 1967. Translated by Mary Teresa Neylan as *Angela Merici and The Company of St. Ursula: According to the Historical Documents*. Rome: Ancora, 1969.

Lemoine, Robert, OSB. *Le monde des religieux*. Vol. 2 of *L'Époque moderne: 1563-1789*. Histoire du droit et des institutions de l'Église en Occident, 15. Paris: Éditions Cujas, 1976.

Lescure, Marie-Henri-François-Charles, de. *Armorial du Gévaudan*. Lyon: A. Badiou-Amant, 1929.

Littré, Emile. *Dictionnaire de la langue francaise*. 7 vols. [Paris]: Gallimard, Hachette, 1959-61.

Mandrou, Robert. *La France aux XVIIe et XVIIIe siècles*. Paris: Presses universitaires de France, 1967.

Marion, Marcel. *Dictionnaire des institutions de la France aux XVIIe et XVIII ^{e} siècles*. Paris: A. Picard, 1923.

Martin, Victor. *Le Gallicanisme et la Réforme catholique: essai historique sur l'introduction en France des décrets du Concile de Trente (1563-1615)*. Paris: Picard, 1919.

Marzin, Louise-Paul. *Marie L'Huilier de Villeneuve, fondatrice des Filles de la Croix, 1597-1650*. Le Puy: Mappus, 1948.

Médaille, Jean-Pierre, SJ. *Maximes de Perfection*, d'après l'édition de N. Jacquard, Clermont, 1672. Edited by Marius Nepper, SJ. Lyon: Roudil, 1962, 1972.

Mousnier, Roland. *Les institutions de la France sous la monarchie absolue: 1598-1789*. 2 vols. Paris: Presses universitaires de France, 1974-1980. Translated by Brian Pearce as *The Institutions of France Under the Absolute Monarchy, 1598-1789*. 2 vols. Chicago: University of Chicago Press, 1979-1984.

Naz, Raoul. *Dictionnaire de droit canonique, contenant tous les termes du droit canonique*. Paris: Letouzey et Ané, 1935-1965.

Nepper, Marius, SJ. *Aux Origines des Filles de Saint-Joseph*. N.p.: Solaro, 1969. Translated by the Federation of the Sisters of St. Joseph, USA., as *Origins: The Sisters of St. Joseph*. [Erie: Villa Maria College, 1975].

Neveux, Hugues, Jean Jacquart, and Emmanuel Le Roy Ladurie. *Histoire de la France rurale*. Vol. 2, *L'âge classique des paysans, 1340-1789*. Edited by Georges Duby and Armand Wallon. 4 vols. Paris: Seuil, 1975.

Payrard, Jean-Baptiste. "Les pénitents du Saint-Sacrement à Chomelix: Documents publiés par l'Abbé Payrard." *Nouveaux Mélanges Historiques* (1885-1886): 187-89.

Poitrineau, Abel. *La Vie rurale en Basse-Auvergne au XVIIIe siècle, 1726-1789*. 2 vols. Paris, Presses universitaires de France, 1965.

———. *Le Diocèse de Clermont*. Histoire des diocèses de France, 9. Paris: Éditions Beauchesne, 1979.

Quétel, Claude. *De par le Roy: Essai sur les lettres de cachet*. Toulouse: Privat, 1981.

Rébelliau, Alfred, ed. *La compagnie secrète du Saint-Sacrement; lettres du groupe parisien au groupe marseillais, 1639-1662*. Edited by Alfred Rébeilliau. Paris: H. Champion, 1908.

Règle et conduite pour les Filles Associées de la maison de l'Instruction de la ville du Puy. Le Puy: Imp. P.B.F. Clet, 1834.

Règles et Constitutions de la Congrégation des Sœurs de la Croix du diocèse du Puy. 1835.

Rivaux, Jean-Joseph. *Vie de la Révérende Mère Marie du Sacré-Cœur de Jésus, Supérieure générale de la congrégation de Saint-Joseph de Lyon*. Lyon: Briday, 1878. Translated by Sisters of St. Joseph, Lindsay, Ont., as *History of the Reverend Mother Sacred Heart of Jesus, née Tezenas of Montcel*. Montreal: Messenger Press, 1910.

Rivet, Bernard, and Emmanuel Le Roy Ladurie. *Une ville au XVIe siècle: Le Puy-en-Velay*. Le Puy: Cahiers de la Haute-Loire, 1988.

Rossel, André, and Pierre-François Aleil. *Découverte du costume auvergnat*. Paris: Éditions Hier et demain, 1974.

Saint-Marthe, Denis de, and Barthélemy Hauréau. *Gallia Christiana in provincias ecclesiasticas distributa*. 16 vols. Paris: Ex Typographia Regia, 1716-1865.

Sales, François de, Saint. *Introduction à la Vie Dévote*. In *Œuvres*. Edited by André Ravier and Roger Devos. Paris: Gallimard, 1969.

――― . *Œuvres de Saint François de Sales Évêque de Genève et docteur de l'Église*. Ed. complète. 27 vols. Annecy: J. Niérat, 1892–1964.

Sœurs de Saint-Joseph. Textes primitifs. Edited by Thérèse Vacher, CSJ, et al. Clermont-Ferrand: Impr. Siman, 1981.

Taveneaux, René. *Le catholicisme dans la France classique: 1610-1715*. 2 vols. Paris: SEDES, 1980.

――― . *La vie quotidienne des jansénistes aux XVIIe et XVIIIe siècles*. Paris: Hachette, 1973.

Teresa of Avila, Saint. *The Collected Works of St. Teresa of Avila*. Translated by by Kieran Kavanaugh and Otilio Rodriguez. 3 vols. Washington: Institute of Carmelite Studies, 1976-.

Thérèse d'Avila, Sainte. *Oeuvres complètes*. Translated by Gregoire de Saint Josseph. Paris: Éditions du Seuil, 1949.

Vachet, Ad[olphe]. *Les paroisses du Diocése de Lyon: archives et antiquités*. Lérins: Abbaye de Lérins, Imprimerie M. Bernard, 1899.

Venard, Marc. *L'Église d'Avignon au XVIème siècle*. Thèse de doctorat, Université de Paris IV, 1977. 5 vols. Lille: Service de reproduction des thèses, Université de Lille III, 1980.

Vic, Claude de, Joseph Vaissette, and Ernest Roschach. *Histoire générale de Languedoc avec des notes et les pièces justificatives par dom Cl. Devic & dom J. Vaissete*. 15 vols. Toulouse: Privat, 1872-92.

Voyer d'Argenson, Marc René de, and H. Beauchet-Filleau. *Annales de la Compagnie du St-Sacrement*. Marseille: Typ. & lith. Saint-Léon, 1900.

Willaert, Léopold. *Après le Concile de Trente: La Restauration catholique, 1563-1648*. Vol. 18 of *Histoire de l'Église, depuis les origines jusqu'à nos jours*. Edited by Augustin Fliche and Victor Martin. Paris: Bloud & Gay, 1960.

Wolf, Pierre. "Étude sur les Constitutions primitives des Sœurs de Saint-Joseph." Fédération française des Sœurs de Saint-Joseph, 1978-1979.

Journals

Achard, Auguste. "L'hospice de Sauxillanges (1664-1904)." *Revue d'Auvergne* 21 (1904): 29-46, 128-32, 188-208, and 285-92.

Albe, Edmond. "La Confrérie de la Passion: contribution à l'histoire de la Compagnie du Saint-Sacrement." *Revue d'histoire de l'Église de France* 3 (1912): 654-70.

Aleil, Pierre-François. "Le Refuge de Clermont, 1666-1792." *Bulletin historique et scientifique d'Auvergne* 86 (1973): 13-69.

Brucker, Joseph. "Nouvelles découvertes sur la compagnie du Saint-Sacrement: VI." *Études* 121 (1901): 187-205.

Cavallera, Ferdinand. "L'héritage littéraire des Pères Médaille." *Revue d'ascétique et de mystique* 11 (April, 1930): 185-95.

Charvin, Dom G. "Henry Oswald de La Tour d'Auvergne, Abbé de Cluny, 1715-1747." *Revue Mabillon* 151-152 (June-December, 1948).

Creusen, J., SJ. "Les Instituts religieux à vœux simples." *Revue des communautés religieuses* (May, 1940): 52-62; and (June, 1940): 34-43.

Dubois, J. "La carte des diocèses de France avant la Révolution." *Annales: économie, société, civilisation* (1965): 680-91.

Fouilloux, Abbé. "Gilbert de Veny d'Arbouze." *Bulletin historique et scientifique d'Auvergne* (1884): 130-40.

Imbert, Jean. "Les prescriptions hospitalières du Concile de Trente et leur diffusion en France." *Revue d'histoire de l'Église de France* 42 (1956): 5-28.

Luirard, Monique, and Odile Massardier. "Un village forézien à la veille de la Révolution: Saint-Genest-Malifaux (1760-1789)." *Cahiers d'histoire* 27 (1982): 259-82.

Pomarat, Michel. "Barthélemy Eyraud, Seigneur de Chaumarès, secrétaire de la reine Anne d'Autriche." *Bulletin historique, scientifique, littéraire, artistique & agricole illustré* 40 (1984).

Prunel, N. "Y eut-il des Compagnies de Dames du Saint-Sacrement au XVIIᵉ siècle?" *Revue pratique d'apologétique* (15 January 1911): 607-610.

Rostagnat, M.-L. "Les visites pastorales de Mᵍʳ Camille de Neufville." *Cahiers d'histoire mondiale* 5 (1960): 251-75.

Vacher, M. Th. "Histoire des Constitutions imprimées des Sœurs de Saint-Joseph, de 1694 jusqu'au milieu du XIXᵉ siècle." *Bulletin de la Fédération française des Sœurs De Saint-Joseph* (1985).

NOTES

1. The book by Alan Tallon, *La Compagnie du Saint-Sacrement* (Paris: Cerf), 1990, came my attention only after I had delivered the manuscript to the publisher. I was therefore unable to use it in the research for the present work. [See also Jean-Pierre Gutton, *Dévots et société au XVIIe siecle: Construire le ciel sur la terre*. Paris: Eds. Belin, 2004.]

2. The translation omits the section "Catalogues et inventaires," *Des "Régulières" dans le siècle*, 374-75. —Trans.

Index

A Note on French surnames: Names with de are alphabetized under the main element (Sales, Francis de). Names with La or de La are alphabetized at La (La Planche, Lucrèce de, Dame de Joux). Names with du are alphabetized at du (du Ranc, Daniel, Lord de Joux). Surnames with more than one element (Claude Spert de Volhac) are double-posted or cross-referenced at both elements.

Carrère, Adrien, 19
Cartier, Marguerite, 264
Cavallera, Ferdinand, 19
Chabron, Guillaume, 103
Chaleyer, Anna, 8, 13–14, 18, 25, 58, 329, 331
Champagnat, Thérèse, 235
Champanhac house, 87
Champeix house, 250, 253
Champflour, Jean-Baptiste de, 286, 287
Chantal, Jeanne de, 32, 107
chapels: at Clermont-Ferrand house, 279, 288; country houses not containing, 248; at Craponne house, 213, 253; at Le Puy house, 367; maintenance of, 338; primitive Constitutions not mentioning, 68, 242; in "principal houses," 253, 255, 258; profession and reception of habit in, 236, 301; in Vienne Constitutions, 143, 148
Charantus, Claude, 35–36
Chardin, Jean-Baptiste, 234
charity and humility, 48–52, 64, 70, 73, 96, 105–6, 109, 264, 314, 345, 368–70
Charity, Daughters of, xxxv, xxxvii, xxxviii, 255
Charpin, Balthazard de, 93
Charren, Sister Marie de Jésus, 286
Charroin, Agathe, 86, 303
Chastel, Clauda, 10–11; age at founding of congregation, 17; in contract of association of goods, 8, 329, 330, 331; as *demoiselle de service*, 68; family background, 10–11, 12, 17; as founding sister, 8, 58; at Langogne, 102; Médaille, possible encounters with, 53; social class of, 10–11, 120
Chastel, Marie, 11
Chateauneuf, Jeanne de Saint-Prié de (Sister des Anges), 263
Chateauneuf, Pierre de, *Sieur* de Saint-Laurans, 17

Chateauneuf-Randon, Anne-Guérin de, 17
Châtellier, Louis, 96
Chazau, Catherine de, 90
Cheylard house, 102, *131,* 138, 222
Chézard de Matel, Jeanne, 93
Chomelix house, 102, 222, 250, 291–92
Chometier, Sister, 218–19
Ciber, *Monsieur,* 301
Circa Pastoralis, xix–xx, xxi
city vs. country sisters and houses, 99–101, 247–48, *249,* 290, 305
civic administrators, relationship with: Clermont-Ferrand house, 275–78, 286–87; Craponne house, 214, 348–50; Le Puy house, 59–62, 64, 326–27; Lyon house, 206–12; Sauxillanges house, 222; Vienne house disputes, 186–92, 196–204
Clavel, Abbé, 212, 229n133, 264
Clermont-Ferrand, *Bon Pasteur* house, 273–89; architecture and construction of, 245, 276; authority and legal status attached to running of, 205; Burdier, Mother Jean, influence of, 288; civic administrators, relationship with, 275–78, 286–87; customs book of 1775 showing schedule of prayer and work at, 278–82; ecclesiastical authority, relationship with, 287, 288–89; education of poor girls at, 138, 276, 278, 285–86; elite boarding school at, 138, 277, 278, 280, 285; establishment of, 137, 274–78; habit worn at, 238, 288; housing of sisters at, 245, 246; insane women confined at, 280, 284; *Le Loge* or *maison de force* within, 275, 280, 282, 283; novitiate at, 275; number of sisters at, 246, 276, 277, 281, 289; penitents at, 278–85; poor, preventive services for, 276, 286, 287; as "principal house," 250, 289; schedule of prayer and work at, 262;

separate house for sisters, lack of,
245, 246; separation from Vienne,
205, 223, 275, 288; single *agrégée*
at, 298; spiritual fathers at, 287;
superiors of, 286–87; Vienne
Constitutions at, 287–88; Vienne
house, houses established by, 138,
275
cloister. *See* enclosure
Colombines, Marquise of, 251
Combes, Marie de, 136
community life of Sisters of St. Joseph,
231–72; *agrégées,* 294–98;
congregational body, authority of,
222–24; daily communal reflection
on morning meditation, 256; daily
schedule (*See* schedule of prayer and
work); dress (*See* habit of Sisters of
St. Joseph); houses (*See* houses and
institutions of Sisters of St. Joseph);
meaning of "community," 295;
Médaille on, 231; superiors,
responsibilities of (*See* superiors);
temporal goods, sharing (*See*
temporal goods); weekly communal
reflection on state of congregation
and works of zeal, 265
Compagniat, Jeanne, 282
Company of Mary Our Lady
(Compagnie de Marie Notre-Dame),
xxx–xxxiii, xxxviii, 4, 241, 254
Company of the Blessed Sacrament,
311; Capponi family and, 90; date of
origins of Sisters of St. Joseph and,
52–54; documents of, parallels of
Sisters of St. Joseph texts with,
45–54; episcopal suspicion of, 93;
Eucharistic devotion of, 47–49;
Eucharistic Letter and, 48, 104, 105,
106, 109; foundation of St. Joseph
houses and, 94; founding of, 27–28;
Ladies' Companies, 28–30, 45,
47–48, 52–53; Lyon's Maison forcée
des Recluses and, 206; *maisons de
refuge,* involvement with, 35, 283;

Maupas, Henry de, and, 32, 33, 35,
36, 93, 312; Médaille and, 27–30,
45; Protestant converts, interest in,
87; as secret society, 27–28, 30, 45,
48–52; Sisters Hospitallers of St.
Joseph de La Flèche and, 108,
117n108; suppression of, 30
competing religious and apostolic roles,
141–42, 167–68, 314–17; "1693 A"
version of Vienne Constitutions,
145–50, 191, 202–4; major
modification of vocation in Vienne
Constitutions, 161–62; in three "first
editions" of Vienne Constitutions,
145–50; two manuscript documents
and letter from Médaille compared,
142–45, 336–40; unity of roles,
difficulty in conveying, 158
Comport, Jehanne, 34–35, 68, 79–80n83
Conditae a Christo Ecclesiae, xlin63
Condren, Charles de, 31
conferences: Maupas, Henry de,
Conference of, 97, 101–2, 290;
spiritual, 265; of superiors, 178–79
Confraternity/Congregation of Mercy,
67, 120, 121, 164, 179, 242, 243,
313, 314, 368
congregational body, authority of,
222–24
consciousness, examen of, 265, 277n96
constitutions, defined, 382
Constitutions of other congregations:
Company of Mary Our Lady
(Compagnie de Marie Notre-Dame),
xxx–xxxii; reliability as source,
xxxix; Sisters of St. Charles of Le
Puy, xxxv–xxxvi
Constitutions of Sisters of St. Joseph,
66–70; *agrégées* in, 289–90, 294–95,
300, 316; Company of the Blessed
Sacrament documents, parallels with,
47; comparison of manuscripts of,
351–55; Eucharistic Letter and,
104–5, 106–7; founding of
congregation as recounted in, 7–8,

186–92, 196–204; congregational separation from, 205, 223–24; dowries brought to, 190, 196, 197, 198, 200, 204; enclosure of, 168, 204–5, 315; establishment of, 102–3, 186; growth and development of congregation, role in, 136–38; habit in, 238–39; hospital or Hôtel-Dieu of Vienne, involvement with, 185–92, 204–5, 244; housing for hospital sisters, 244, 245; Le Puy gathering of 1693 and, 145; Maison de Providence, 186–91; necrologies of, 263–64; novitiate of, 187, 195–96, 198, 221; poor, care of, 189–90, 192–94, 197, 198, 200, 203, 205; as "principal house," 250; receptions and professions in, 236; royal letters patent for, 149, 191, 202–5; schedule of prayer and work at, 261, 262, 263–64; social status at, 195–96, 199–200; superiors of, 185–205; work of sisters at, 138

Villars, Henry de: Constitutions, approval of, 24, 145, 149, 340–41; houses approved by, 88; new establishments started by existing sisters under, 136; protection of houses of congregation by, 93, 94; Satillieu house and, 236; superiors and, 177, 180, 186, 195; Vienne house, establishment of, 102, 137, 186

Villars, Louise de, 93

Villars, Pierre de, 93

Ville (Villevocance) house, 305

Villeneuve, Marie L'Huillier de, xxi, 75, 166

Villeroy, François Paul de Neuville de, 208–9

Vincent de Rambion, Françoise de, 196, 207

Vinols, Caprais de, 212, 251

Vinols, Charlotte de (Sister Saint-Charles), 212–16, 218, 220, 222, 223, 253, 264, 290

Visitation Order: apostolic vocation of, xxx; Carmelites, daily schedule based on, 254–55; enclosure required for, xxi; as "great design" compared to "little design" of St. Joseph, 107–8; housing requirements, 241; influence on Sisters of St. Joseph, 119, 121; in Le Puy-en-Velay, 4–5; Lyon, Maison des Filles Pénitentes in, 206, 211; Lyon, patronage of Archbishop of, 93; Marquemont, patronage of Archbishop de, 31; Maupas, Henry de, and, 32; schedule of prayer and work of Sisters of St. Joseph schedule compared to, 255–60, *256–57,* 267; Spiritual Directory of, 74–75; spiritual fathers, authority of, 177; in Vienne Constitutions, 147, 151–55, 166, 167

Viverols house, 136, 250, 251, 264

vocal prayer, 255, 258–59, 278–79

vocation. *See* mission and vocation of Sisters of St. Joseph

Volhac, Claude Spert de, 35

vows: comparison of vows of Sisters of St. Joseph and Scholastics of Society of Jesus, 344–45; of first sisters, 58–59, 60, 99; profession formulae and rituals, 236; protestation of humility and charity and, 345; of sisters in "principal houses," 65, 67, 120, 153, 168, 174–75, 184–85, 236, 244, 277, 290, 298–99, 300, 301; of *sœurs agrégées,* 99, 153, 154, 237, 290, 298–302, 304, 345–46; superiors and, 175; temporal goods, disavowal of, 175; in Vienne Constitutions, 147, 153–54, 160, 165; Visitation Order's influence on, 153–54

Ward, Mary, 119

Wars of Religion in France, 3

widows' clothing, congregation's adoption of, 68, *128,* 148, 233, 234, 236, 237

About the Author

Marguerite (Sister Thérèse) Vacher, a native of Arfeuilles (Allier), France, became a member of the Congregation of the Sisters of St. Joseph of Clermont in 1944. After receiving the Diplôme de Psychologue de l'Ecole de Psychologues Praticiens from the l'Institut Catholique in Paris, she spent the first part of her professional life as a psychologist and director of her congregation's school for mentally handicapped children in Clermont-Ferrand. Since 1965 she has been involved in research, teaching, and writing for the French Federation of the Sisters of St. Joseph and earned the Doctorat d'Histoire moderne in 1989 from the Université Lyon 2–Lumière under the direction of Jean-Pierre Gutton. In addition to a number of shorter articles, her publications include the critical edition of *Sœurs de Saint-Joseph: Textes primitifs* (1981) and *Des "régulières" dans le siècle: Les sœurs de Saint-Joseph de Saint-Joseph du P. Médaille aux XVIIe et XVIIIe siècles* (1991). In 1993 the Congregation of Clermont-Ferrand was incorporated into the new Institut Saint-Joseph. Sister Thérèse Vacher resides in Clermont-Ferrand, continuing her research as well as her long dedication to work with the Spiritual Exercises of St. Ignatius in connection with Jesuits of the French Province in Lyon.

Breinigsville, PA USA
04 April 2010
235486BV00001B/2/P